501 Quilting Motifs

DESIGNS FOR HAND
OR MACHINE QUILTING

FROM THE EDITORS OF

Quiltmaker

The Quilts You Want to Make—We Show You How

MAGAZINE

Martingale®
& COMPANY

501 Quilting Motifs:
Designs for Hand or Machine Quilting

That Patchwork Place® is an imprint of Martingale & Company®.

Martingale & Company
19021 120th Ave. NE, Suite 102
Bothell, WA 98011-9511 USA
www.martingale-pub.com

Credits

President & CEO: Tom Wierzbicki
Editor in Chief: Mary V. Green
Managing Editor: Tina Cook
Developmental Editor: Karen Costello Soltys
Copy Editor: Marcy Heffernan
Design Director: Stan Green
Production Manager: Regina Girard
Illustrator: Laurel Strand
Cover & Text Designer: Stan Green

Mission Statement

Dedicated to providing quality products and service to inspire creativity.

This Symbol Means the Design Is Digitized for Quilting

Many of the designs in *Quiltmaker's* extensive library of motifs are available for use on computer-guided quilting machines. Visit quiltmaker.com to purchase. Formats available include Statler Stitcher, CompuQuilter, and IntelliQuilter.

Quiltmaker, ISSN 1047-1634, is published bimonthly by Creative Crafts Group, LLC, 741 Corporate Circle, Suite A, Golden, CO 80401, www.quiltmaker.com.

Printed in China
16 15 14 13 12 11 8 7 6 5 4 3 2 1

Library of Congress Cataloging-in-Publication Data is available upon request.

ISBN: 978-1-60468-054-6

Table of Contents

Welcome

Welcome to *501 Quilting Motifs: Designs for Hand or Machine Quilting*. This book includes beautiful quilting motifs to enhance patchwork or appliqué. You'll find a variety of styles and sizes. Variations on each motif provide alternatives for your projects. We include an extensive index that allows you to search for a motif alphabetically or by size. We hope you find this collection an inspiring resource as you create the rich surface textures of your quilt.

How to Use This Book

Please note that the measurements for the quilt blocks and borders are *finished* sizes into which the motifs can fit. Seam allowances are already hidden by the time you get to the quilting step.

To find a motif to fit a specific space, refer to the "Size Index" on page 202 for suggestions. When you need quilting inspiration, just leaf through the pages.

Selecting Motifs

Answering these questions will help narrow down motif possibilities.

What is the style of my quilt? For a formal, traditional quilt, look for circular motifs, feathers, or flowers. You can enhance the formal style of your quilt by centering motifs on each plain block.

If you're leaning toward an informal, casual look, less-defined shapes work well. You may want to position motifs randomly or use a combination of motifs in different areas to enhance the style.

Do I want to enhance or contrast the lines of the quilt top? If your quilt is made up of diagonals that you want to enhance, choose an angular, geometric motif. If you want to soften the appearance of the diagonal lines, choose a gentler and more rounded motif.

What size space do I need to fill? The "Size Index" will help you find a motif to fit the space to be quilted. If the motif you choose doesn't have an option that fits, see "Adapting Motifs" on page 4.

Does the space I need to fill have a busy print or a plain print? Solid-colored fabric is the perfect place to showcase an intricate quilting motif you love. The same motif on a busy print will get lost, and your quilting will go unnoticed.

Am I machine quilting or hand quilting? Hand quilting allows most any kind of design without limitations. Make sure you find a motif that will showcase all the time you put into the quilting. If machine quilting is your method of choice, you may want to focus on continuous-line patterns. You can complete individual motifs without having to start and stop sewing. If you select a motif that's not a continuous-line pattern, keep in mind that you'll have to begin and end the line wherever it dead-ends. Adapt the motif to make it continuous. Make sure to start and stop any lines of quilting with tiny stitches to anchor them.

How accomplished am I as a quilter? If the thought of quilting even one of those detailed motifs strikes fear in your heart, choosing one for your queen-size quilt project will only mean that the quilt never gets done. Choose something simpler that you will be happy with, saving the detailed motif for a pillow top that requires only one design. If you love to quilt and can't wait to tackle the biggies, go for it!

How much quilting do I need? As with many quilting questions, the answer is "it depends." It depends on the look you're trying to achieve, the batting you use, and how the quilt will be used. In general, plan for a consistent density across your quilt. Expand your vision beyond the border and block seams. Quilt across all the borders or bring a block motif into empty spaces along a border motif. Read your batting manufacturer's instructions to know the minimum amount of quilting required. If you're making a quilt that will be washed frequently, give it the security of a lot of quilting. If you're making a wall quilt, you can get away with less quilting if that's the look you want.

Adapting Motifs

You've found a motif you love, but it isn't exactly what you need. Here are some ways to adapt the motif you can't live without.

Change the Size

The easiest way to adjust the size of a motif is with a photocopy machine. First, make a paper shape that represents the space for the motif. Then reduce or enlarge the motif on the copier until it fits into the paper shape. Layering the two papers and holding them up to a light is a good way to check.

Consider an Alternative Placement

Who says a motif has to fit inside a block? If your motif is too large, perhaps it can break the boundaries of the block and overlap into other areas of the quilt. If it fits the style of the quilt, why not?

Consider Filling in the Space with Other Quilting

If your motif is small and you don't want multiple shapes but need more quilting, use another method such as those shown below to fill in the space.

For a formal look, add a grid behind the motif.

Machine stipple around the motif to cover areas quickly and make the motif stand out.

Echo quilt around the motif to emphasize the shape of the central design.

Make a Motif Continuous

If the motif has more starts and stops than you want to quilt, you can always add more quilting lines.

Add lines for a continuous motif.

Quilt Continuously Between Motifs

Quilt a complementary line to travel from one motif to the next, echo a portion of the motif, or quilt in a seam line to move to the next motif. Consider adding tendrils or curls to fill spaces between motifs.

Add lines and shapes to fill spaces.

Transferring Motifs

Mark your quilt before layering and basting. The most common way to transfer a design is to trace the quilting motif onto tracing paper. Place the tracing paper under the quilt top with a light source under it. A portable light box works well. Lightly mark the design on the quilt top with the marking tool of your choice. Refer to "Marking Tools" on page 6 for marking options.

If your quilt fabrics are dark, you may prefer to trace around a template rather than use a light box. To make a template, trace the motif on heavy clear plastic using a permanent marker. If the design is closed, simply cut on the marked outer line. For a more intricate motif, use a craft knife to cut out the lines, cutting a wide enough channel to accommodate your marking tool. You can also buy a double-bladed knife made specifically for cutting channels.

Positioning Motifs and Variations

Refer to the instructions below for help with positioning motifs on your block or patch.

Finding the Center

For a centered motif, find the center of the block by folding the fabric in half lengthwise, and then crosswise, and lightly finger-pressing. When unfolded, the creases will help you center the motif for tracing.

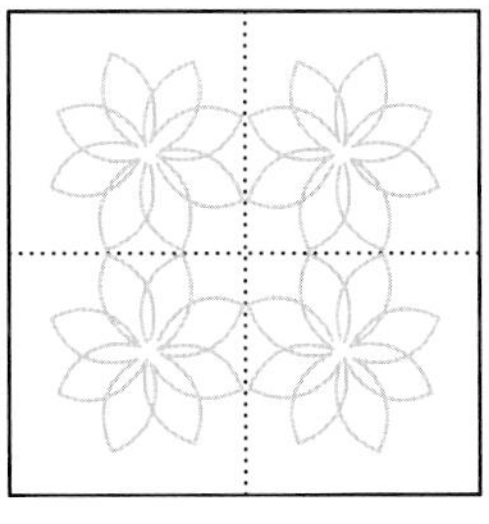

Finding Diagonal Lines

Many variations are lined up with diagonal lines. To position these, cut a piece of tracing paper to the size of the finished block. Fold in half from corner to corner, and then fold in half again. Lightly finger-press. When unfolded, the creases can be used to line up motifs to create the whole design.

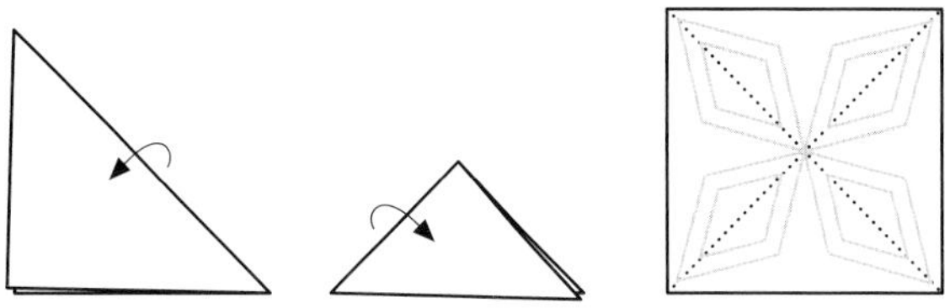

Eight-Point Circles

Some design options rely on circles for motif placement. You will find ¼-circle patterns on page 201. The patterns include all the circle sizes used in this book. To draw a circular motif, first find the center of your tracing paper by folding. Next, open up the paper, align the center marks, and trace the arc. Then, rotating the paper ¼ turn each time, repeat the tracing to make a complete circle.

For example, an 11½" block for the "Rosebush" motif on page 65 has leaves spaced around a circle. To draw this design, place a dot where each fold crosses the circle. Line up the motifs on the dots, trace, and repeat until the circle is complete.

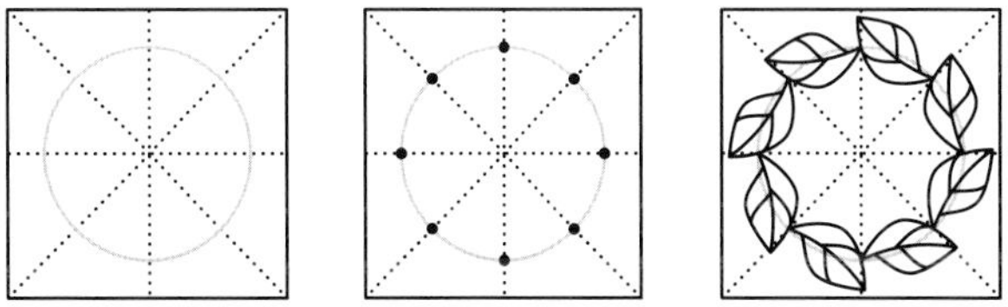

Finding Vertical, Horizontal, and Diagonal Lines

For some designs, you'll need guidelines in several directions. Fold the paper lengthwise and crosswise; then open it out and refold it corner to corner to get horizontal, vertical, and diagonal lines.

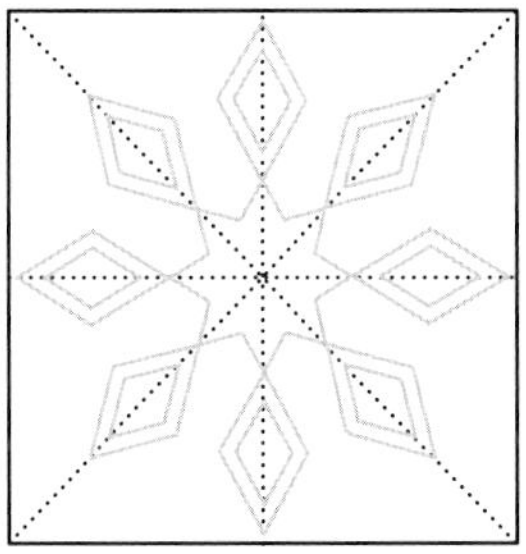

Six-Point Circles

To position some designs, use a combination of the circle and angle patterns on page 201. For example, a variation for the Ivy 1 motif on page 180 uses only three repeats. To draw this design, draw a 4" circle, and then draw lines at 60° angles, as shown. Place three dots on the circle, one at every other intersection of the lines and the circle. Starting at each dot, trace the motif three times. In this case, the circle becomes part of the quilting design. Be sure to trace it when transferring the design to the quilt top.

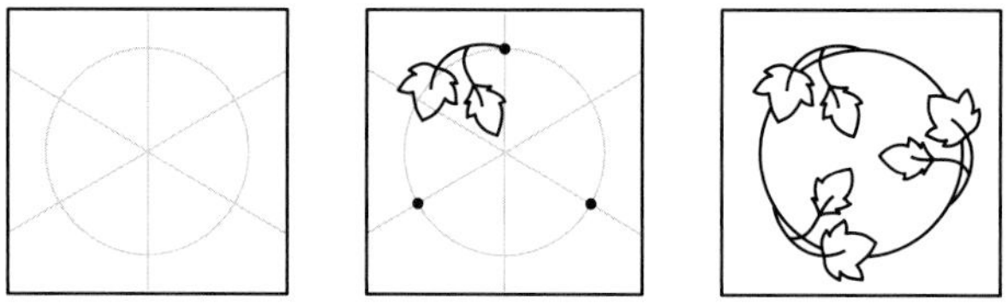

Marking Tools

Every quilter, for one reason or another, will have her favorite way of marking a quilt. This table helps you identify tools to find your own preferences. Test any marking product for removability before using it on your quilt.

Product	Description	Type of Quilting	Advantages	Concerns	Template Required
Pencil	Quilter's colored pencils, mechanical pencils	Hand	Thin line usually disappears under stitching, easily erased	Often not dark enough to be seen for machine quilting	Yes
Chalk	Tailor's chalk, chalk dispensers, chalk pencils	Hand/machine	Comes in a variety of colors, erases easily with rubbing	Can rub off before you want it to	Yes
Soap	Soapstone, soap slivers	Hand	Easily washed out, economical, shows well on dark fabrics	Often not dark enough to be seen on light fabrics and prints	Yes
Markers	Air-erase markers, washable markers	Hand/machine	Good dark line	Some quilters worry about marks reappearing	Yes
Hera marker	Tool that creases the quilt to show markings	Hand/machine	Makes no permanent mark	Can be difficult to see, can wear off before you want it to	Yes
Tape	Masking tape, narrow tape with marked lines	Hand/machine	Peels off easily, marking of quilt top not necessary, can be reused	Only for straight lines or very gentle curves	No
Quilter's guide on machine	Bar attaches to the walking foot on some machines	Machine	Marking of quilt top not necessary	Best for straight lines with a guide to follow	No
Tracing paper	Motif is traced on paper and pinned to quilt top	Machine	Marking of quilt top not necessary	Motif must be traced on every sheet	No

Dolphin Bay

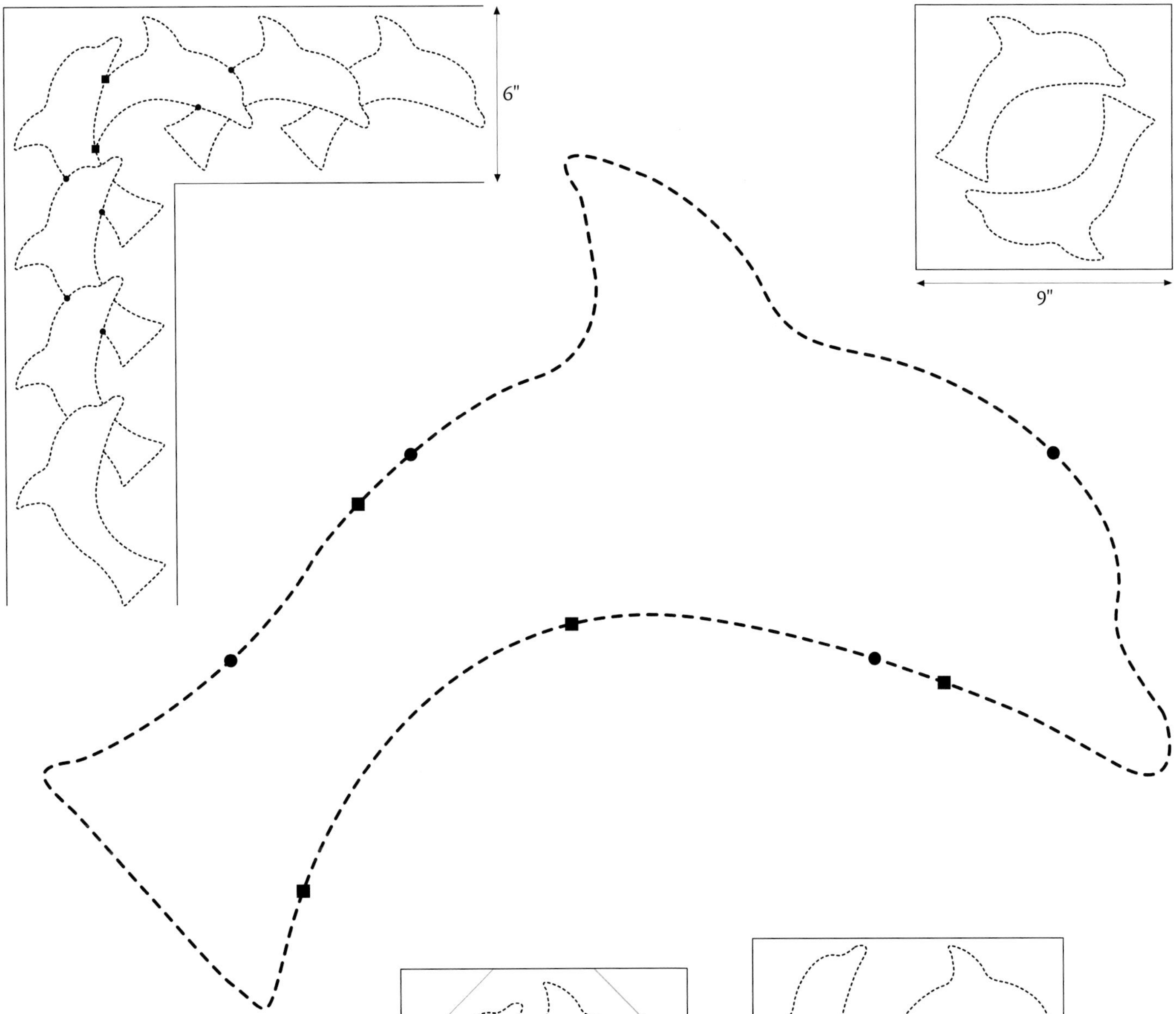

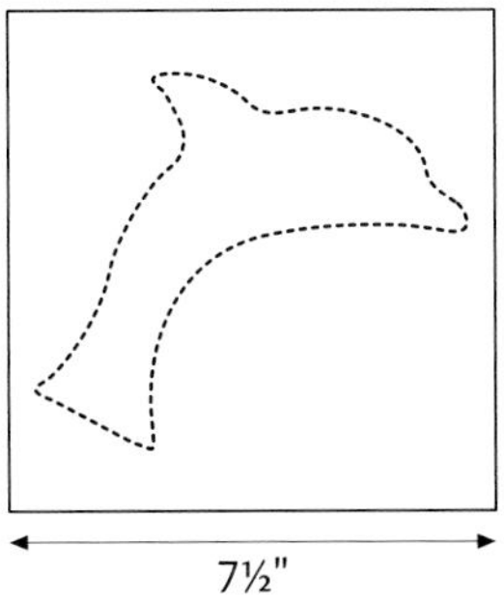

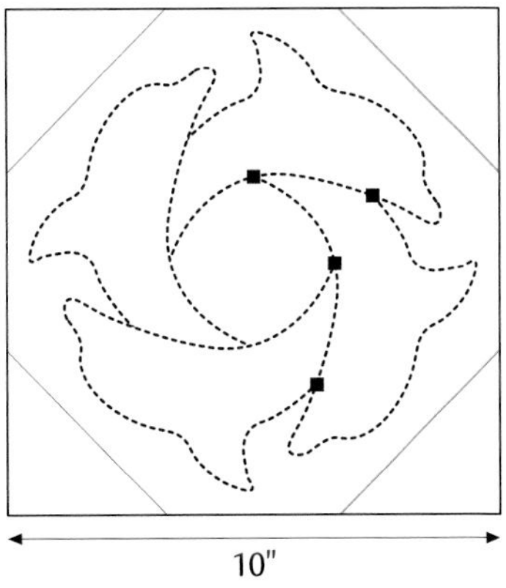

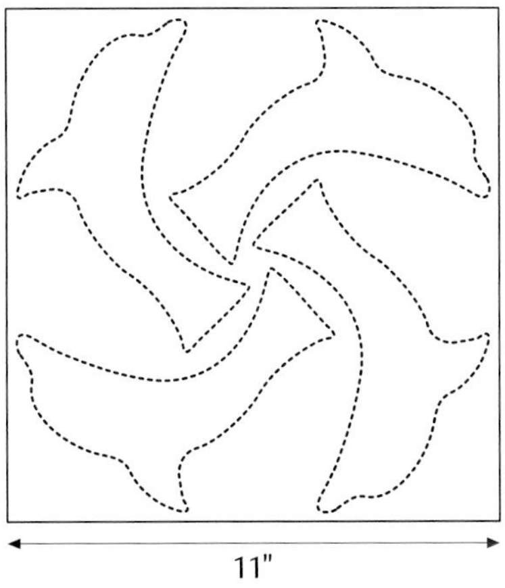

Floating Clouds and Stars

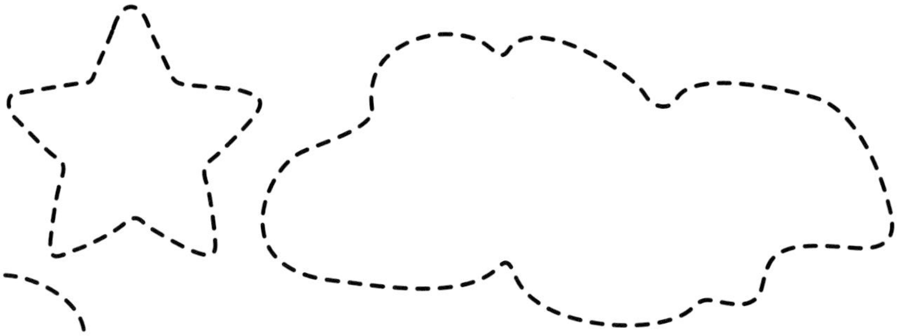

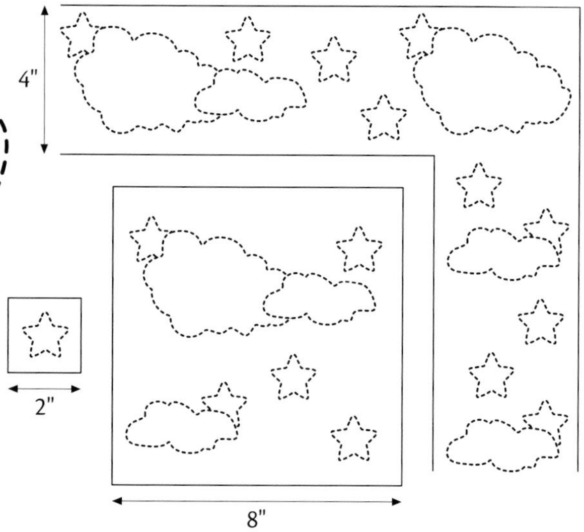

Sunshine

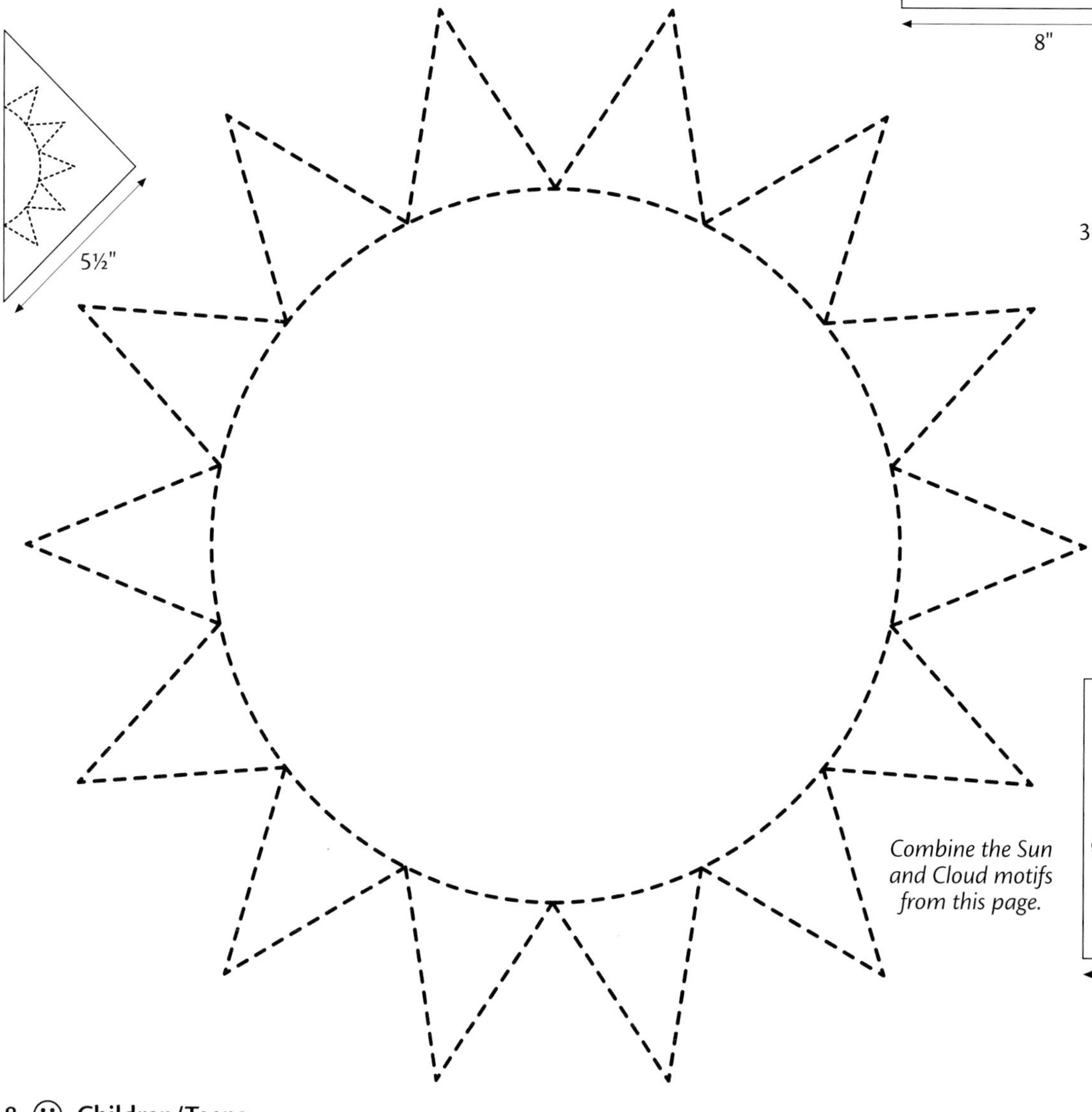

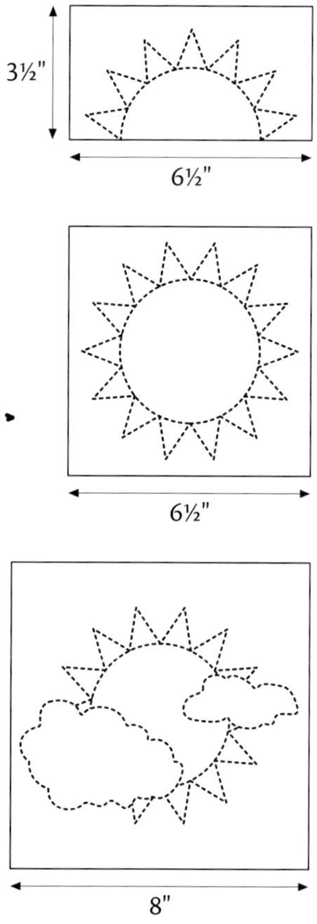

Combine the Sun and Cloud motifs from this page.

Man in the Moon

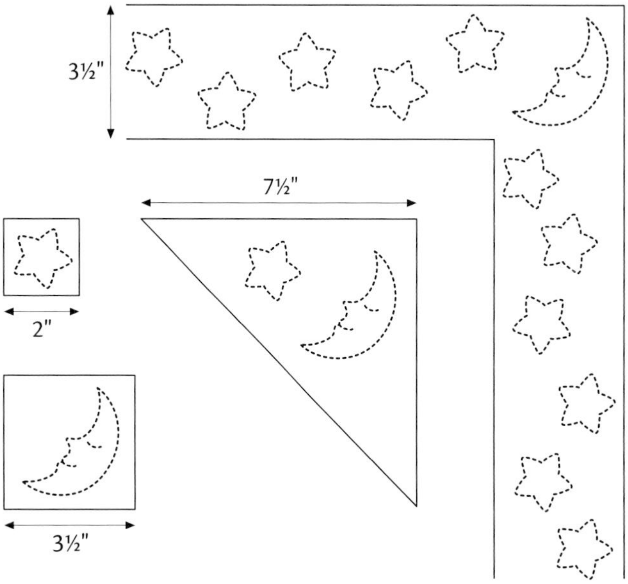

Rainbow Sherbet

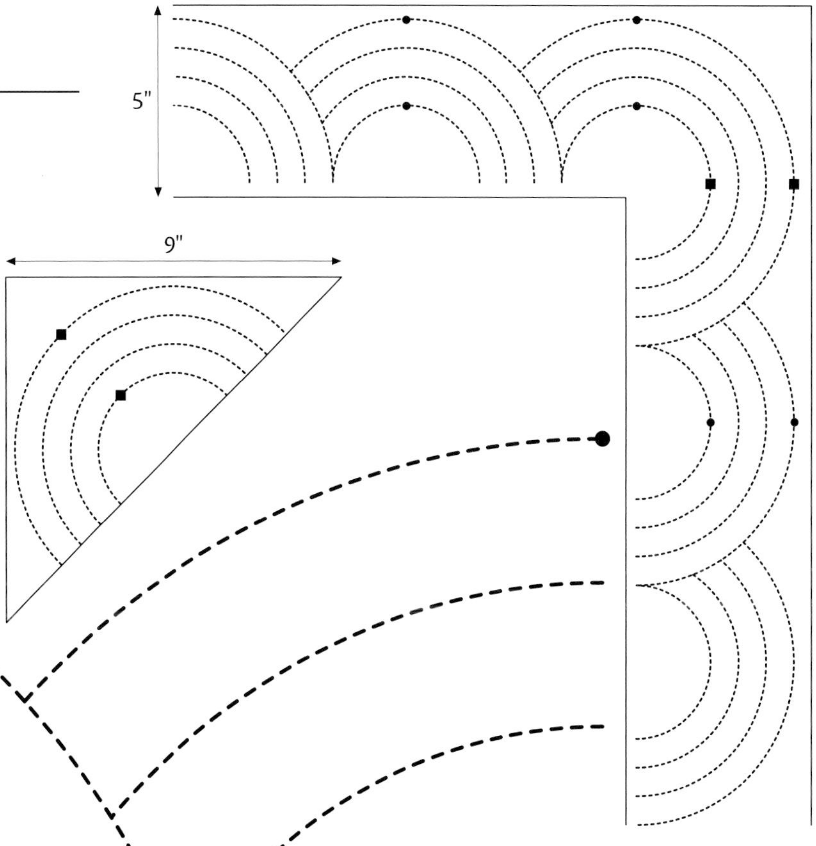

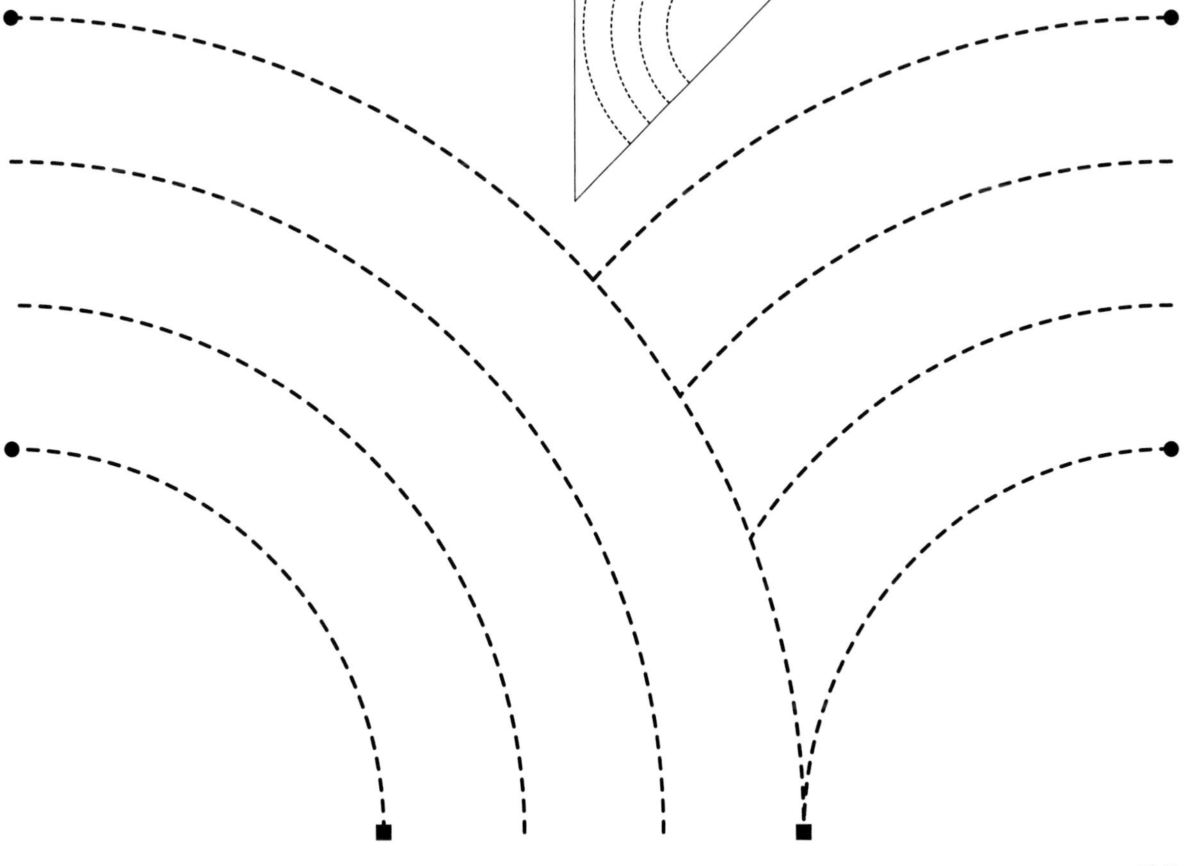

Baby Birds

4½"
3½"
3½"

Teddy Bear

2"
4½"
4"
2"
2"
4"

Reversed motifs are shown in gray.

Duck Stroll

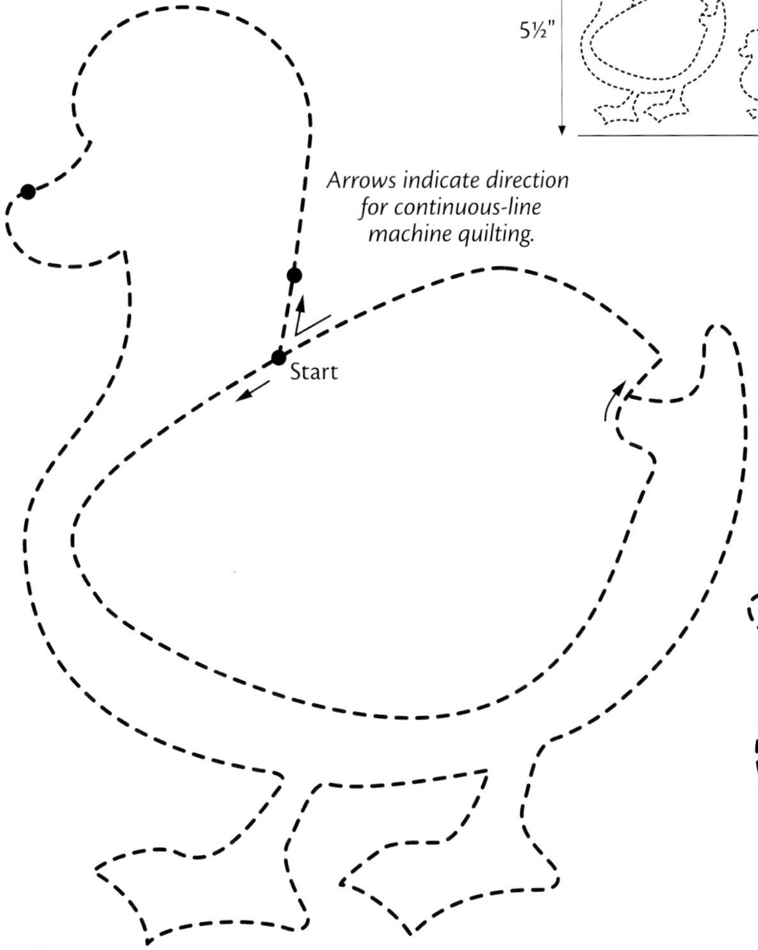
Arrows indicate direction
for continuous-line
machine quilting.
Start

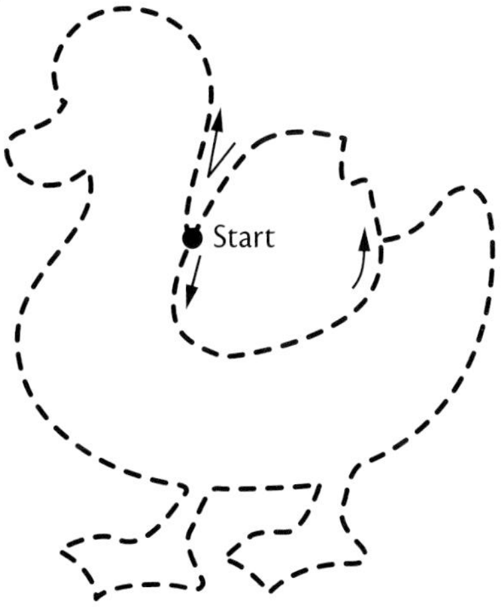
Start

5½"
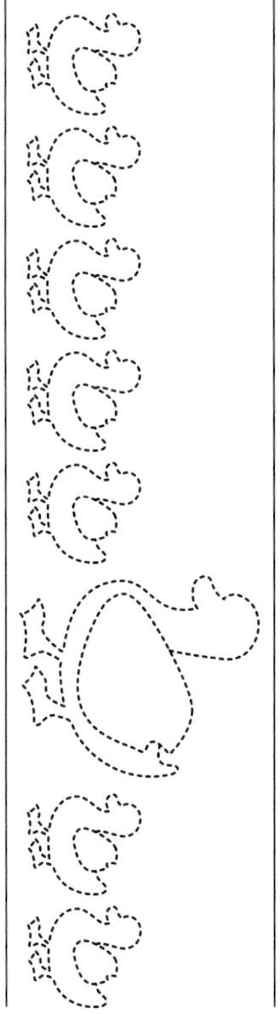

5½"

3"

Fall Frolic

2½"

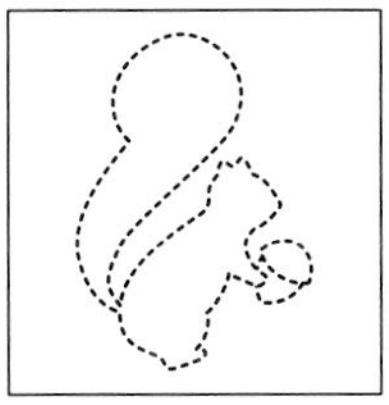

5"

Reversed motif is shown in gray.

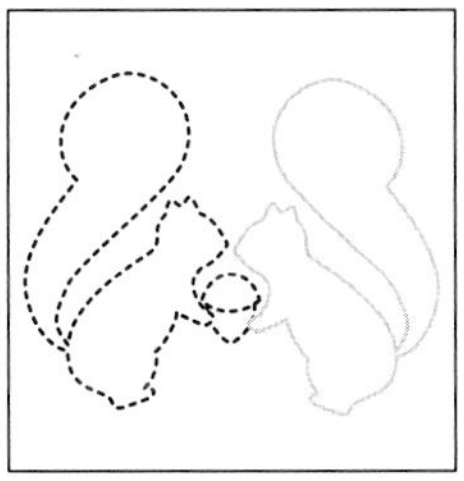

6"

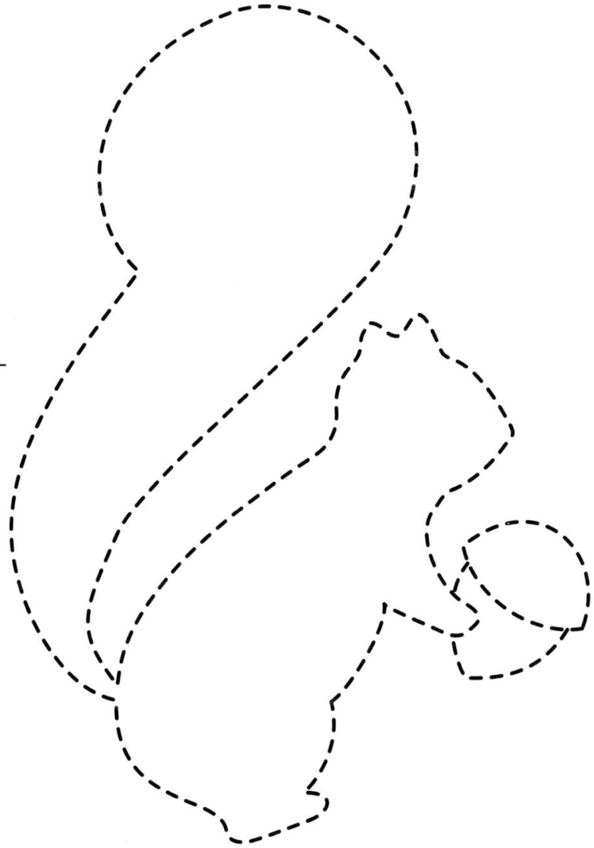

Groovy Flowers

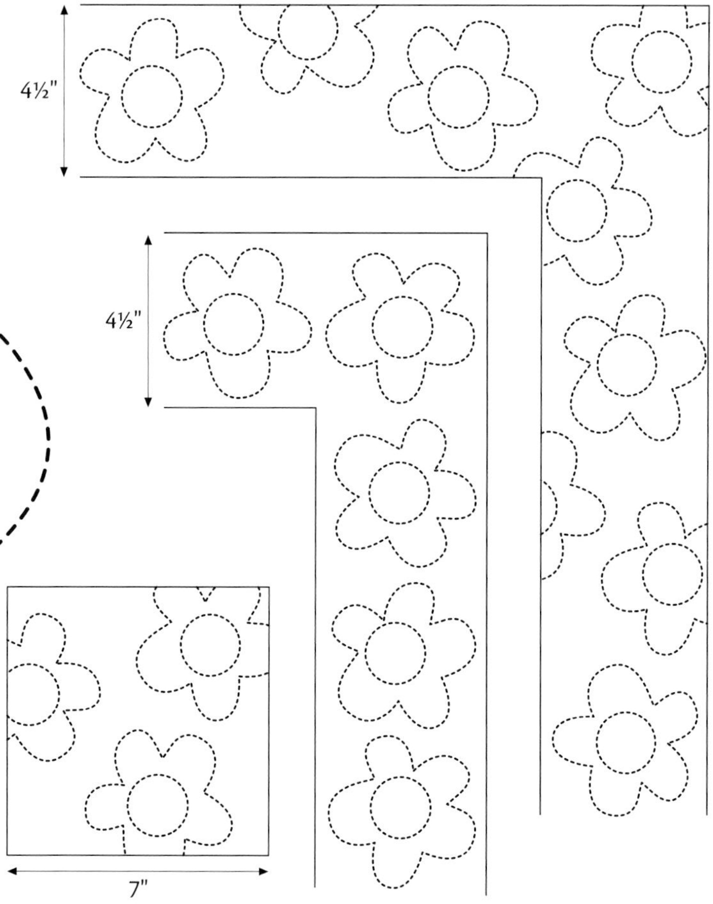

Psychedelic Swirls

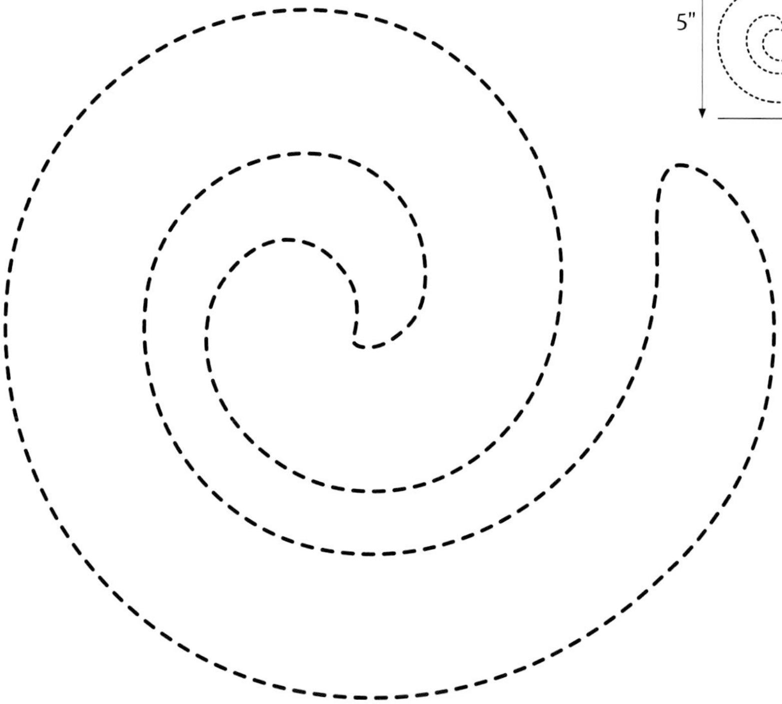

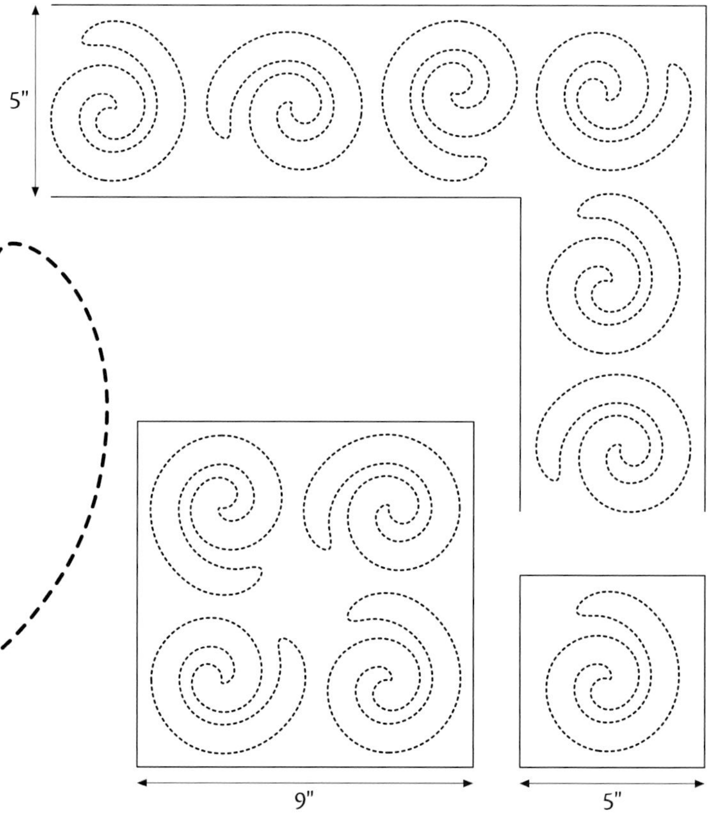

Peace Sign

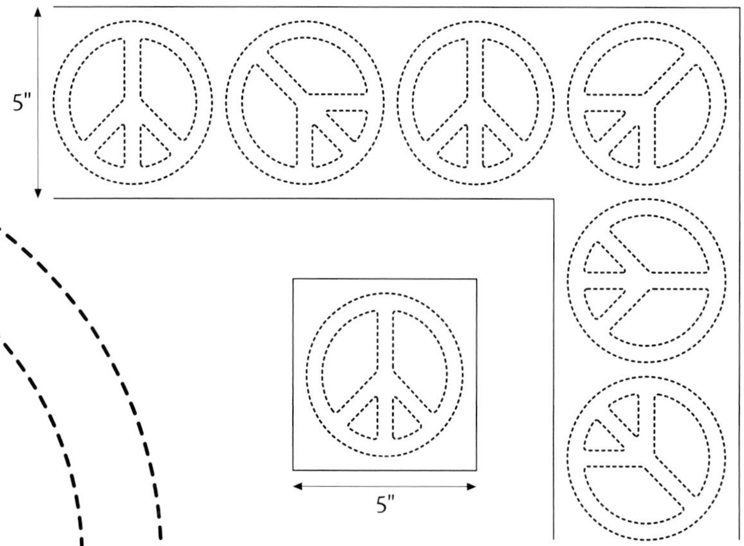

Combine the '60s era designs from these two pages.

Happy Face

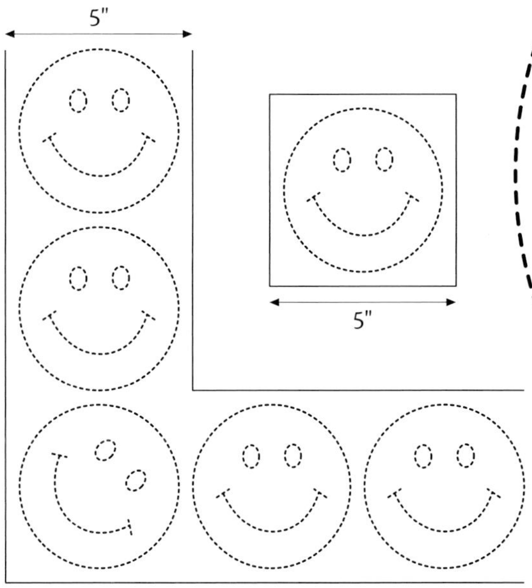

To the Moon

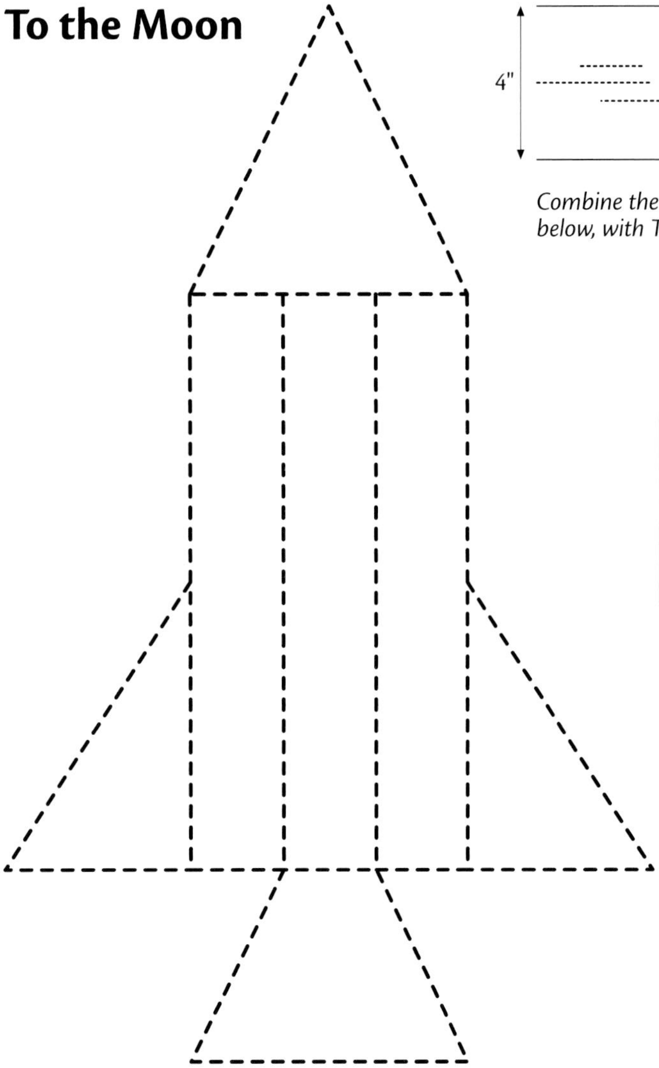

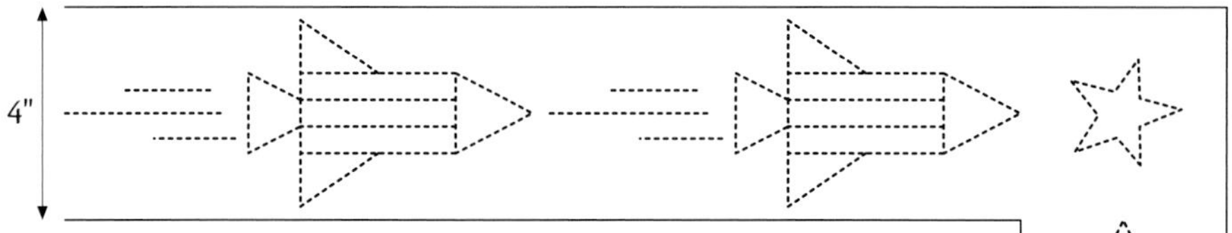

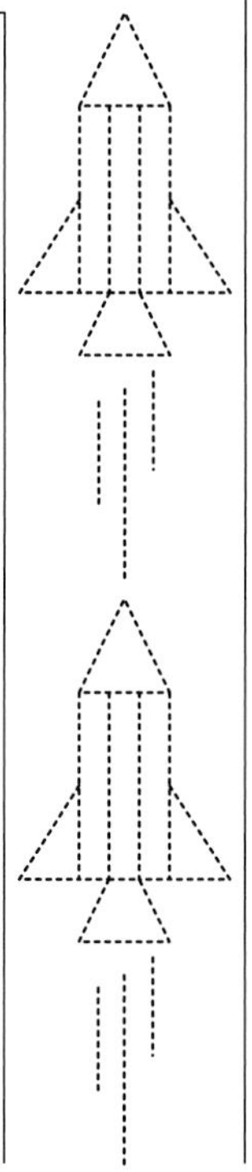

Combine the star and star trail from Stardust, below, with To the Moon to create a border.

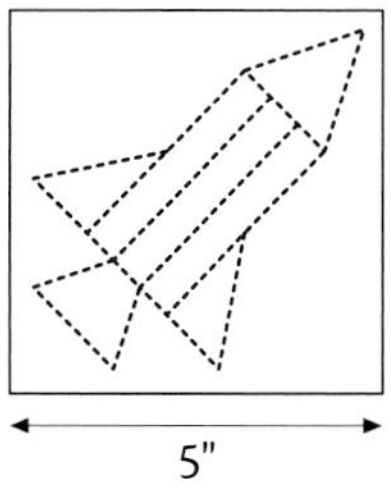

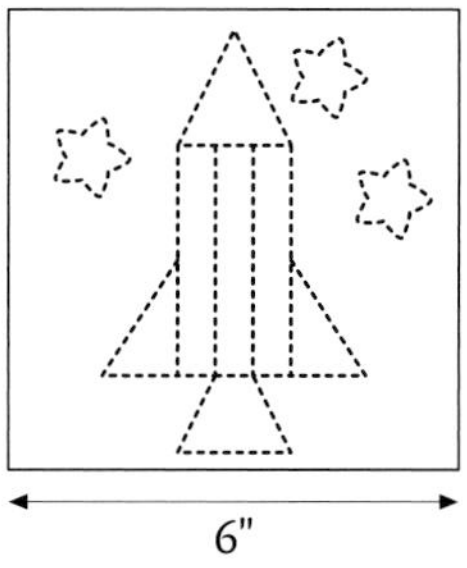

Combine the star from Desert Sunset, page 24, with To the Moon.

Stardust

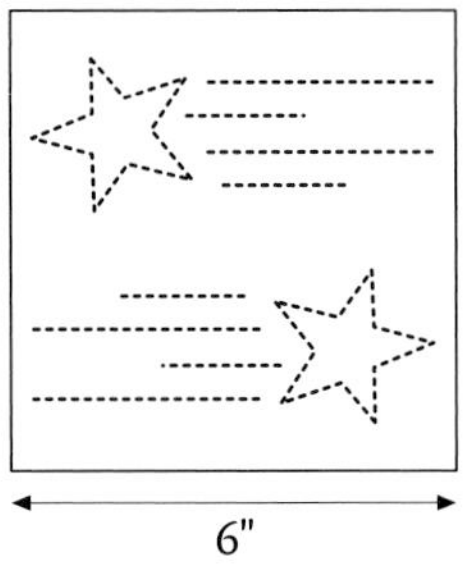

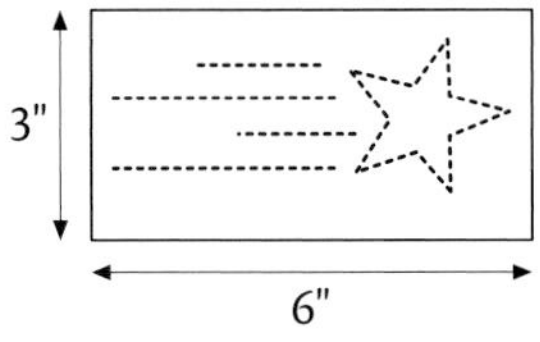

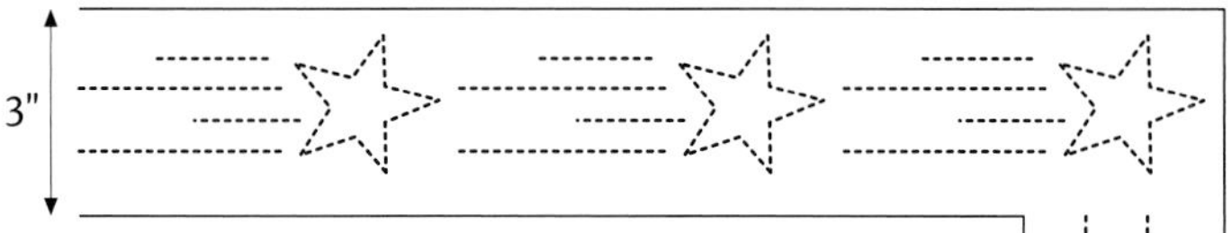

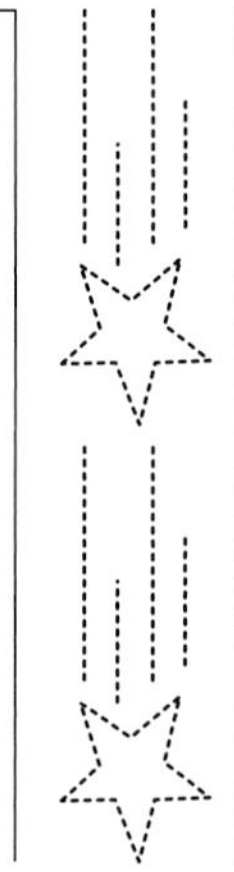

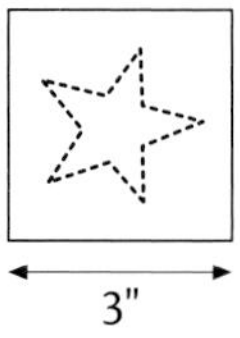

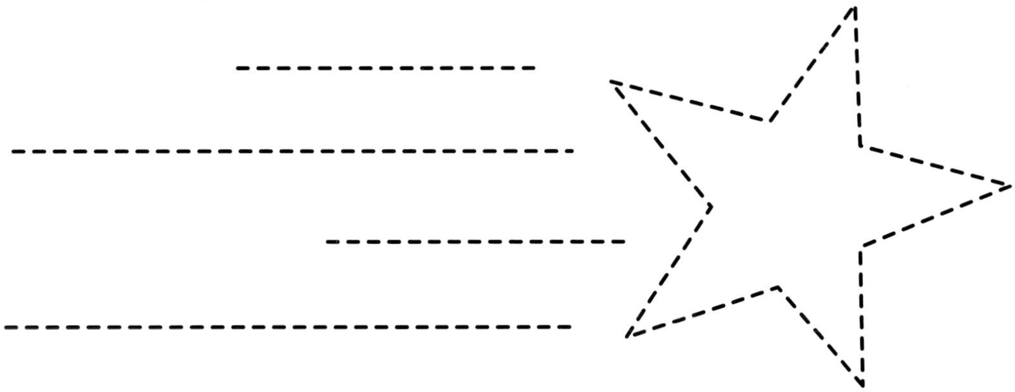

Sea Serpent/Knight

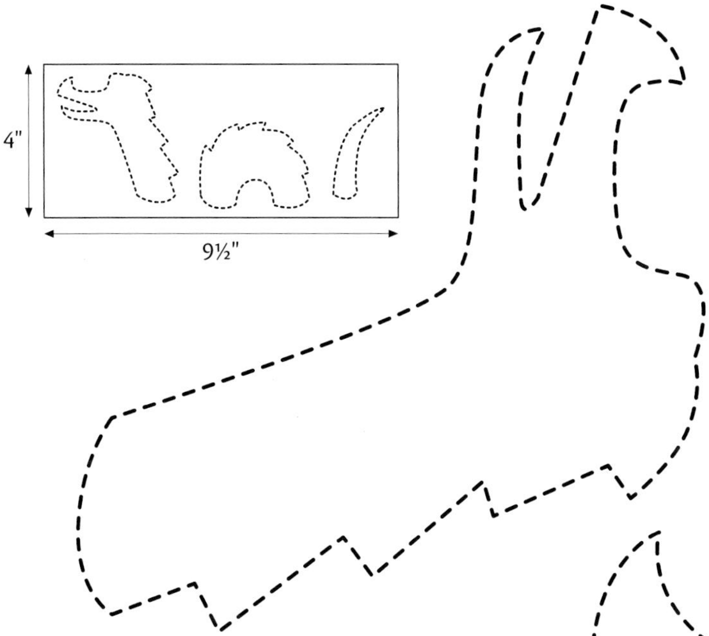

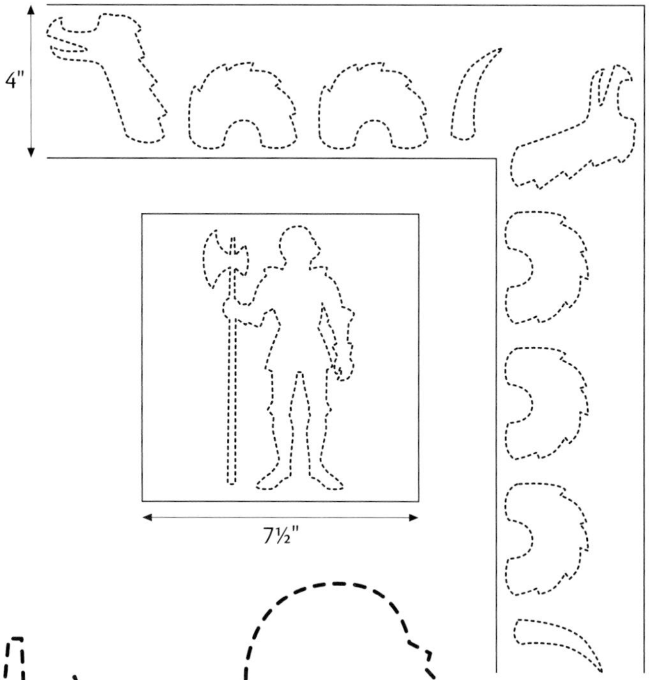

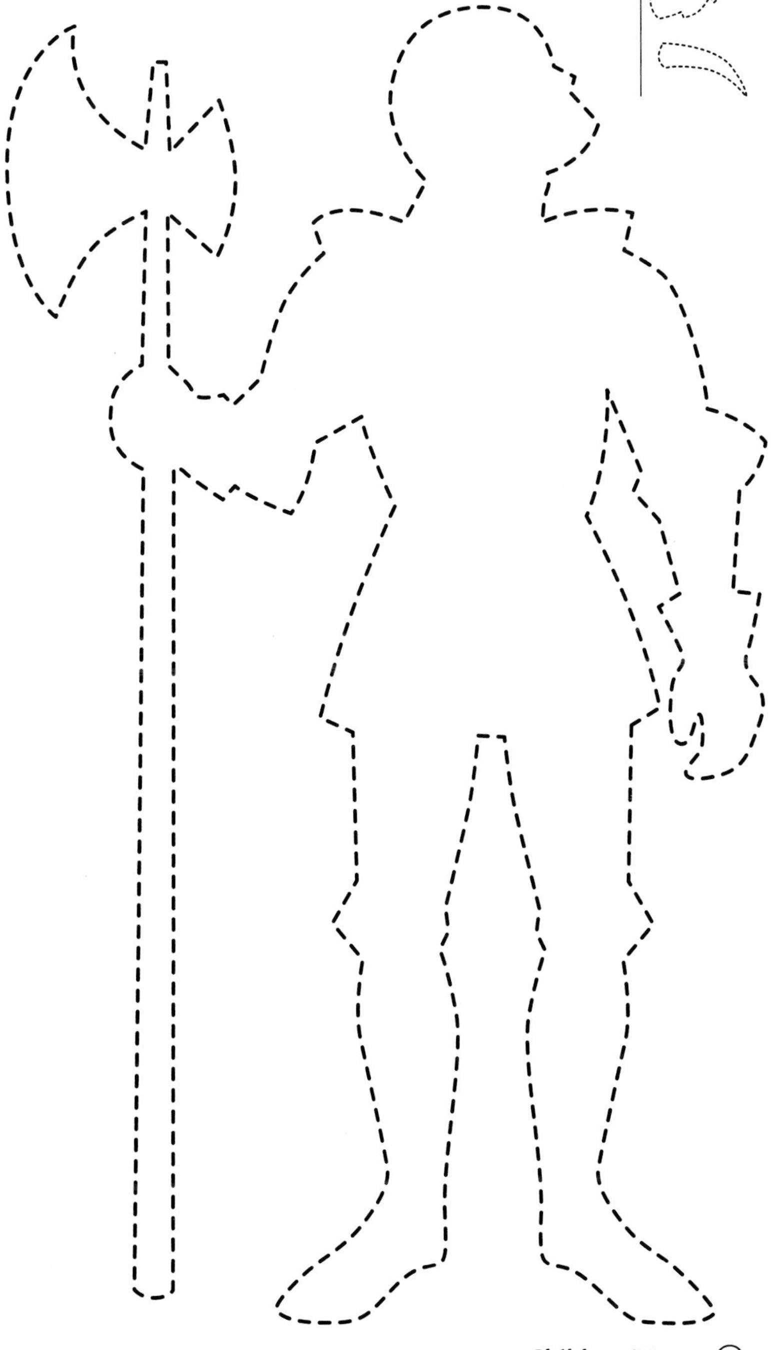

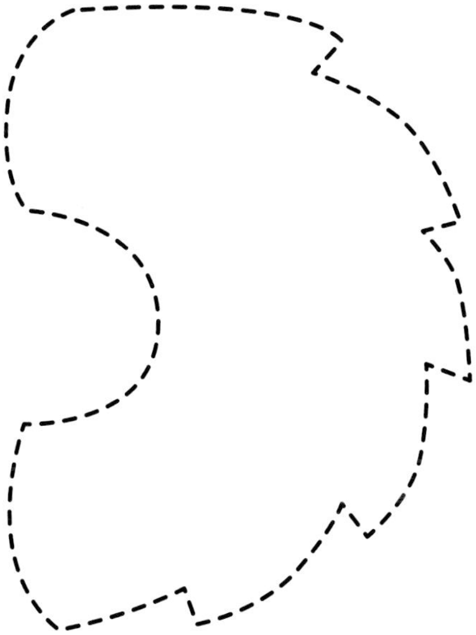

Flying Dragon

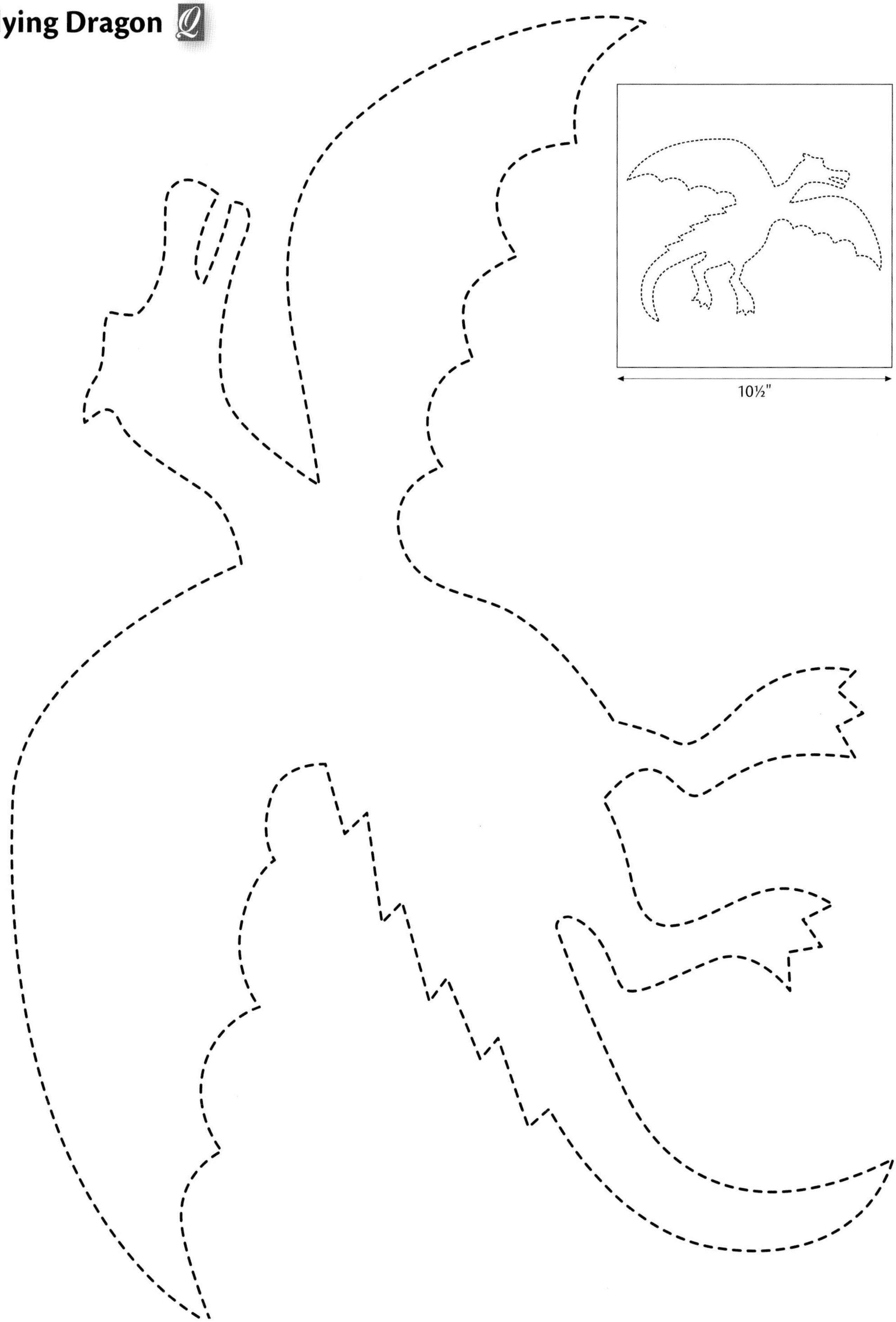

King/Princess

8½"

8½"

Castle

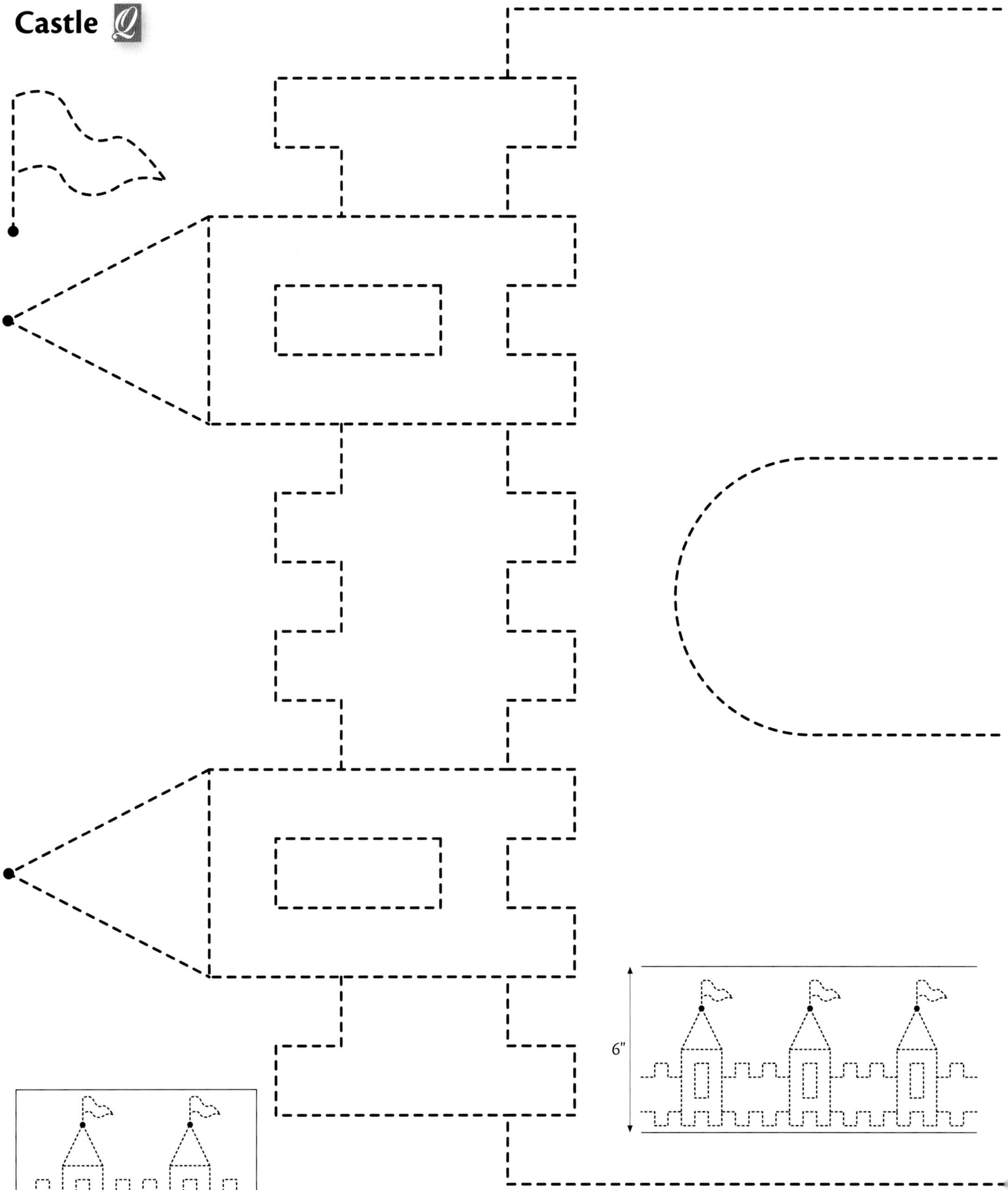

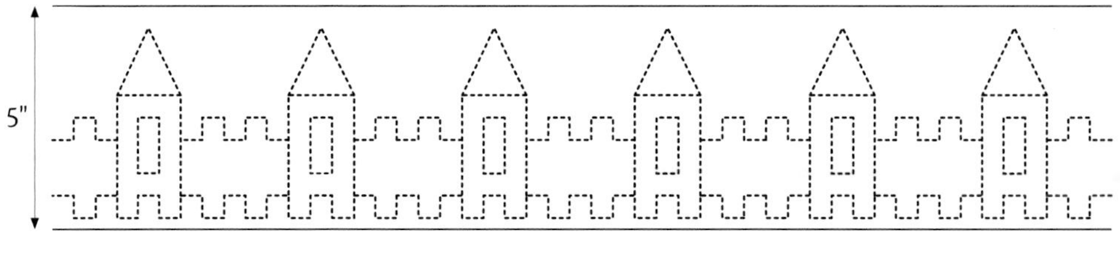

Unicorn/Horse

Elephants on Parade

Gray lines show
connecting tail.

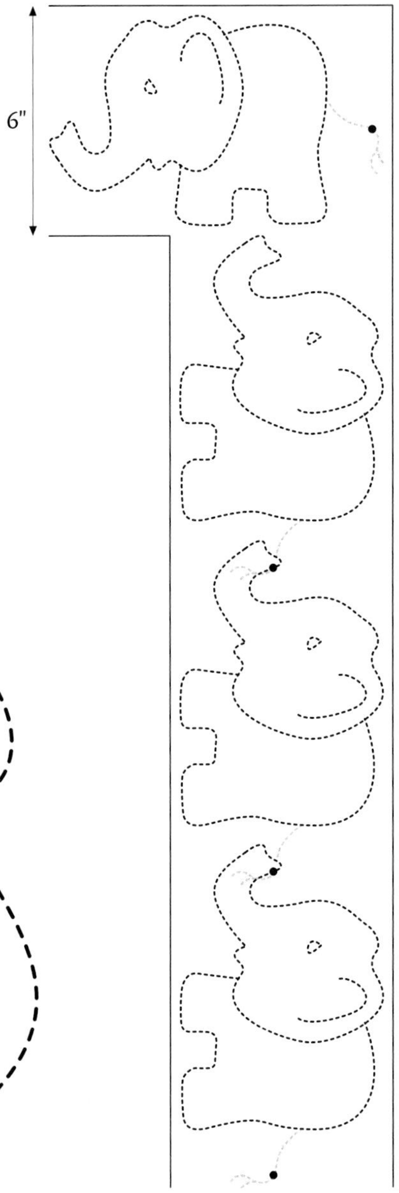
6"

10"

Triple Scoop

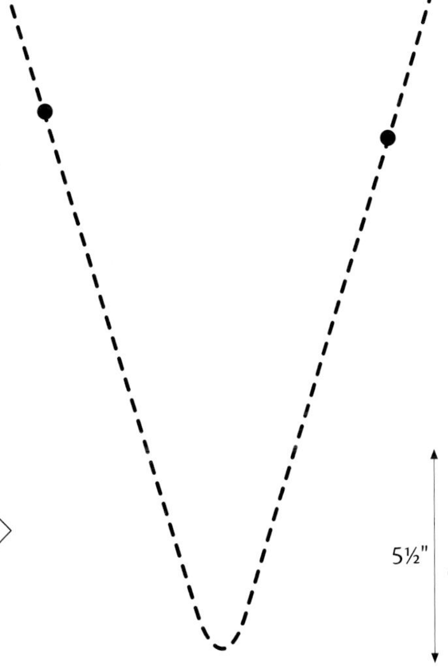

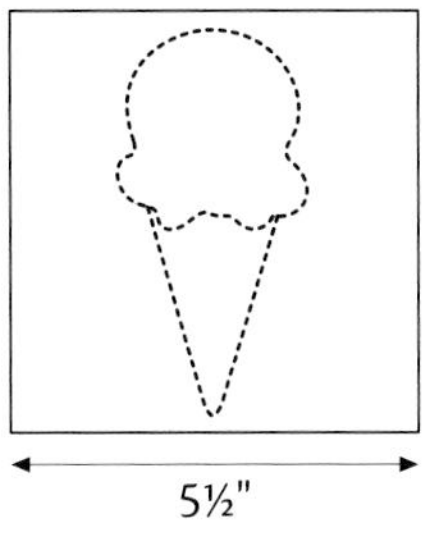

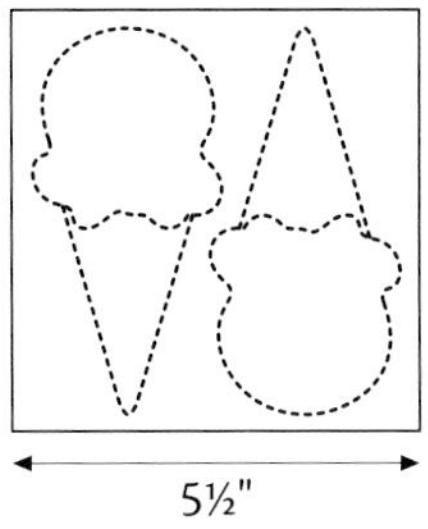

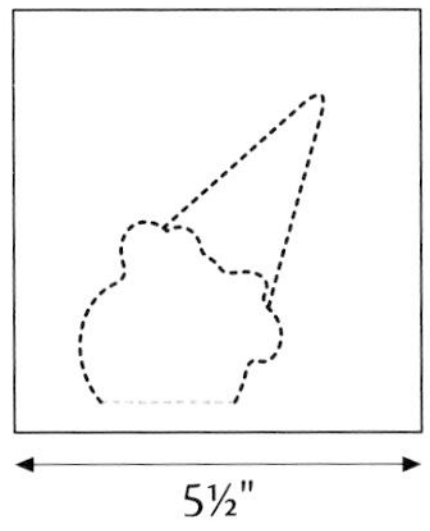

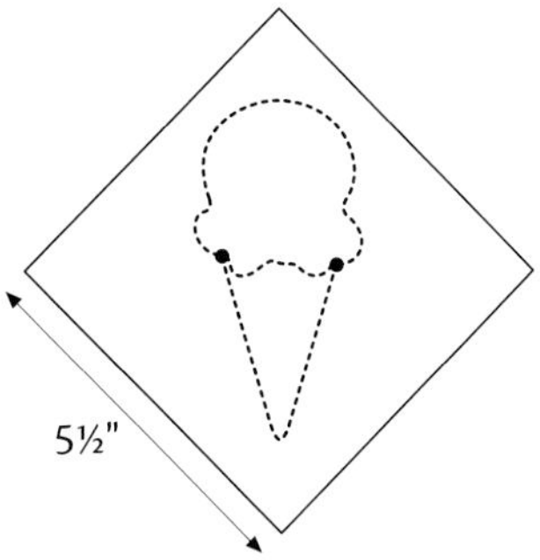

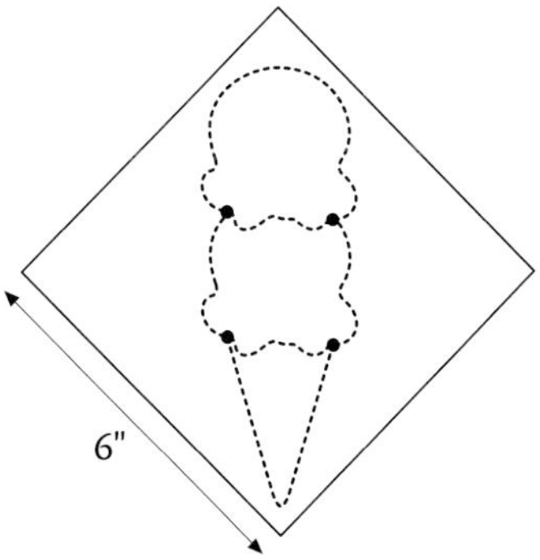

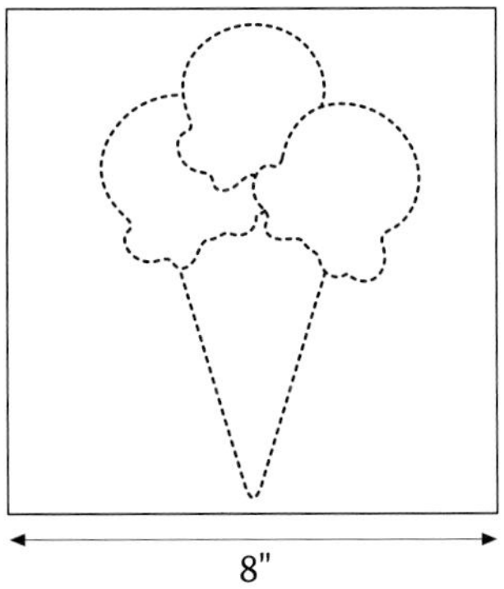

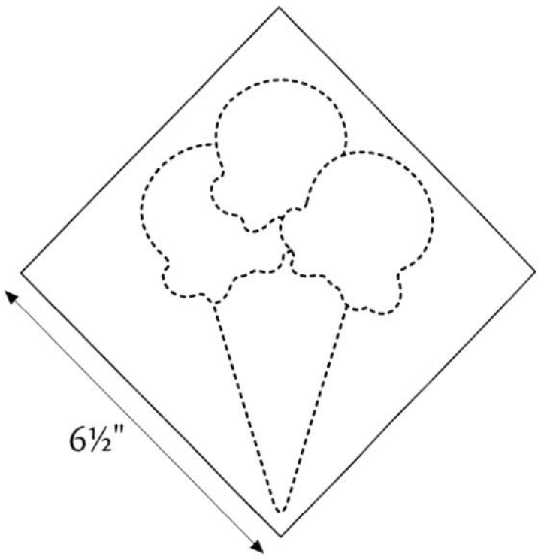

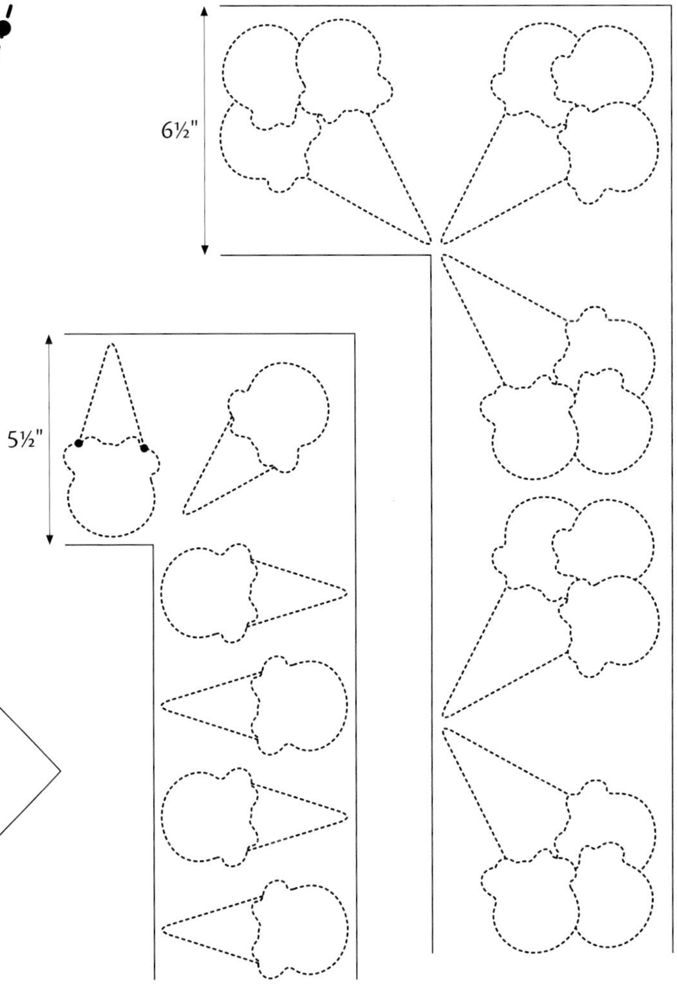

Best Foot Forward

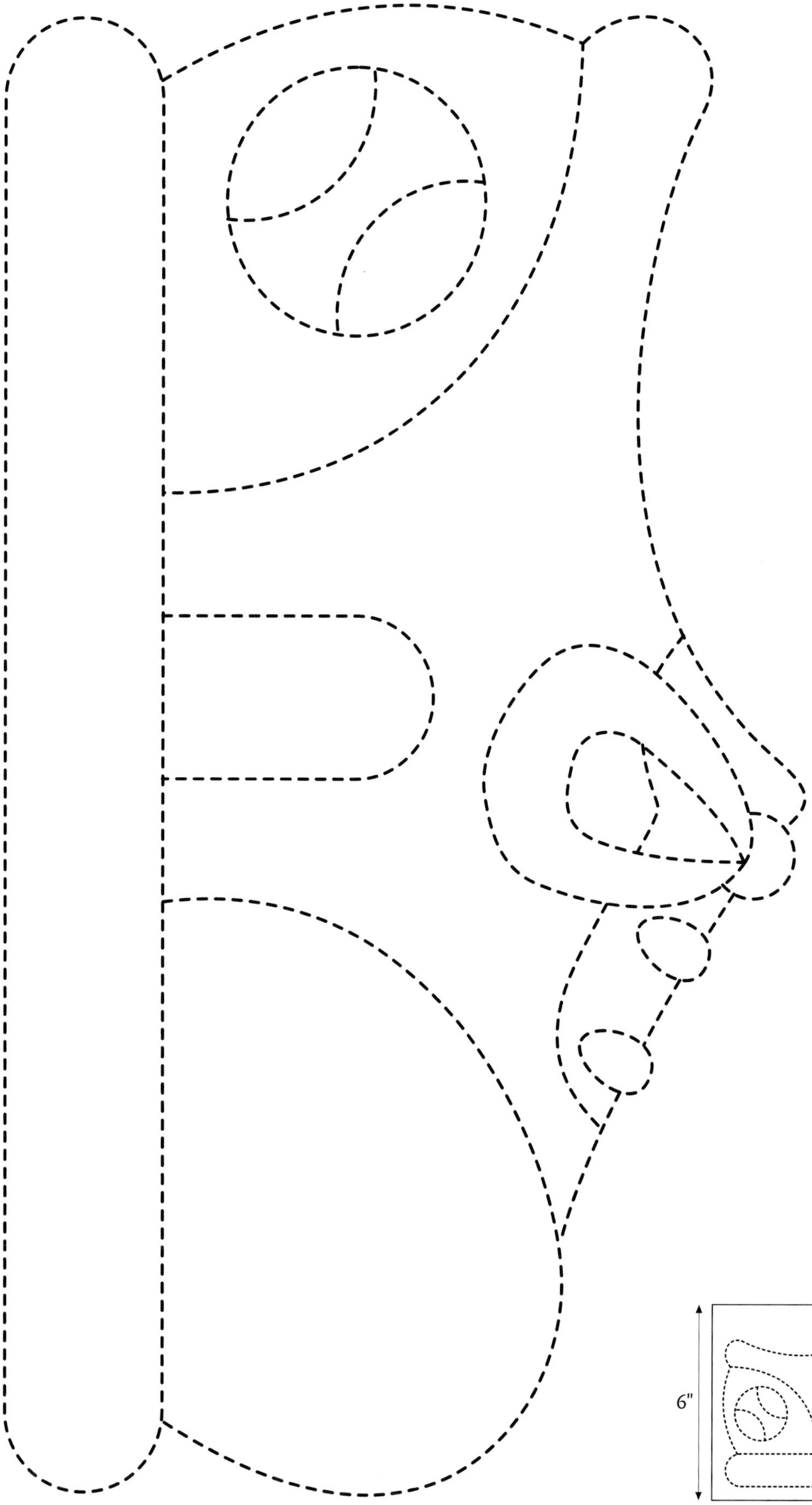

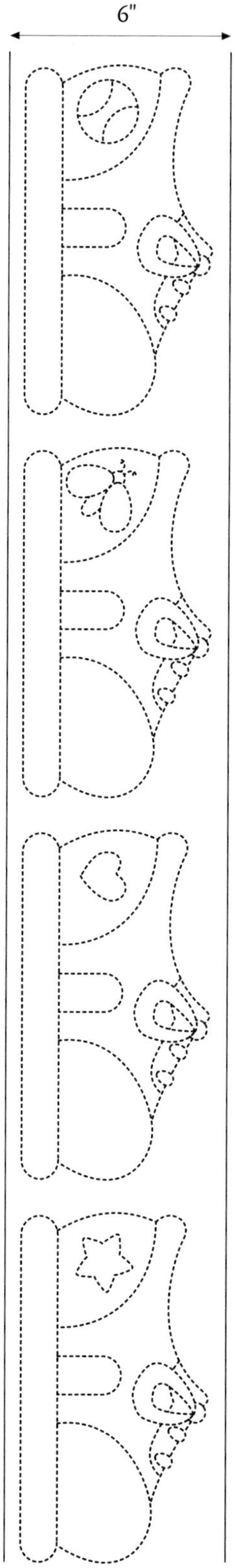

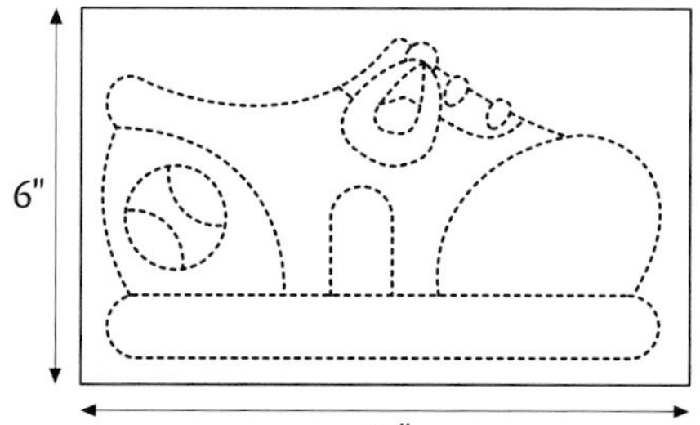

Twinkling Stars

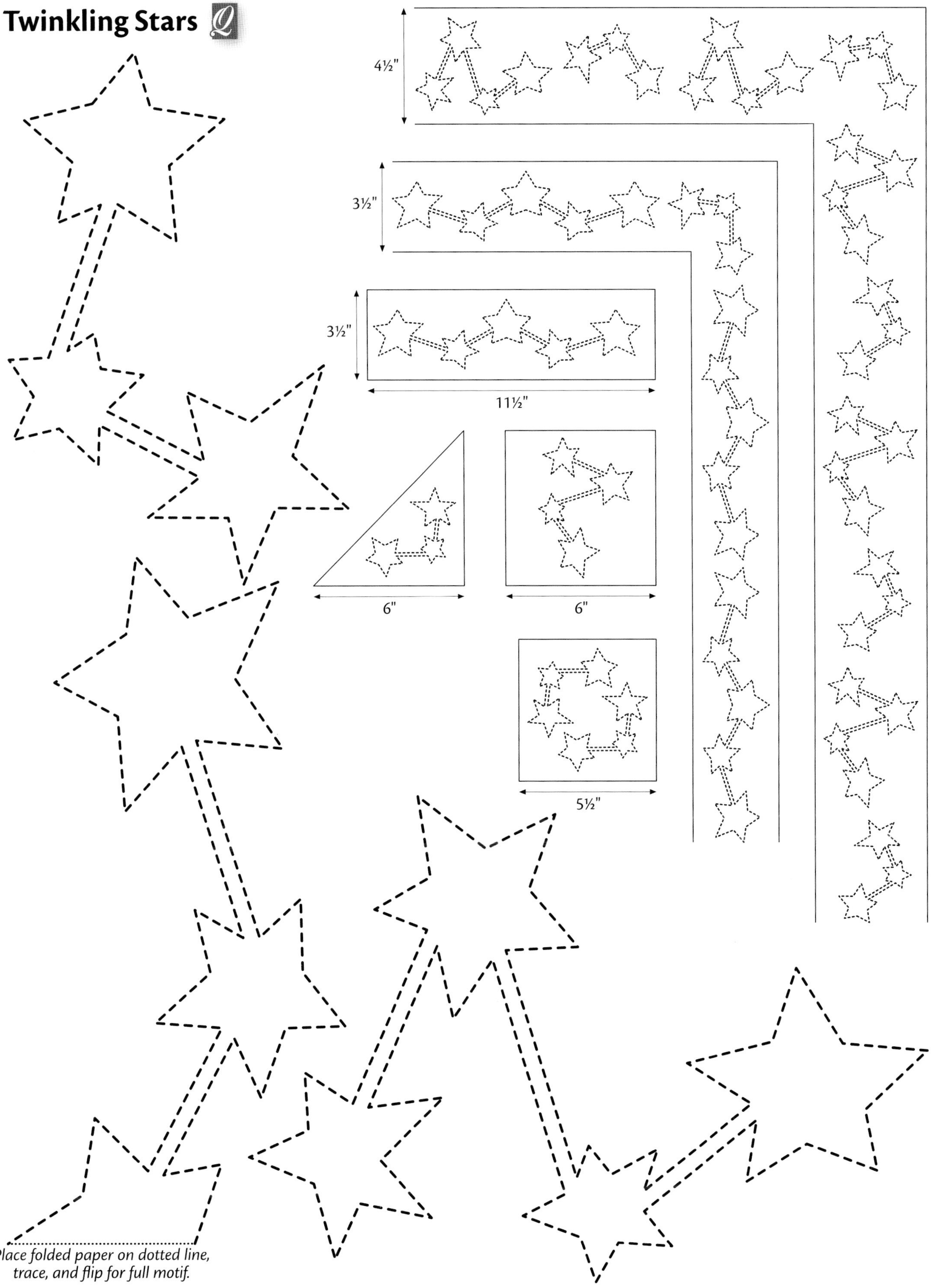
4½"
3½"
3½"
11½"
6"
6"
5½"

Place folded paper on dotted line, trace, and flip for full motif.

Just Ducky

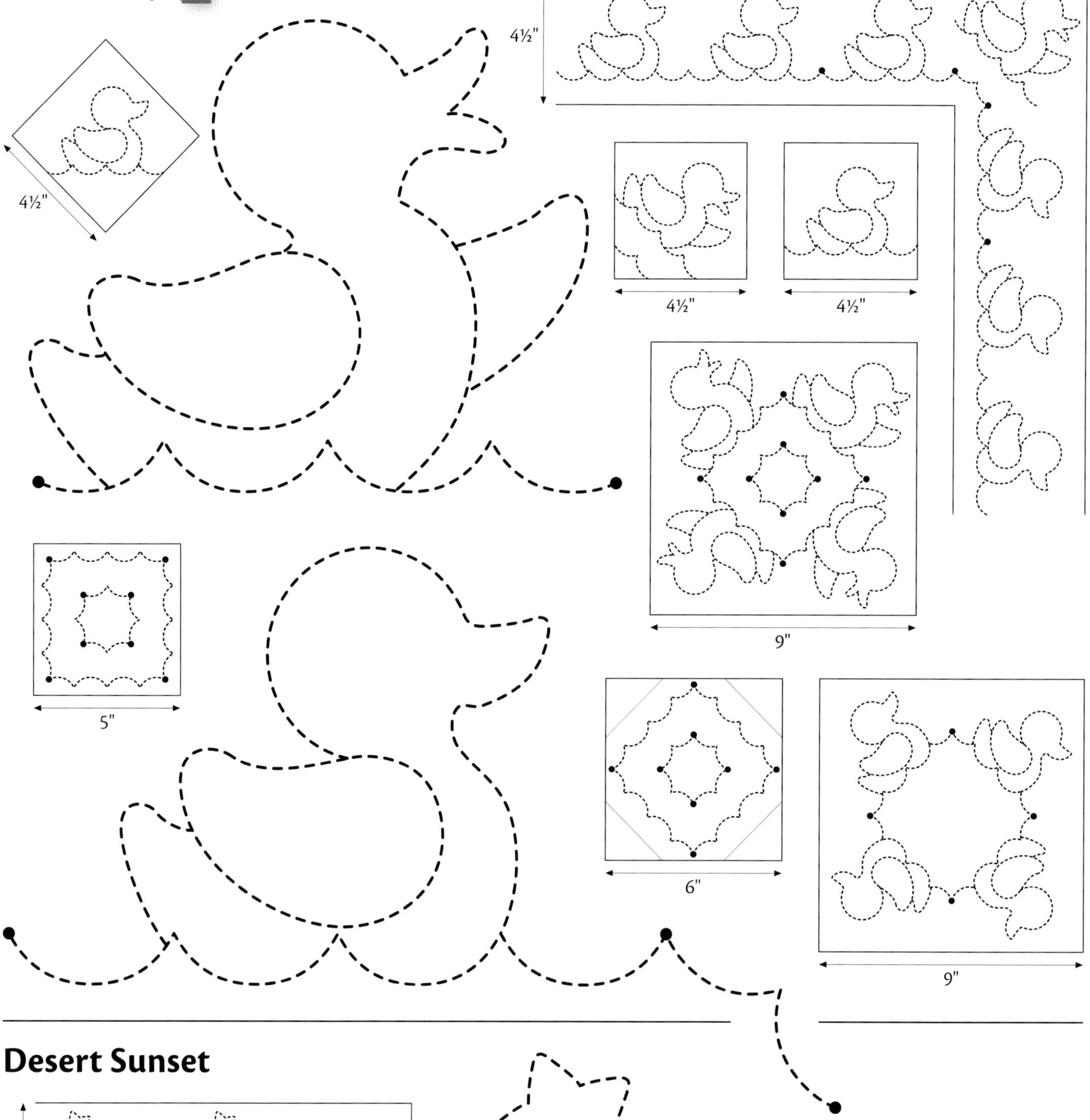
4½"
4½"
4½"
4½"
9"
5"
6"
9"

Desert Sunset

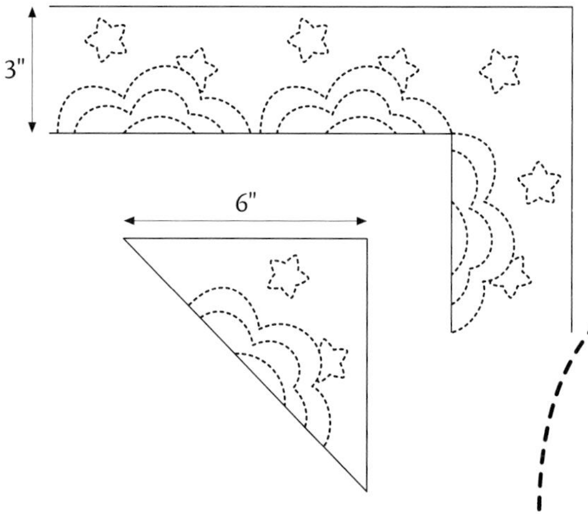
3"
6"

Puppy Romp

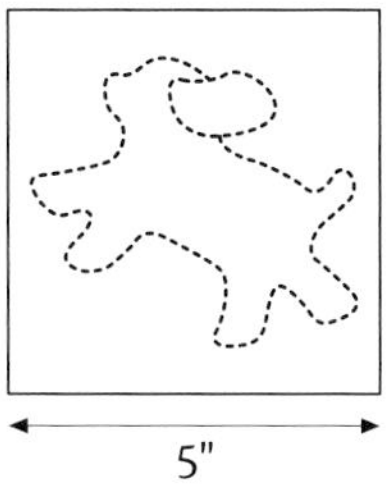

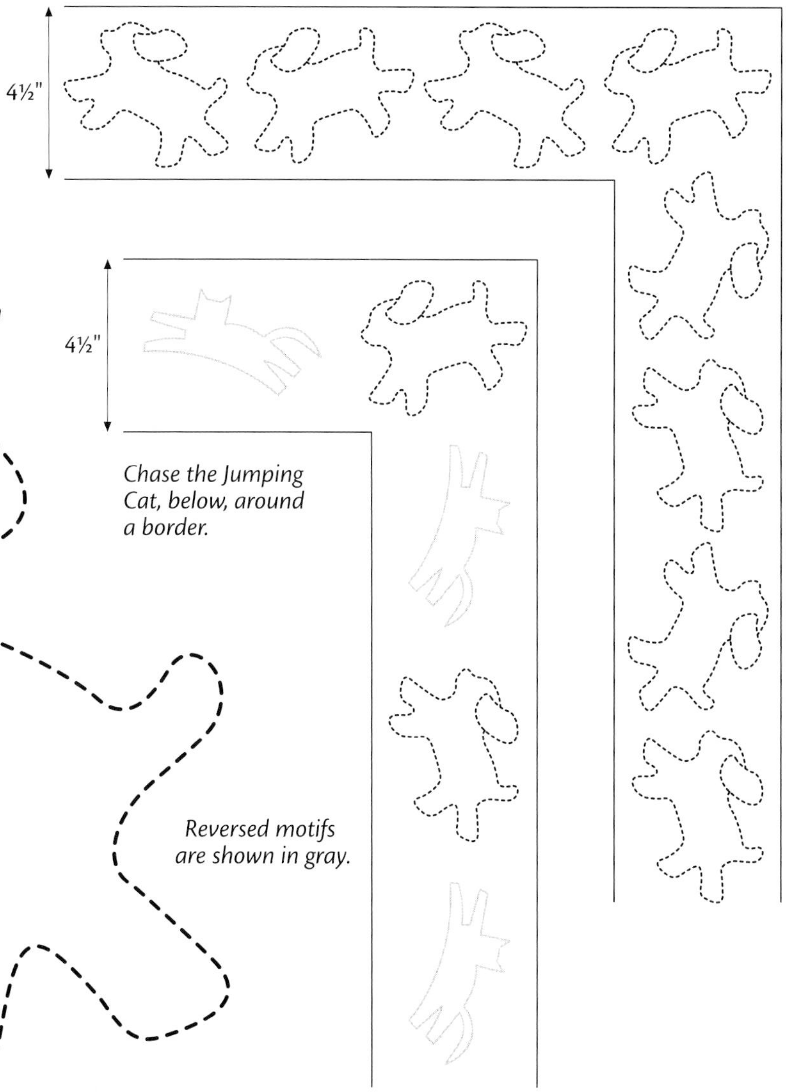

Arrow indicates direction for continuous-line machine quilting.

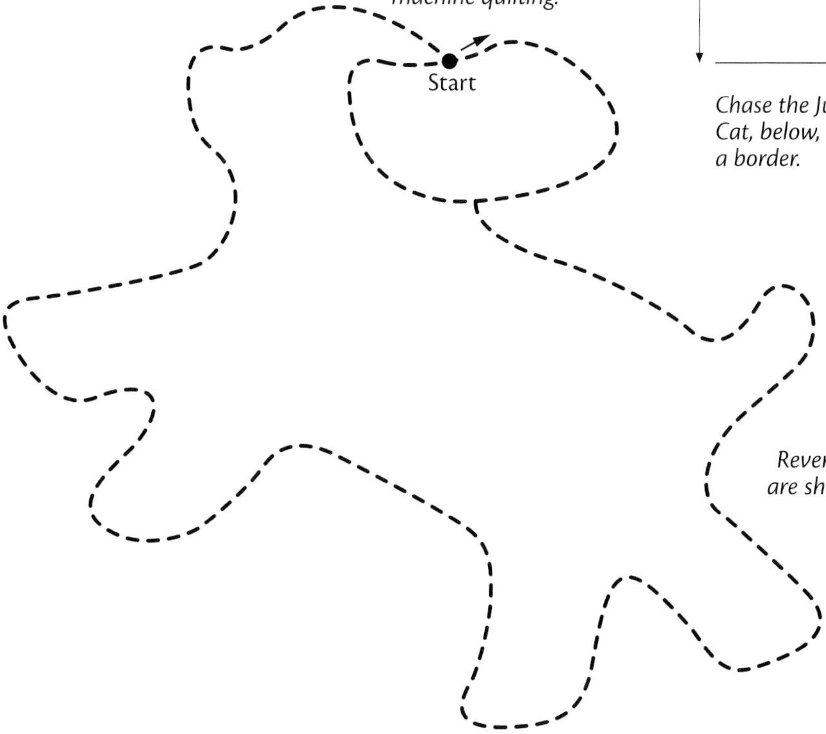

Chase the Jumping Cat, below, around a border.

Reversed motifs are shown in gray.

Jumping Cat

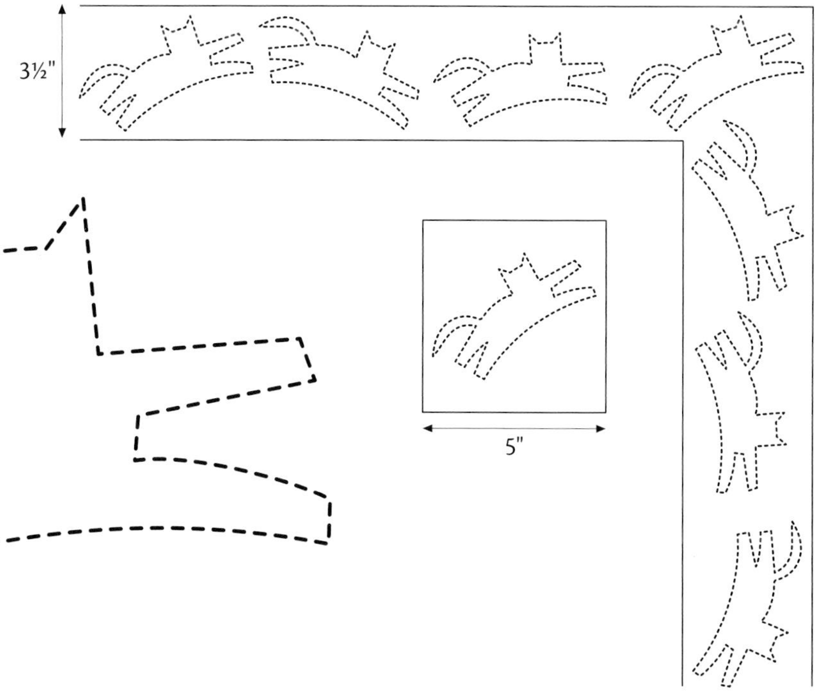

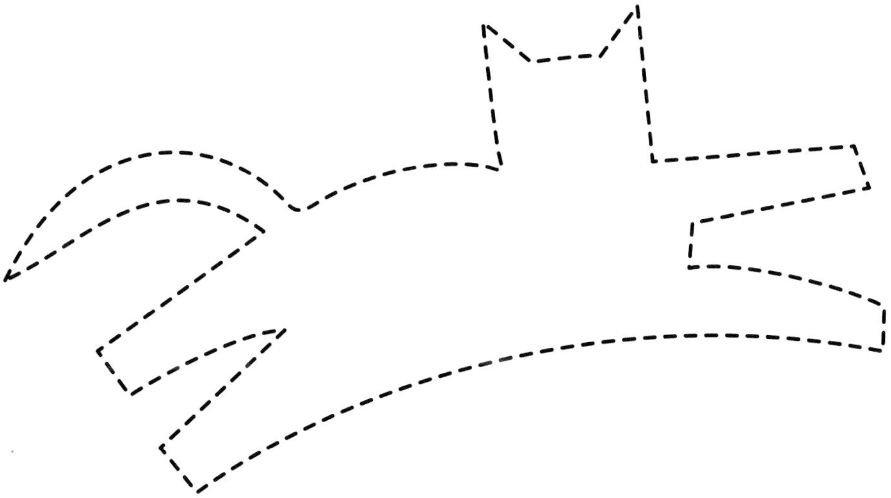

Sheriff's Badge

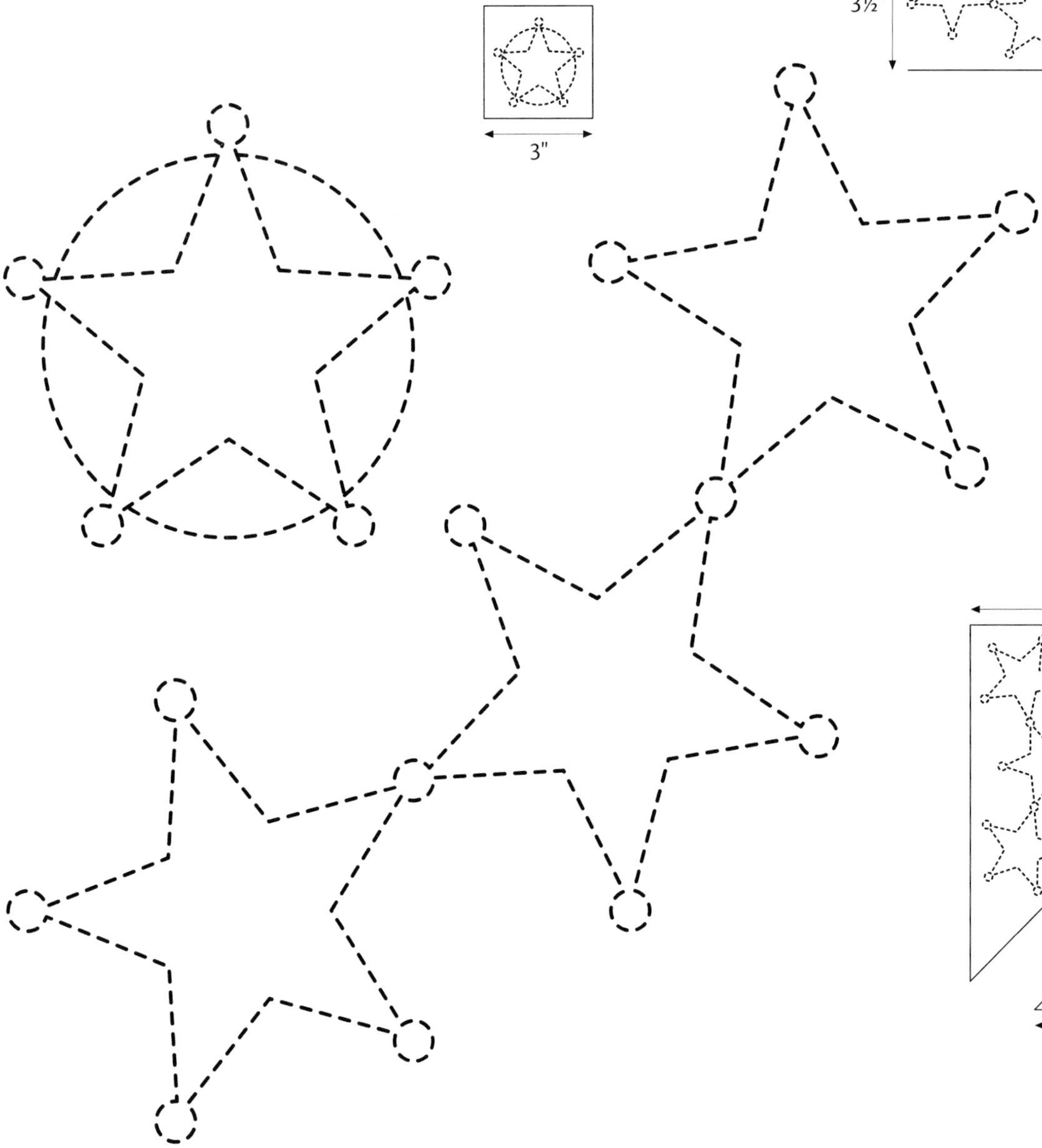

3"

3½"

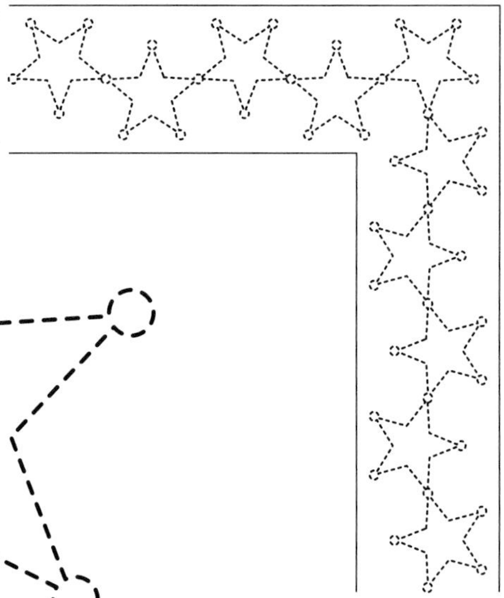

9½"

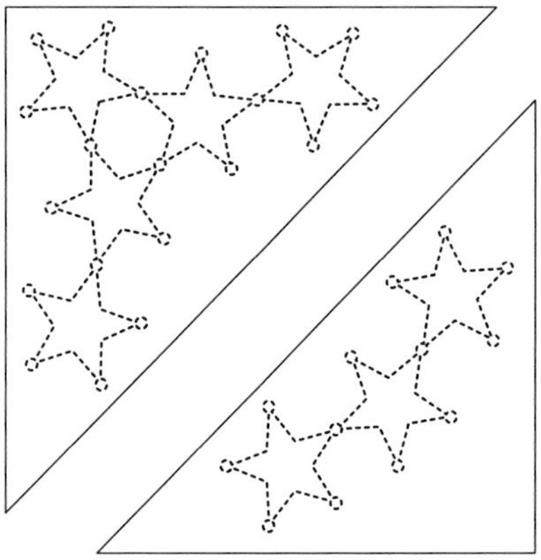

8½"

Crown

4"

7"

8½"

Bicycle

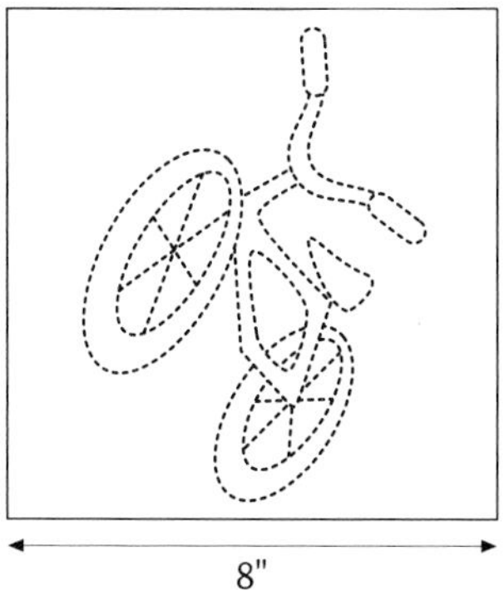

Skateboard

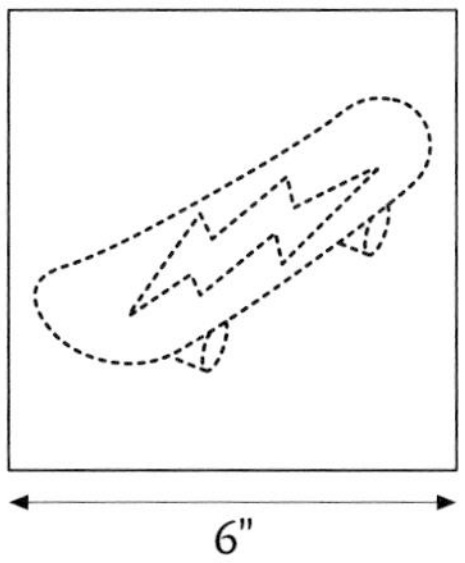

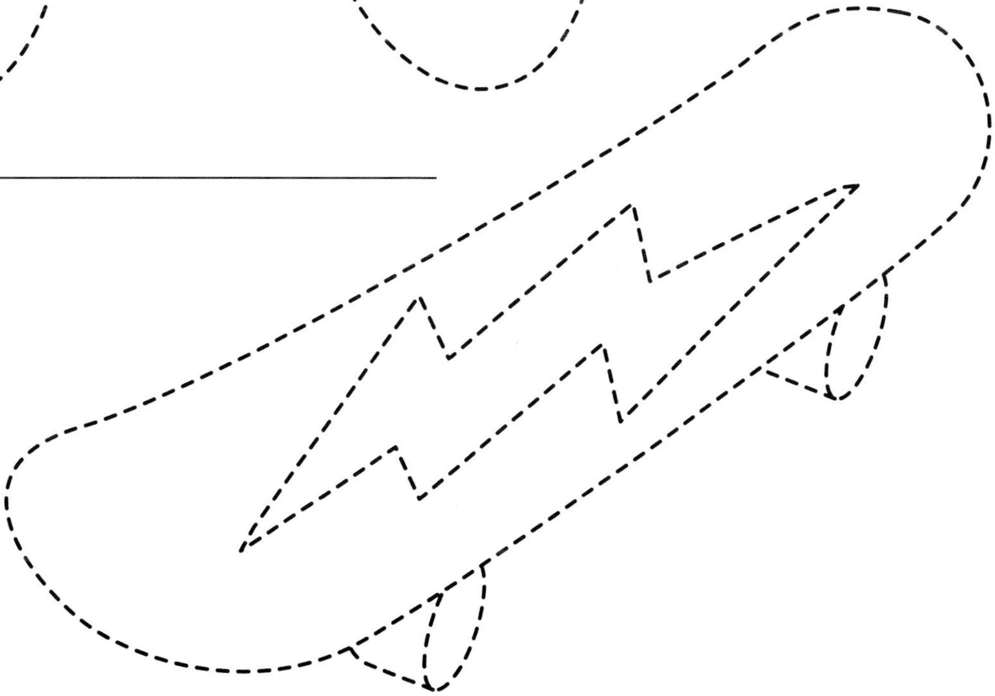

Balloons

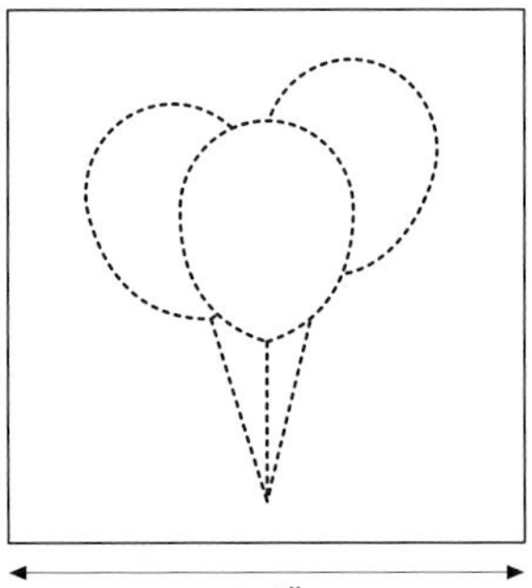

7½"

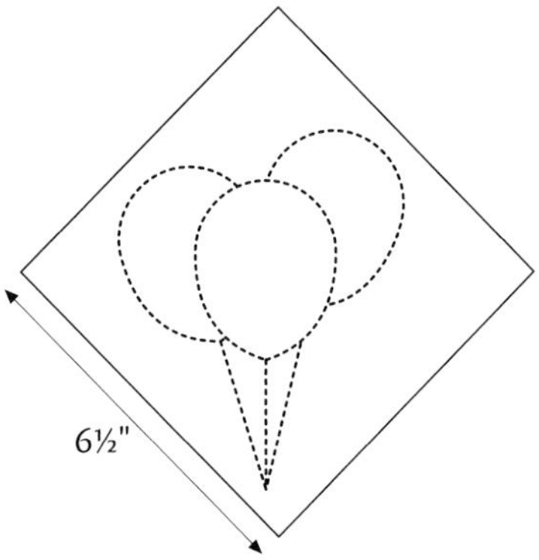

6½"

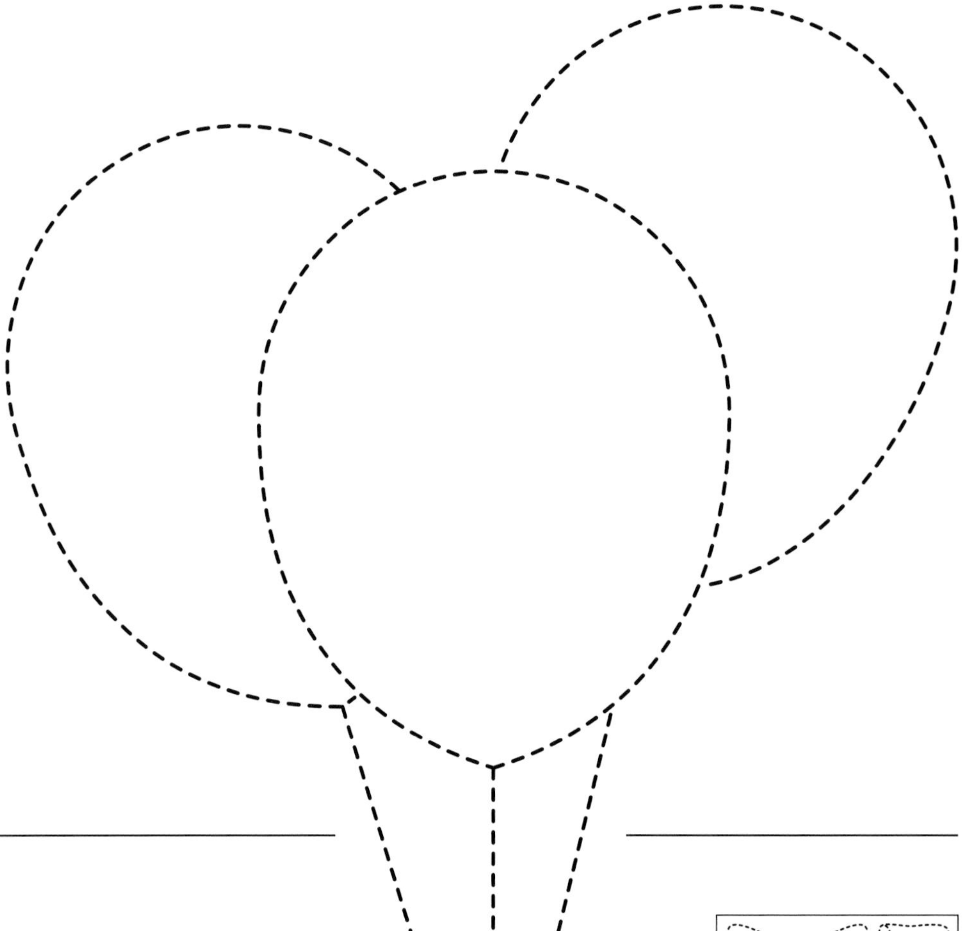

Bonnie Blue Ribbon

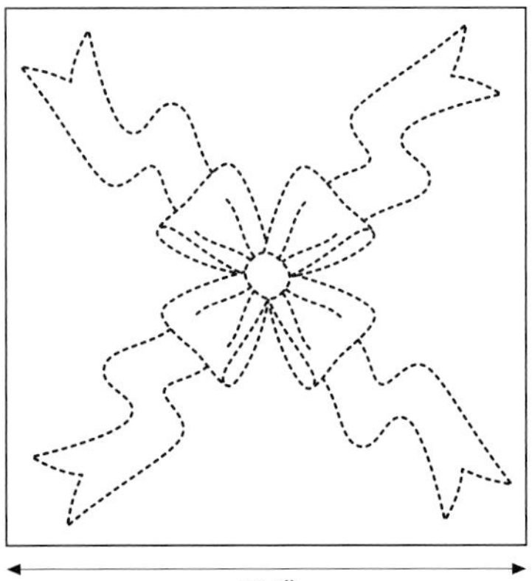

9½"

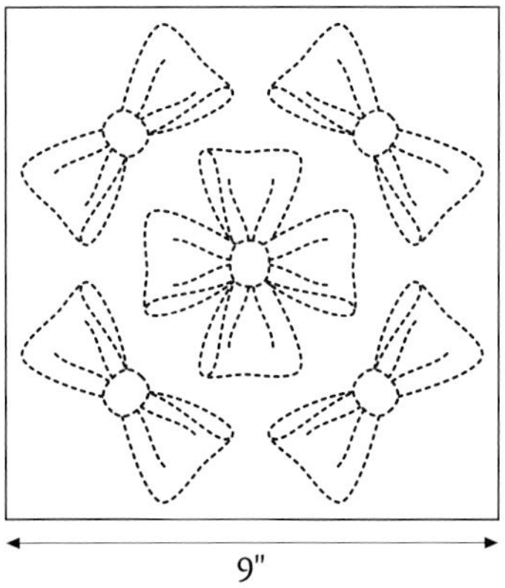

9"

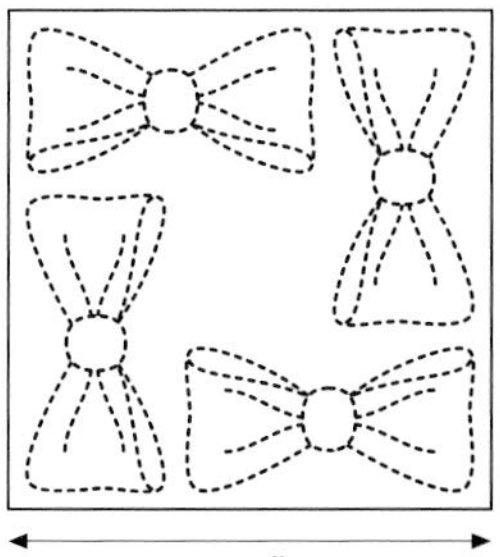

6½"

2½"

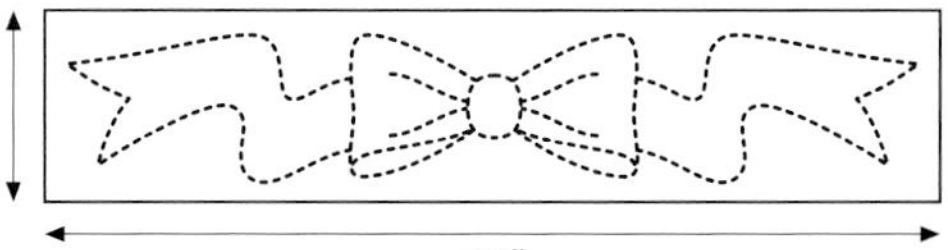

12"

2½"

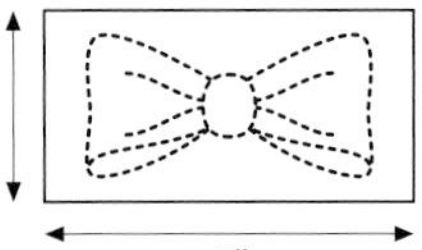

5"

2½"

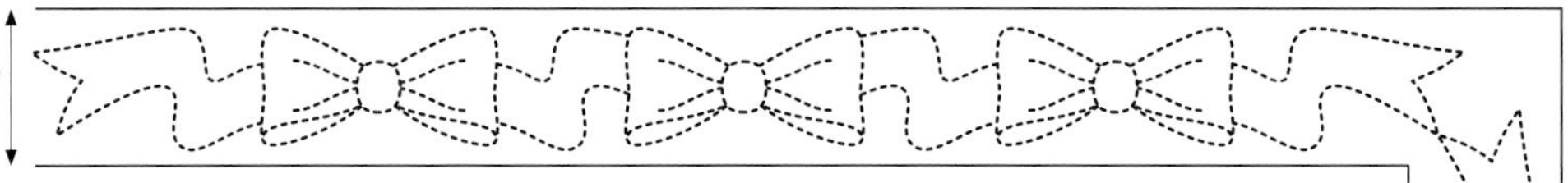

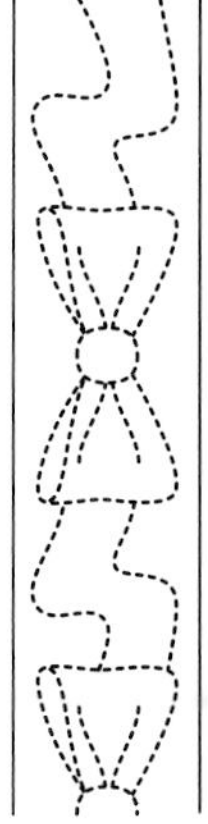

Place folded paper on dotted line, trace, and flip for full motif.

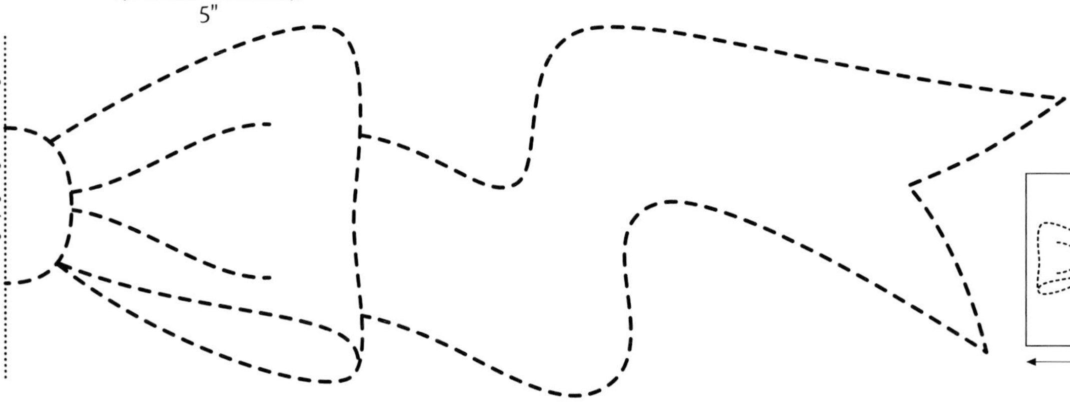

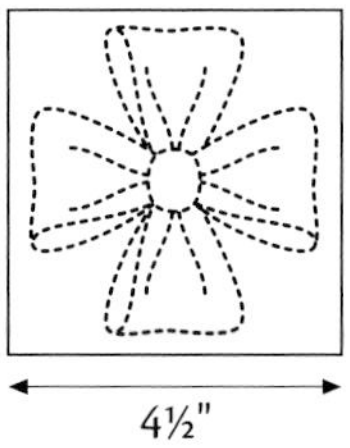

4½"

Two Bunnies

5½"

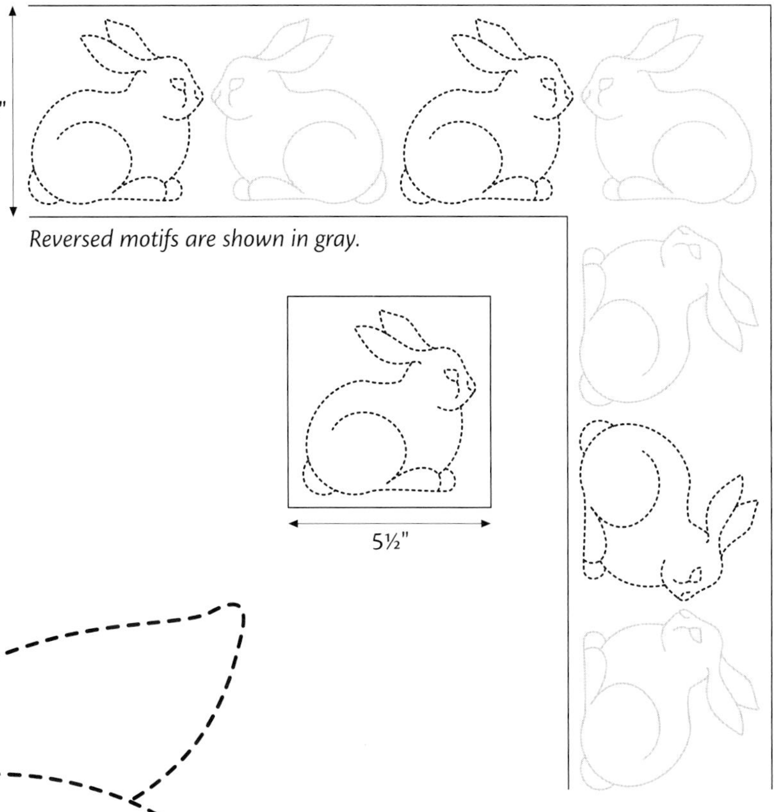

Reversed motifs are shown in gray.

8"

5½"

Butterfly

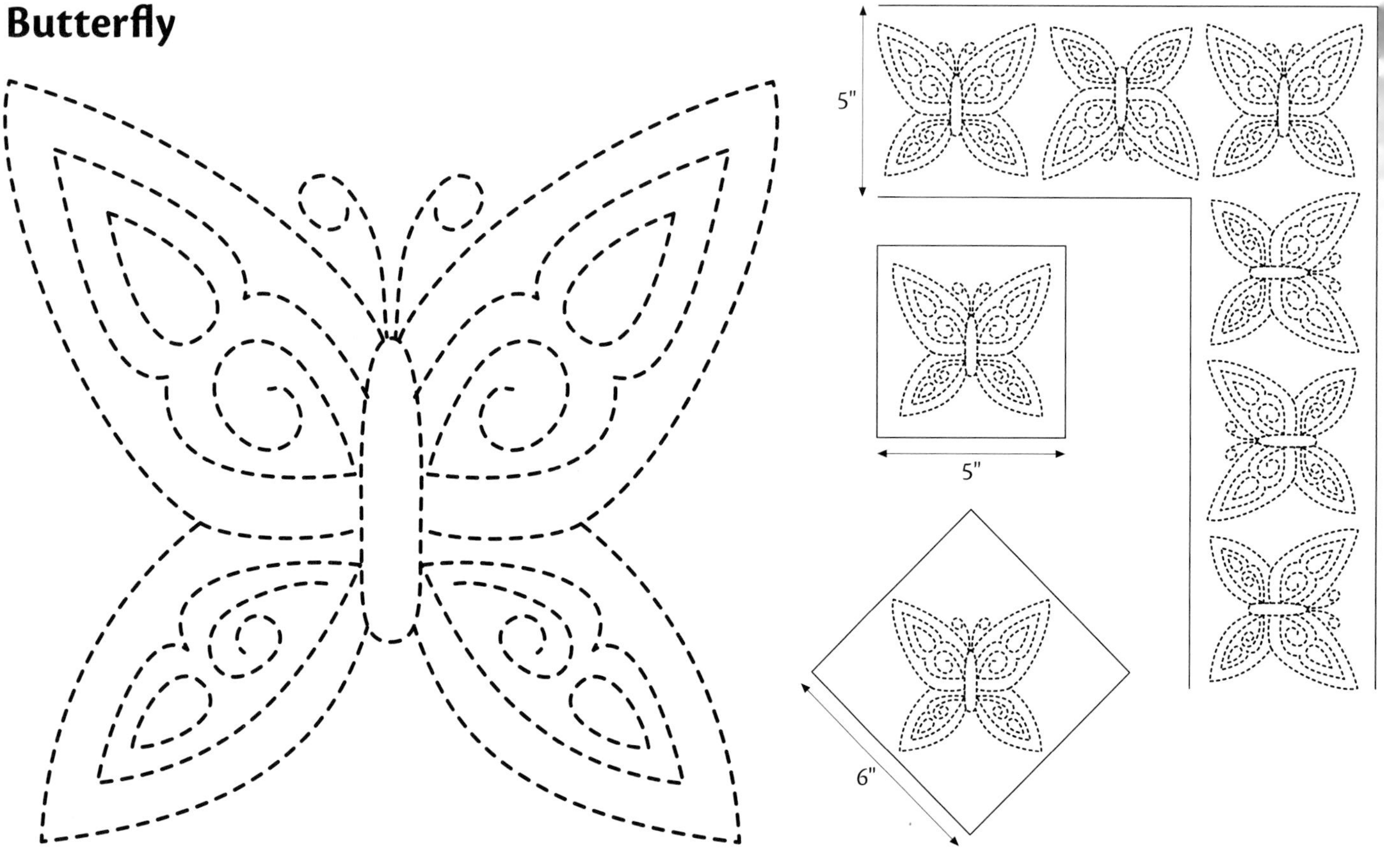

Shooting Stars

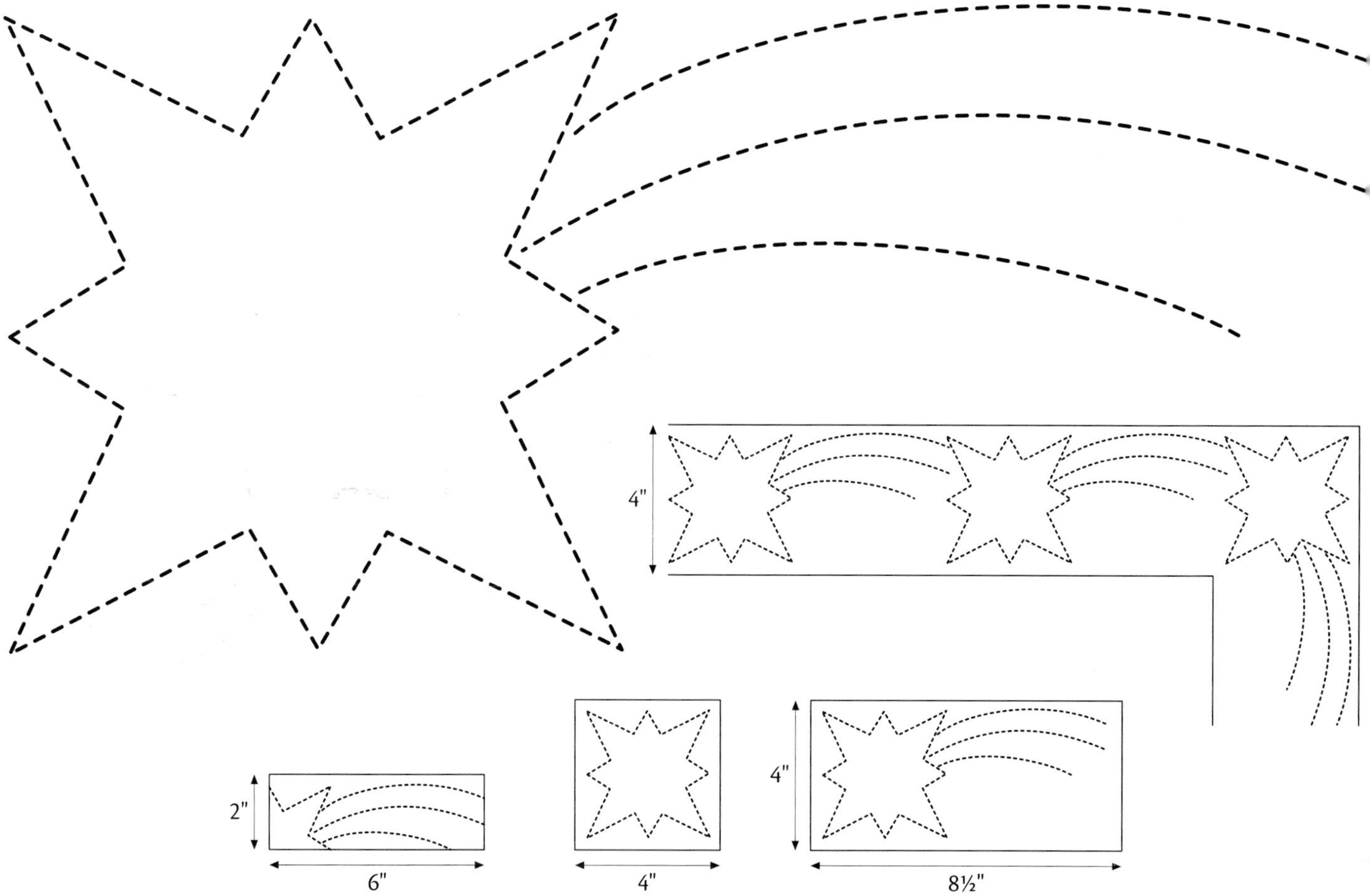

Penguin on Ice

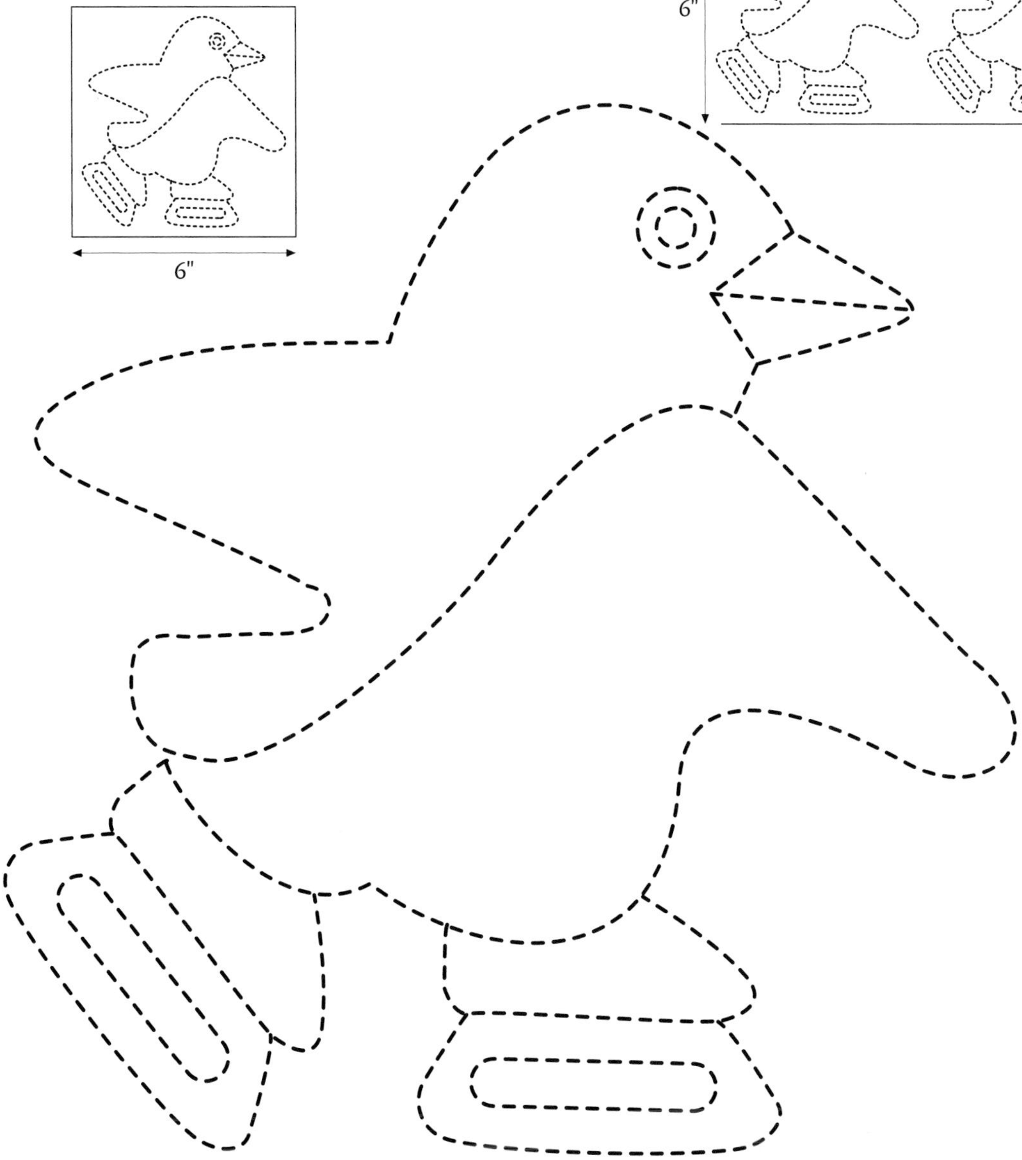

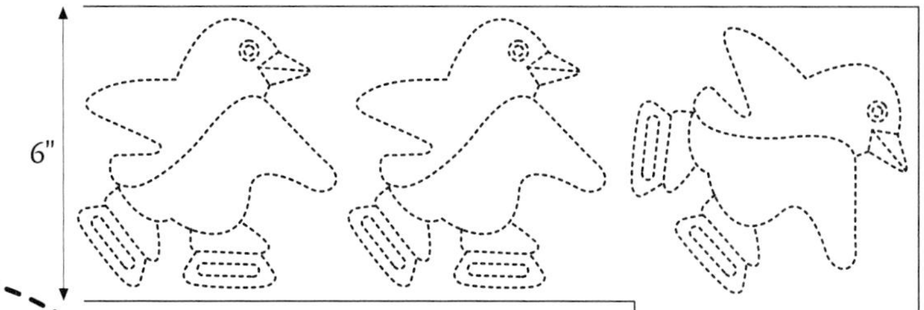

Comet

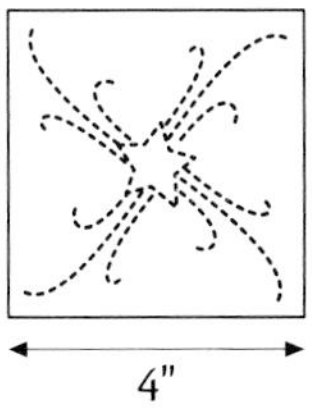

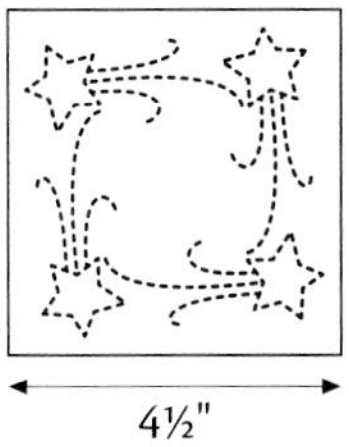

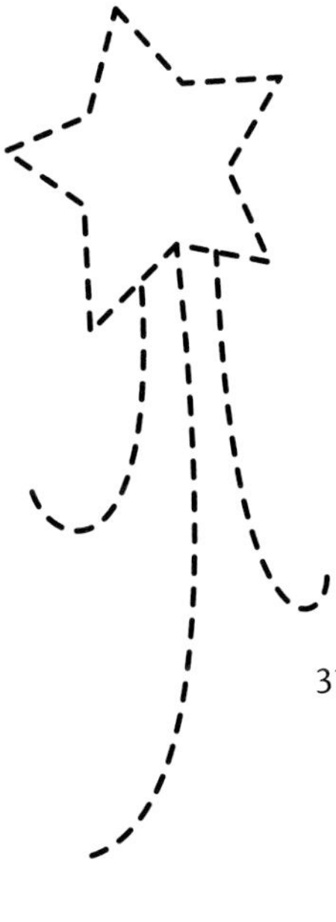

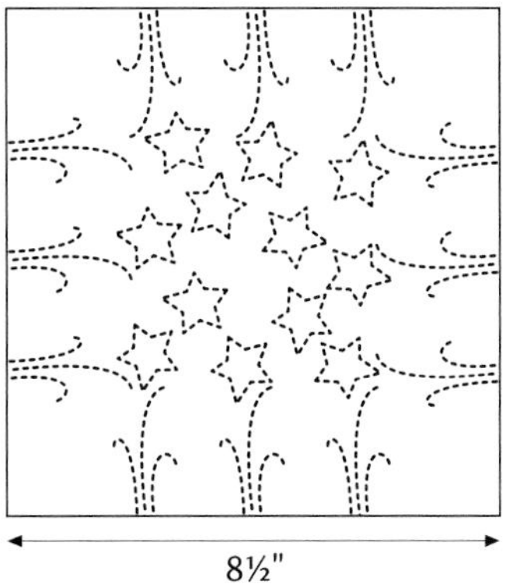

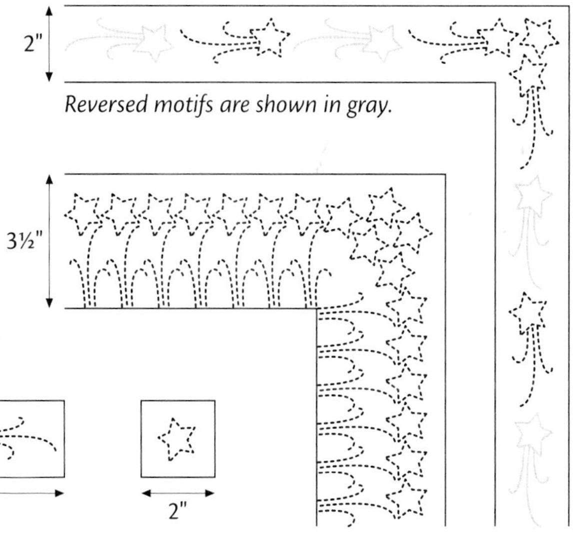

Reversed motifs are shown in gray.

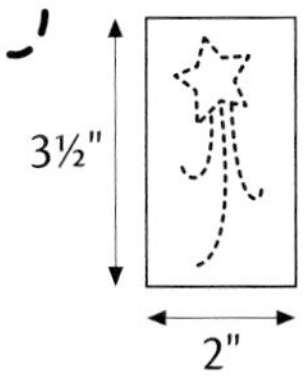

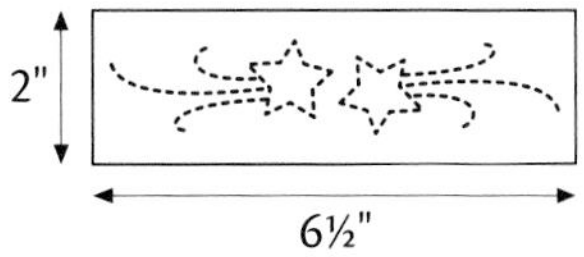

Little Star

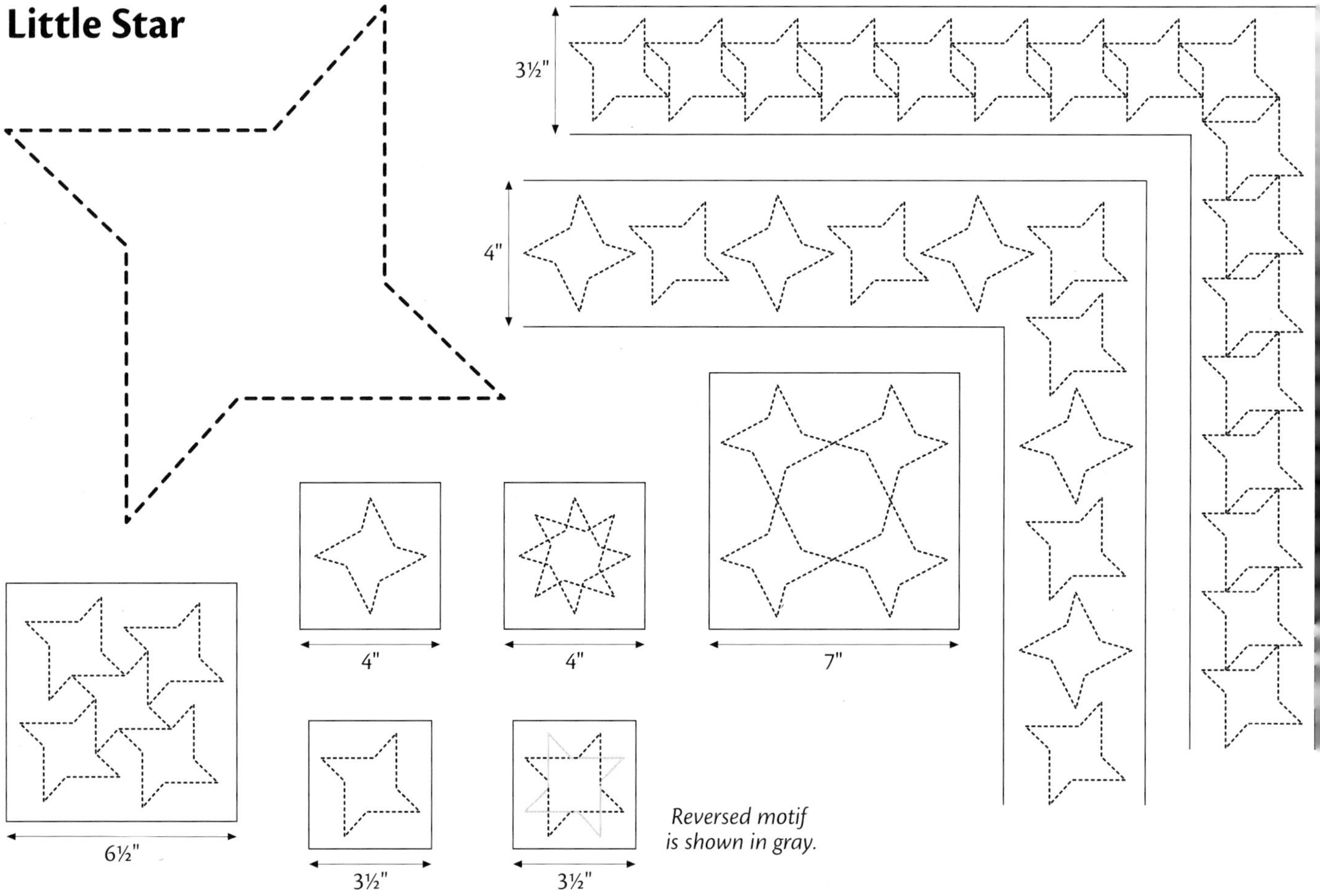
3½"
4"
4"
4"
7"
6½"
3½"
3½"

Reversed motif is shown in gray.

Sizzle

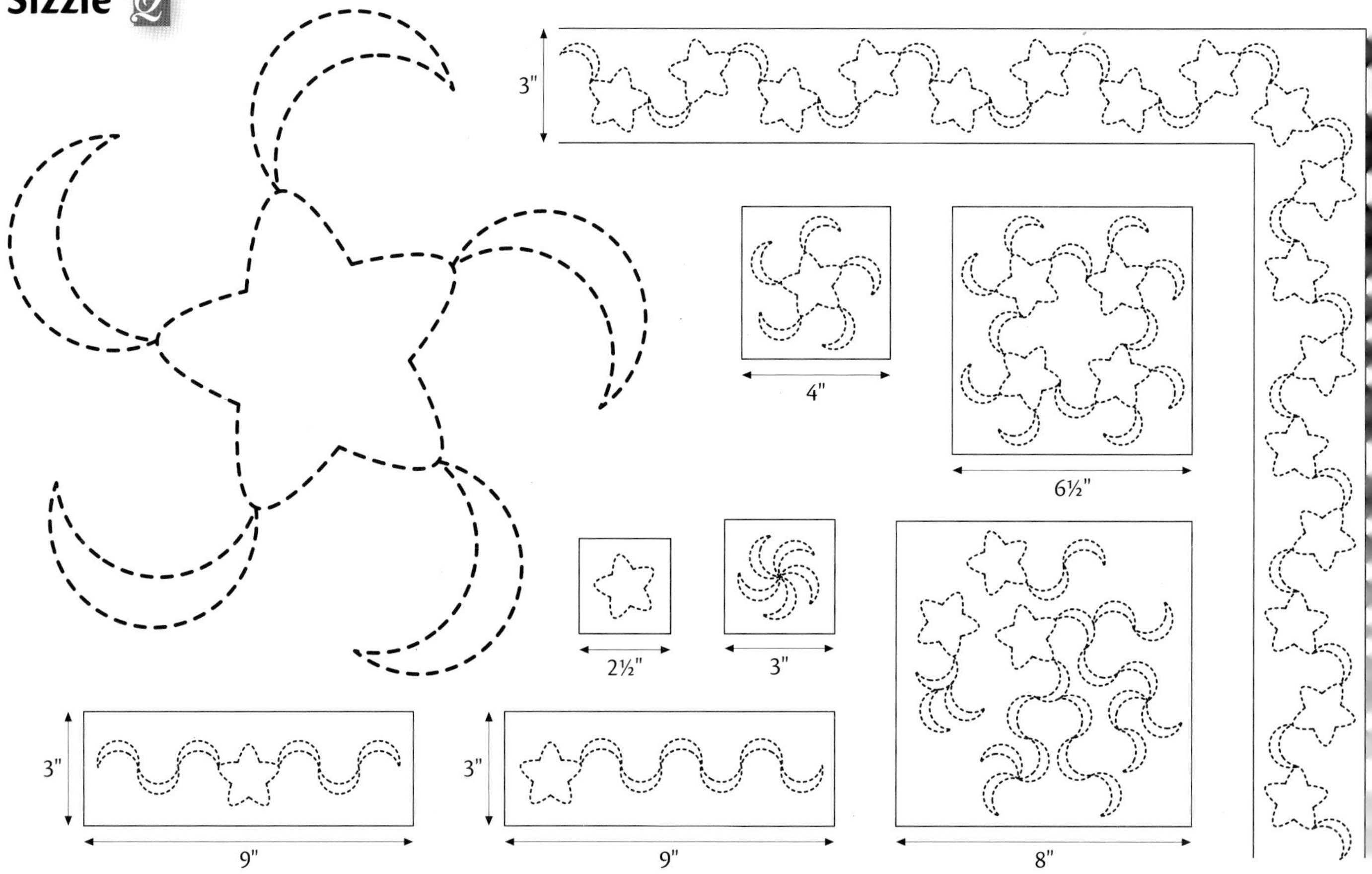
3"
4"
6½"
2½"
3"
3"
9"
3"
9"
8"

Fizz Hearts

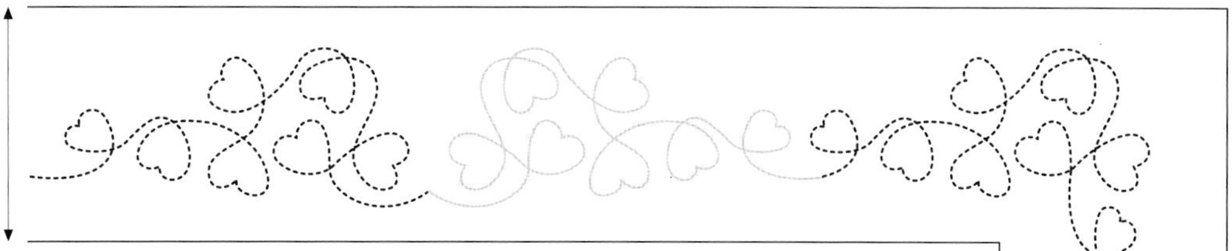

Reversed motifs are shown in gray.

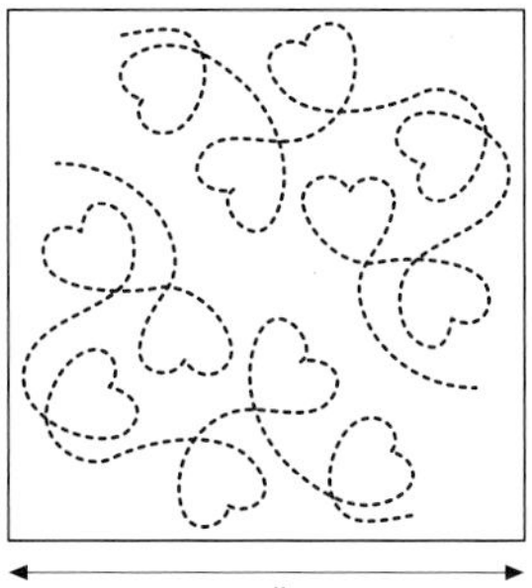

7"

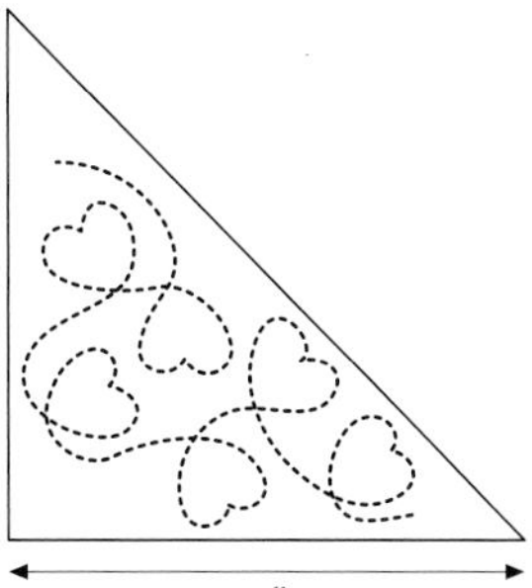

7"

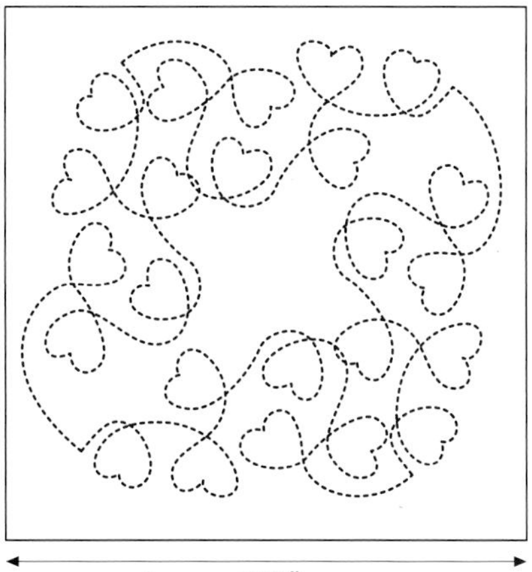

10½"

Fluttering By

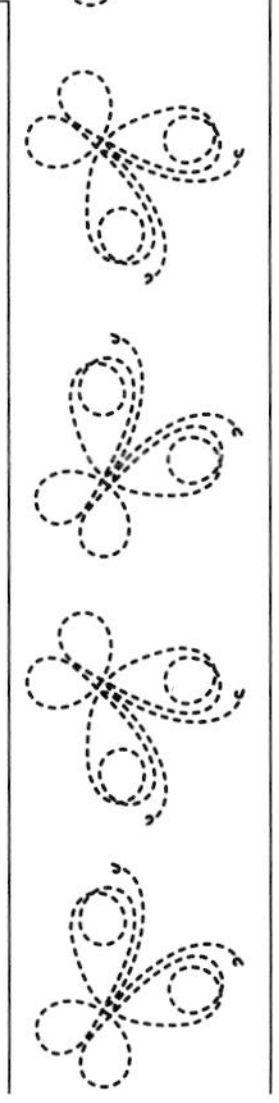

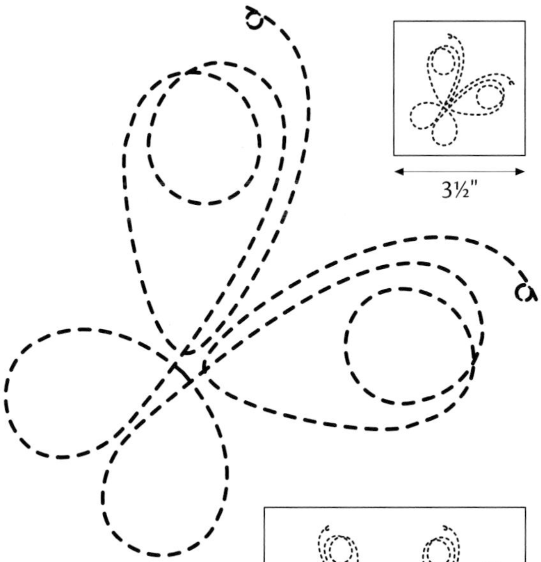

3½"

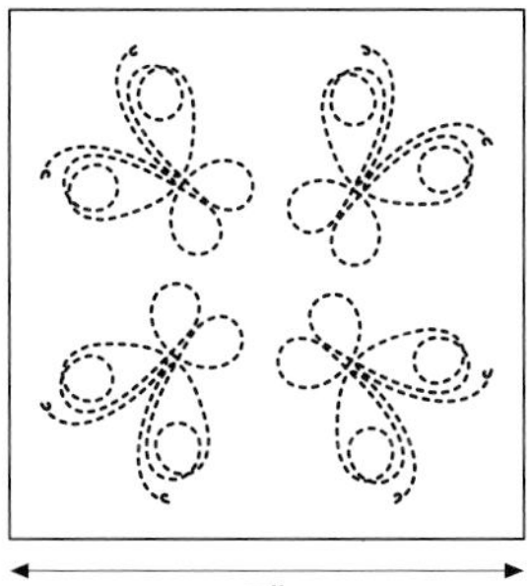

7"

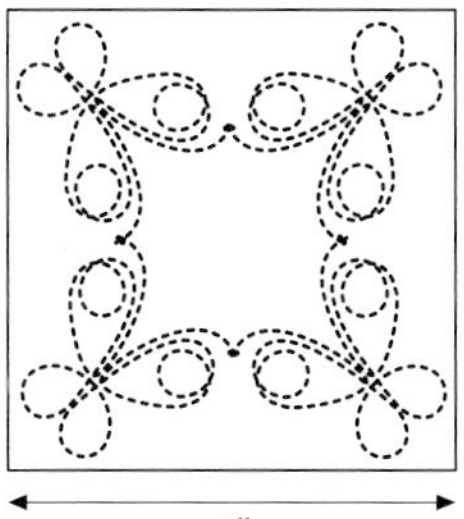

6"

Butterfly Dance

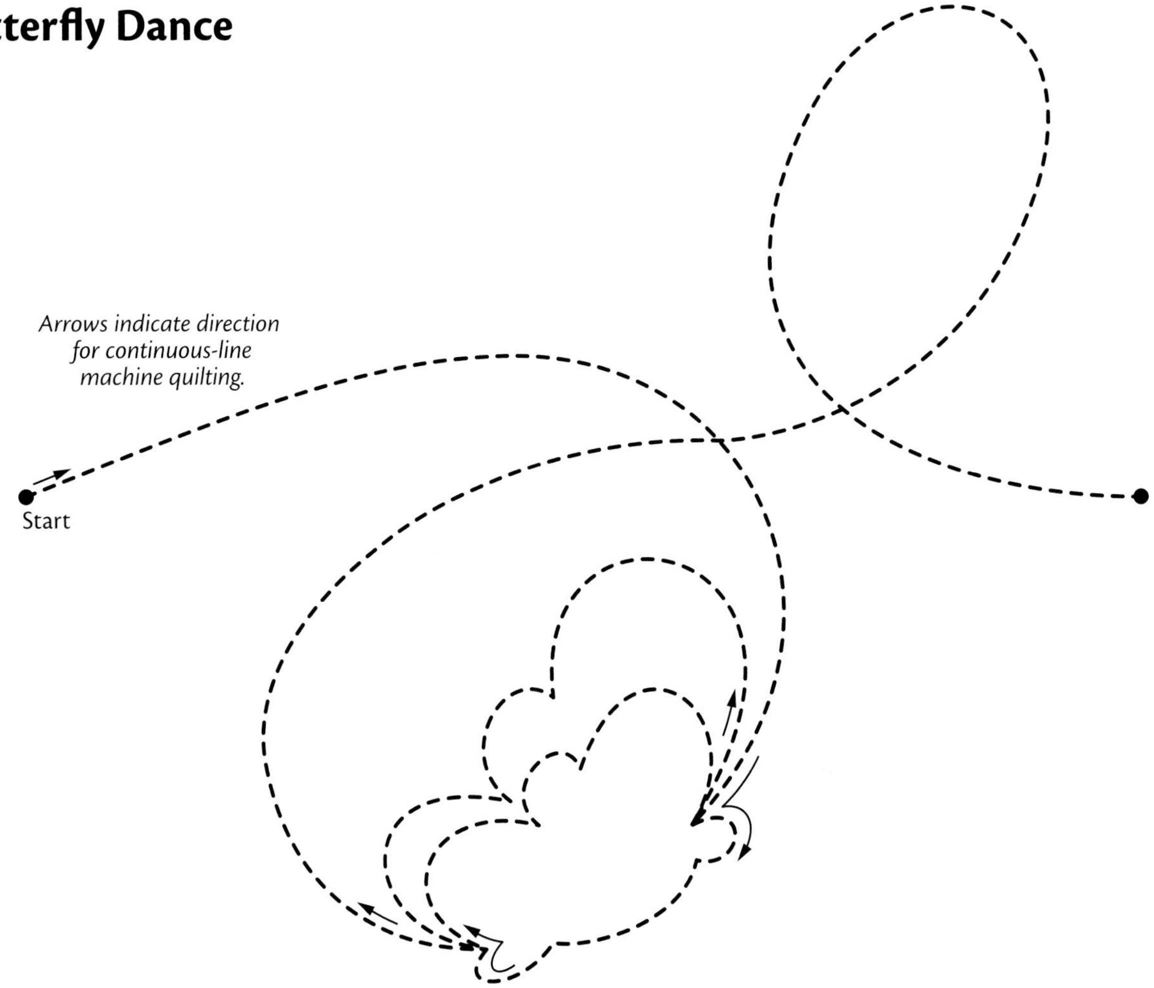

Arrows indicate direction for continuous-line machine quilting.
Start

Reversed motifs are shown in gray.

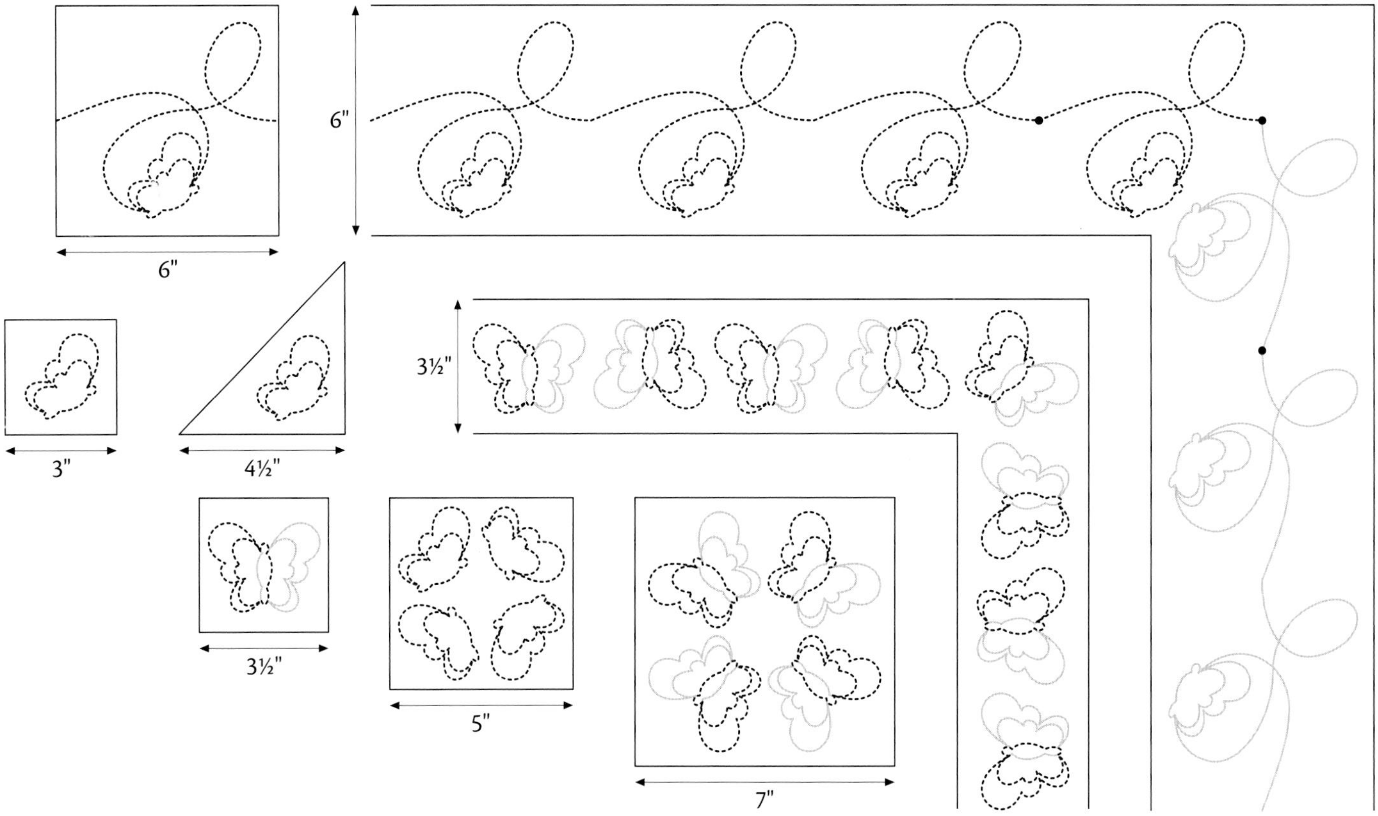

6"
6"
3"
4½"
3½"
3½"
5"
7"

Setting Sail

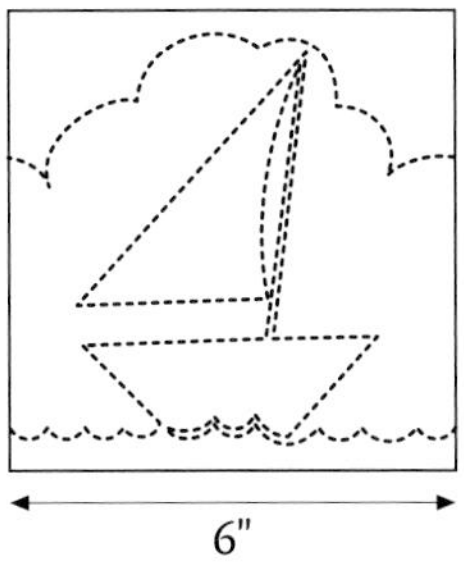

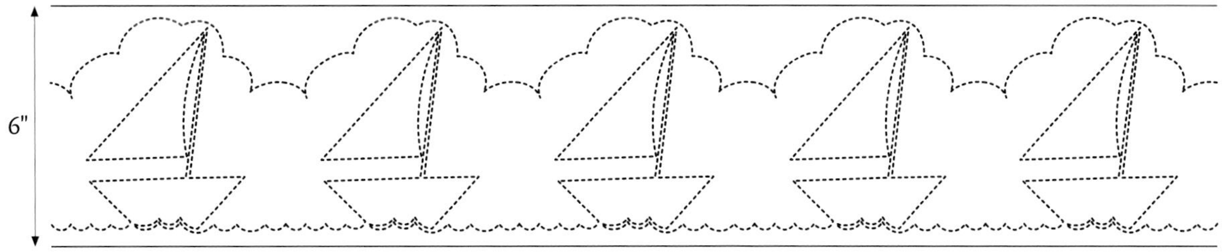

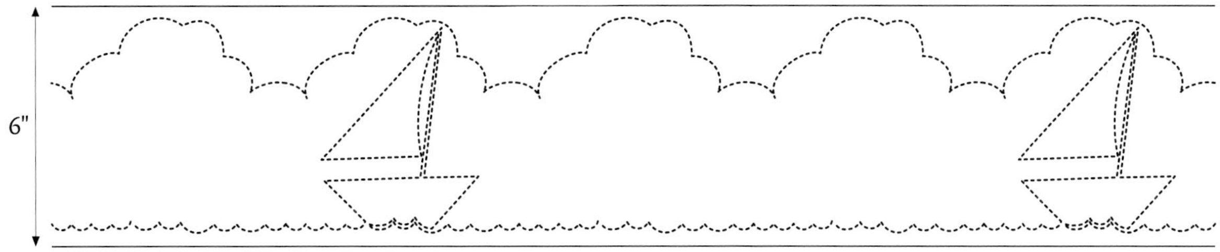

Dog Bone

3½"

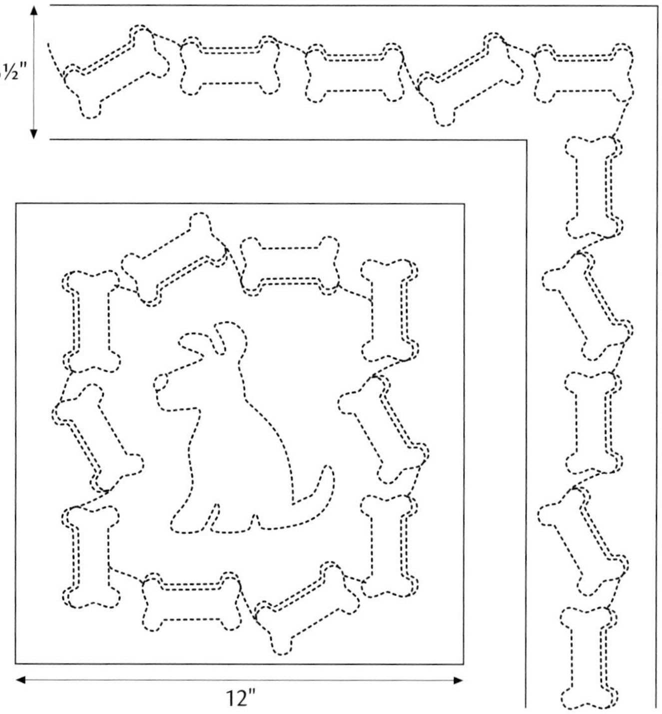

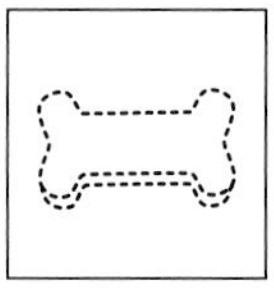

3½"

12"

Combine the Dog Bone motif with Dog, below.

Dog

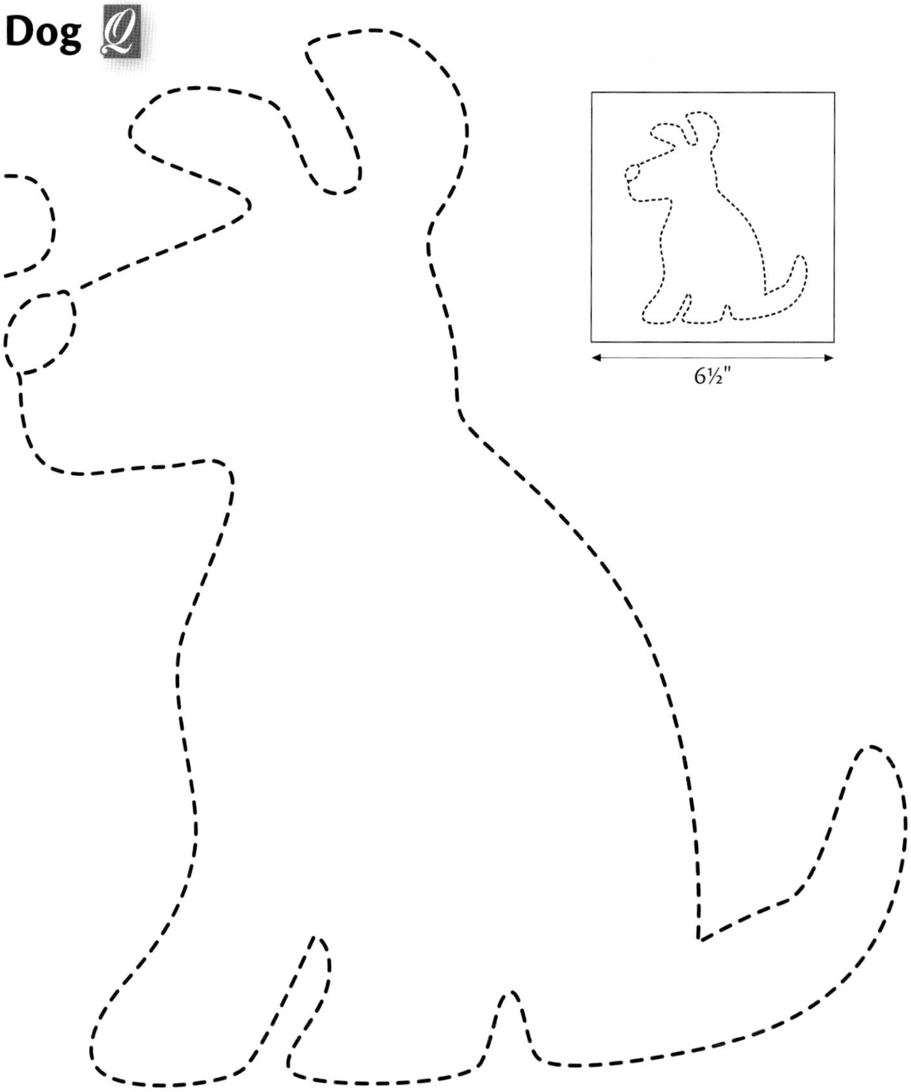

6½"

Flying Colors

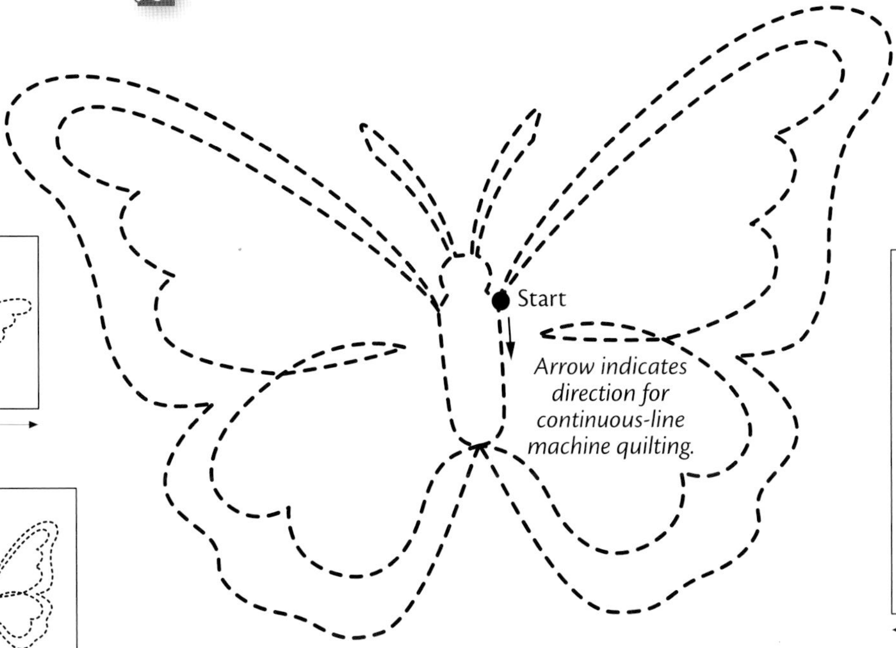
Start
Arrow indicates direction for continuous-line machine quilting.

5½"

4½"

5½"

9½"

3½"

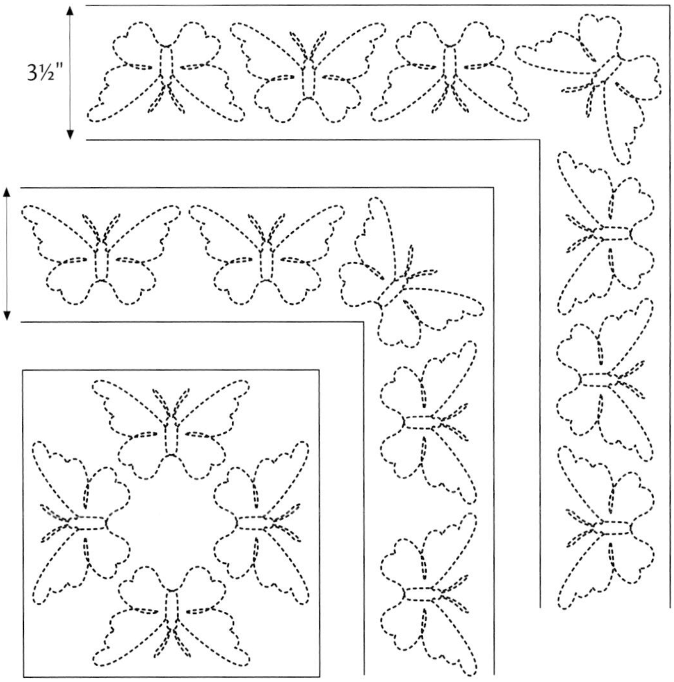

3½"

8"

8½"

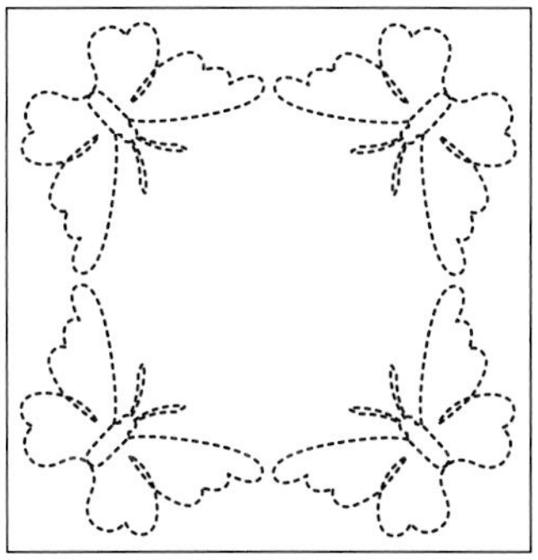

8½"

Owl

5½"

Silver Plume

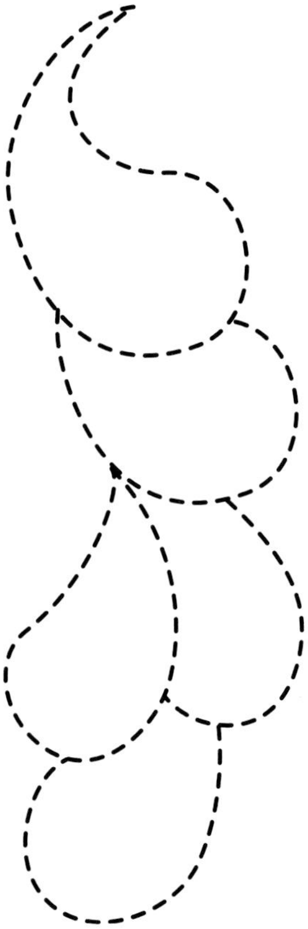

2"
2"
4"
9"

Reversed motifs are shown in gray.

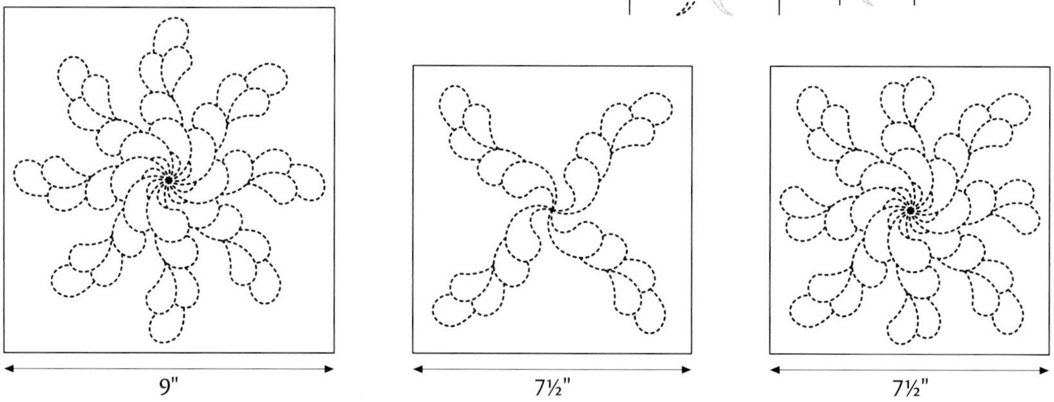
9"
7½"
7½"

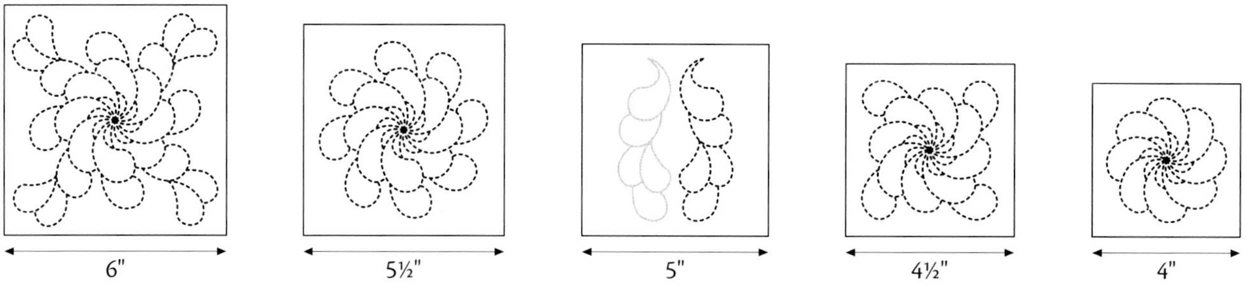
6"
5½"
5"
4½"
4"

Cocheco

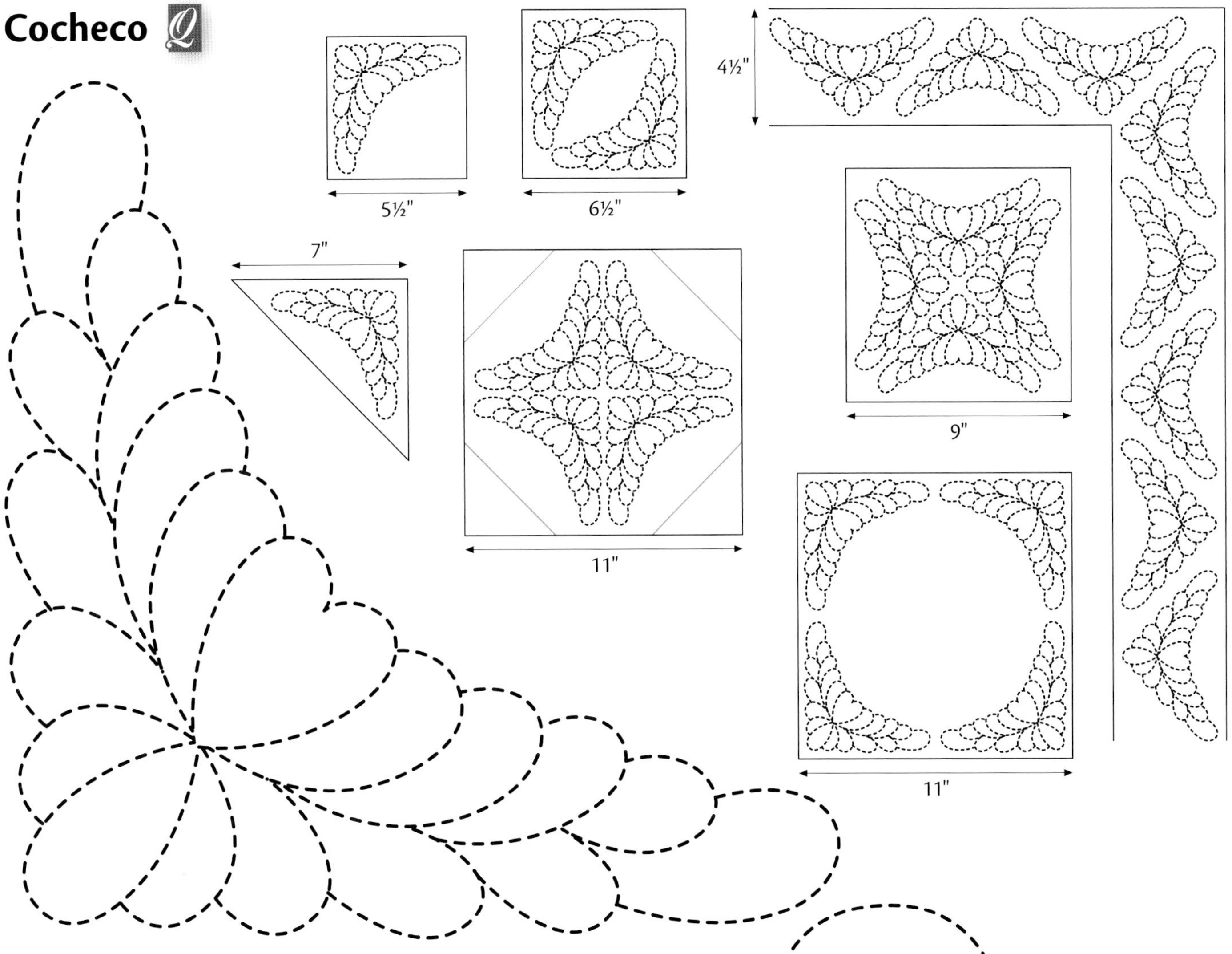
5½"
6½"
4½"
7"
11"
9"
11"

Scalloped Teardrop

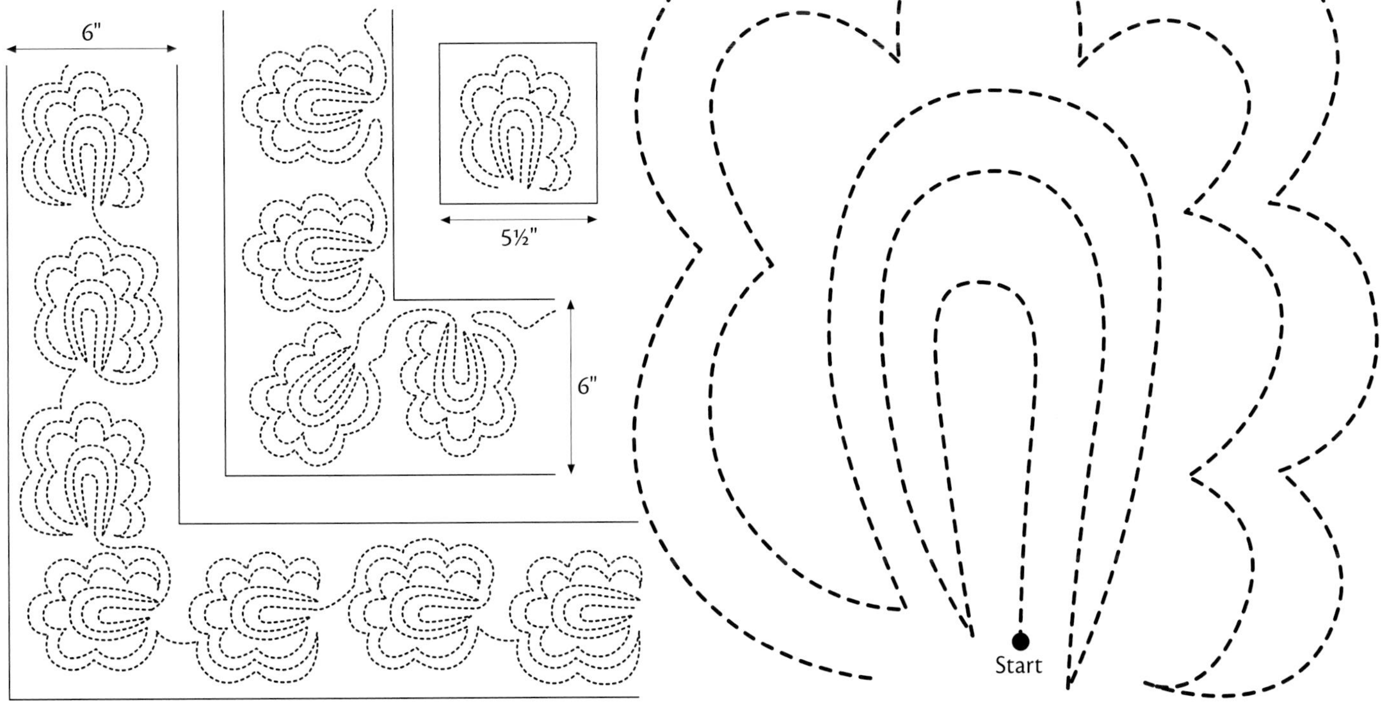
6"
5½"
6"
Start

Double Feather Wreath

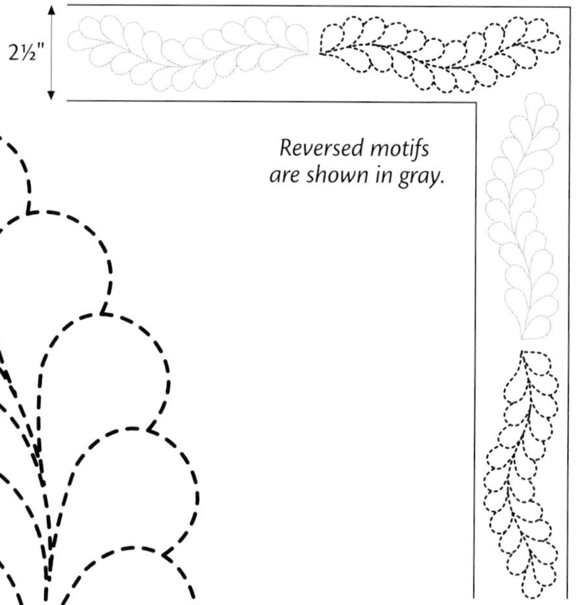

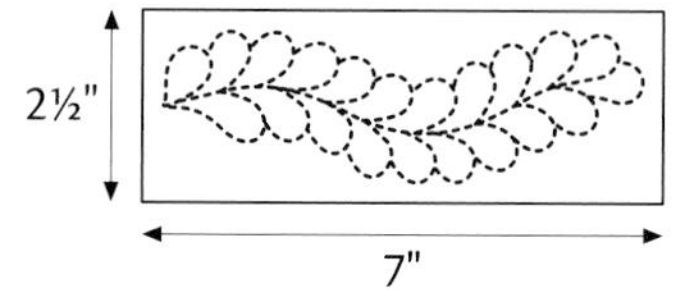

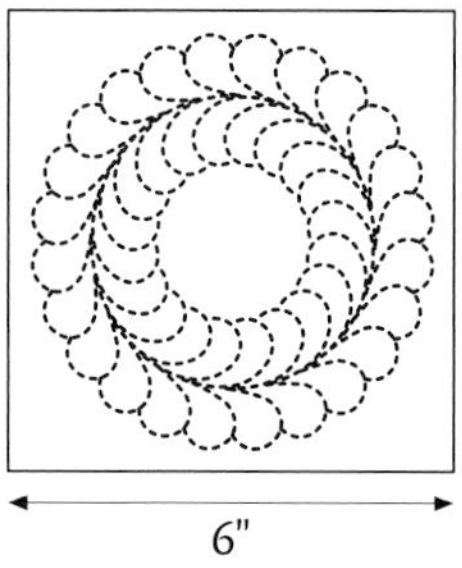

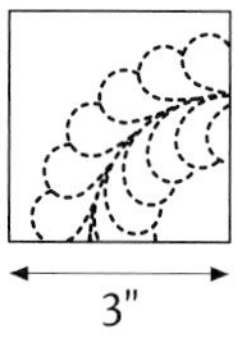

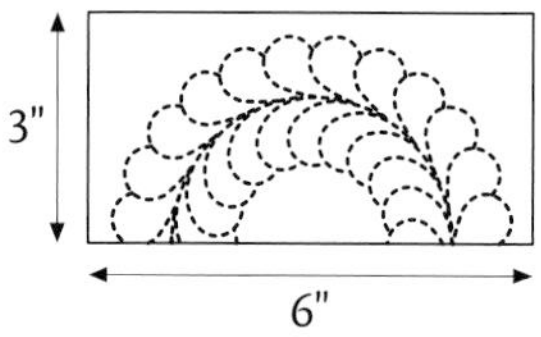

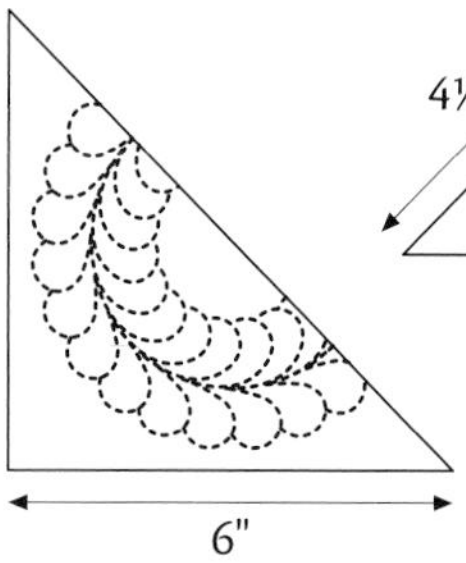

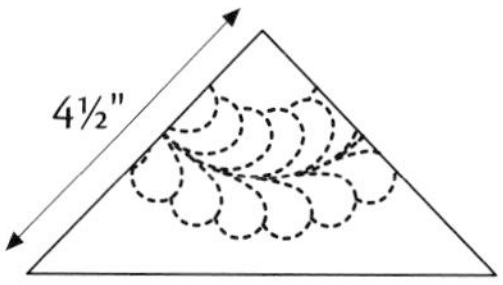

Fancy Feathers

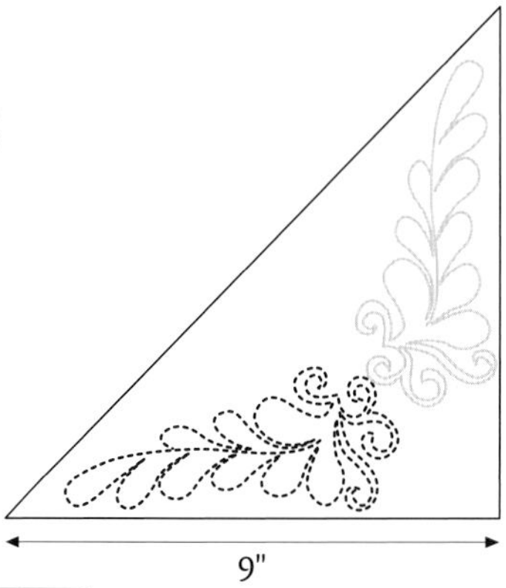

Reversed motifs are shown in gray.

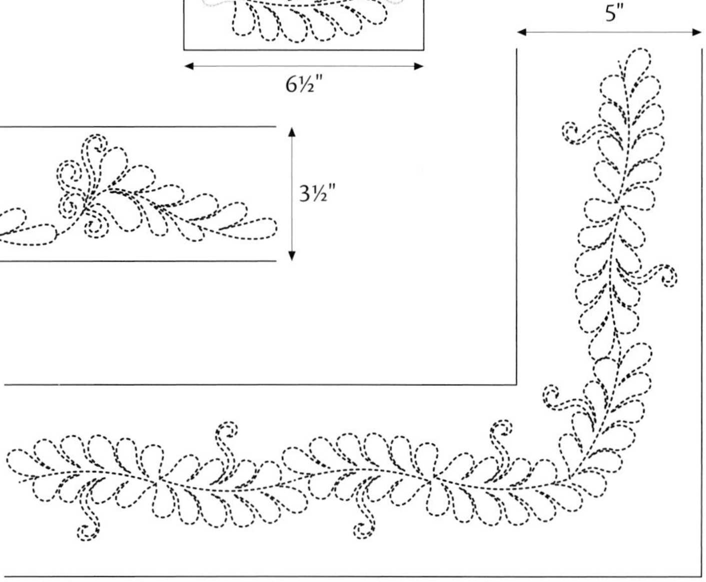

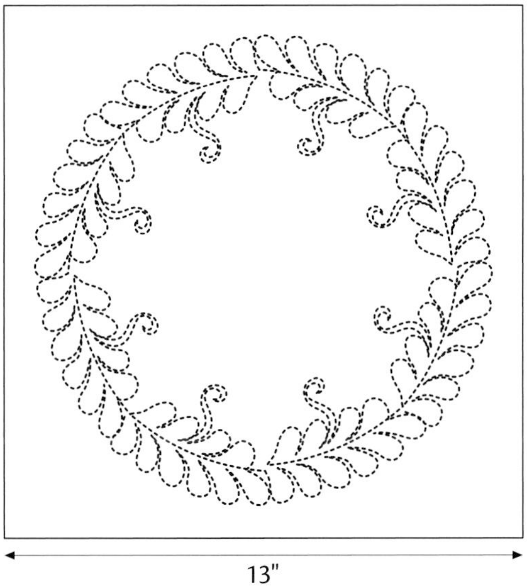

Fanfare

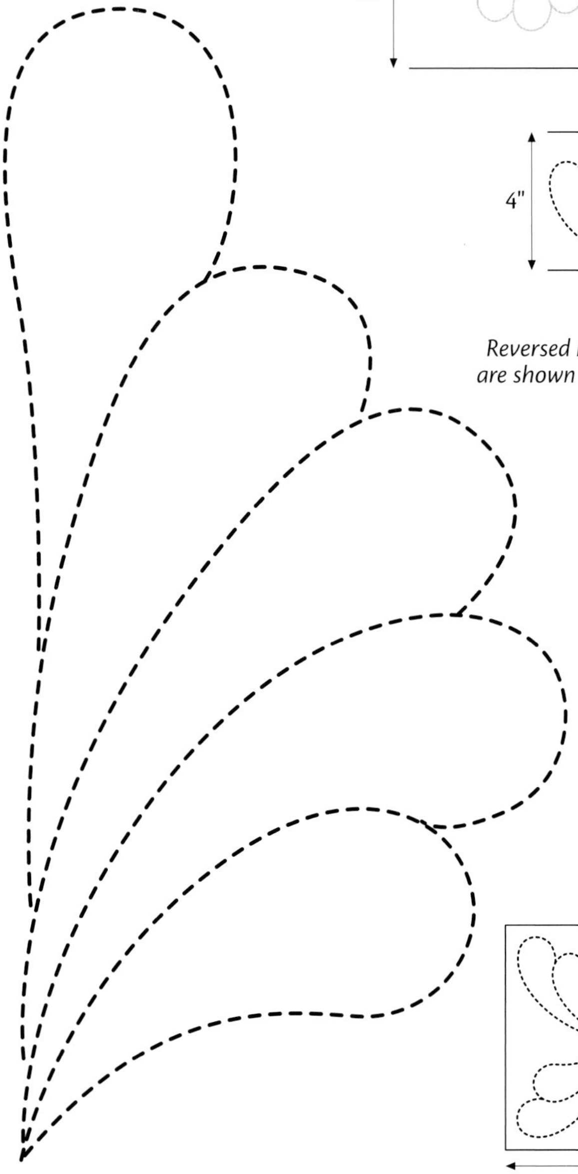

Reversed motifs are shown in gray.

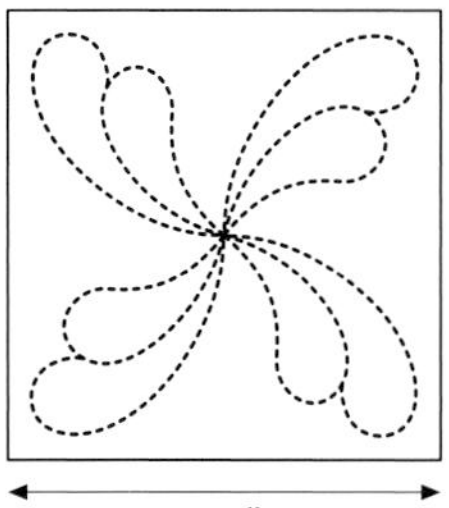

6½"

12"

15"

10"

12"

Feathered Cable

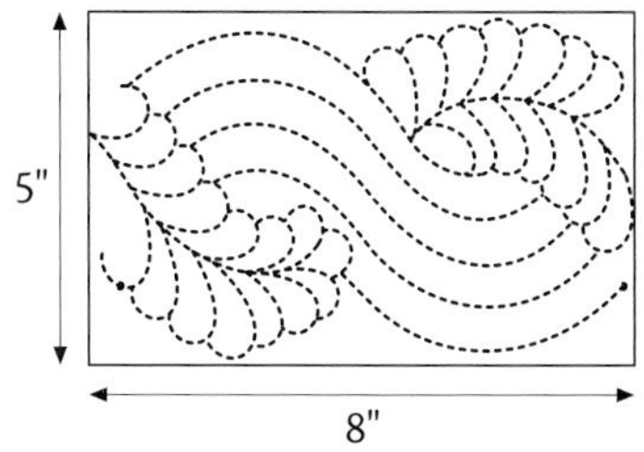

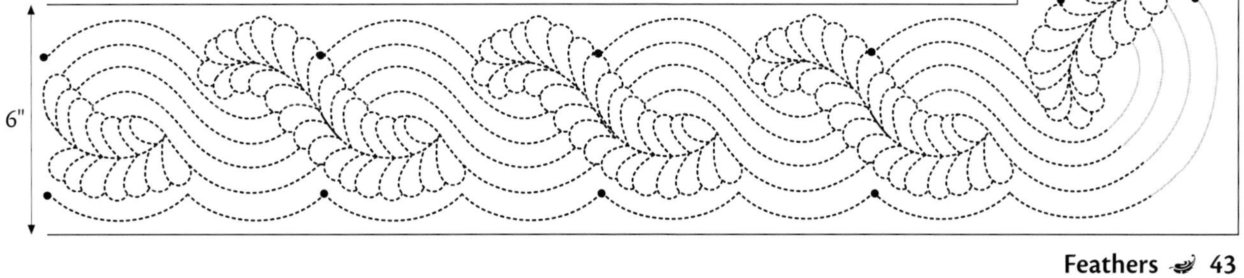

Feather Heart

Place folded paper on dotted line, trace, and flip for full motif.
5"
9½"
9½"
6"
4"
17"
9½"
13½"

Feather Plume

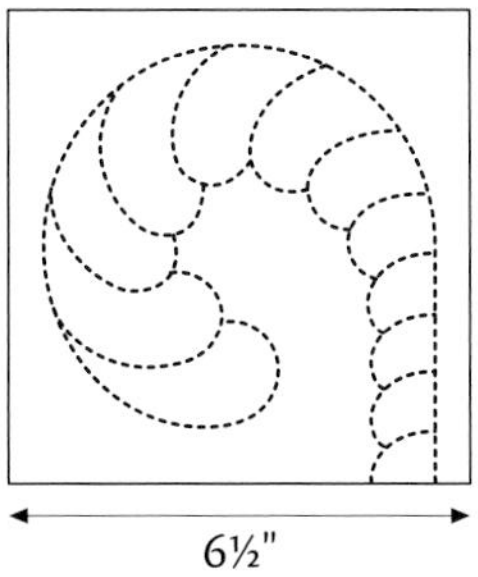

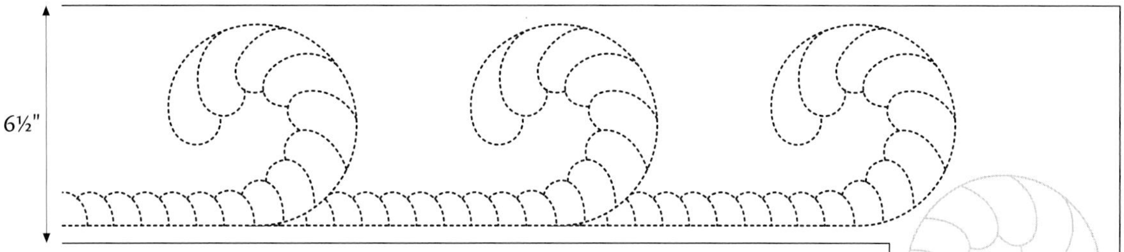

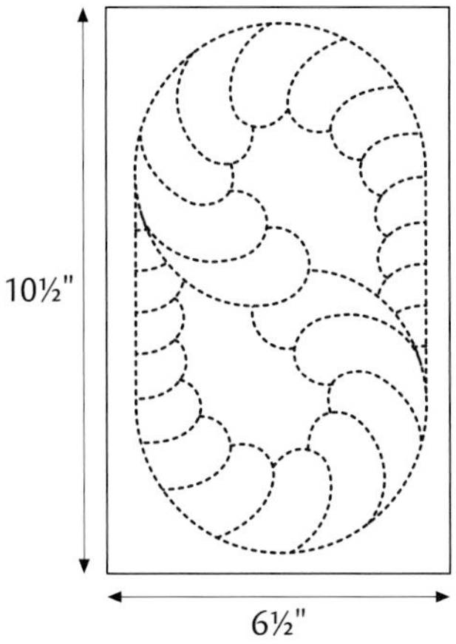

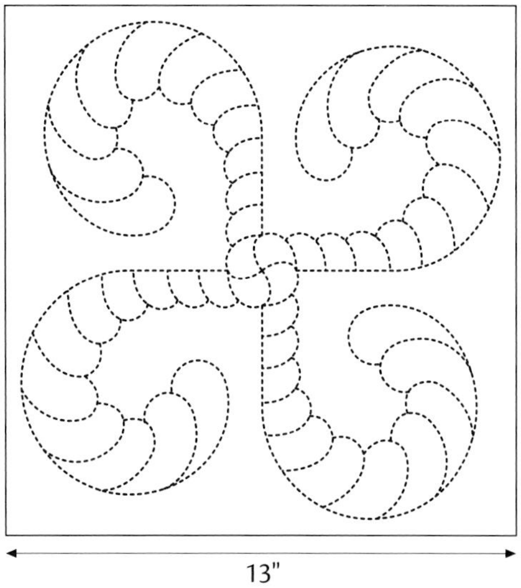

Reversed motifs are shown in gray.

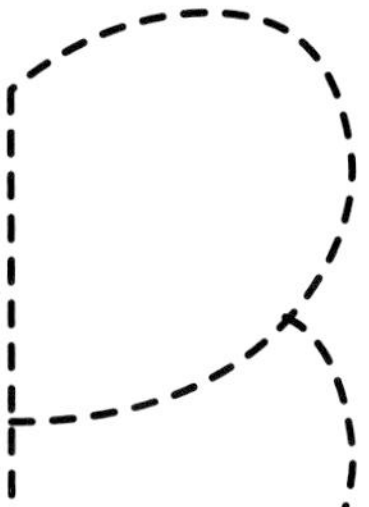

Feather Spray

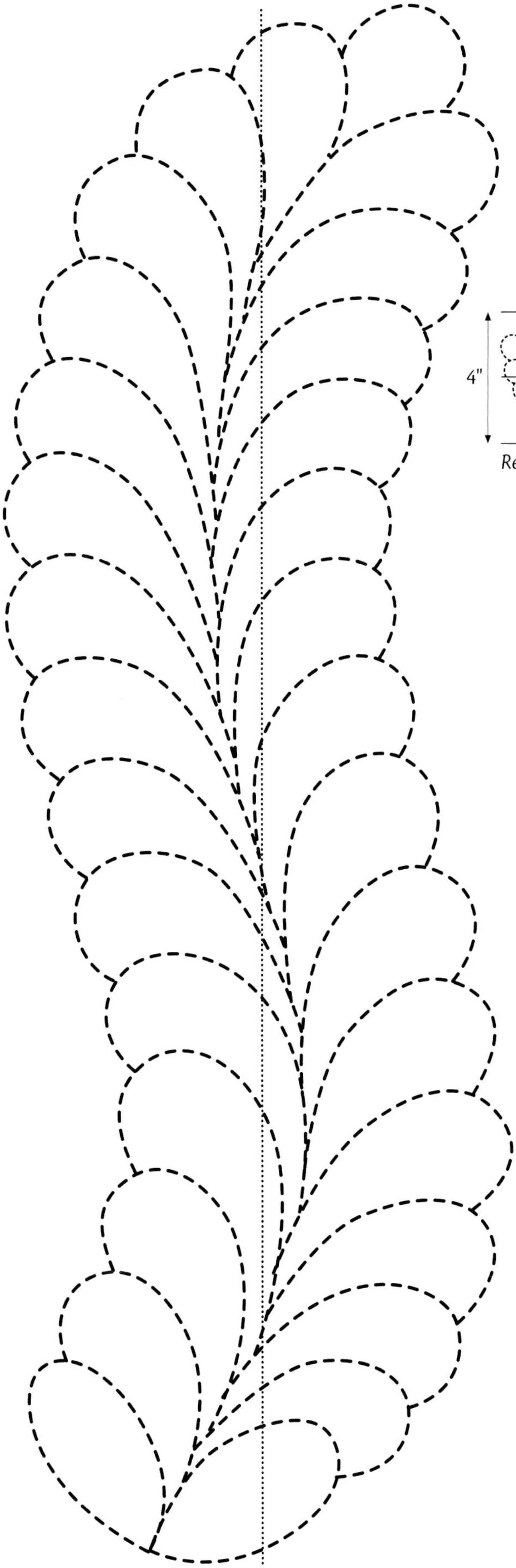

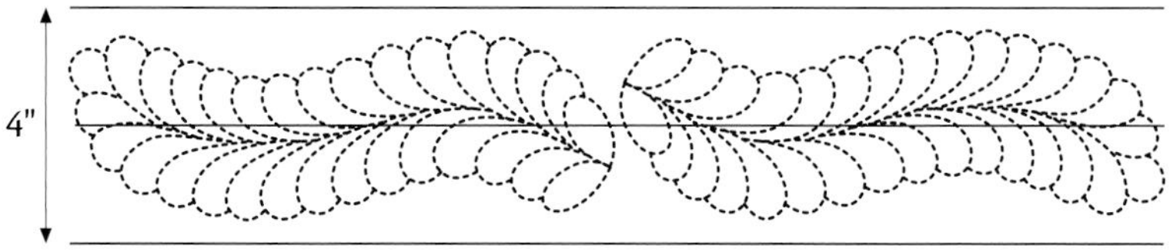

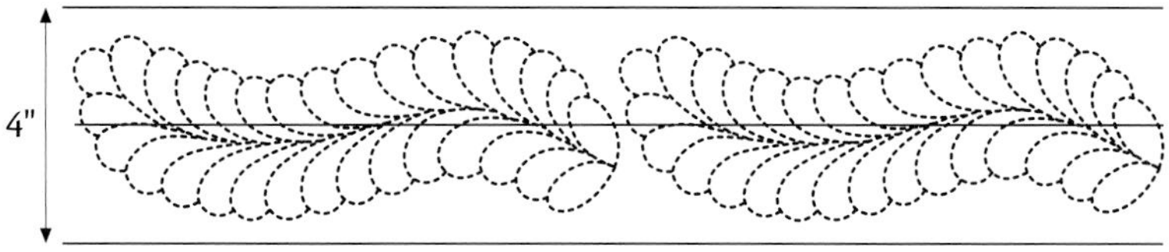

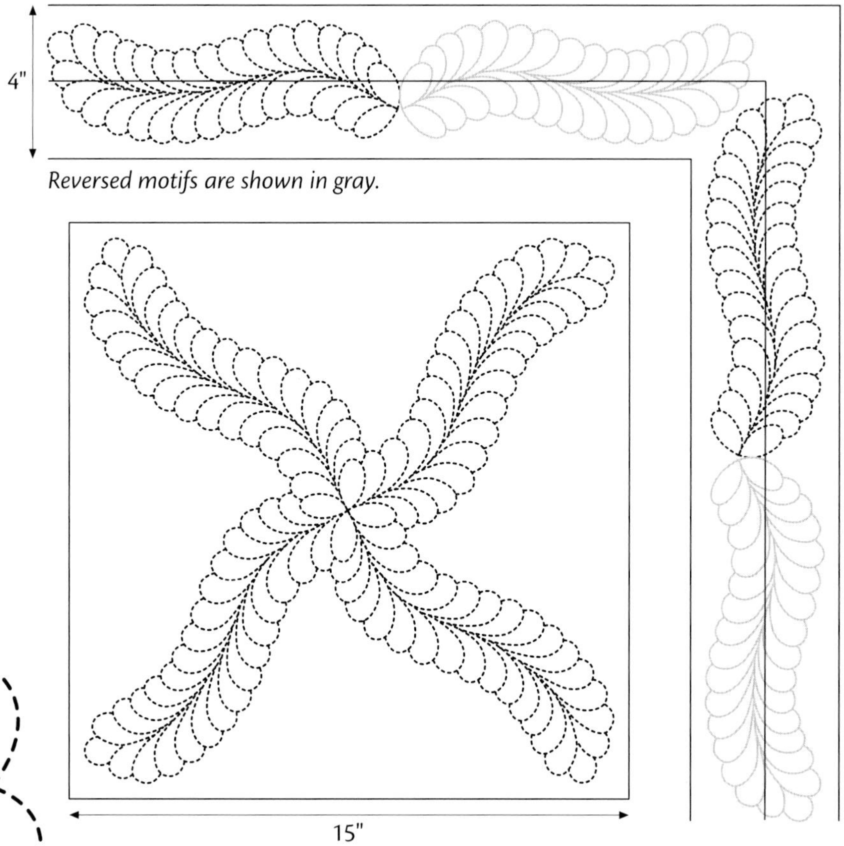

Reversed motifs are shown in gray.

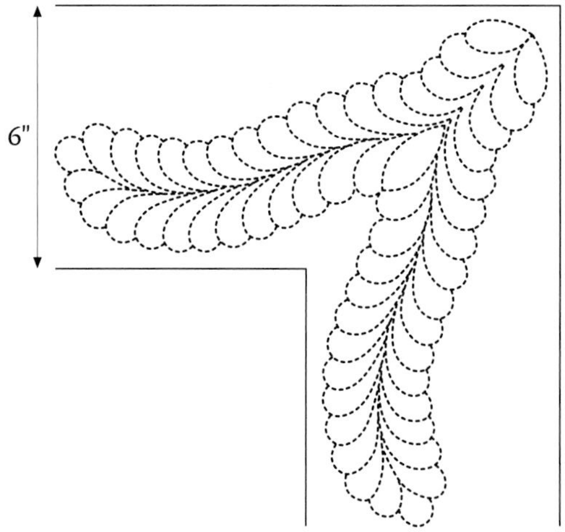

Feather Wreath 1

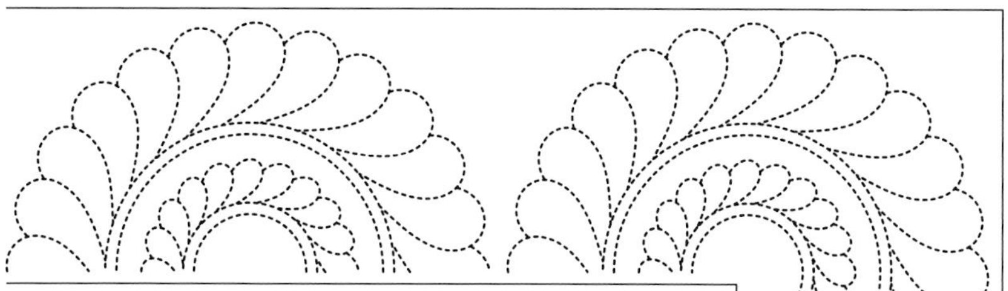
6"

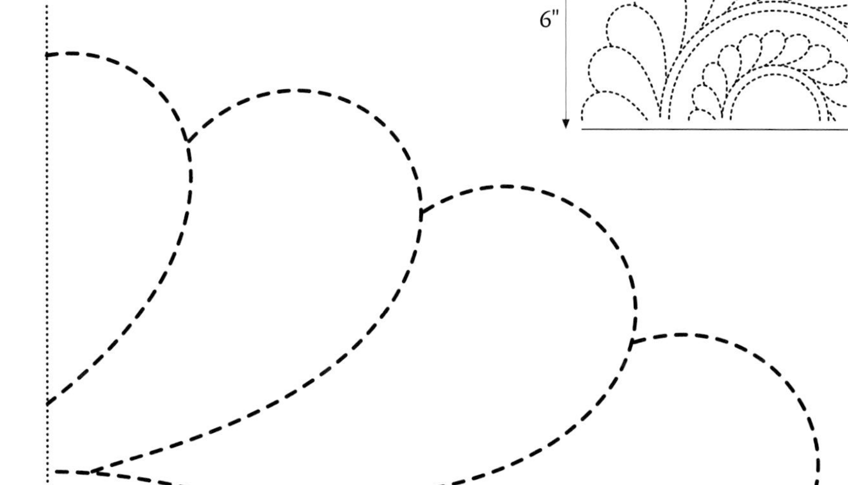

Place folded paper on dotted lines, trace, and rotate for full motif.

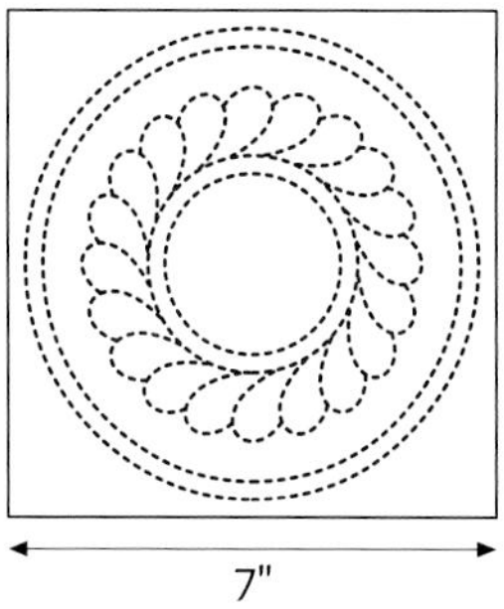
7"

5½"

11½"

11½"

12"

Feather Wreath 2

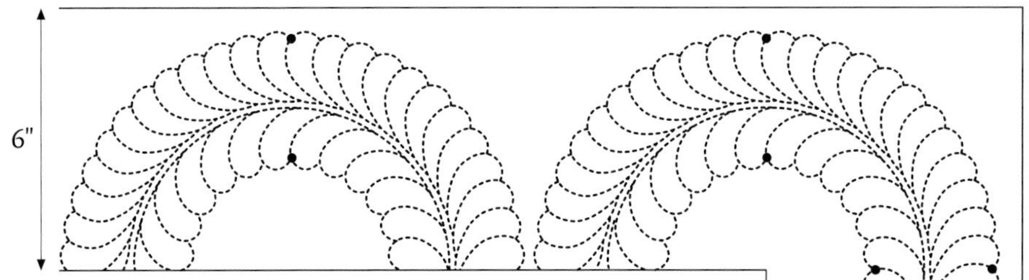

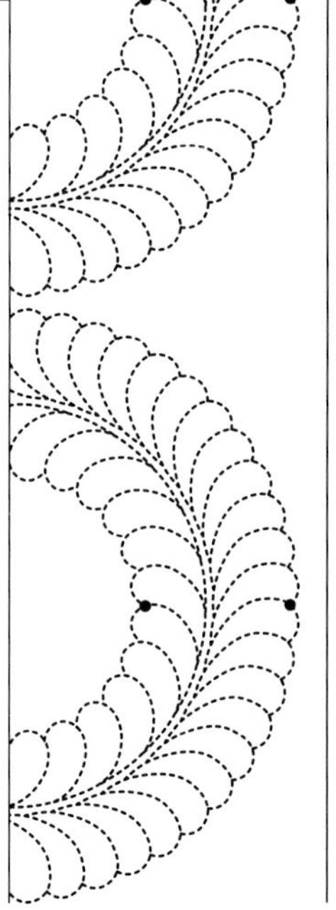

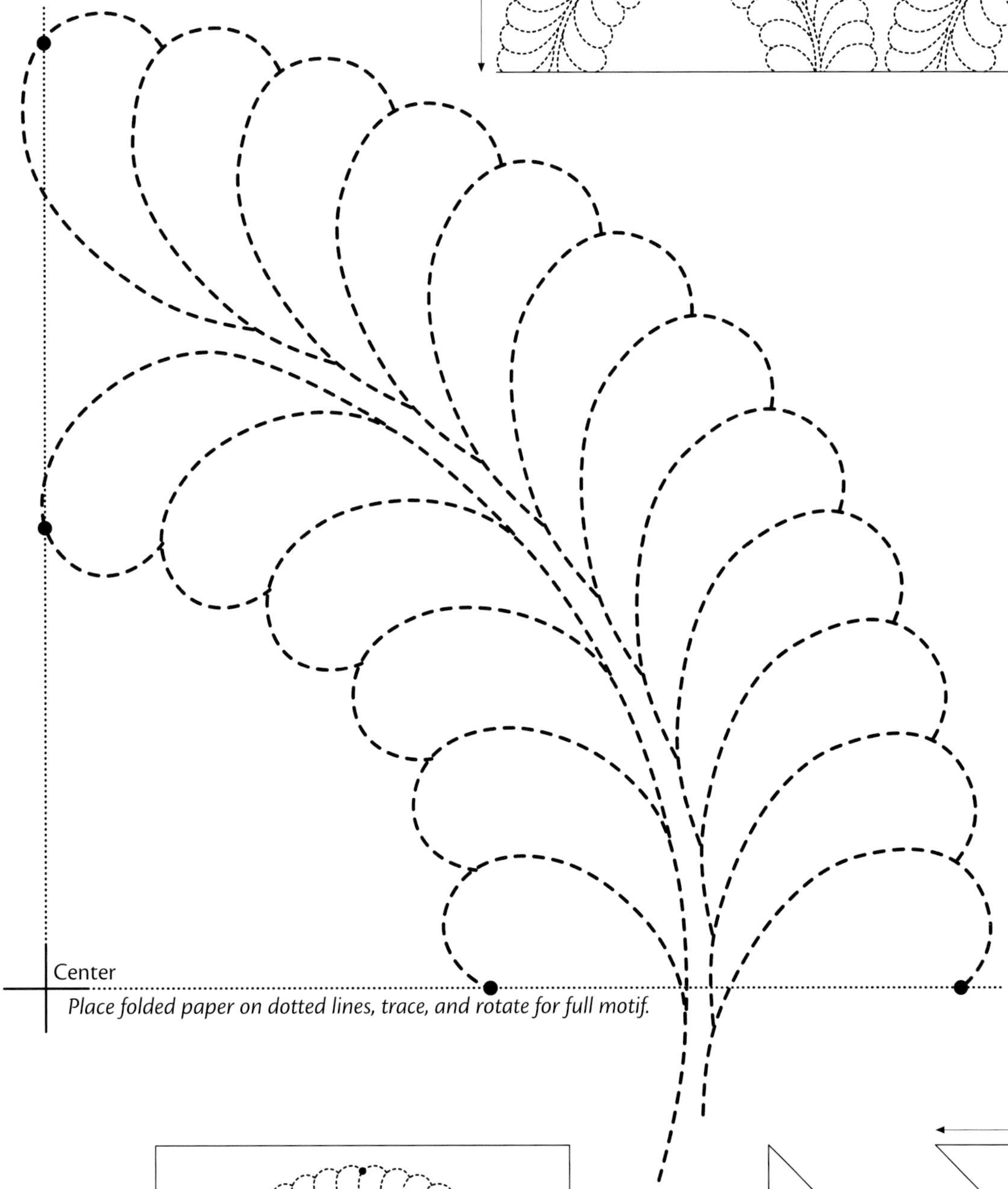

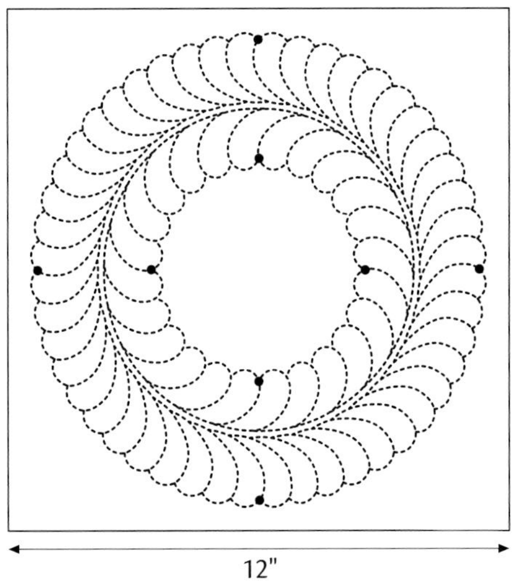

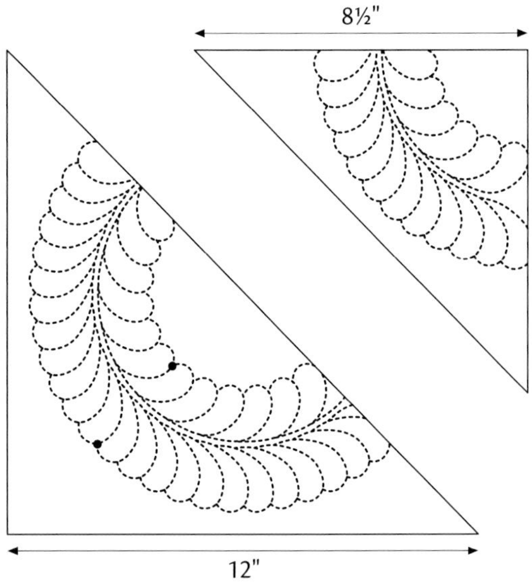

Goose Down

Reversed motifs are shown in gray.

Place folded paper on dotted line, trace, and rotate for full motif.

Kaleidoscope

Place folded paper on dotted line, trace, and flip for full motif.

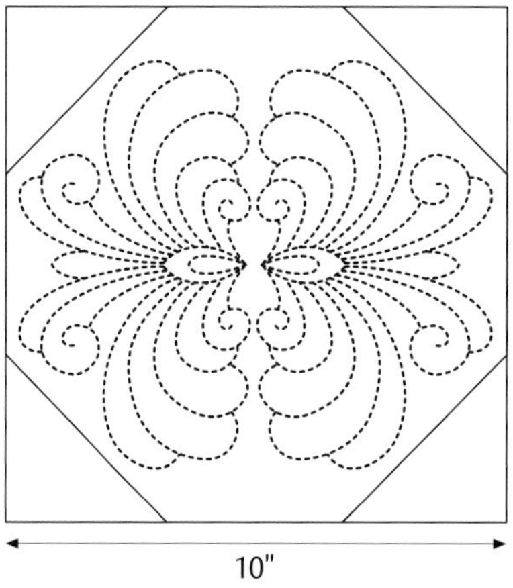

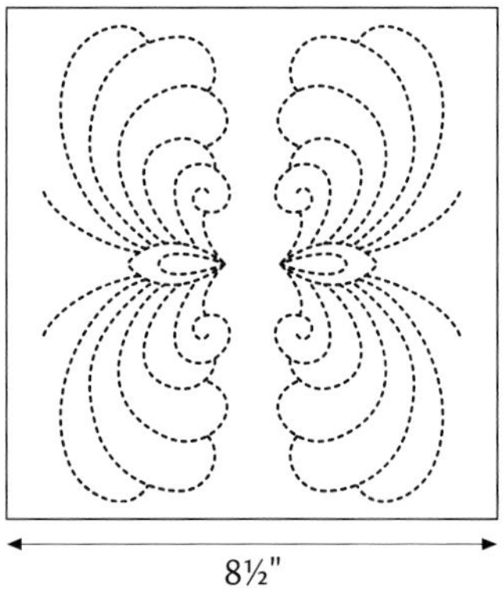

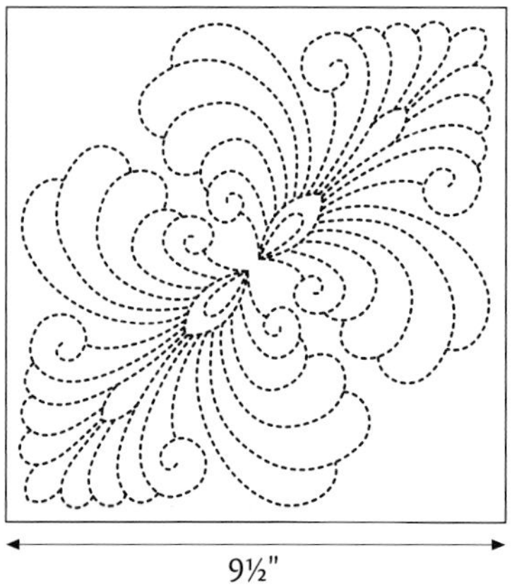

Sun Feathers

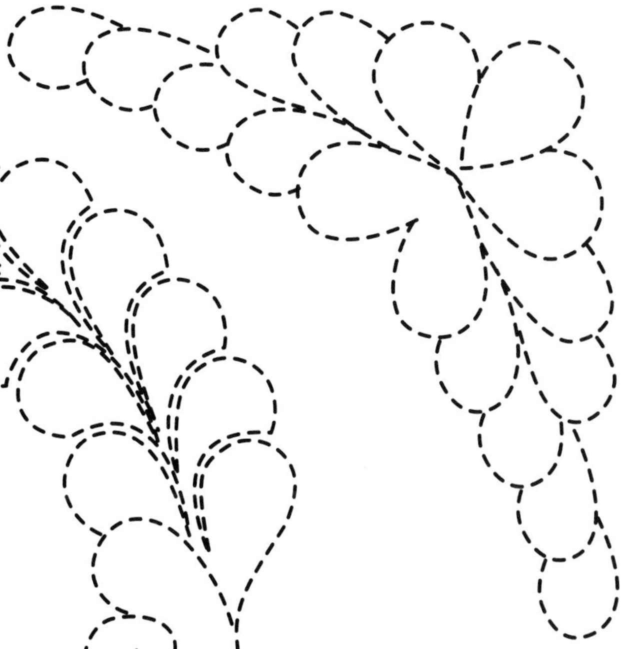

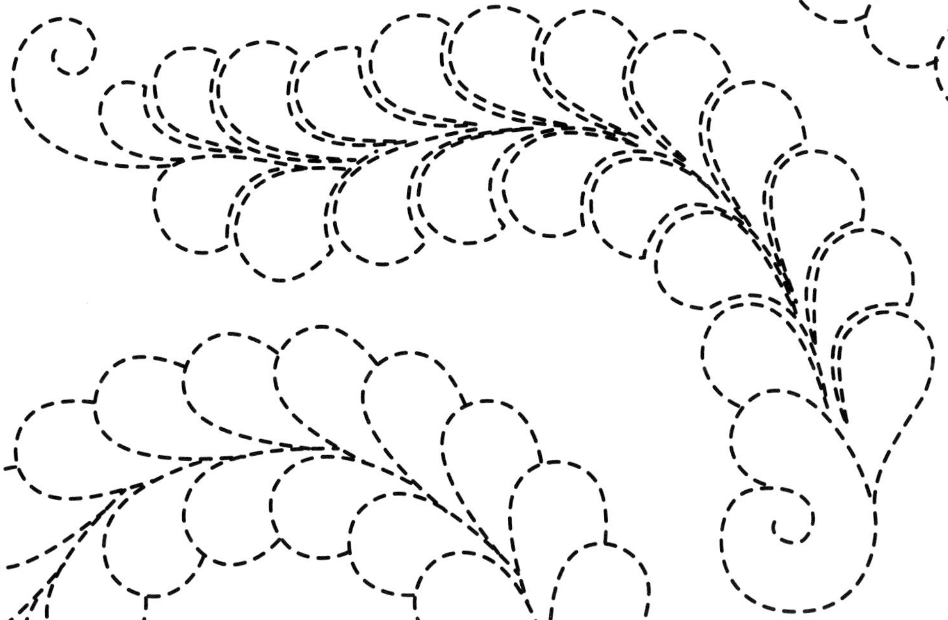

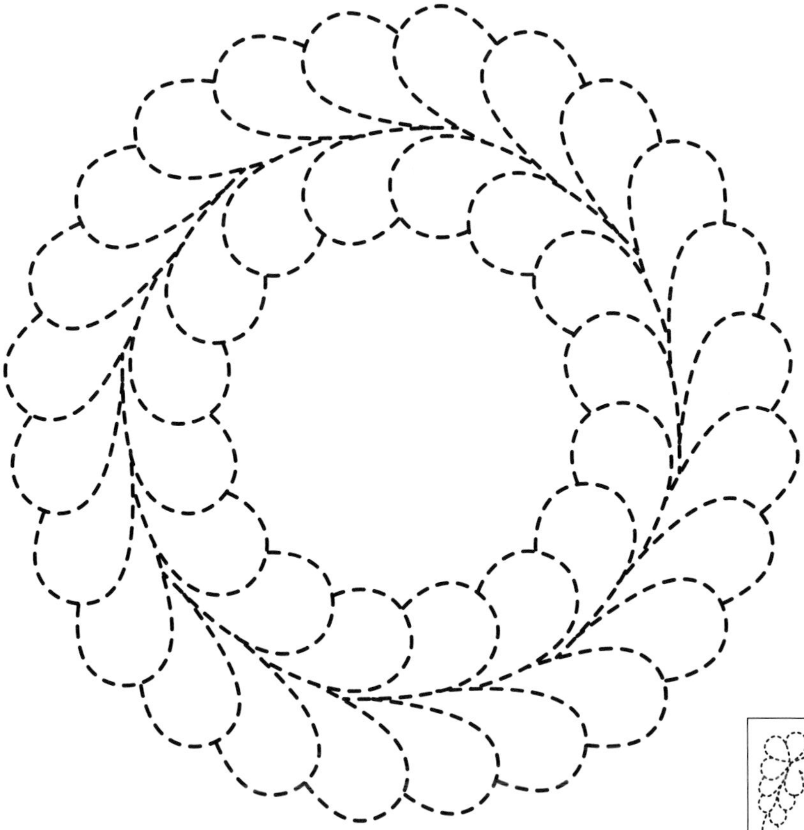

Reversed motifs are shown in gray.

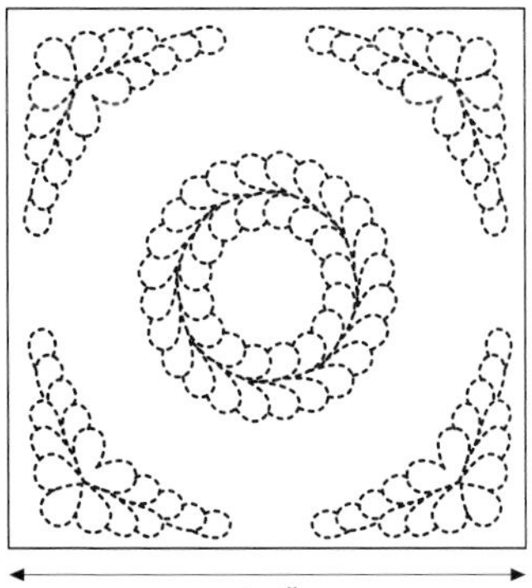

8½"

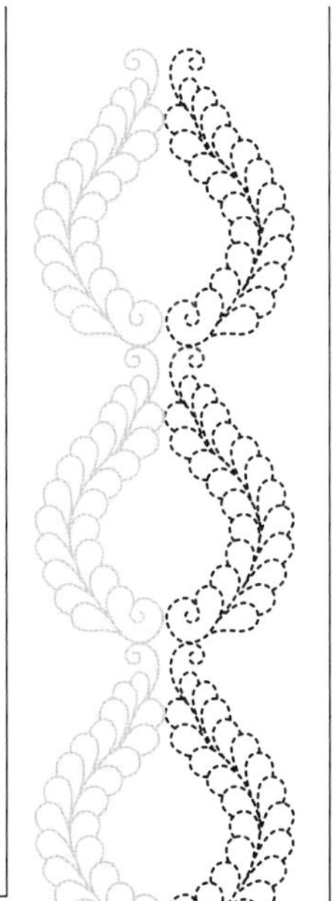

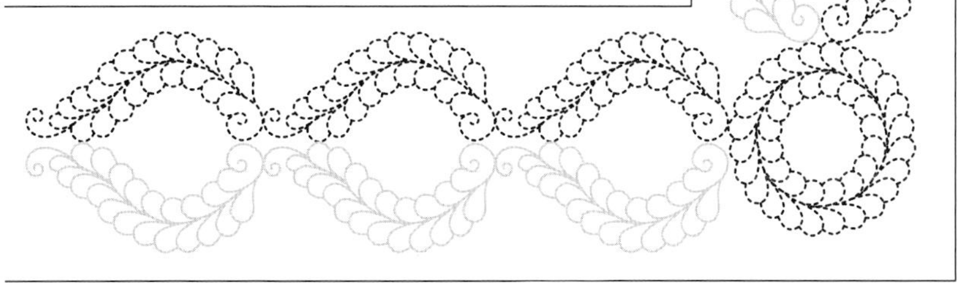

6"

13"

Sweethearts

Place folded paper on dotted line, trace, and flip for full motif.

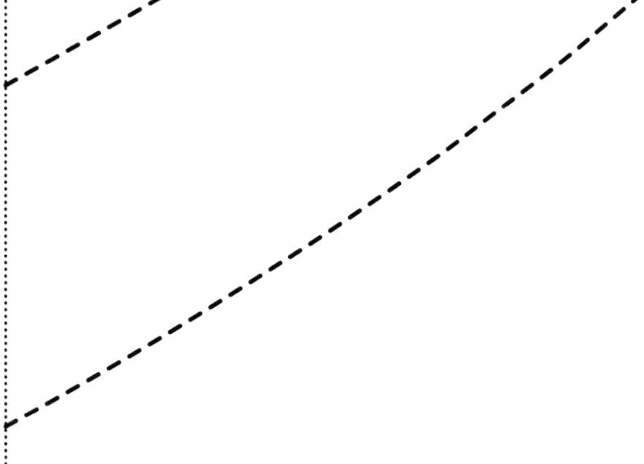

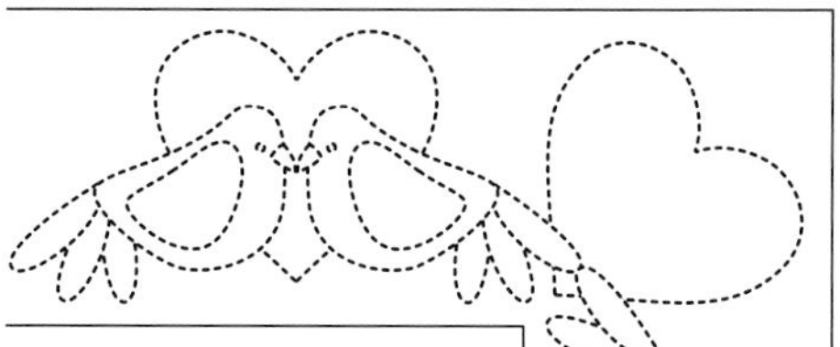

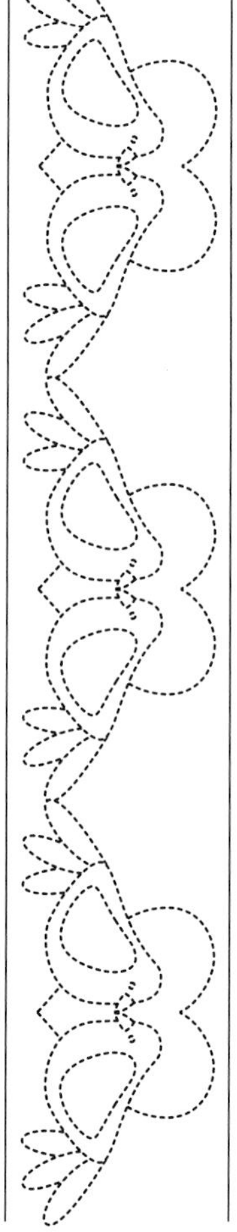

5"

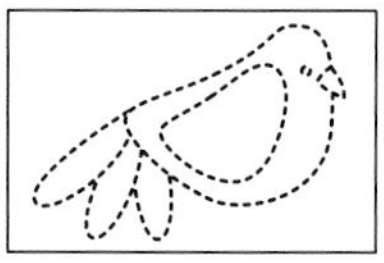

3½"

5½"

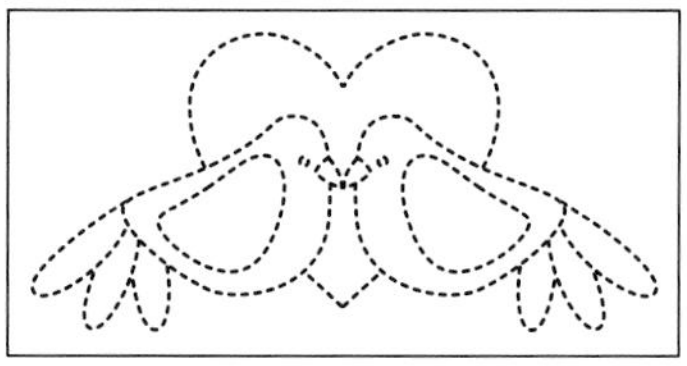

5"

10"

10½"

11"

Sweetheart Swag

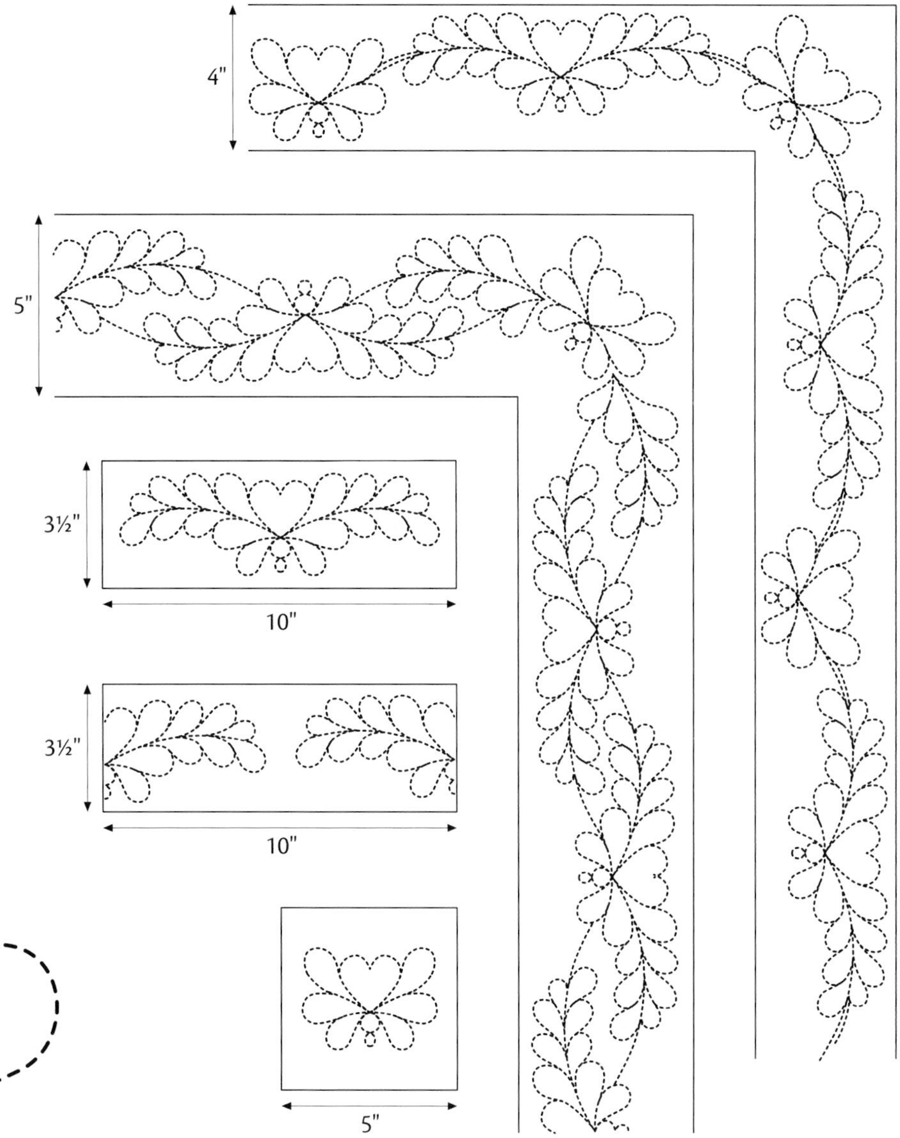
4"
5"
3½"
10"
3½"
10"
5"

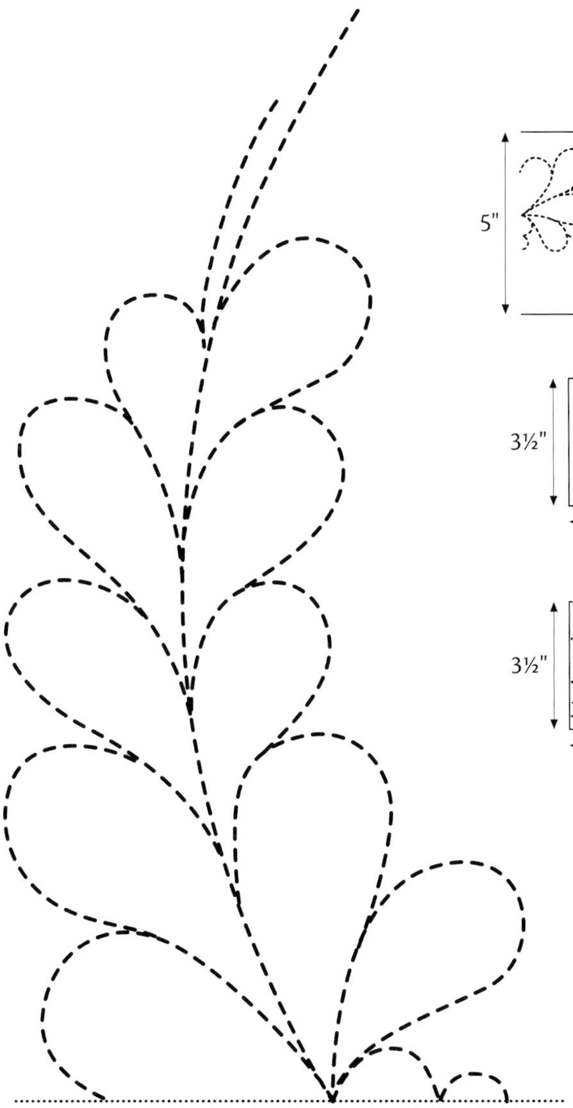

Place folded paper on dotted line, trace, and flip for full motif.

16"

14"

Washington's Wreath

Place folded paper on dotted lines, trace, and rotate for full motif.

Limerick Waves

6½"
14"
13½"
5½"

Reversed motifs are shown in gray.

Feathered Heart

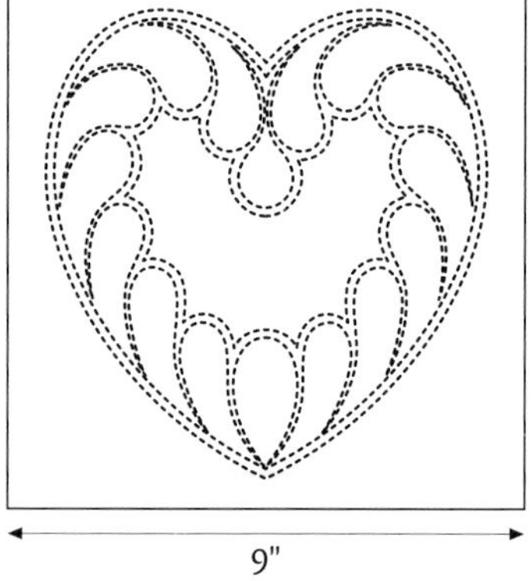

9"

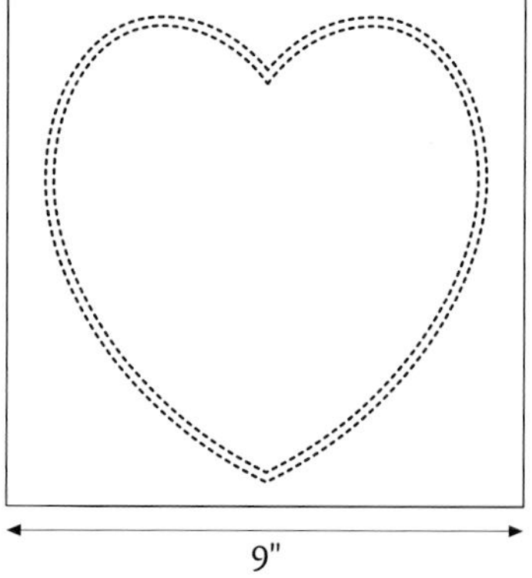

9"

Feathered Heart

16"

17"

16"

Sweet Talk

Reversed motifs are shown in gray.

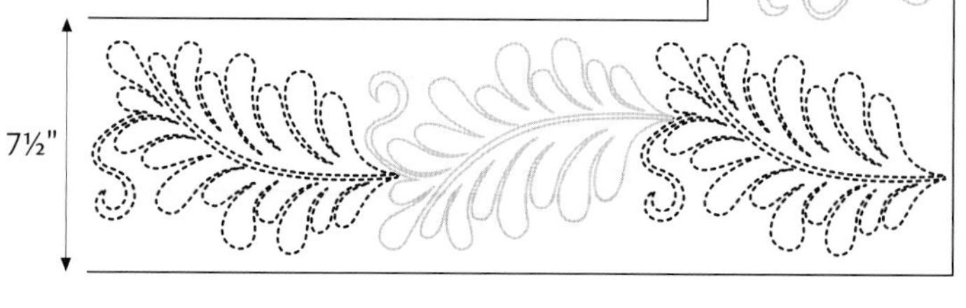

Celebration 1

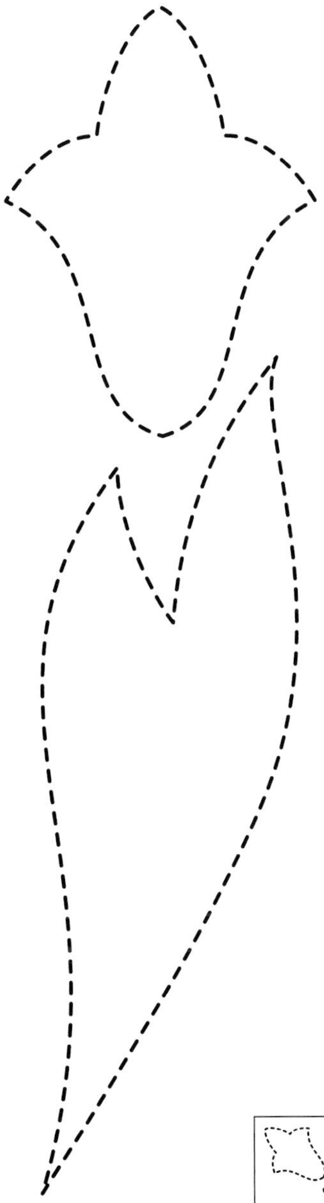

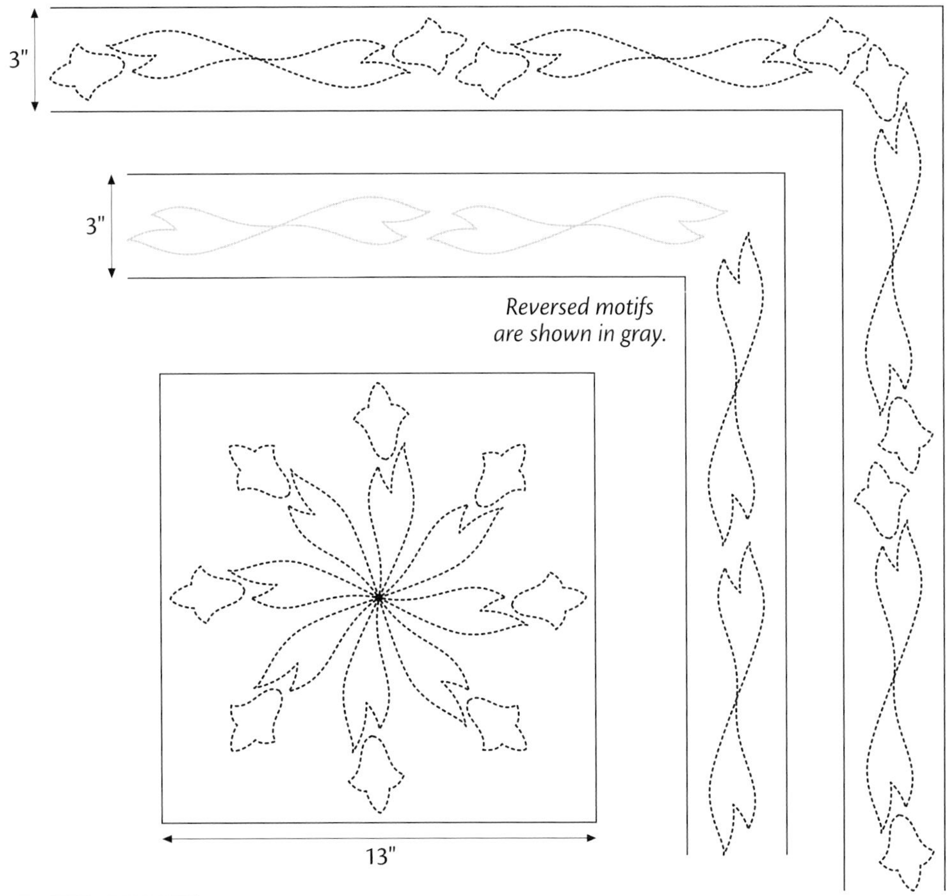

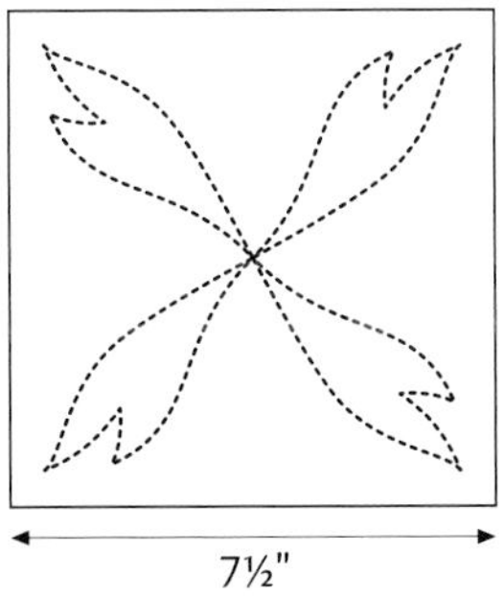

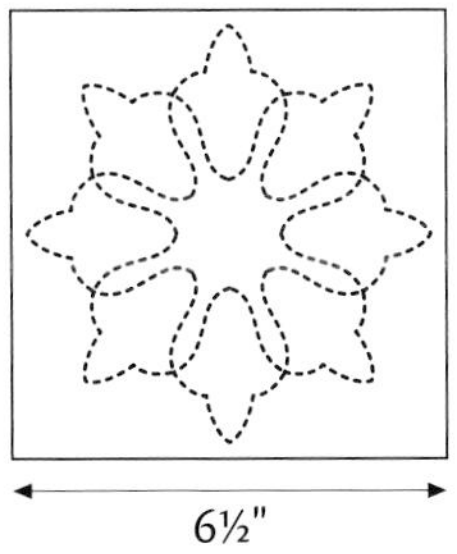

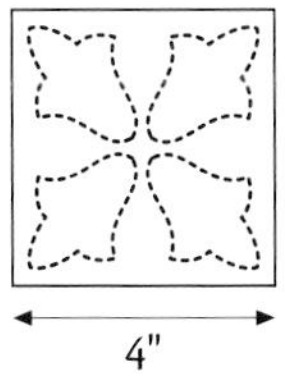

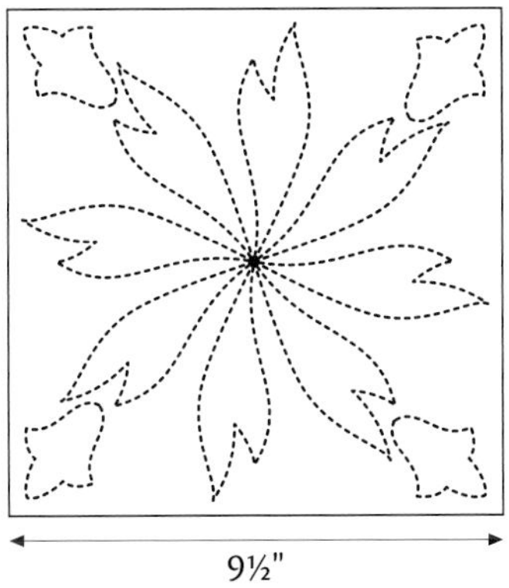

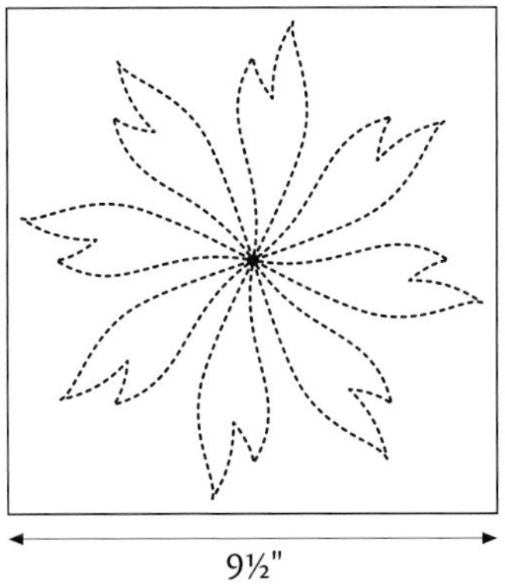

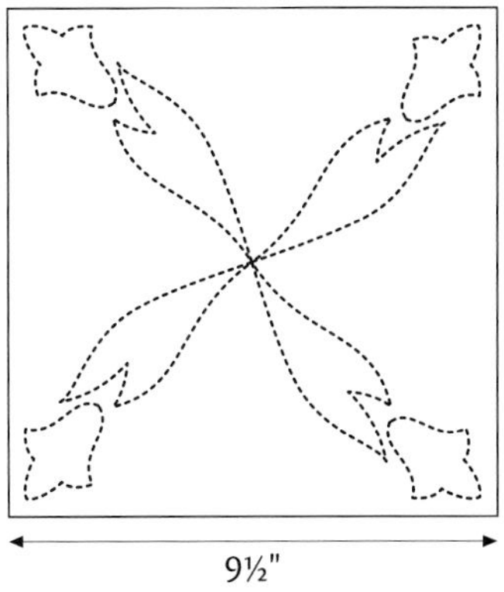

Lida Rose

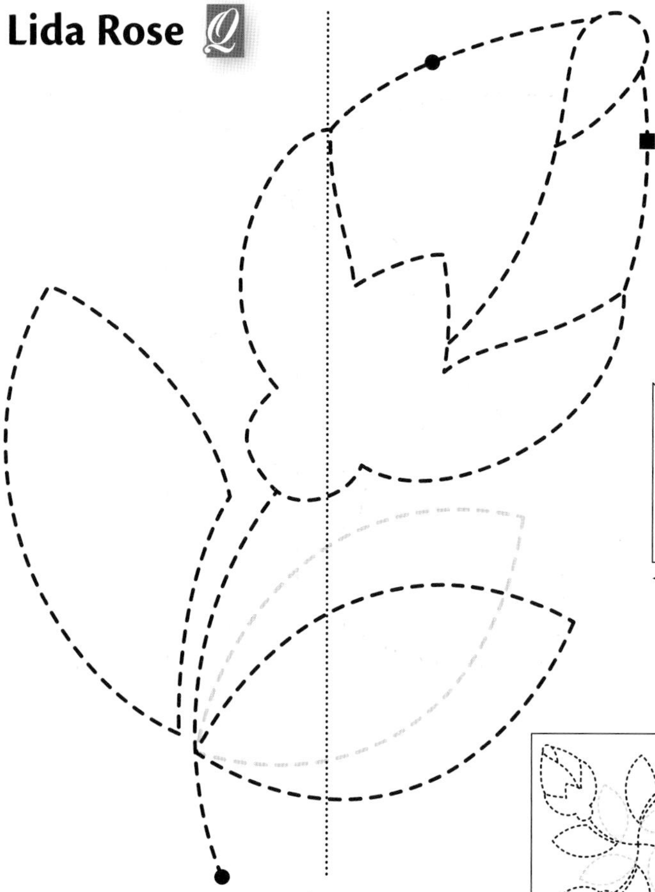

Some layouts require the "tucked-in" leaf shown here in gray.

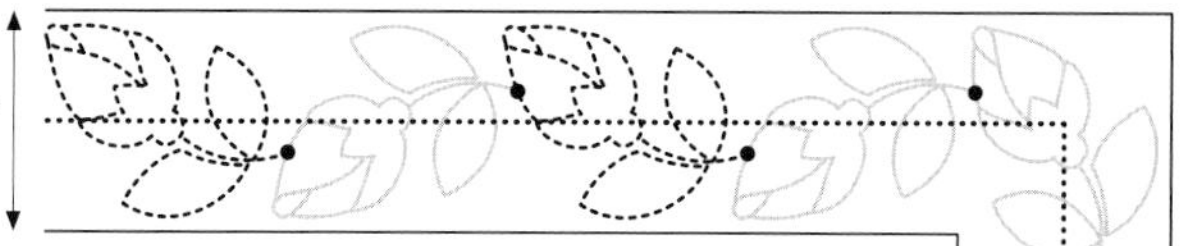

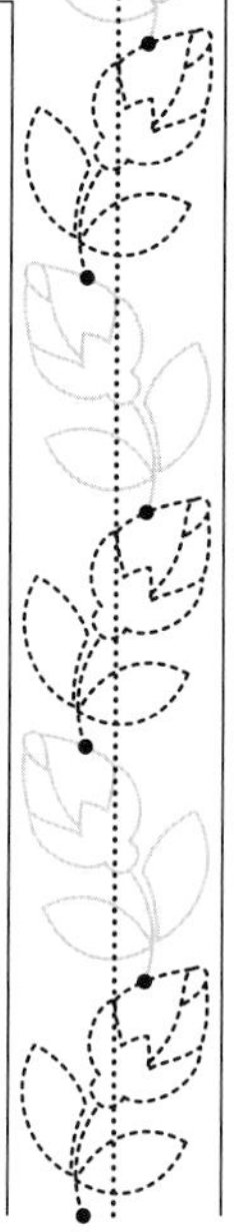

For border, flip every other motif and match dots. Reversed motifs are shown in gray.

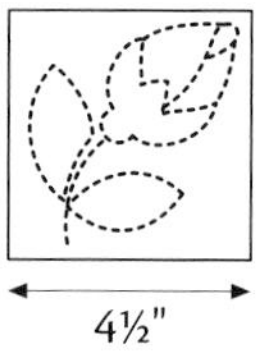

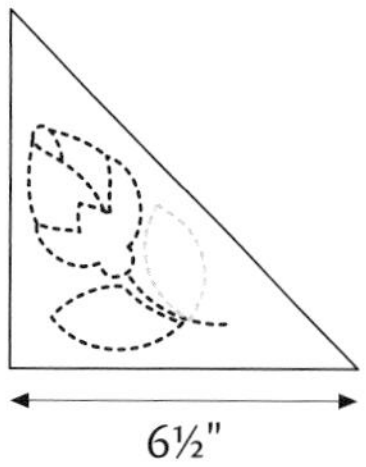

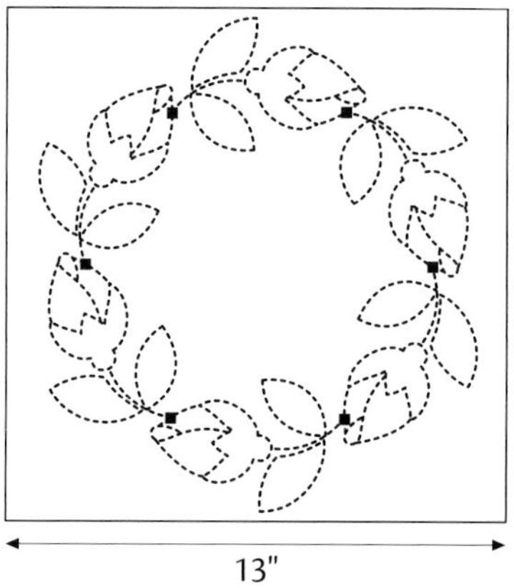

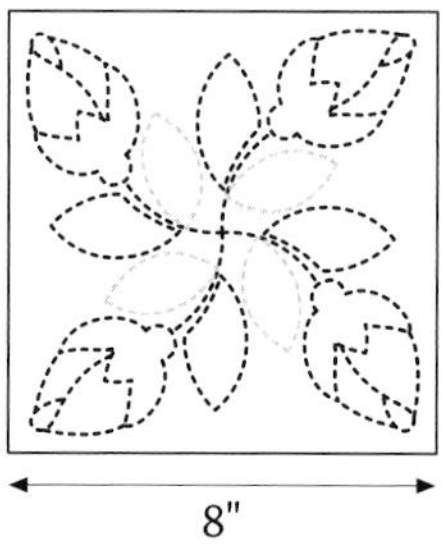

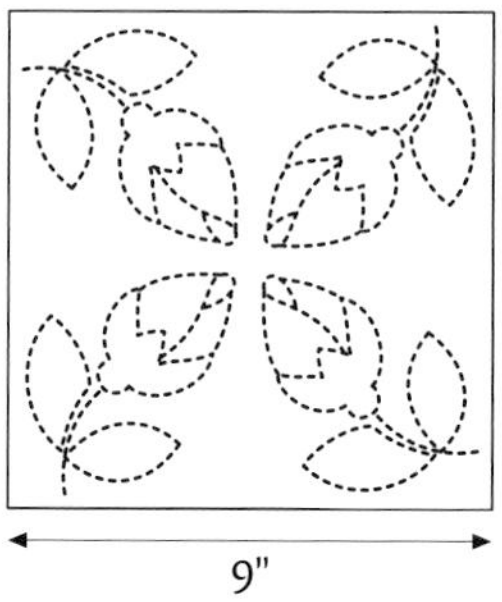

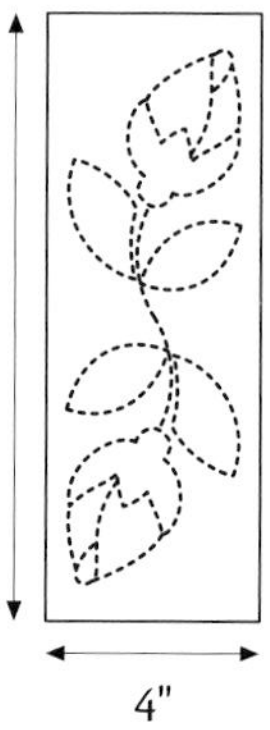

Lantern Lily

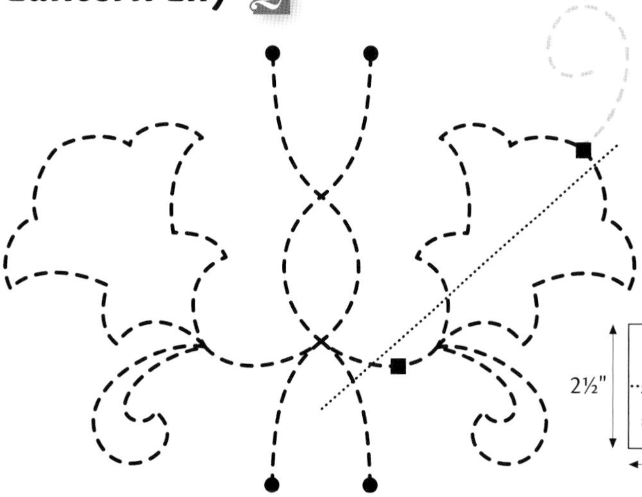

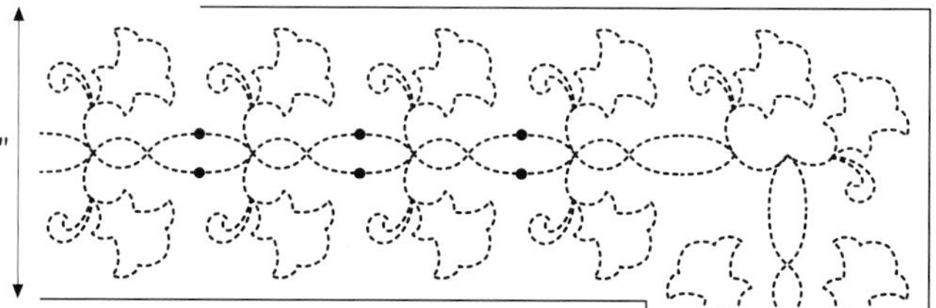

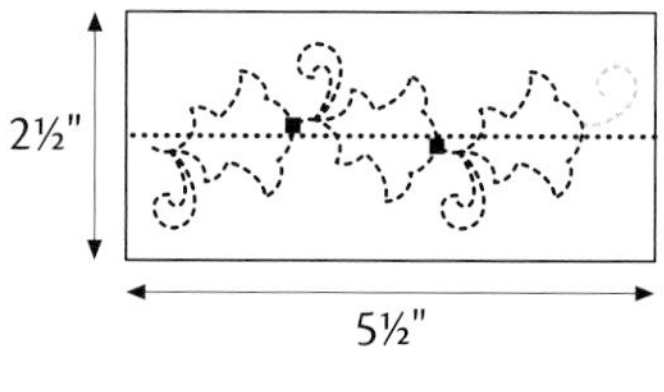

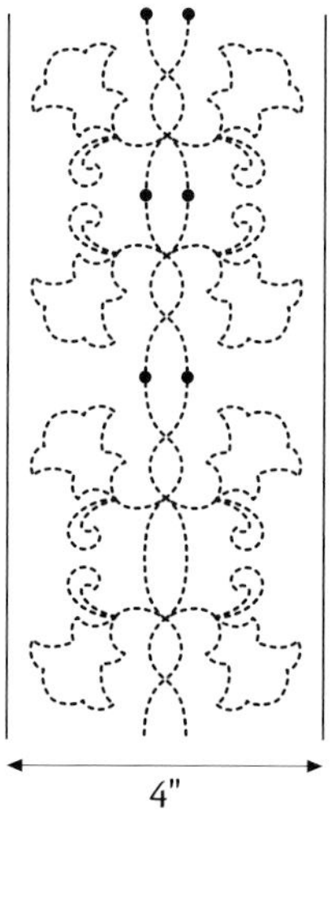

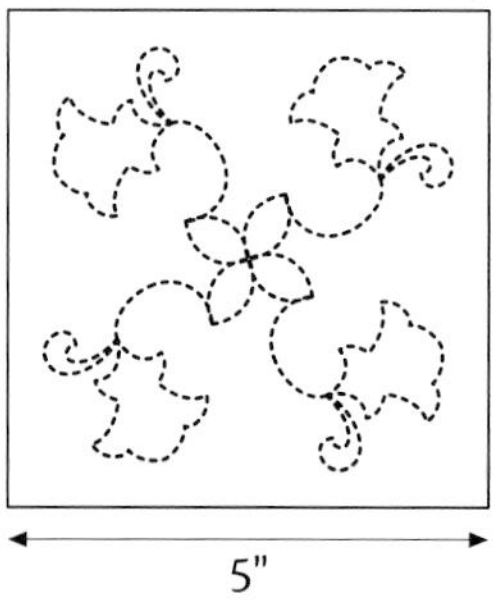

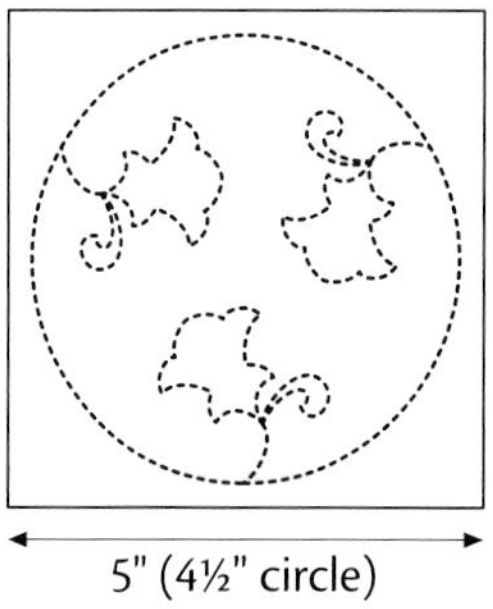

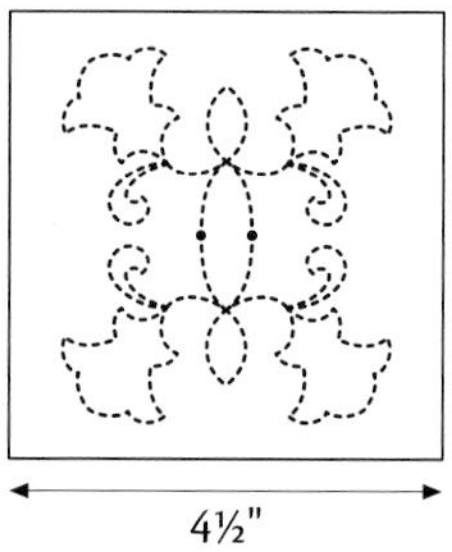

Wild Rose

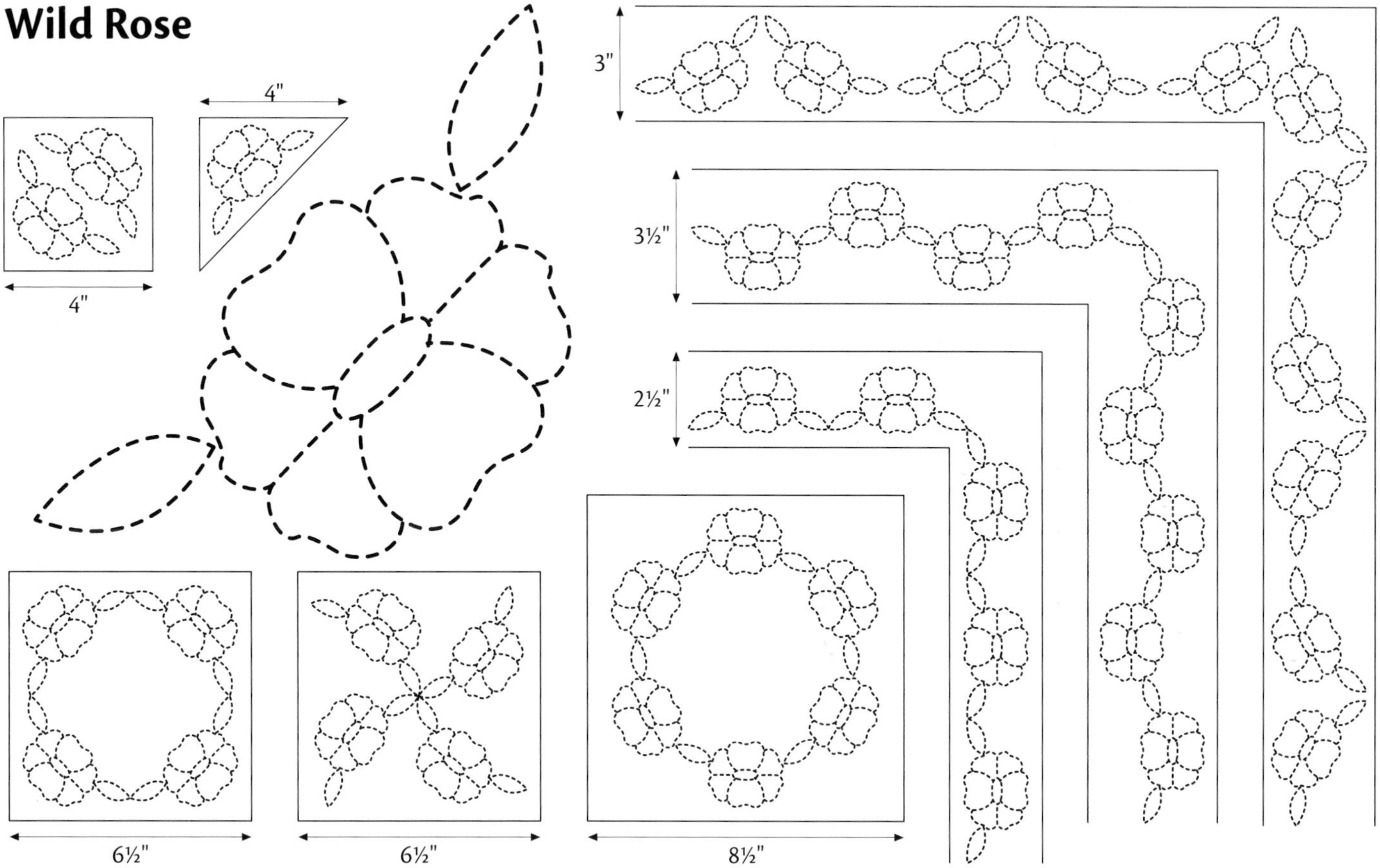

4"
4"
3"
3½"
2½"
6½"
6½"
8½"

Breezy Blossom

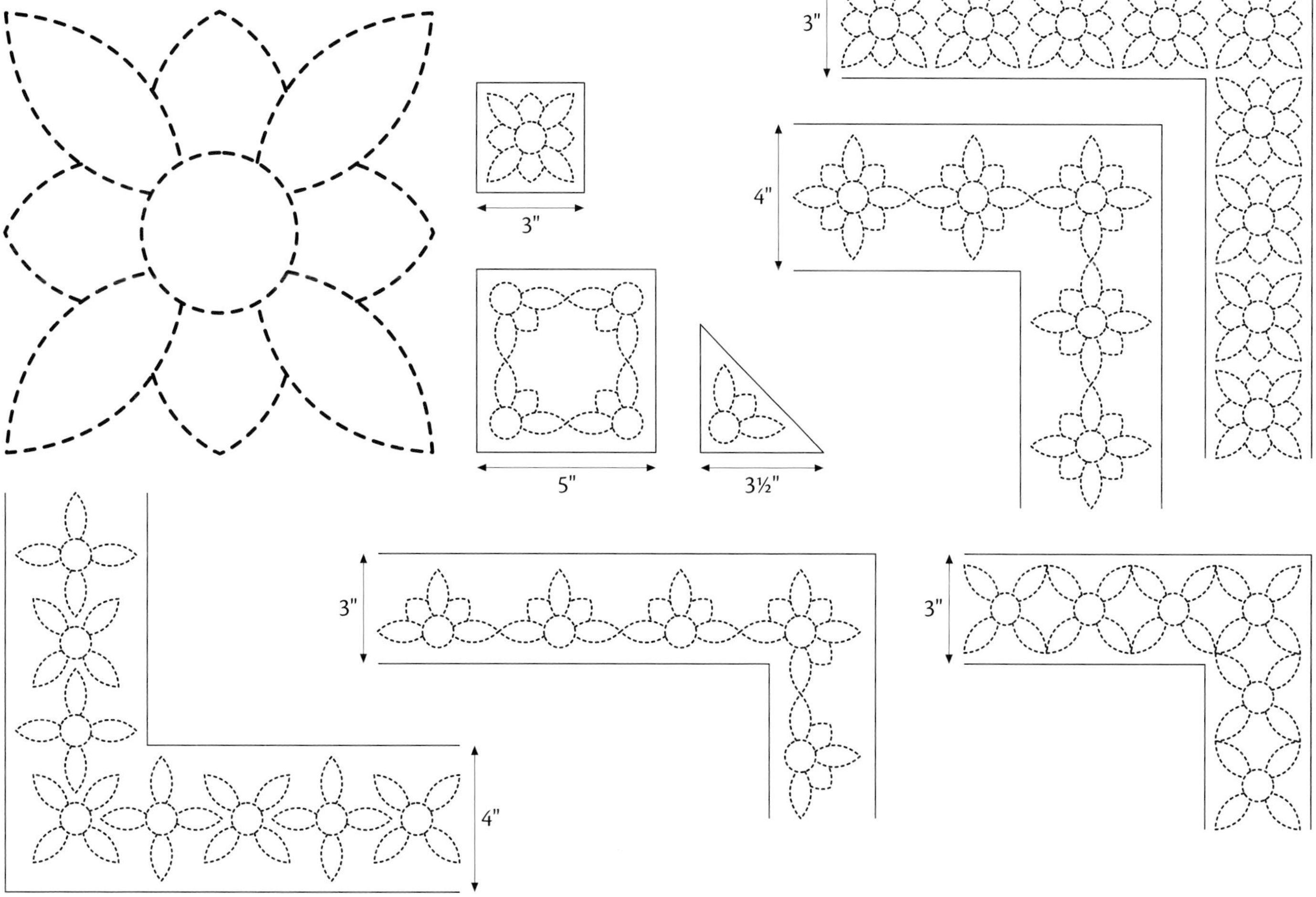

3"
3"
4"
5"
3½"
3"
3"
4"

Spring Promise

2½"
3½"
3½"
5"
2"
2"
2"
2½"
Reversed motifs are shown in gray.
3½"
3½"
4½"
3½"

Feathers and Flowers

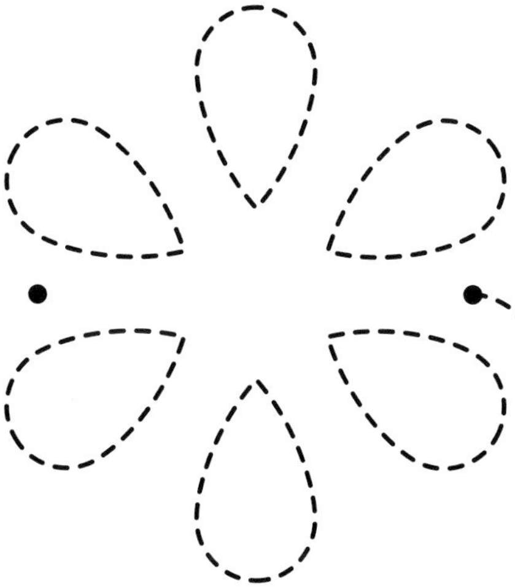

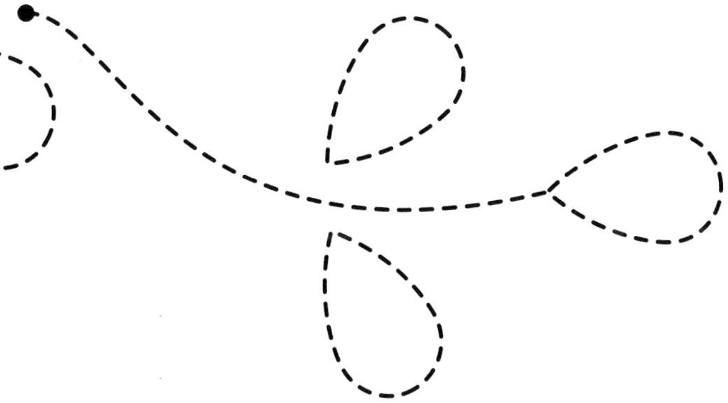

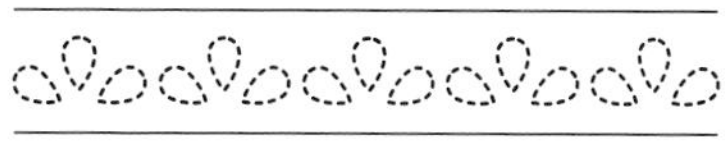

2"

3"

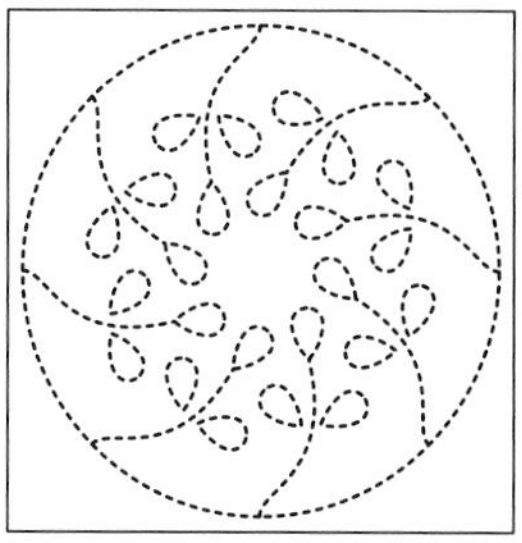

8½" (8" circle)

7½"

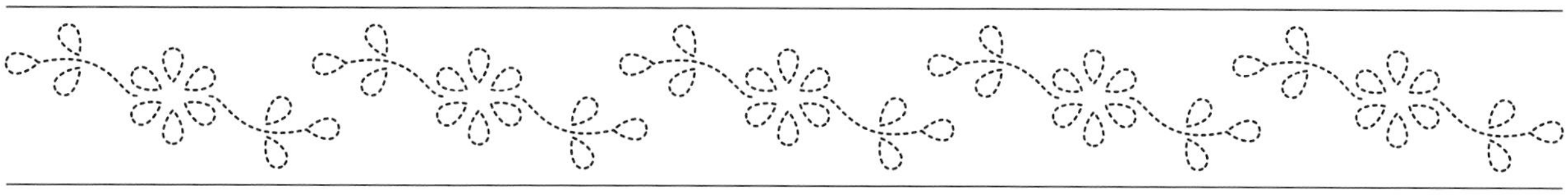

4½"

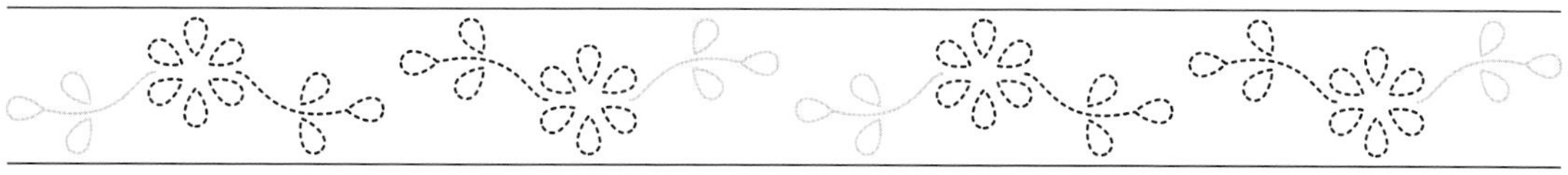

3½"

Reversed motifs are shown in gray.

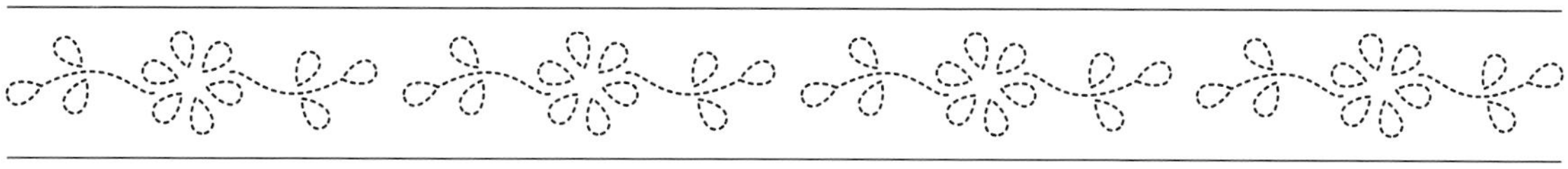

3½"

First Bloom

8"

9½"

6½"

He-Loves-Me

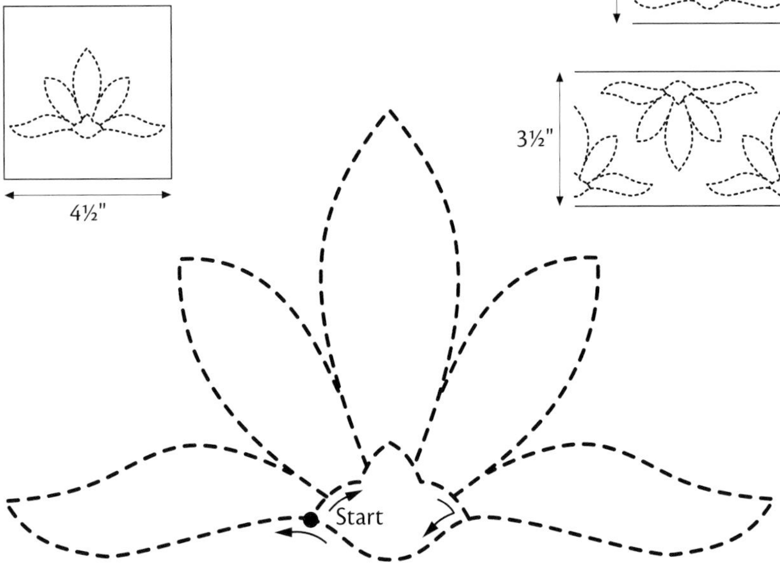

Arrows indicate direction for continuous-line machine quilting.

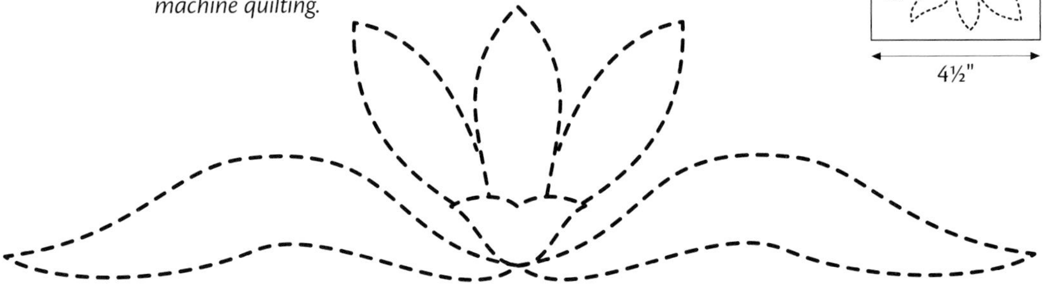

Friendship Blossoms

Reversed motifs are shown in gray.

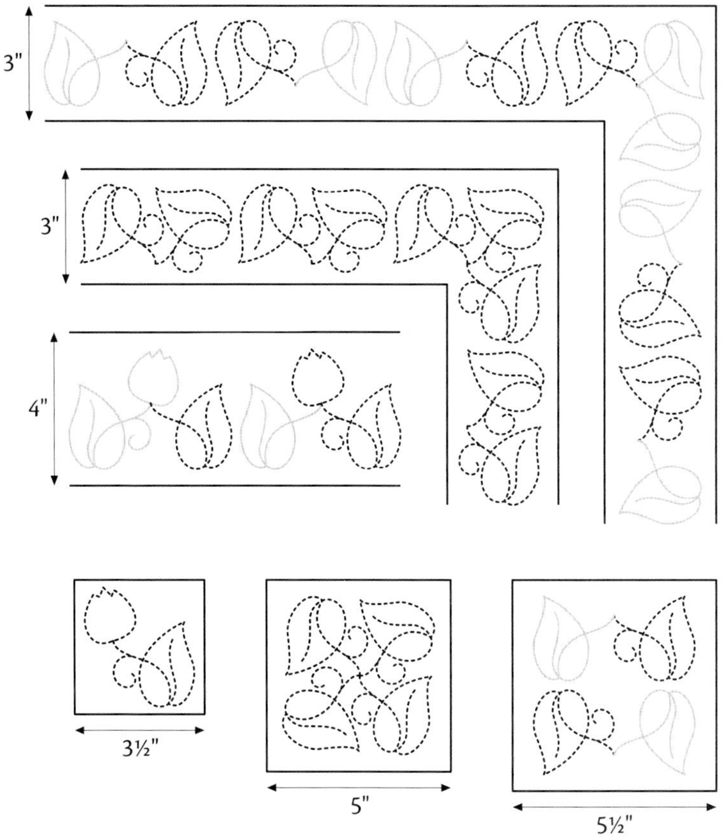

3"
3"
4"
3½"
5"
5½"

Rosebush

Reversed motifs are shown in gray.

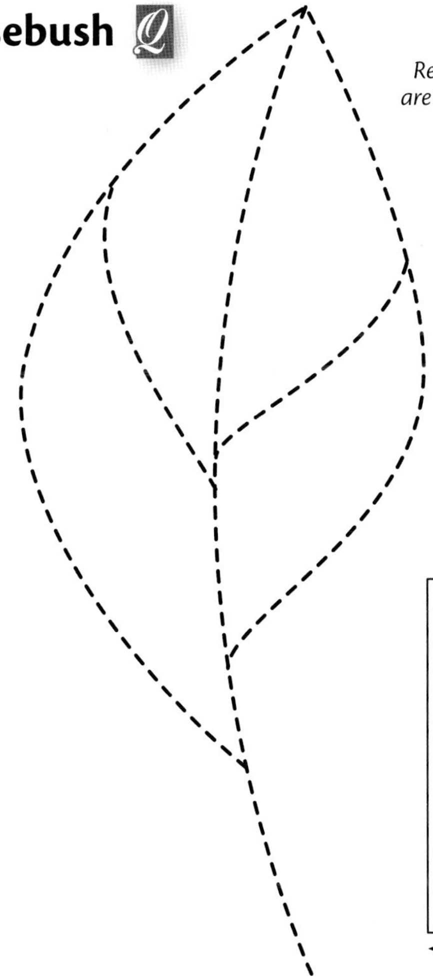

3½"
7"
10½"
11½" (8½" circle)
11½" (8½" circle)

Floating Lily

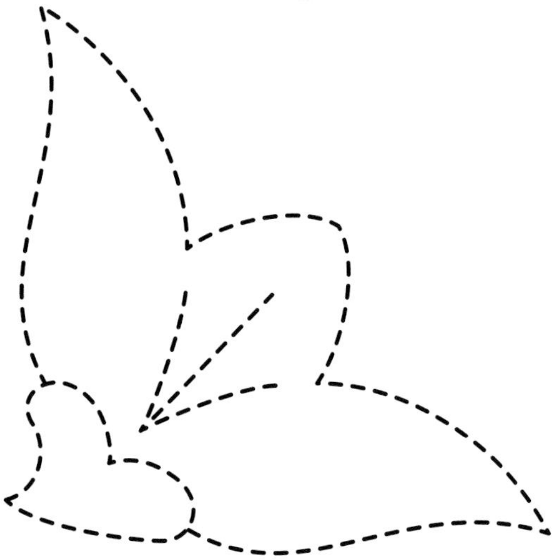

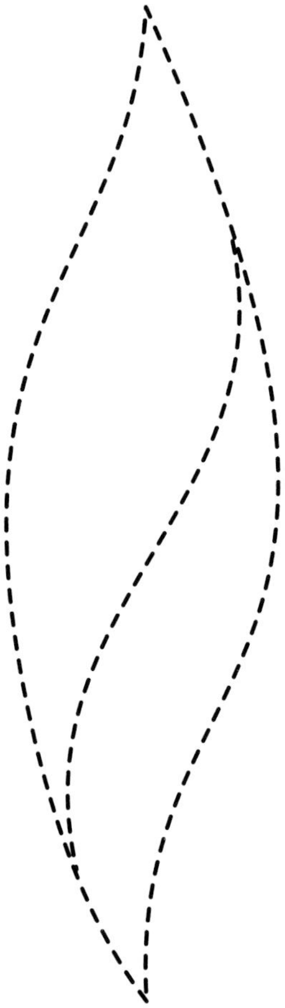

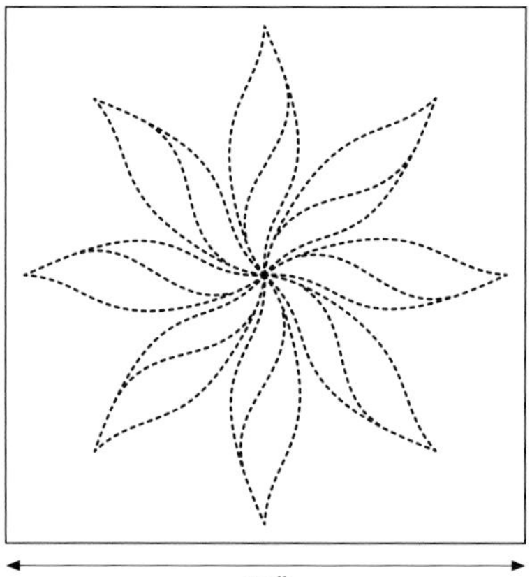

10"

11"

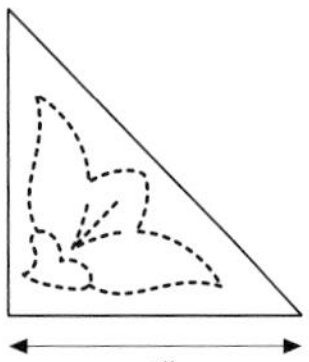

4"

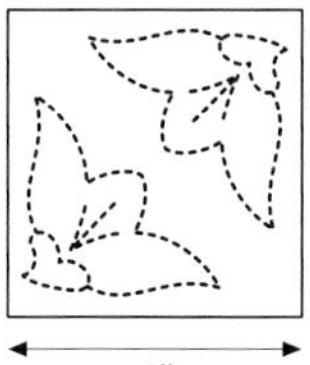

4"

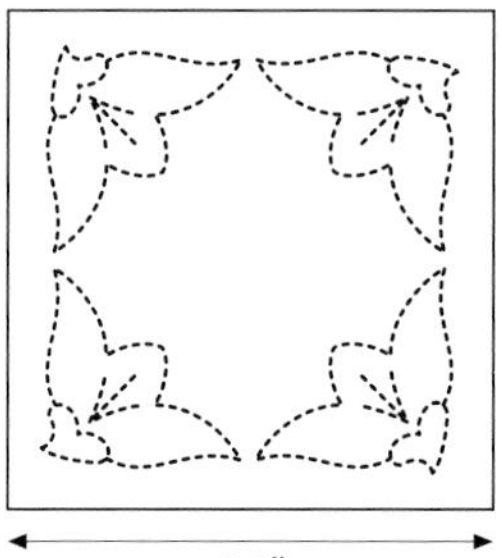

6½"

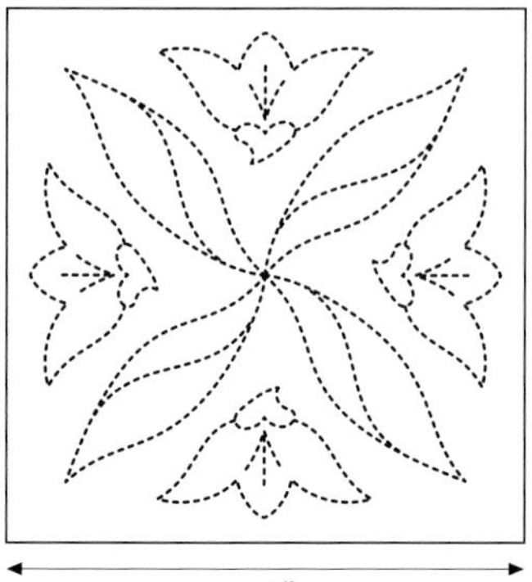

8½"

5½"

5"

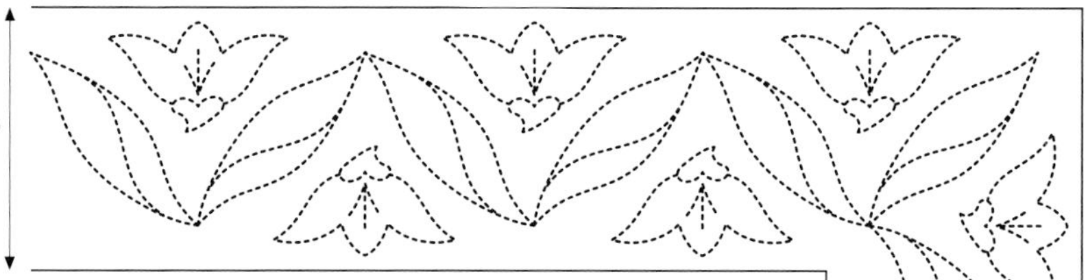

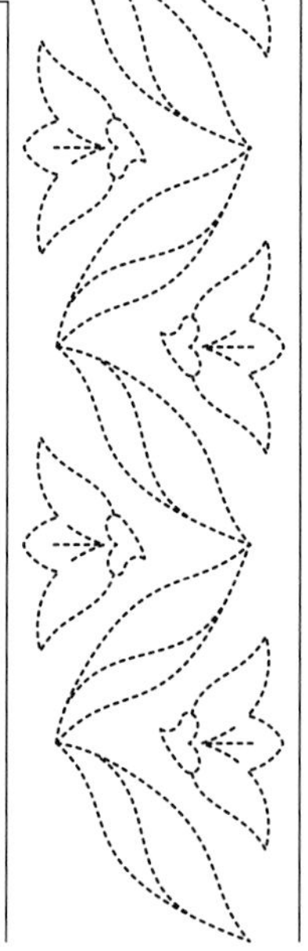

4½"

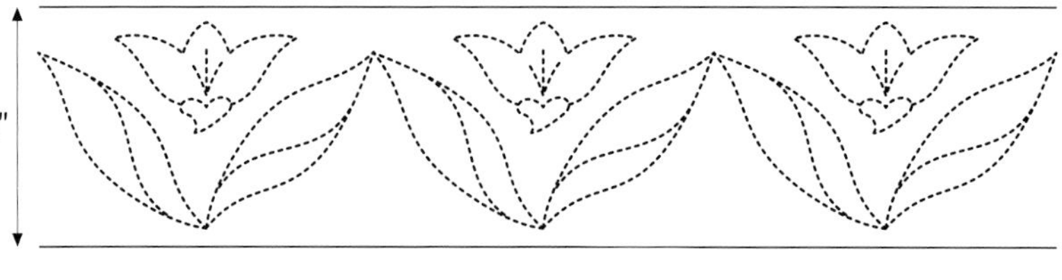

3½"

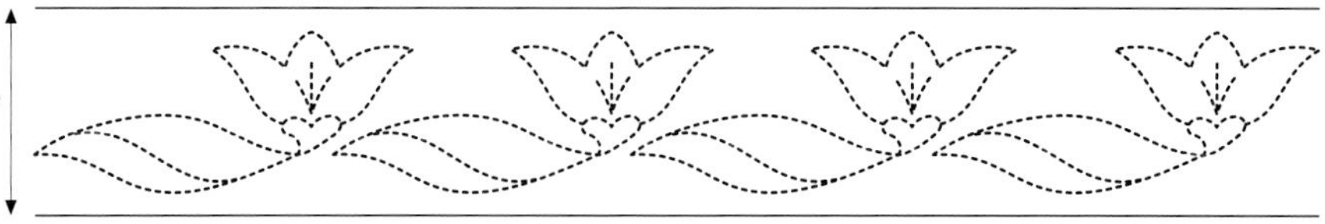

5"

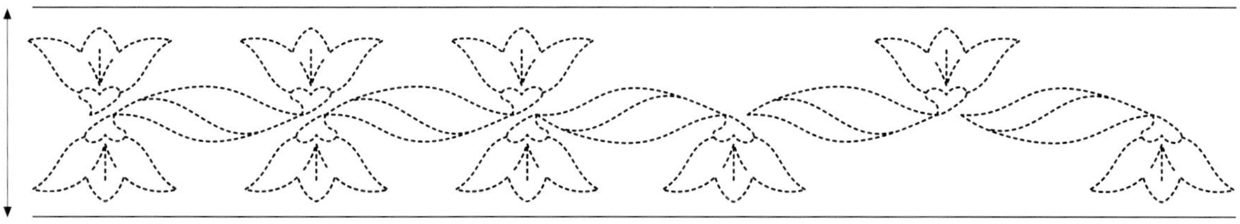

Daisy Field

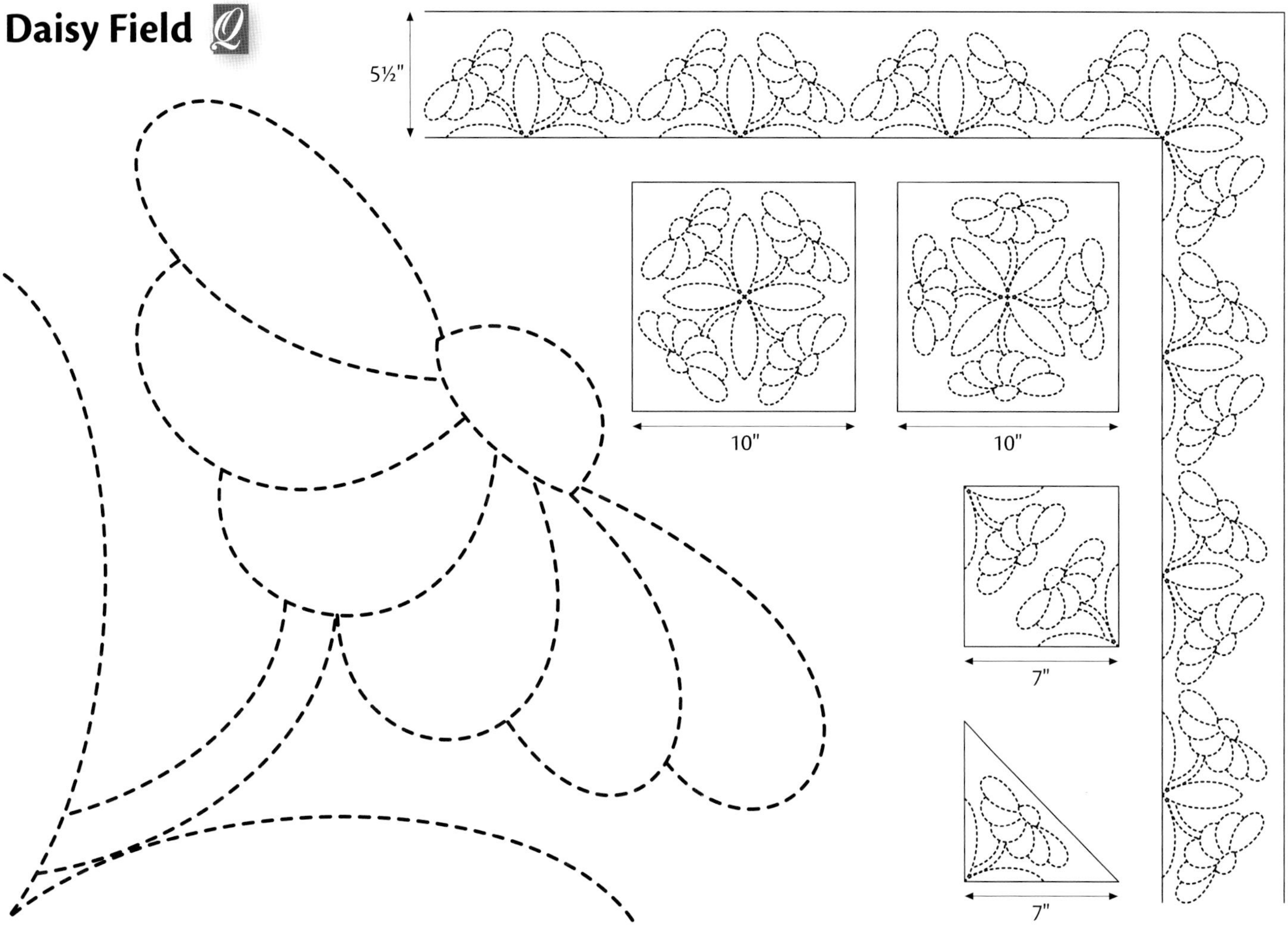

5½"
10"
10"
7"
7"

Lotus Bud

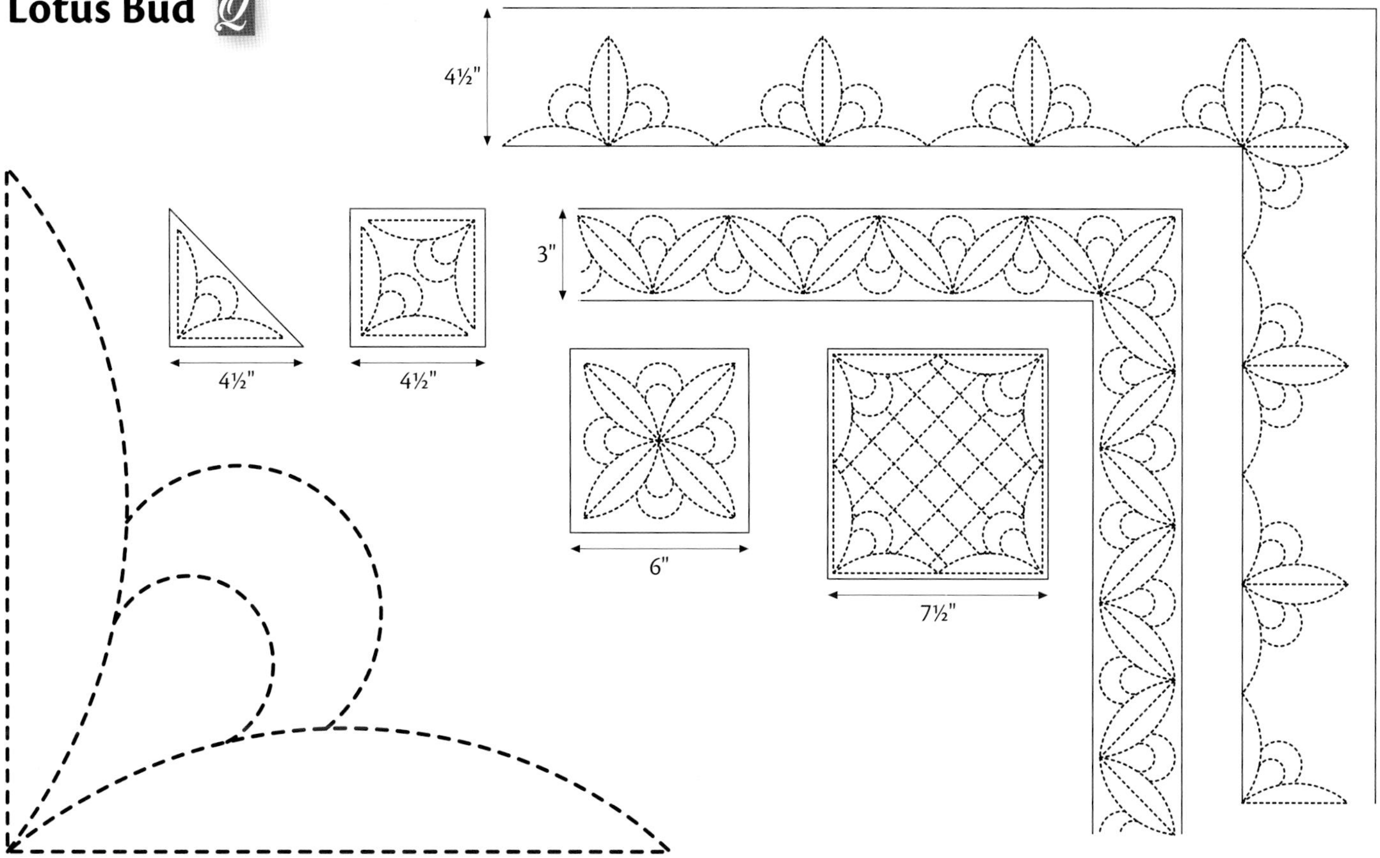

4½"
3"
4½"
4½"
6"
7½"

Persian Rose

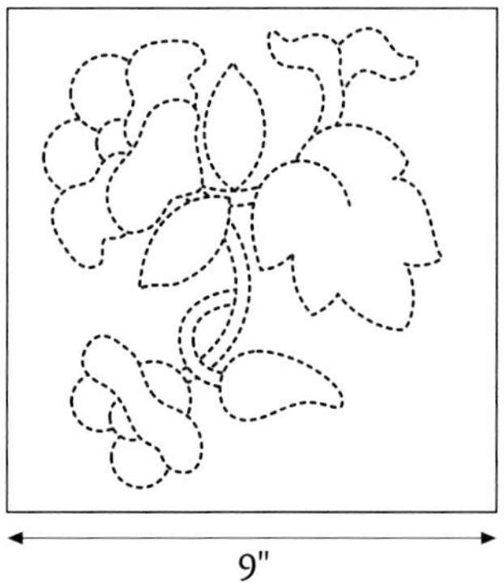

Reversed motifs are shown in gray.

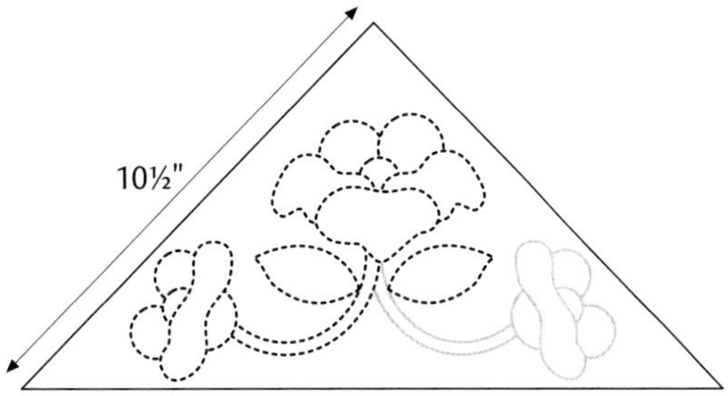

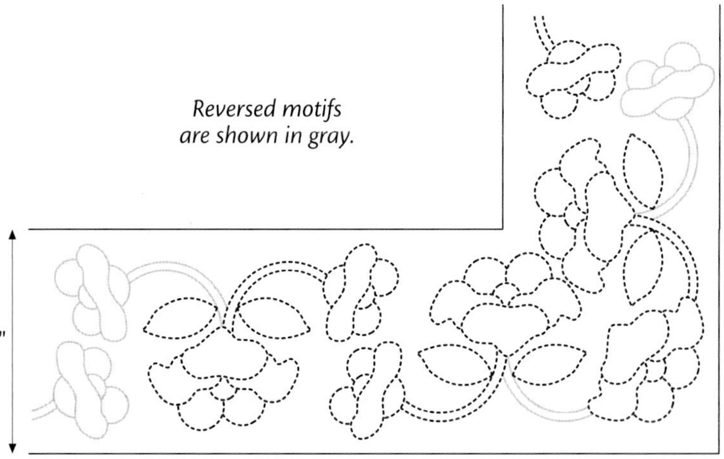

Floral Delight

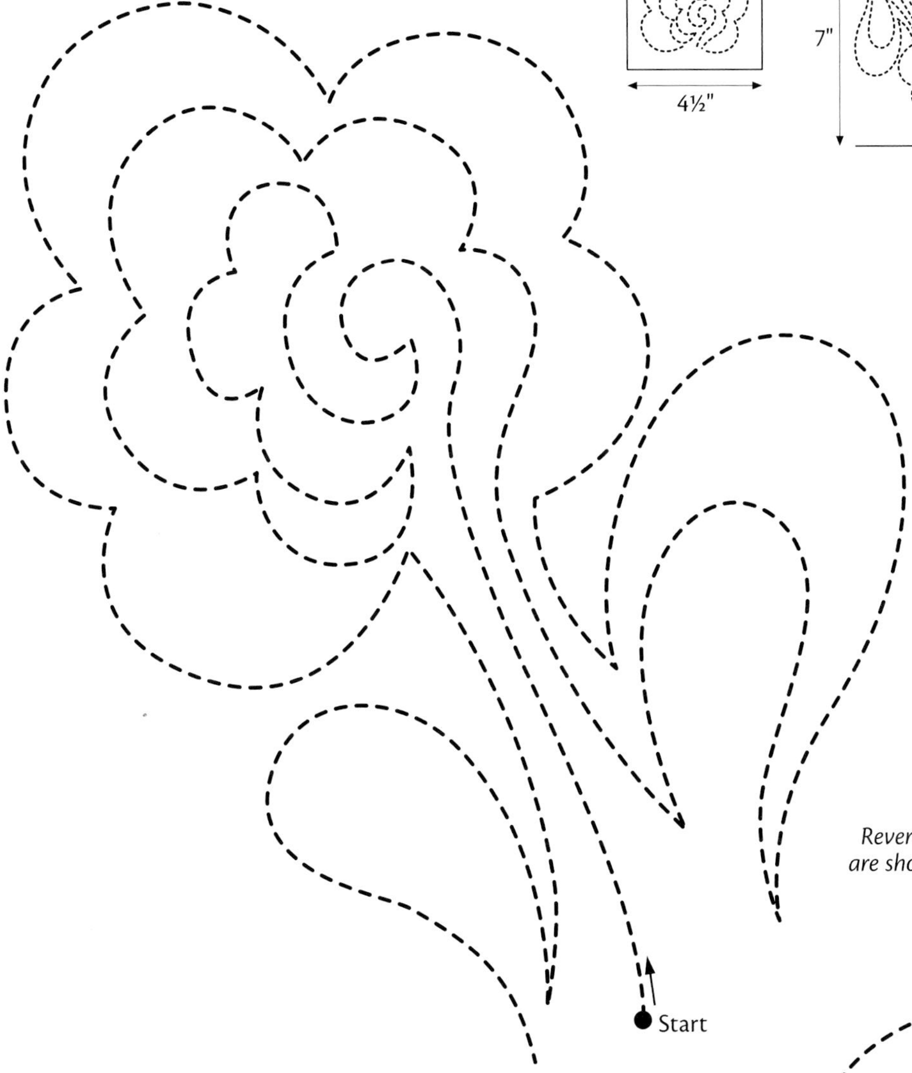

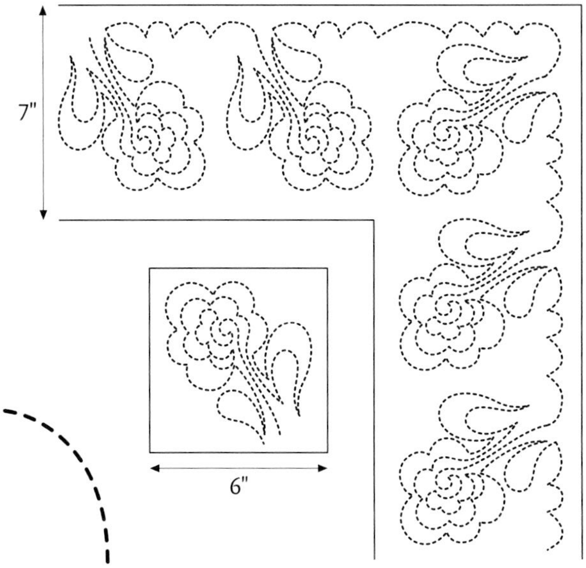

Reversed motifs are shown in gray.

Pinwheel Posey

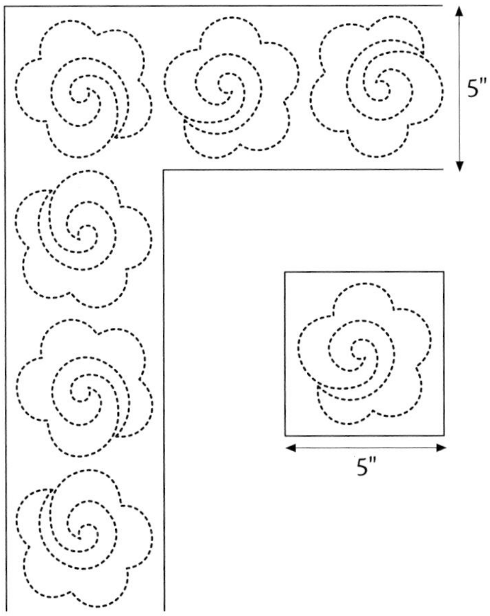

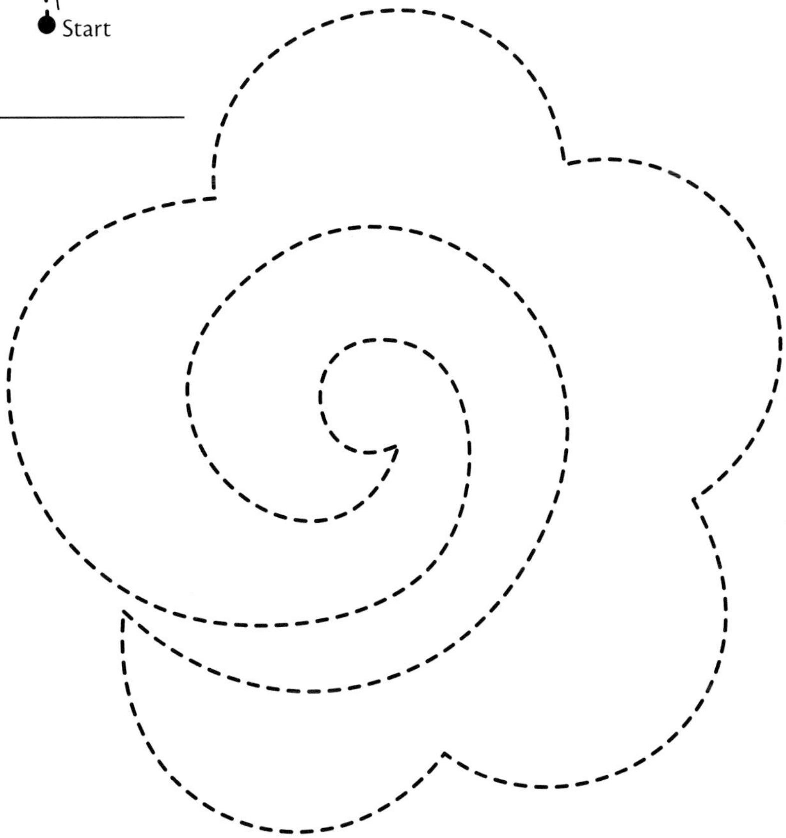

Tropical Fling

6"
12½"
End
9½"
Arrows indicate direction for continuous-line machine quilting.
Start
13"

Lily Bud

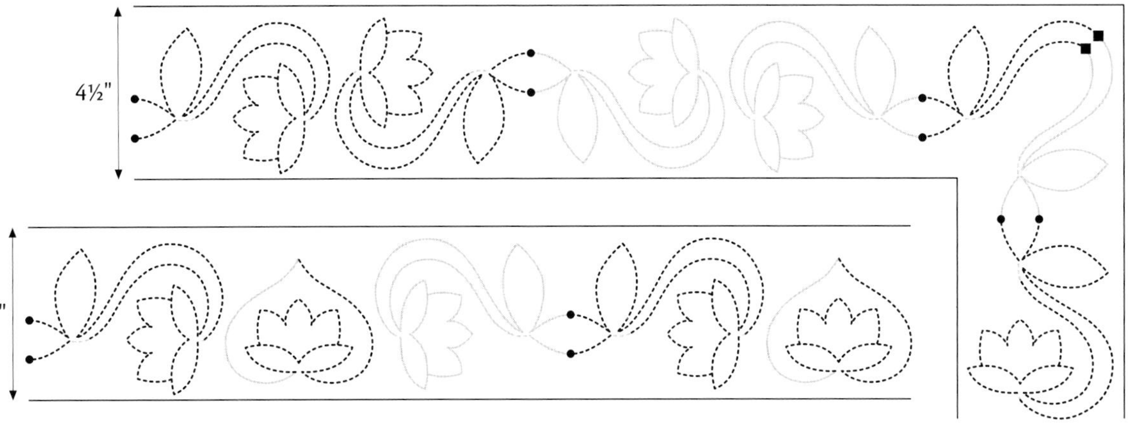

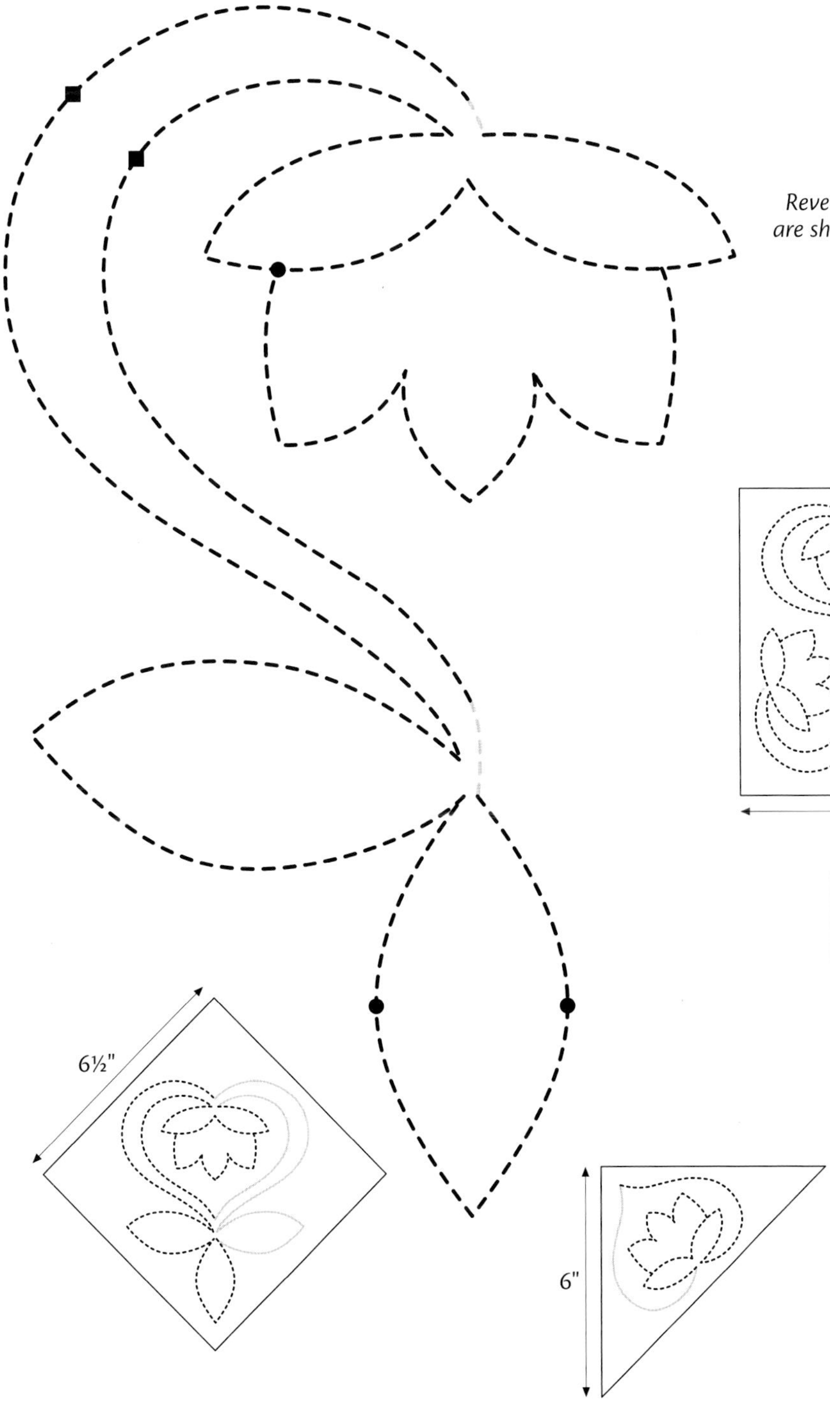

Reversed motifs are shown in gray.

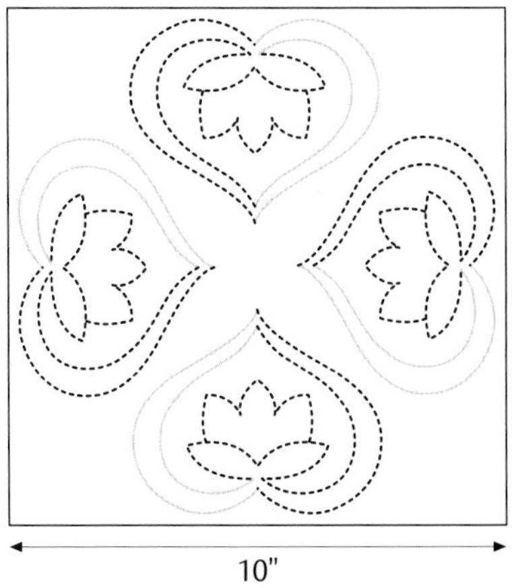

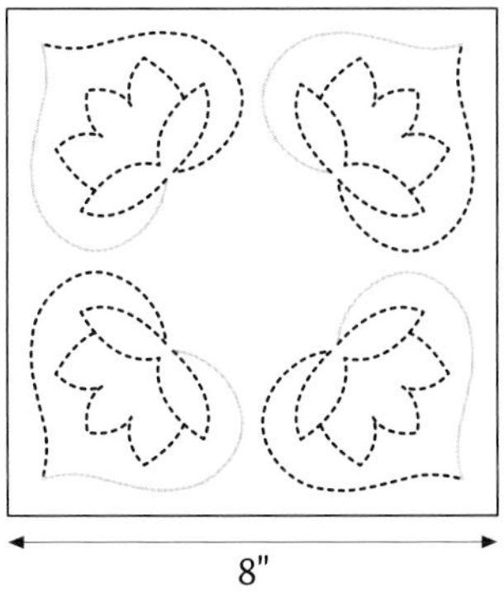

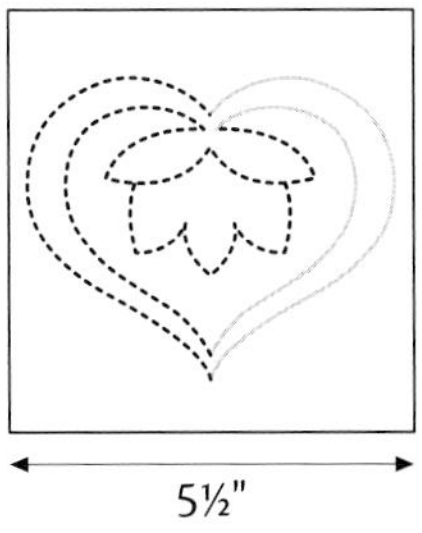

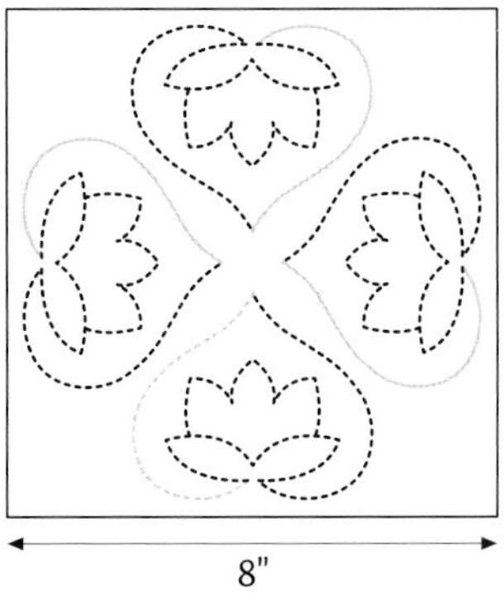

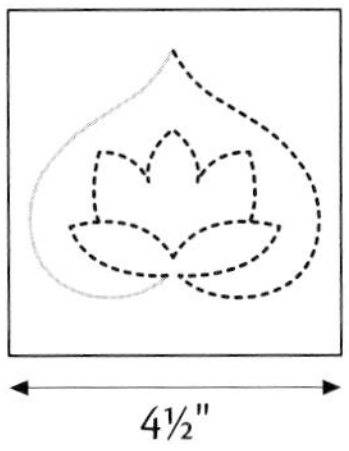

Jaunty Jump-Ups

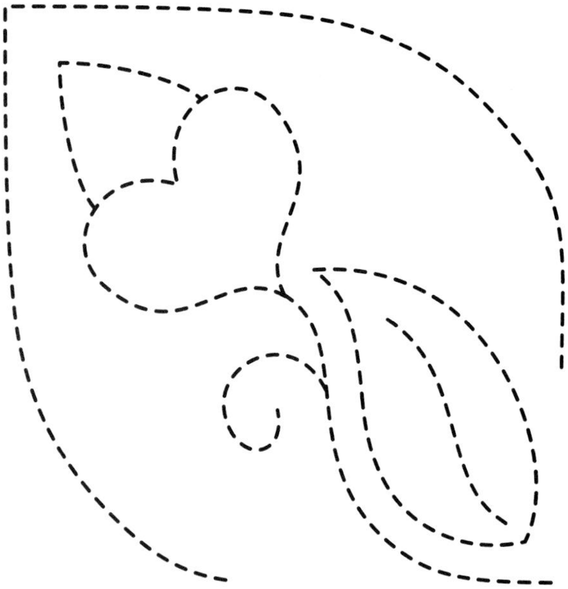

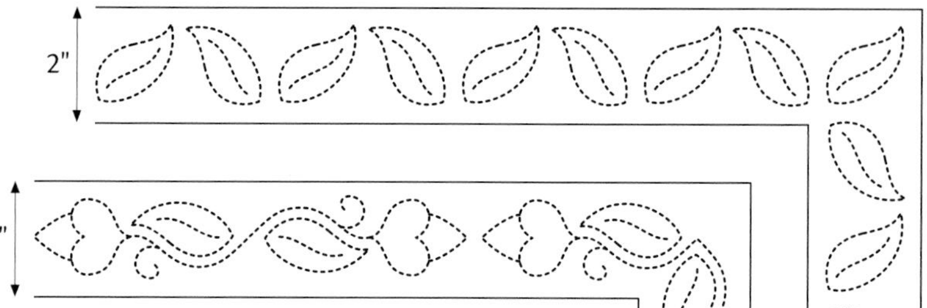

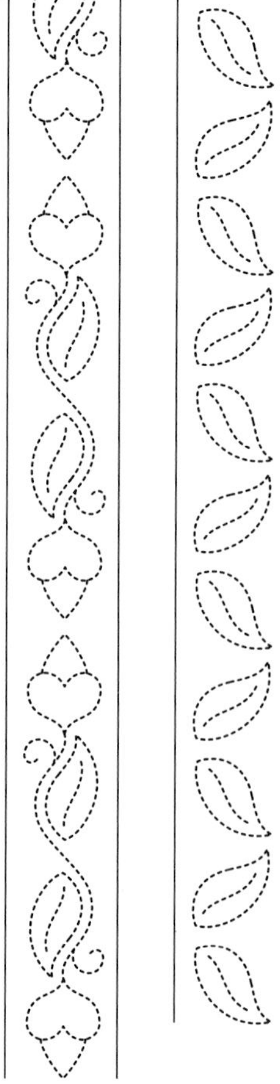

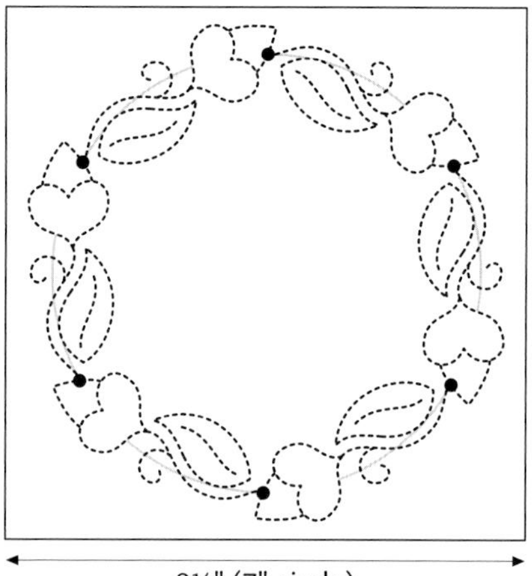

8½" (7" circle)

8½"

6"

6½"

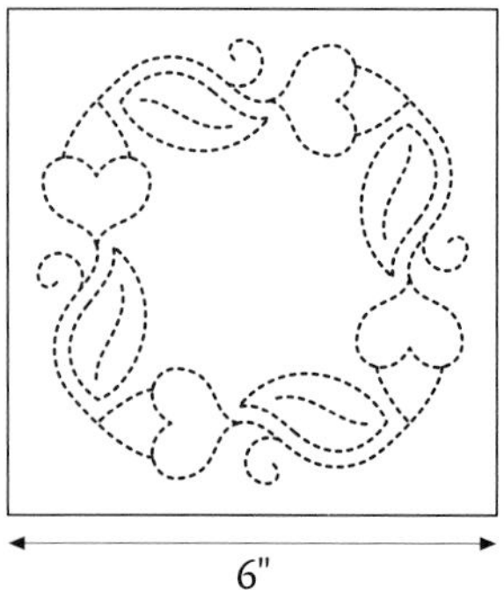

6"

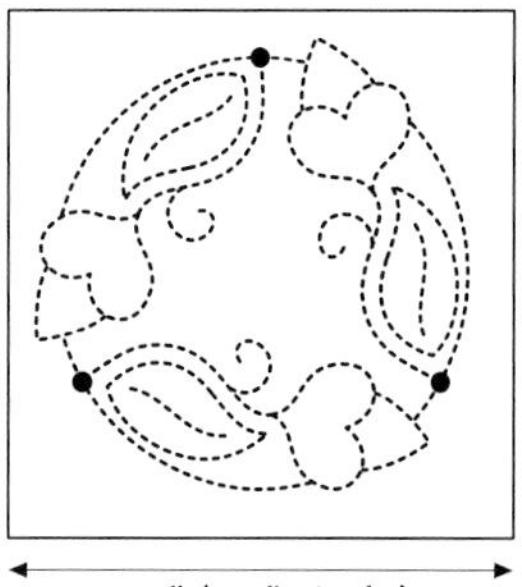

5½" (4½" circle)

7"

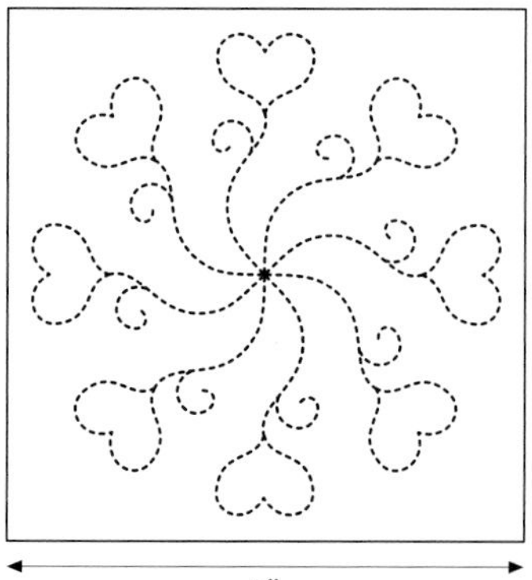

7"

6"

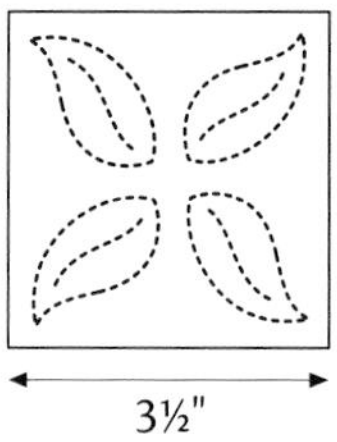

3½"

Harvest Bloom

9"

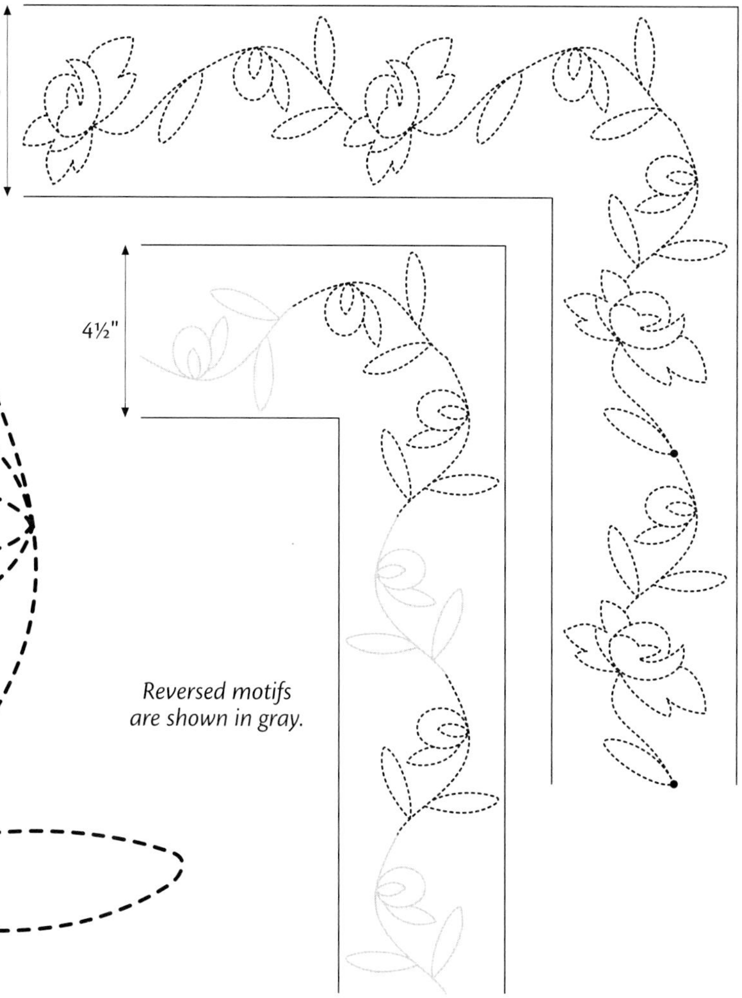

5"

4½"

Reversed motifs are shown in gray.

6½"

6½"

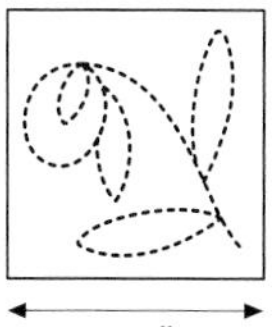

3½"

5"

6"

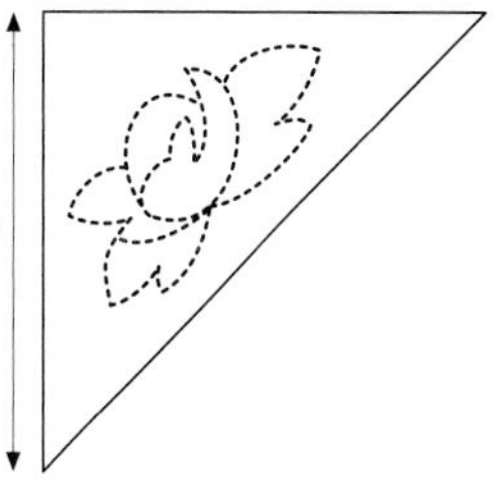

Shasta Daisy

4"

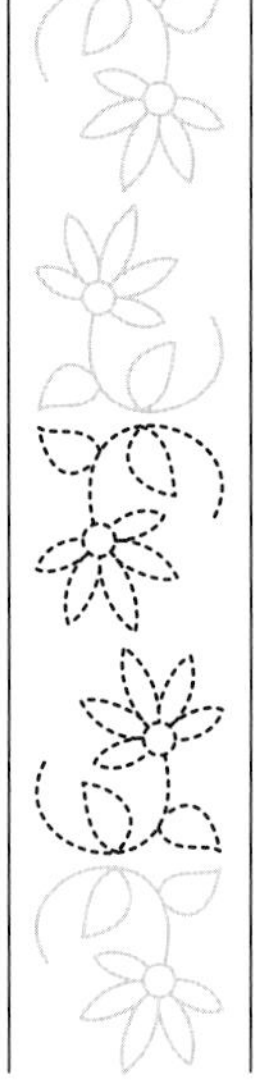

4"

Reversed motifs are shown in gray.

5"

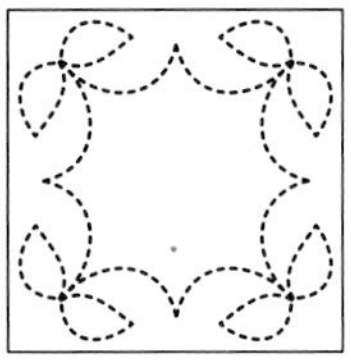

5½"

5½"

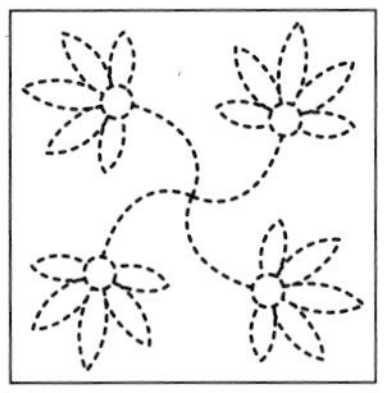

6"

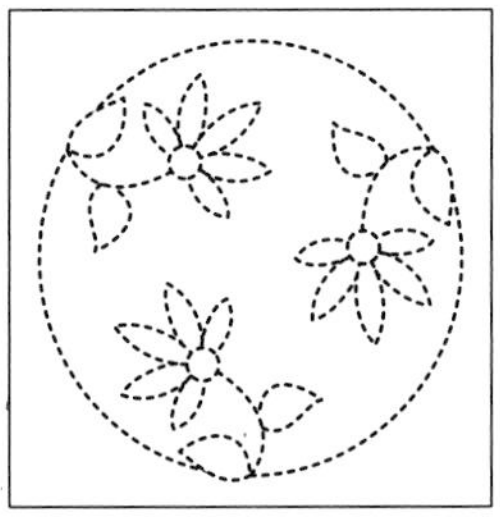

8" (7" circle)

Silver Bells

9"

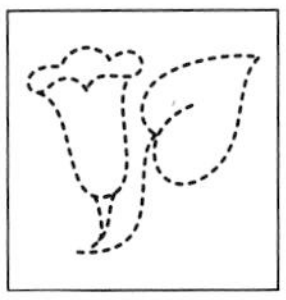

4½"

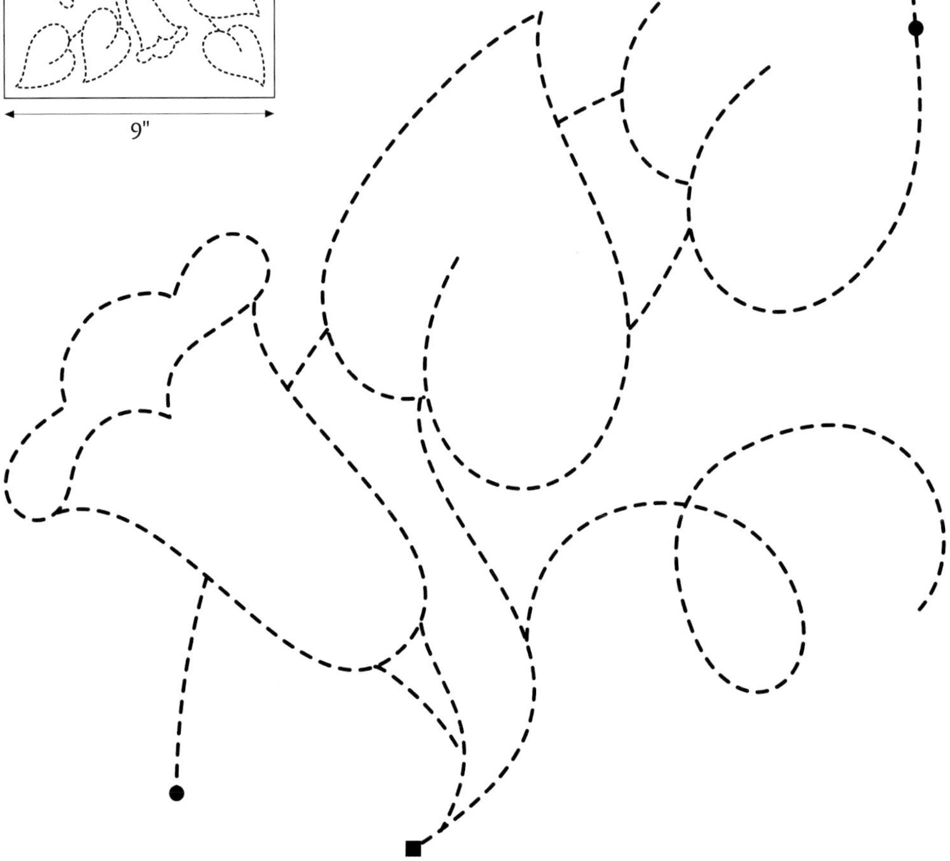

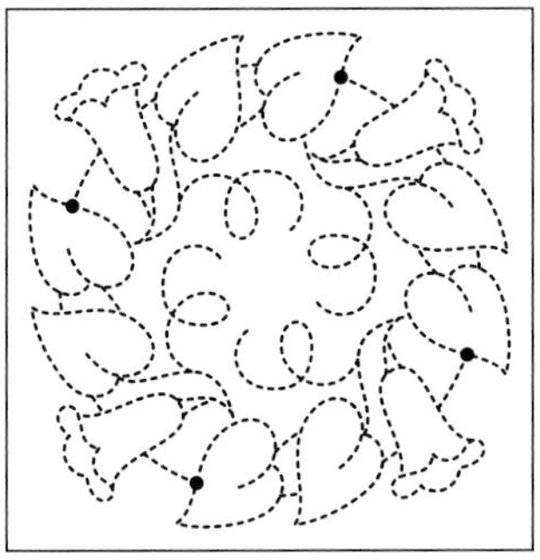

10"

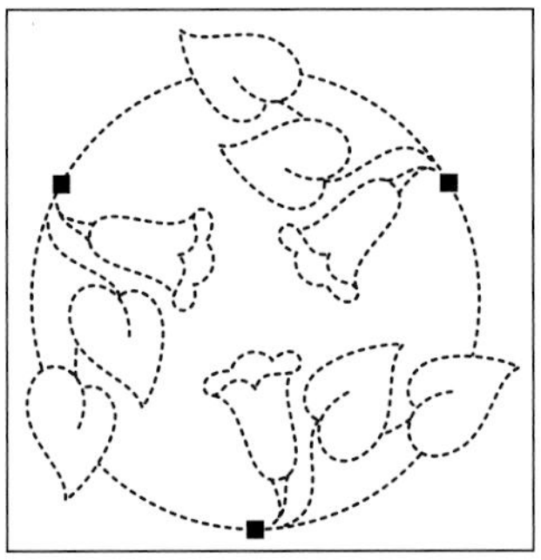

10" (8½" circle)

9"

Star Flower

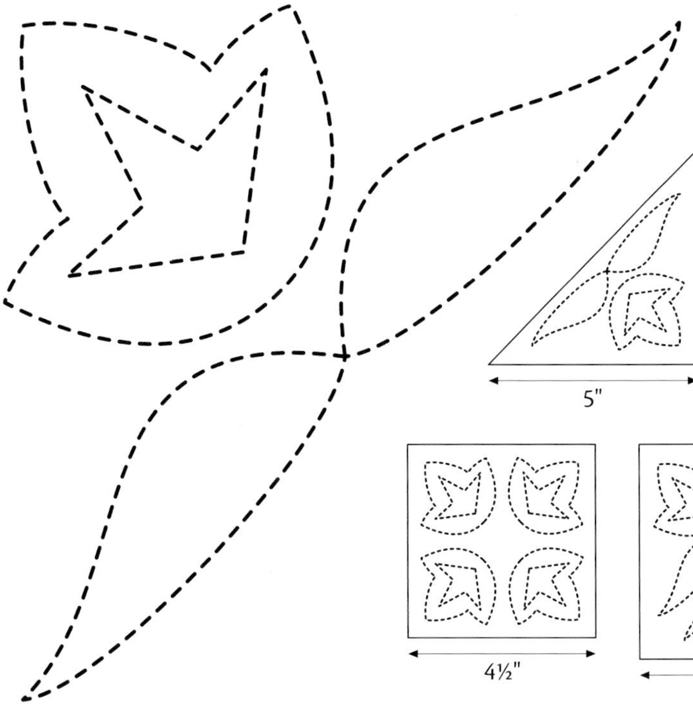

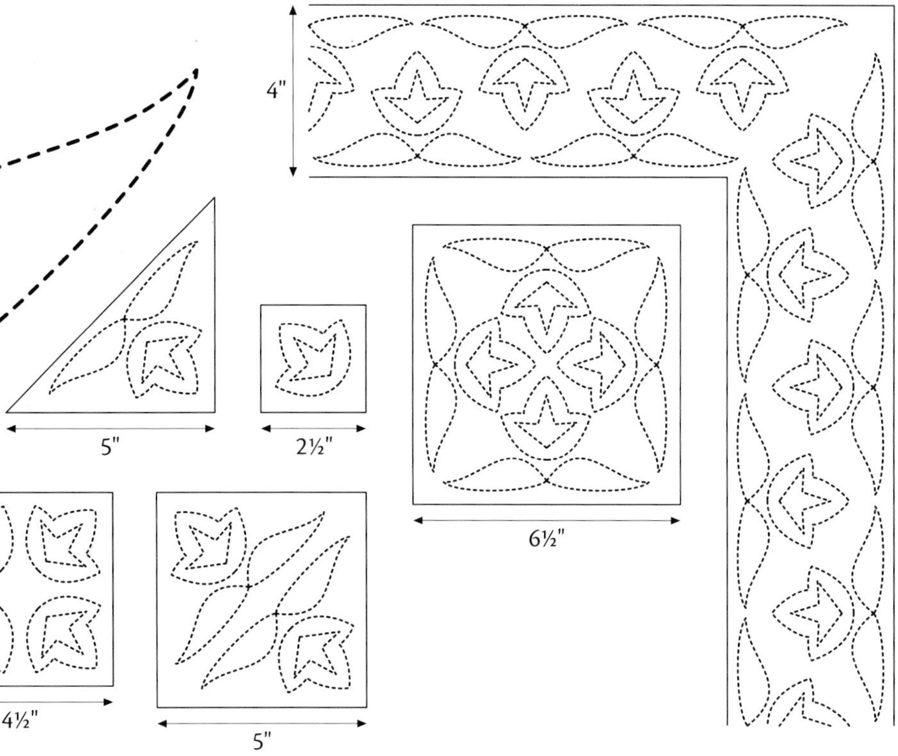
4"
5"
2½"
6½"
4½"
5"

Springtime

2½"

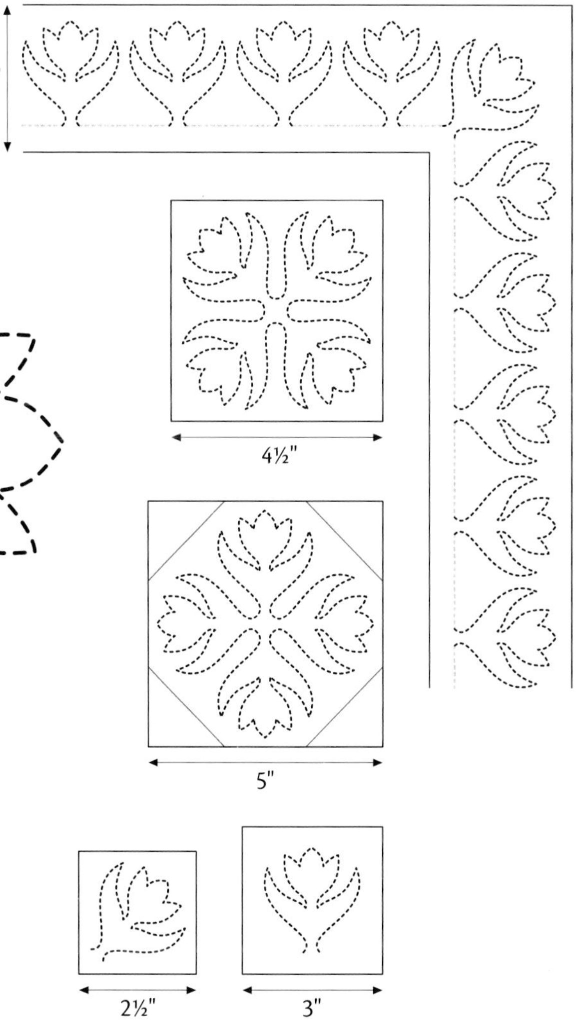
3"
4½"
5"
2½"
3"

Rose Beauty

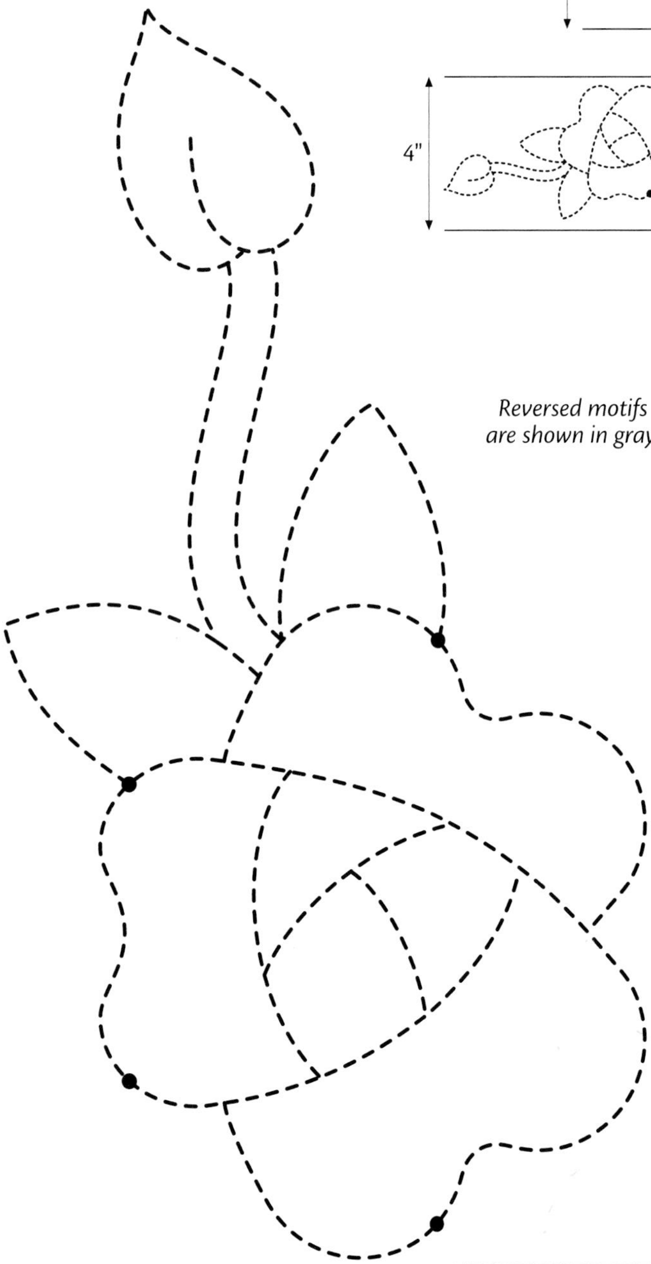

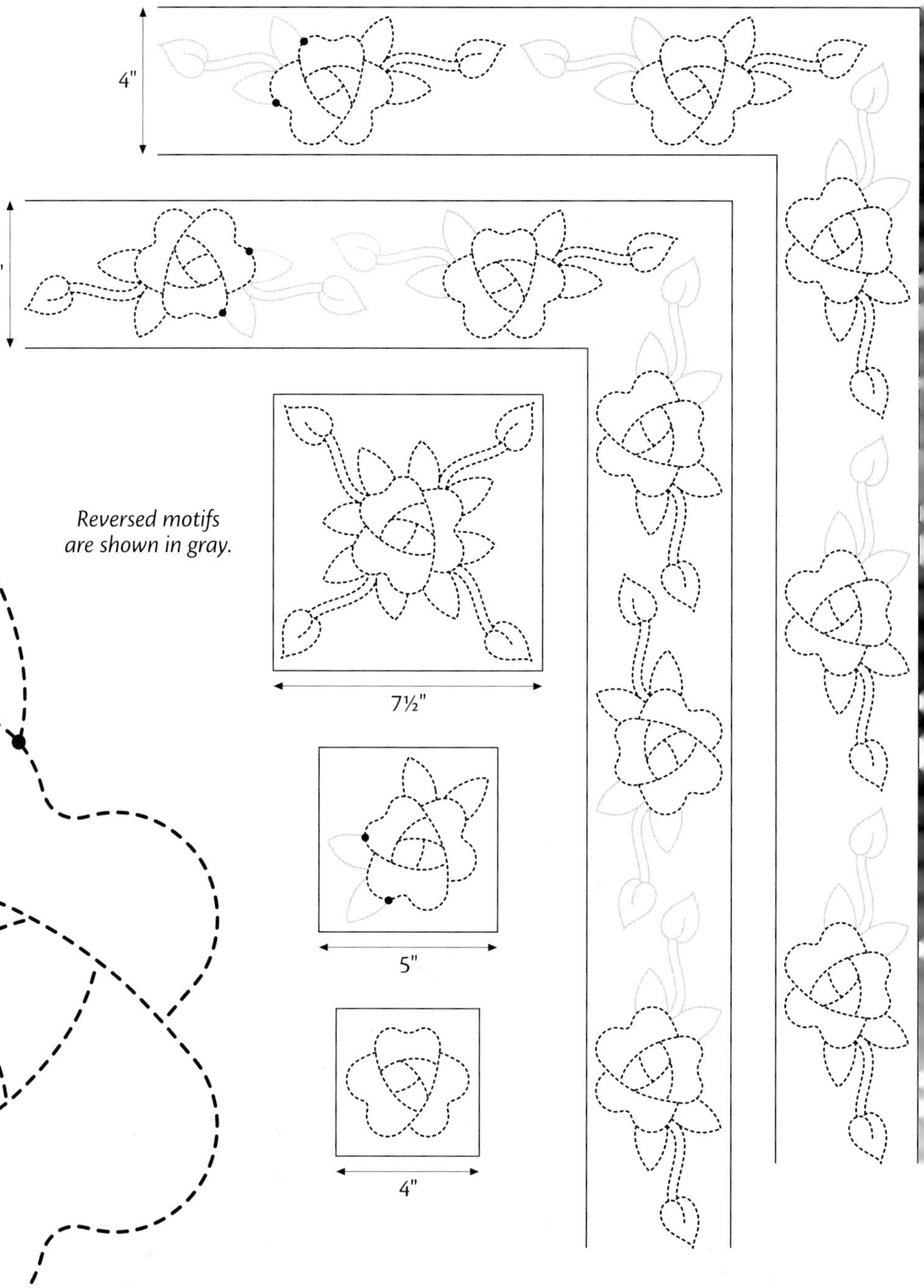

4"

4"

Reversed motifs are shown in gray.

7½"

5"

4"

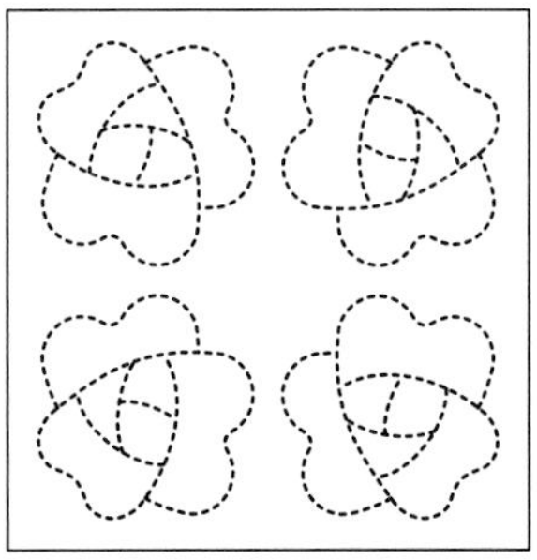

7½"

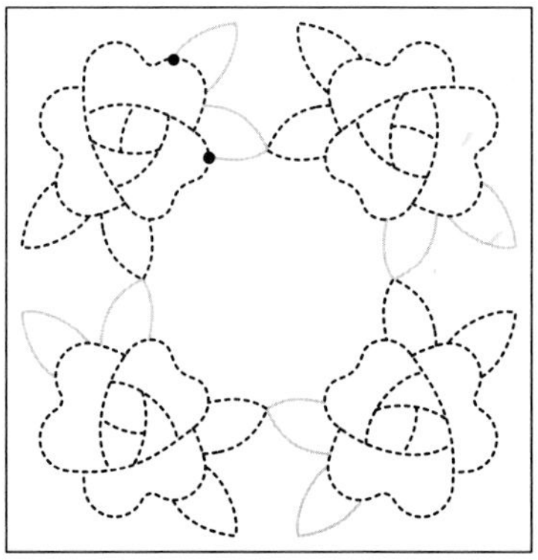

9½"

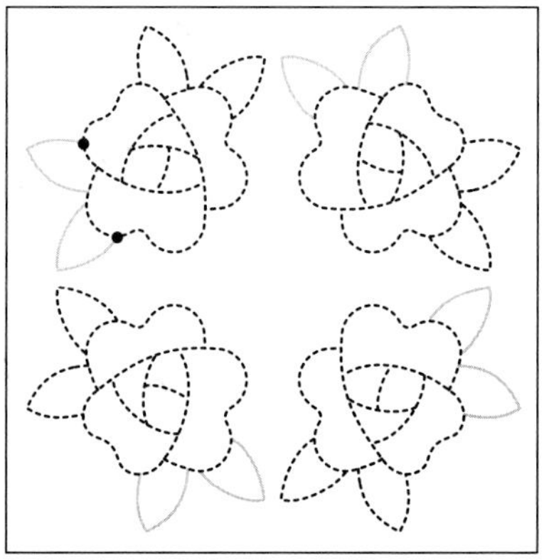

10"

Sparkling Flower

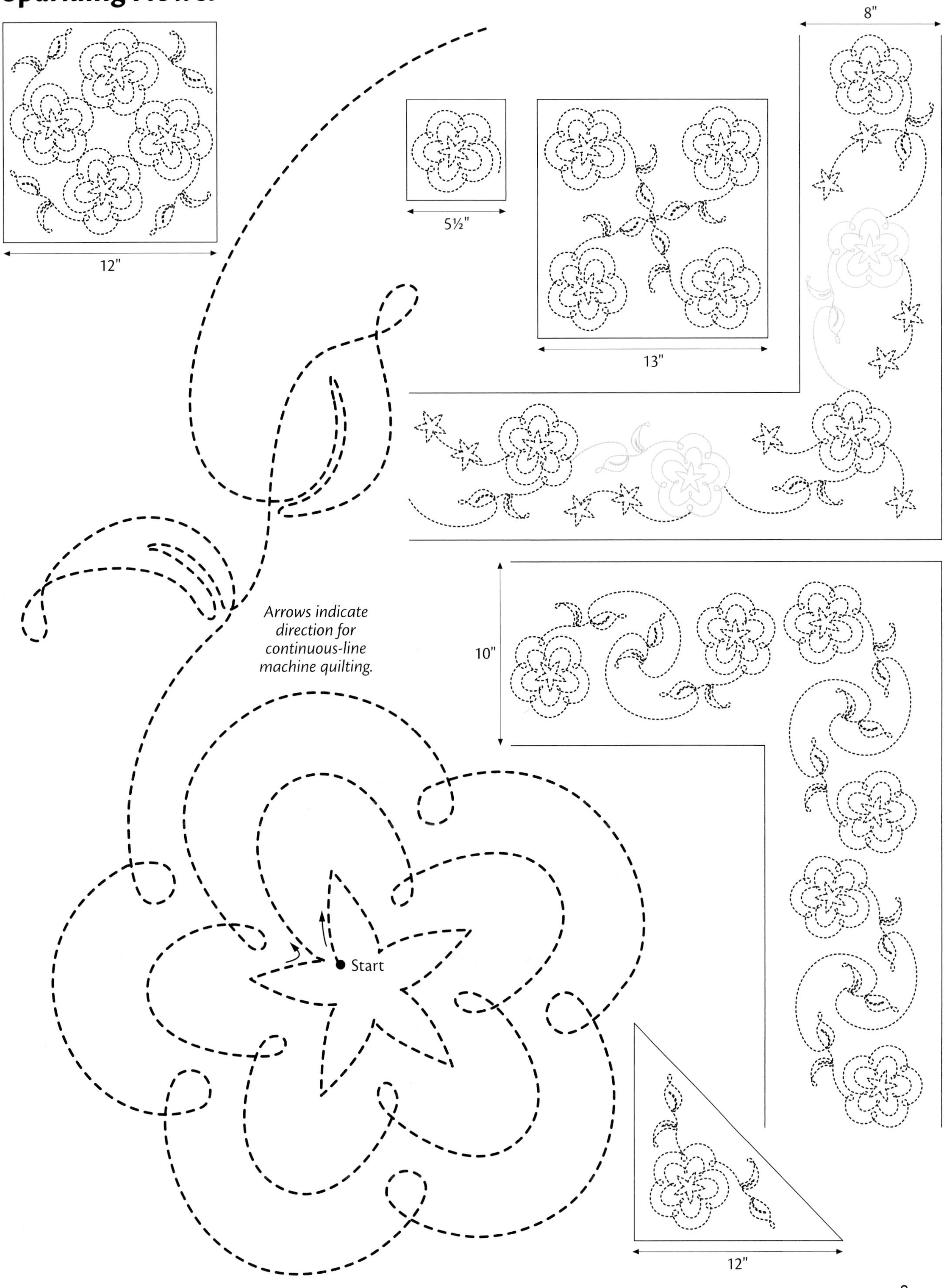
12"
8"
5½"
13"
Arrows indicate
direction for
continuous-line
machine quilting.
10"
Start
12"

Buttercup

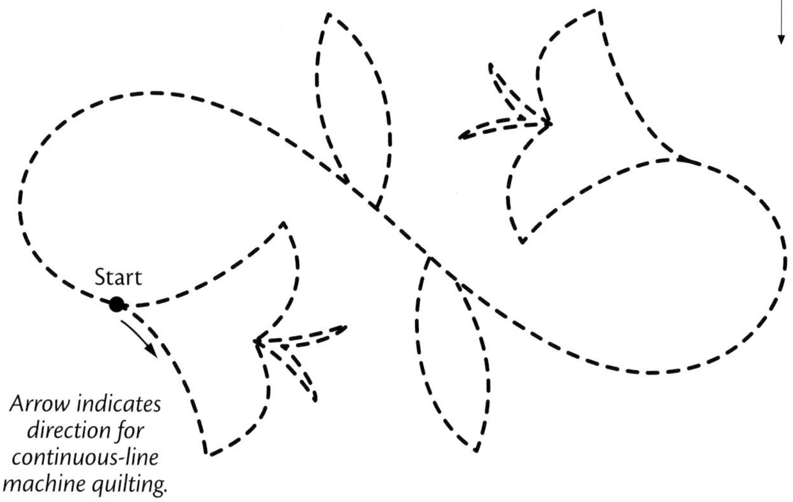

Start
Arrow indicates direction for continuous-line machine quilting.

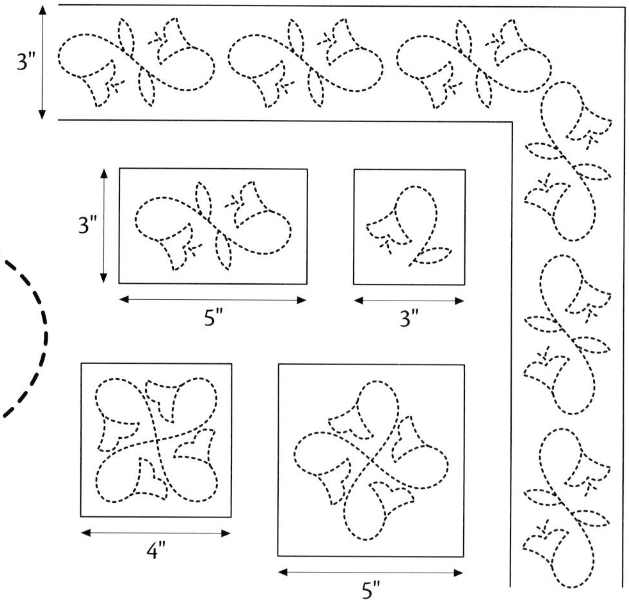

3"
3"
5"
3"
4"
5"

Flower of Youth

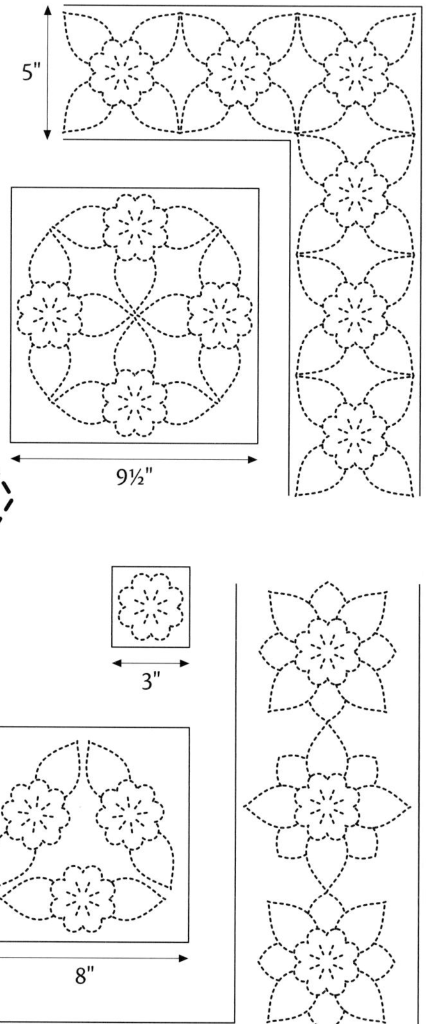

5"
9½"
3"
8"

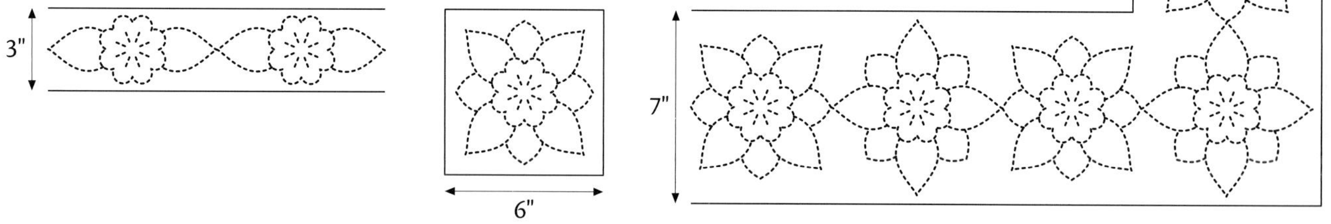

3"
6"
7"

Happy Days

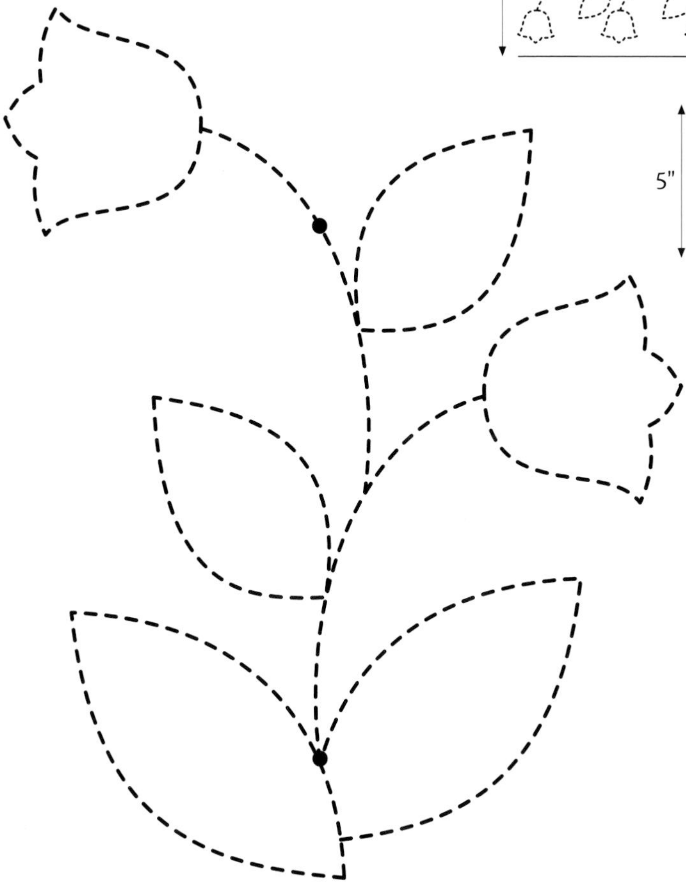

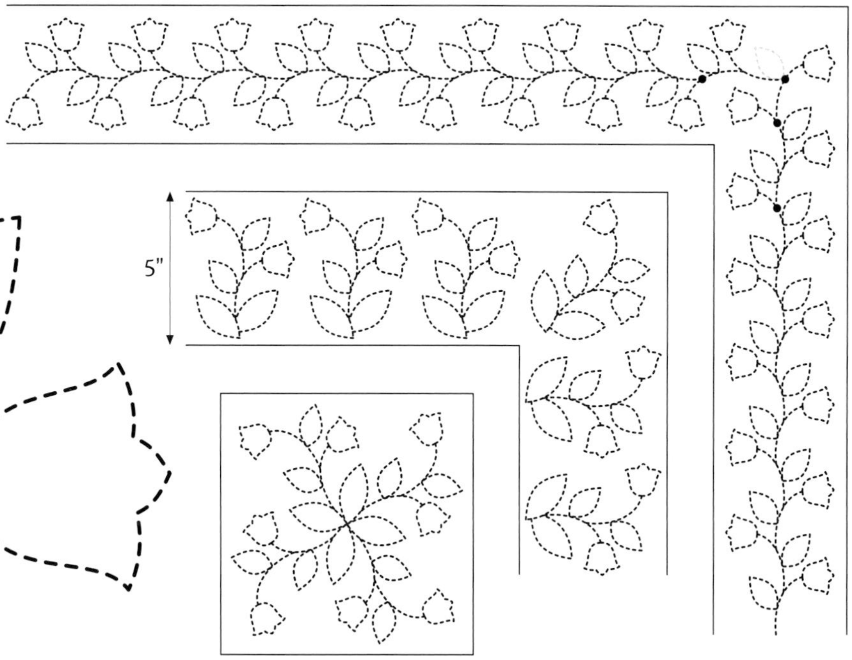

4½"

5"

8½"

5"

6"

7½"

Petite Fleur

6"

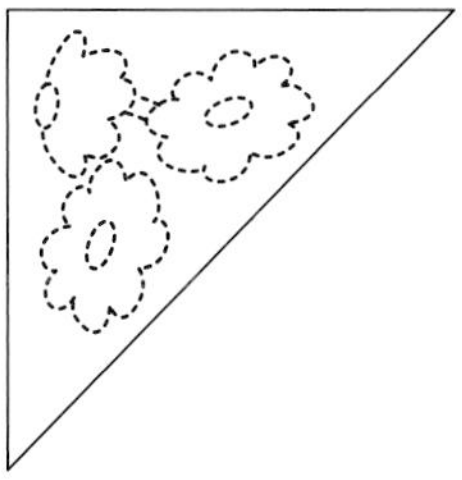

6"

4"

5"

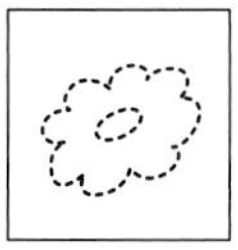

3"

Belle Fleur

6½"
9½"
4"
4"
5"
9½"
8½"

Reversed motifs are shown in gray.

Daisy Delight

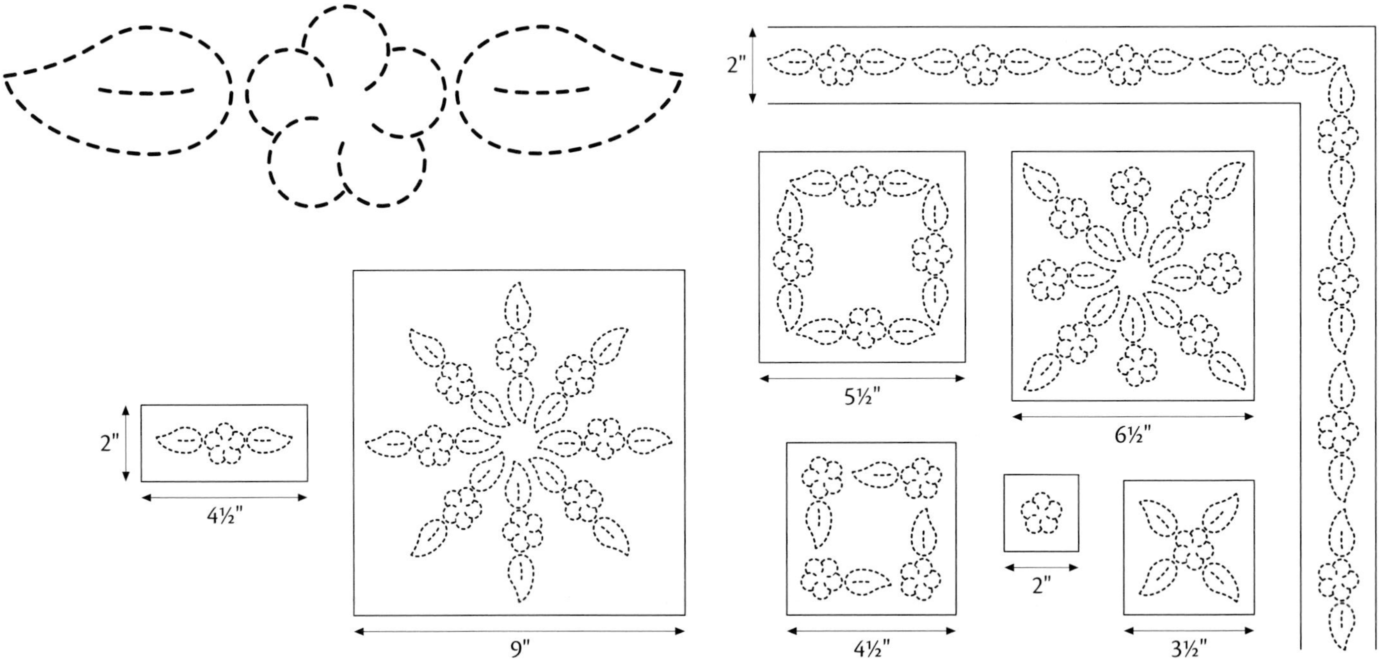

2"
2"
4½"
9"
5½"
6½"
4½"
2"
3½"

Grandma's Trellis

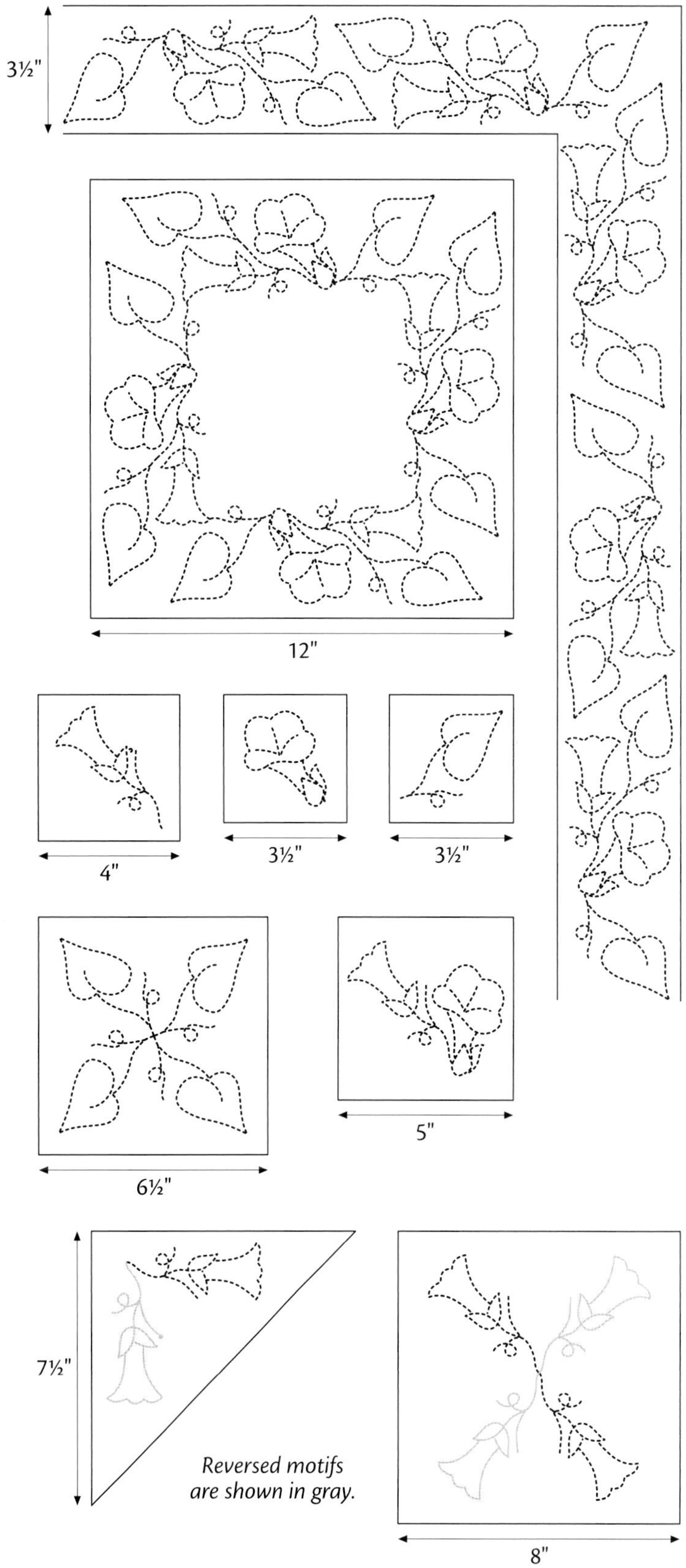
3½"
12"
4"
3½"
3½"
6½"
5"
7½"
8"

Reversed motifs are shown in gray.

Shy Violet

Reversed motif is shown in gray.

Budding Beauty

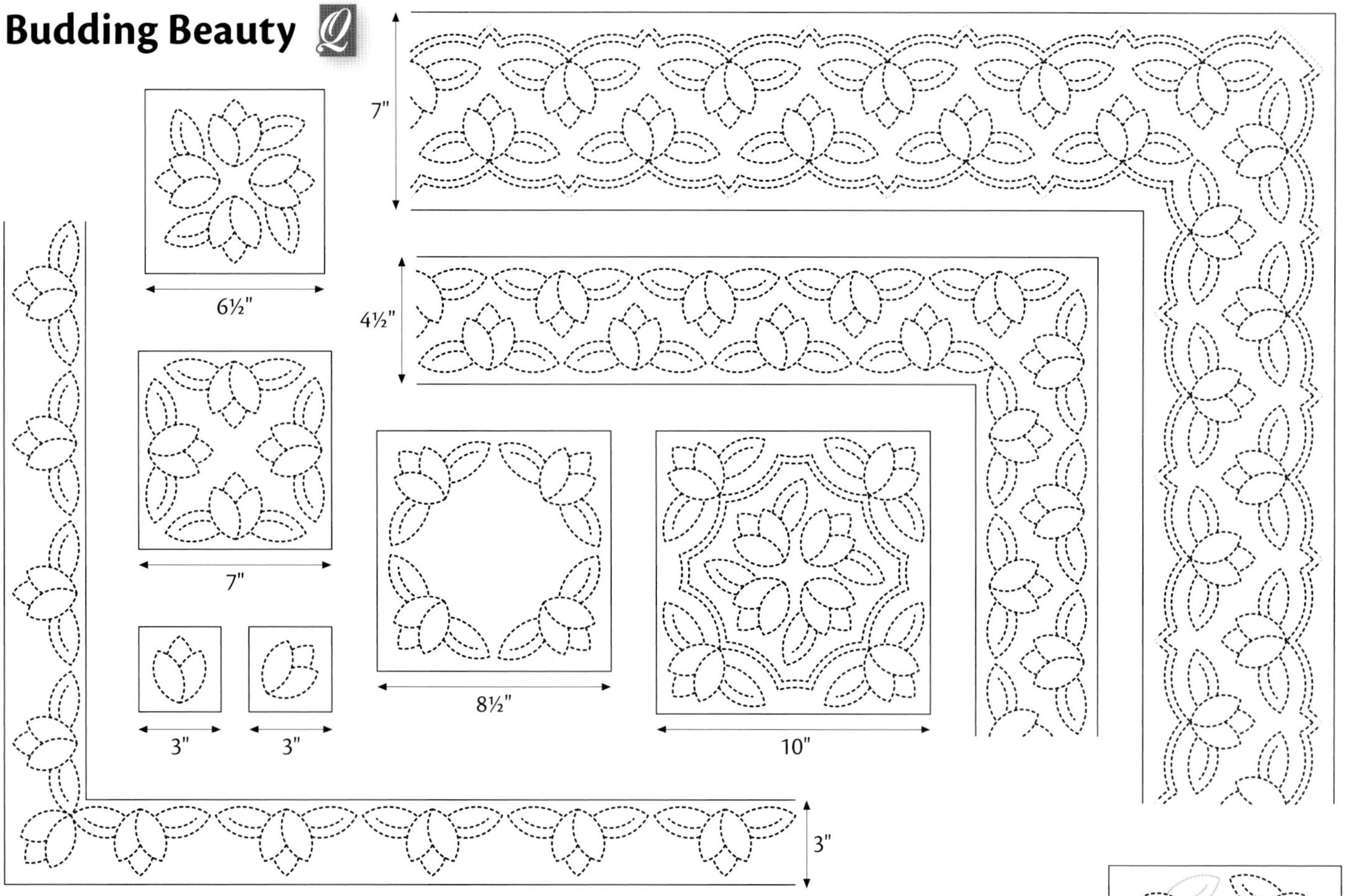

7"
6½"
4½"
7"
8½"
10"
3"
3"
3"

Center

Place folded paper on dotted lines, trace, and rotate for full motif.

Reversed motifs are shown in gray.

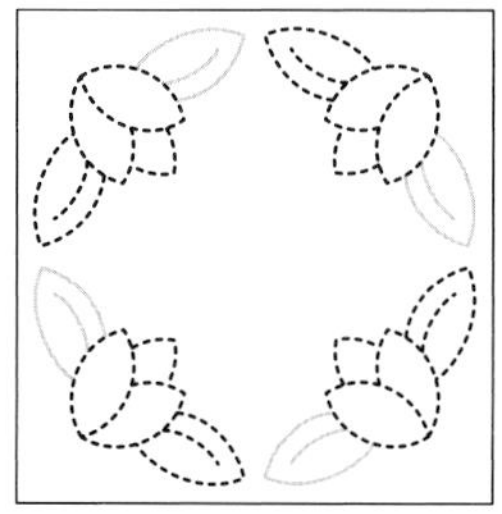

8½"

8½" (5½" circle)

8½"

Evening Flower

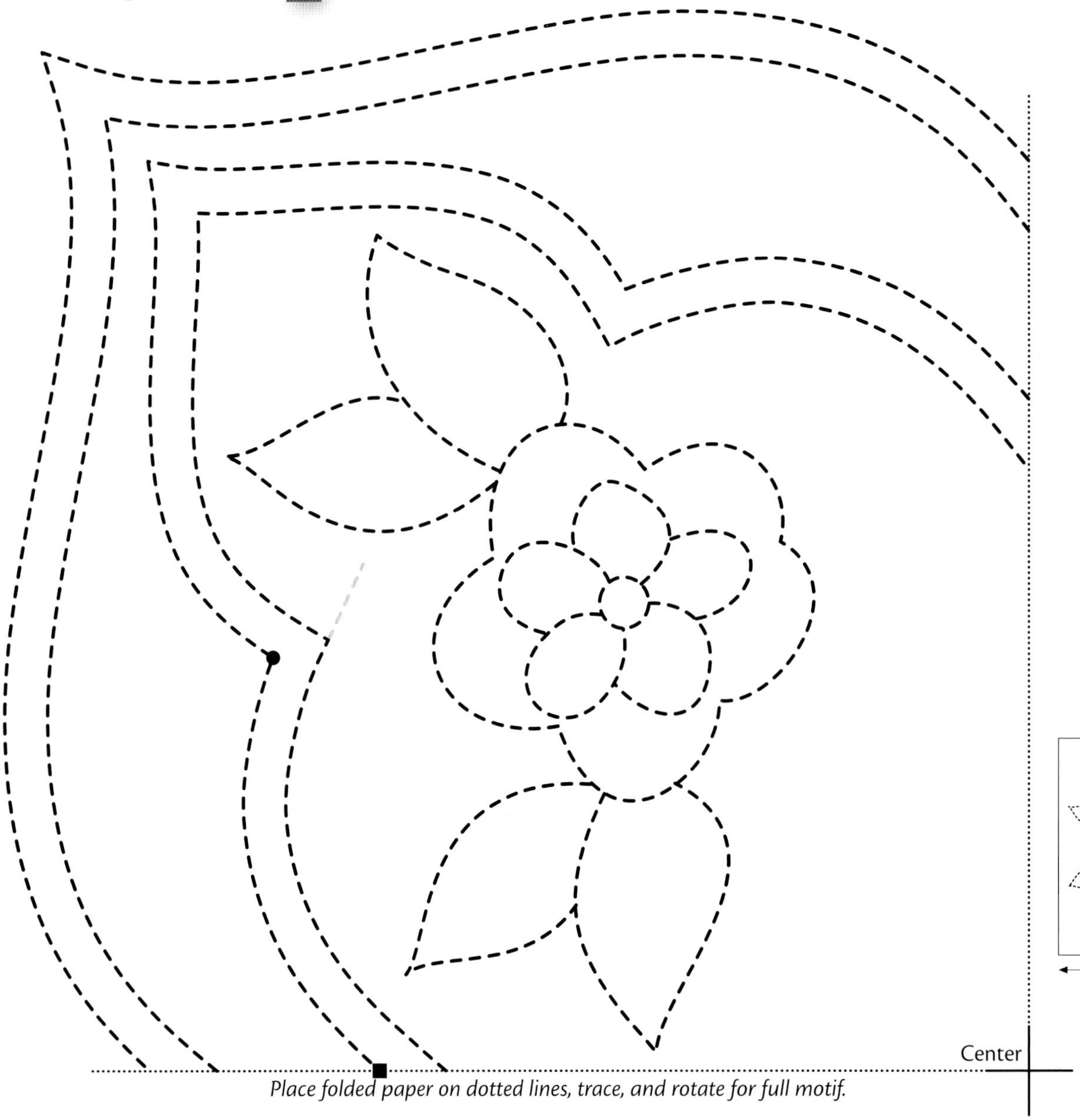

Place folded paper on dotted lines, trace, and rotate for full motif.

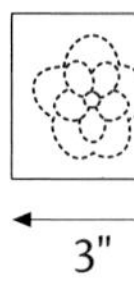

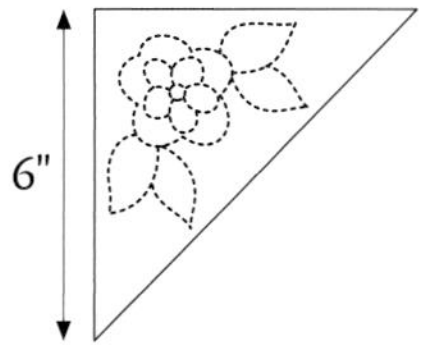

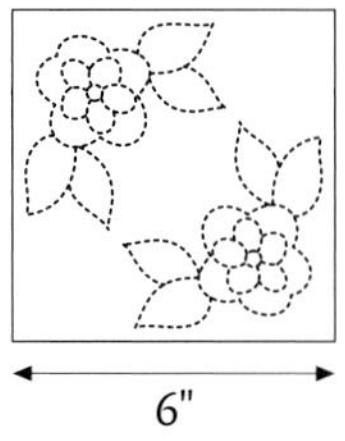

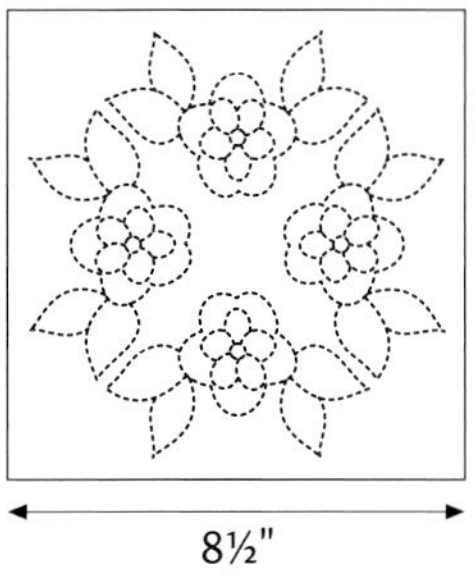

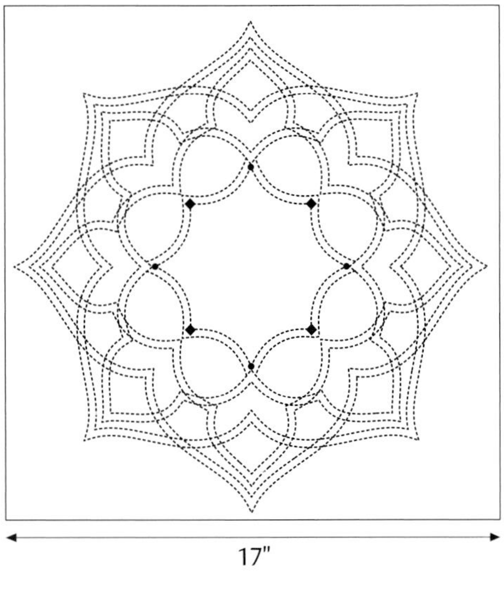

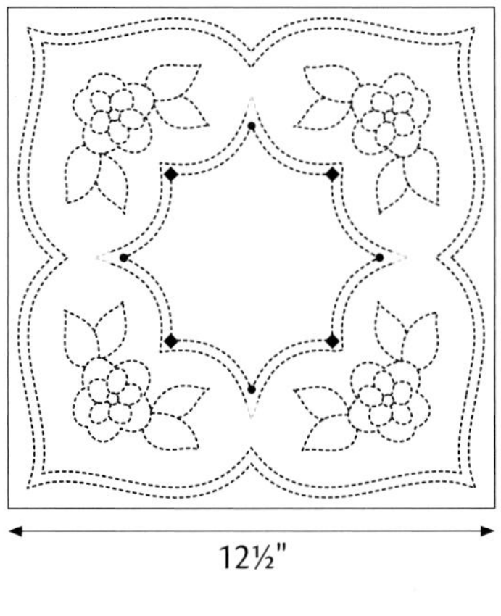

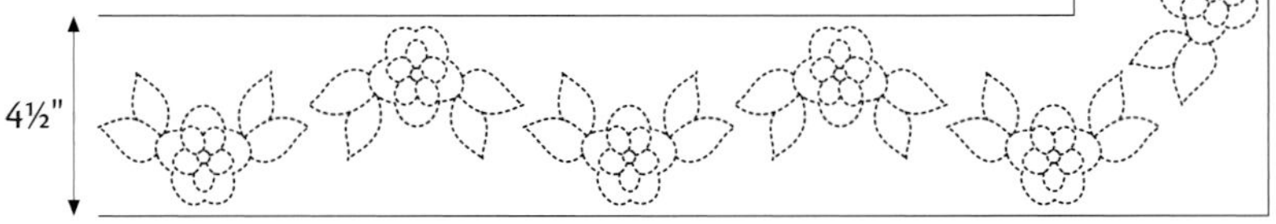

Floral Spray

Start
4½"
4½"
15"
13½"
6½"
10½"
9"
6½"
3½"

Arrows indicate direction for continuous-line machine quilting.

Reversed motifs are shown in gray.

Morning's Glory

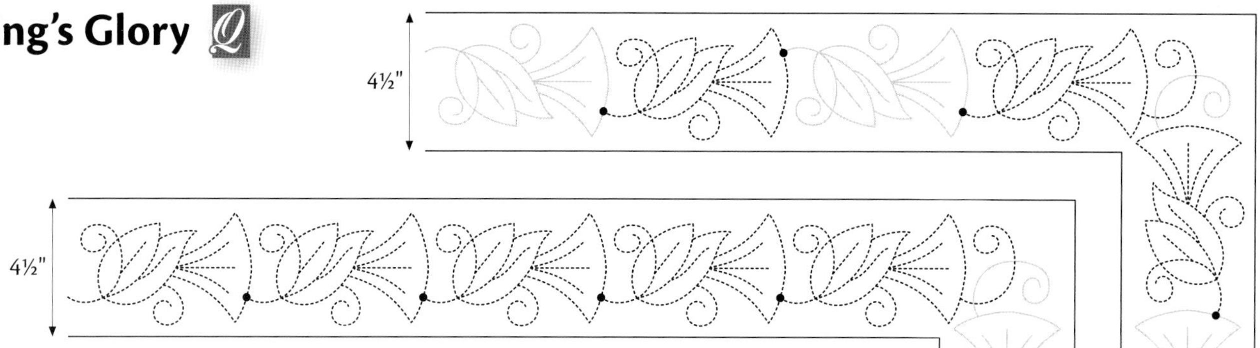

Reversed motifs are shown in gray.

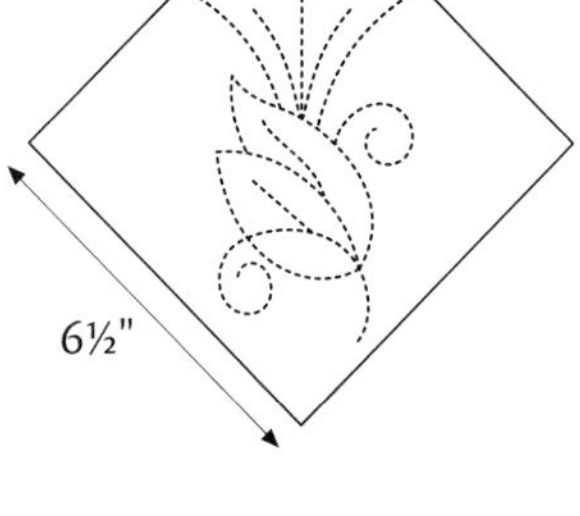

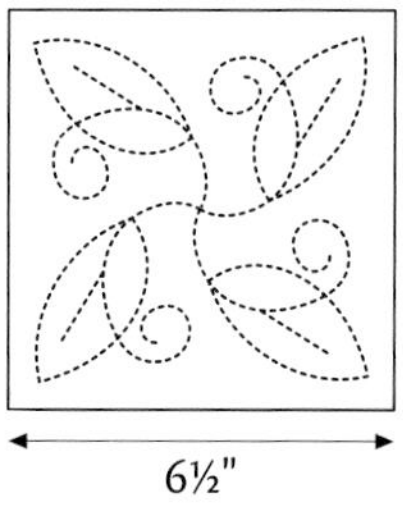

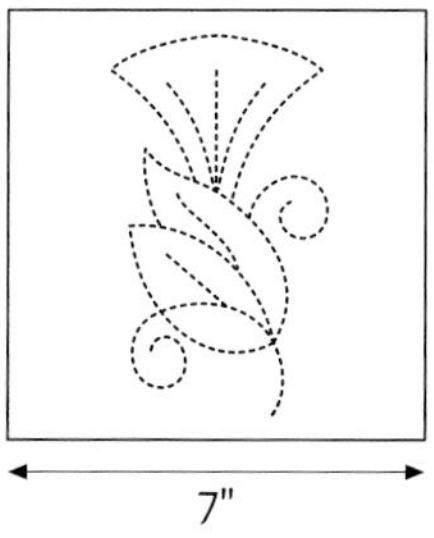

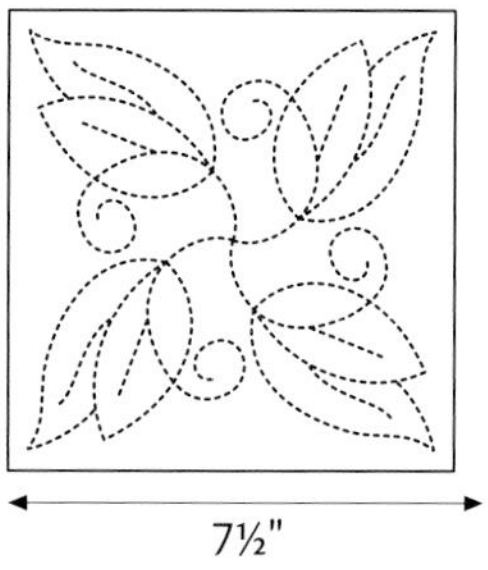

Floral Medley

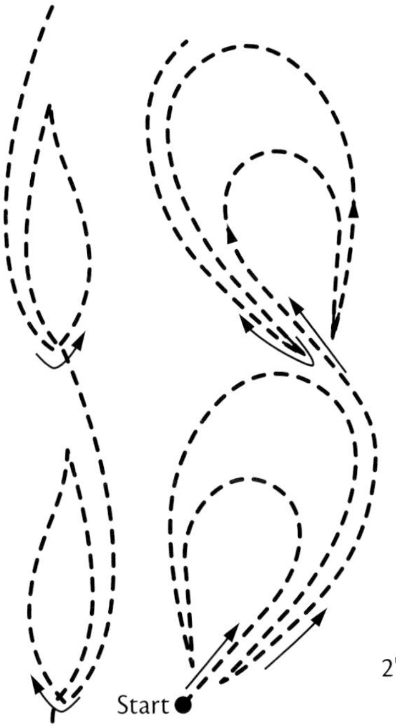

Arrows indicate direction for continuous-line machine quilting.

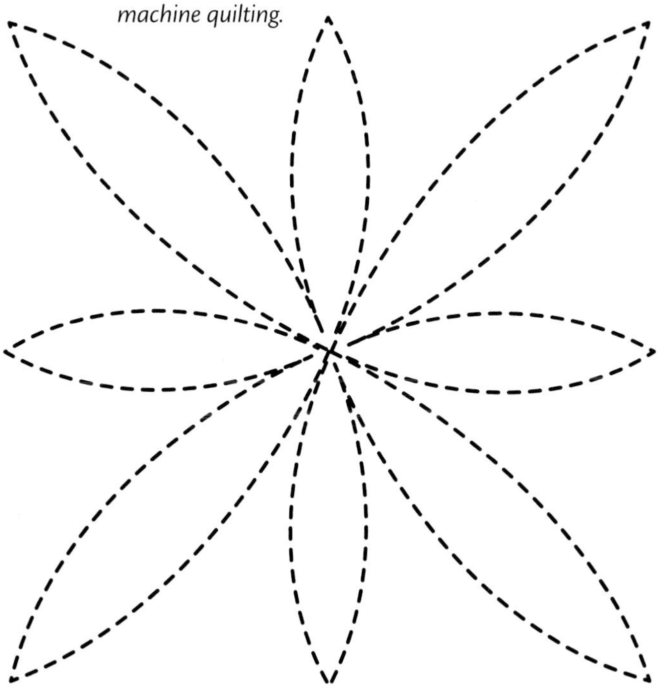

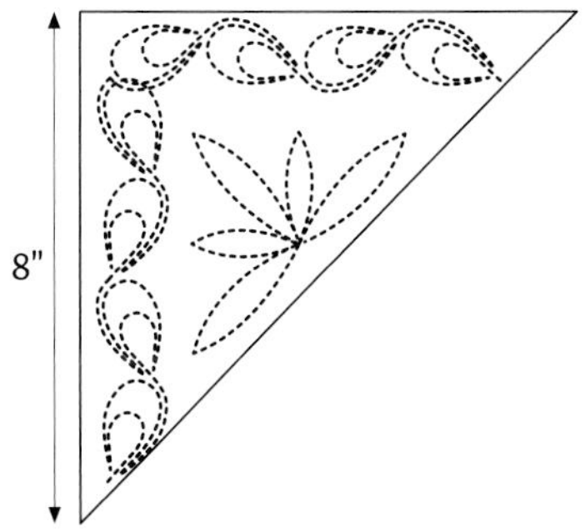

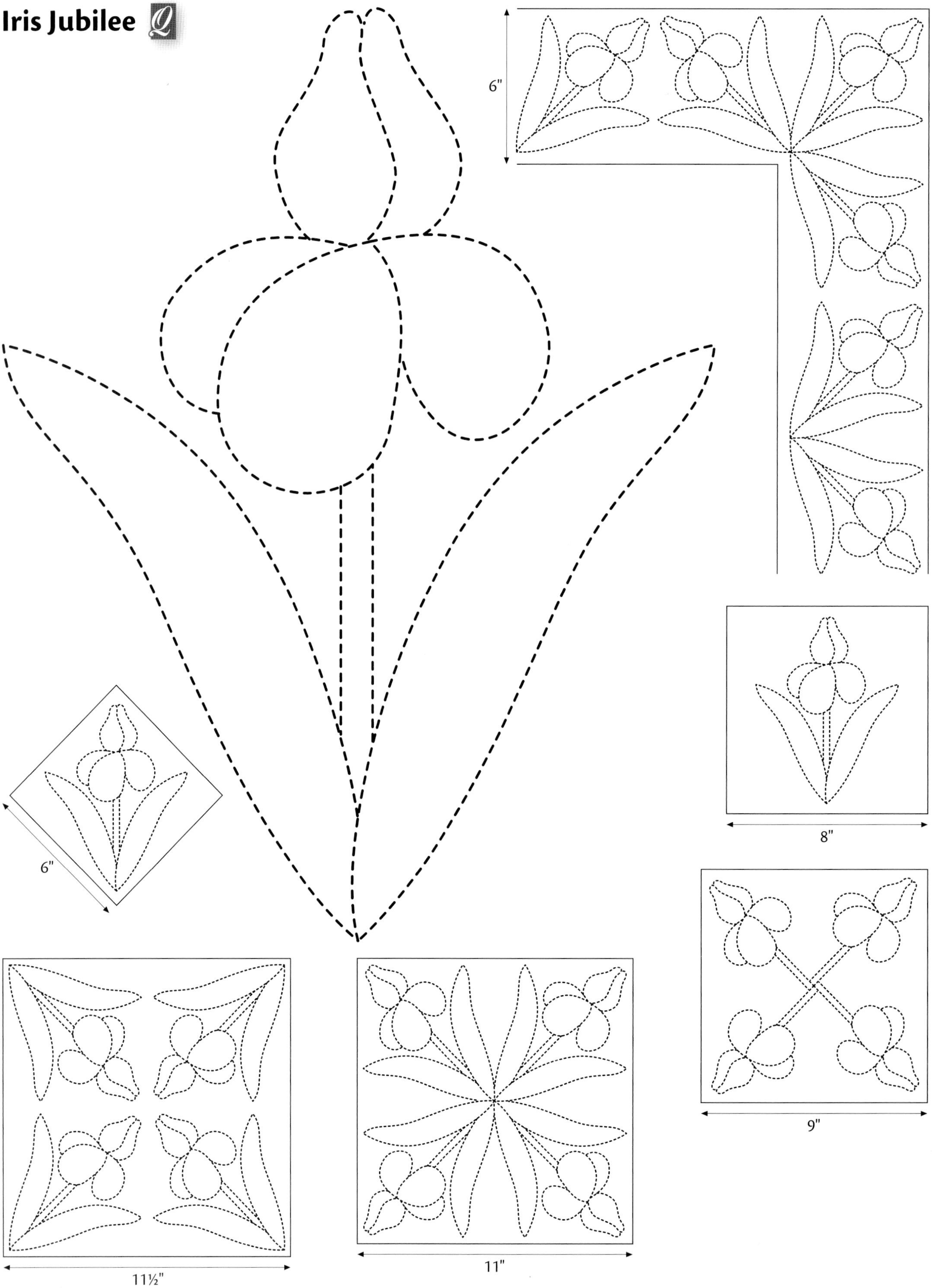
6"
8"
6"
9"
11½"
11"

Blossom Vine

Reversed motifs are shown in gray.

Daffodil Fancy

5½"
5½"
10"
10"
5½"
8"
5"
2½"
2½"

Reversed motifs are shown in gray.

Rondo

Reversed motifs are shown in gray.

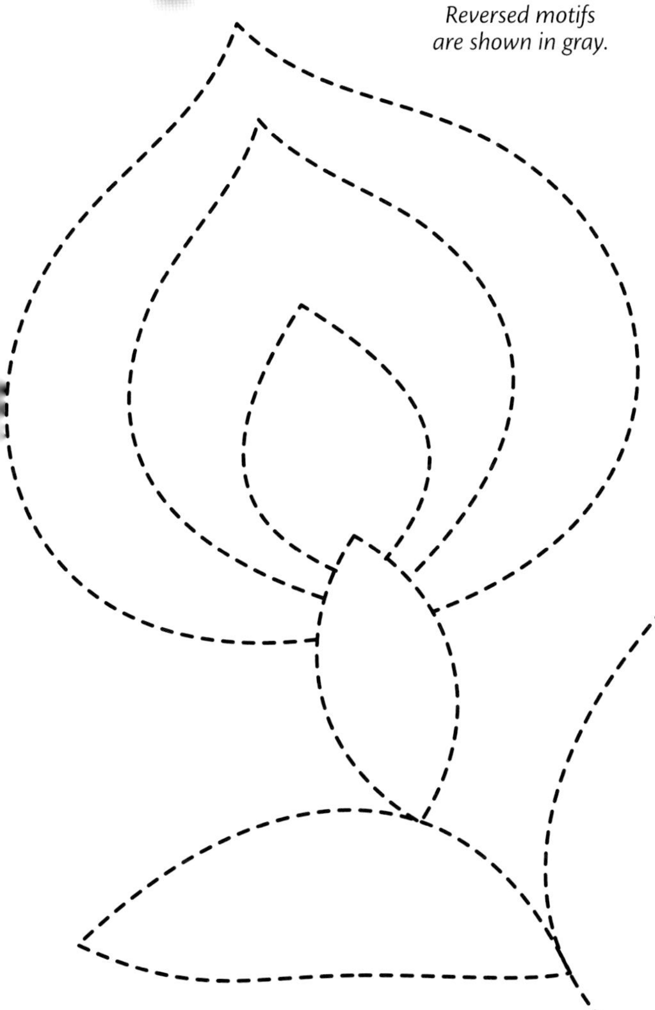

6"

4"

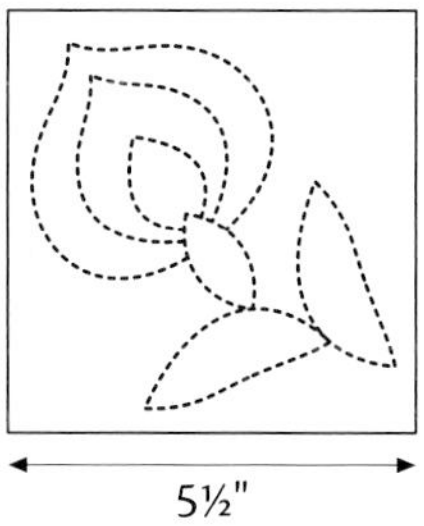

5½"

7"

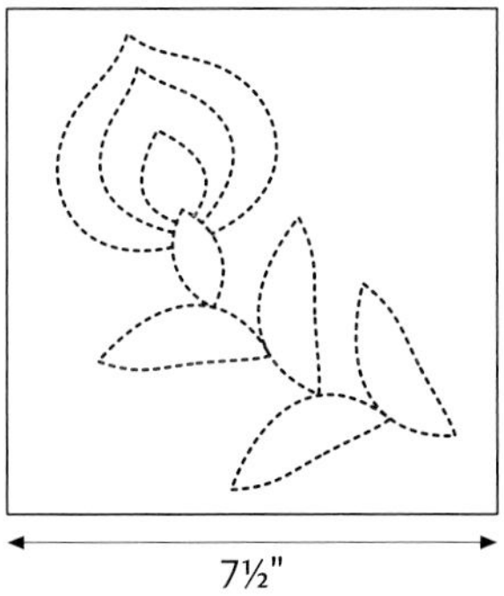

7½"

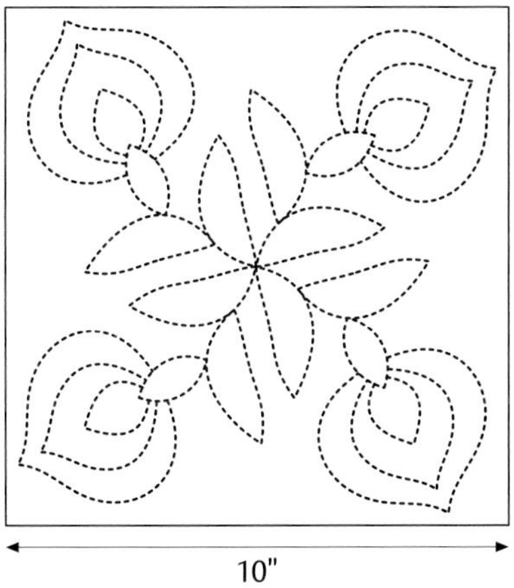

10"

13"

Dandy Daisy

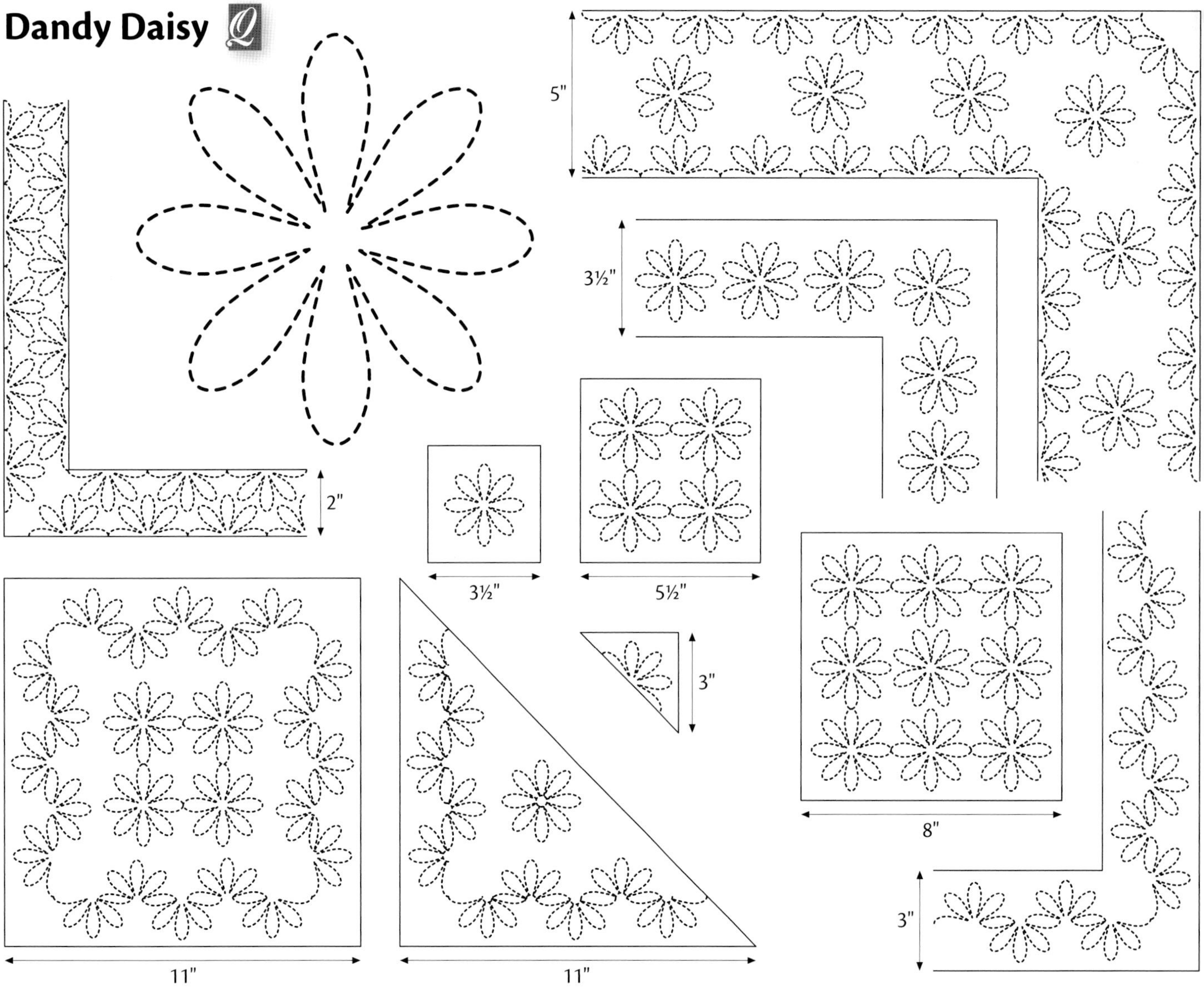
5"
3½"
2"
3½"
5½"
3"
8"
11"
11"
3"

Petite Daisy

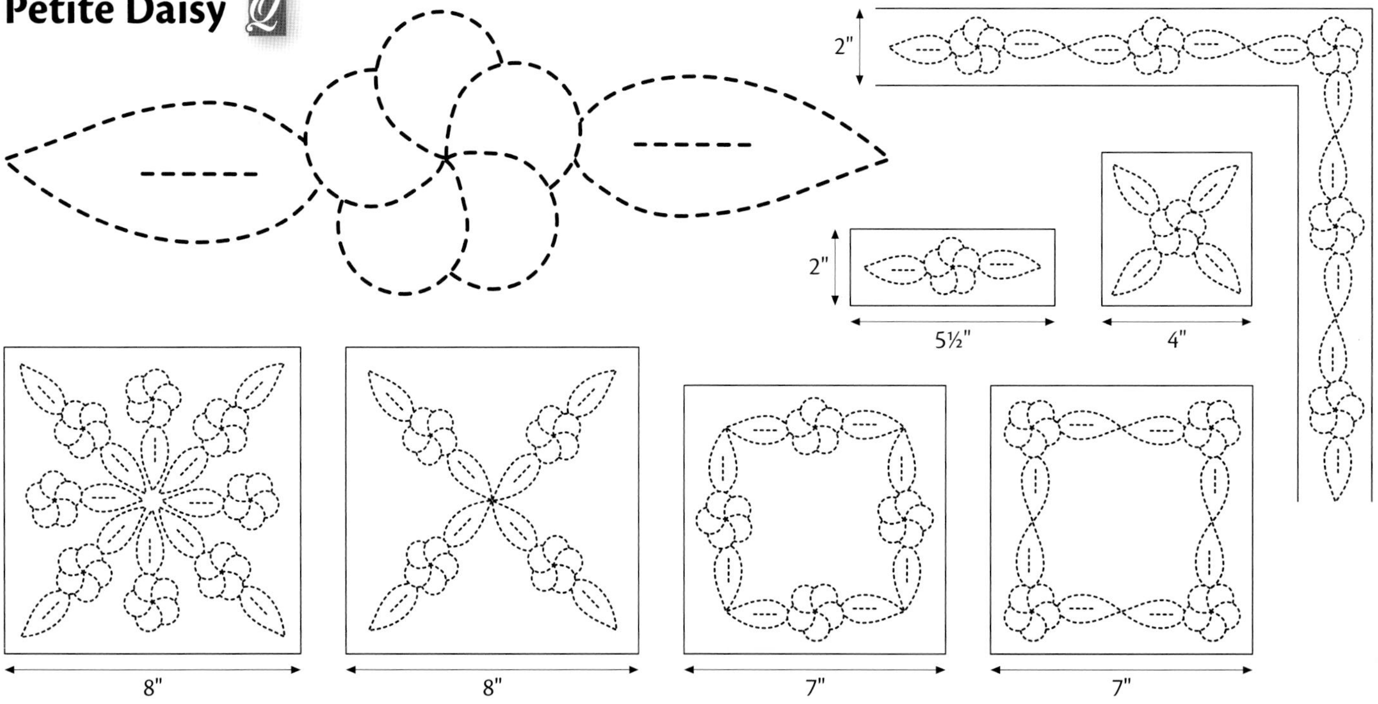
2"
2"
5½"
4"
8"
8"
7"
7"

Fanciful Flowers

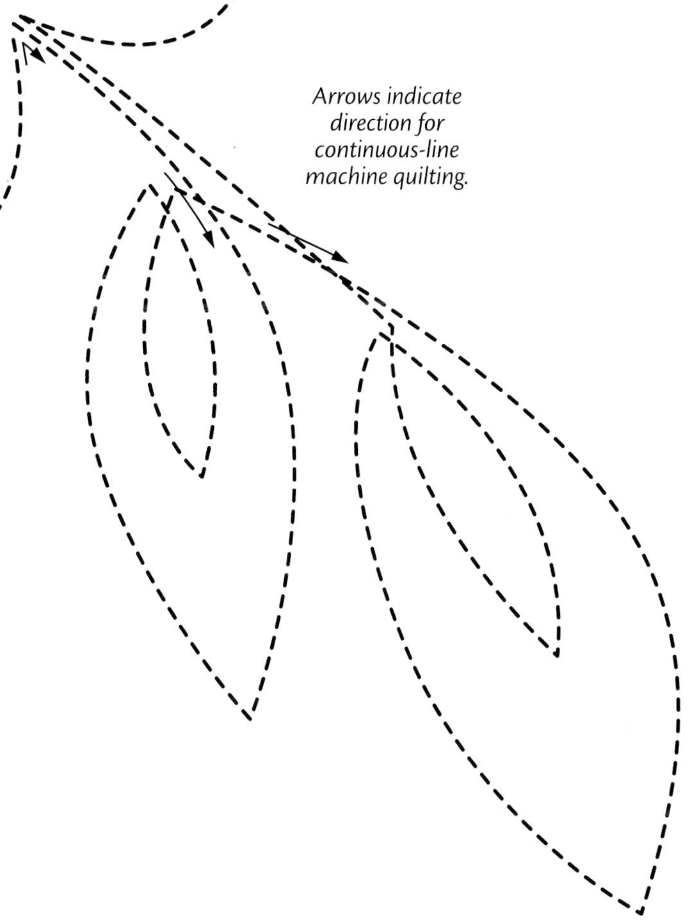
Start
Arrows indicate direction for continuous-line machine quilting.

6½"

4"

12"

Wandering Summer

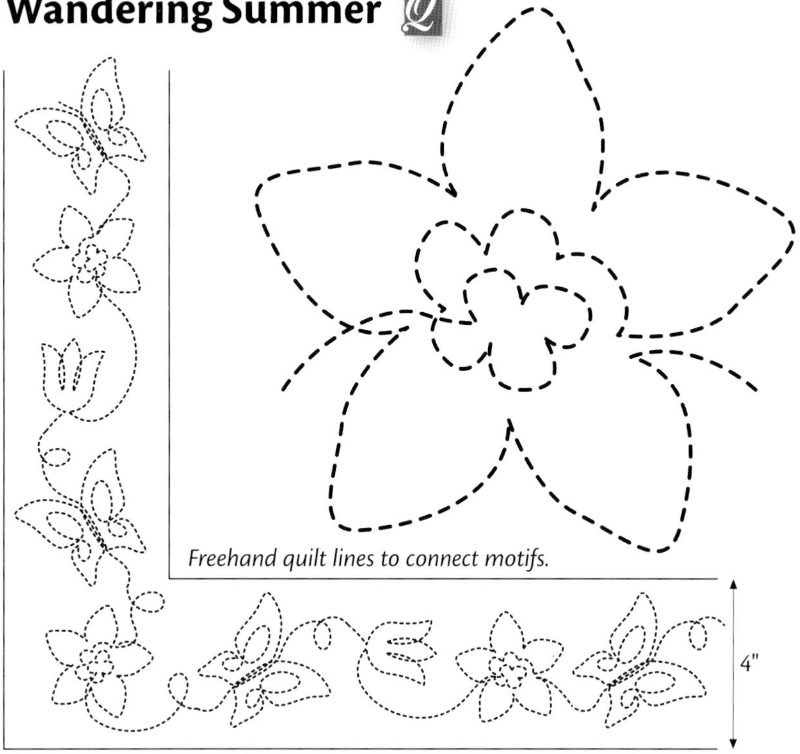

Freehand quilt lines to connect motifs.
4"

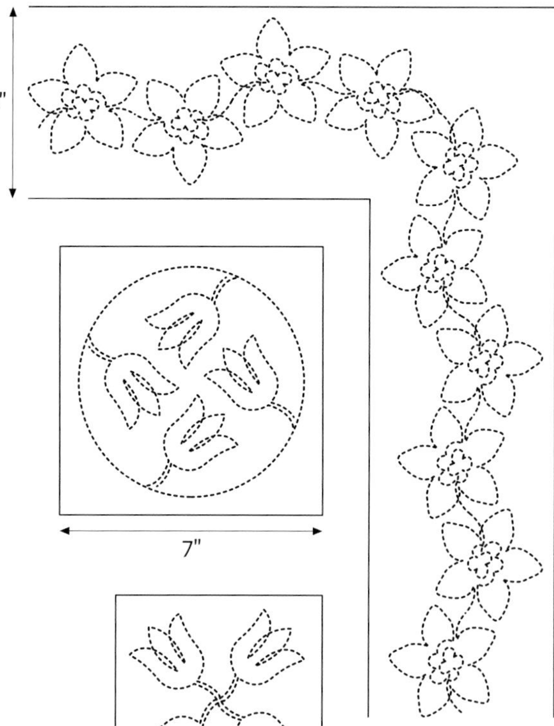

5"
7"

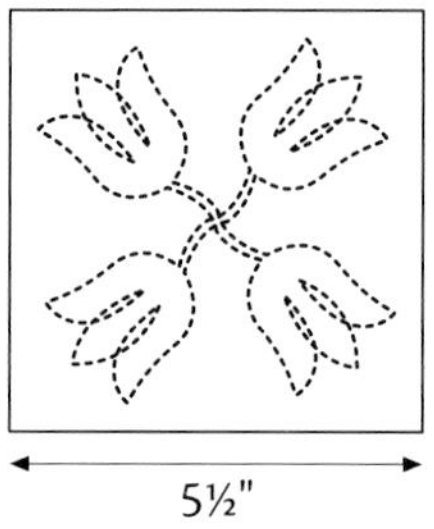

5½"

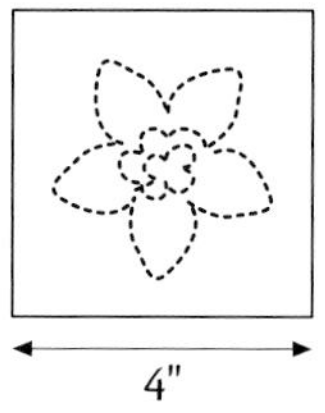

4"

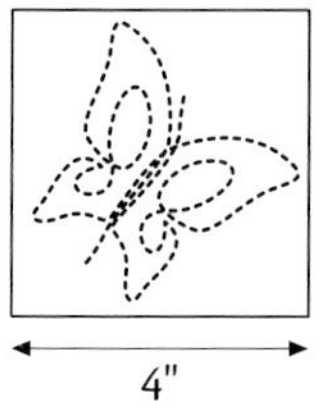

4"

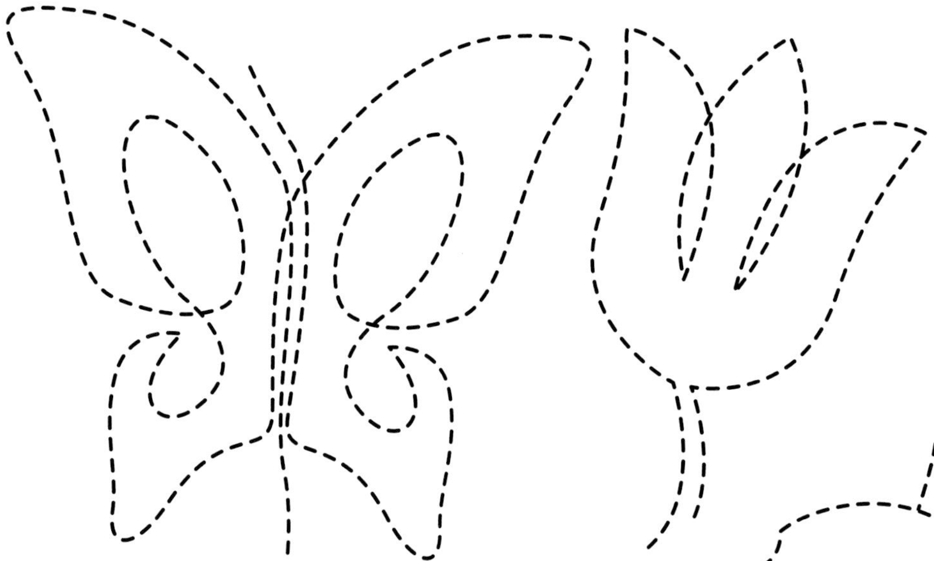

Dogwood

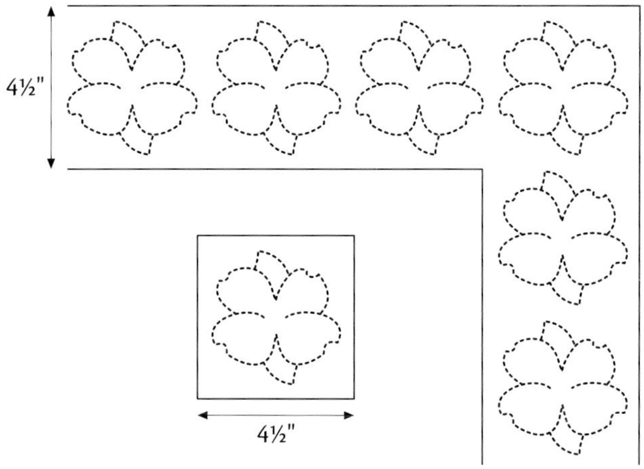

4½"
4½"

Tulip Wreath

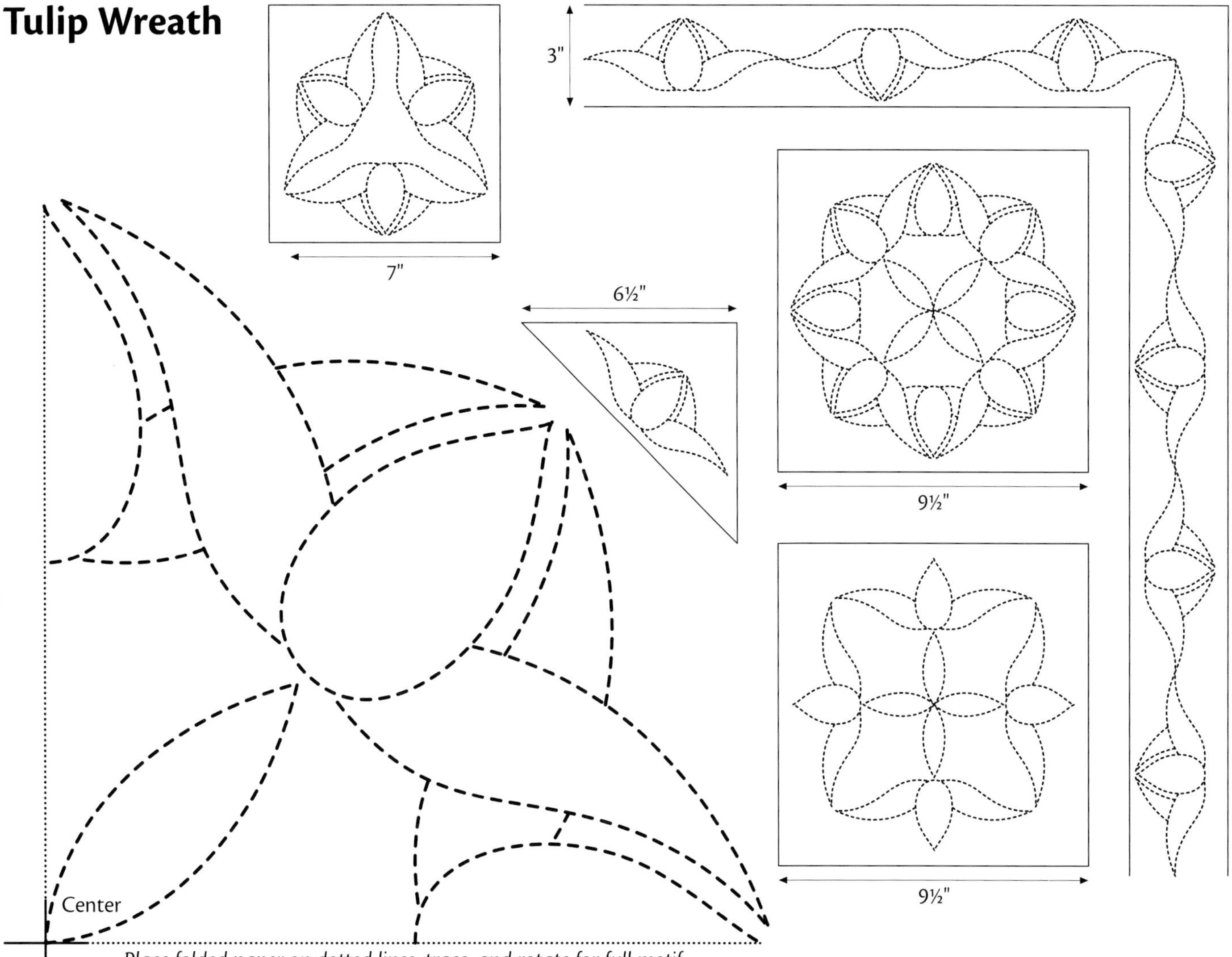

3"
7"
6½"
9½"
9½"
Center

Place folded paper on dotted lines, trace, and rotate for full motif.

Snow Blossom

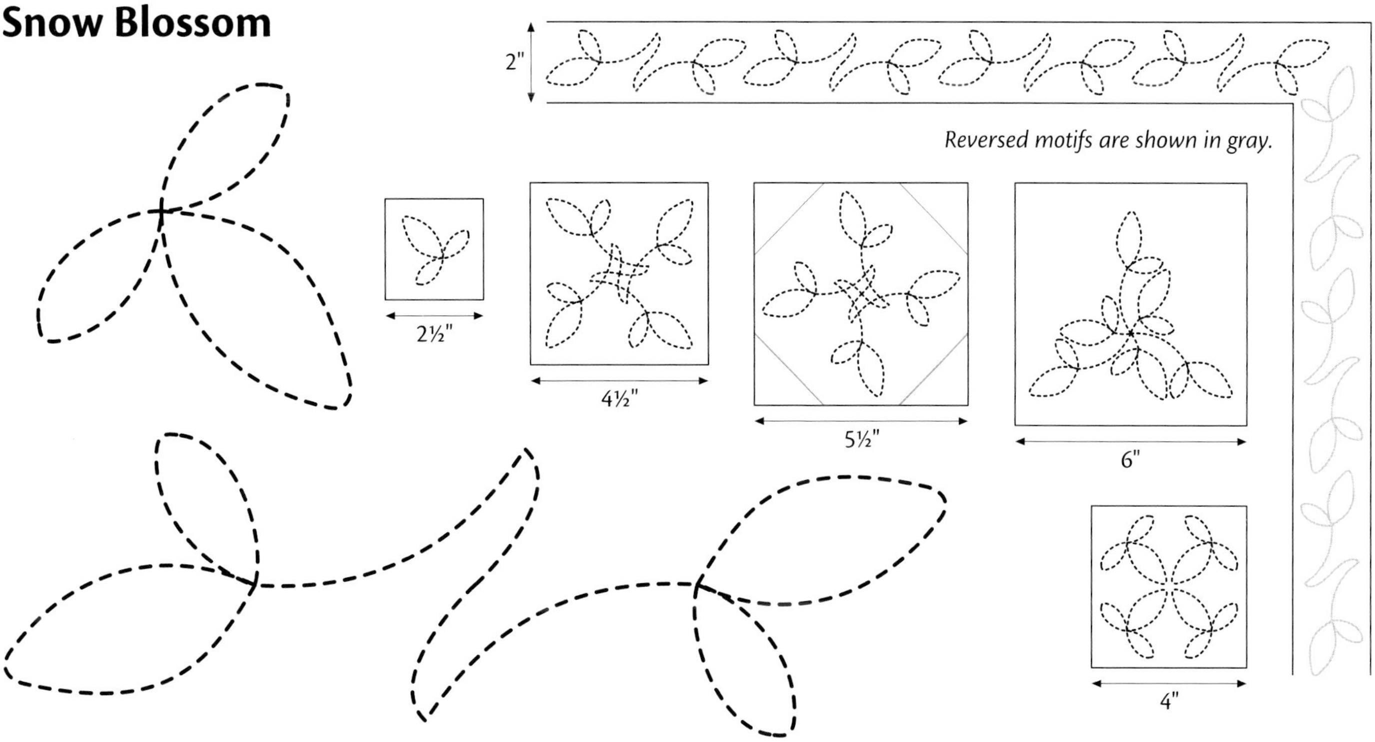

2"
2½"
4½"
5½"
6"
4"

Reversed motifs are shown in gray.

Sundae Surprise

12½"

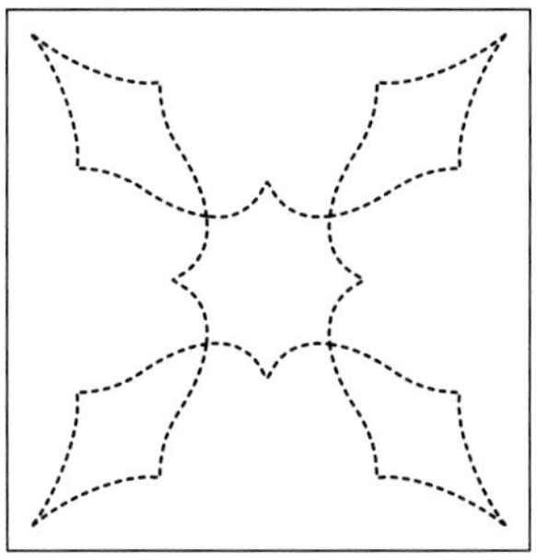

8½"

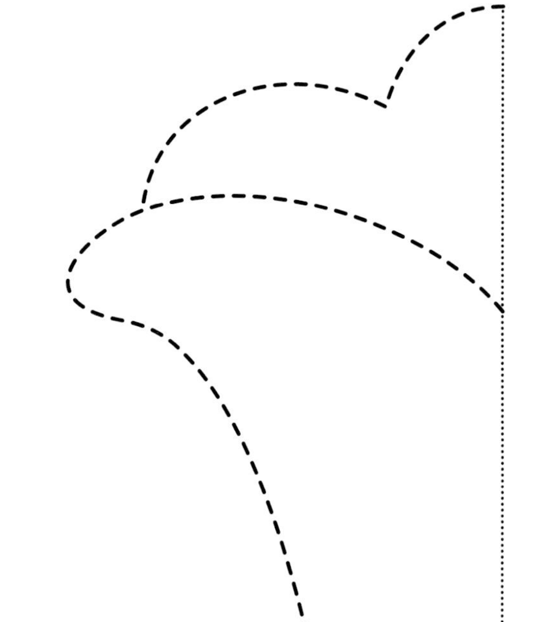
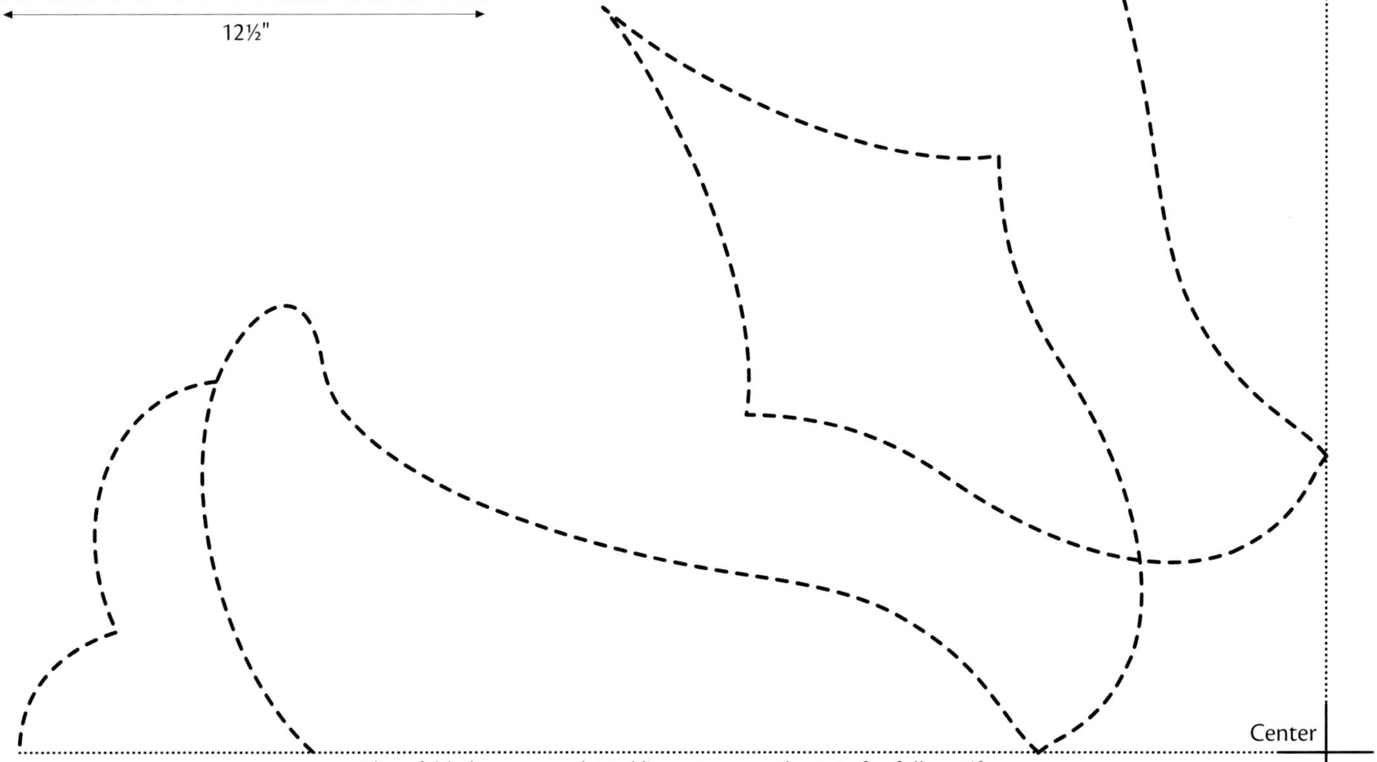

Place folded paper on dotted lines, trace, and rotate for full motif.

12"

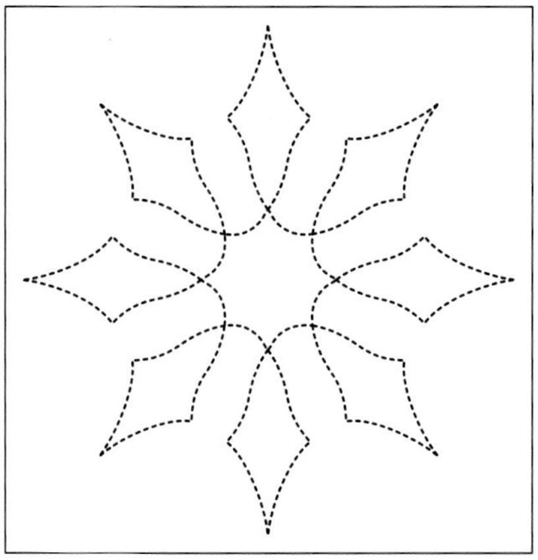

12"

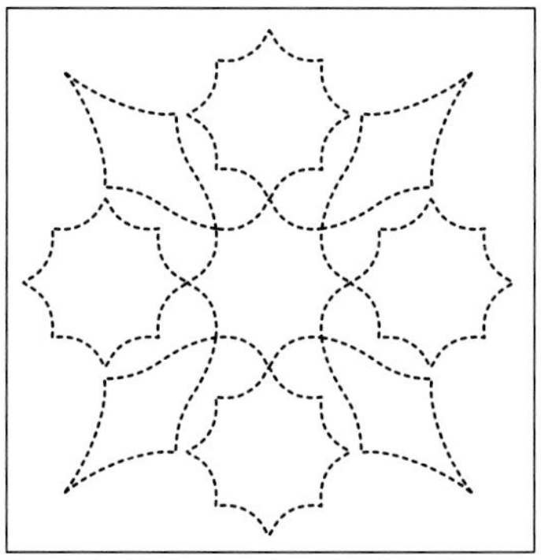

10"

Butterfly Garden

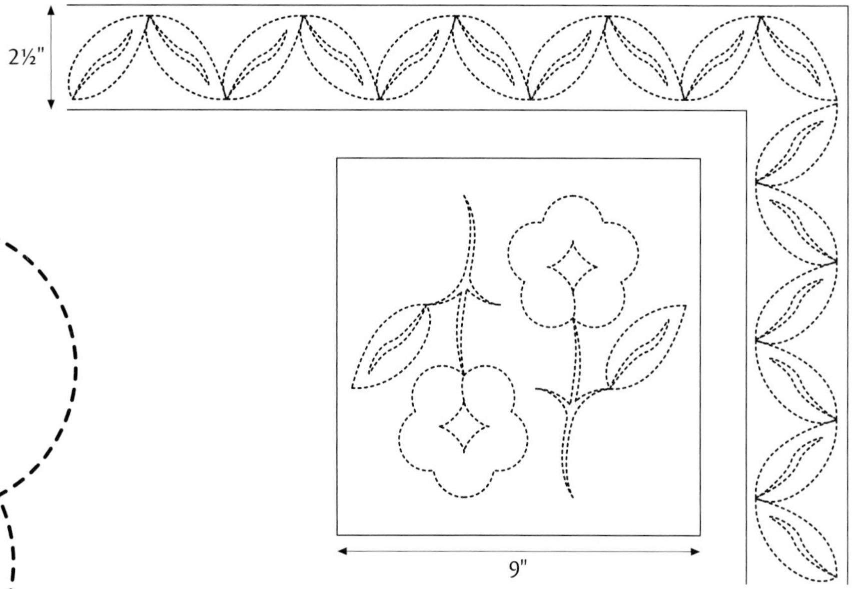
2½"
9"

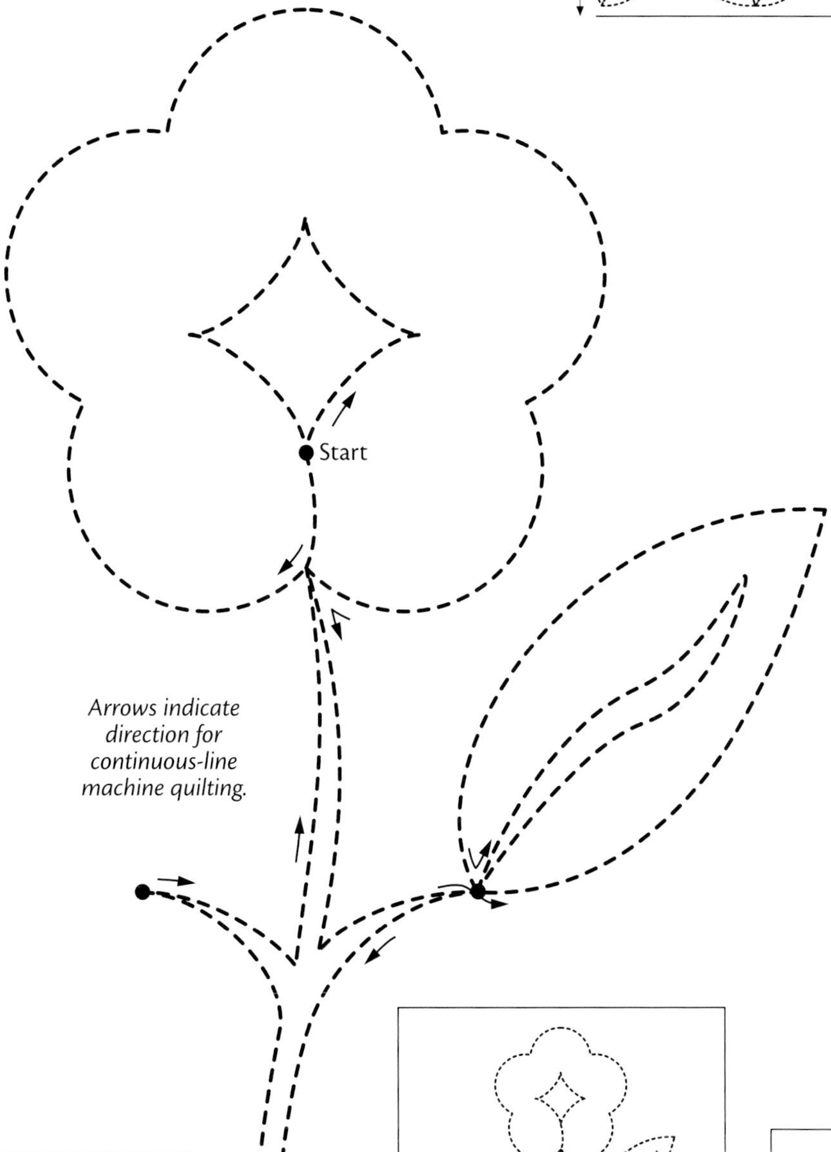
Start
Arrows indicate direction for continuous-line machine quilting.

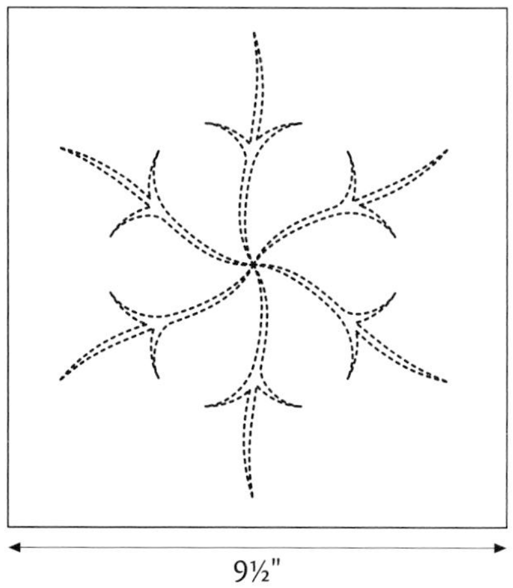
9½"

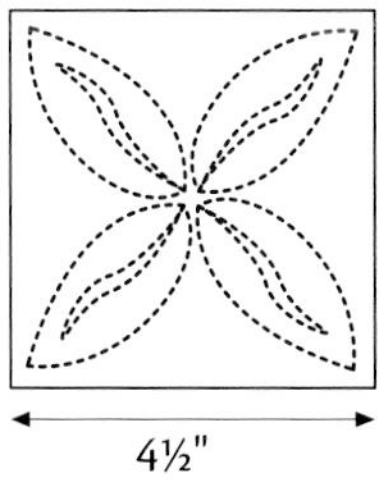
4½"

8"

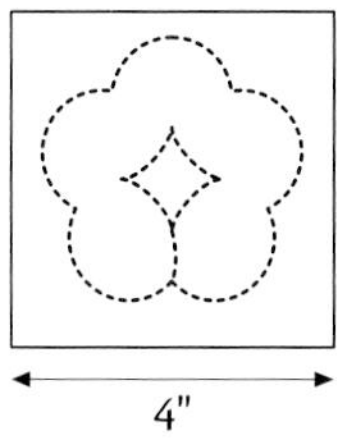
4"

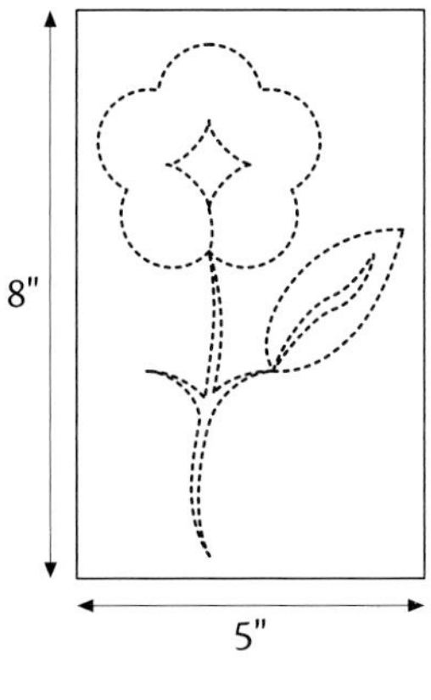
8"
5"

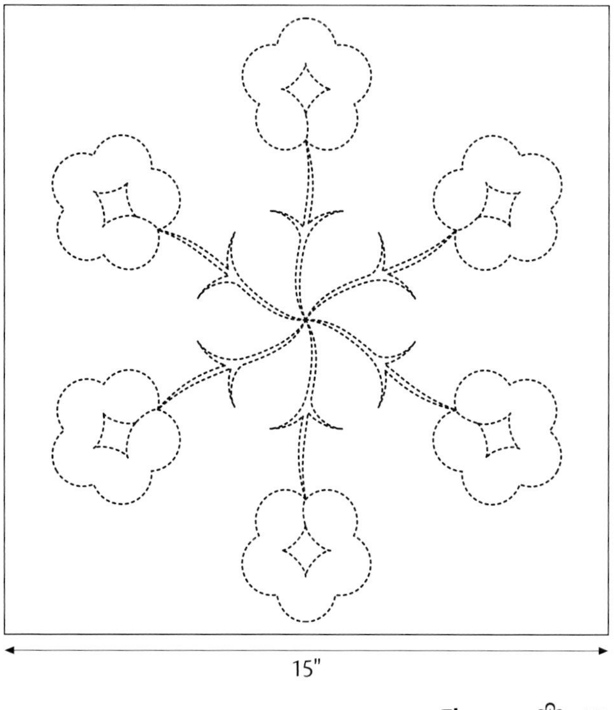
15"

Sunflower

Climbing Vine

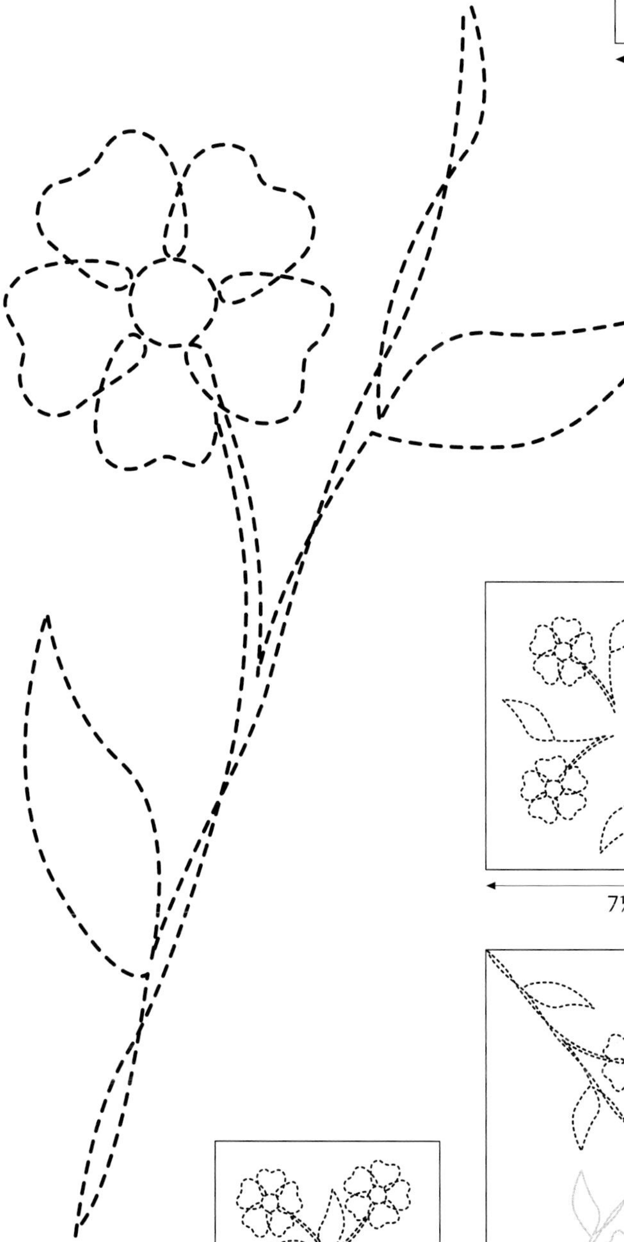

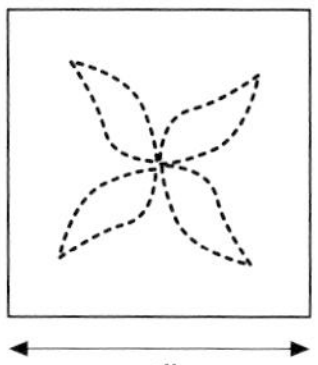

4"

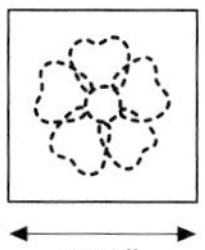

2½"

14"

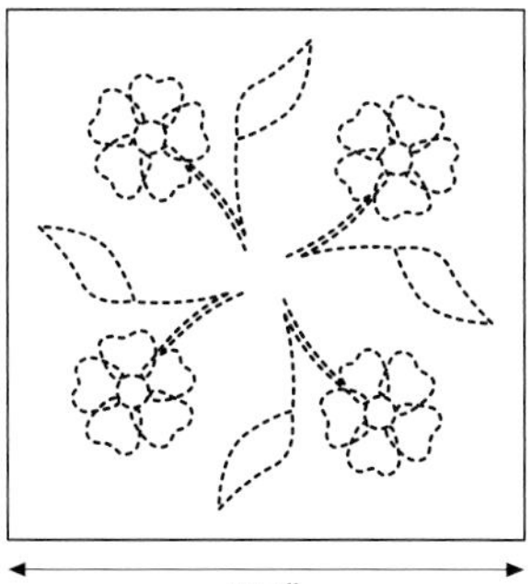

7½"

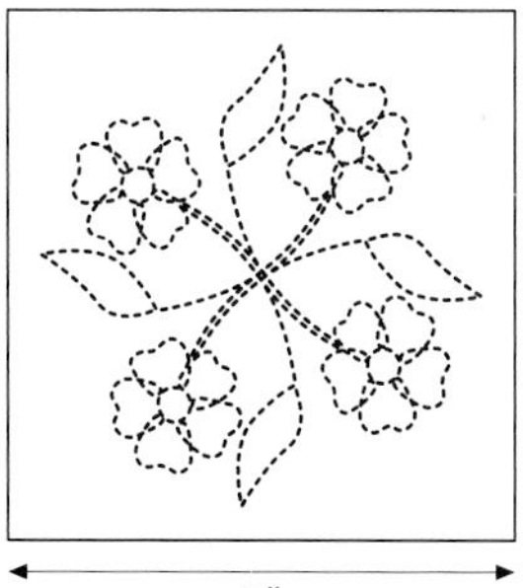

7"

11"

Reversed motifs are shown in gray.

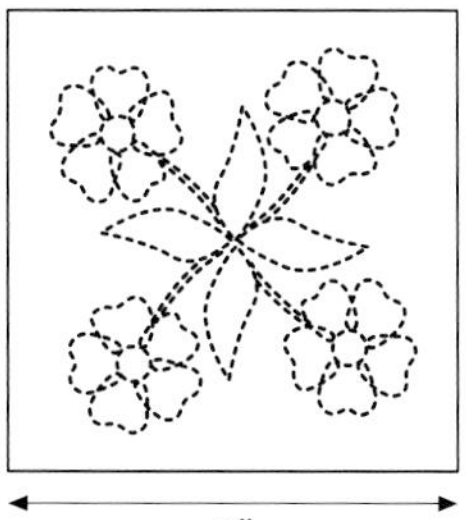

6"

5½"

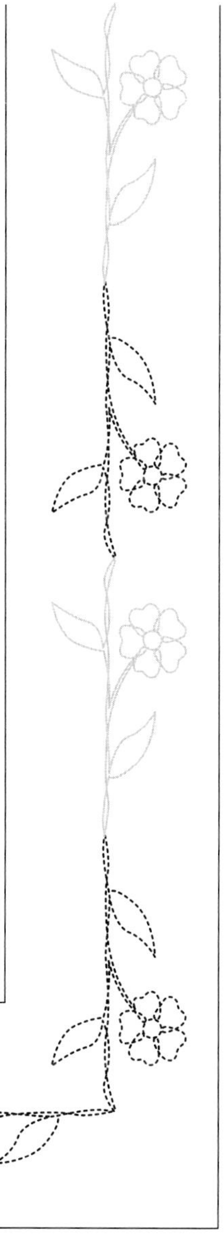

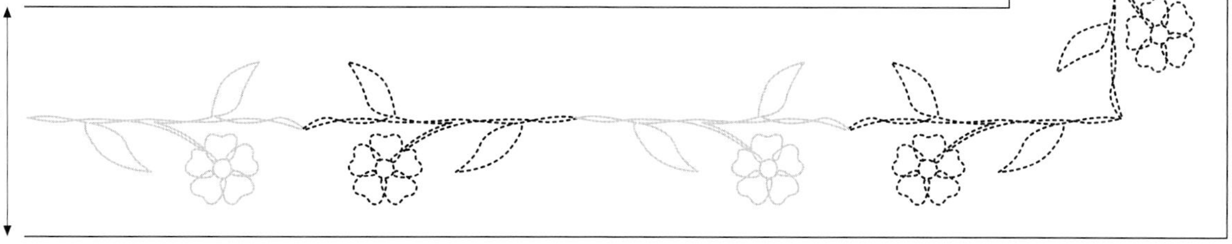

Glorious Morning

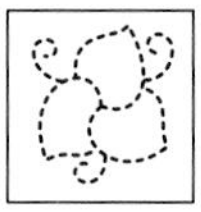

2½"

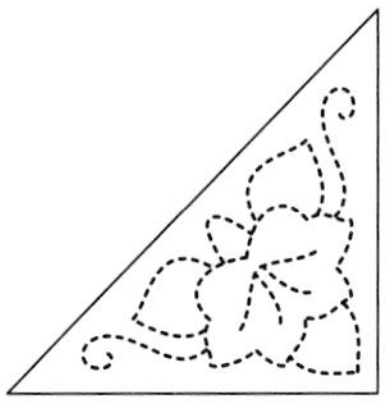

5"

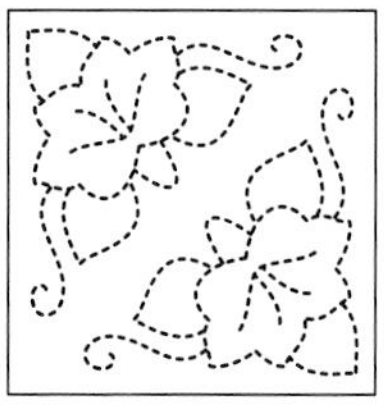

5"

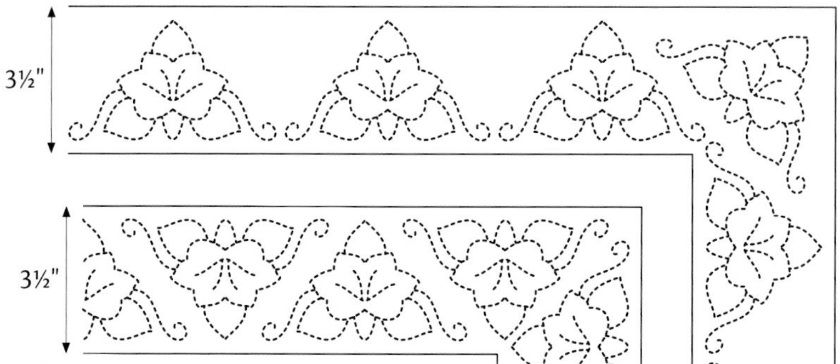

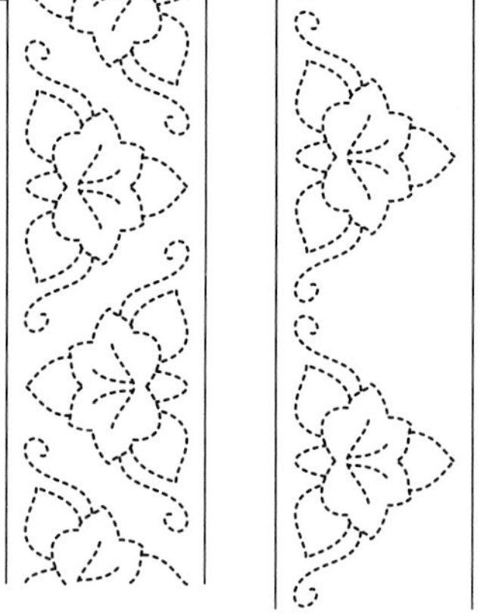

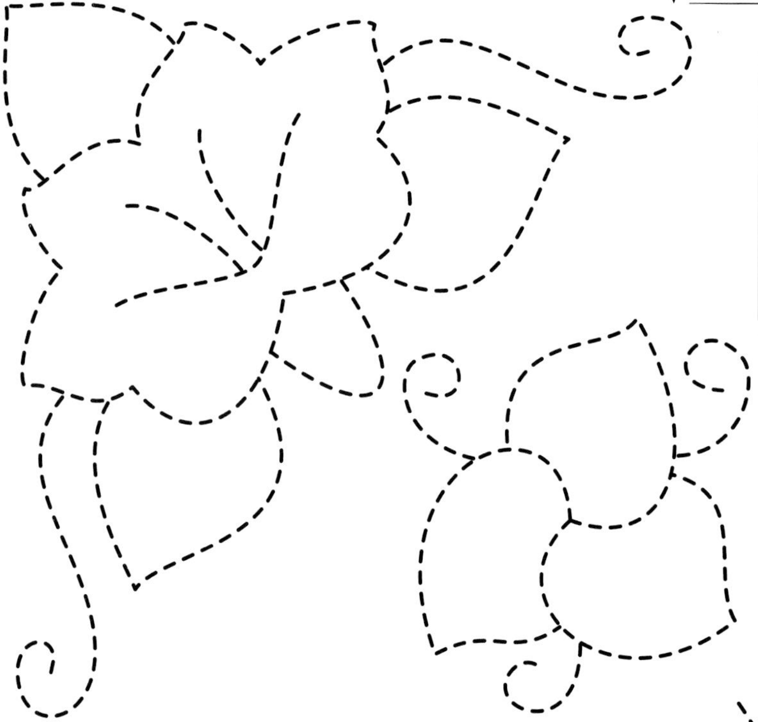

7"

4"

8½"

Wandering Flower

10½"

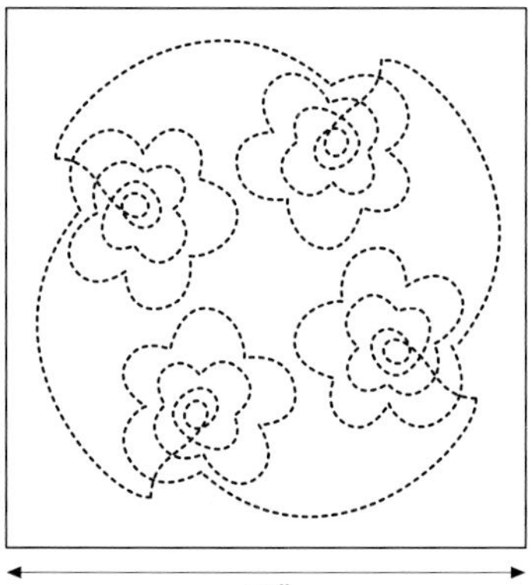

13"

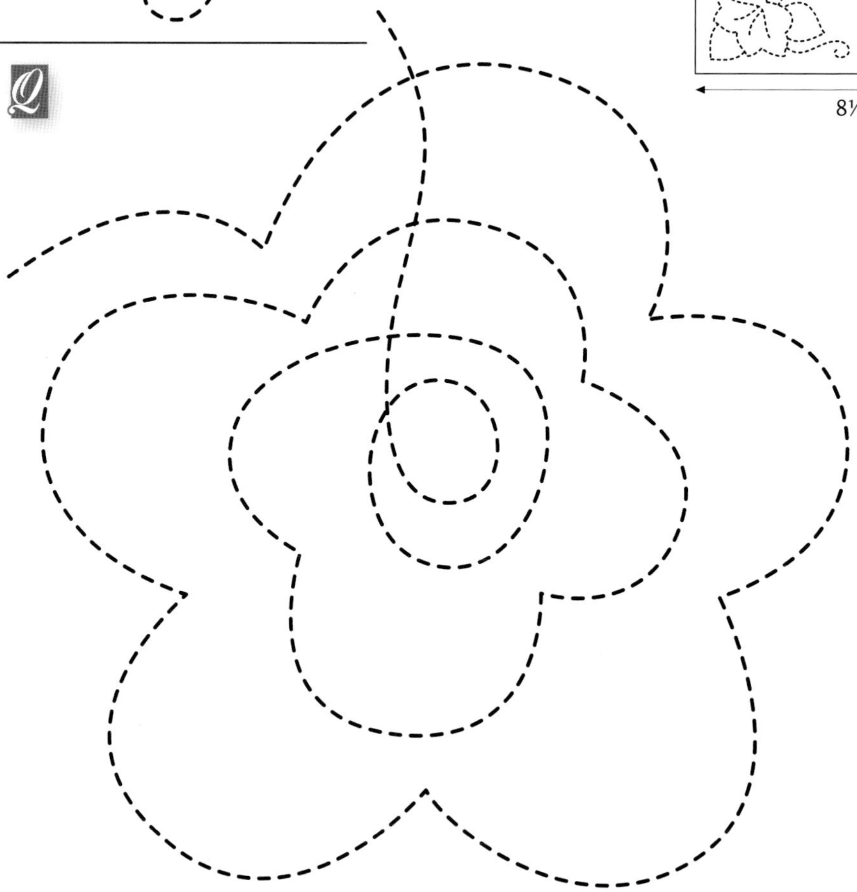

Tulip

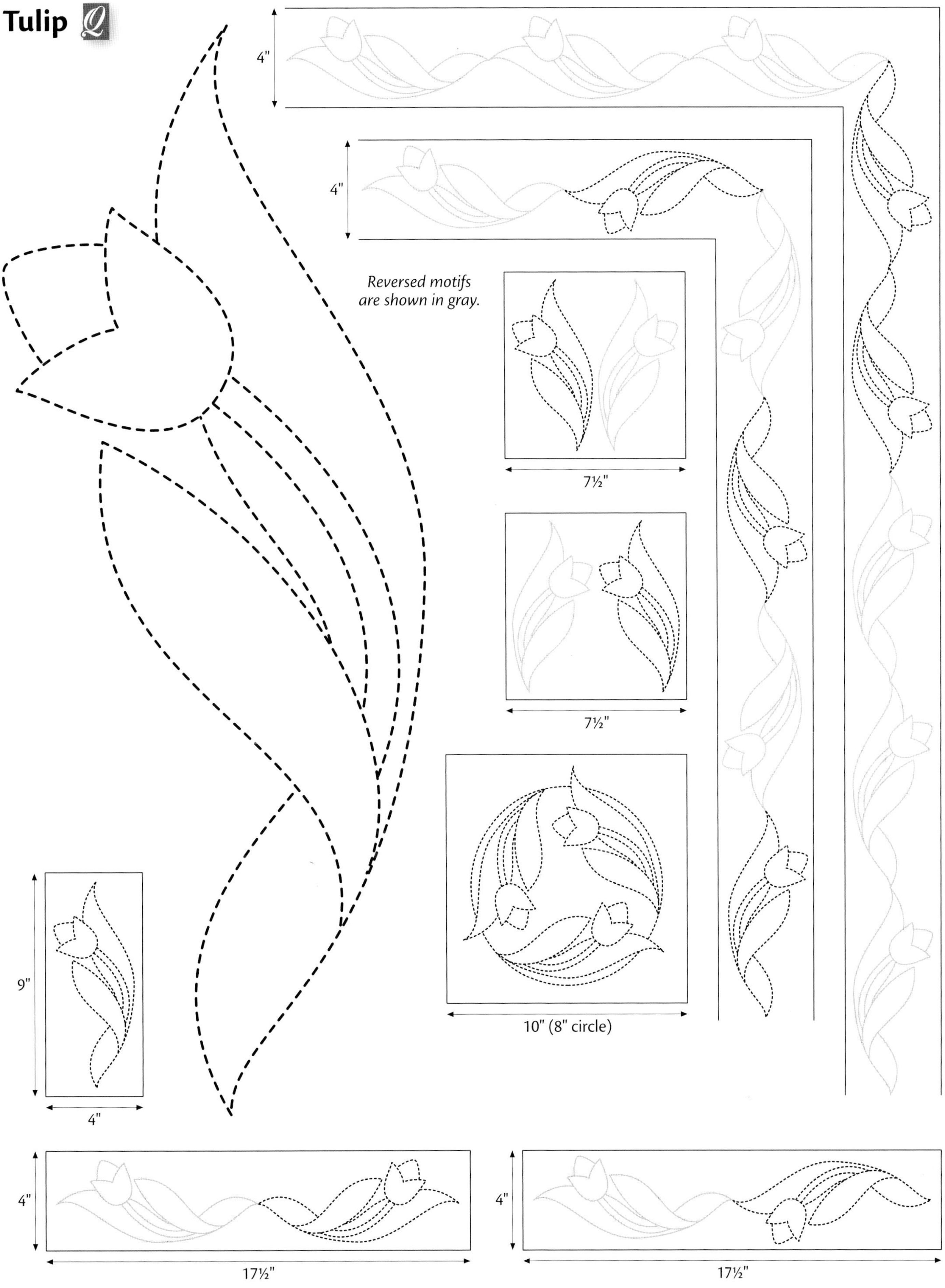
4"
4"
Reversed motifs are shown in gray.
7½"
7½"
10" (8" circle)
9"
4"
4"
17½"
4"
17½"

Garden Party

Foods

Teacher's Pet

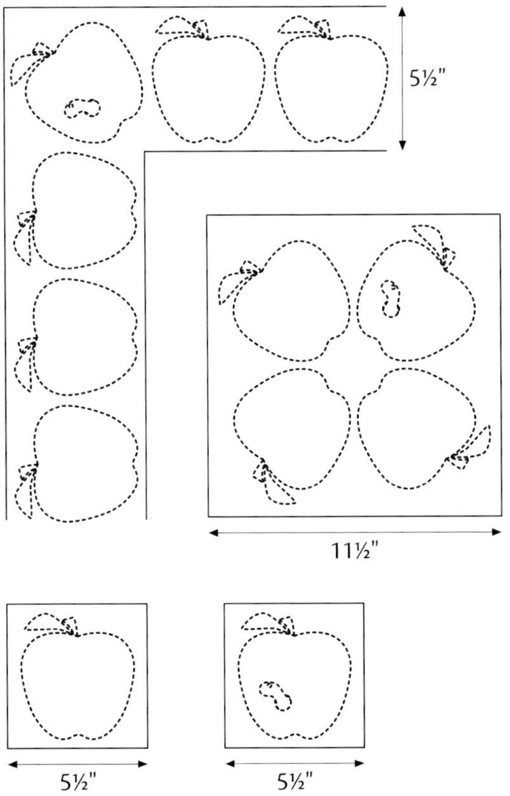
5½"
11½"
5½"
5½"

Catch of the Day

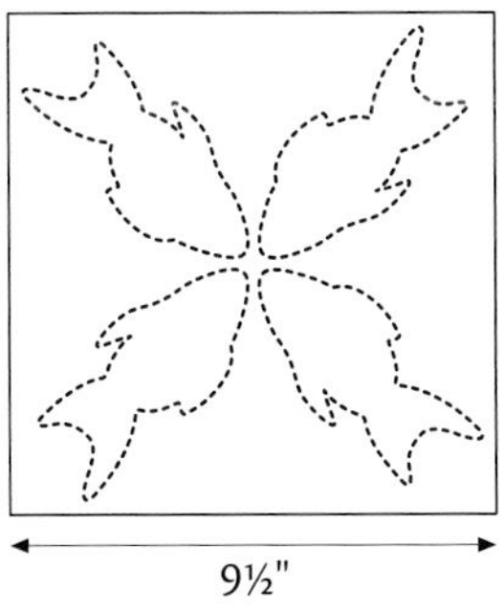
9½"

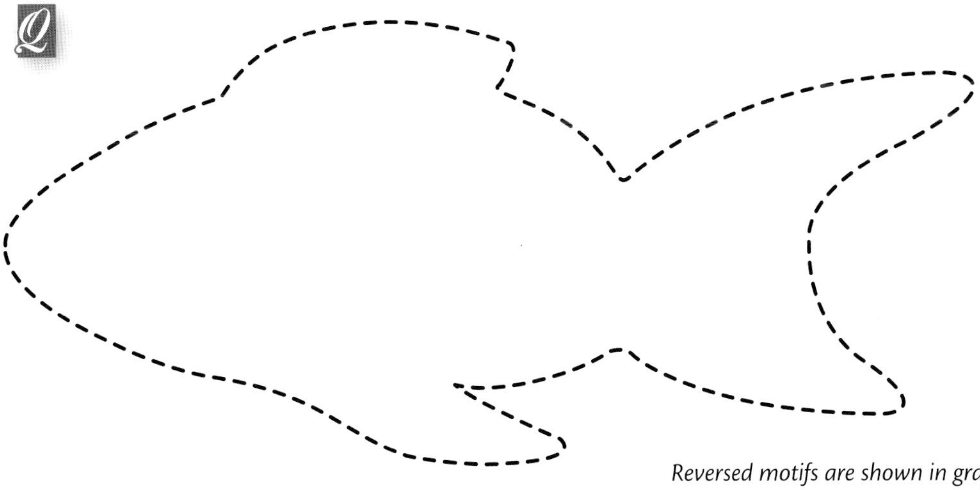

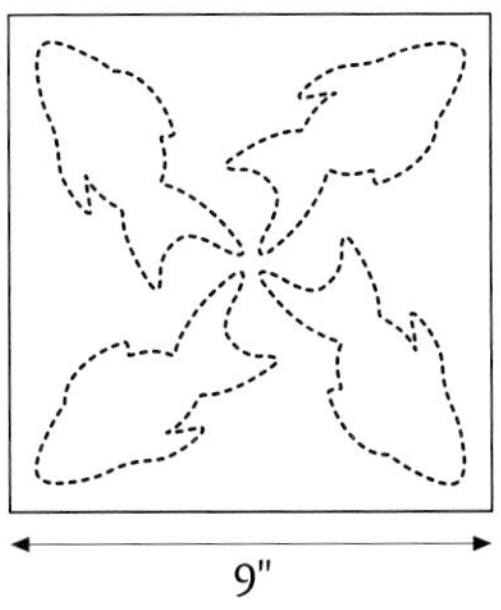
9"

Reversed motifs are shown in gray.

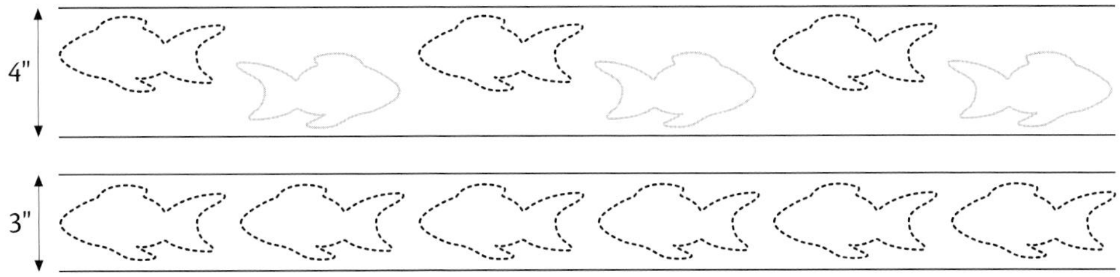
4"
3"

Ravishing Radishes

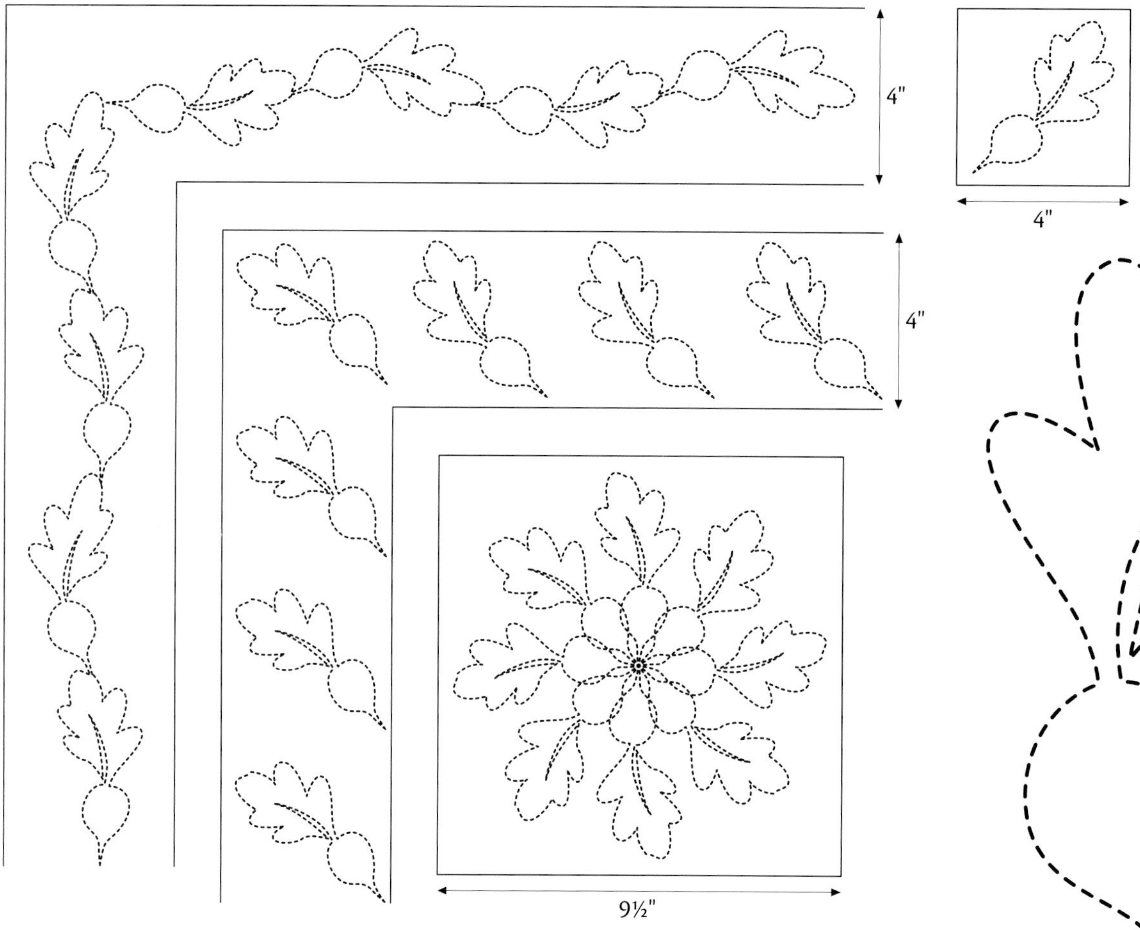
4"
4"
4"
9½"

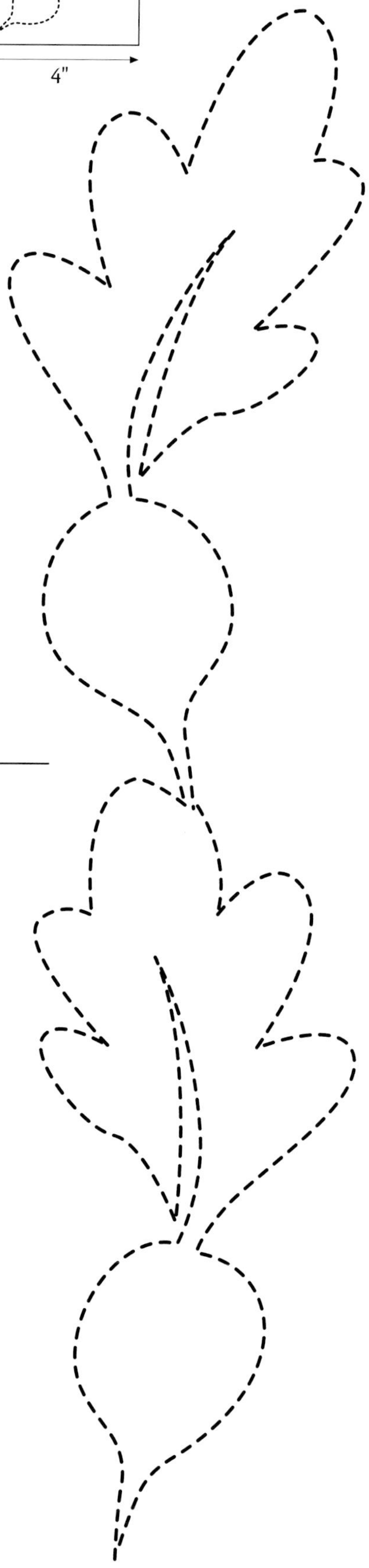

Lemon Twist

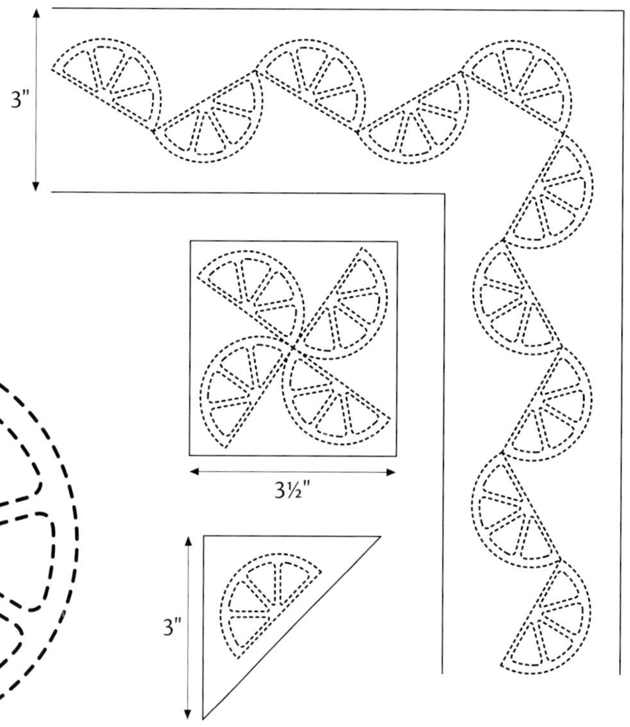
3"
3½"
3"

Berry Blossom

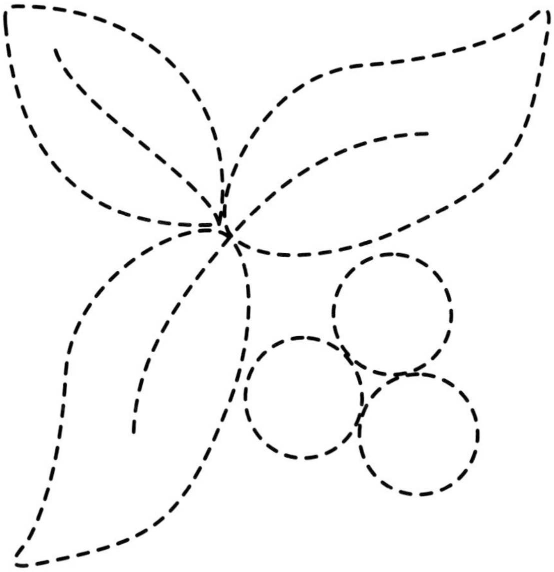

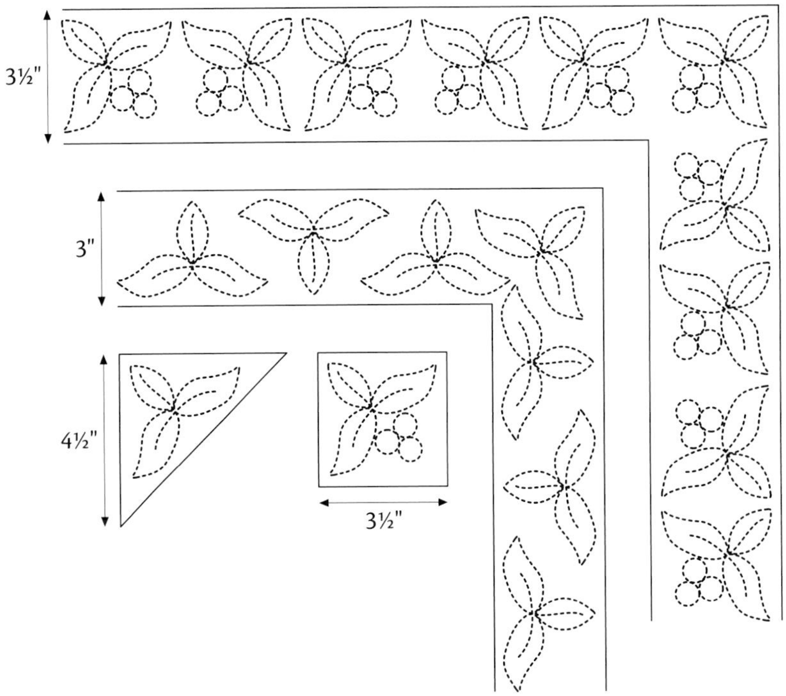

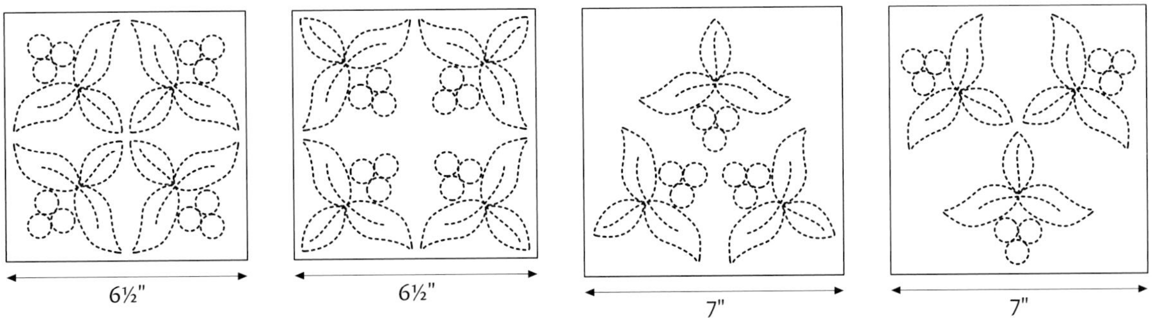

Peach Harvest

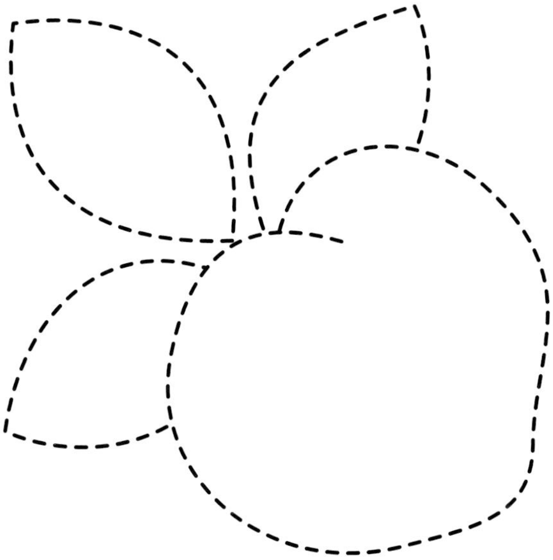

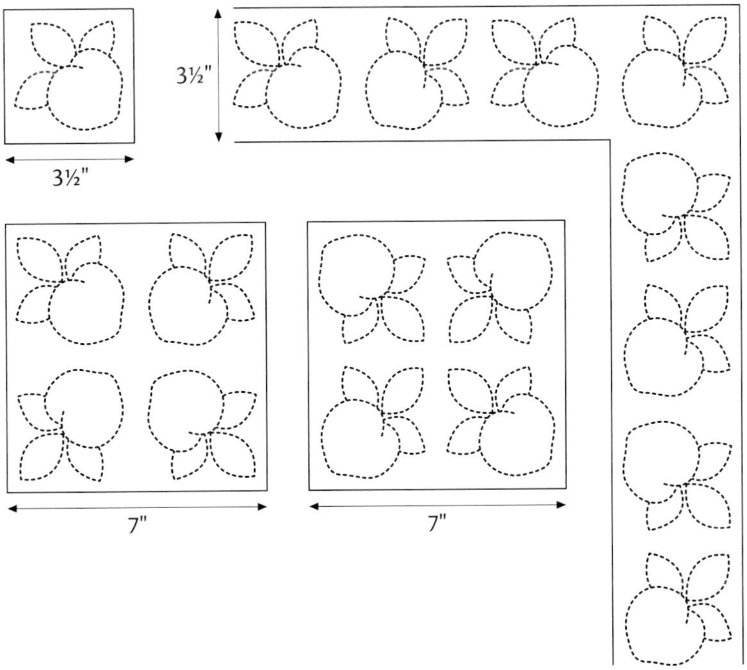

Herbal Medley

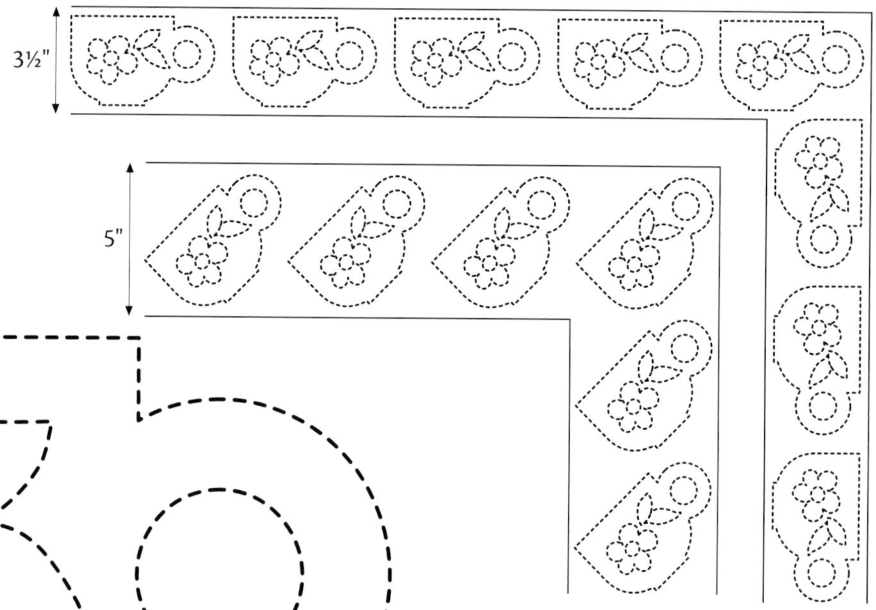

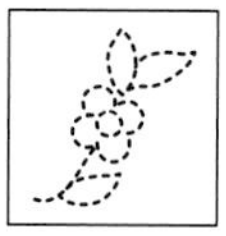

3½"

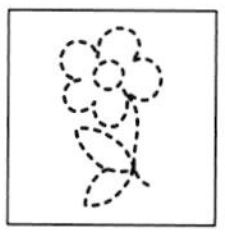

3½"

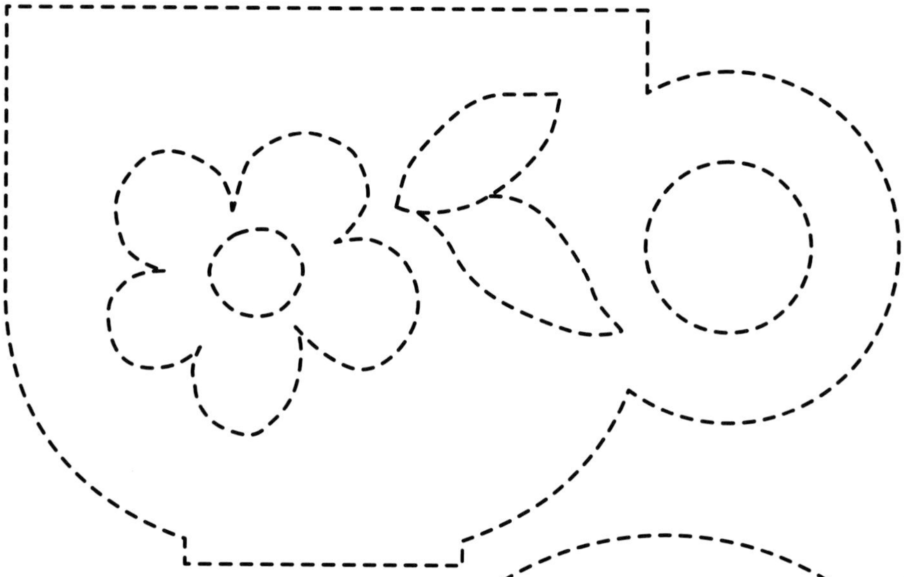

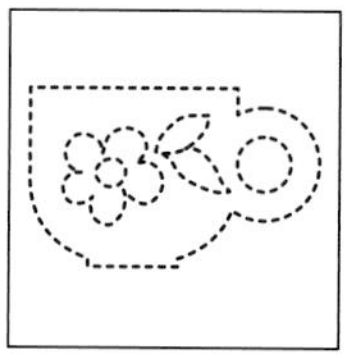

5½"

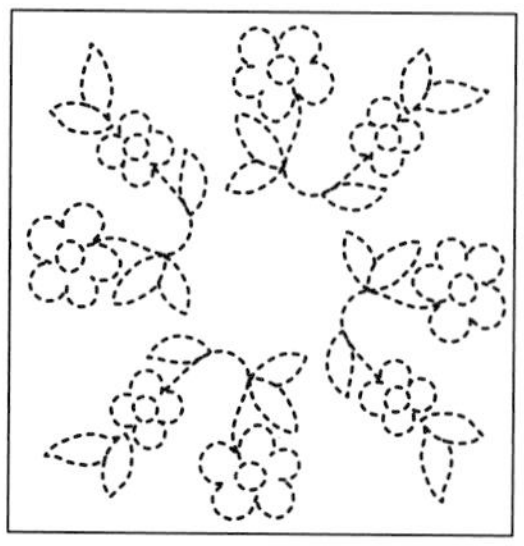

8½"

5"

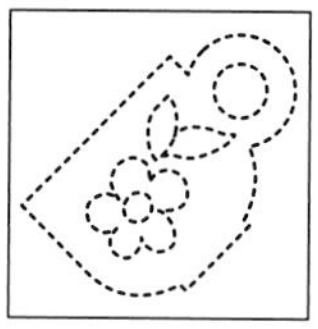

5"

5"

6"

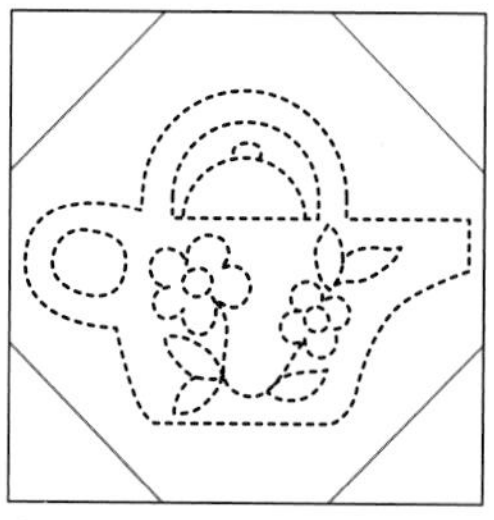

8"

Granny Smith's

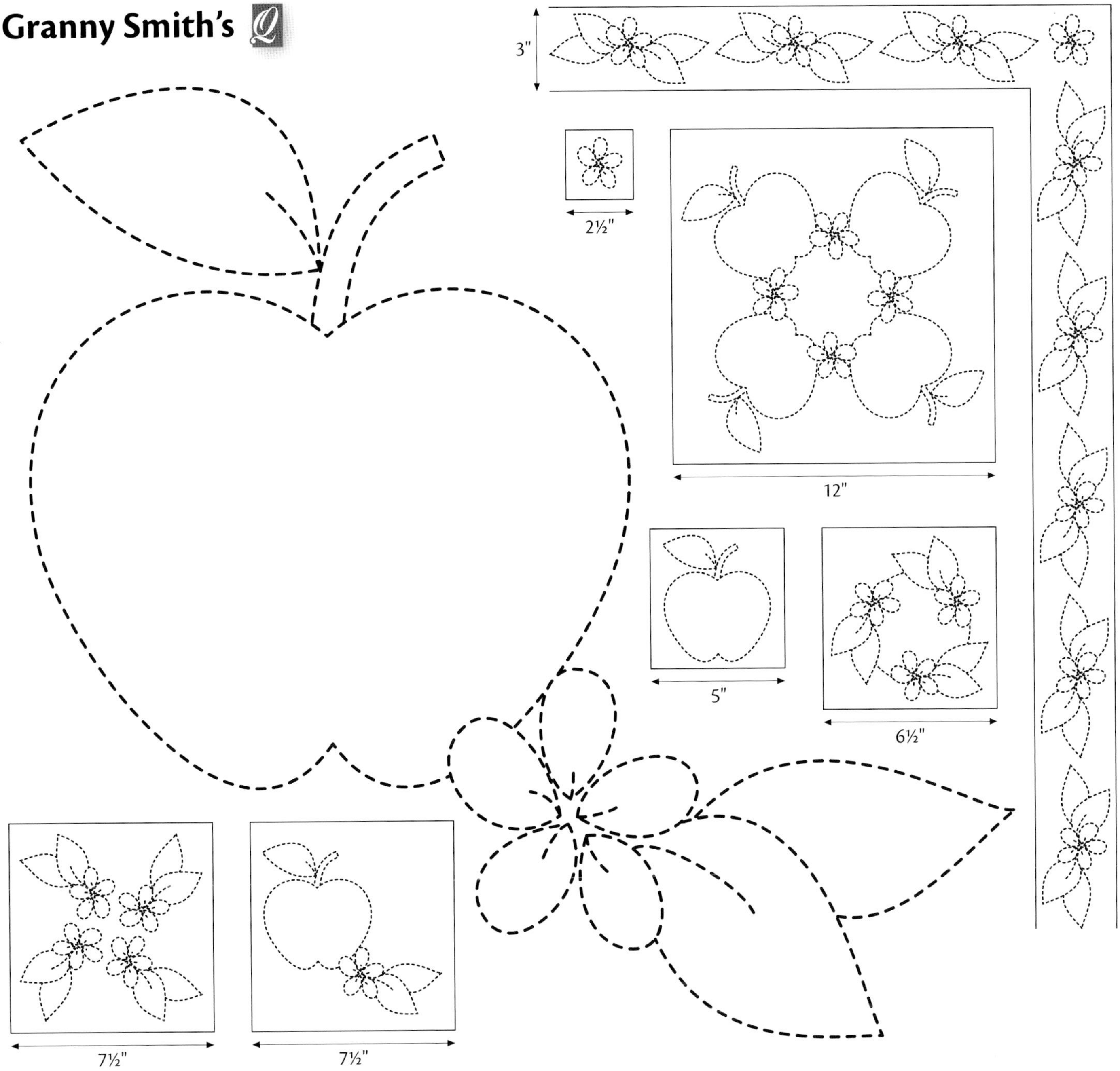
3"
2½"
12"
5"
6½"
7½"
7½"

Bite o' Melon

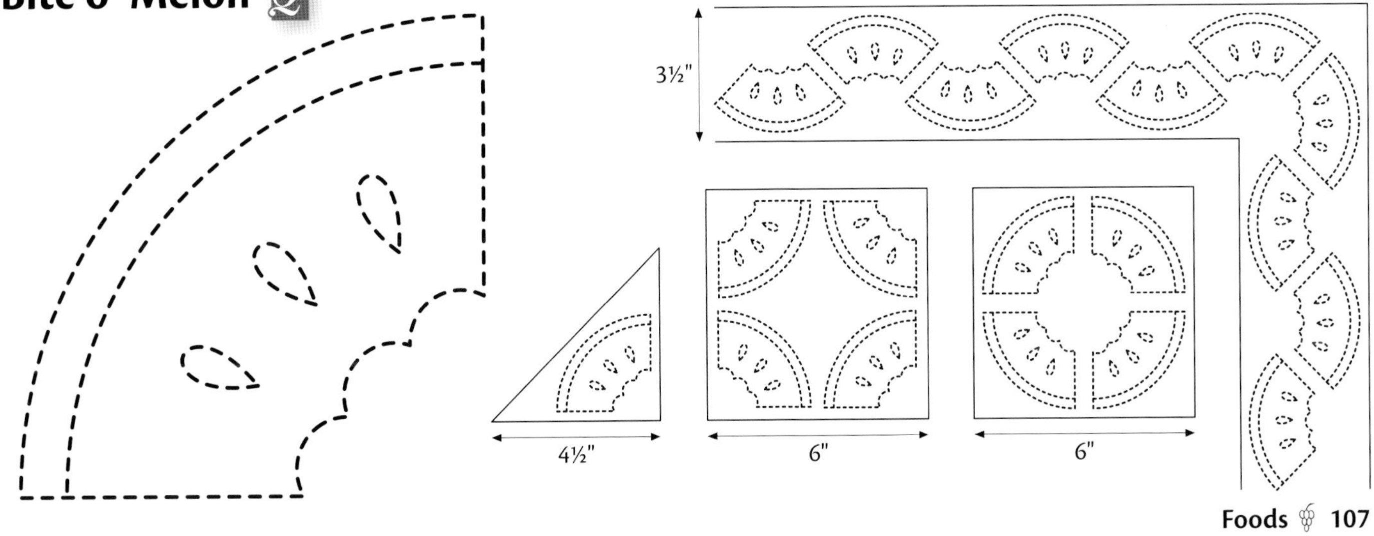
3½"
4½"
6"
6"

Strawberry Fields

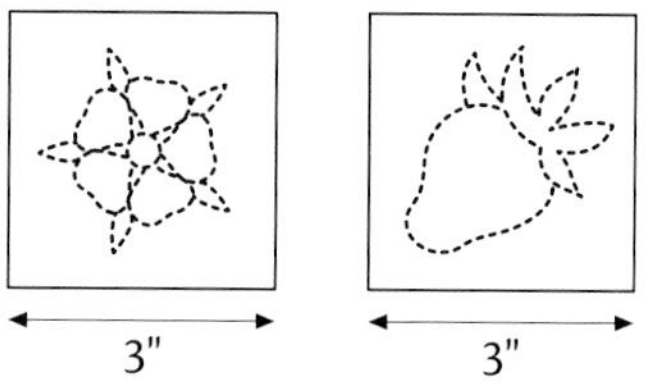

Reversed motifs are shown in gray.

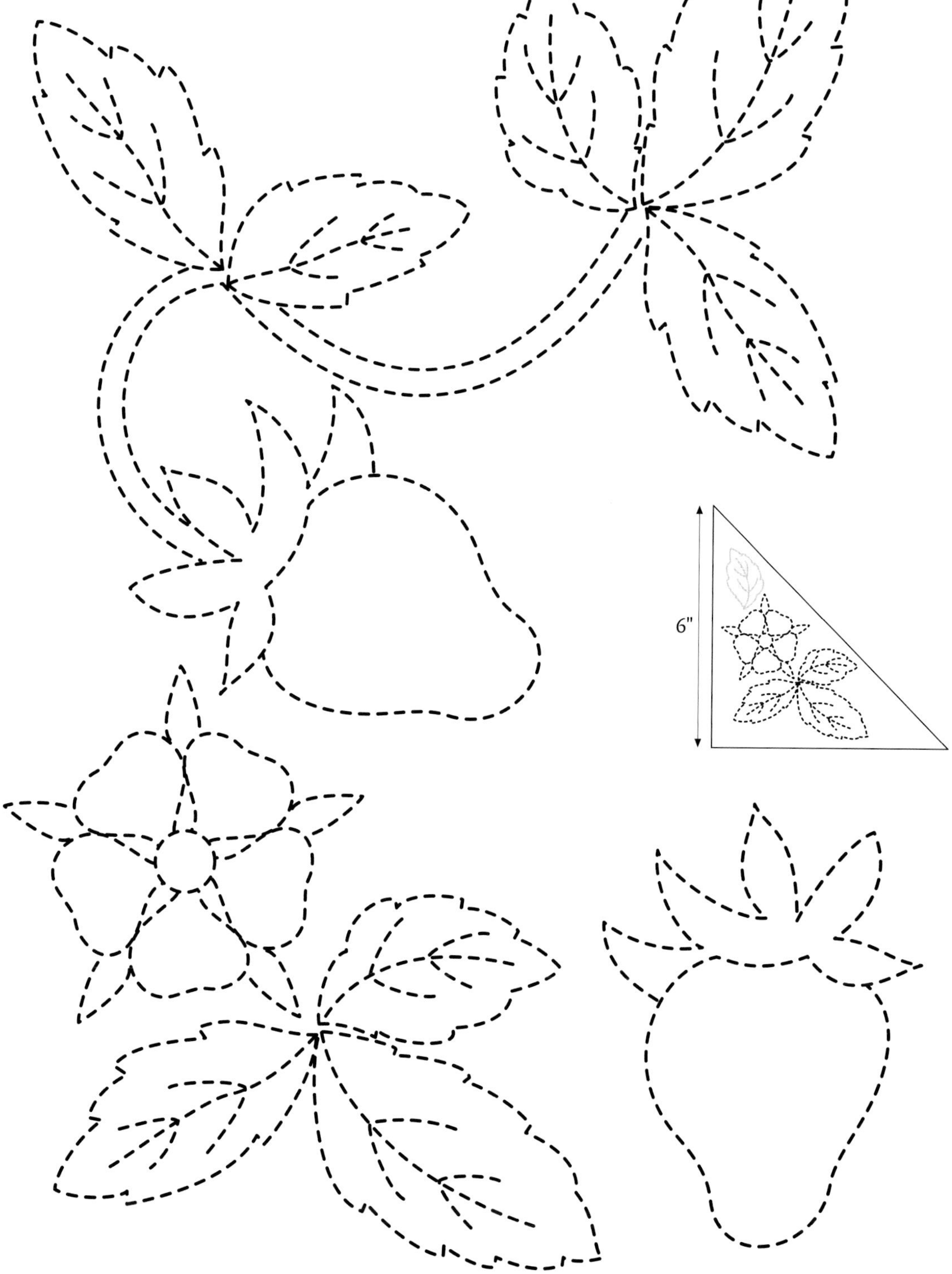

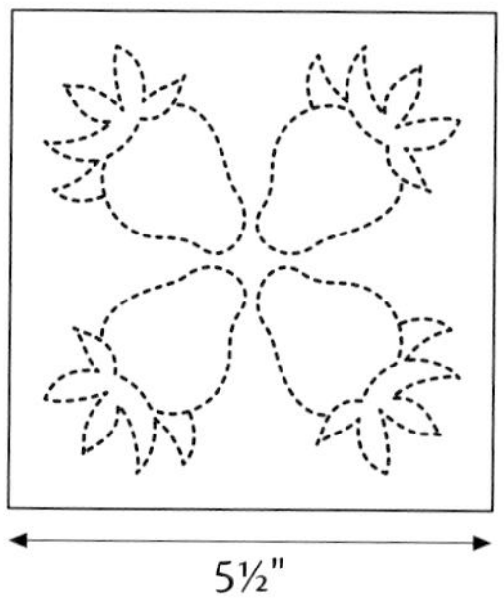

Cherry

15"

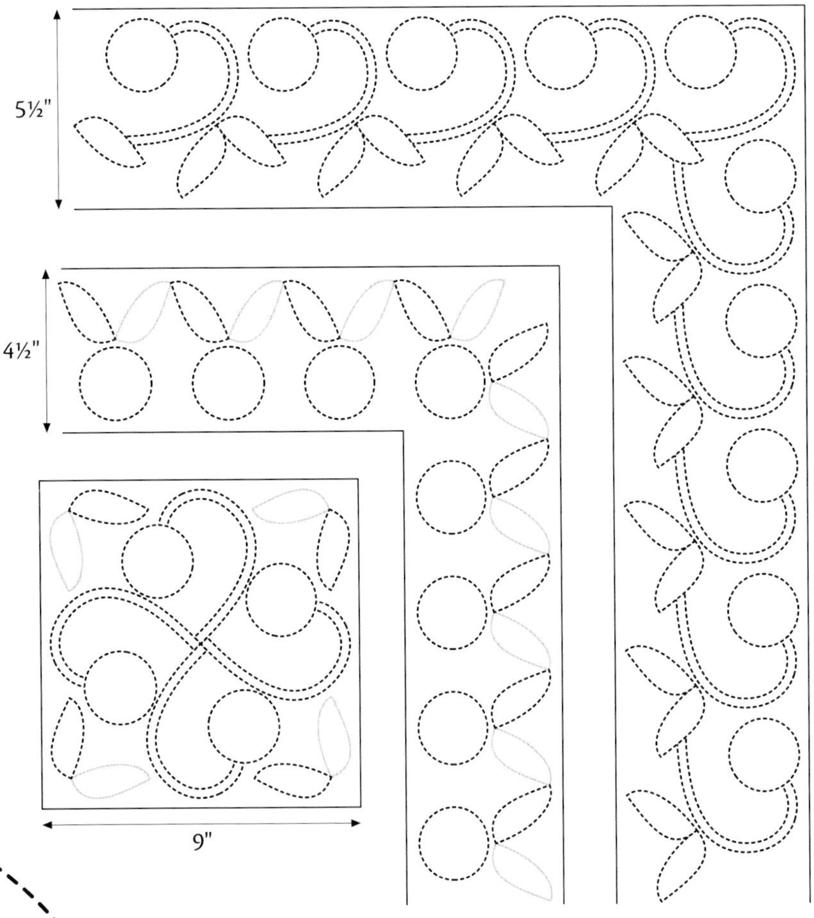

9"

Reversed motifs are shown in gray.

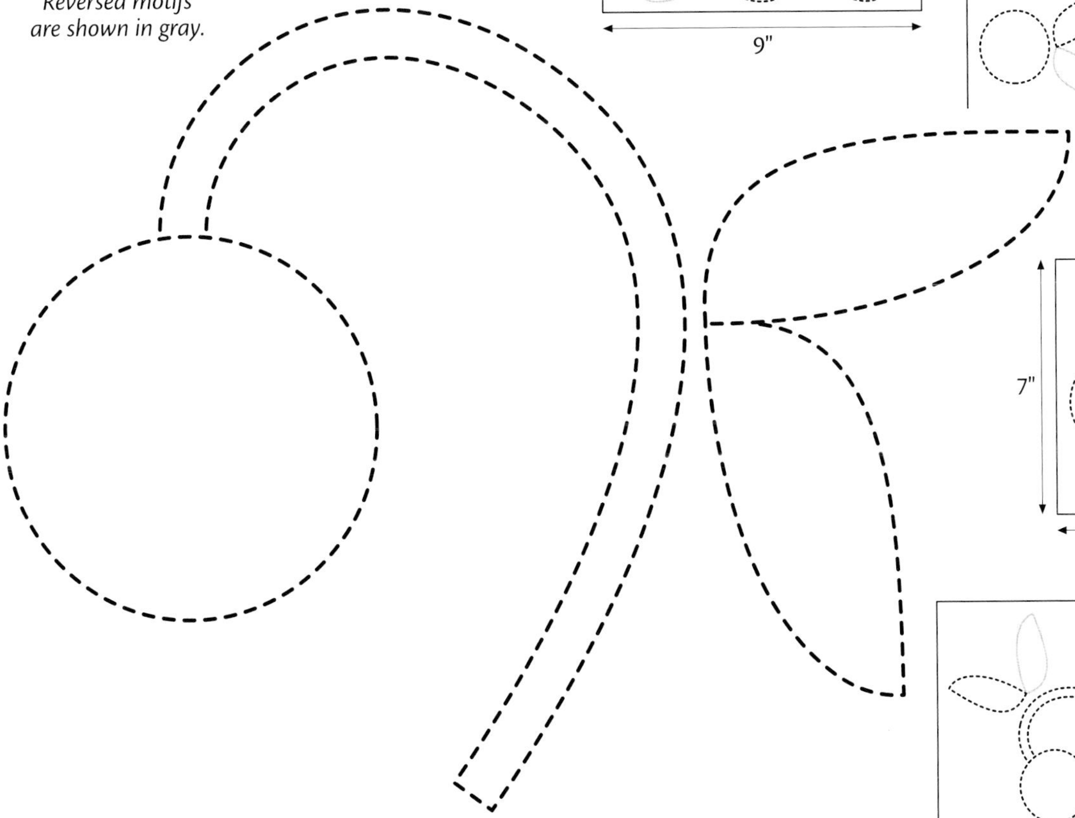

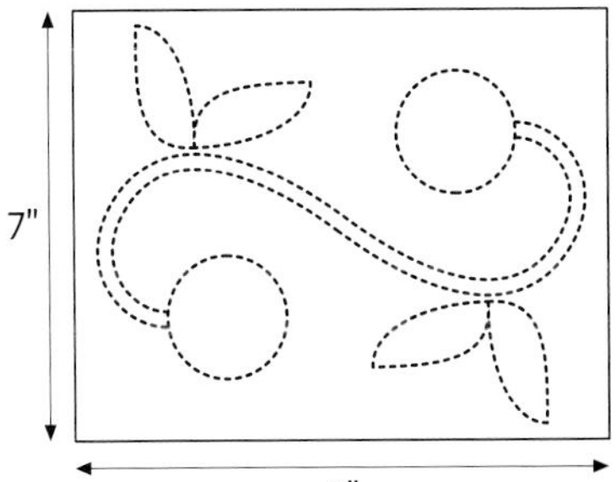

9"

12½"

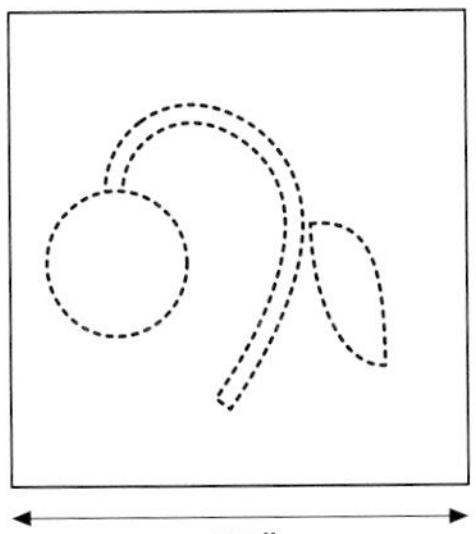

6½"

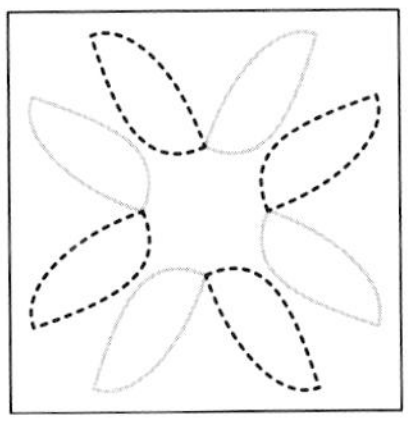

5½"

5½"

Rippling Waves

Dancing Curls

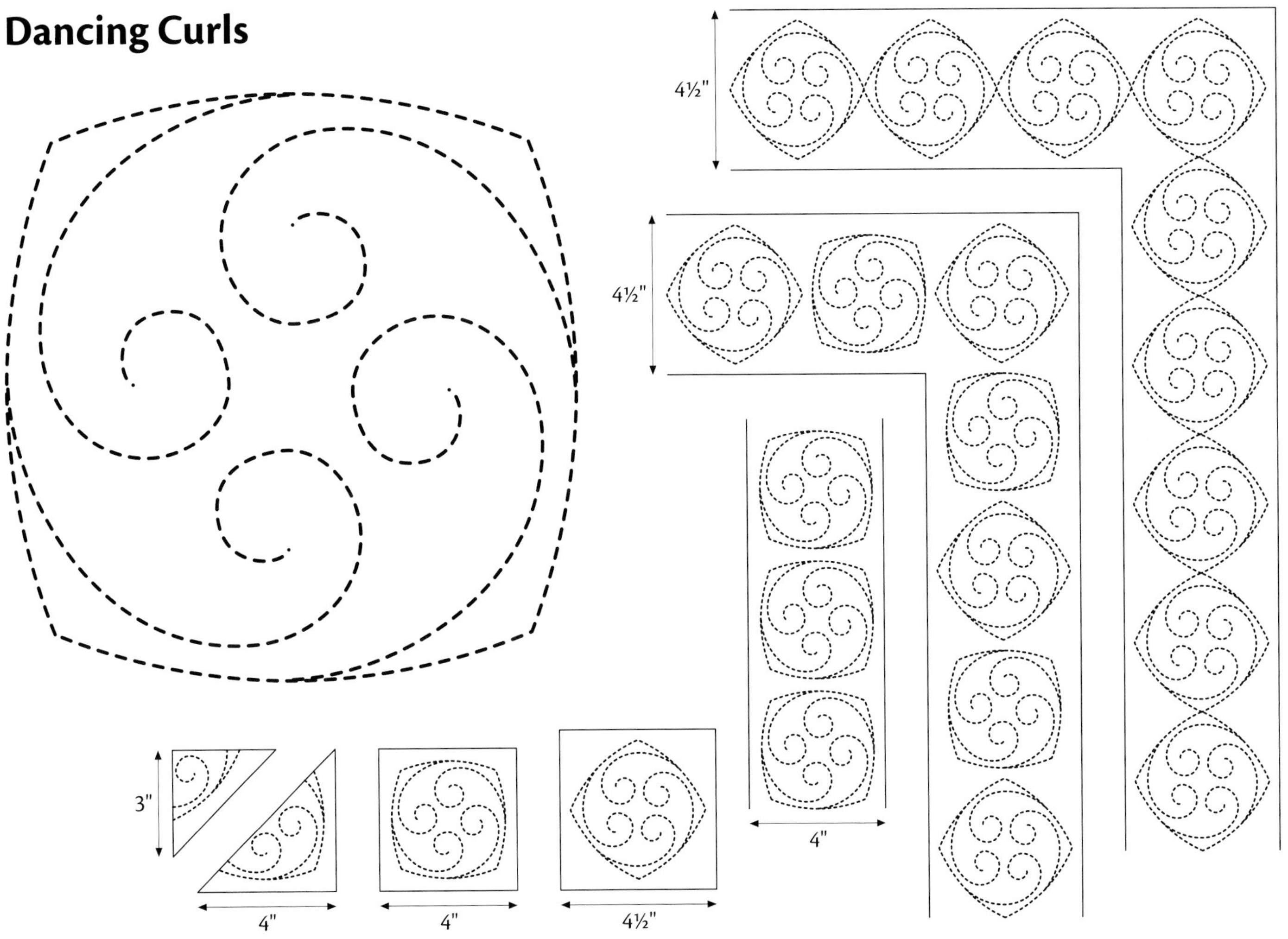

Wavelet

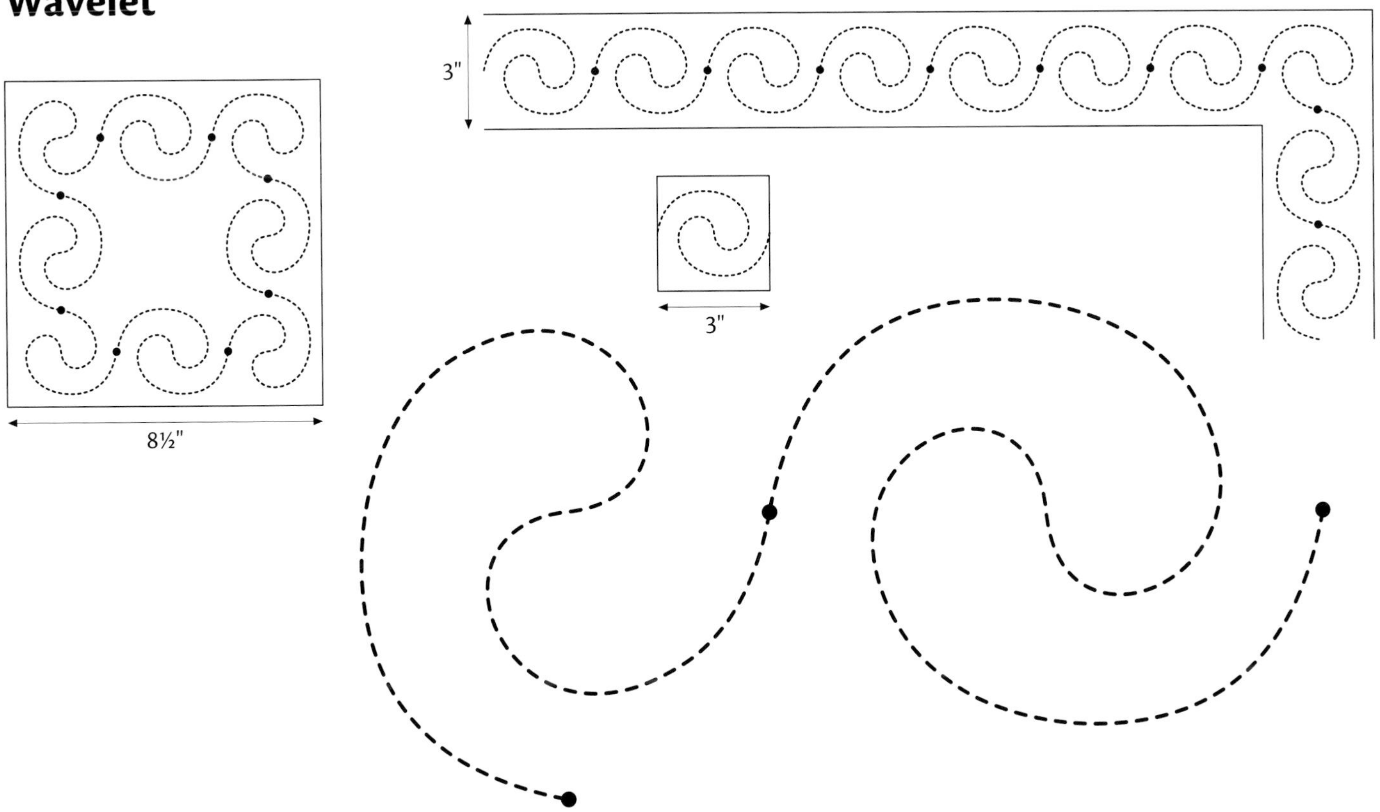

Whirlabout

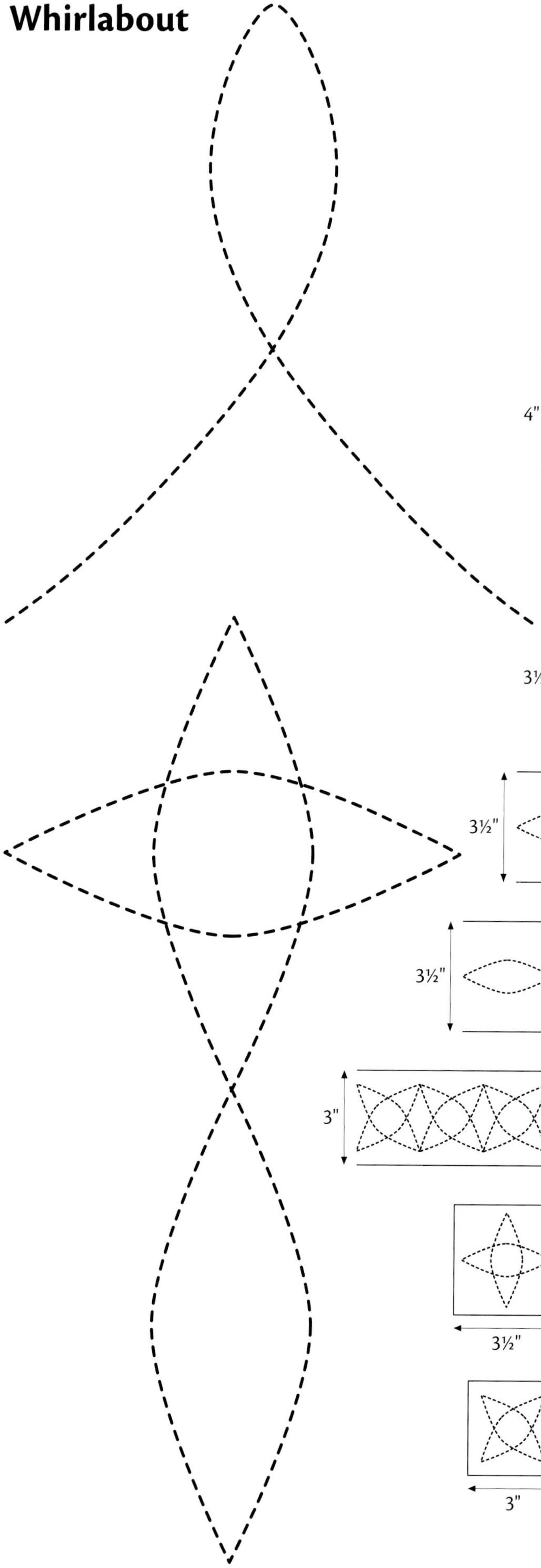

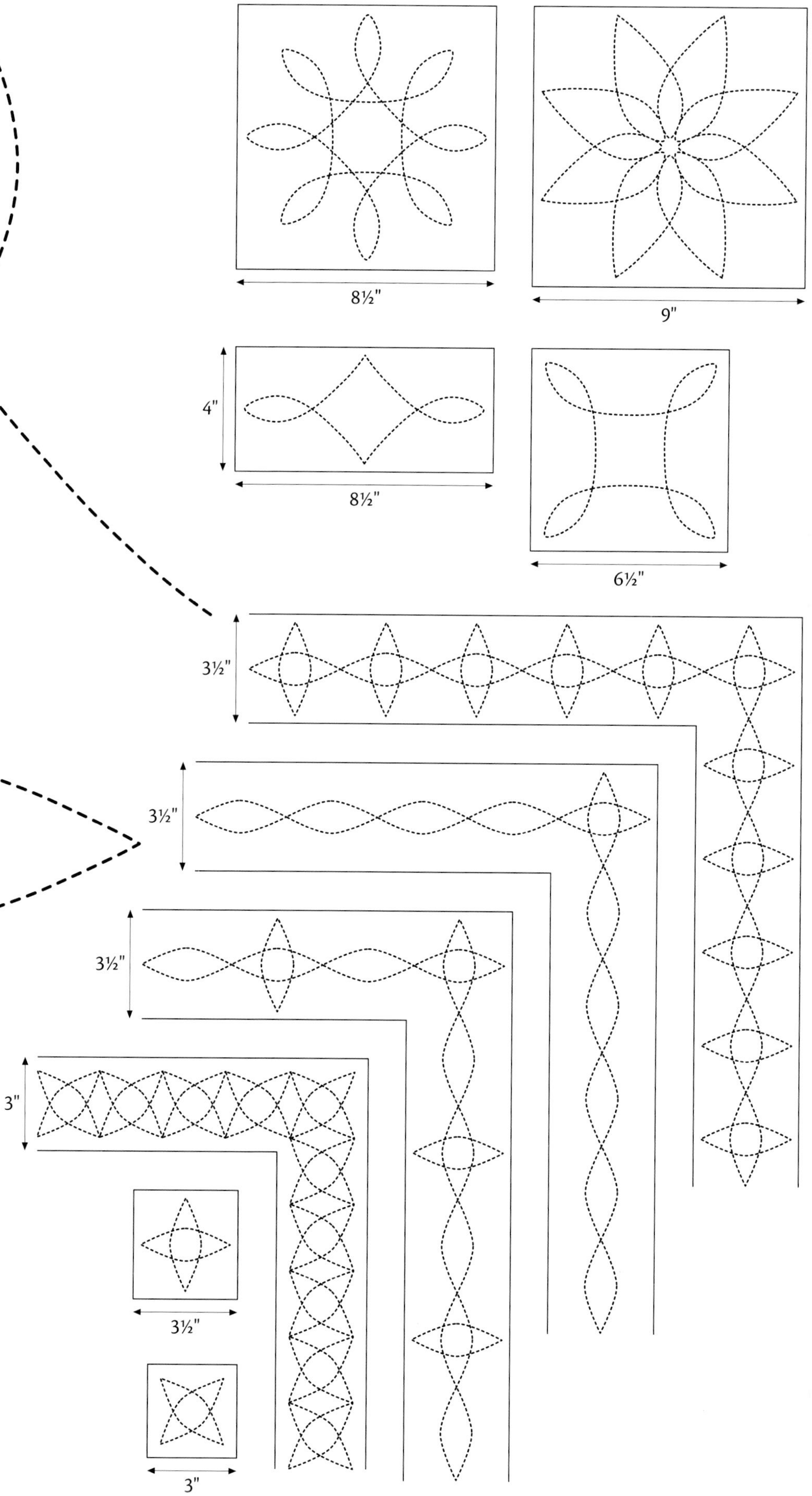

Candle Flame

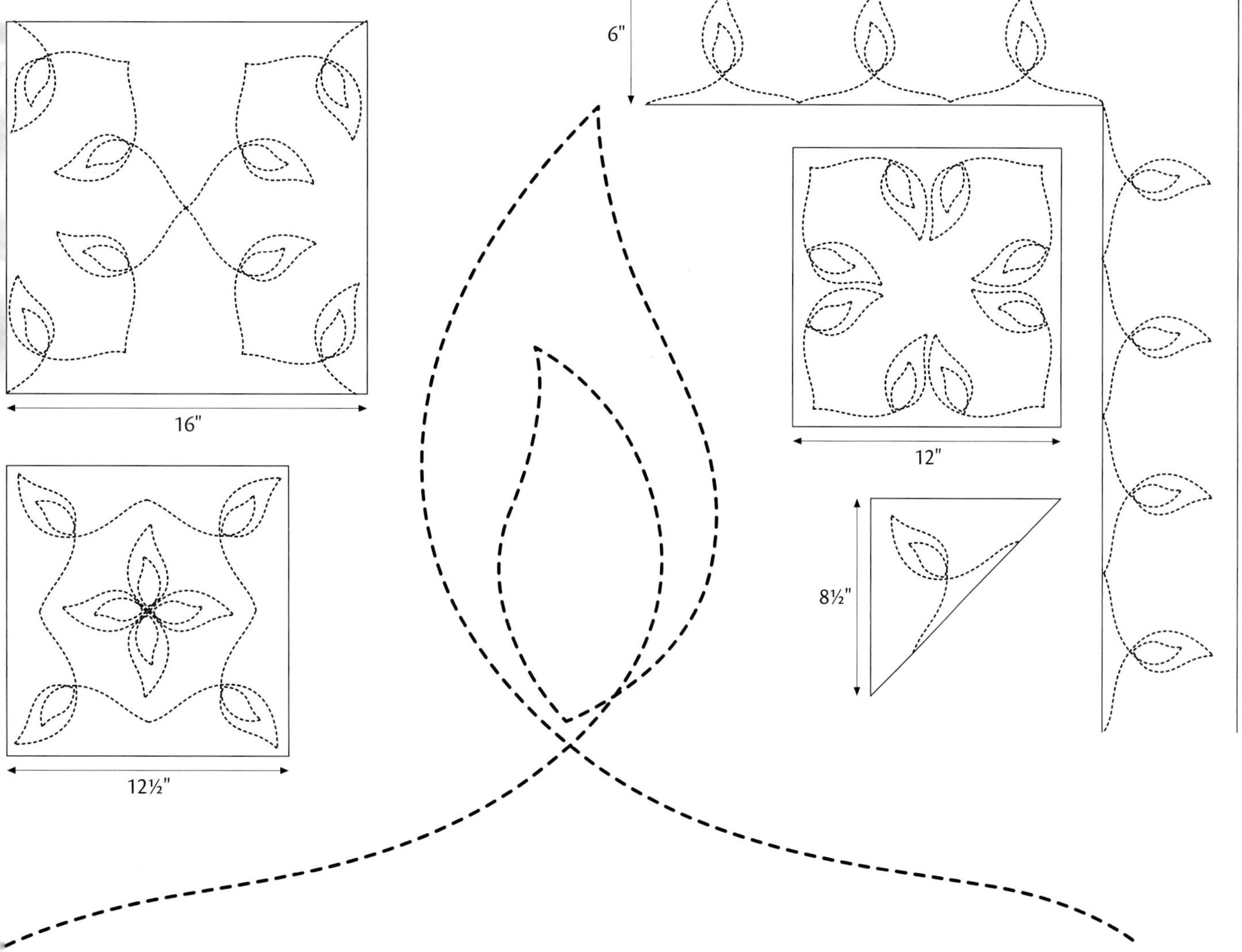

Ribbon Reel

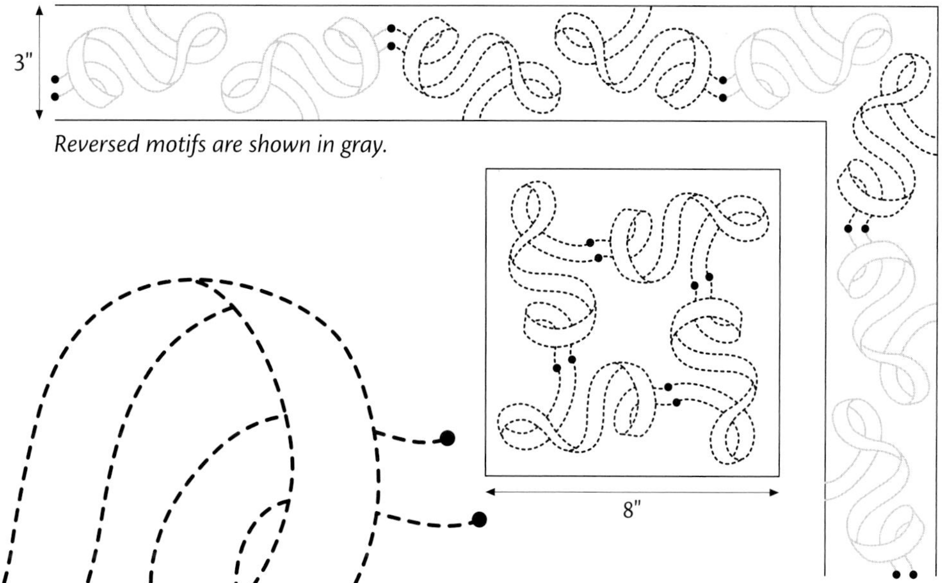

Reversed motifs are shown in gray.

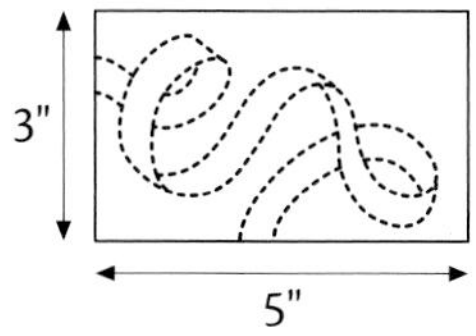

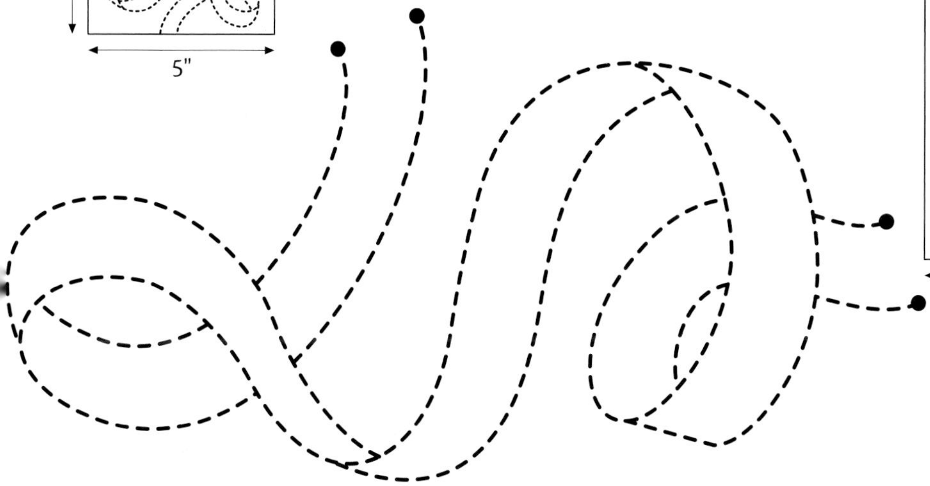

Autumn Breeze

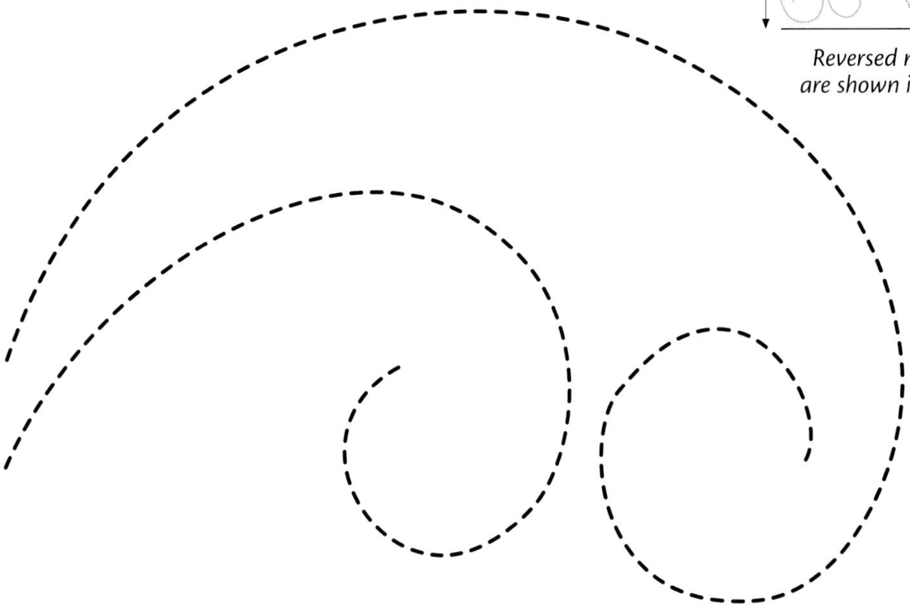

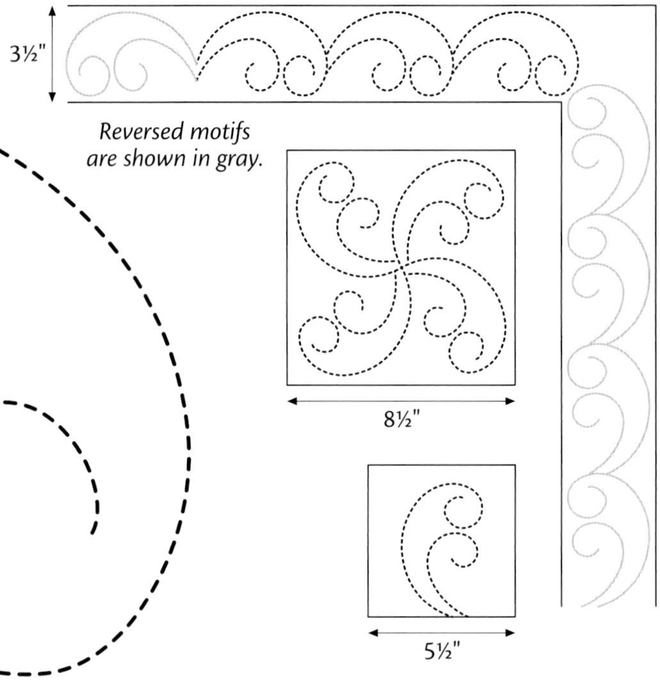

Reversed motifs are shown in gray.

Celebration 2

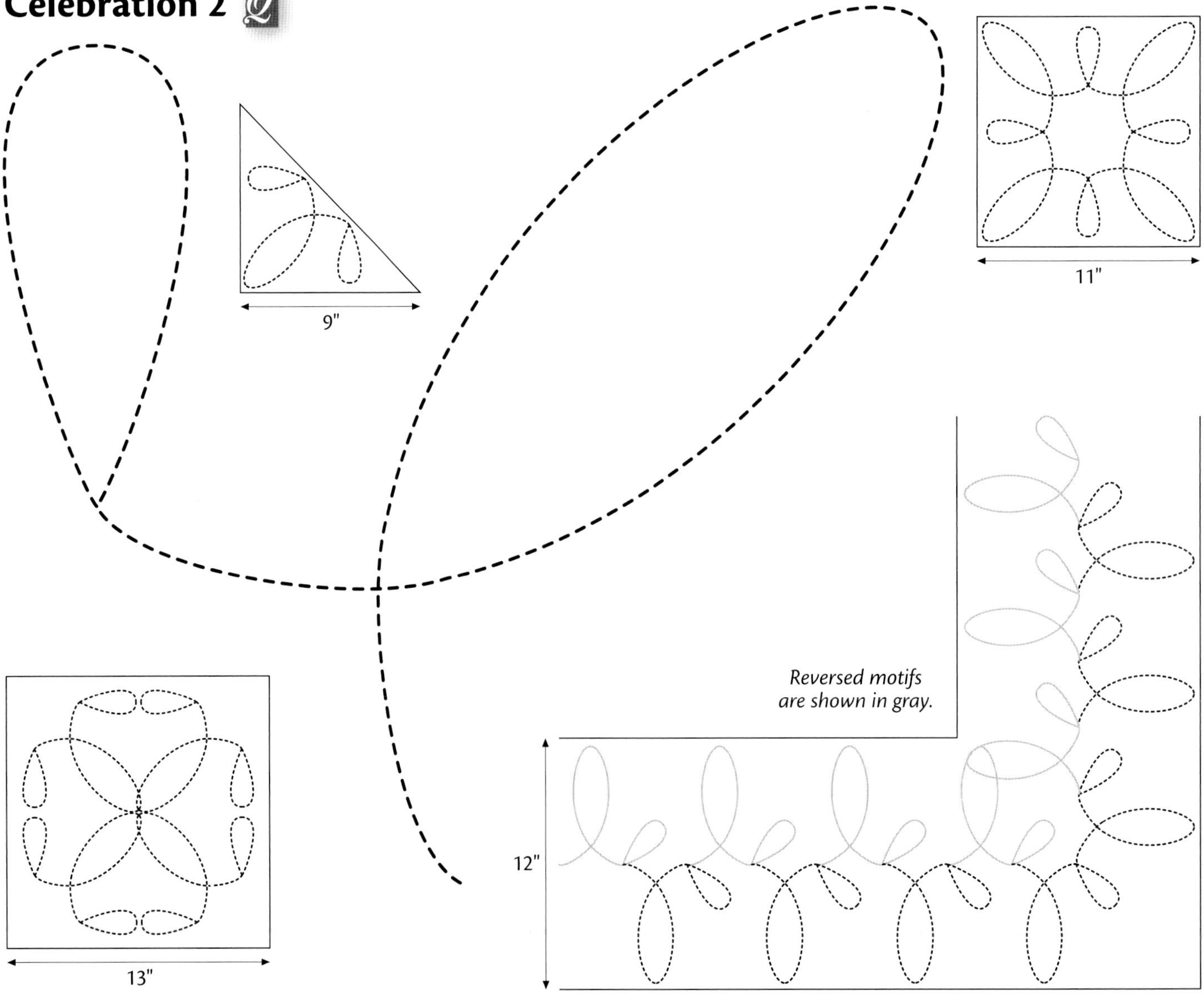

Reversed motifs are shown in gray.

Yukon Cable

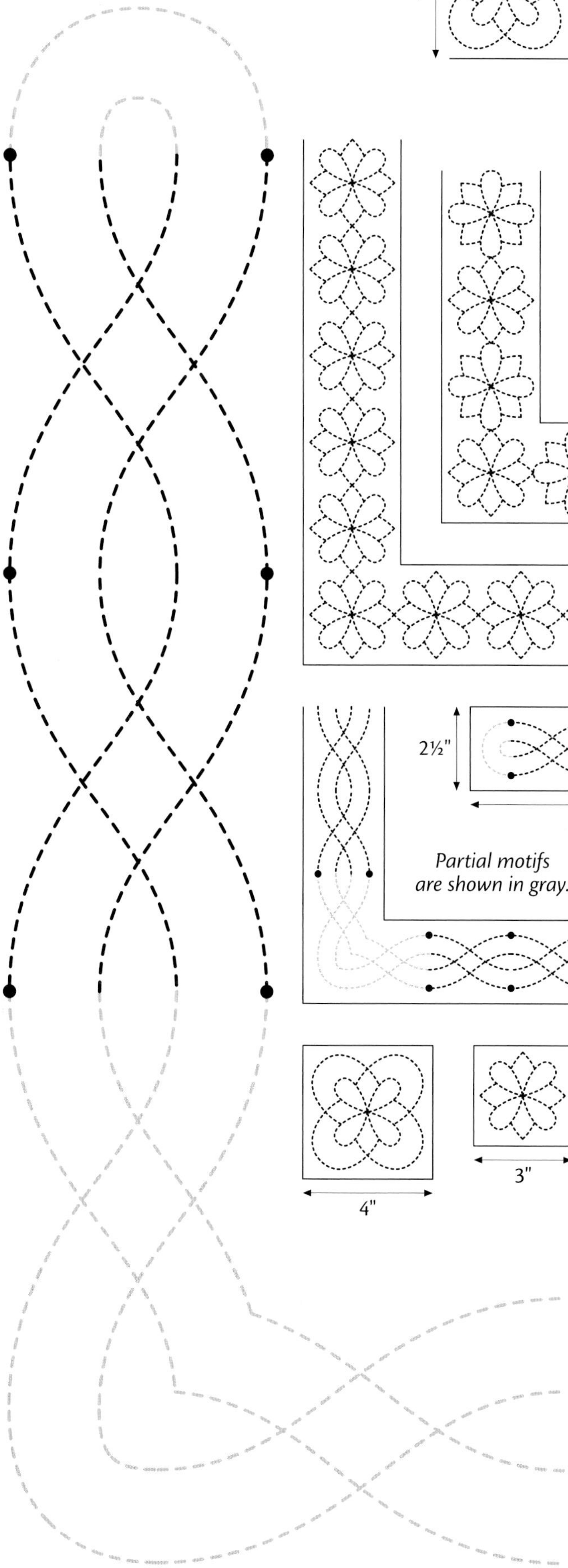

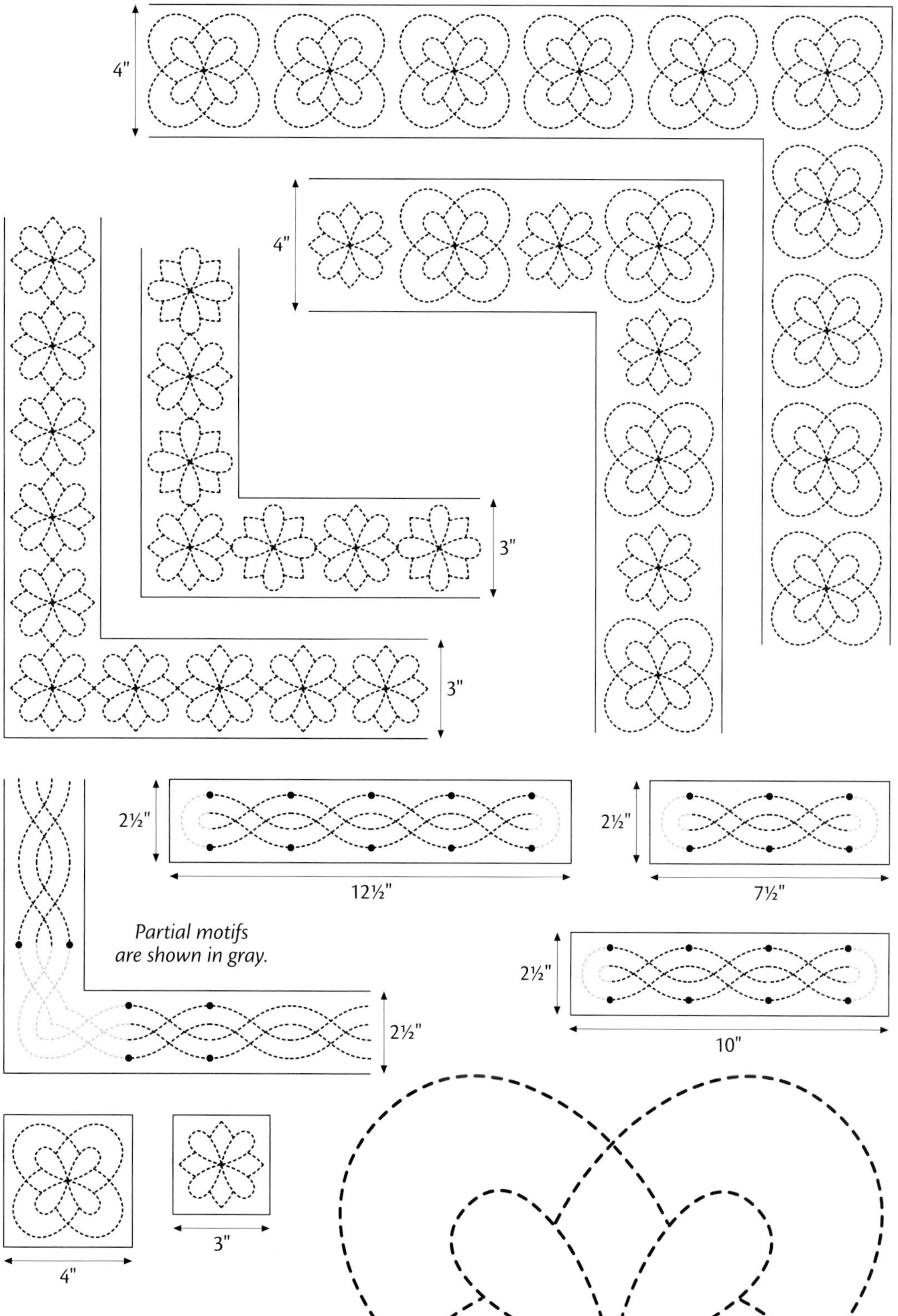
4"
4"
3"
3"
2½"
12½"
2½"
7½"
Partial motifs are shown in gray.
2½"
10"
2½"
4"
3"

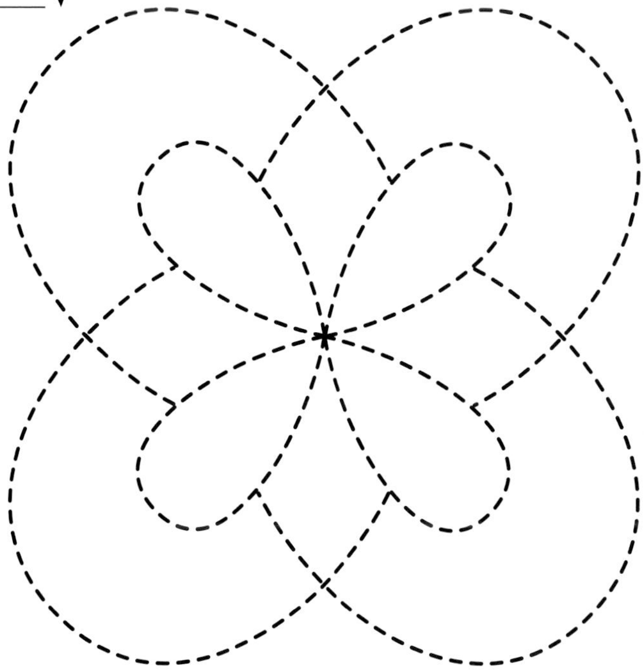

Ribbon Dance

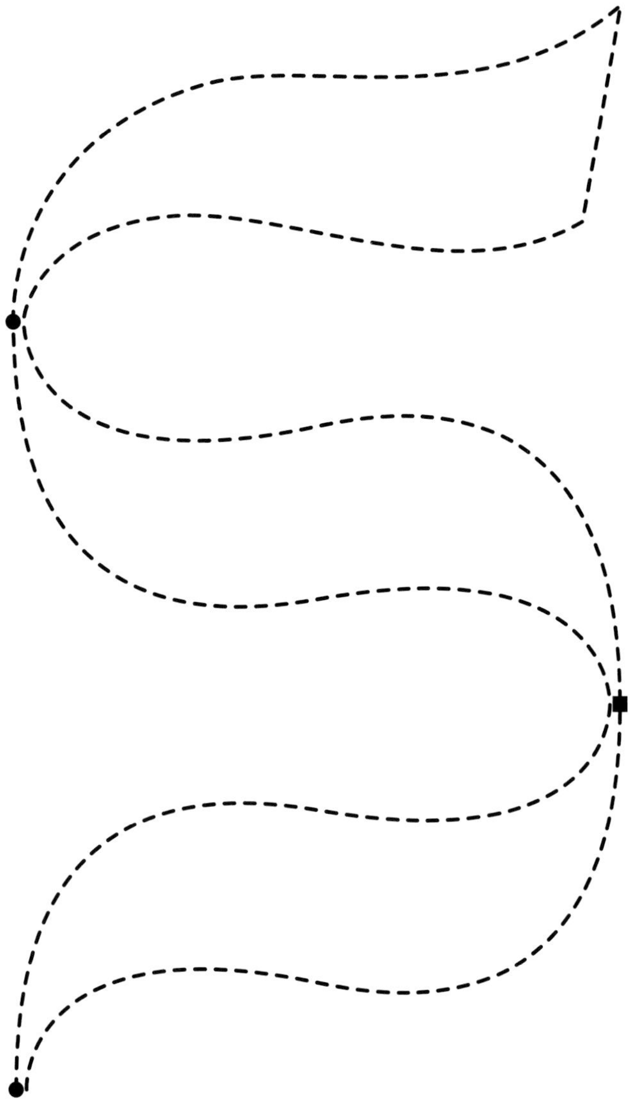

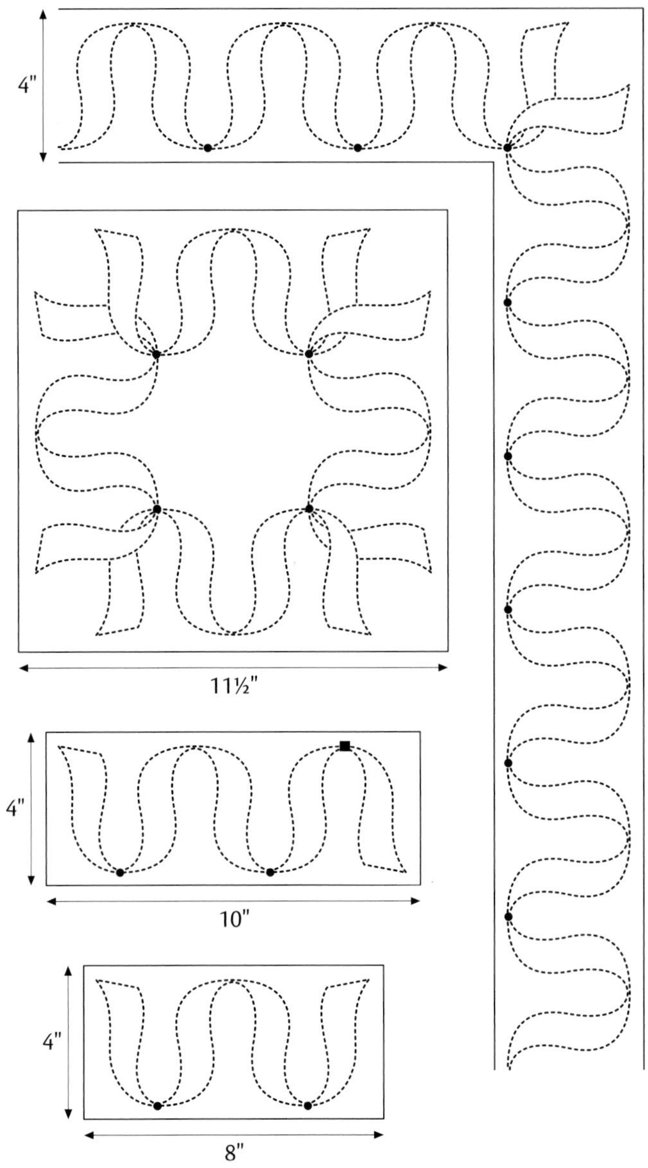
4"
11½"
4"
10"
4"
8"

Wind Swirl

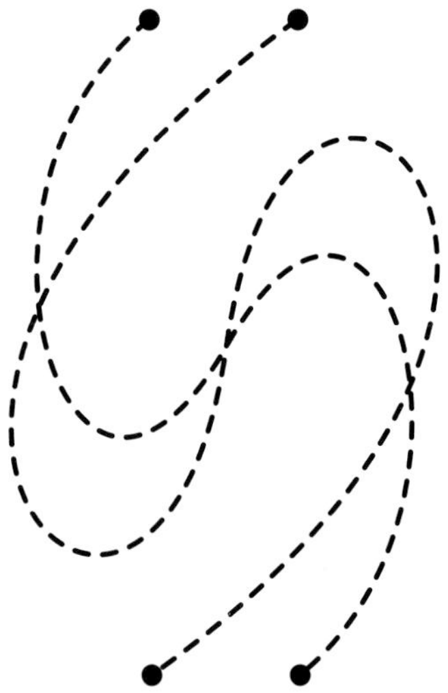

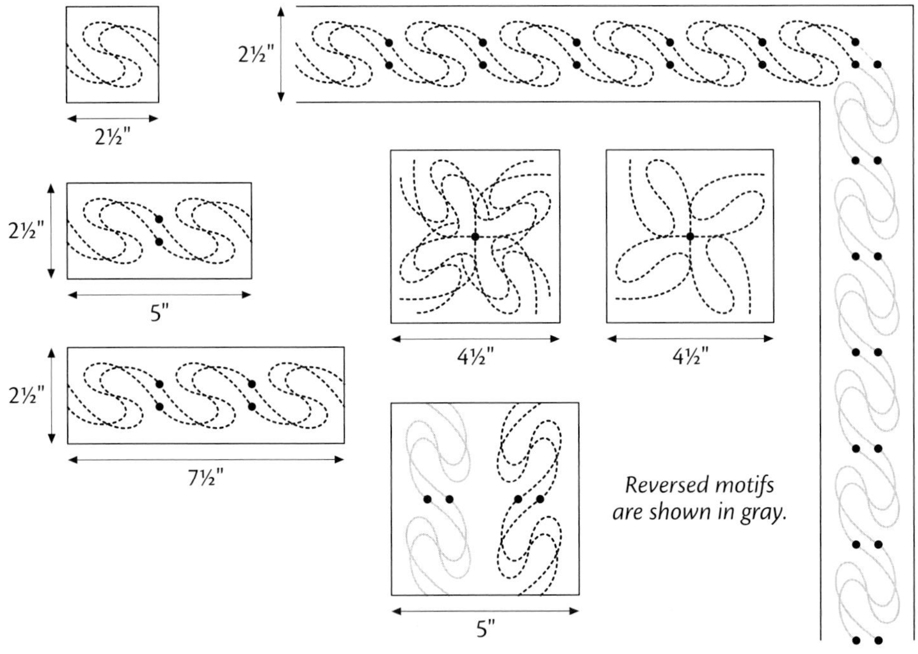
2½"
2½"
2½"
2½"
5"
2½"
7½"
4½"
4½"
5"
Reversed motifs are shown in gray.

Furrow Cable

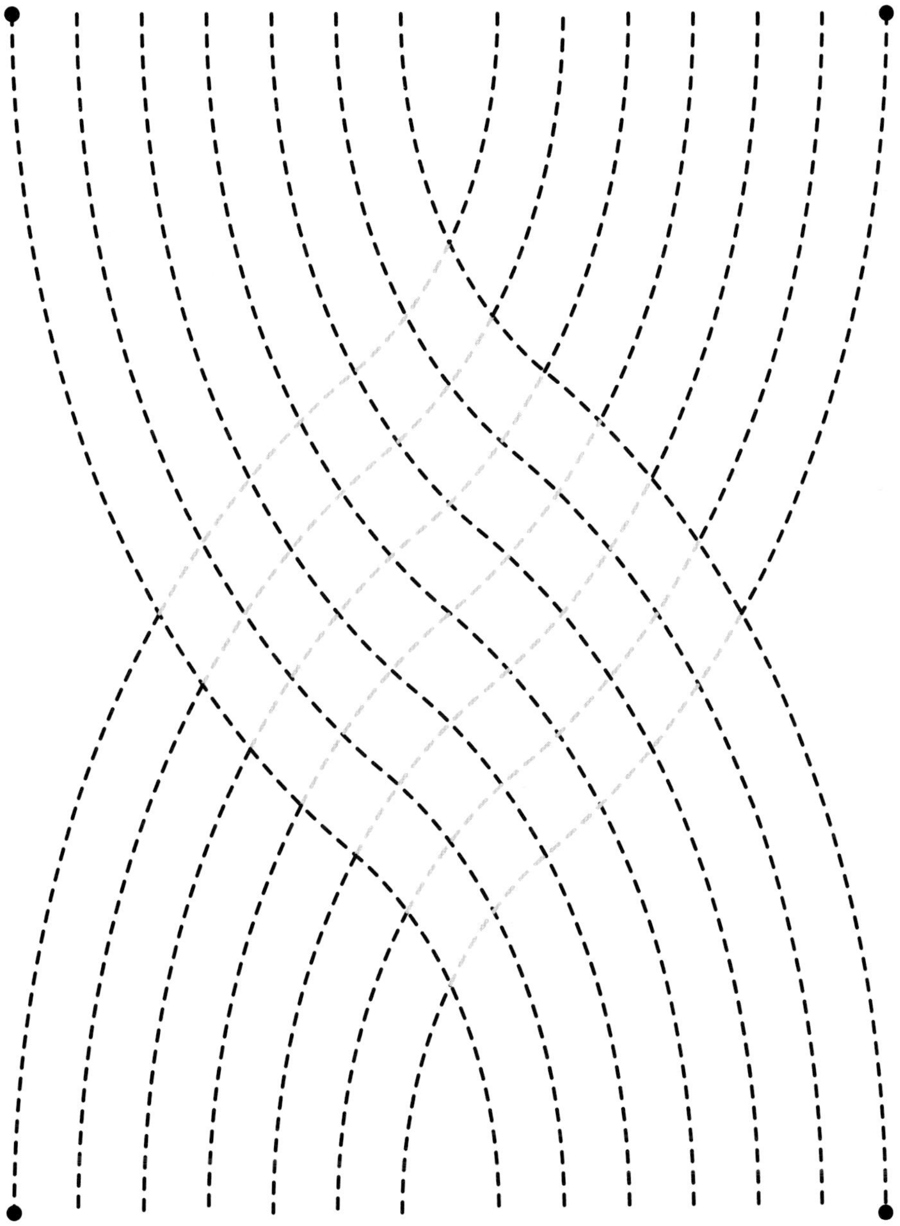

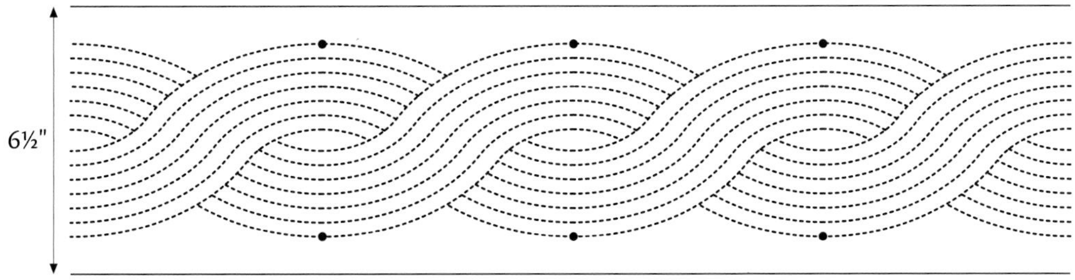

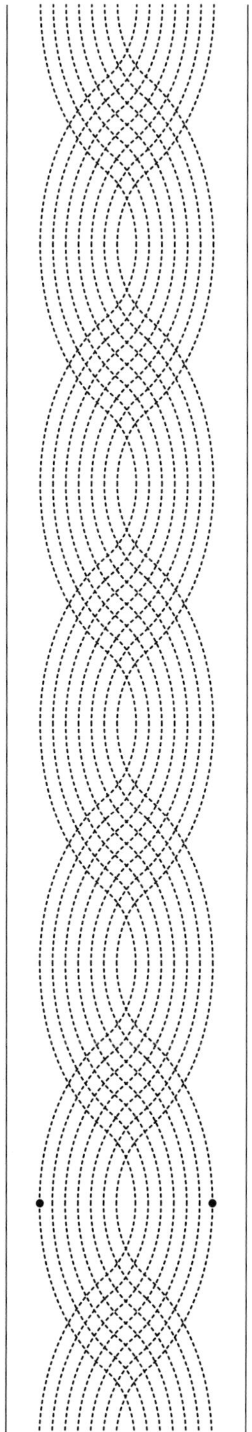

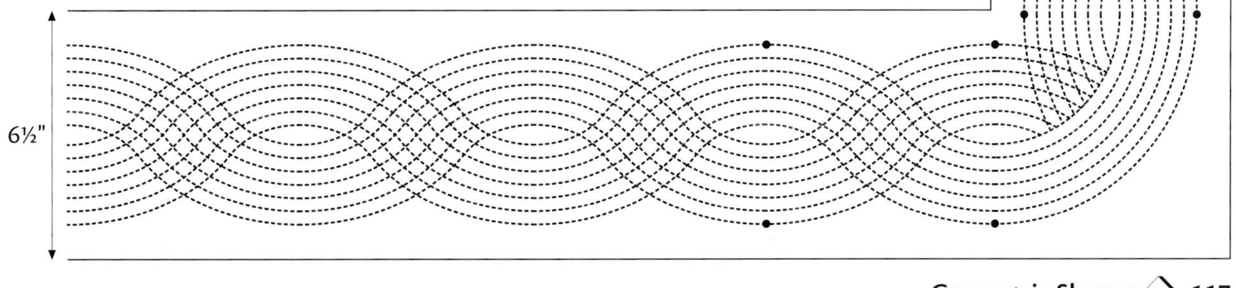

Fish Splash

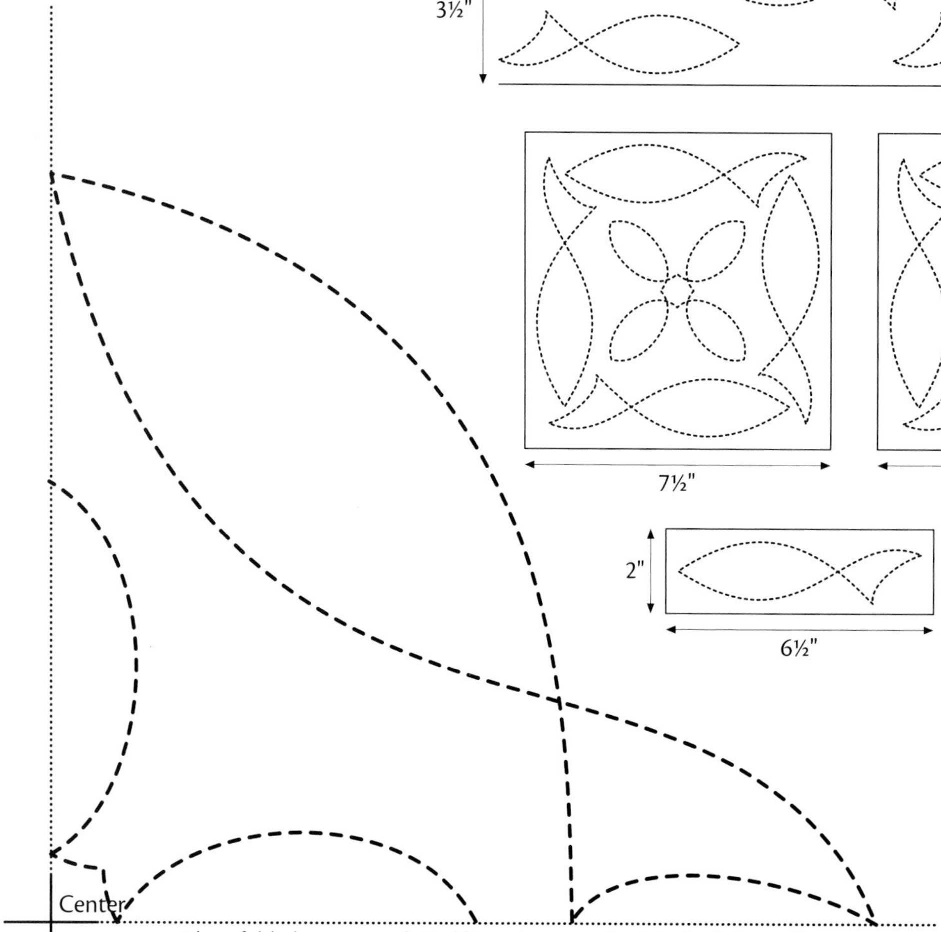
Center

Place folded paper on dotted lines, trace, and rotate for full motif.

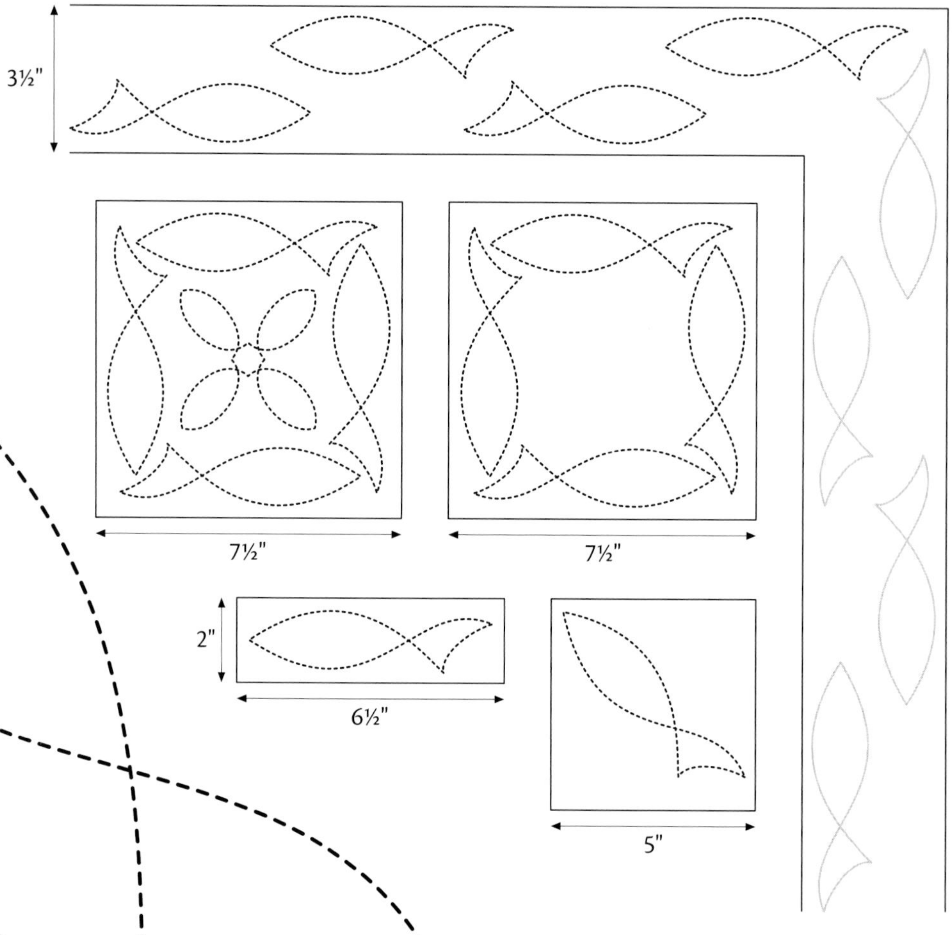
3½"
7½"
7½"
2"
6½"
5"

Reversed motifs are shown in gray.

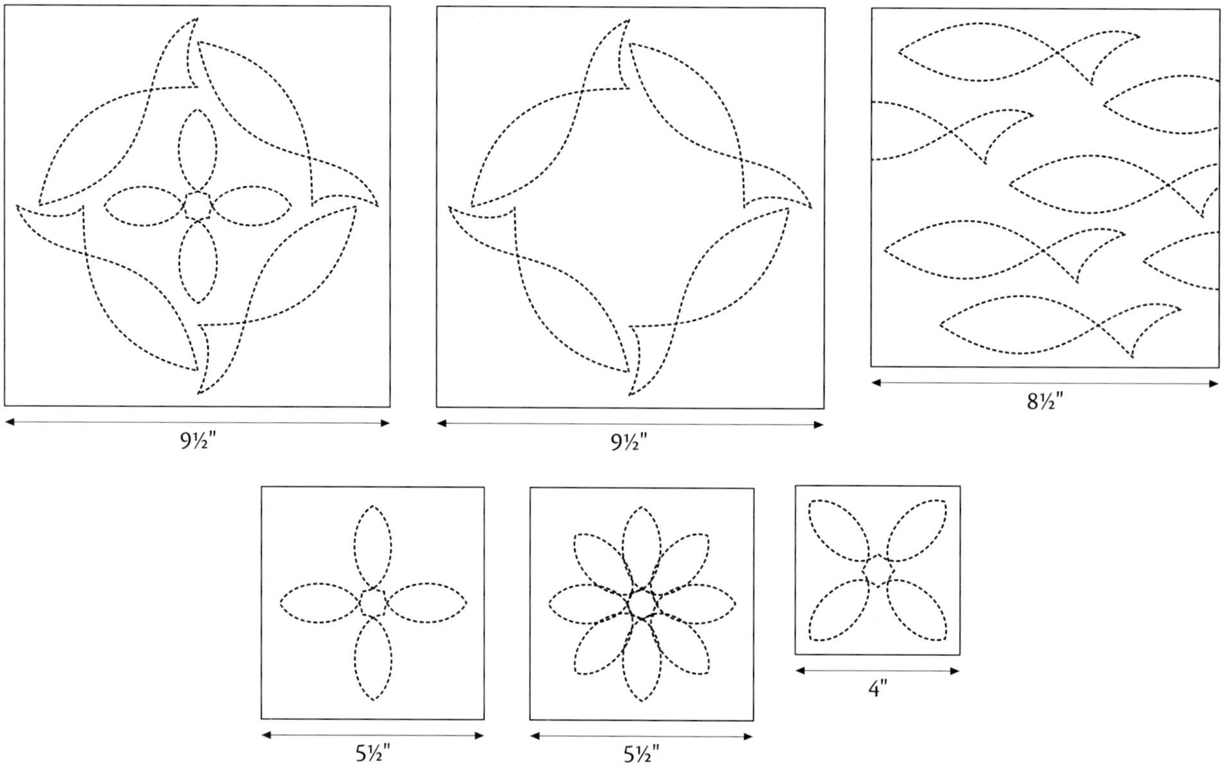
9½"
9½"
8½"
5½"
5½"
4"

Celtic Knot

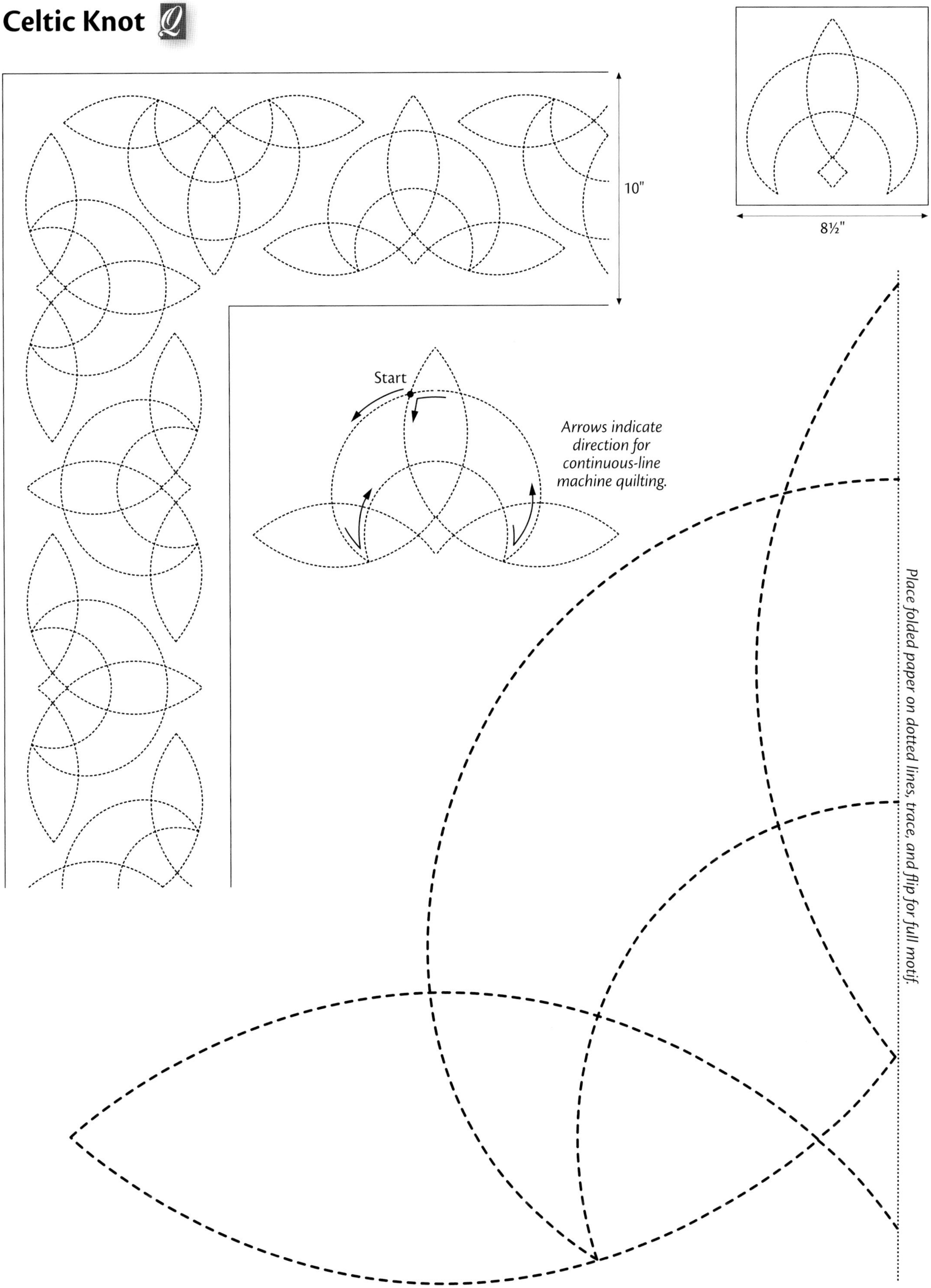
10"
8½"
Start
Arrows indicate direction for continuous-line machine quilting.
Place folded paper on dotted lines, trace, and flip for full motif.

Arrowhead

3½"

2"

10½"

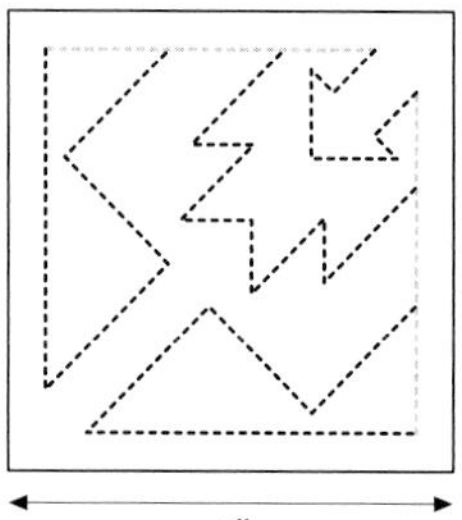

6"

7"

9½"

10½"

Celestial

Celtic Chain

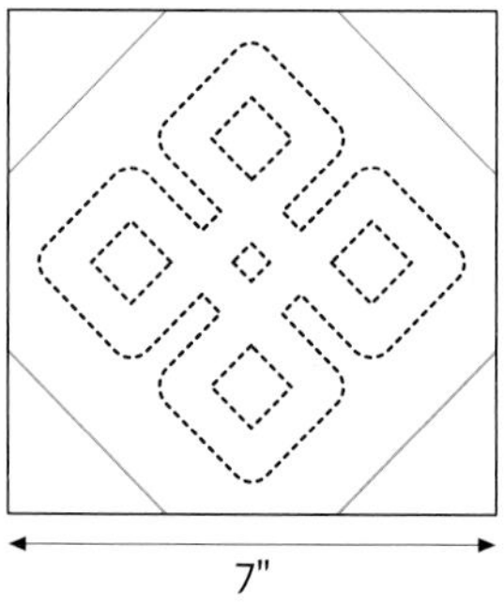

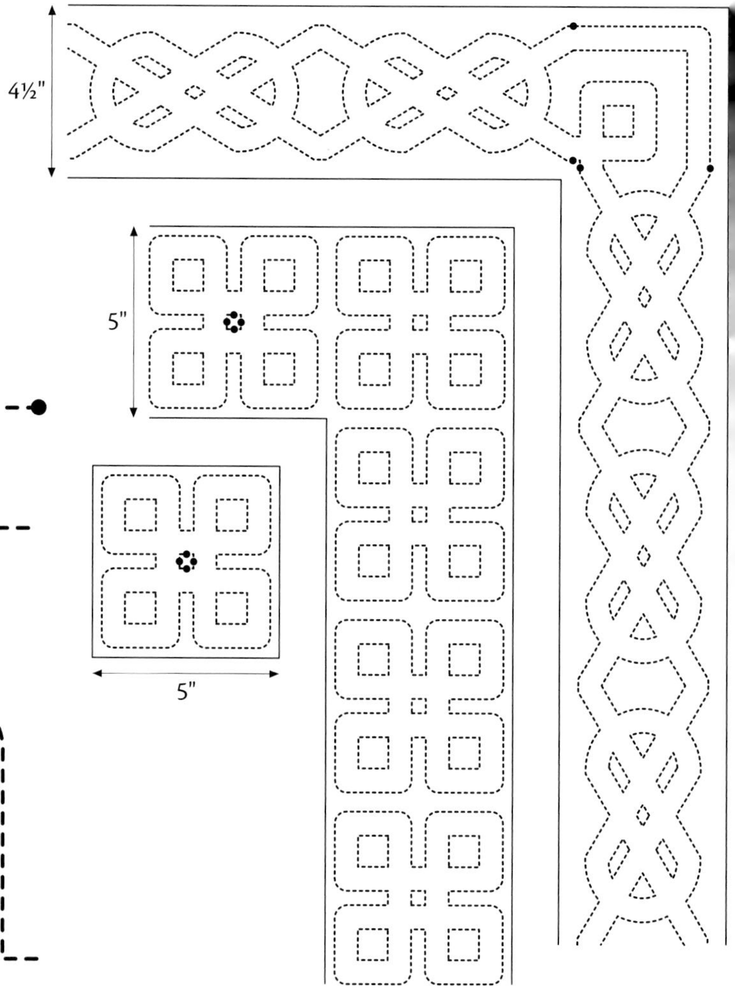

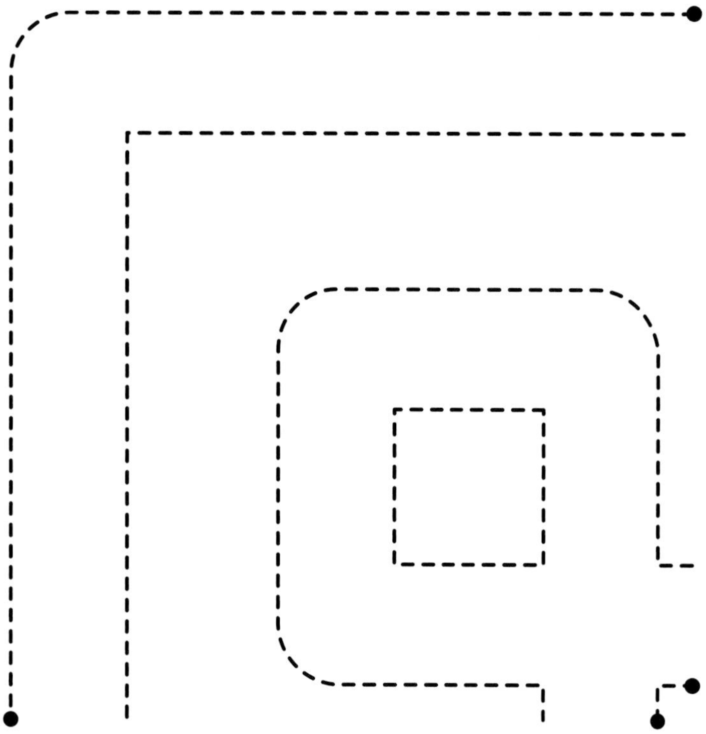

Golf Ball

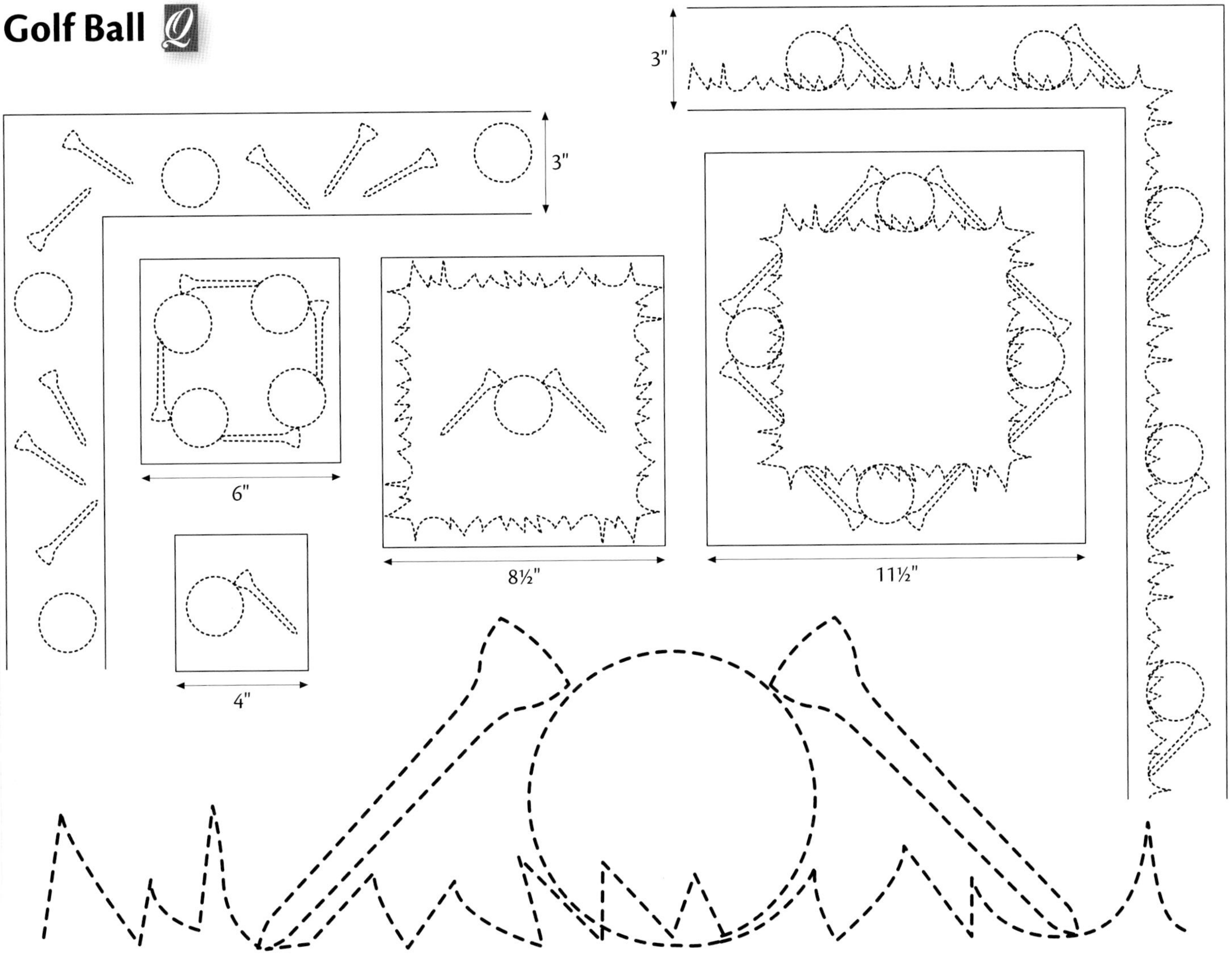
3"
3"
6"
8½"
11½"
4"

Guatemala

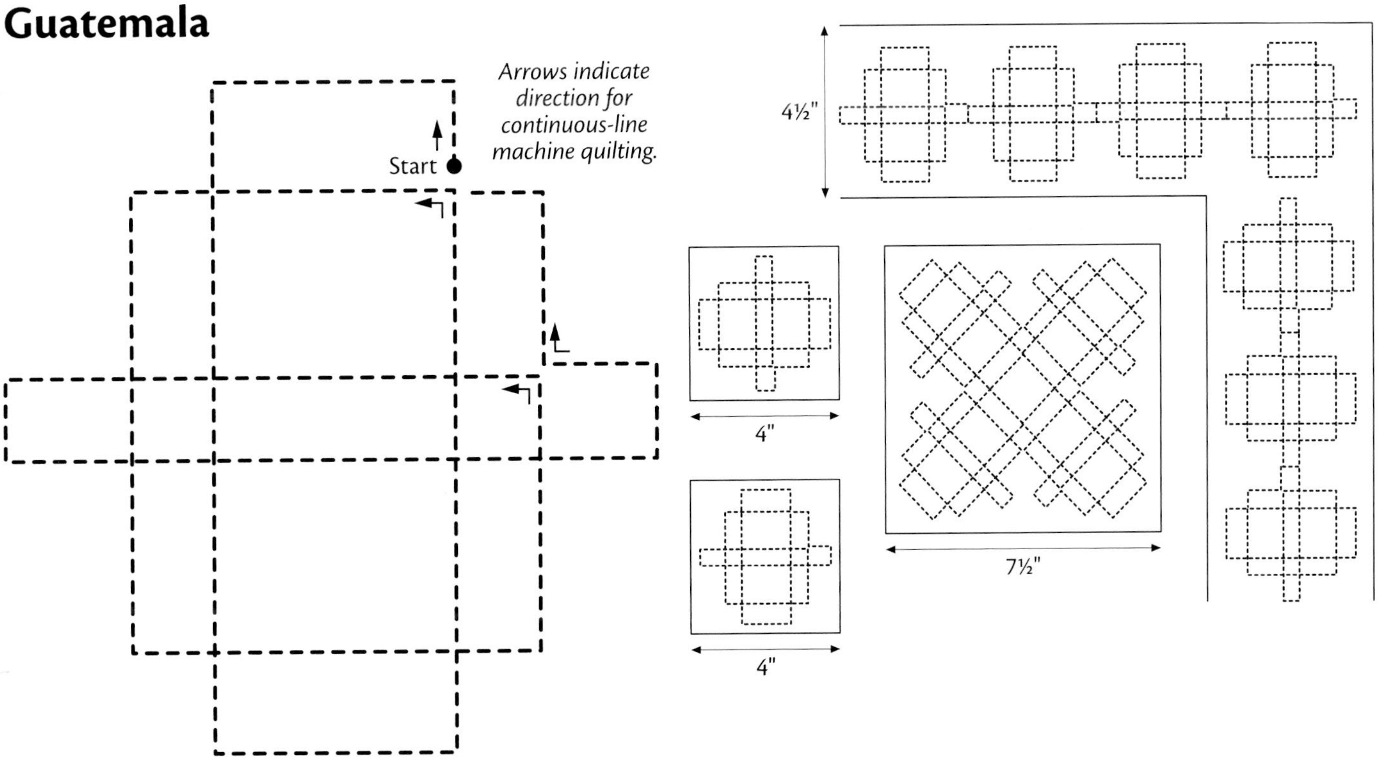
Arrows indicate direction for continuous-line machine quilting.
Start
4½"
4"
7½"
4"

Loops and Swirls

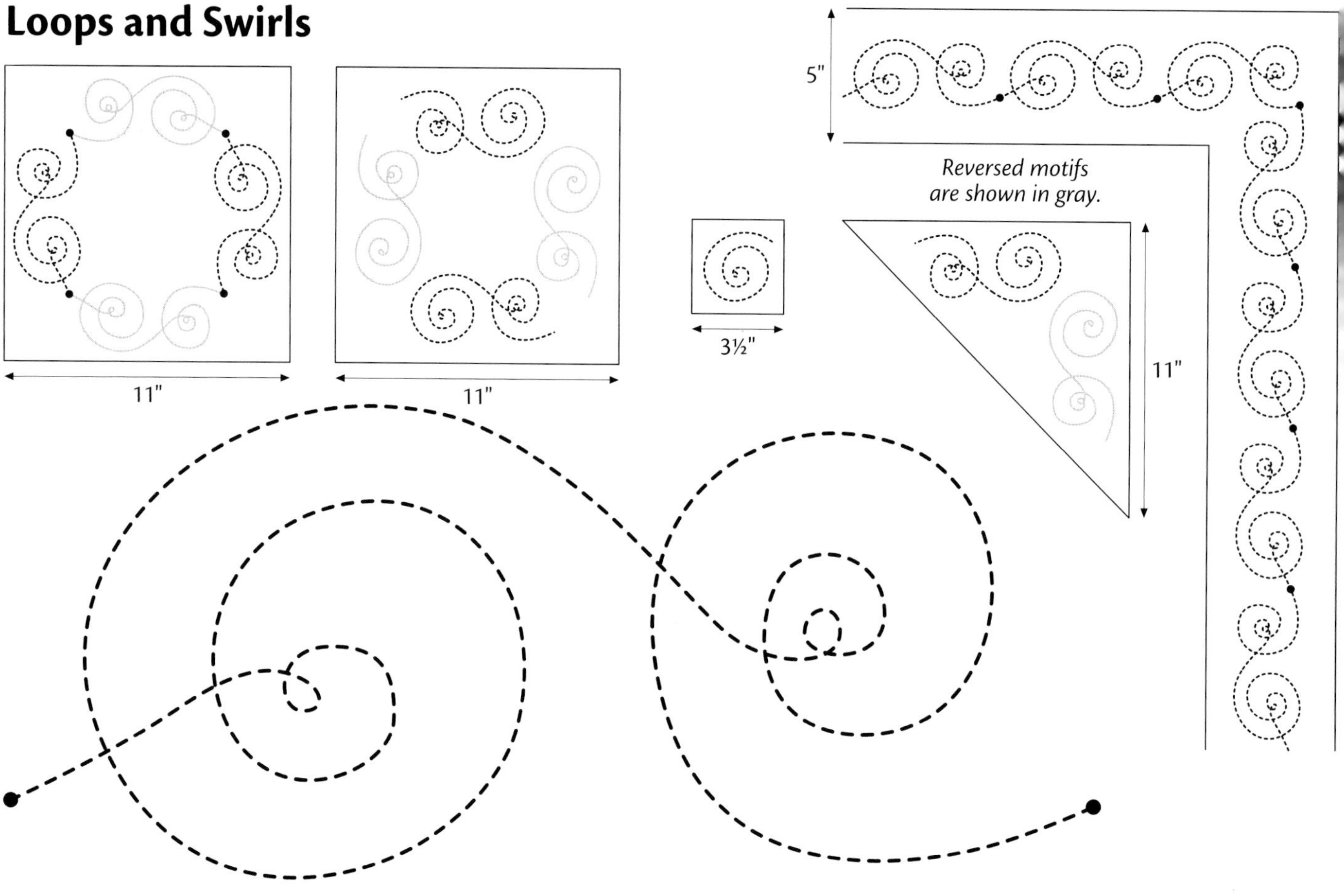
5"
Reversed motifs are shown in gray.
11"
11"
3½"
11"

Windmill

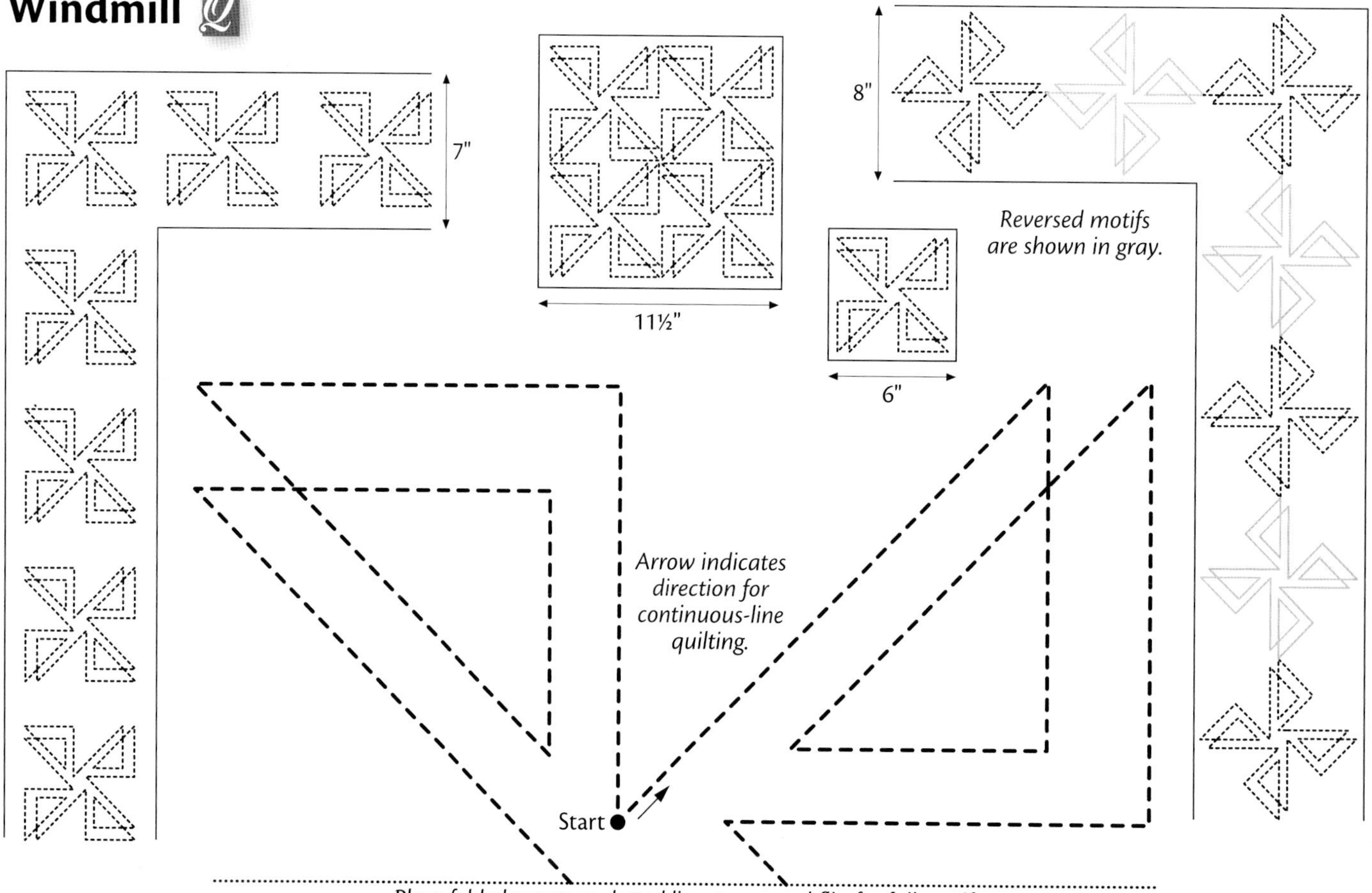
7"
8"
11½"
Reversed motifs are shown in gray.
6"
Arrow indicates direction for continuous-line quilting.
Start

Place folded paper on dotted line, trace, and flip for full motif.

Spirals and Scrolls

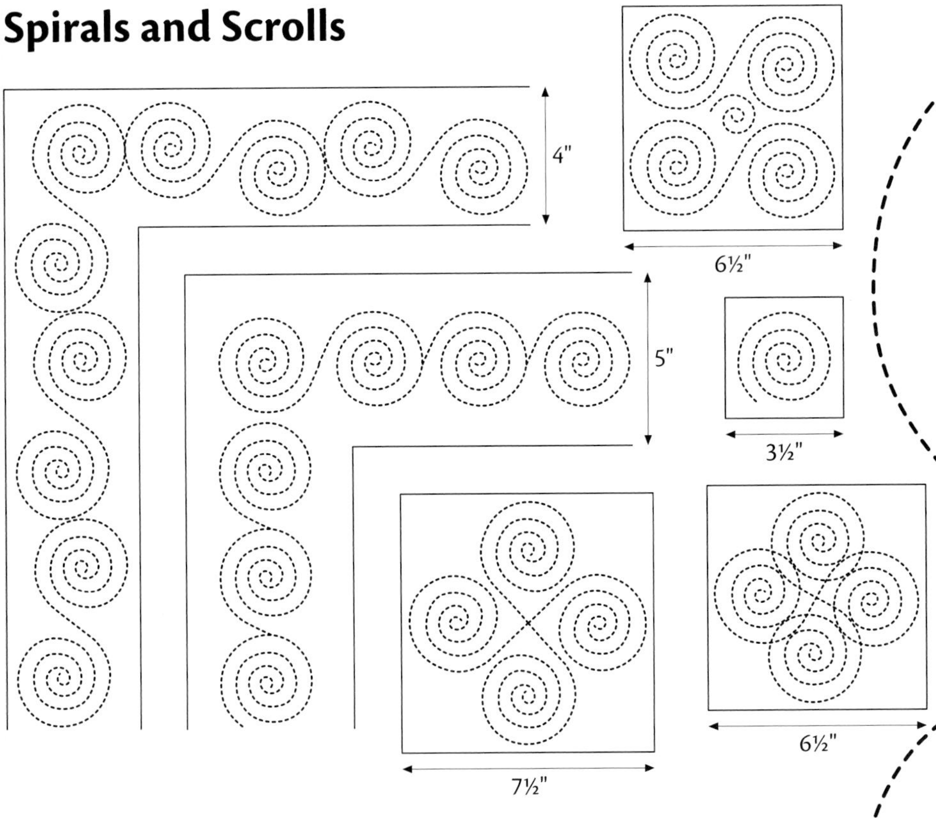
4"
6½"
5"
3½"
7½"
6½"

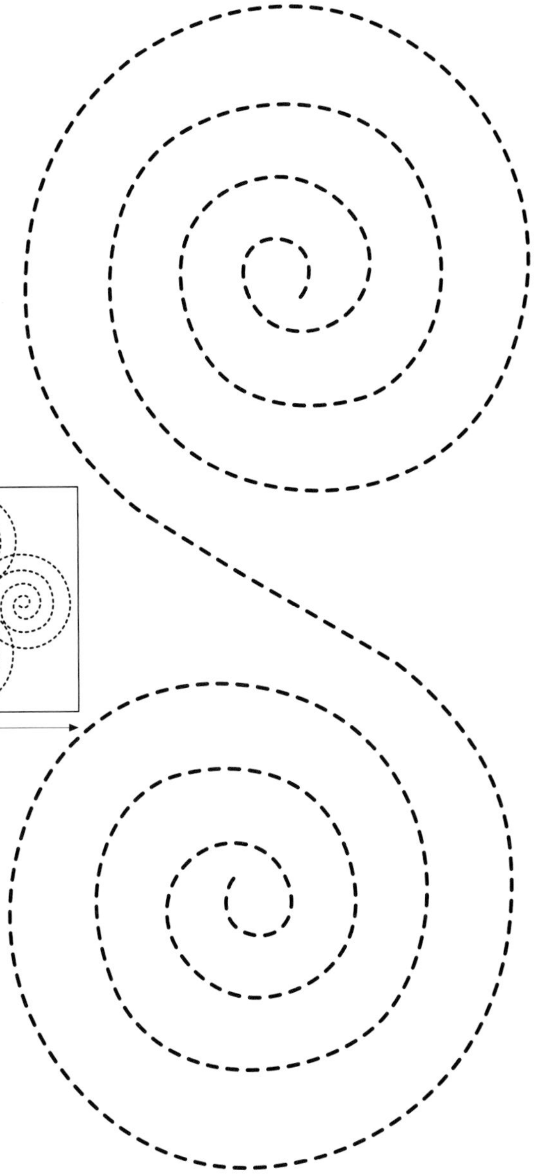

Paisley

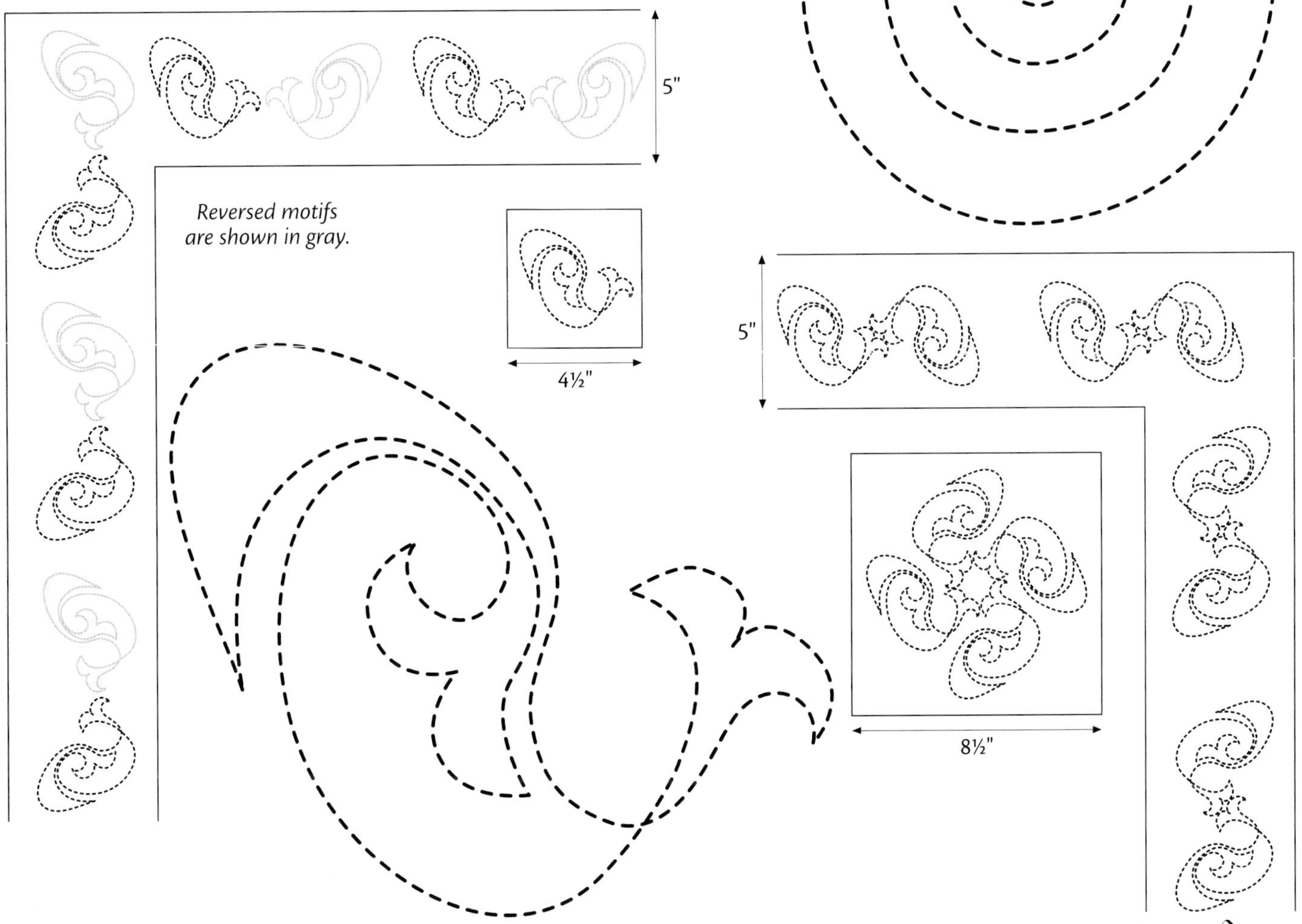
5"
4½"
5"
8½"

Reversed motifs are shown in gray.

Diamond

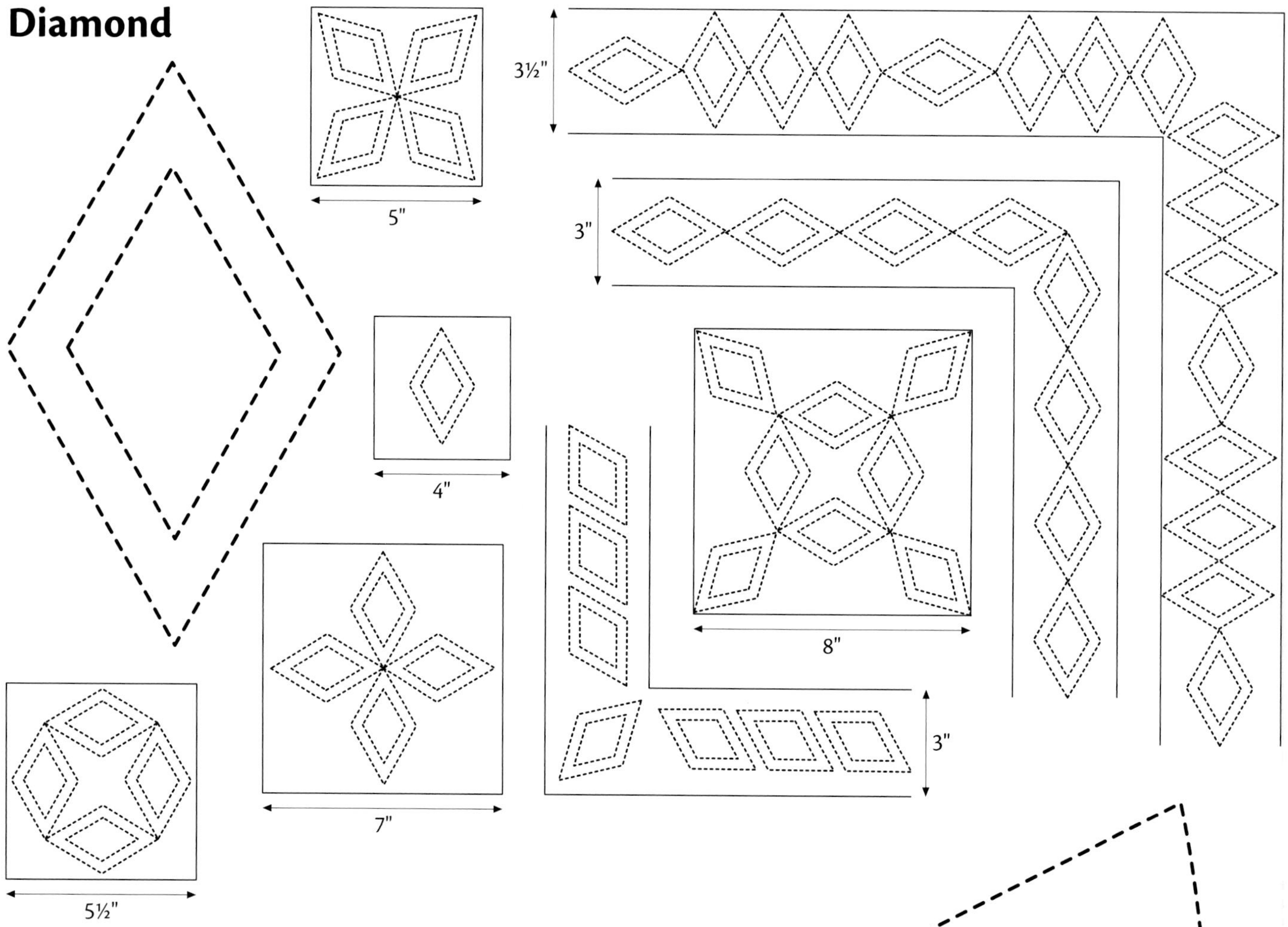
5"
3½"
3"
4"
8"
7"
3"
5½"

Whirlybows

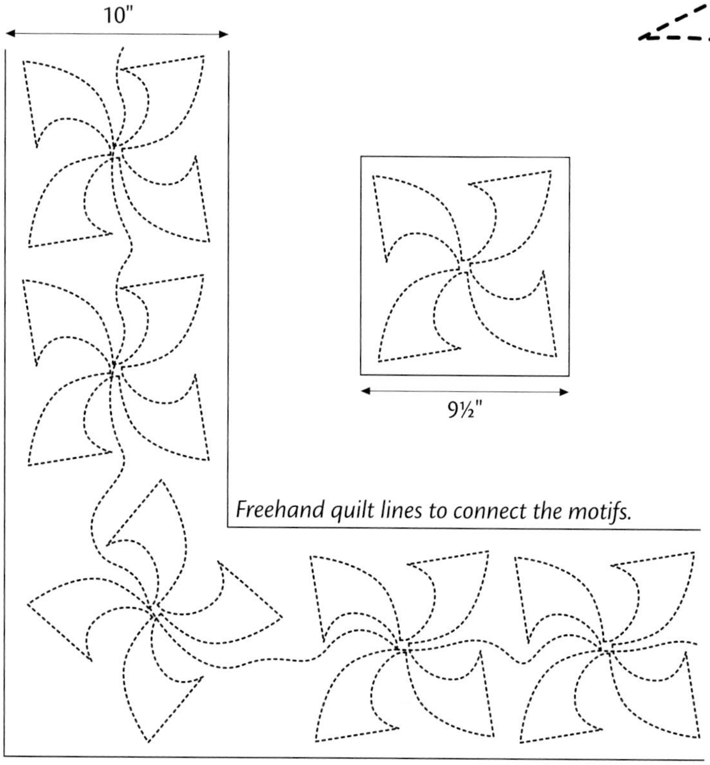
10"
9½"
Freehand quilt lines to connect the motifs.

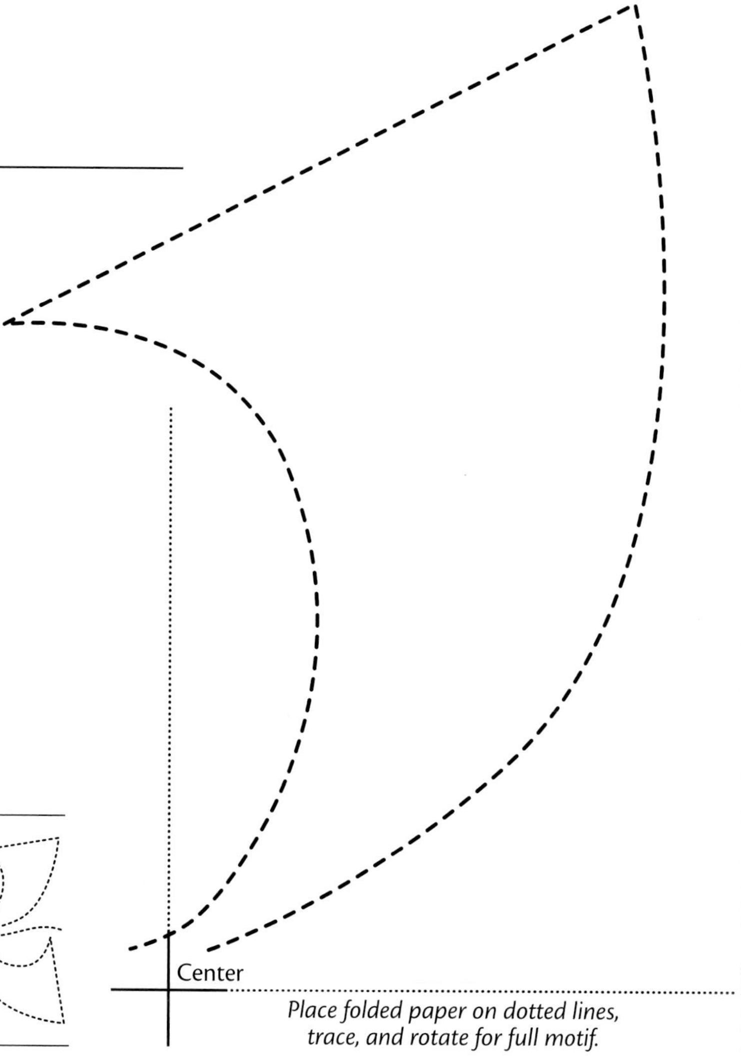
Center

Place folded paper on dotted lines, trace, and rotate for full motif.

Hanover

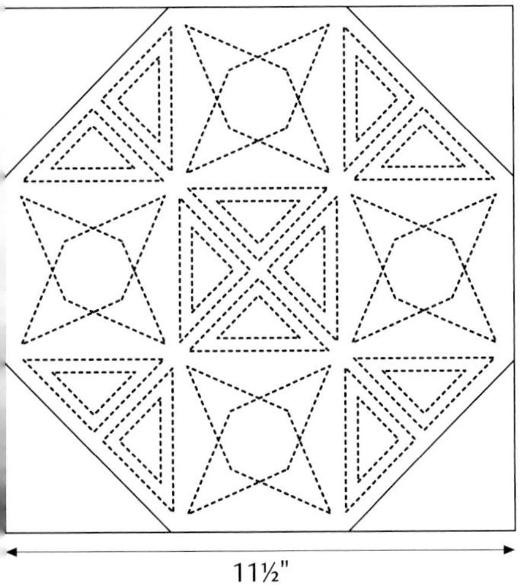

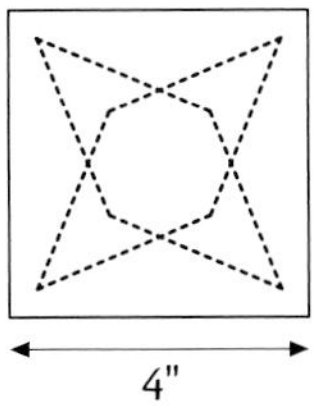

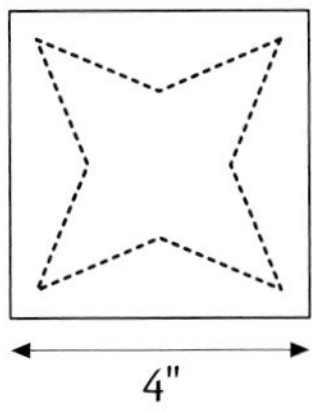

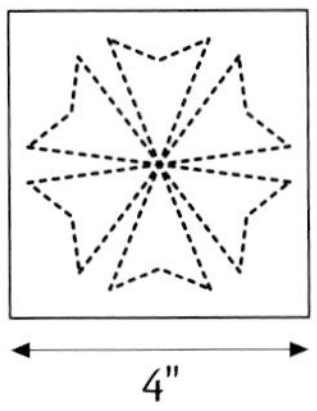

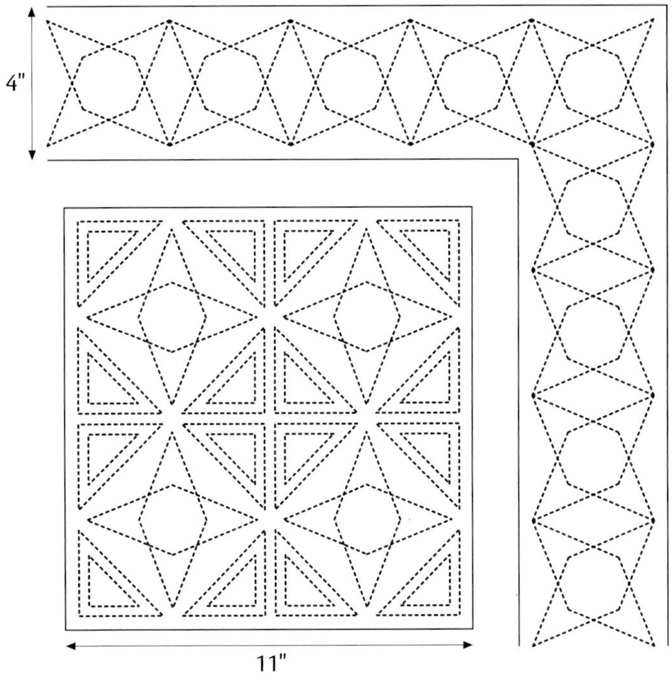

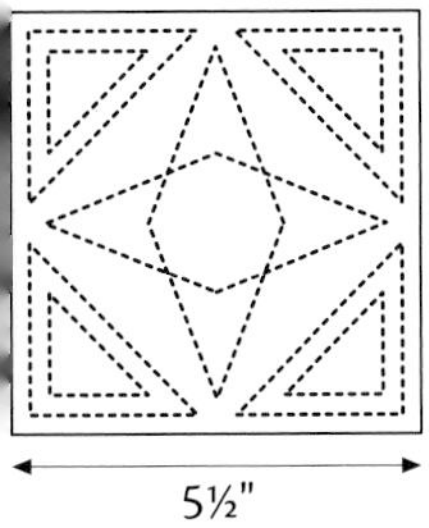

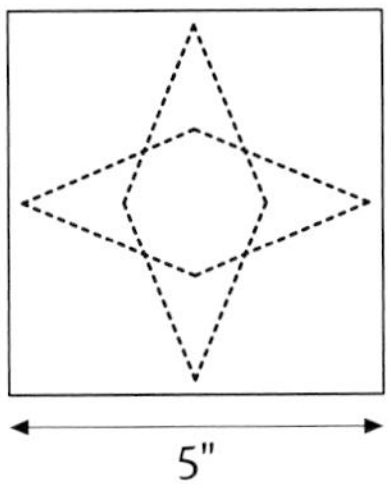

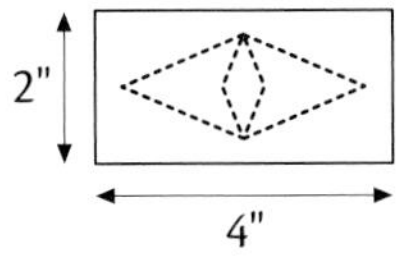

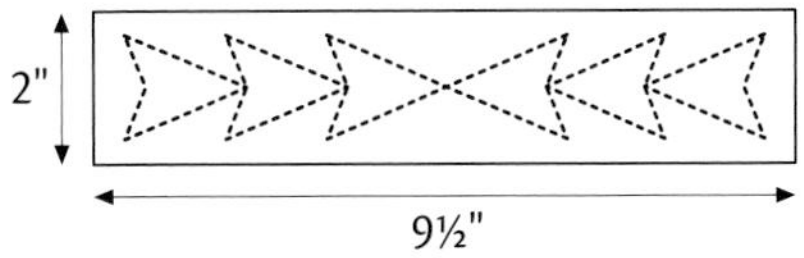

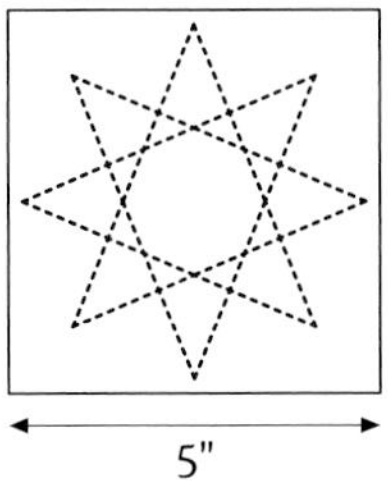

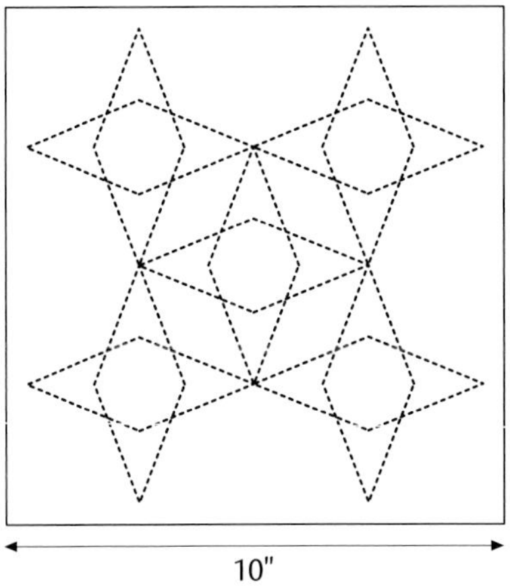

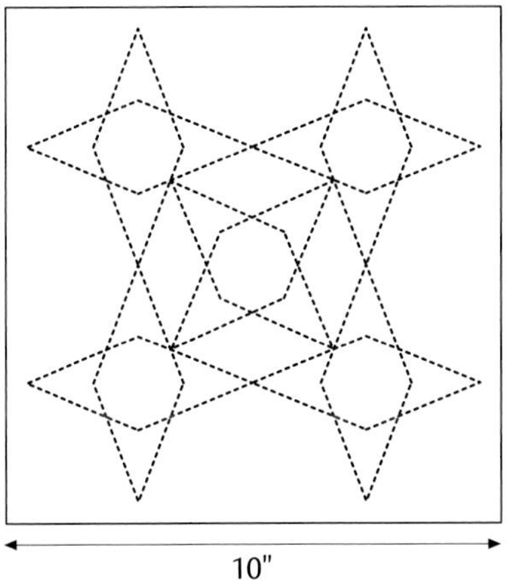

Cable Border

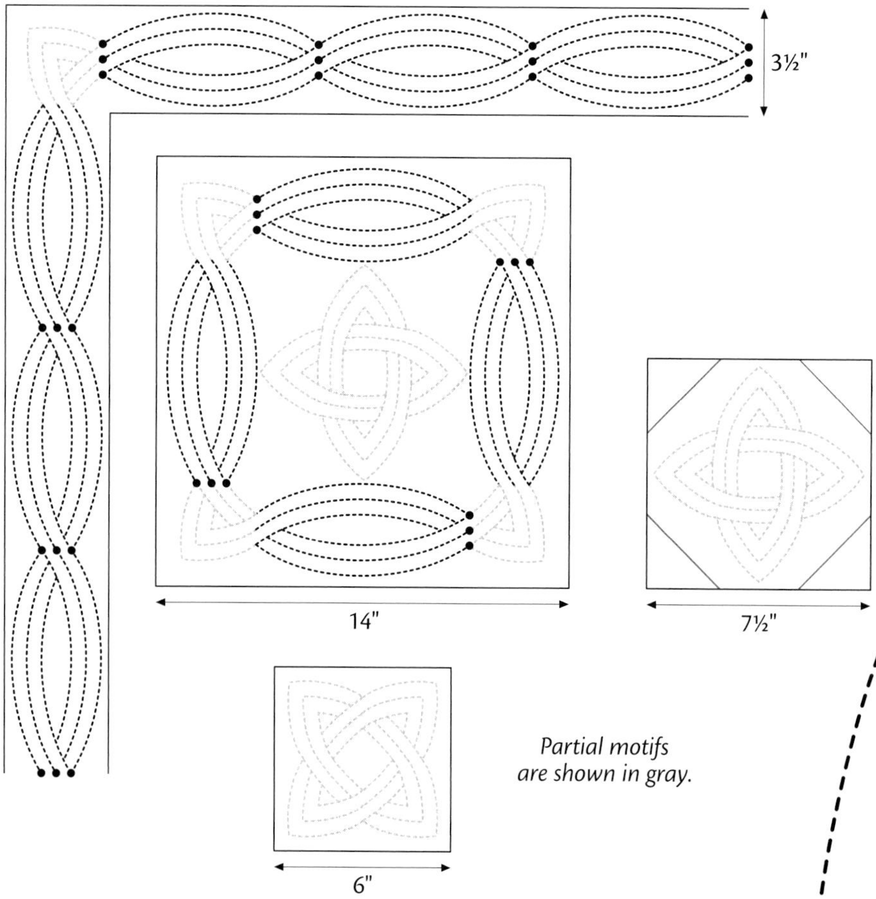

Partial motifs are shown in gray.

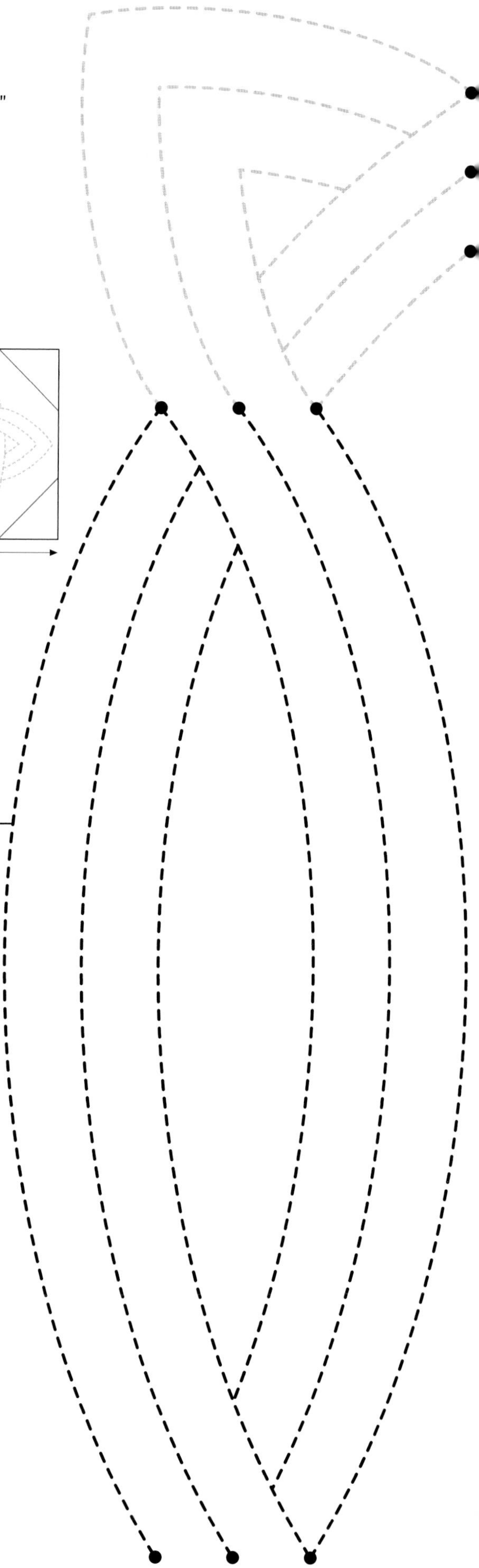

Saw Blade

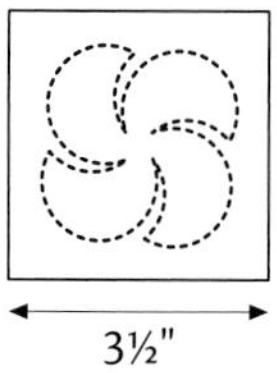

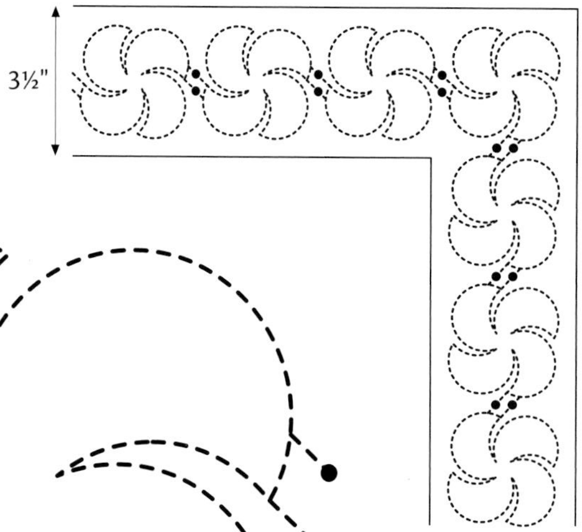

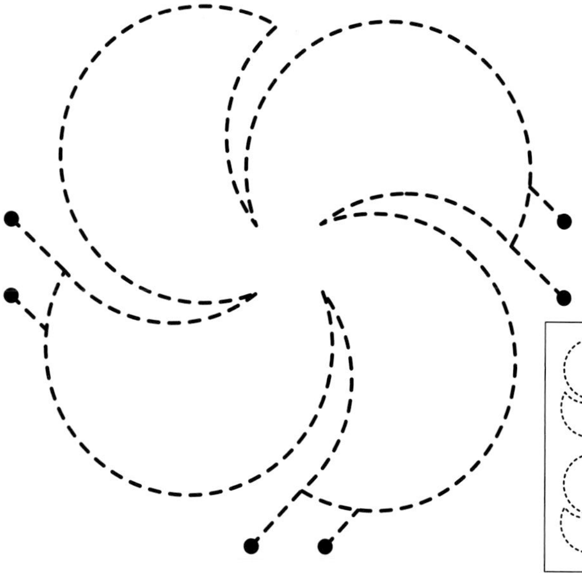

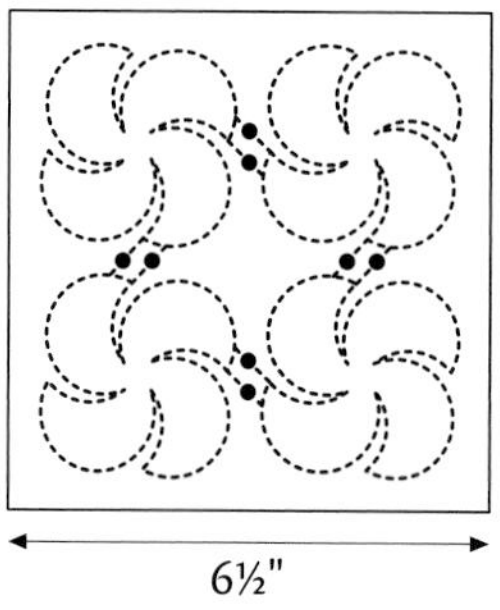

Shadowbox

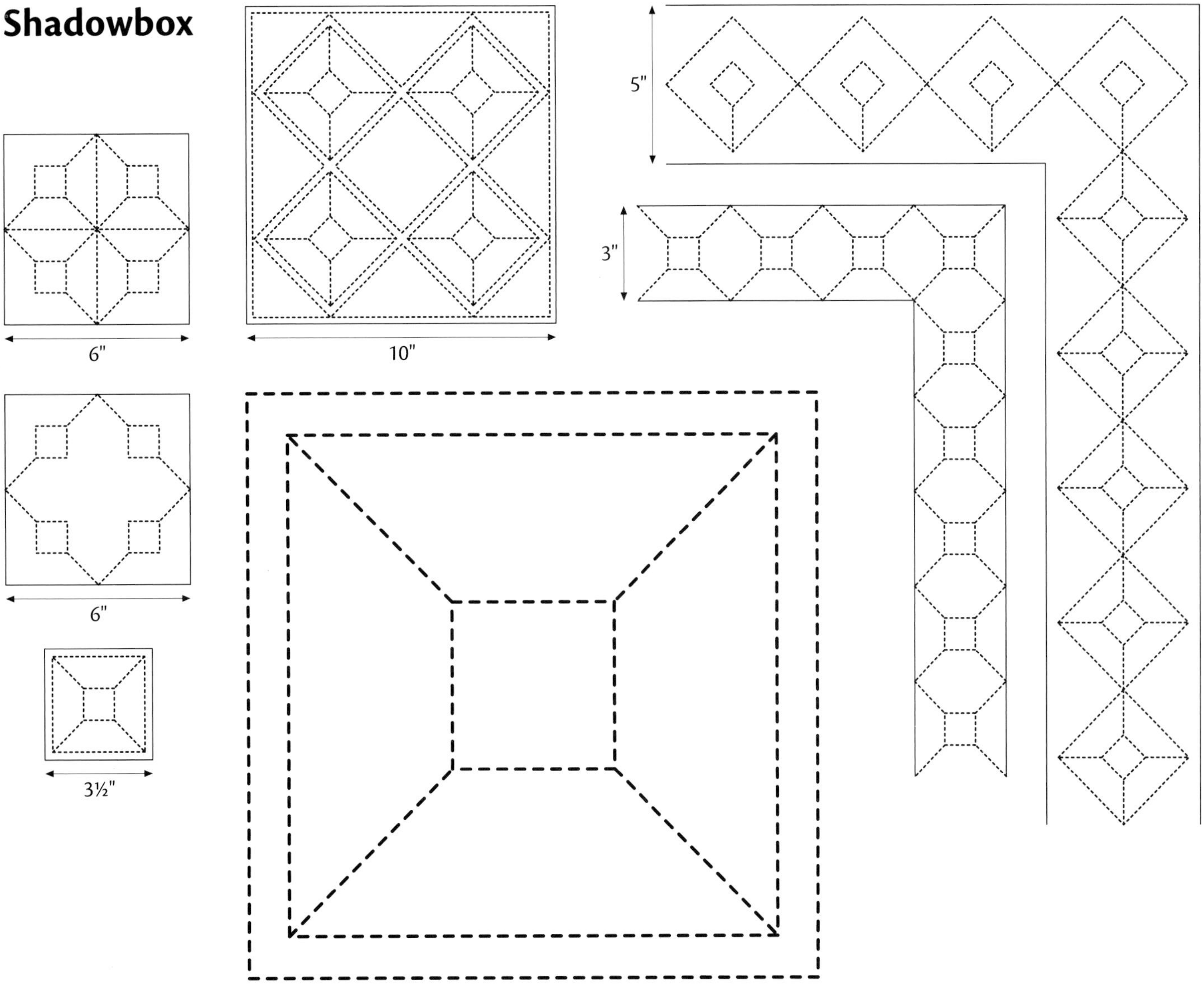
5"
3"
6"
10"
6"
3½"

Star in the Window

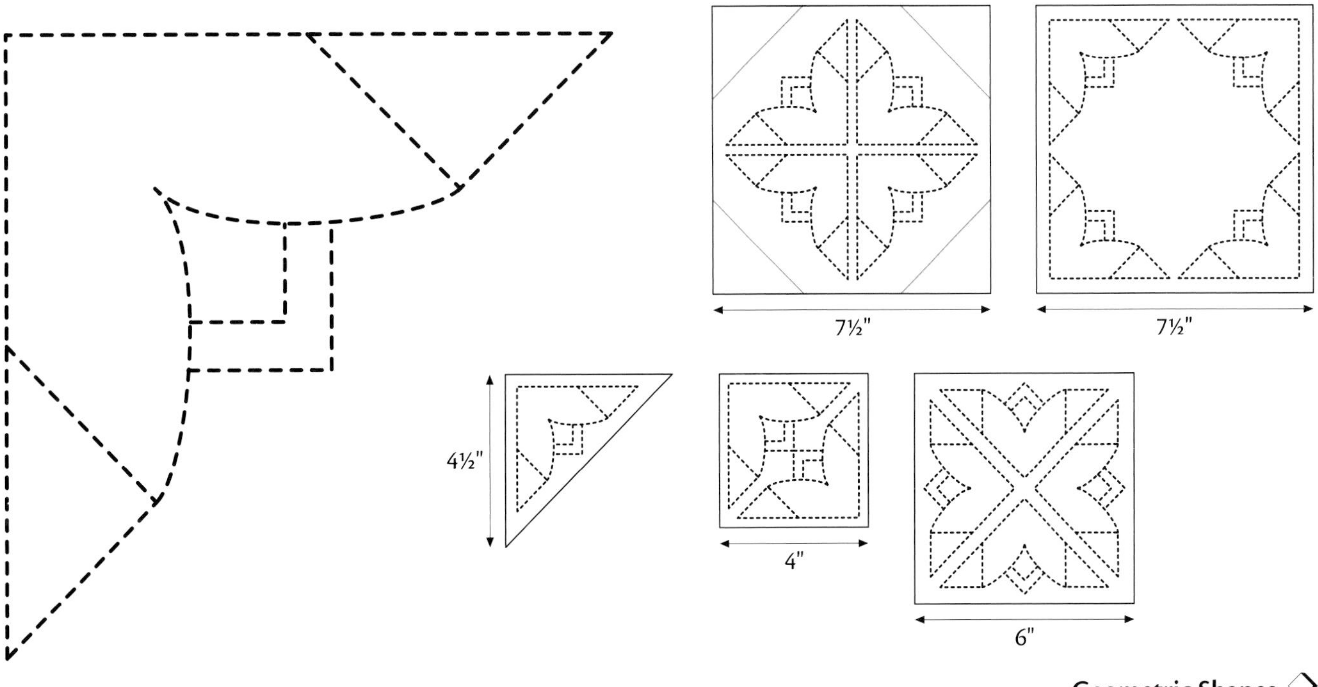
7½"
7½"
4½"
4"
6"

Lattice Blossom

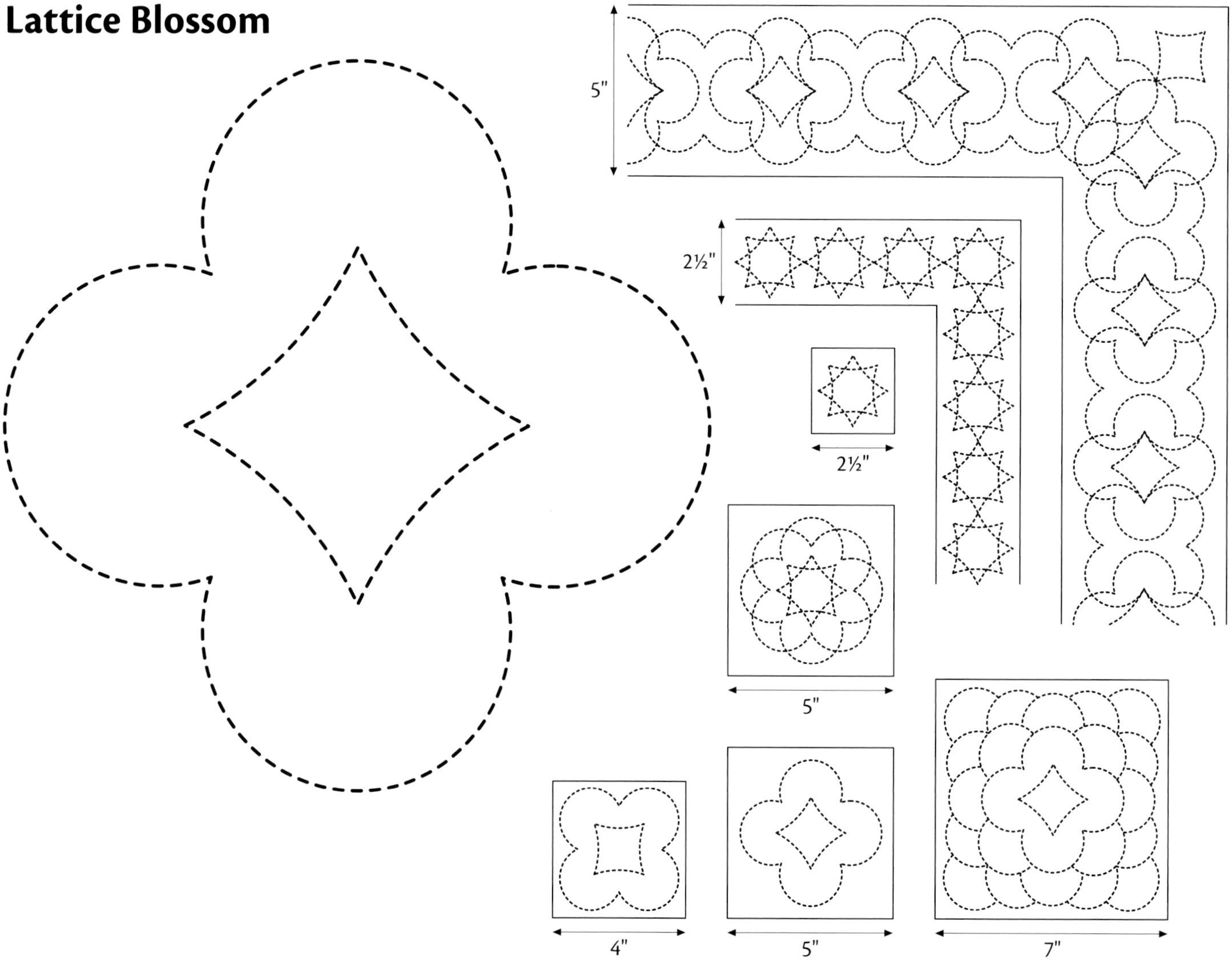

West Wind

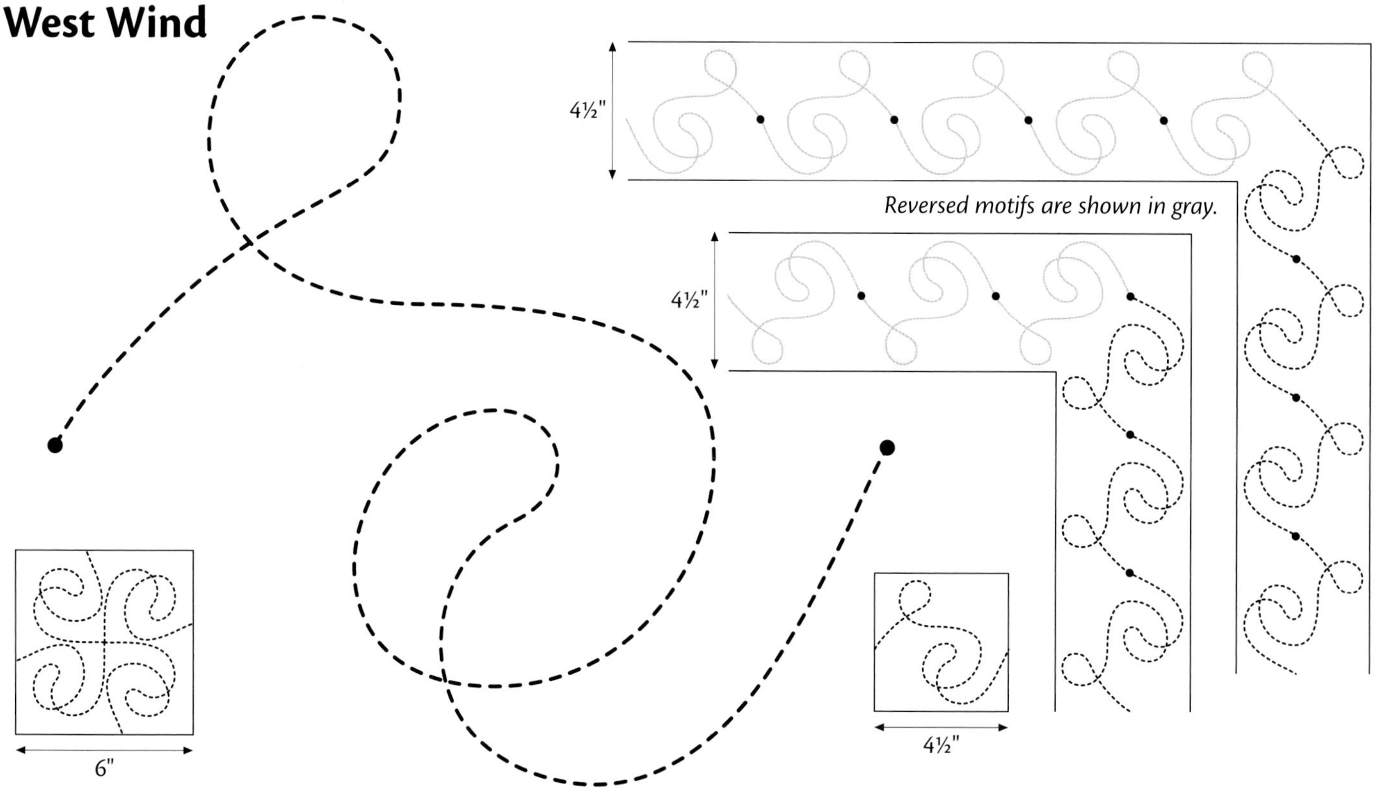

Reversed motifs are shown in gray.

Explorers

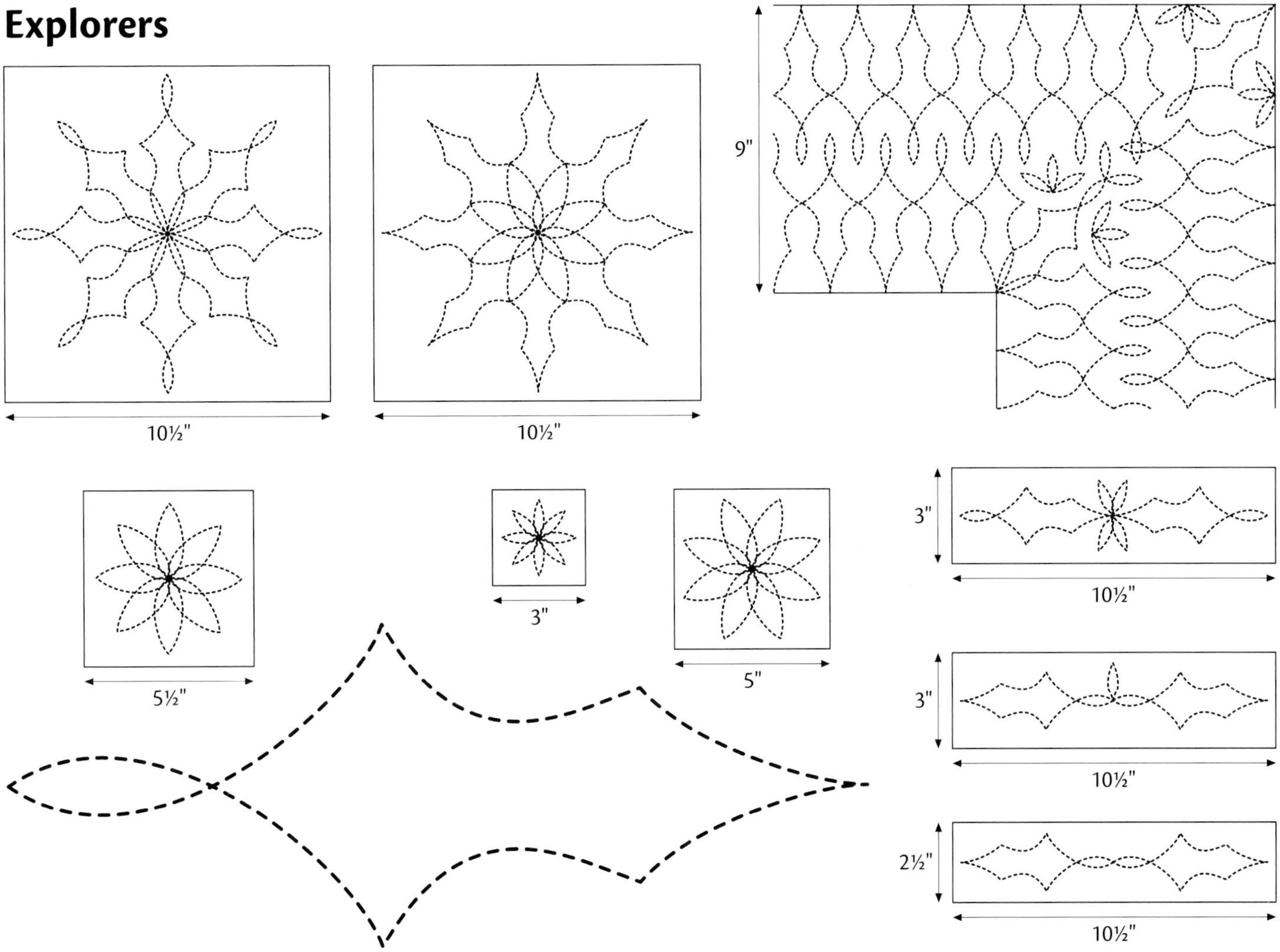

Spiraling Squares

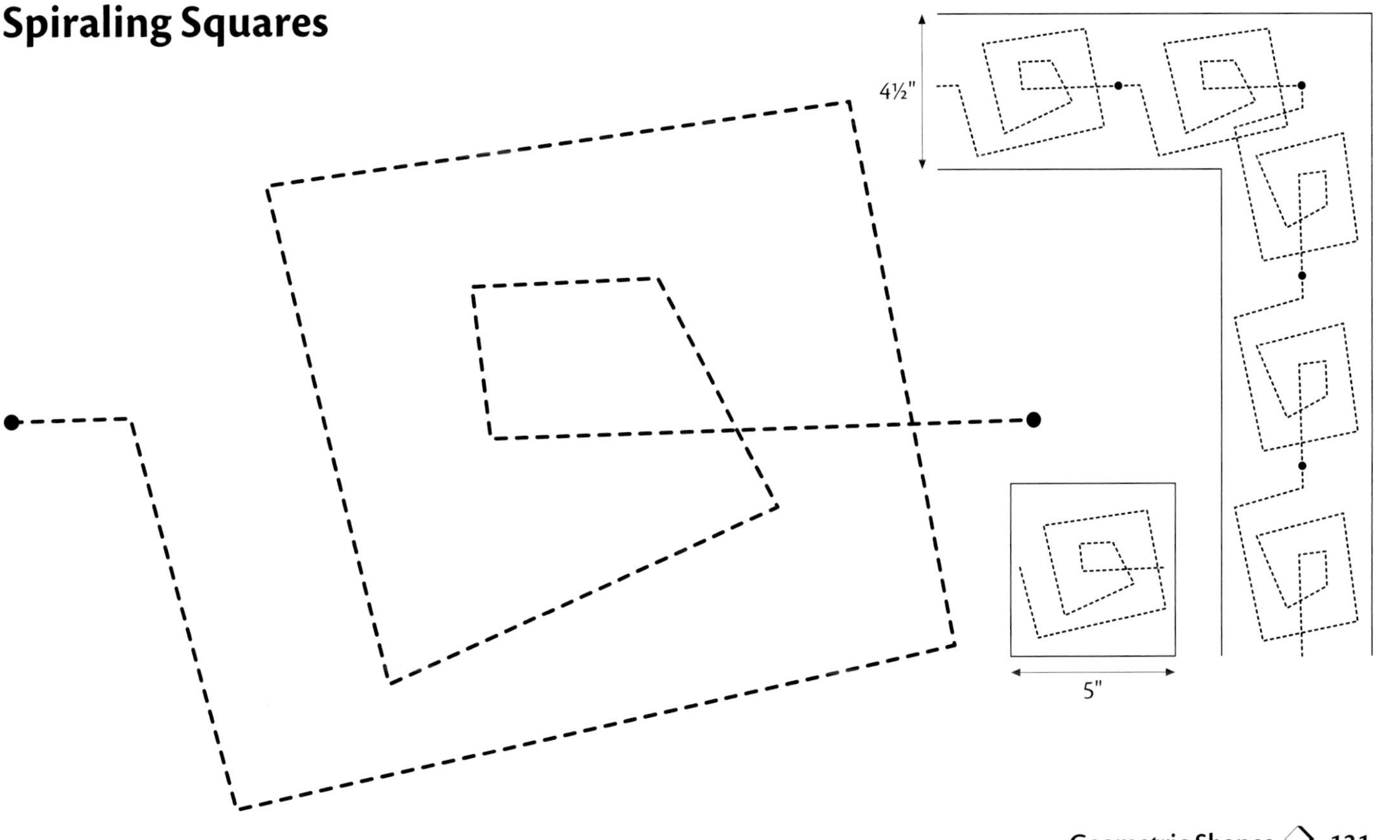

Twirl Around

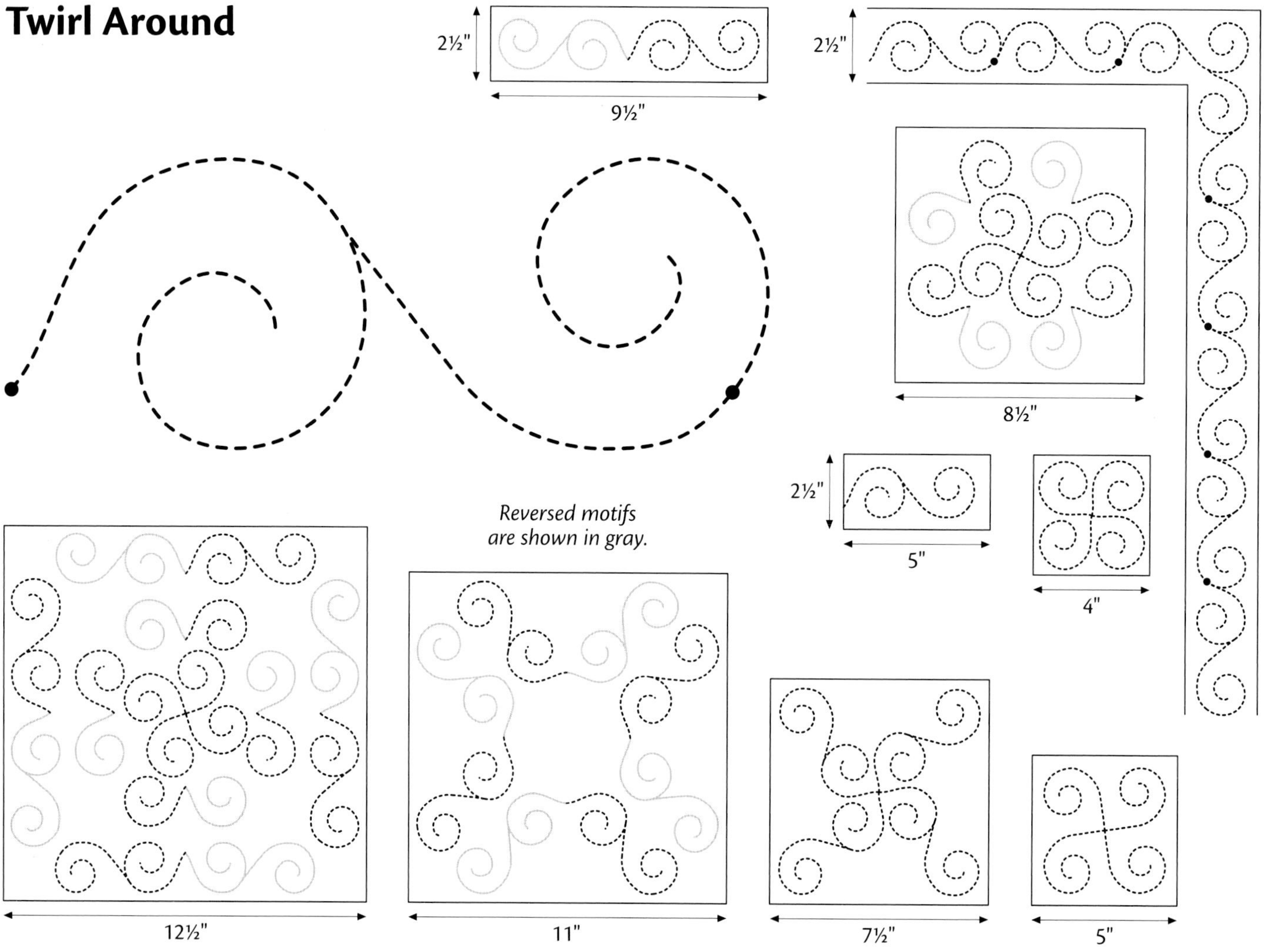

2½"
9½"
2½"
8½"
2½"
5"
4"
12½"
11"
7½"
5"

Reversed motifs are shown in gray.

High Seas

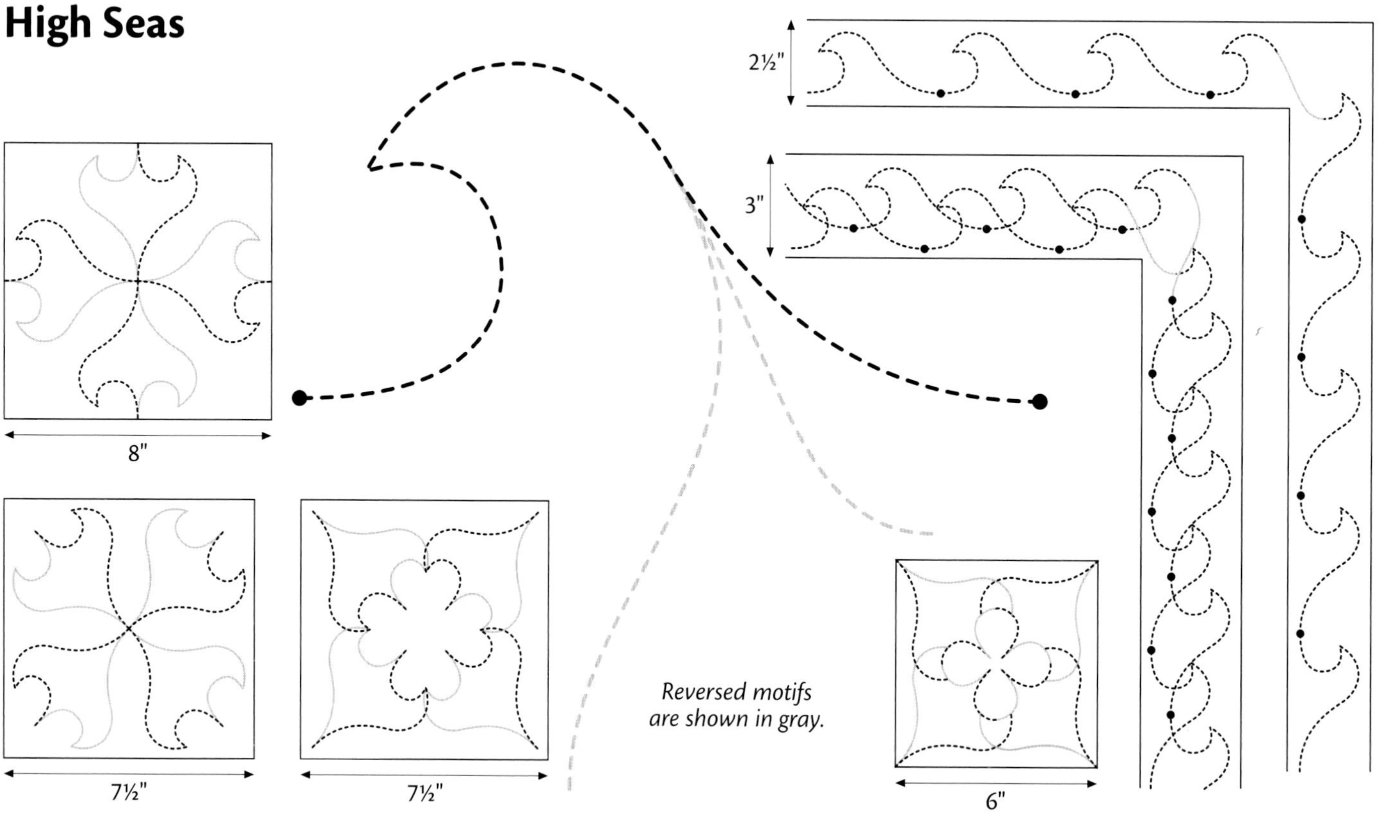

2½"
3"
8"
7½"
7½"
6"

Reversed motifs are shown in gray.

Today's Touch

4"
3"
4"
5½"
5½"
4"
11"
6"
10½"
7½"

Whirligig

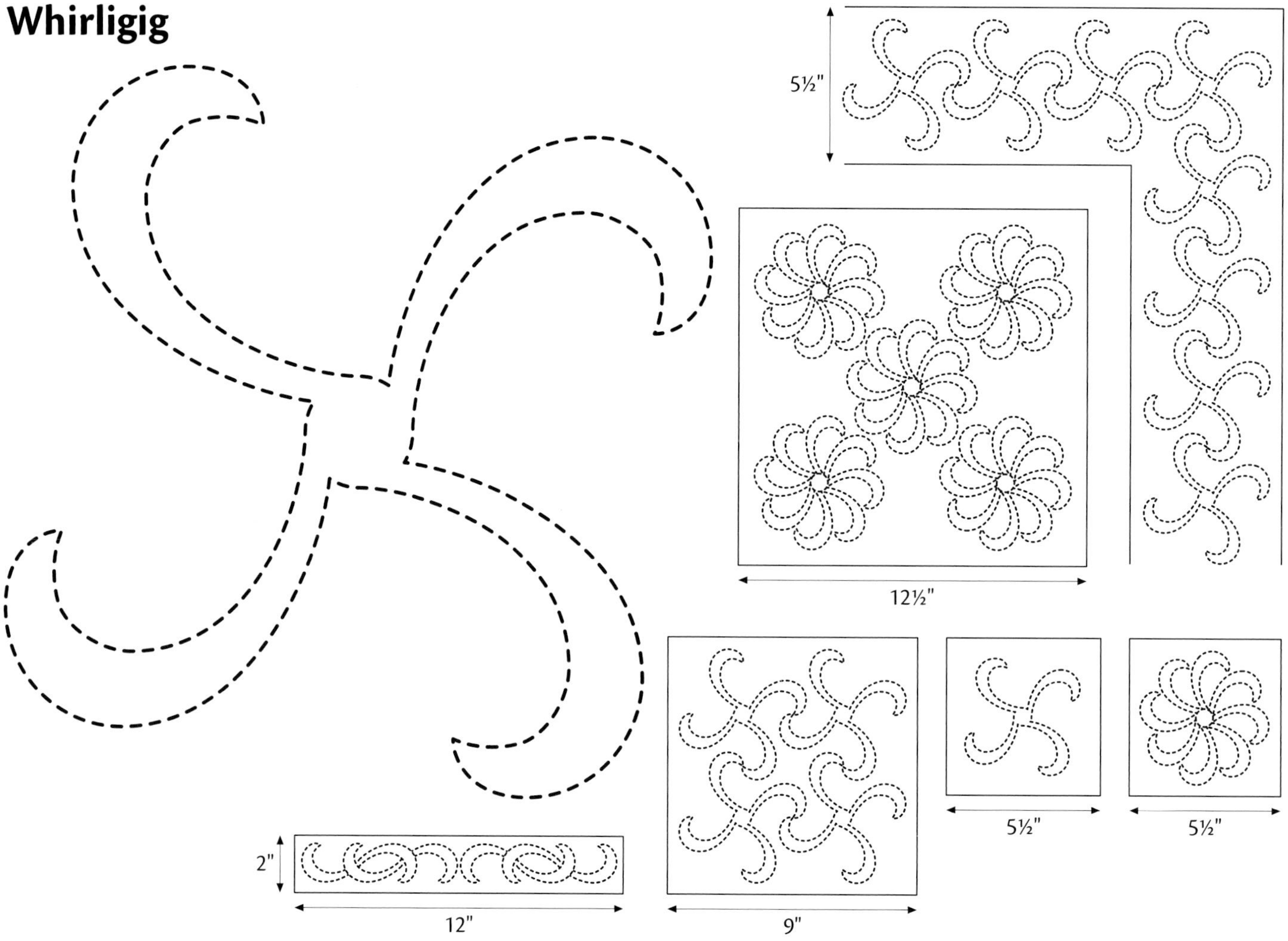

5½"
12½"
2"
12"
9"
5½"
5½"

Ritzy

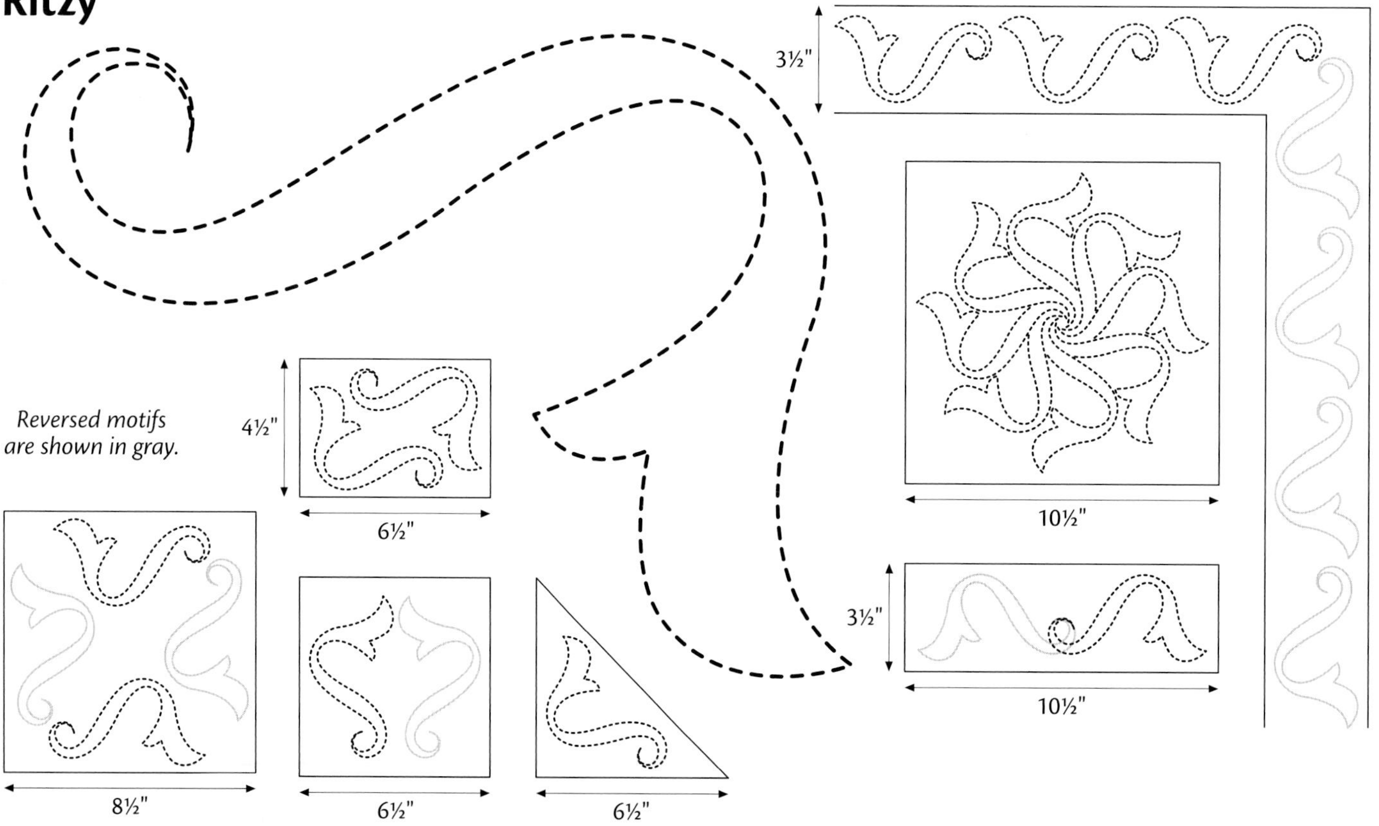

3½"
4½"
6½"
10½"
3½"
10½"
8½"
6½"
6½"

Reversed motifs are shown in gray.

Fleur-de-Lis

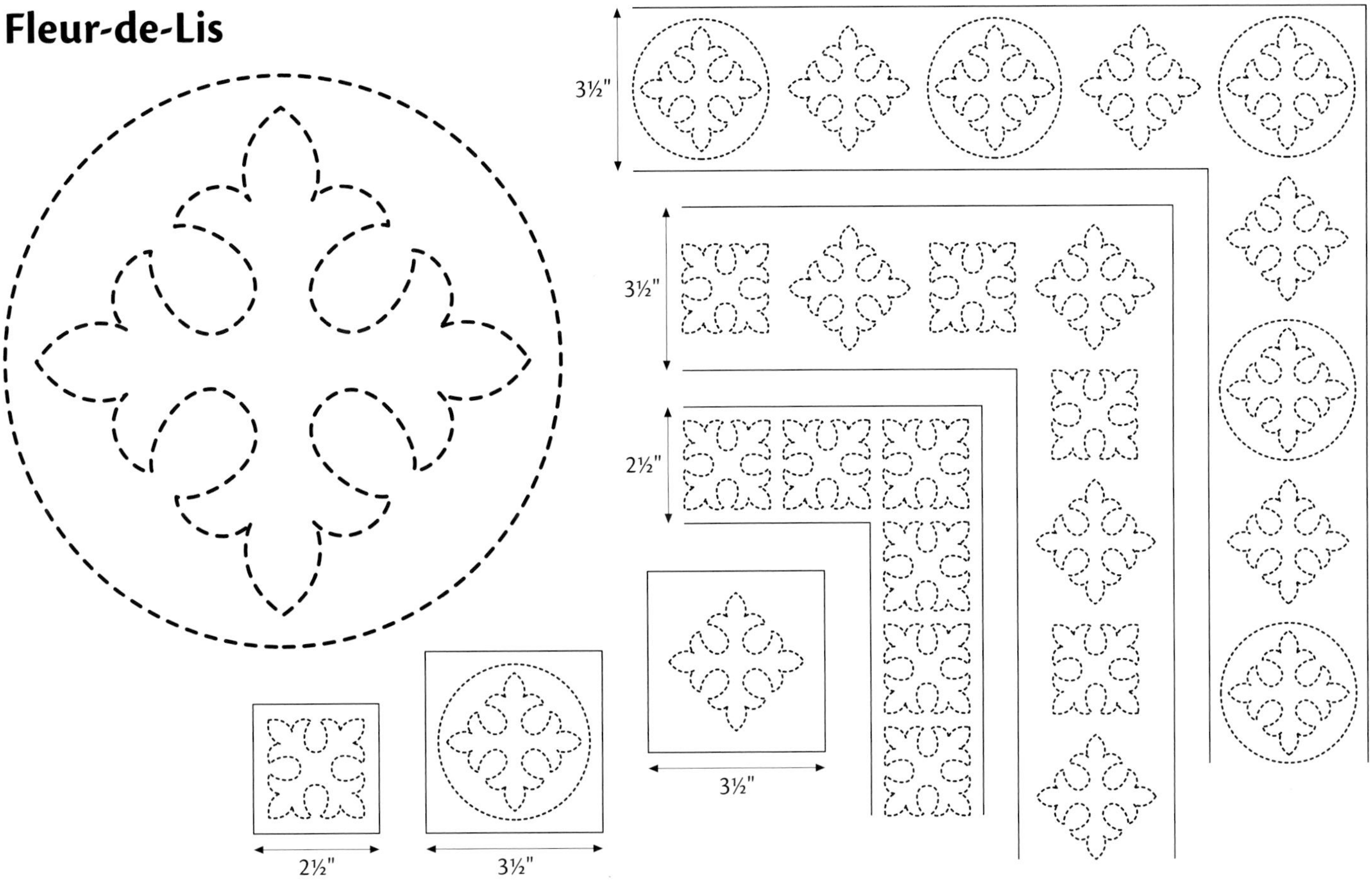
3½"
3½"
2½"
2½"
3½"
3½"

Gibraltar

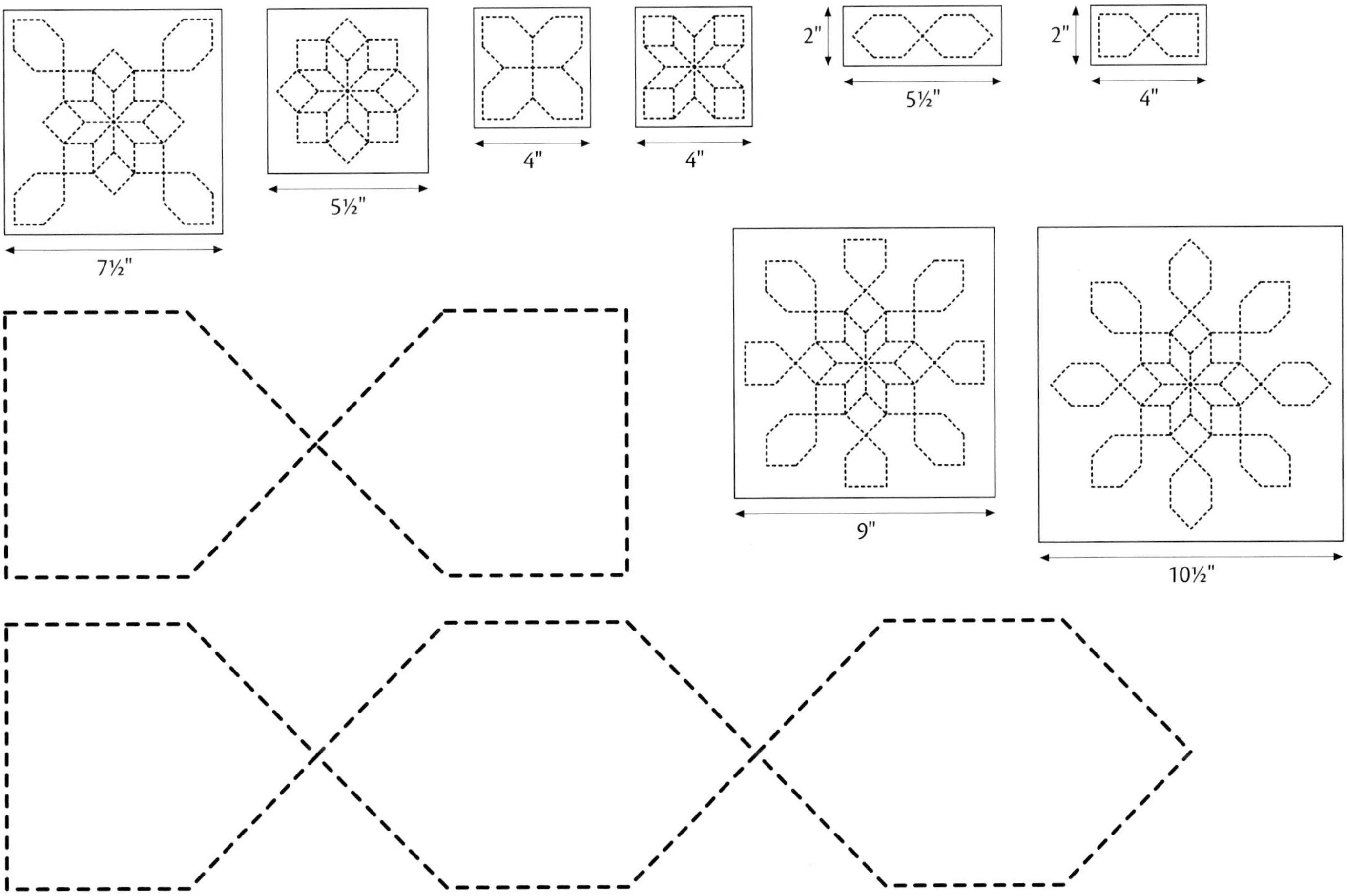
7½"
5½"
4"
4"
2"
5½"
2"
4"
9"
10½"

Lemon Peel

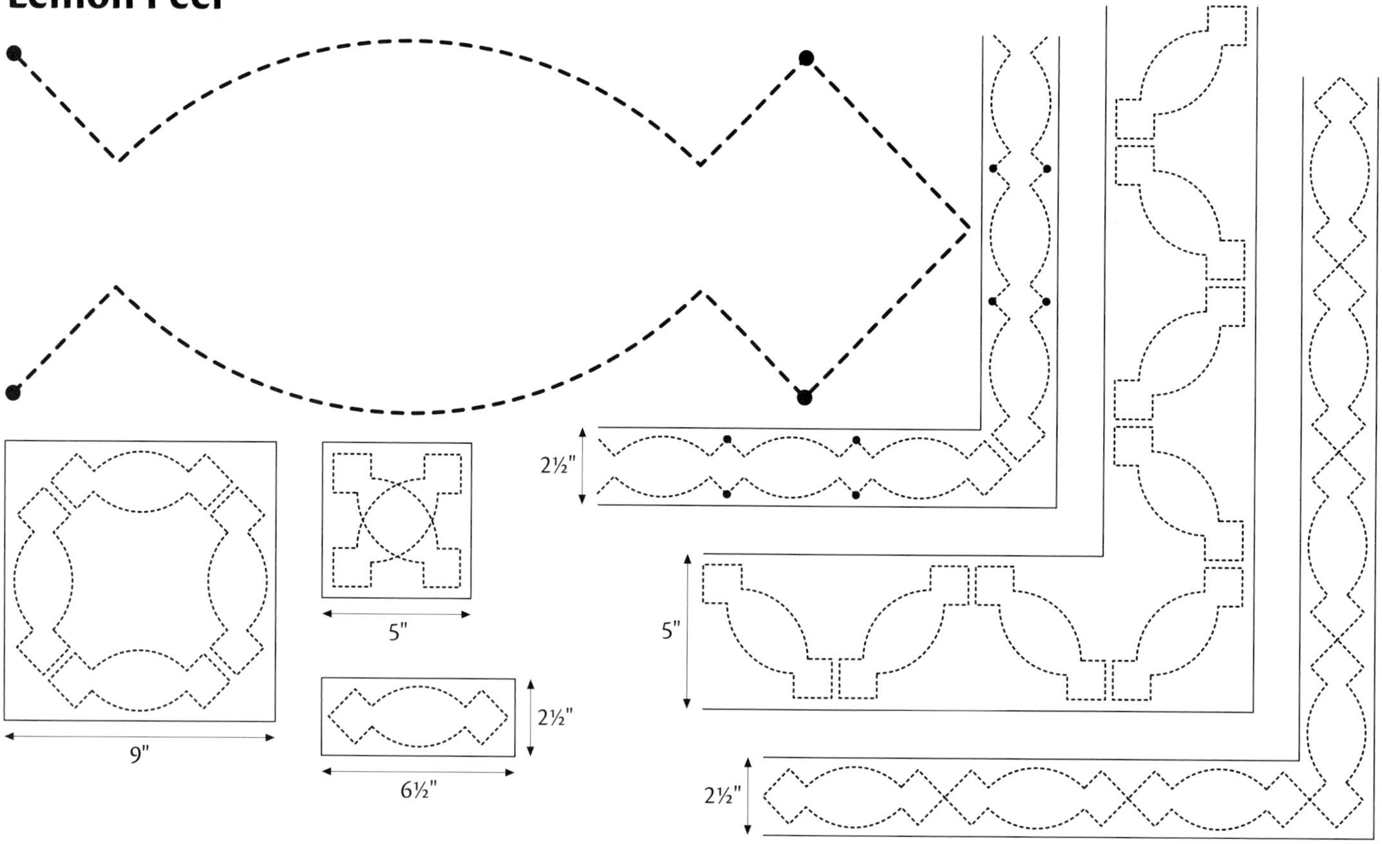
2½"
5"
9"
6½"
2½"
5"
2½"

Bows and Borders

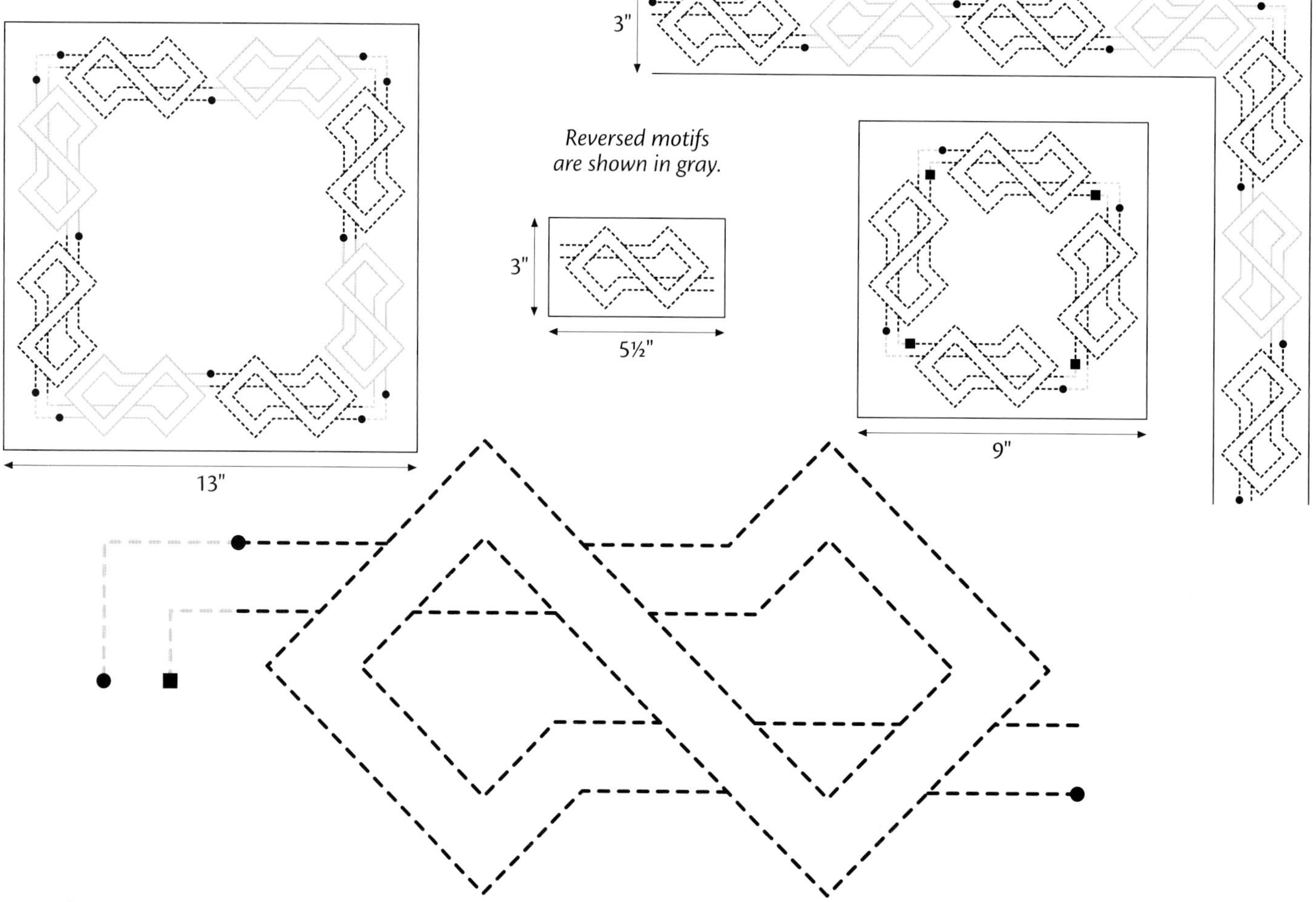
3"
13"
3"
5½"
9"

Reversed motifs are shown in gray.

Between Times

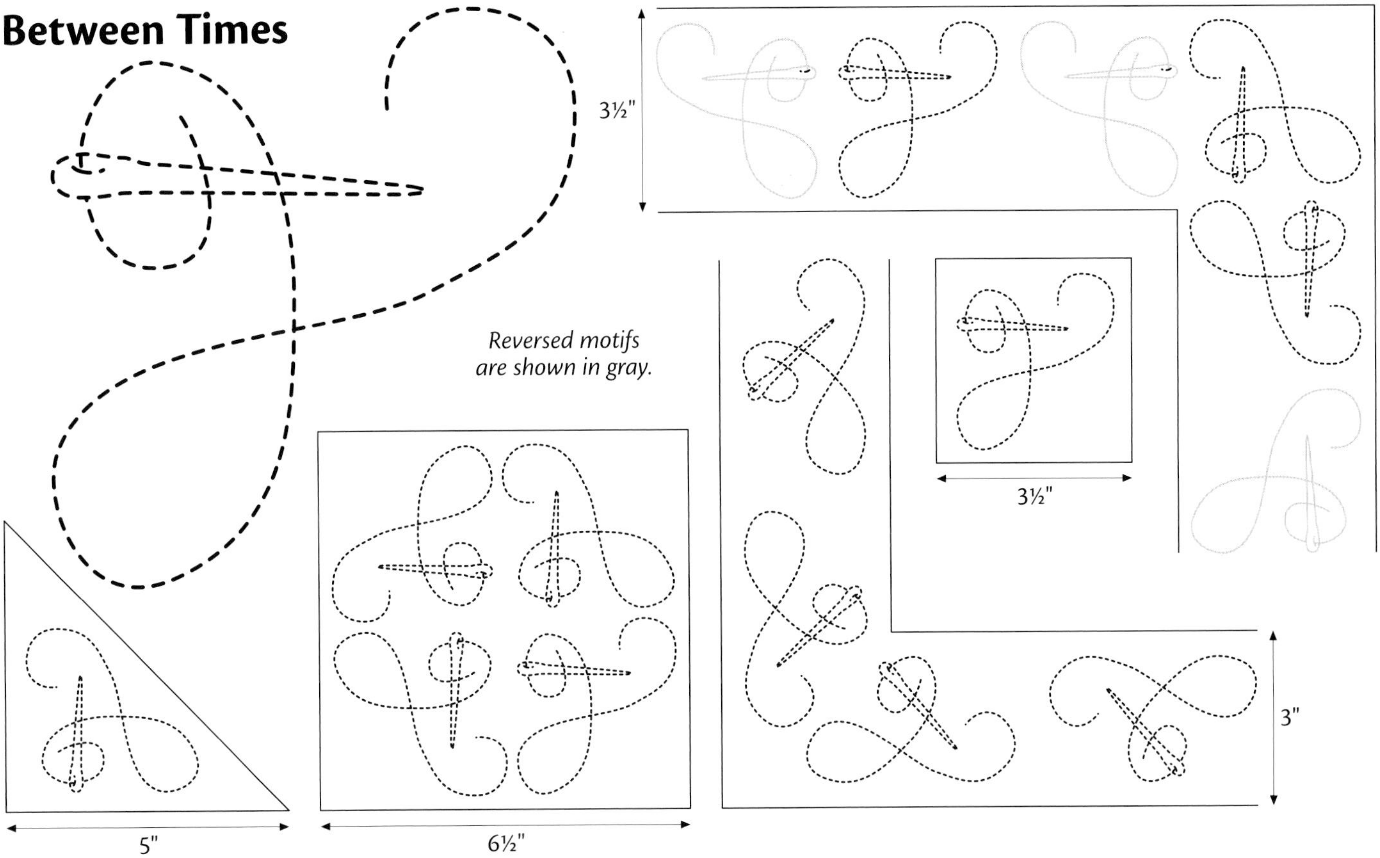
3½"
3½"
3"
5"
6½"

Reversed motifs are shown in gray.

Twirly Tucks

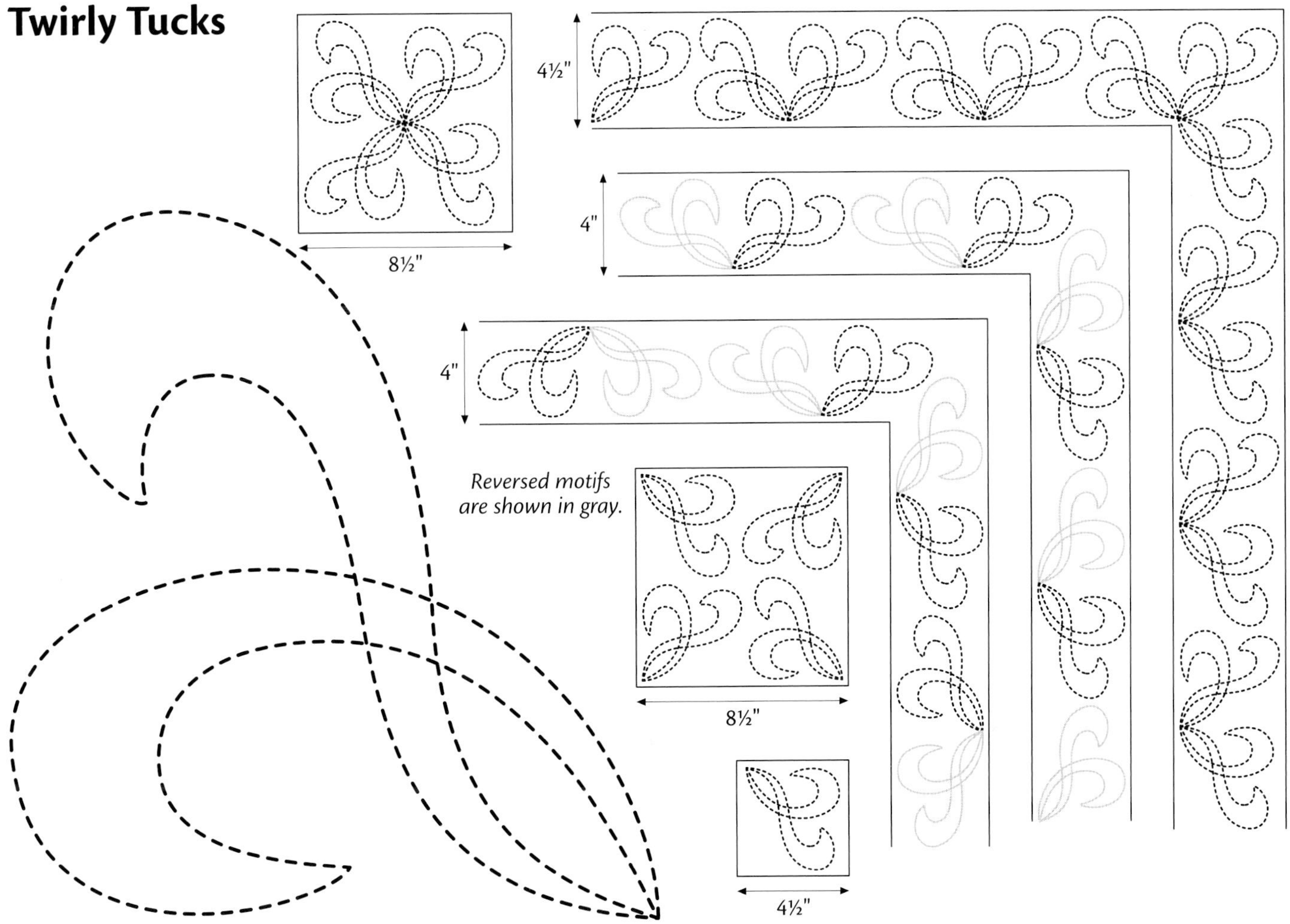
4½"
4"
4"
8½"
8½"
4½"

Reversed motifs are shown in gray.

Swirl

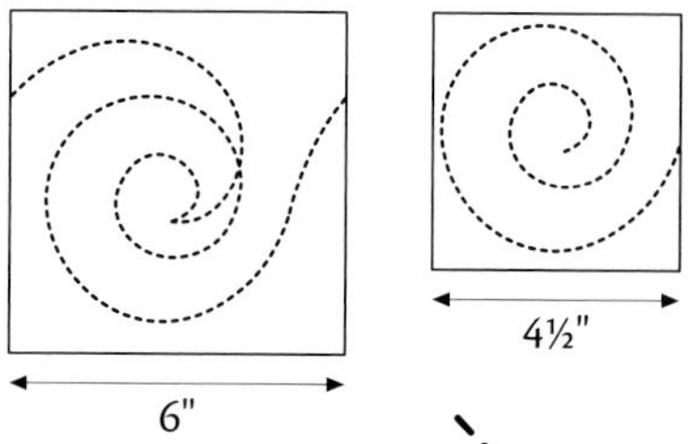

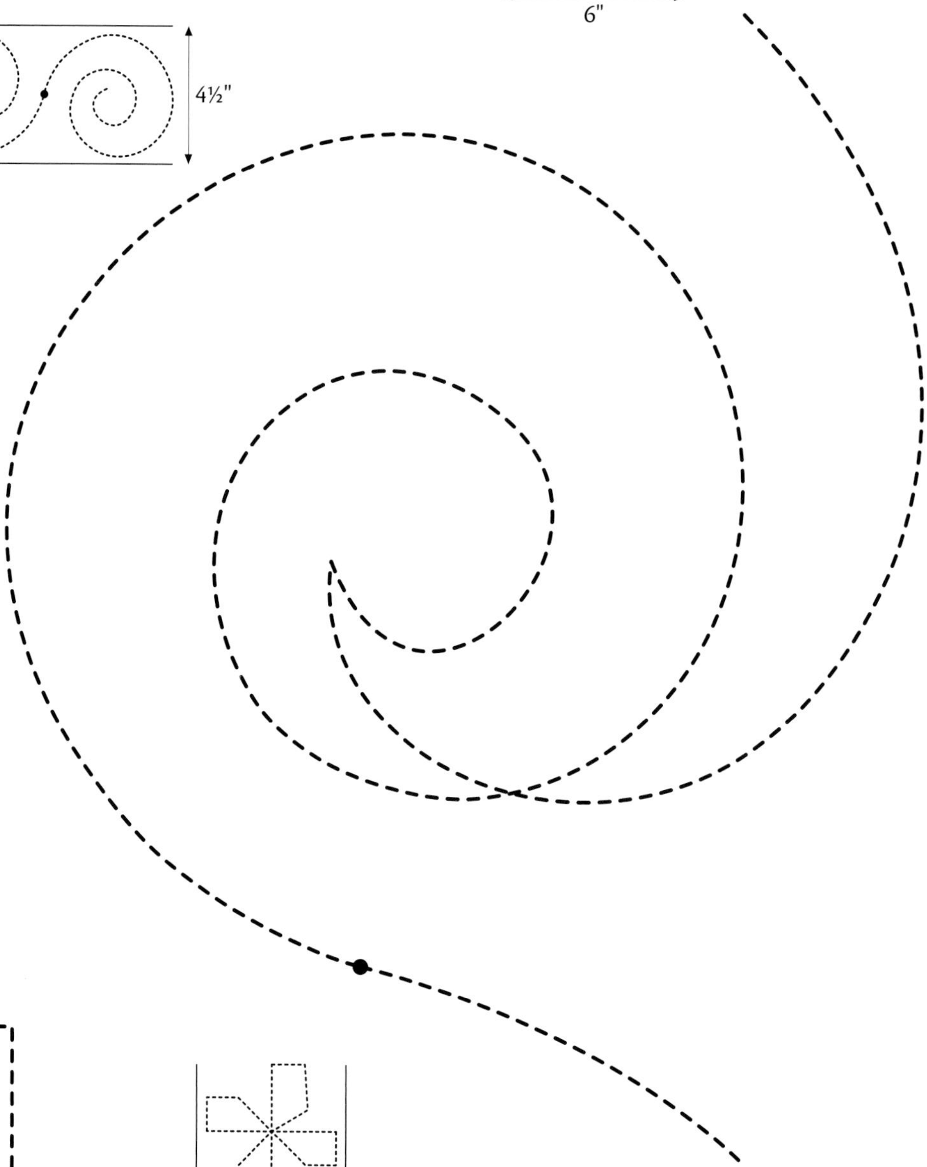

Palace Steps

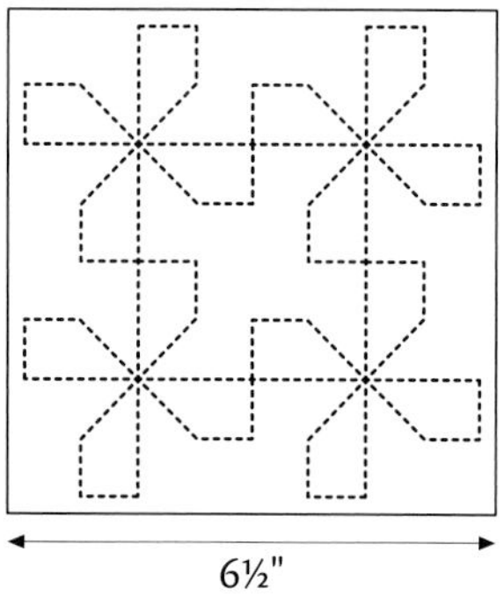

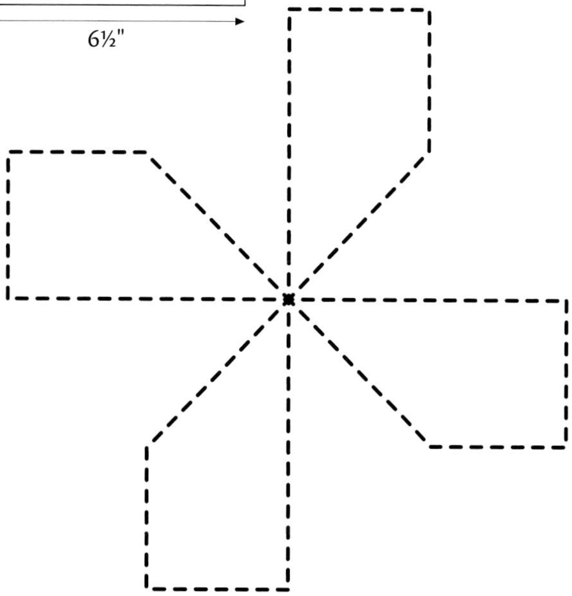

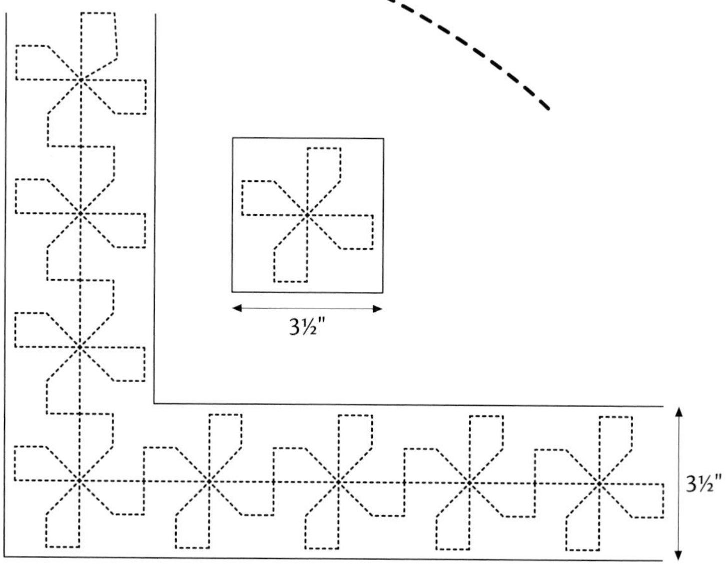

Lacy Lock

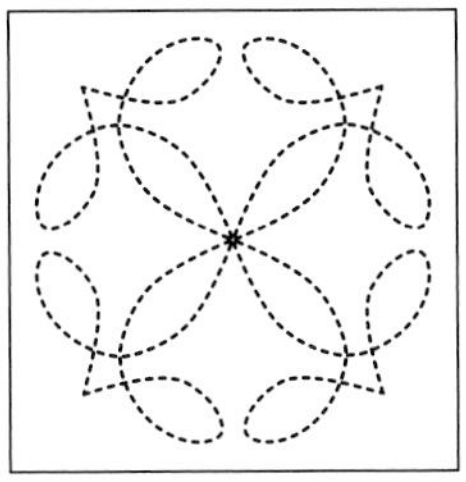

6"

6"

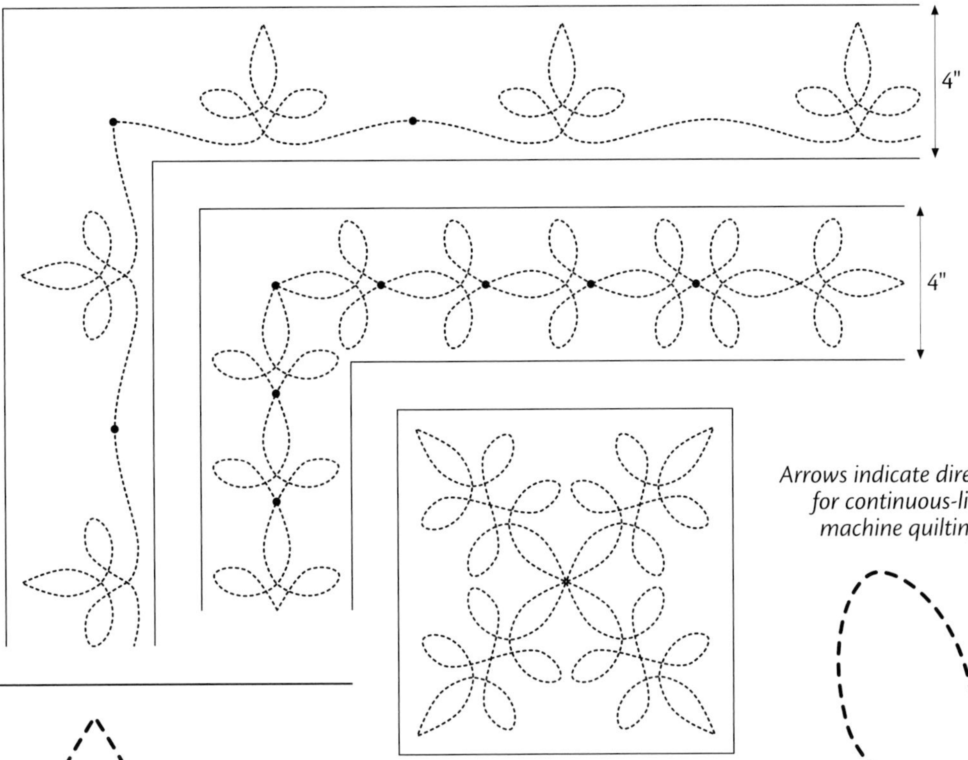

9"

Arrows indicate direction for continuous-line machine quilting.

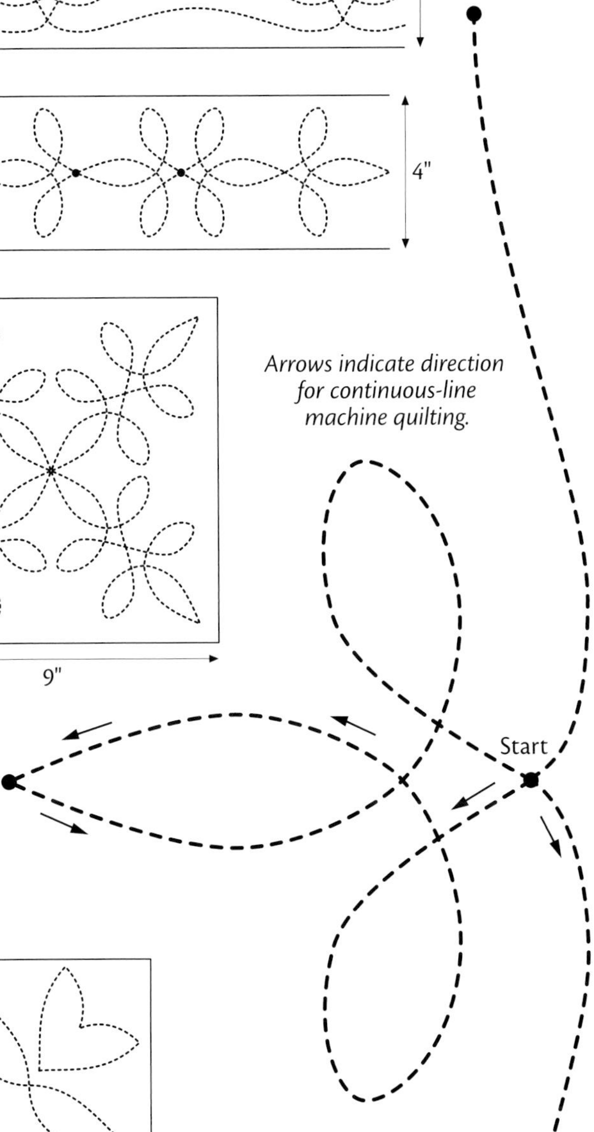

Fantasia

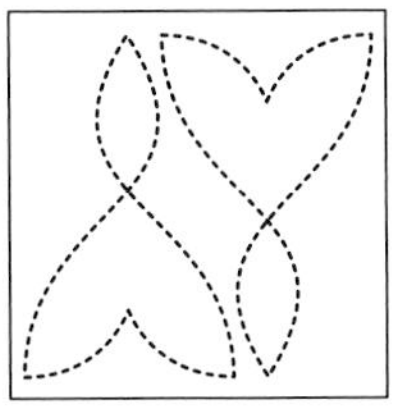

7"

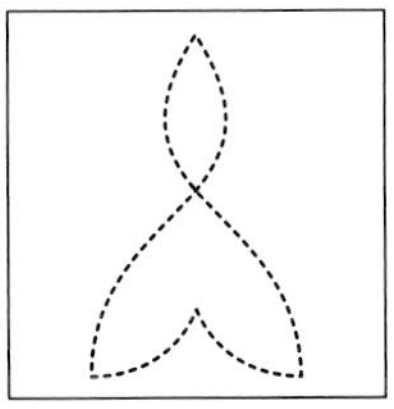

7"

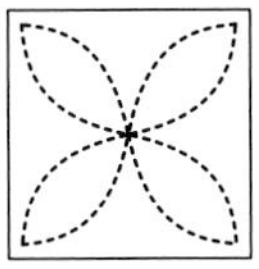

4½"

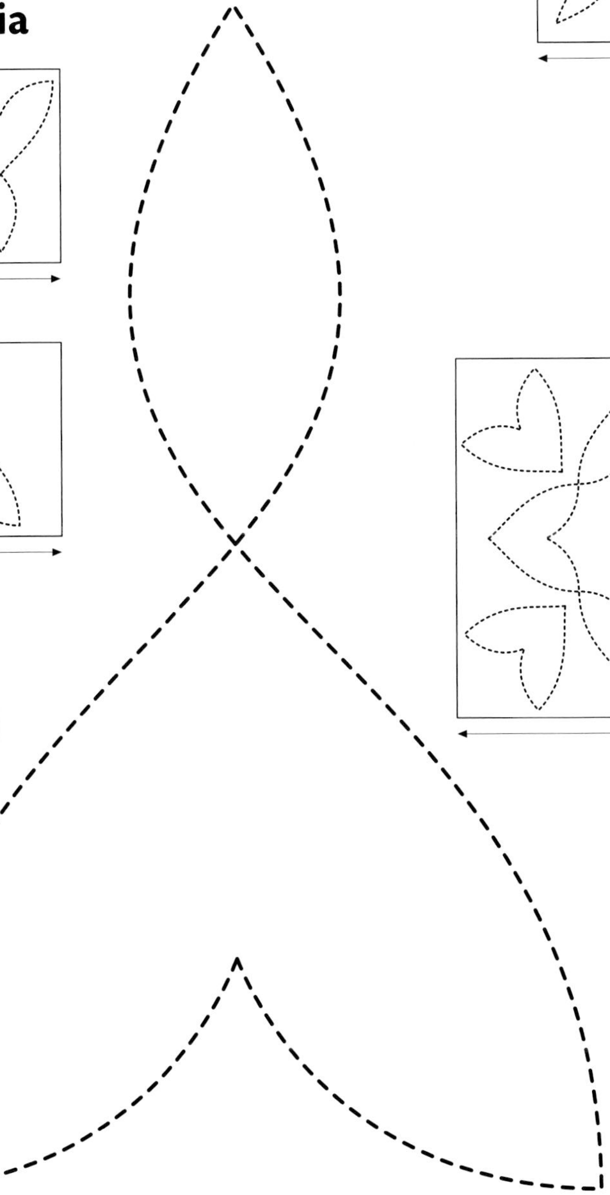

13"

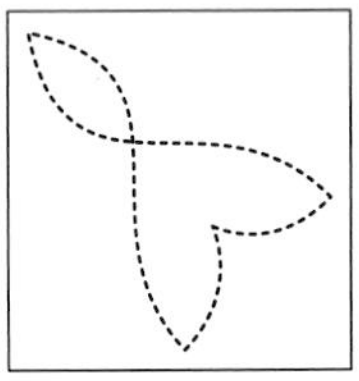

6½"

12"

Starblossom

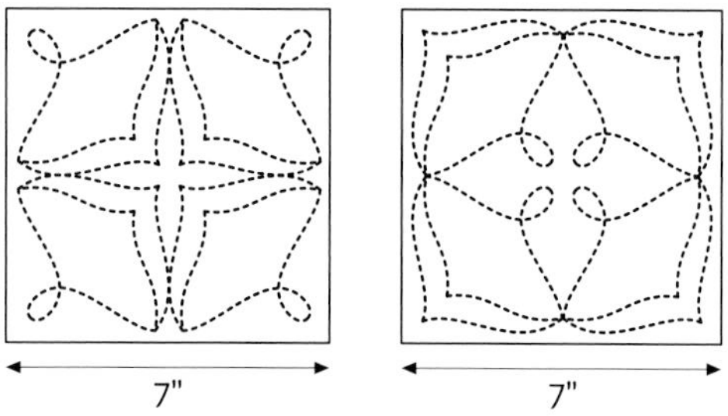

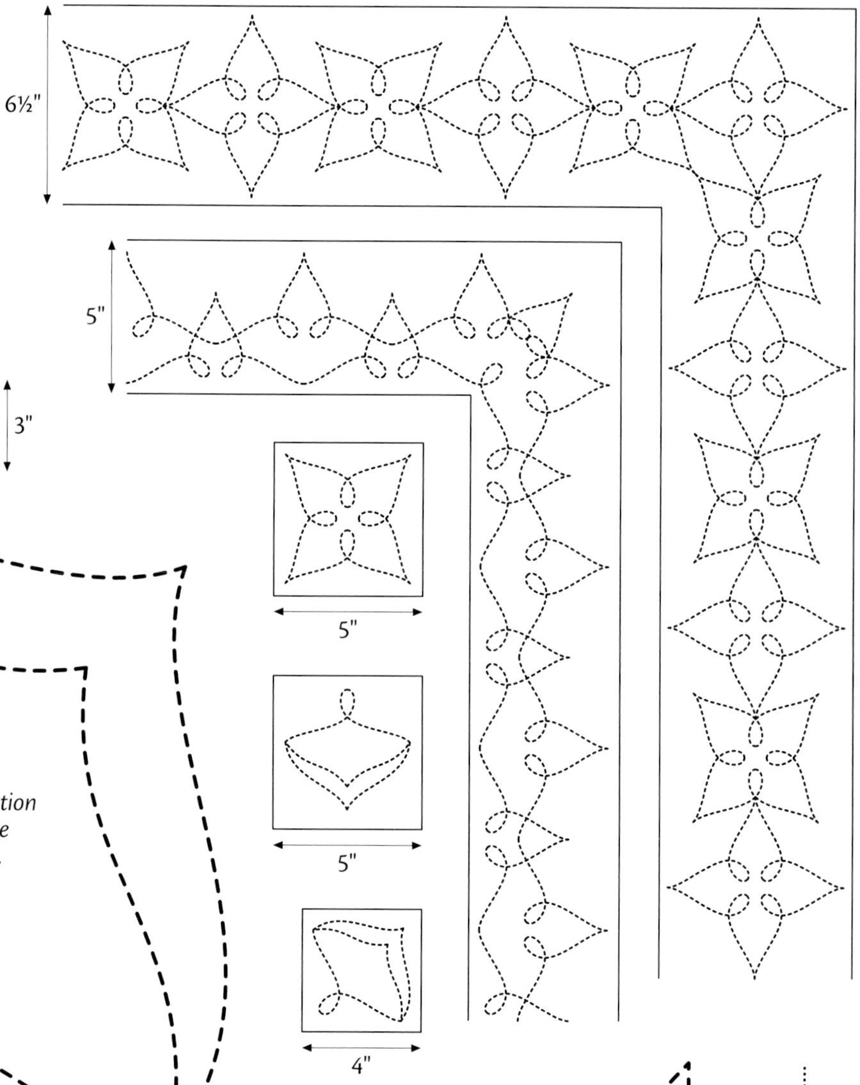

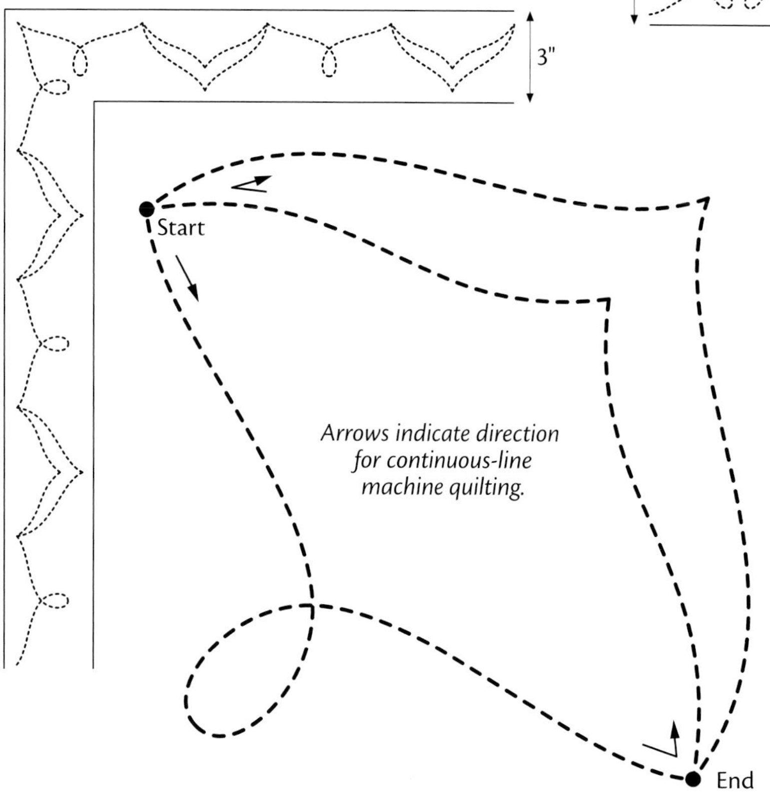

Pyramids of the Sun

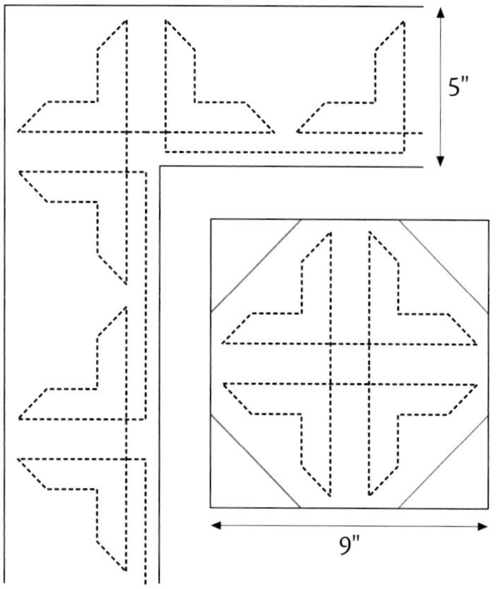

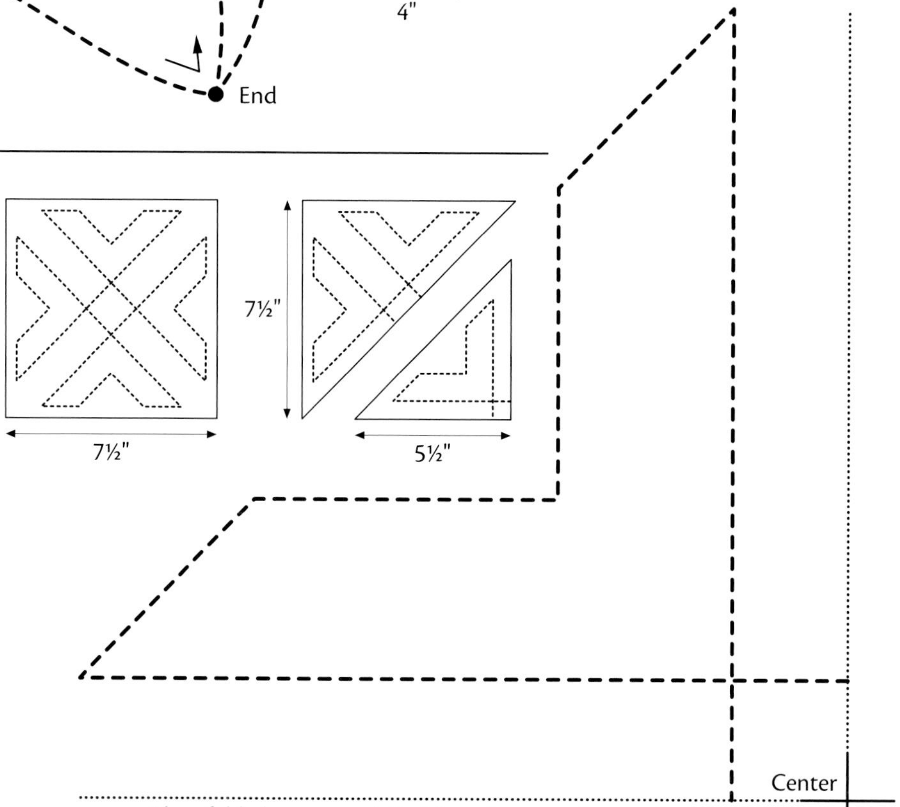

Place folded paper on dotted lines, trace, and rotate for full motif.

Graceful

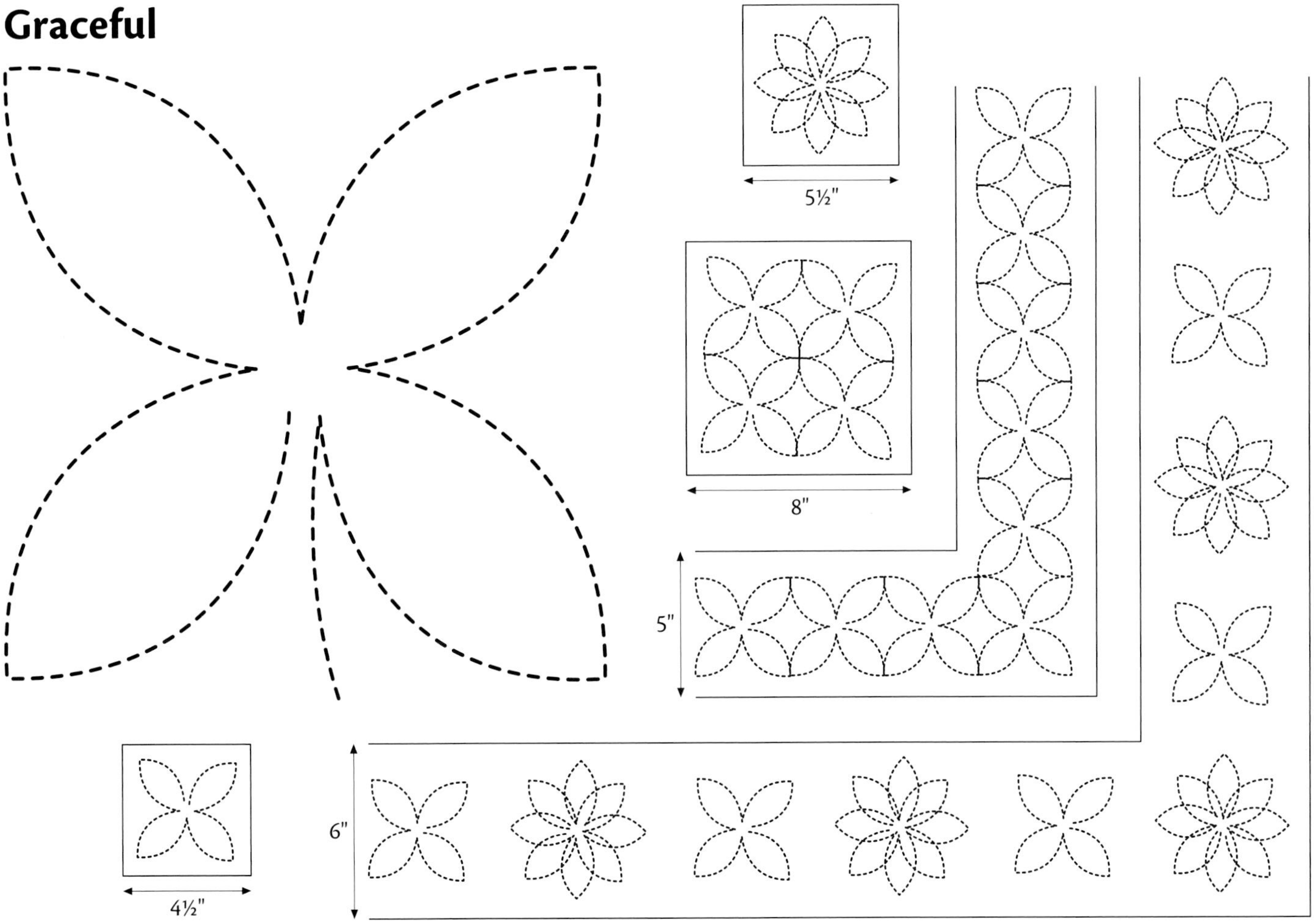
5½"
8"
5"
6"
4½"

Win Again

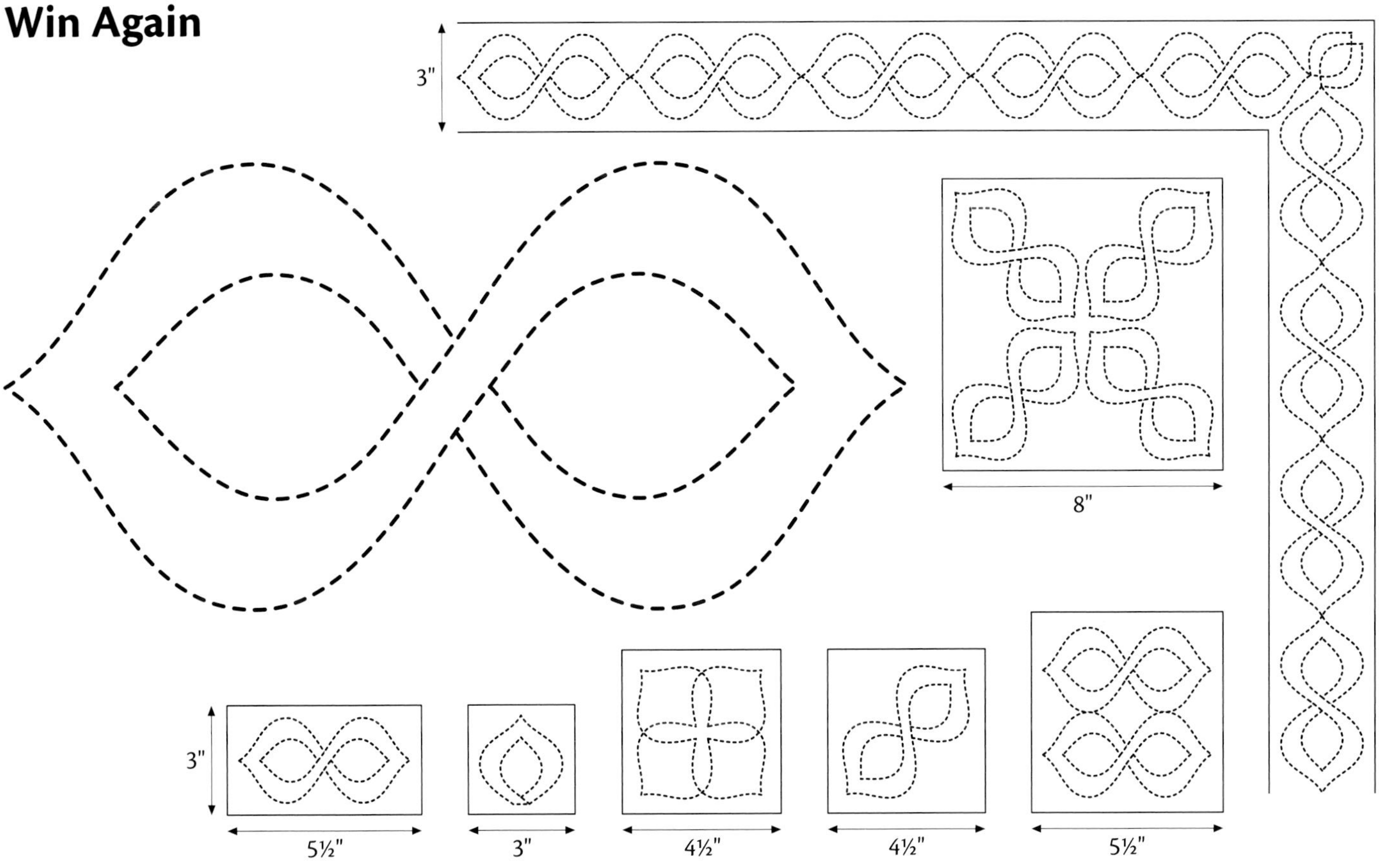
3"
8"
3"
5½"
3"
4½"
4½"
5½"

Irish Cable

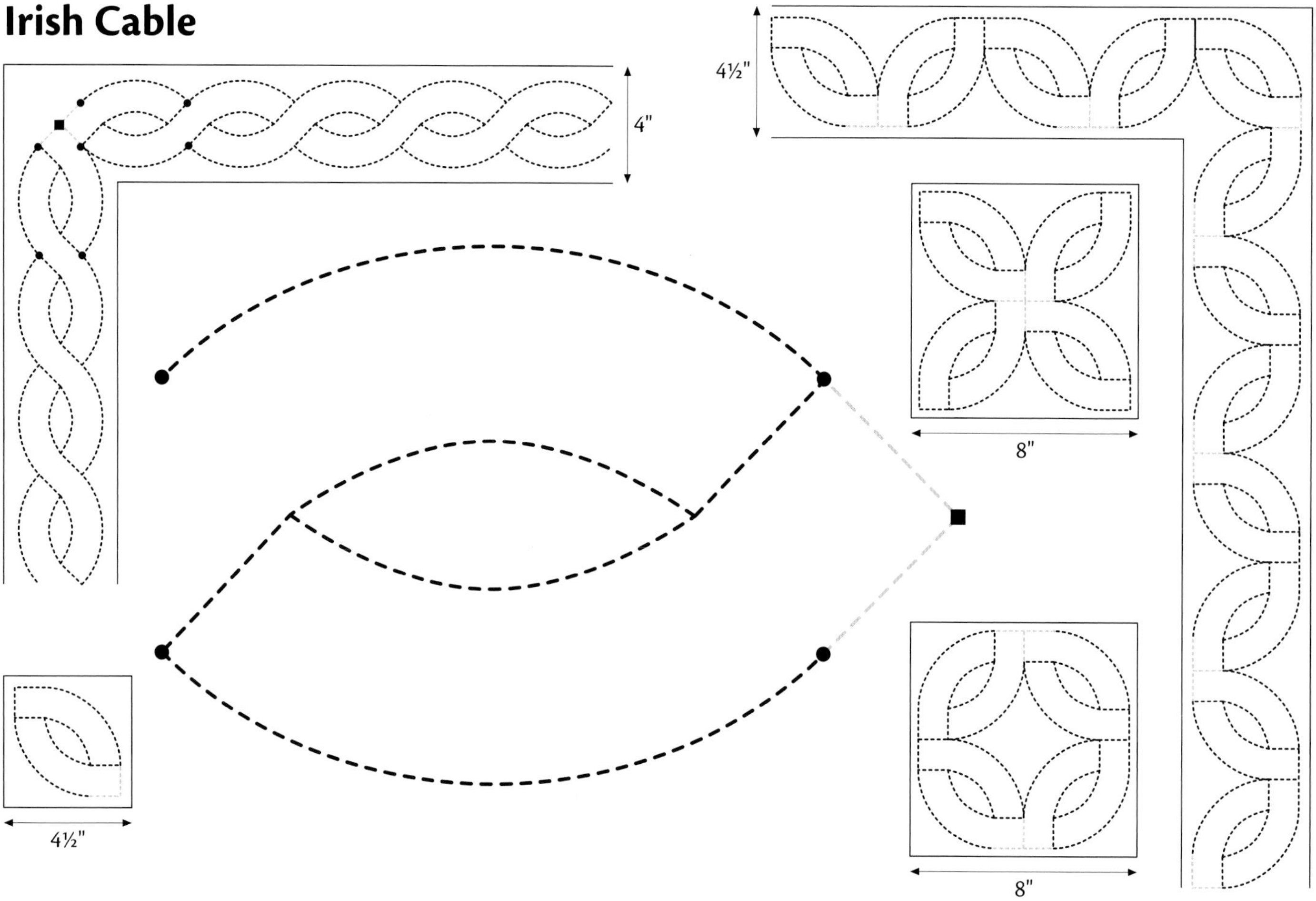
4"
4½"
8"
8"
4½"

Windswept

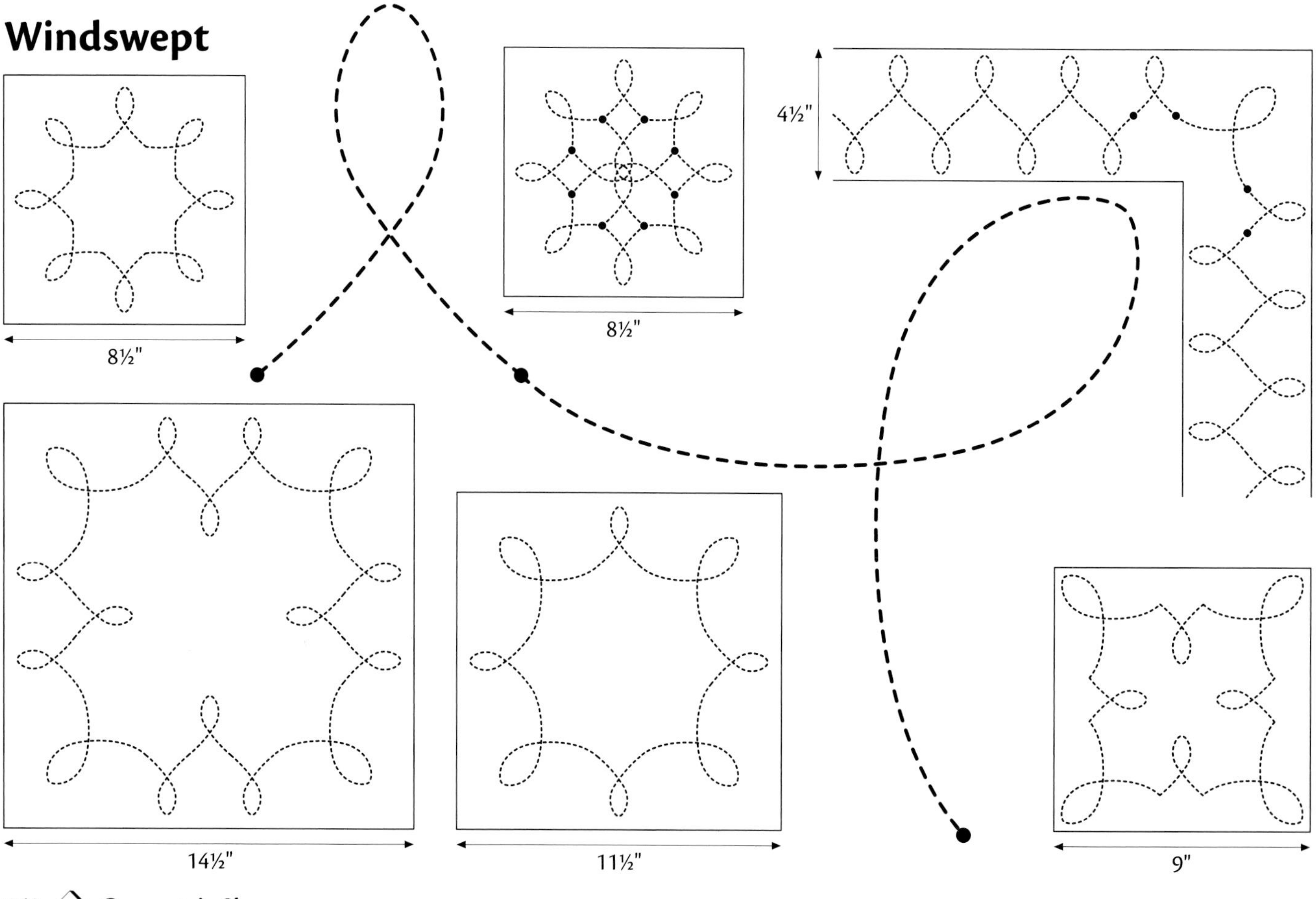
4½"
8½"
8½"
14½"
11½"
9"

Main Street

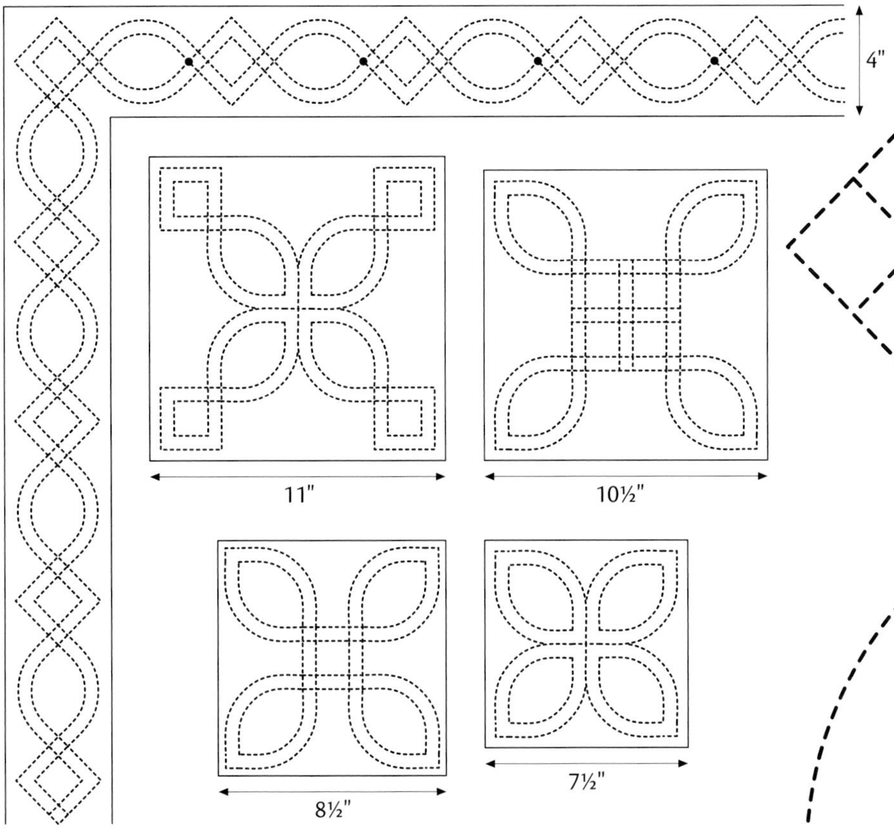
4"
11"
10½"
8½"
7½"

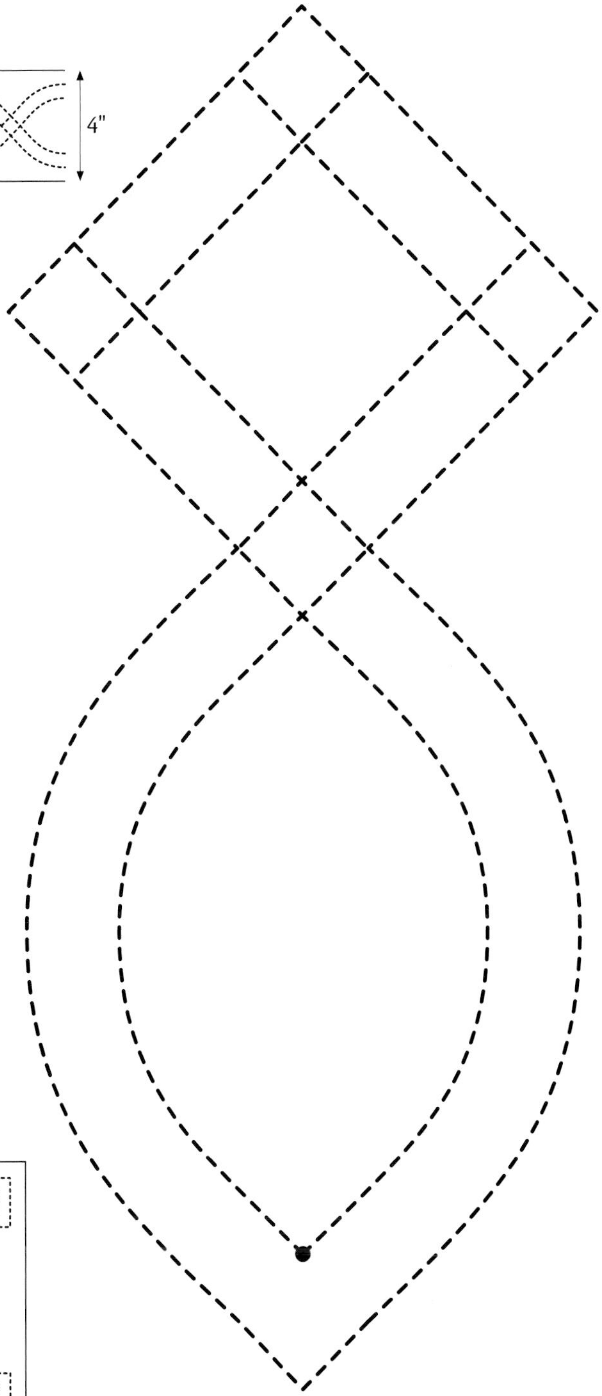

Continuous Cable

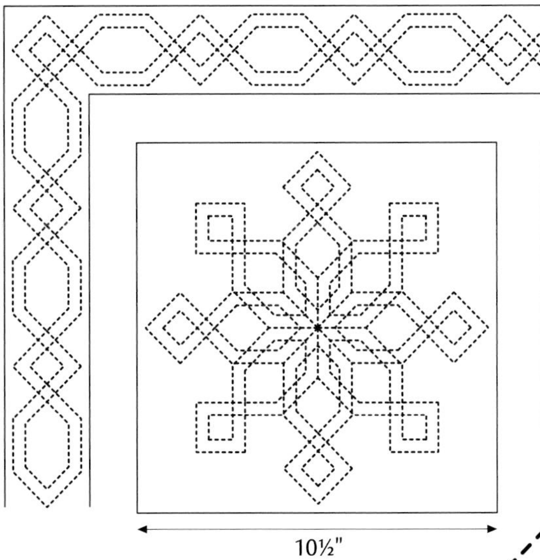
2½"
10½"

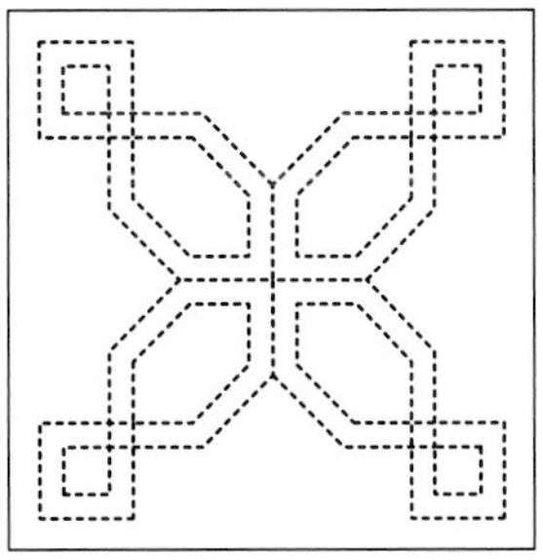

8"

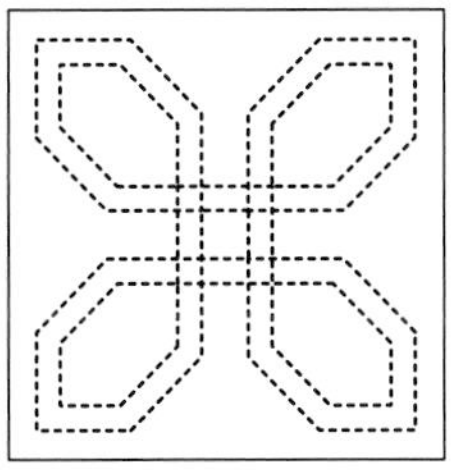

6½"

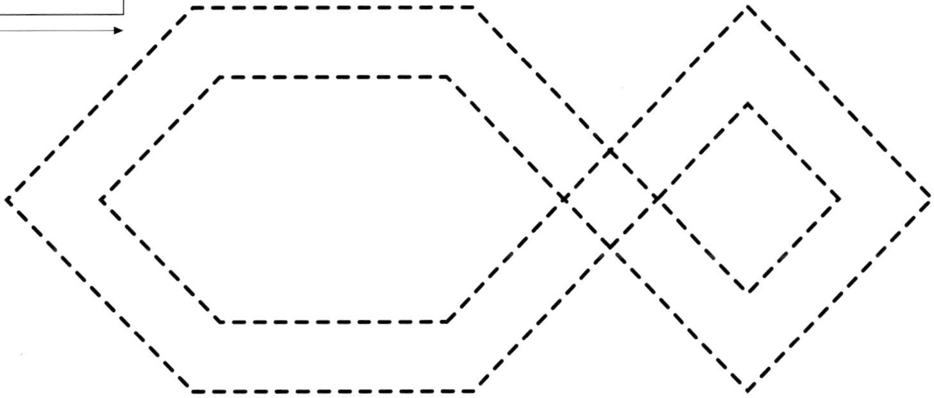

Chinook

9½"
4"
4"
Reversed motifs are shown in gray.
4½"
5"
5"
8½"

Cat Tails

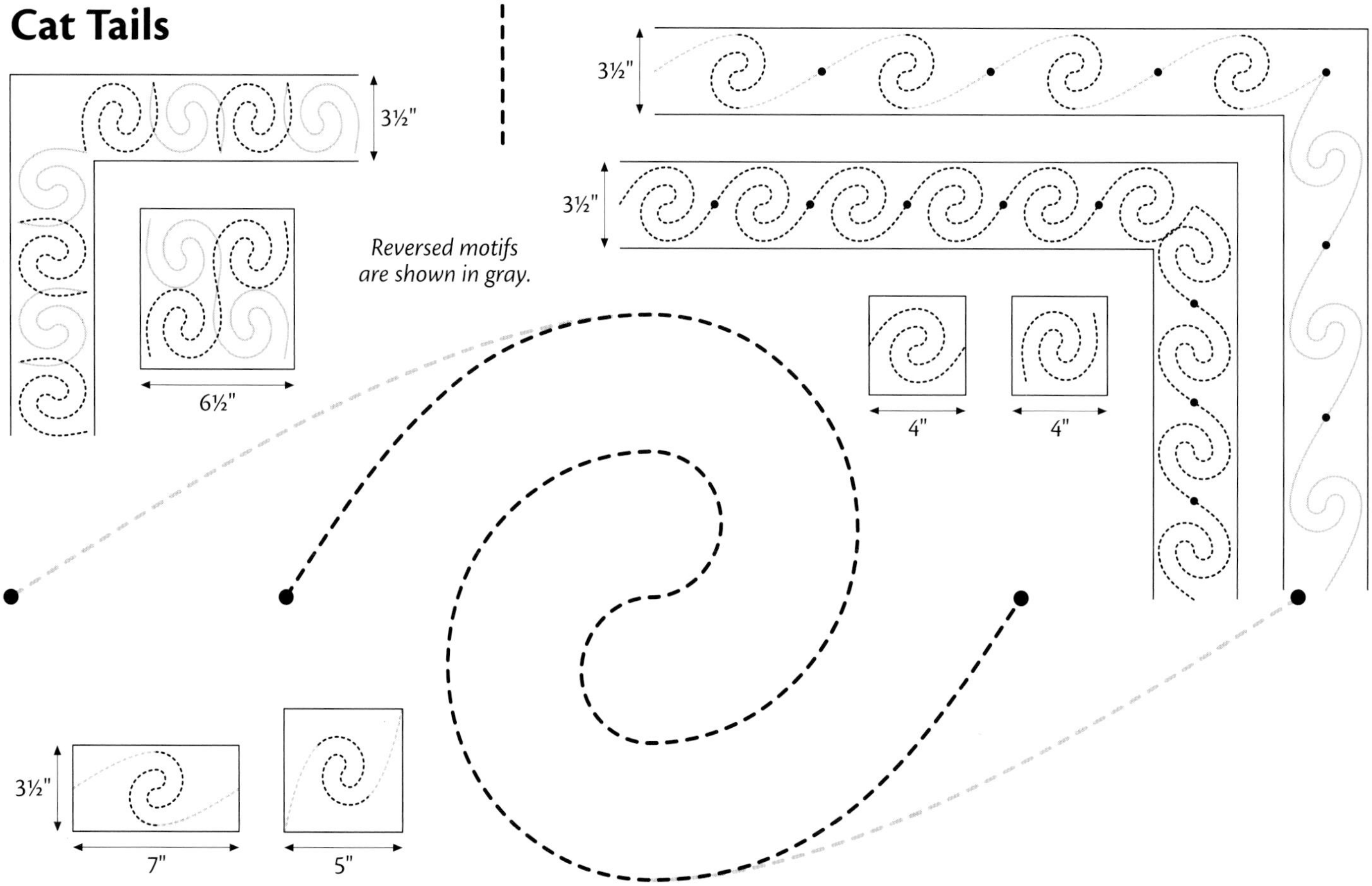

3½"
3½"
3½"
Reversed motifs are shown in gray.
6½"
4"
4"
3½"
7"
5"

Hearts

Kissing Hearts

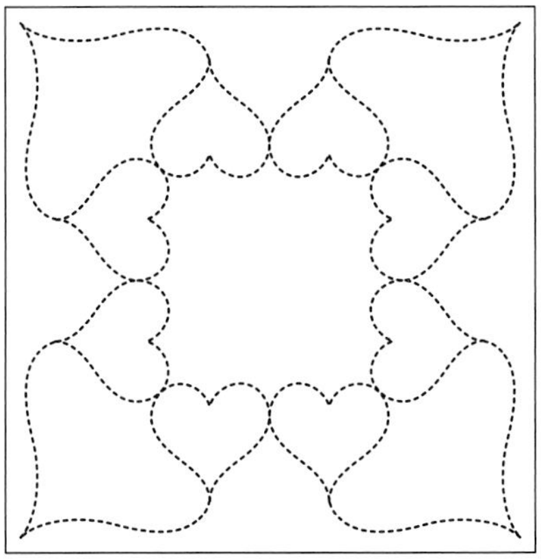

13"

7½"

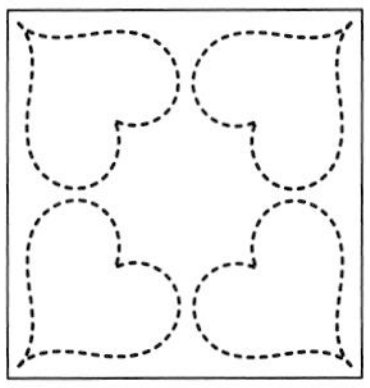

6"

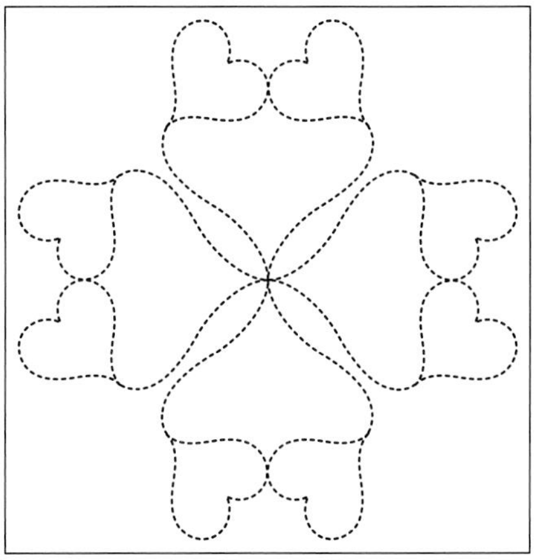

14"

Hearts in Bloom 1

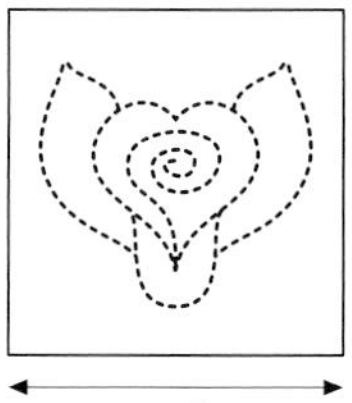

4½"

6"

6½"

8½"

4"

8"

3½"

For single heart shape, trace the heart that forms the flower.

Hearts in Bloom 2

6½"
10½"
9"
8½"

Flower and Beehive

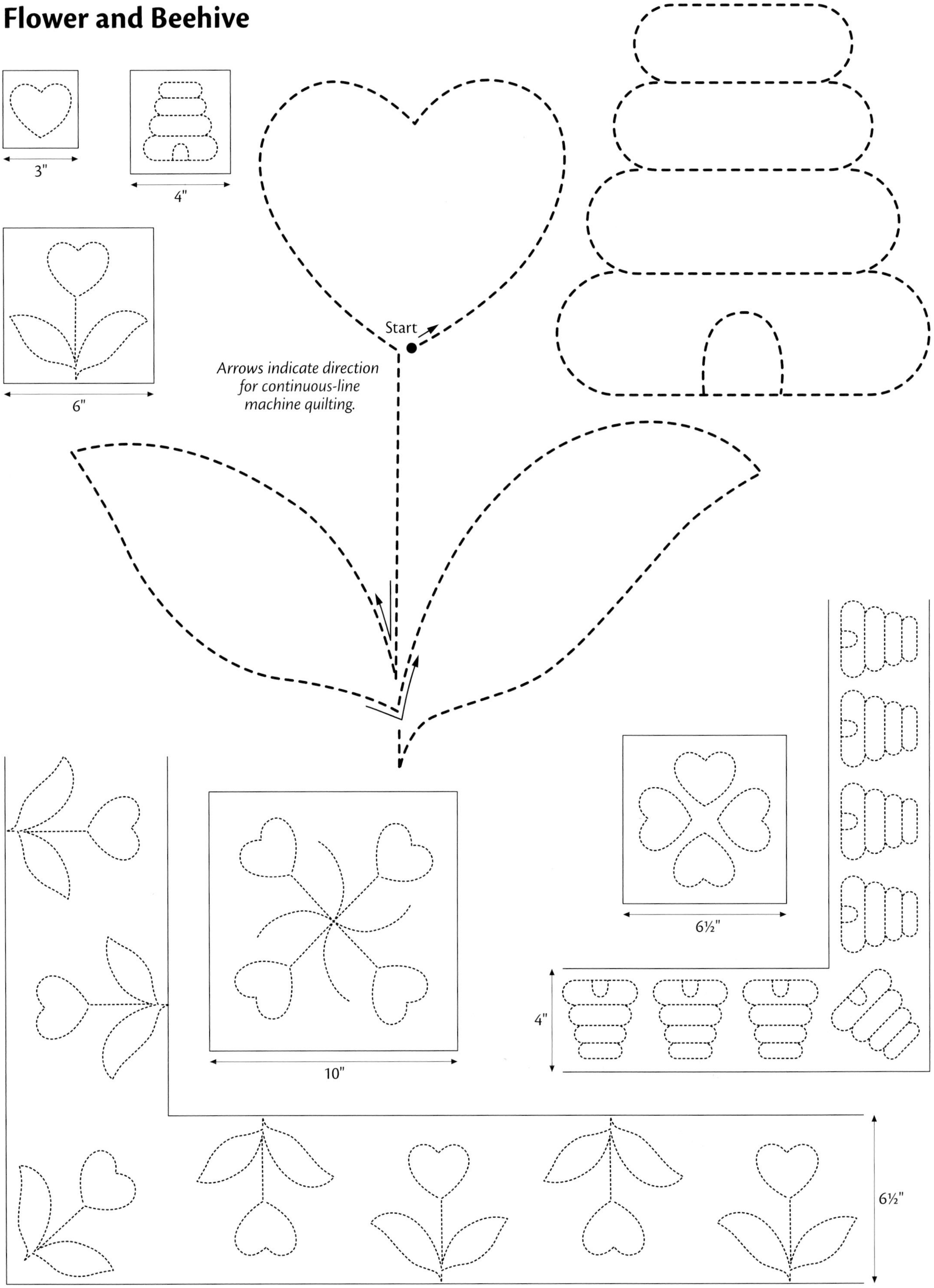
3"
4"
6"
Start
10"
6½"
4"
6½"

Arrows indicate direction for continuous-line machine quilting.

Love's Bloom

Place folded paper on dotted lines, trace, and rotate for full motif.

6"

10½"

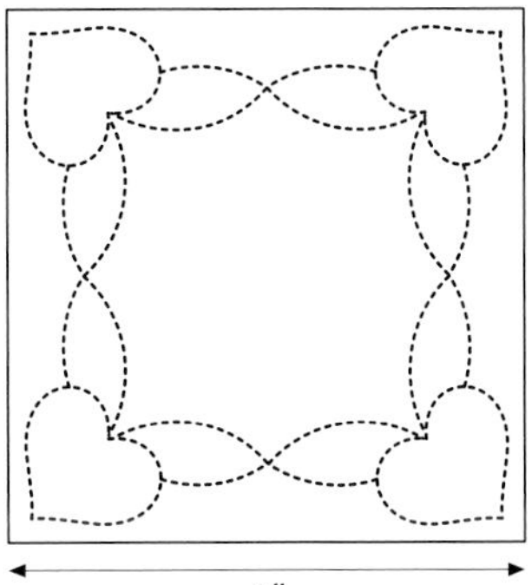

8"

7½"

April Love

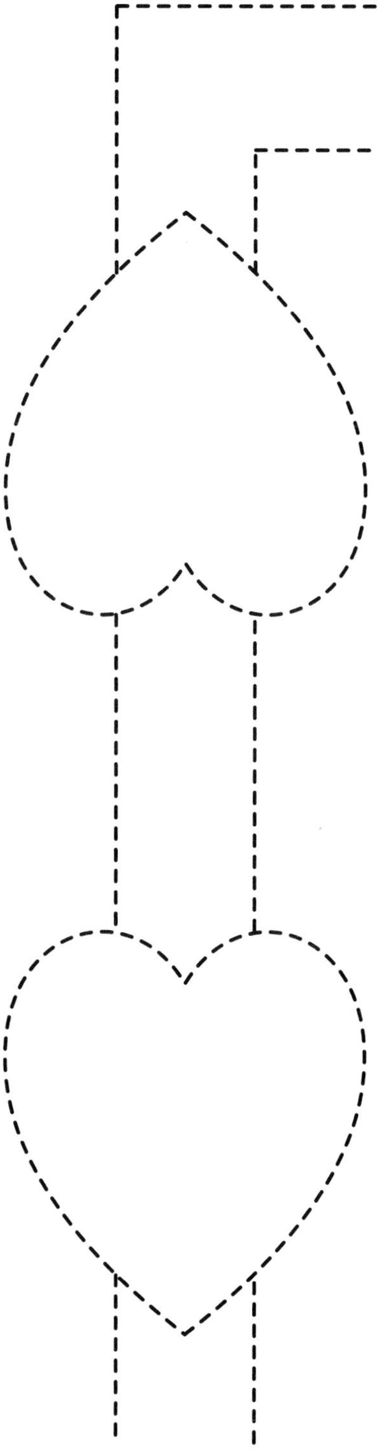

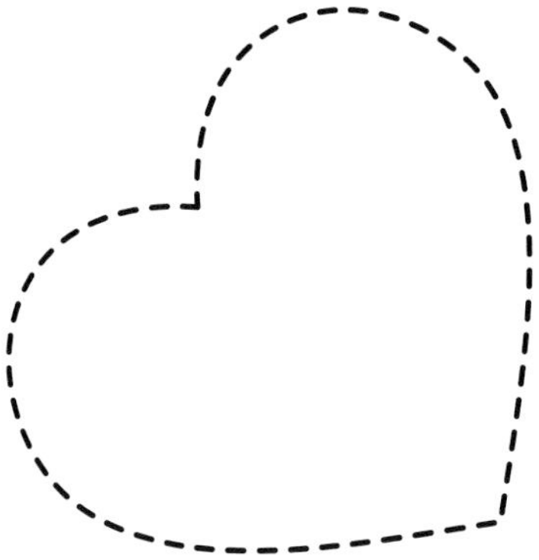

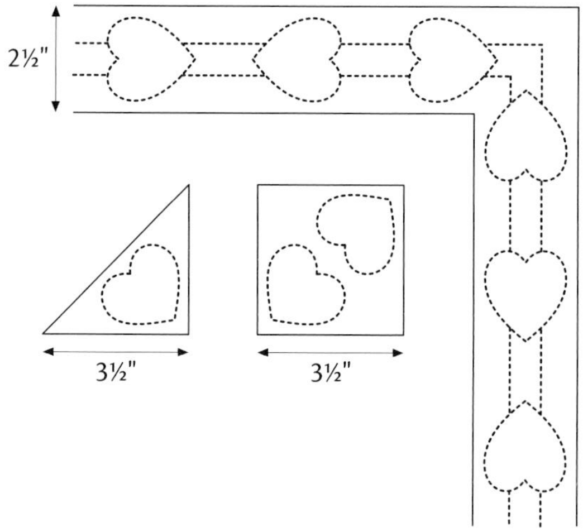

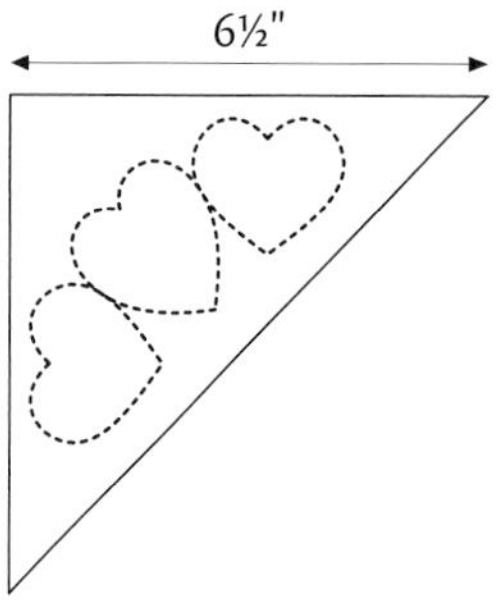

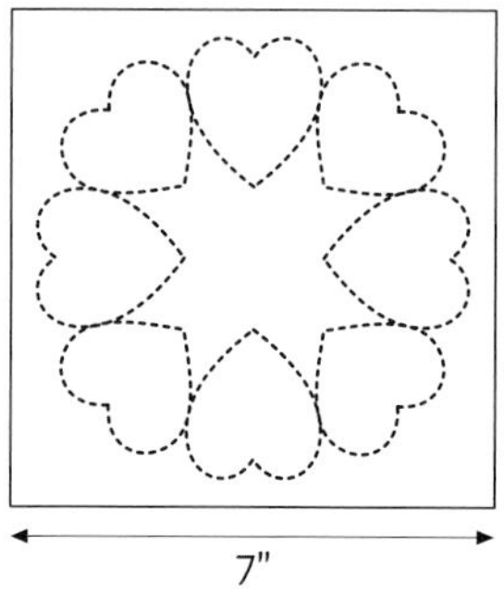

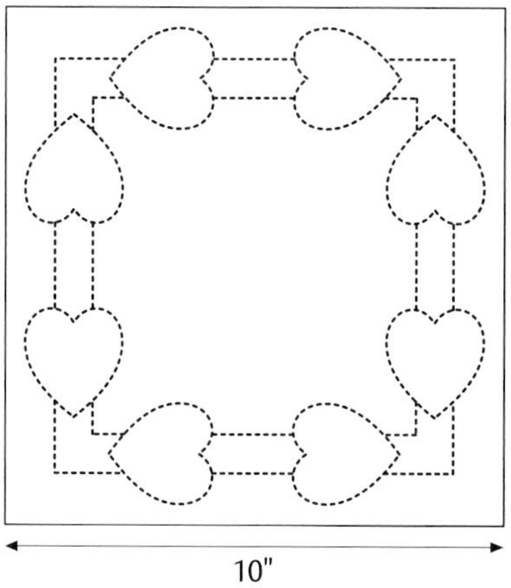

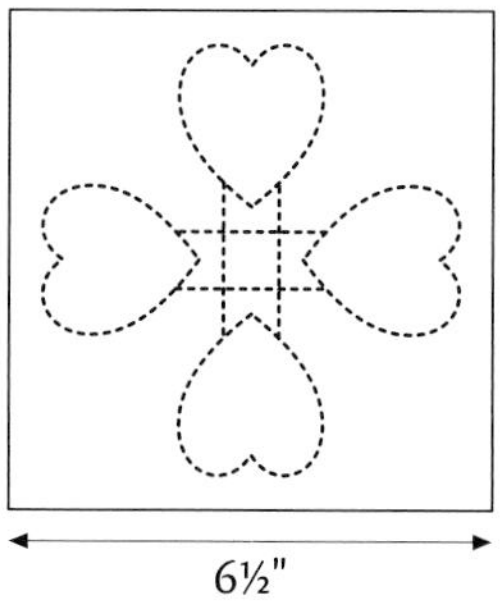

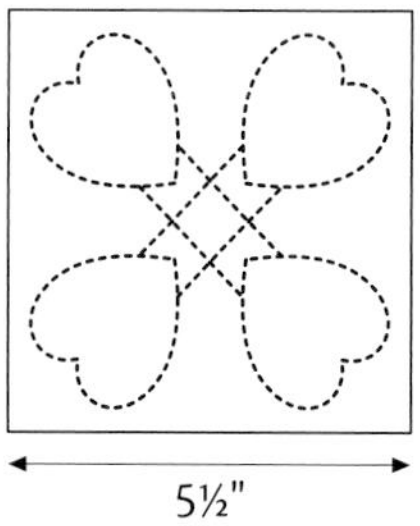

Hearts and Flowers

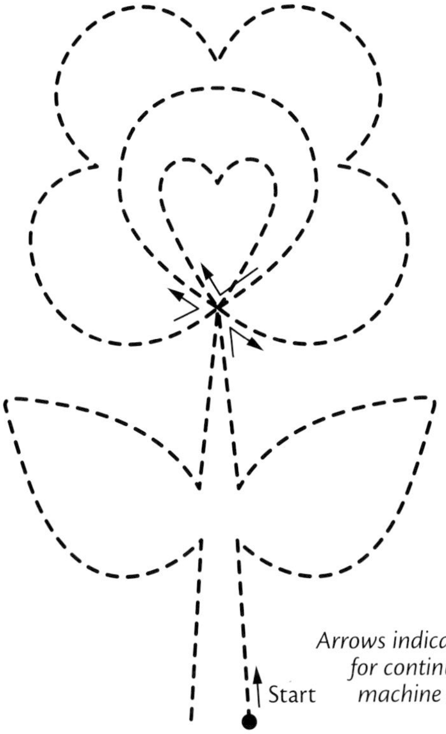

Start

Arrows indicate direction for continuous-line machine quilting.

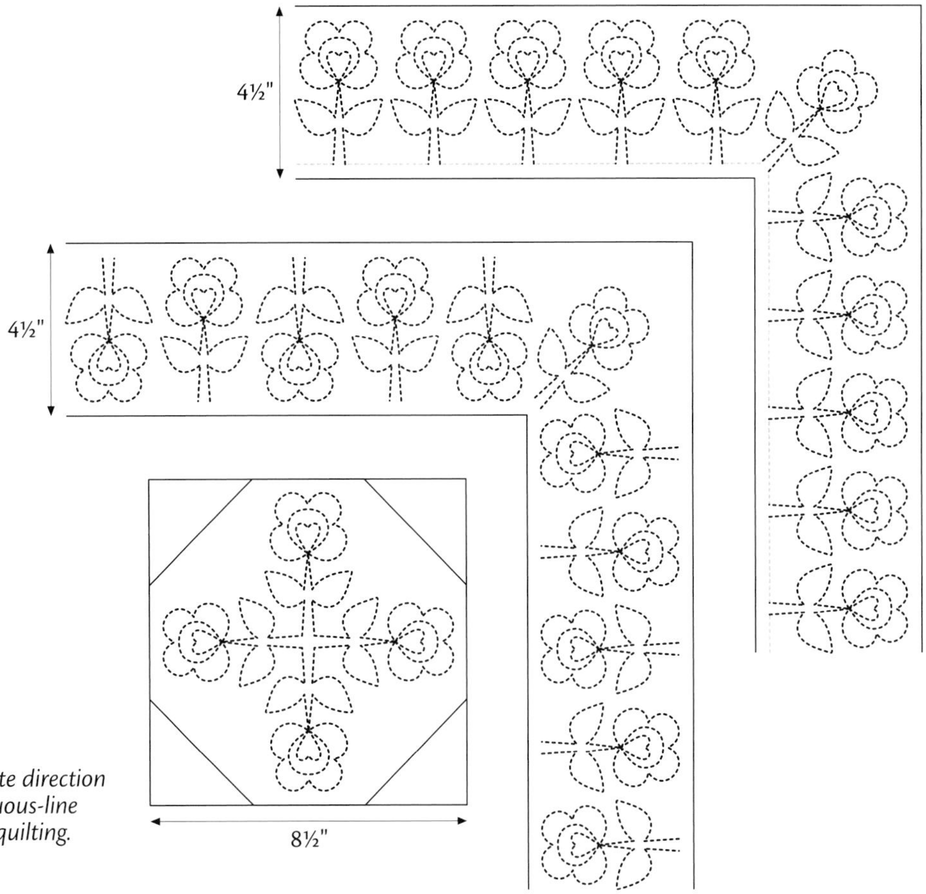

4½"
4½"

8½"

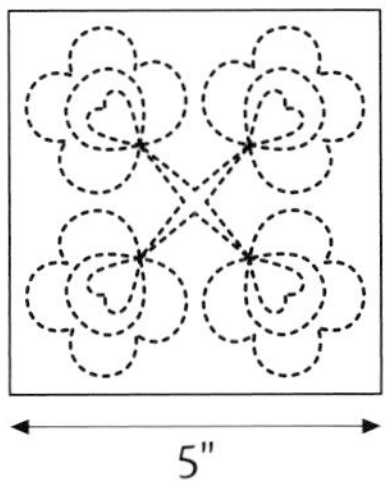

5"

5½"

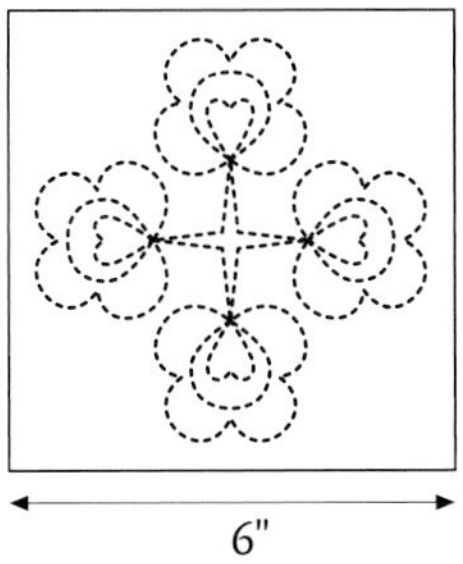

6"

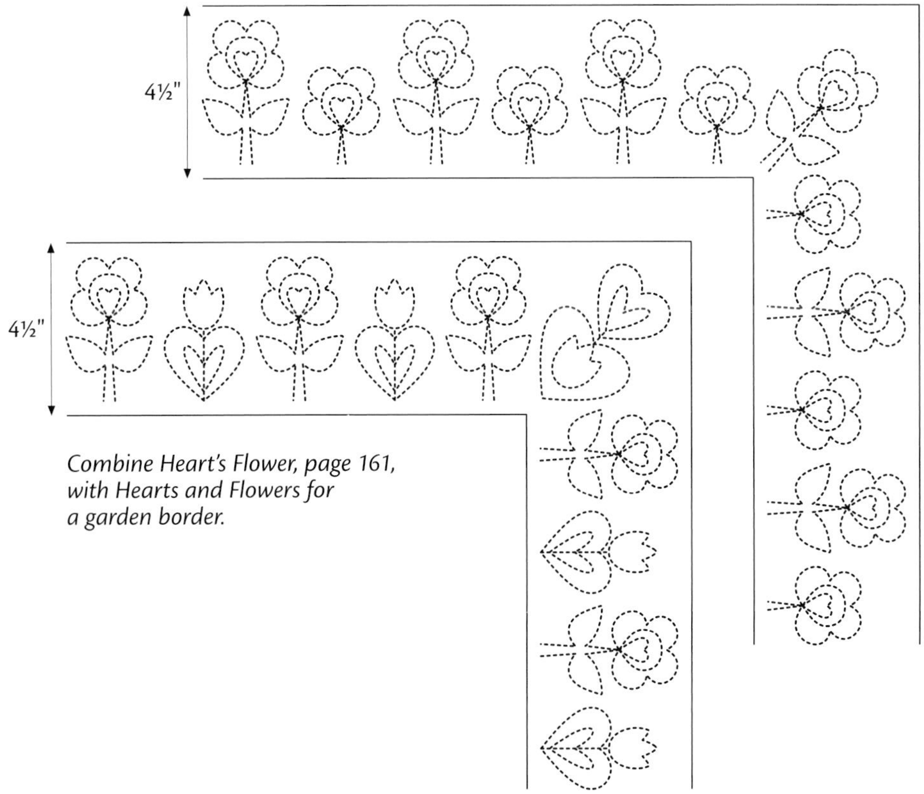

4½"
4½"

Combine Heart's Flower, page 161, with Hearts and Flowers for a garden border.

Hearts and Swags

Place folded paper on dotted lines, trace, and rotate for full motif.

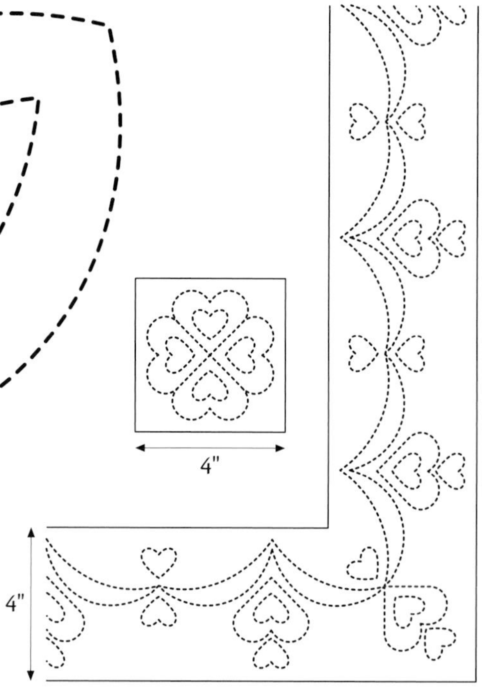

4"

5½"

5½"

5½"

15"

11"

11"

10"

Floral Heart

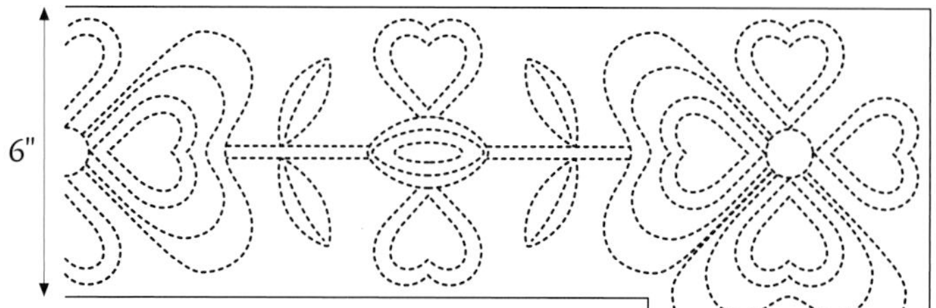

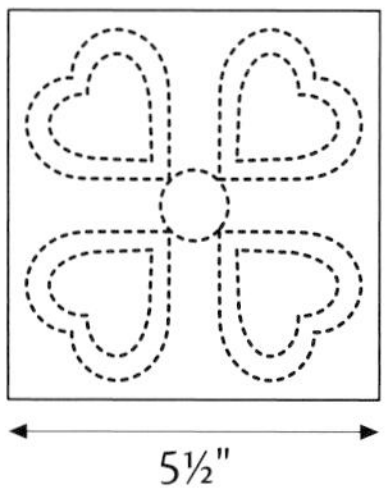

Loving Hearts

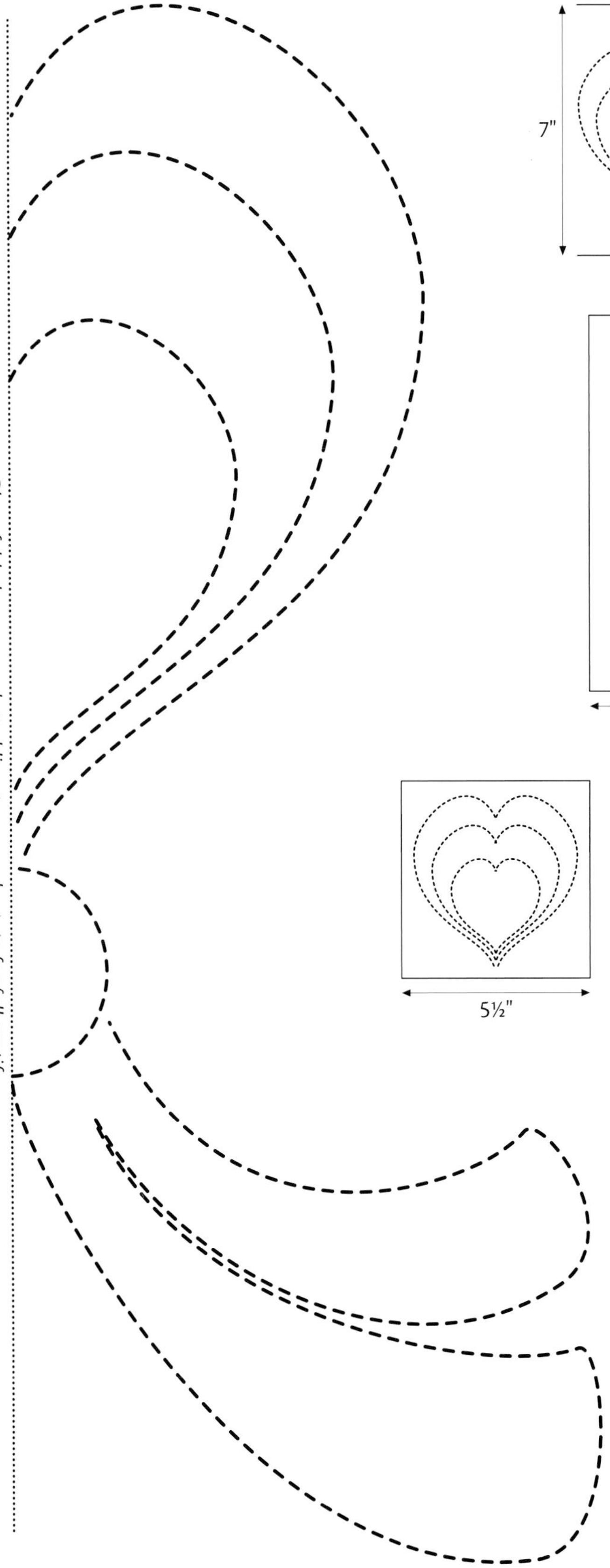

Place folded paper on dotted line, trace, and rotate for full motif.

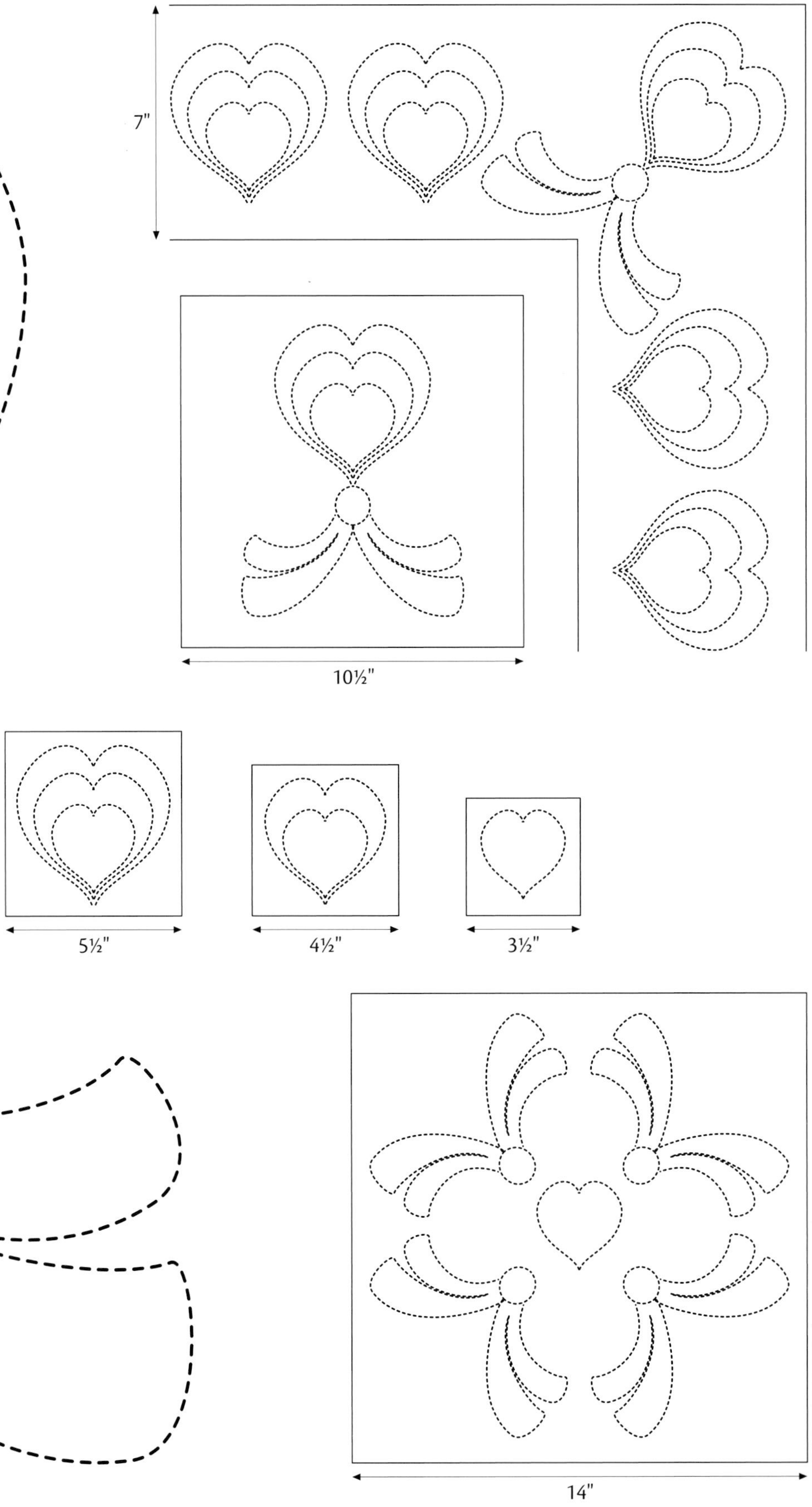

7"
10½"
5½"
4½"
3½"
14"

Amish Traditions

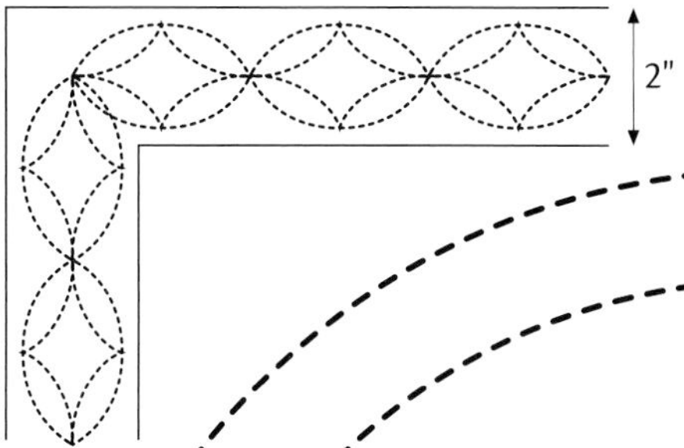

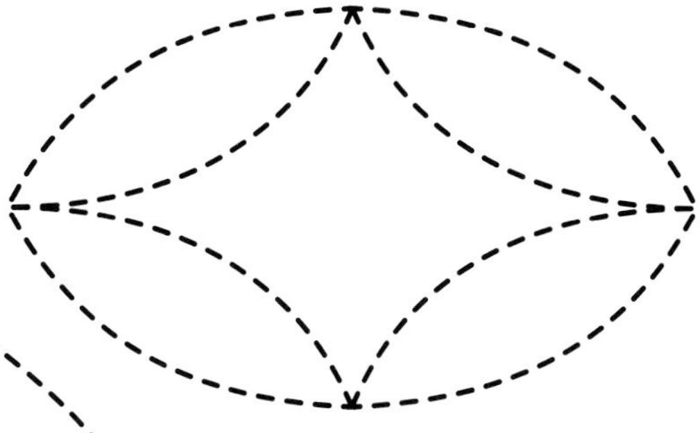

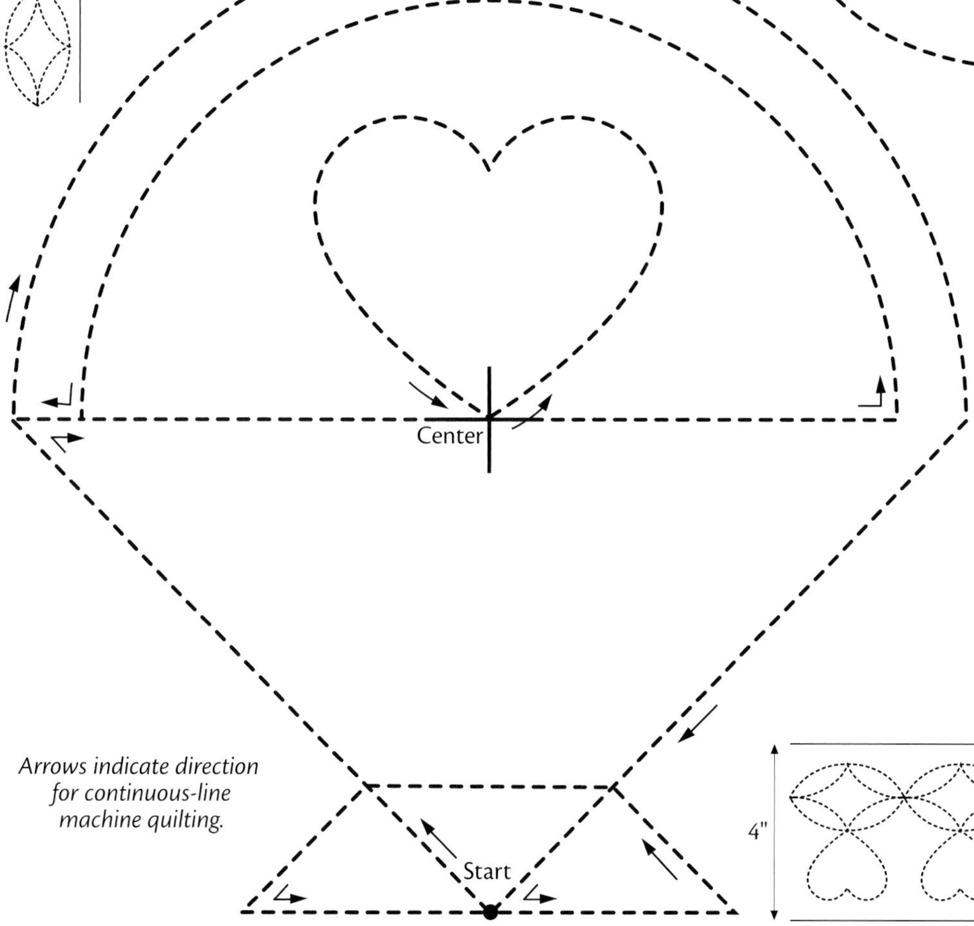

Arrows indicate direction for continuous-line machine quilting.

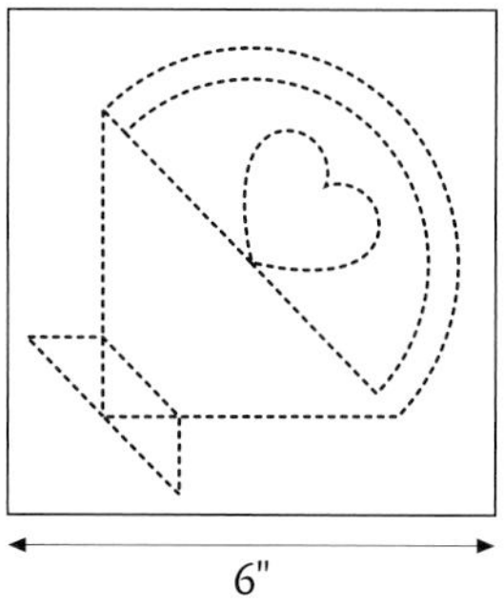

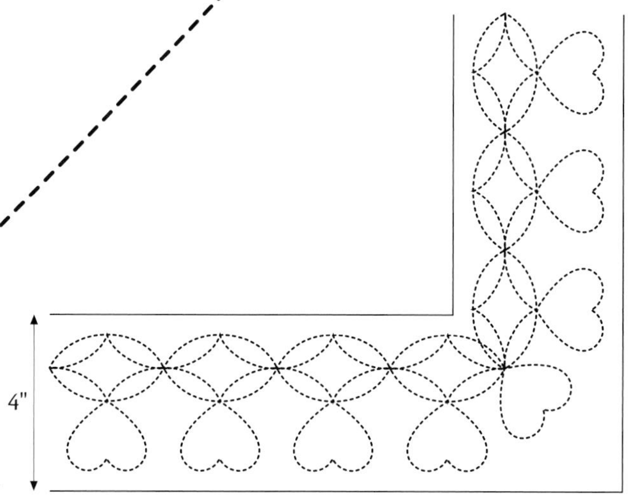

Hearts Abloom

Reversed motifs are shown in gray.

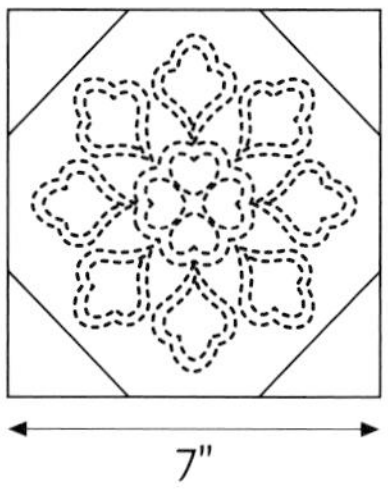

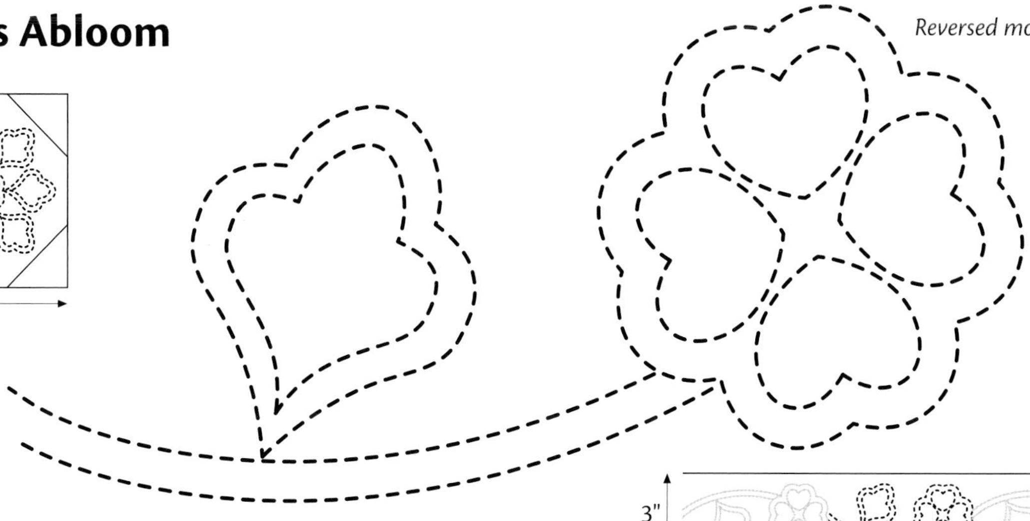

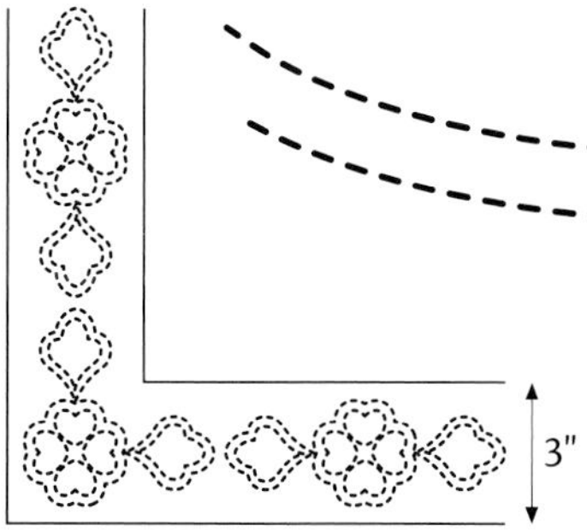

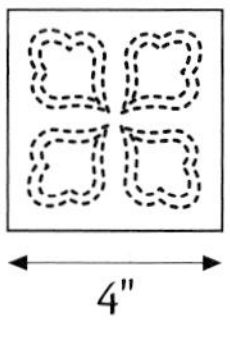

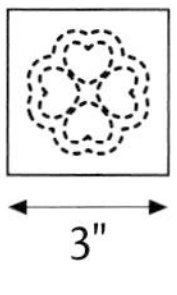

Grace Notes

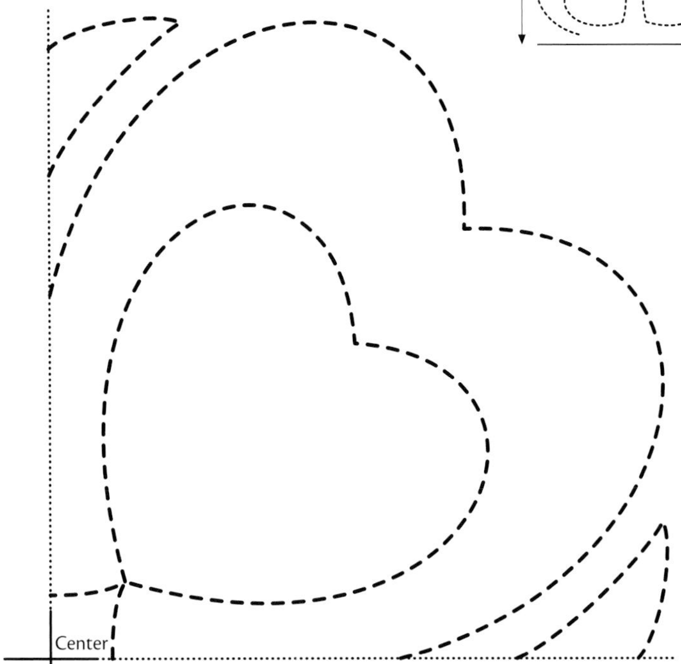
Center

Place folded paper on dotted lines, trace, and rotate for full motif.

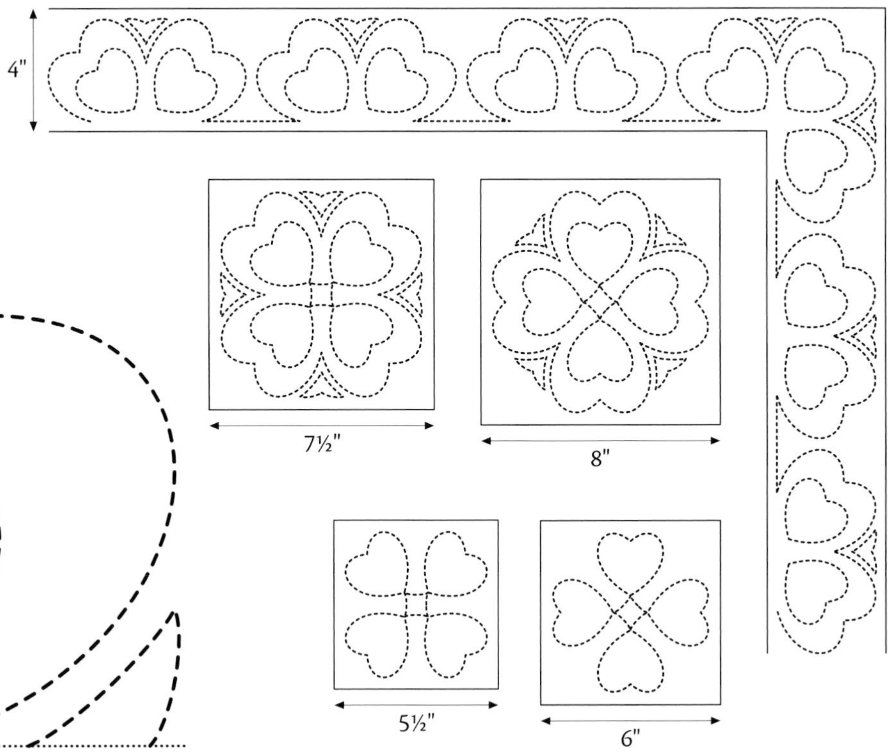
4"
7½"
8"
5½"
6"

Heartsong

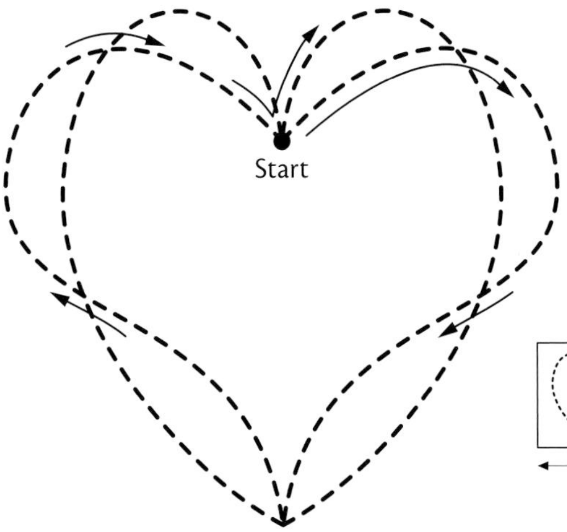
Start

Arrows indicate direction for continuous-line machine quilting.

3"
3"
3"
4"
3"
3"
3"
5"
5"
5"

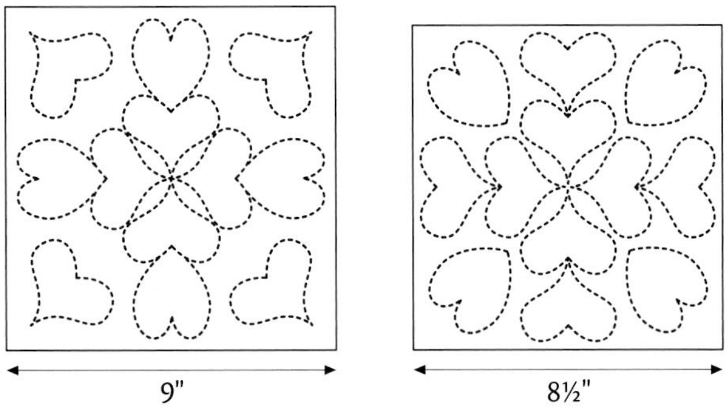
9"
8½"

Ribbons of Love

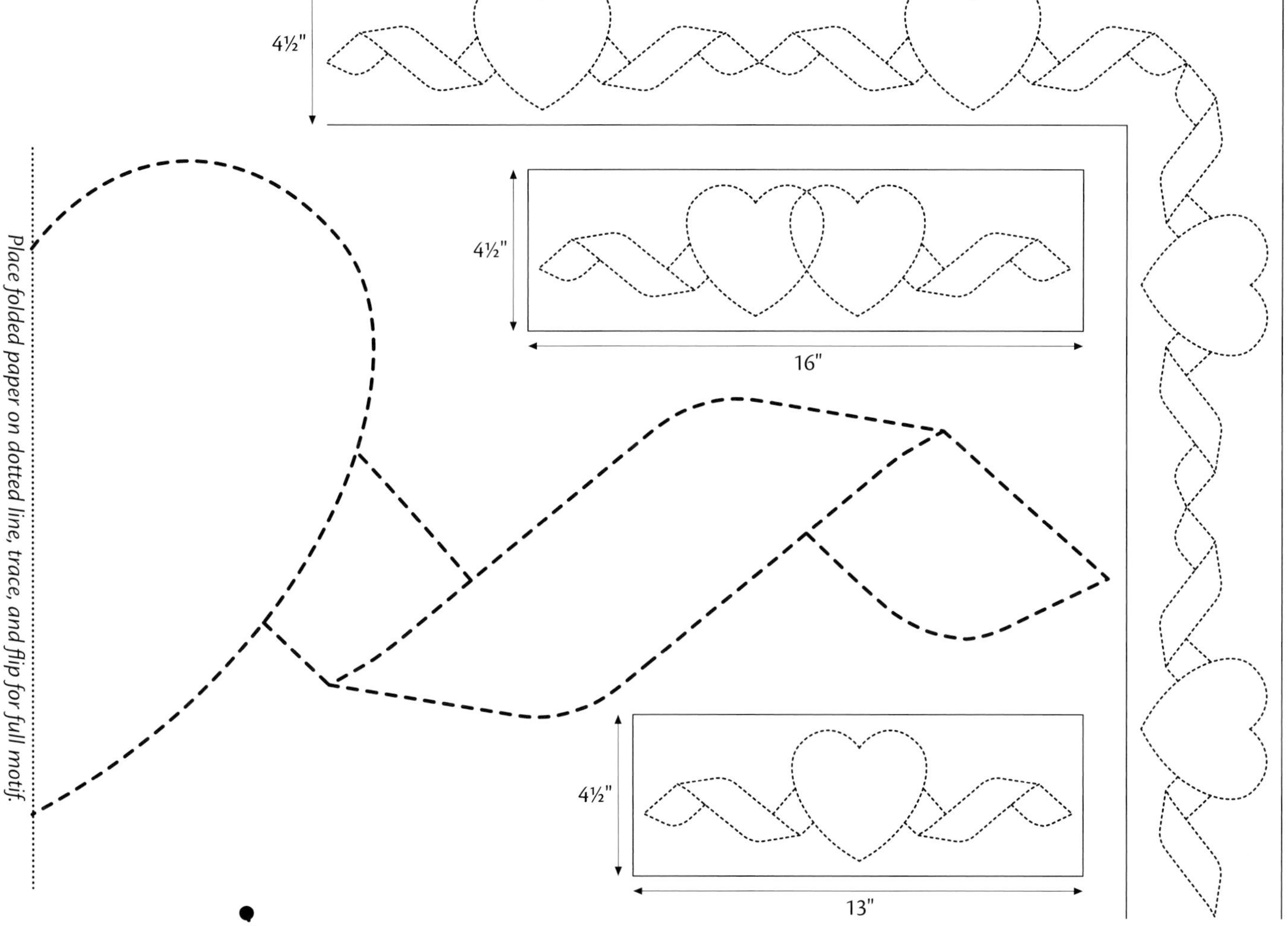

Heart Strings

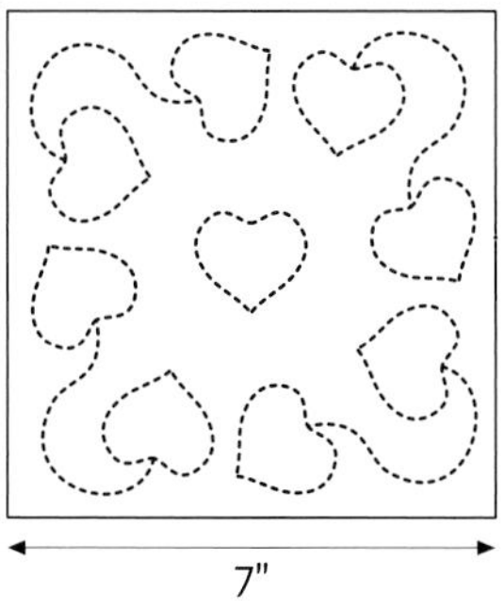

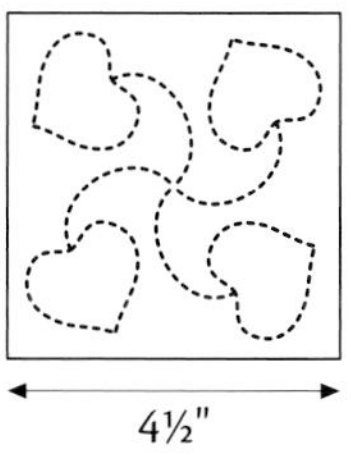

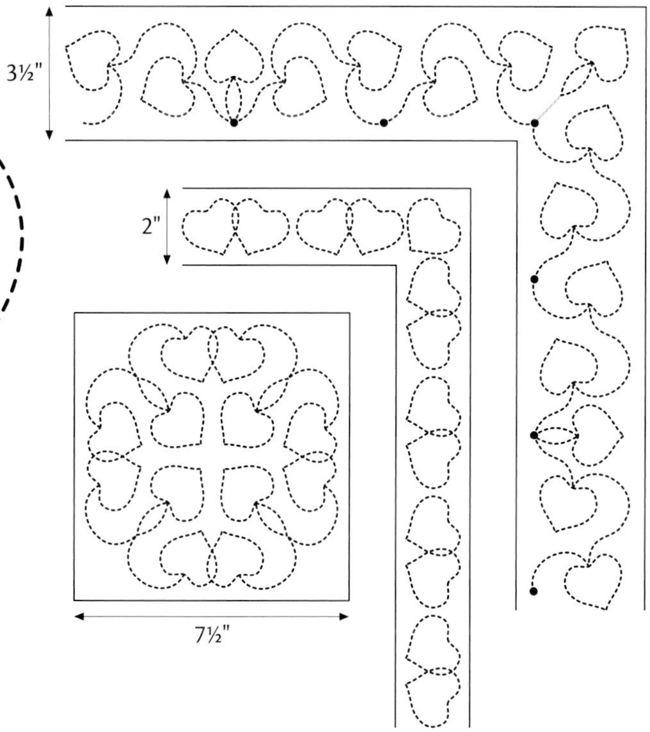

Rhythm and Bows

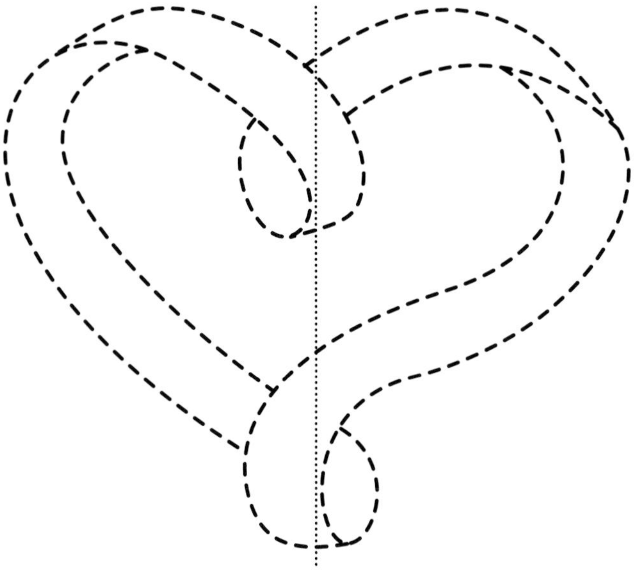

7½"

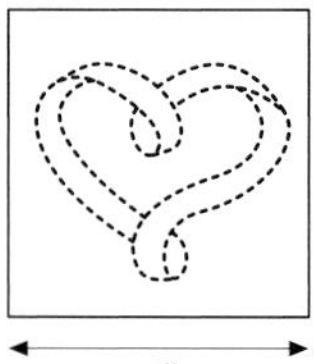

4"

Place folded paper on dotted line, trace, and flip for full motif.

3½"

11½"

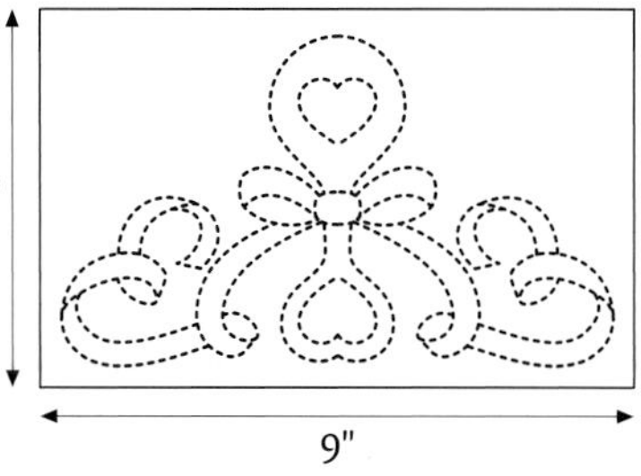

5½"

9"

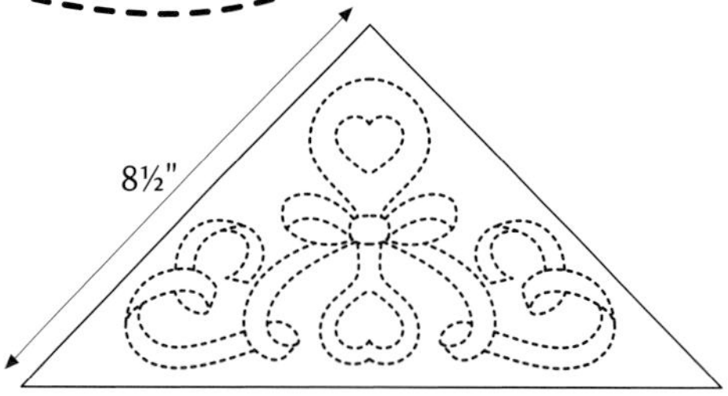

8½"

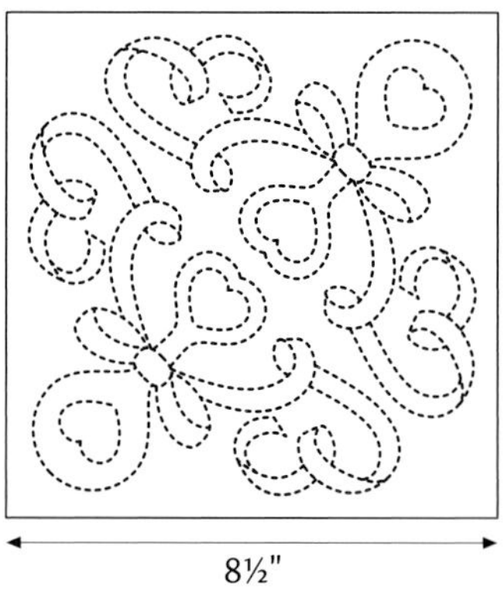

8½"

Hearts Around

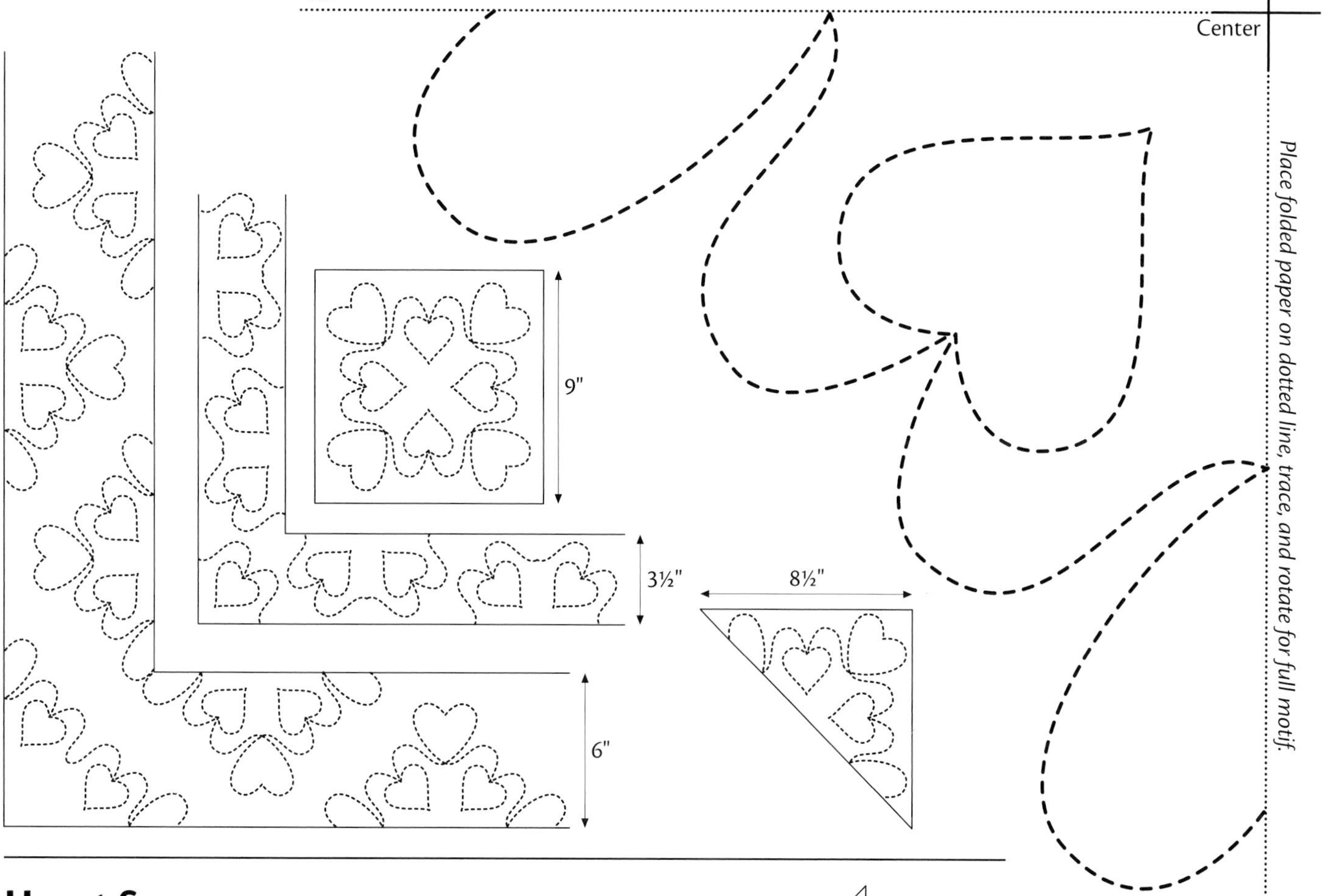
Center
Place folded paper on dotted line, trace, and rotate for full motif.
9"
3½"
8½"
6"

Heart Songs

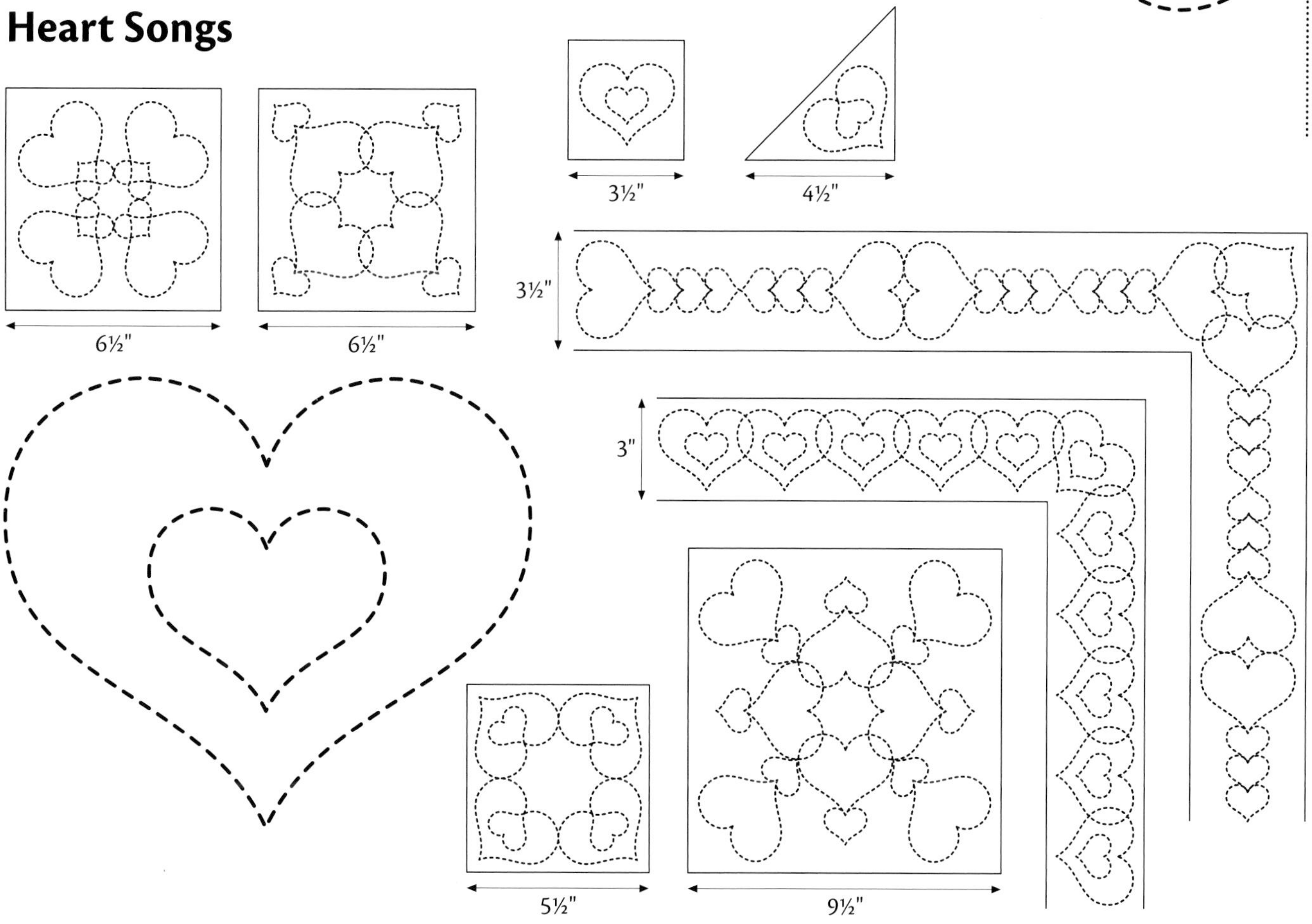
3½"
4½"
6½"
6½"
3½"
3"
5½"
9½"

Caesar's Heart

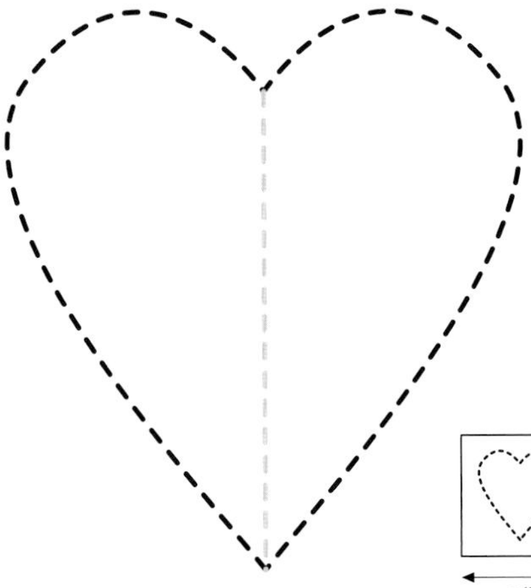

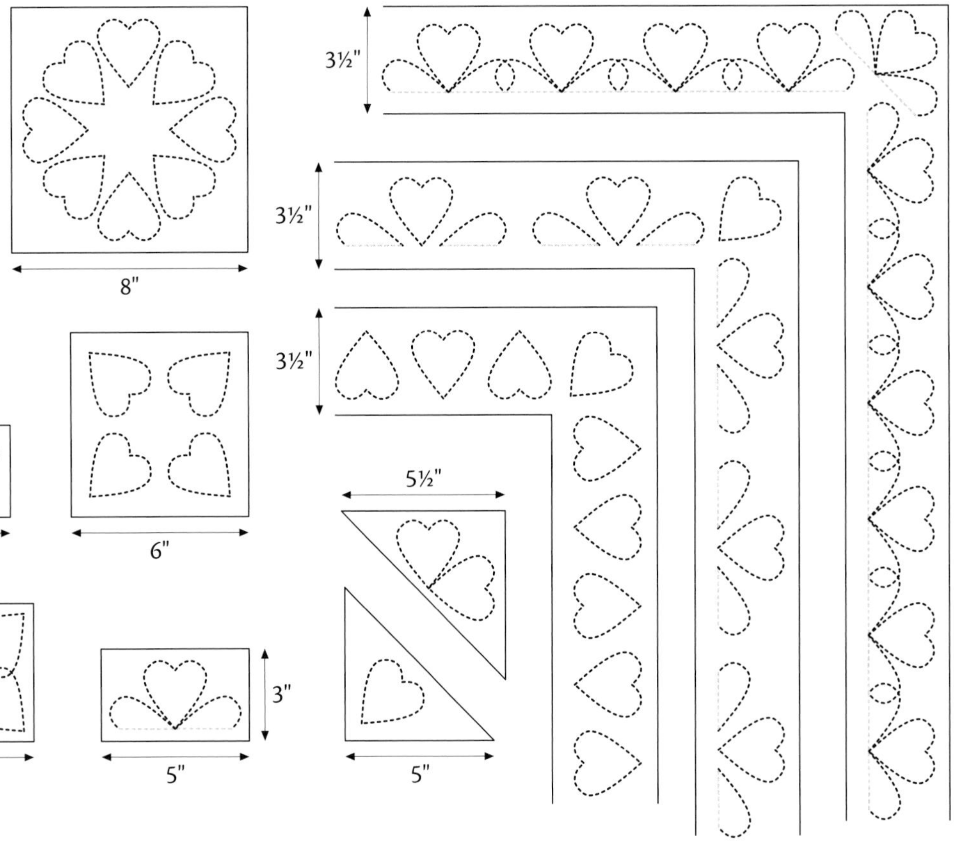

3½"
3½"
3½"
8"
6"
5½"
5"

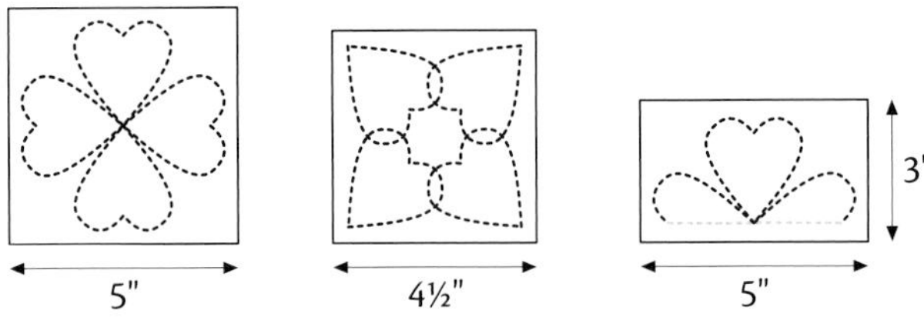

3"
5"
4½"
5"
3"

Triple Heart

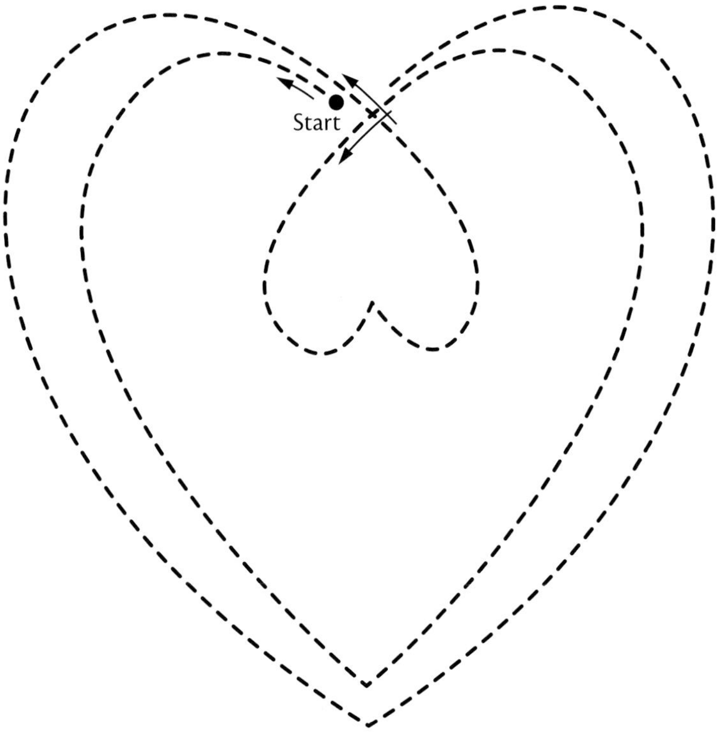

Start

Arrows indicate direction for continuous-line machine quilting.

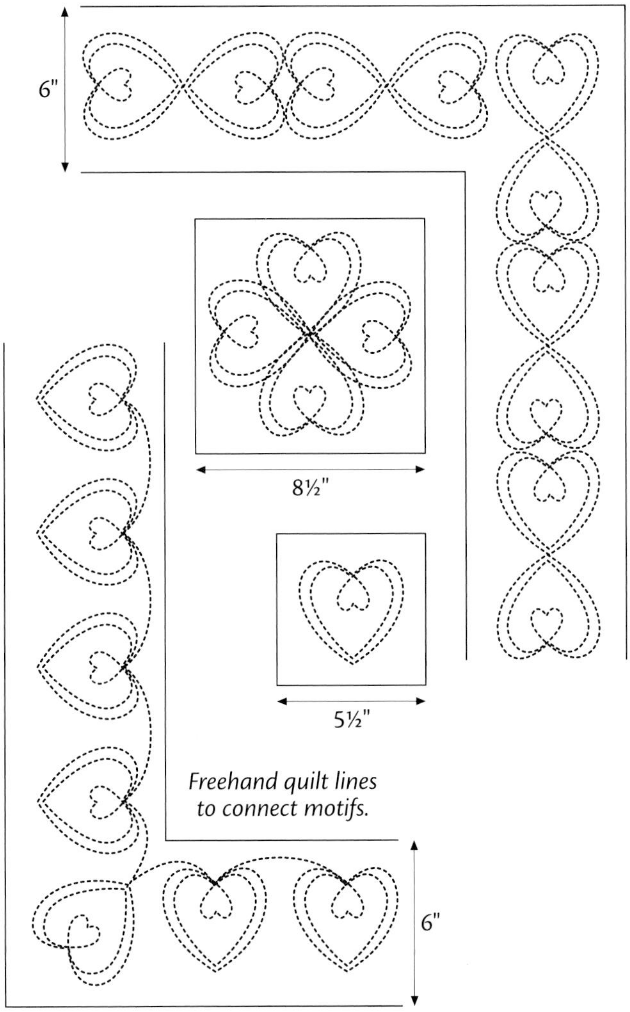

6"
8½"
5½"
Freehand quilt lines to connect motifs.
6"

Hearts Aflutter

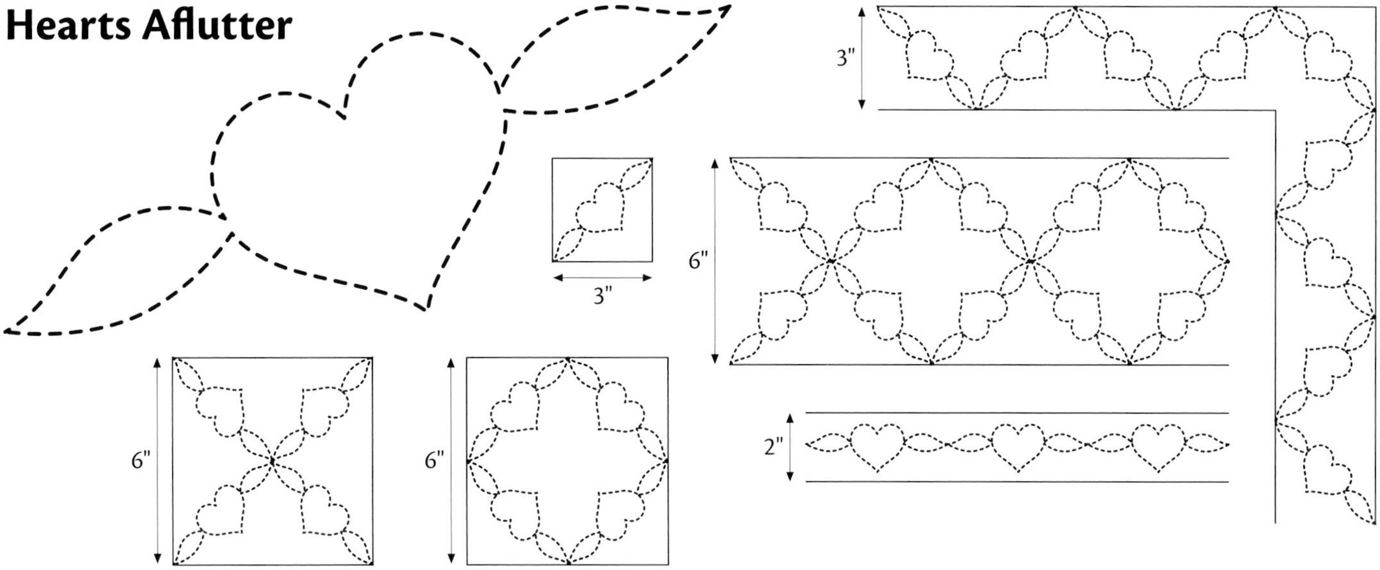

Heart's Flower

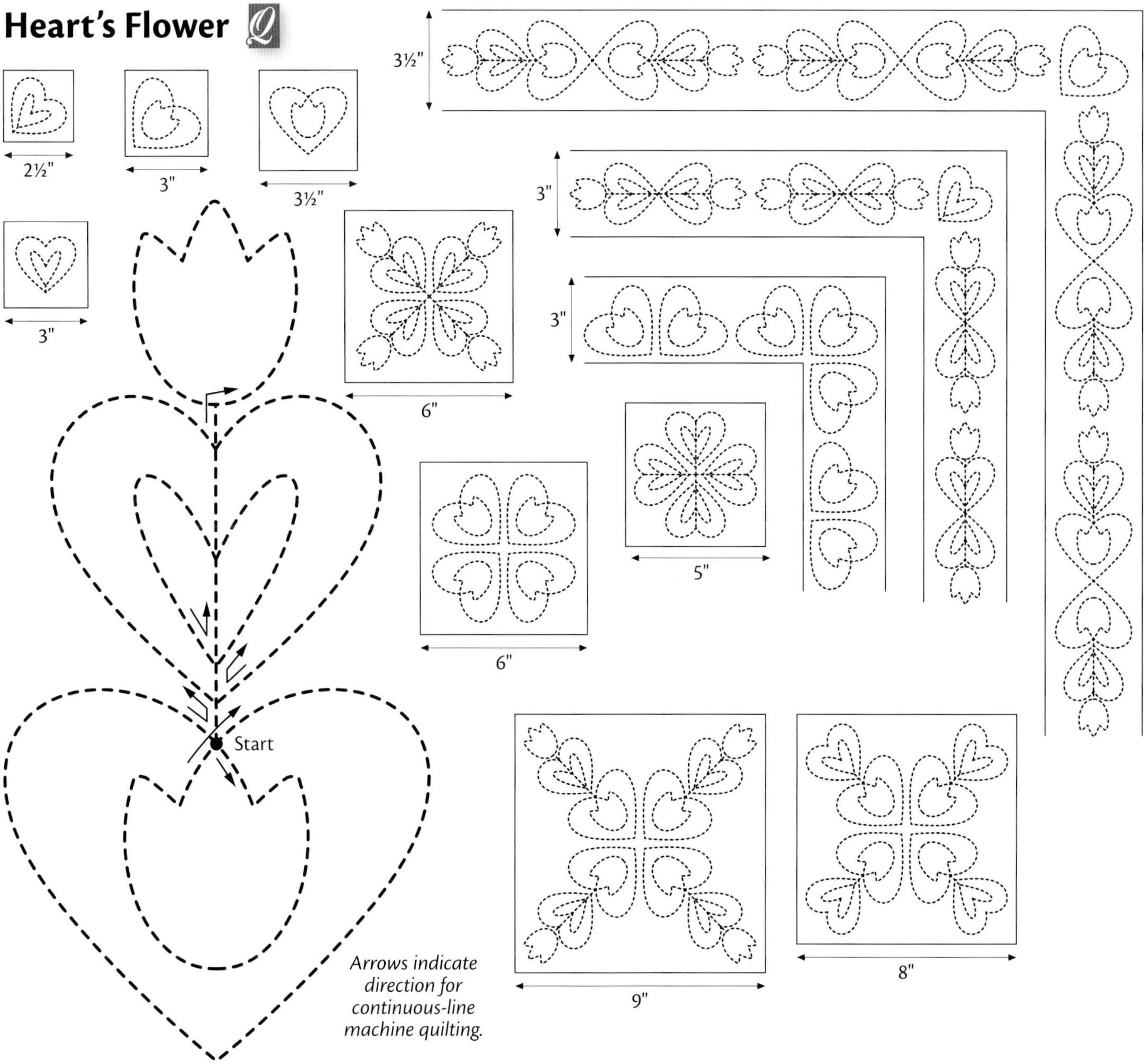

Arrows indicate direction for continuous-line machine quilting.

Spring Delight

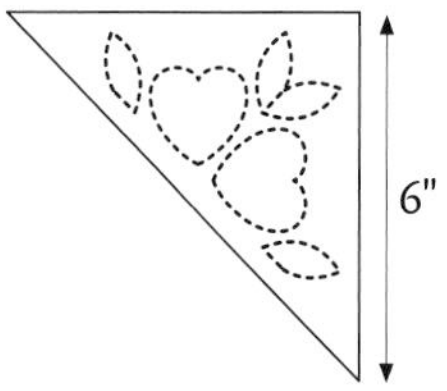
6"

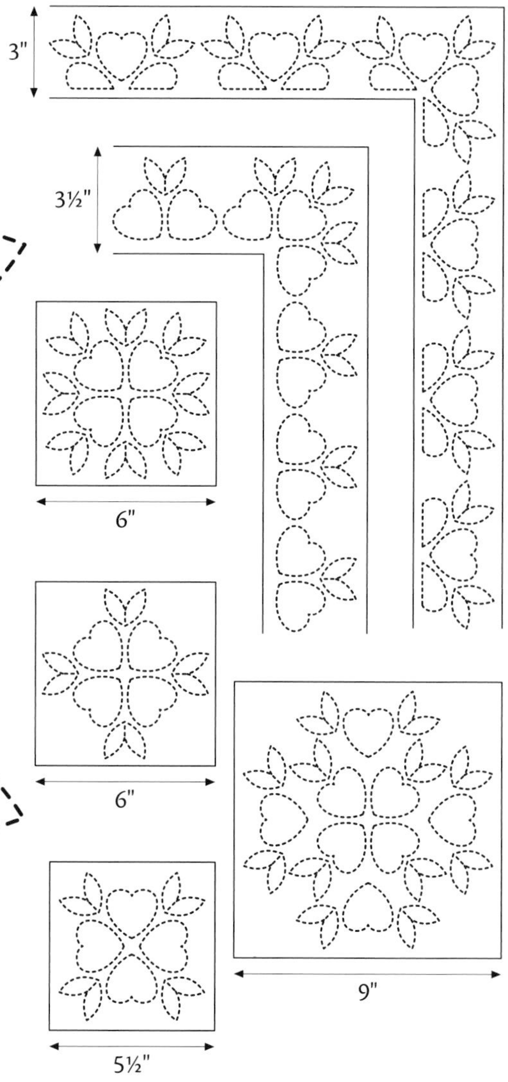
3"
3½"
6"
6"
9"
5½"

Country Baskets

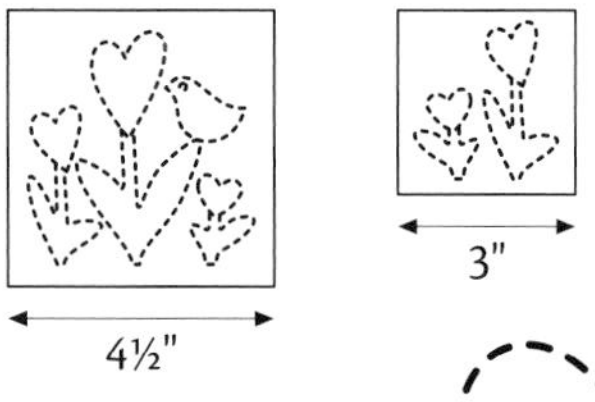
4½"
3"

Start

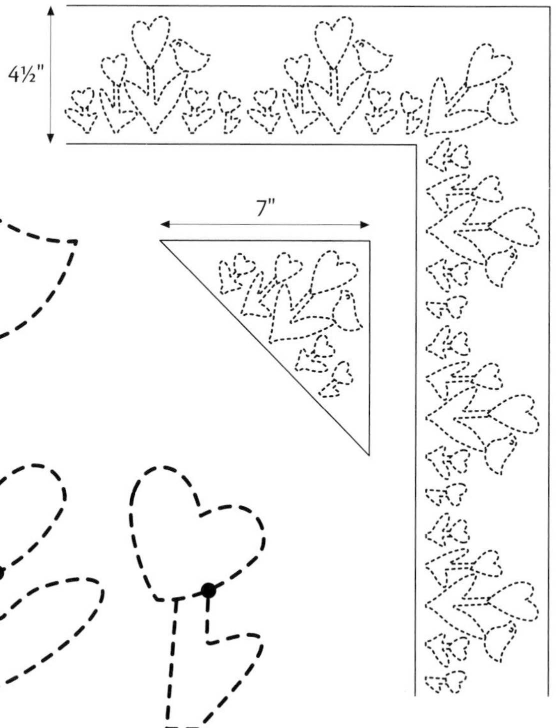
4½"
7"

Bows and Bells

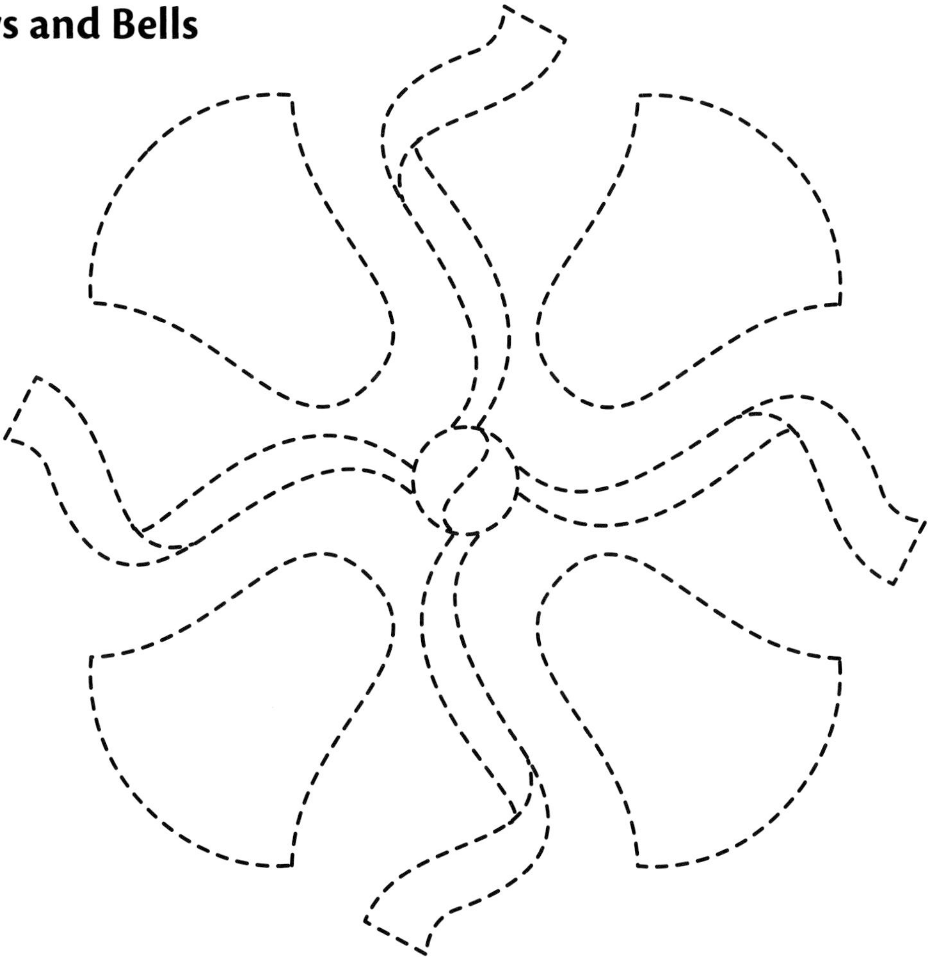

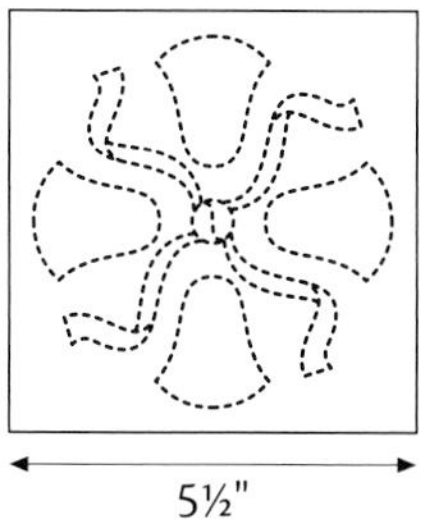
5½"

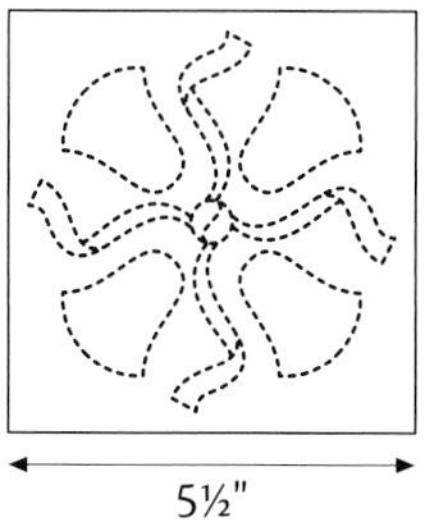
5½"

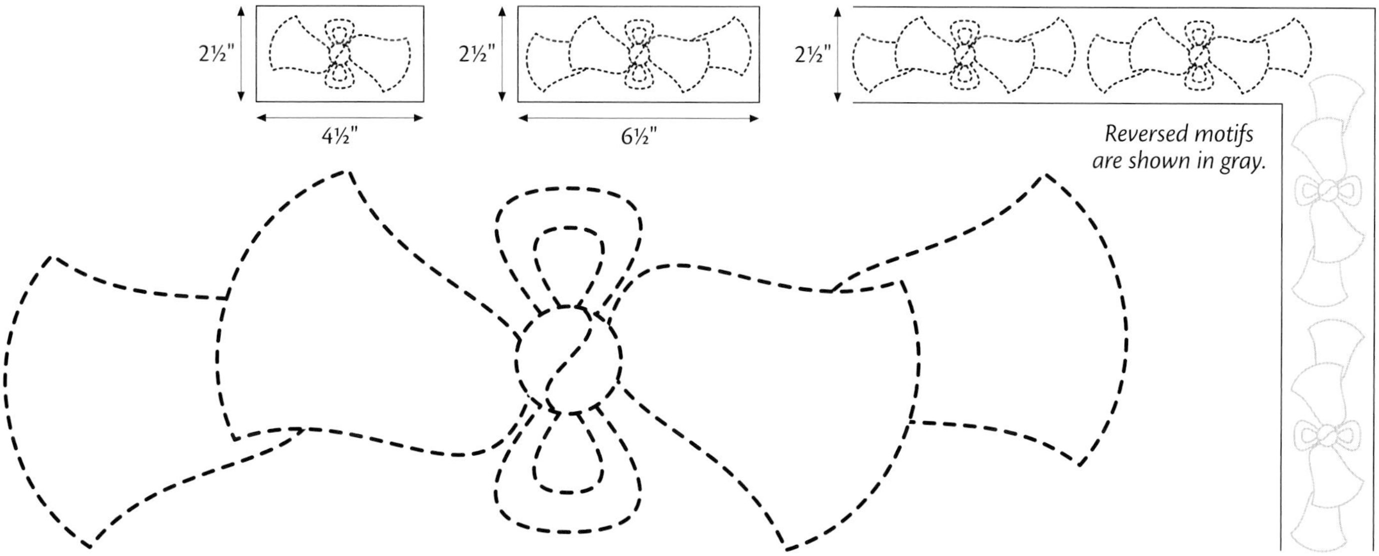
2½"
4½"
2½"
6½"
2½"
Reversed motifs
are shown in gray.

Simply Snowflakes

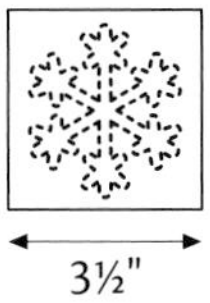

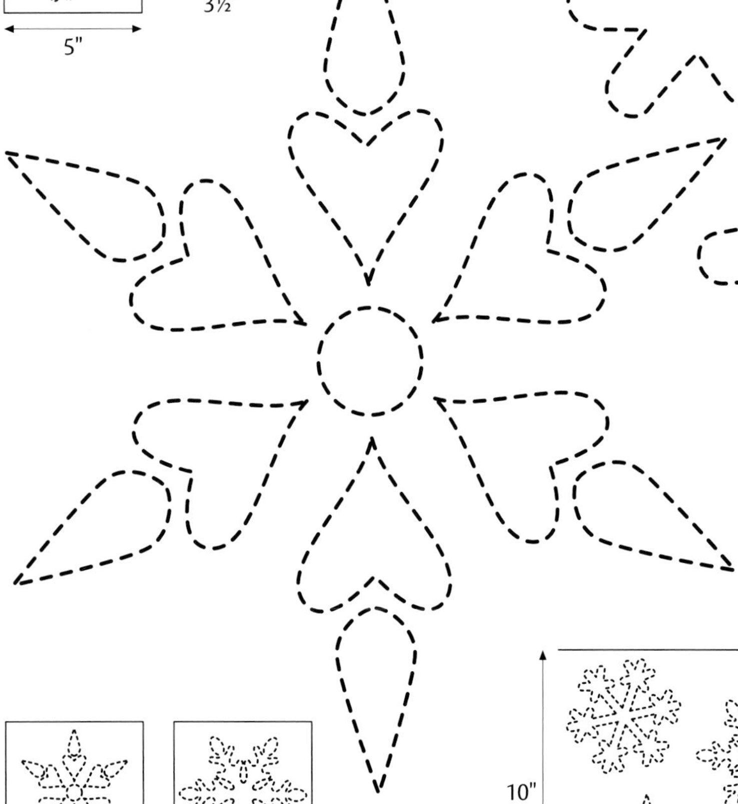

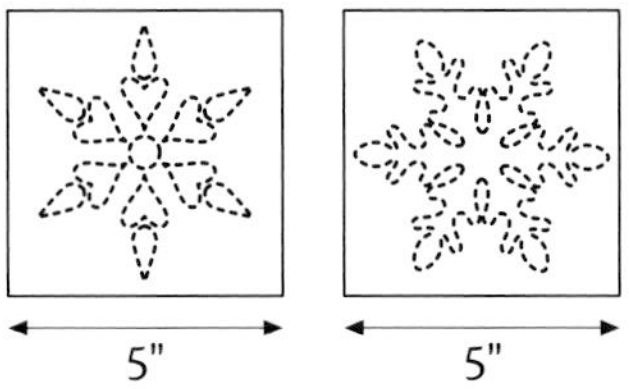

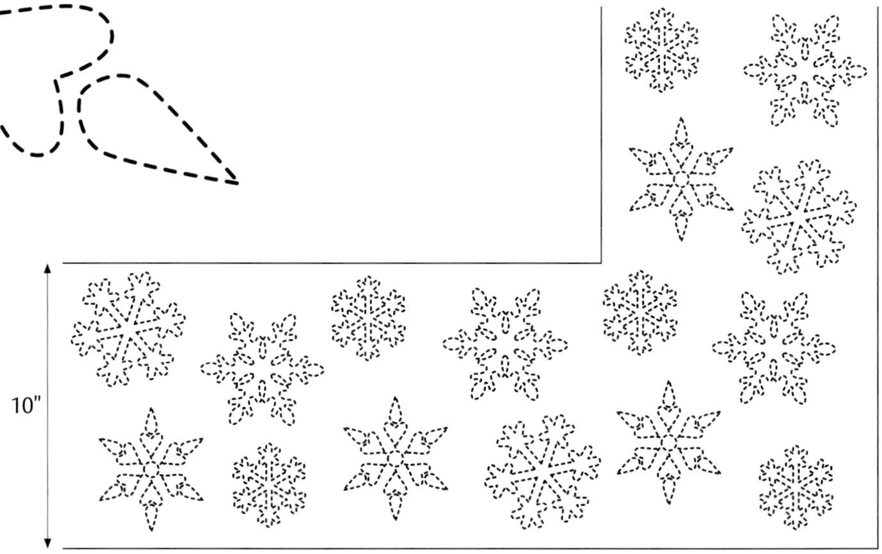

Holiday Hearts

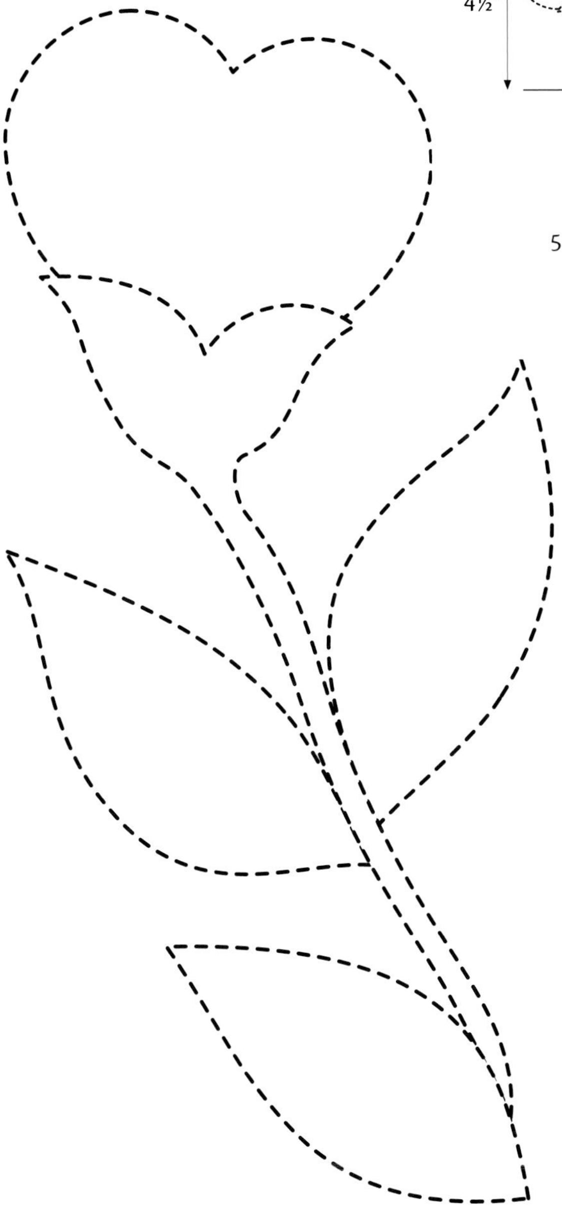

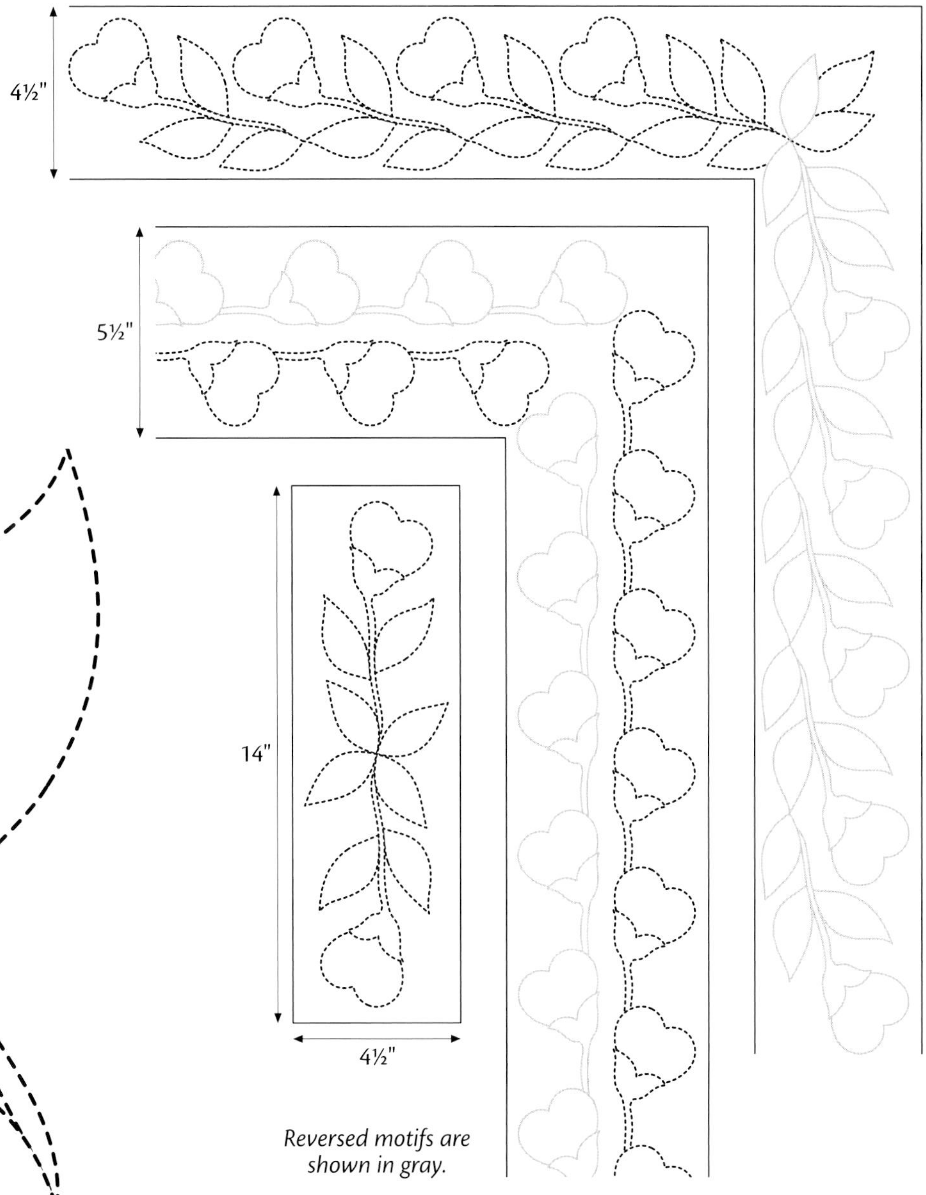

Reversed motifs are shown in gray.

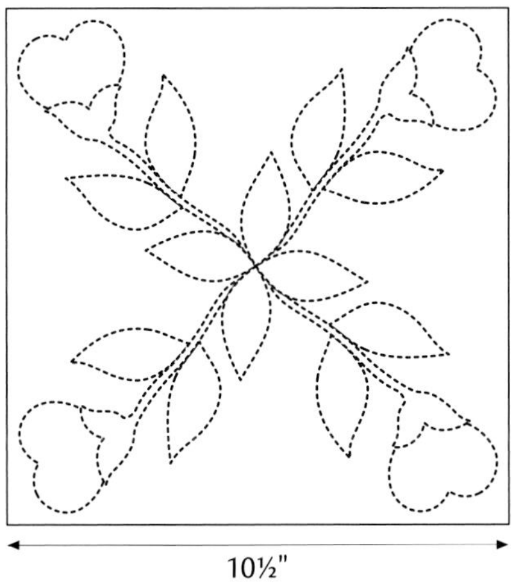

Patch-o'-Pumpkins

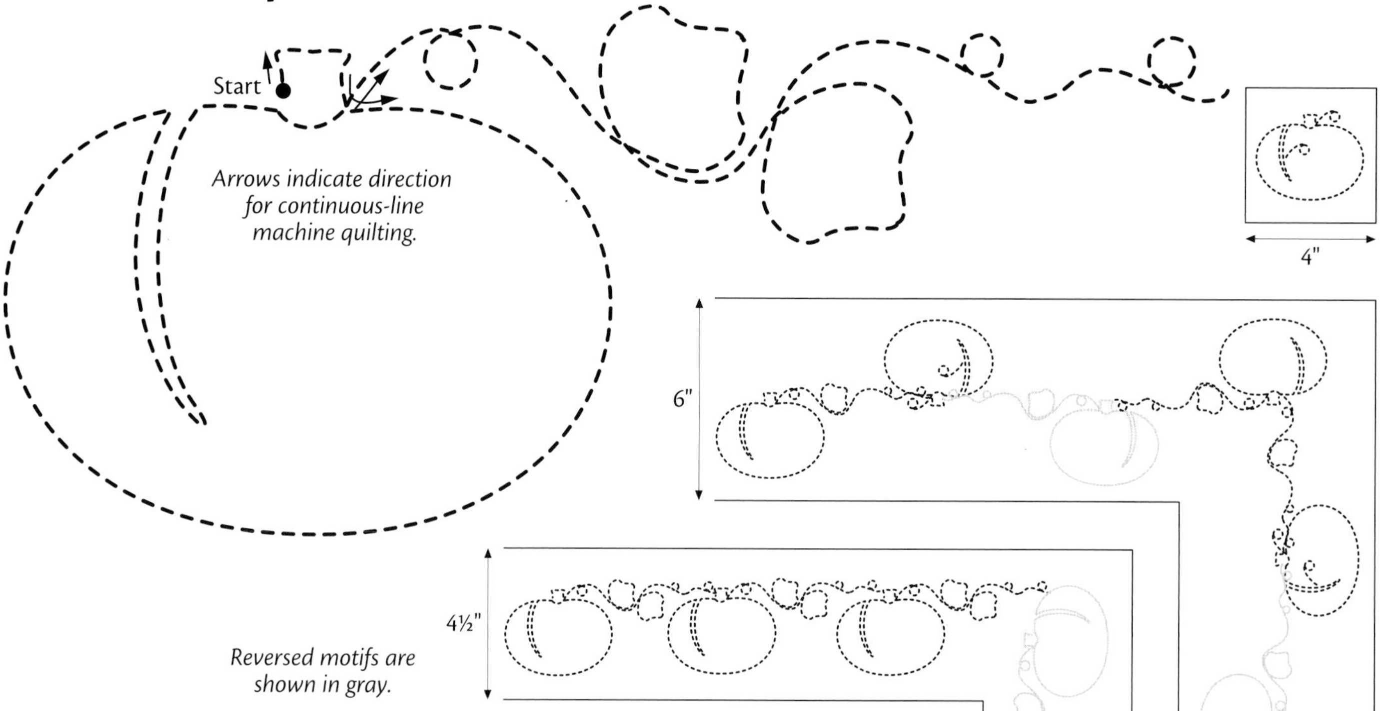
Start
Arrows indicate direction
for continuous-line
machine quilting.
4"
6"
4½"
Reversed motifs are
shown in gray.

Oak and Acorn

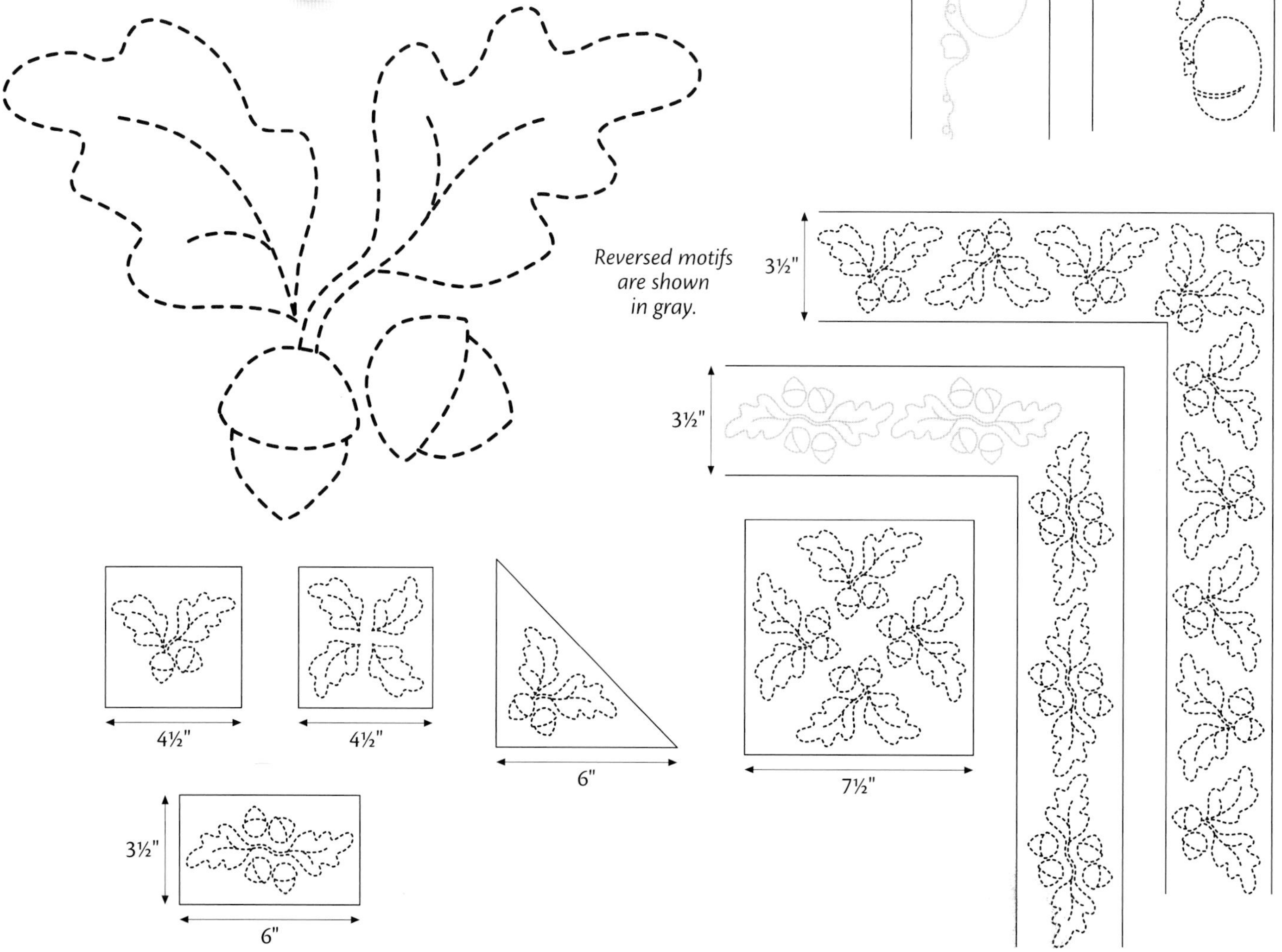
Reversed motifs
are shown
in gray.
3½"
3½"
4½"
4½"
6"
7½"
3½"
6"

Pumpkin Vine

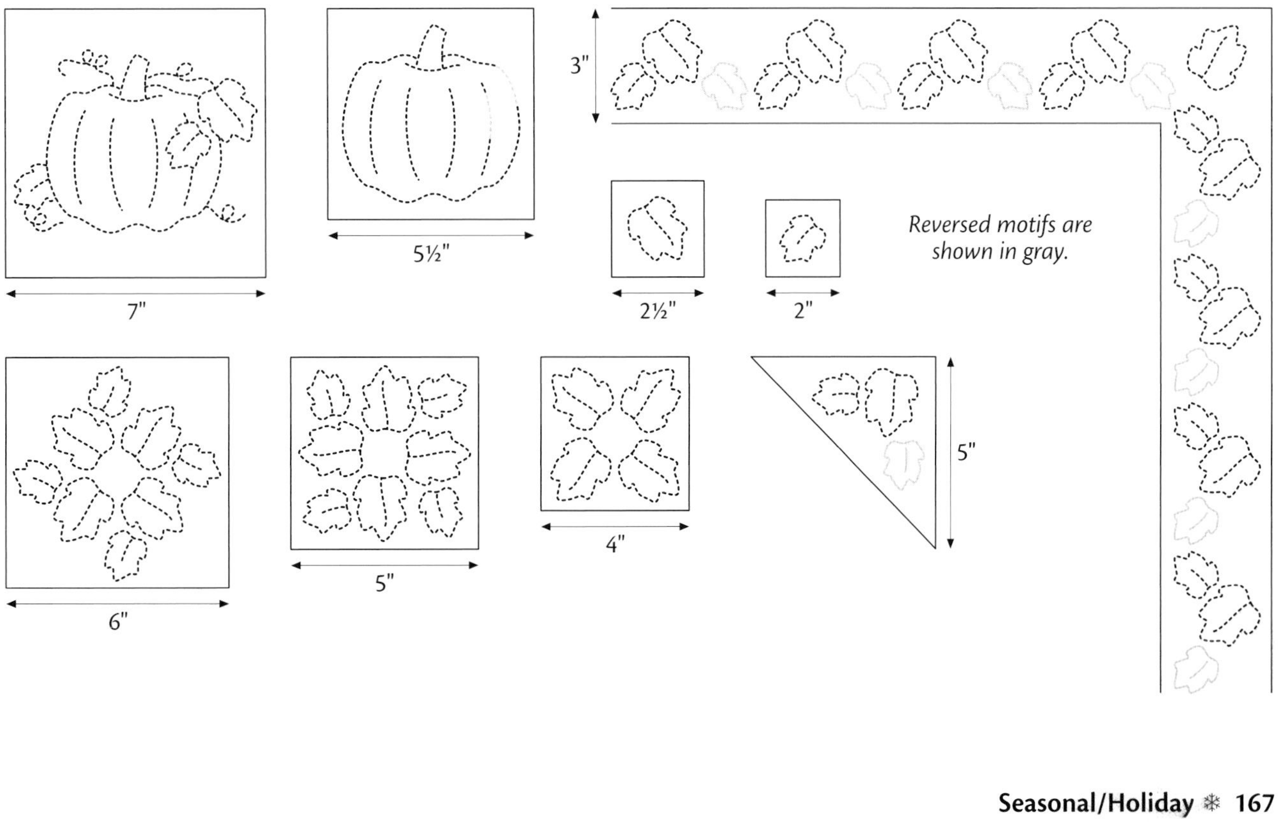
3"
7"
5½"
2½"
2"
Reversed motifs are shown in gray.
6"
5"
4"
5"

Starburst

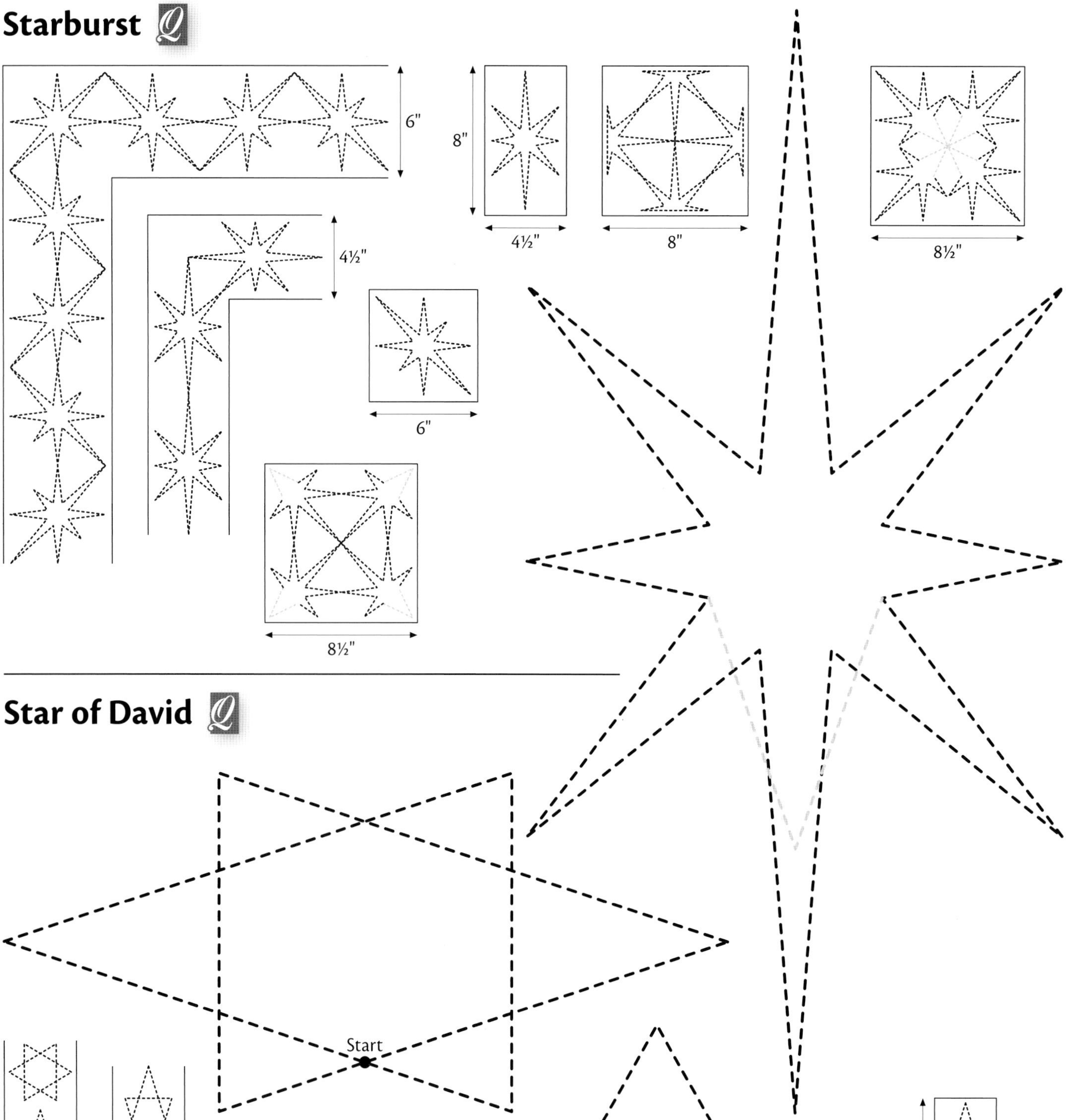
6"
4½"
8"
4½"
8"
8½"
6"
8½"

Star of David

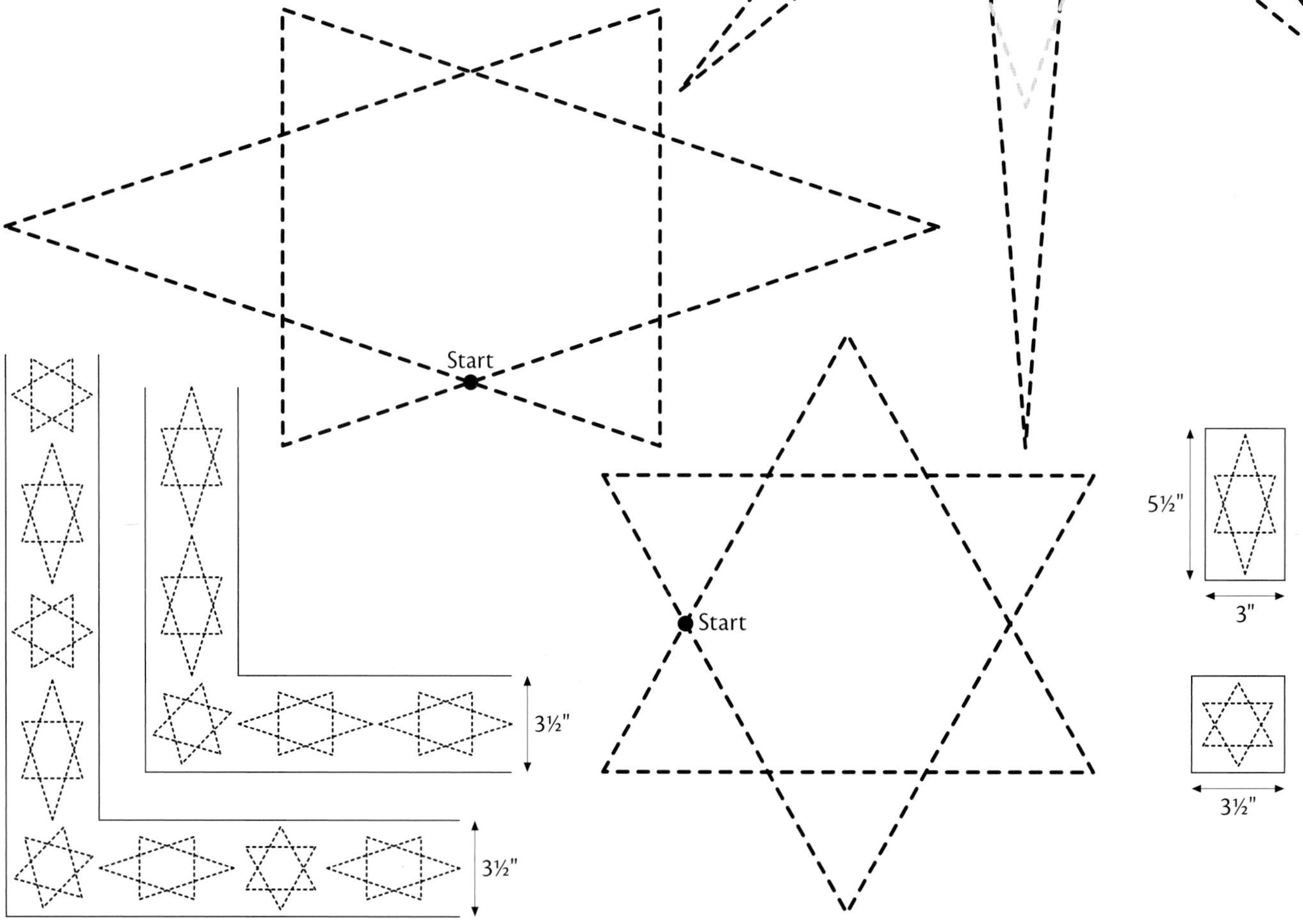
Start
Start
5½"
3"
3½"
3½"
3½"

Piney Woods

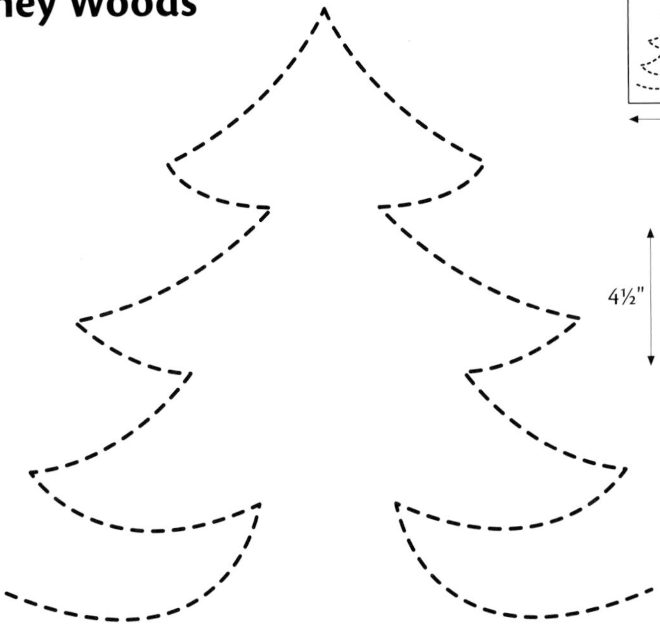

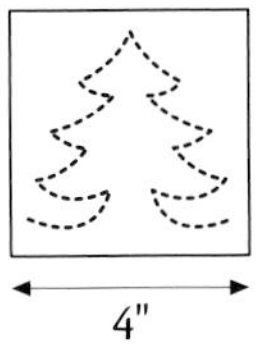

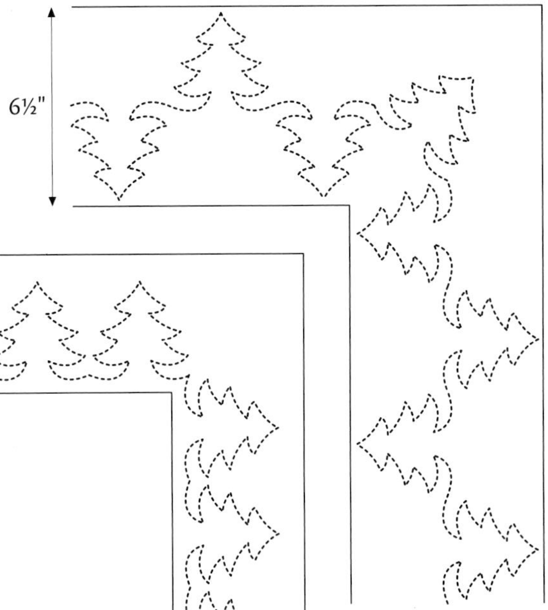

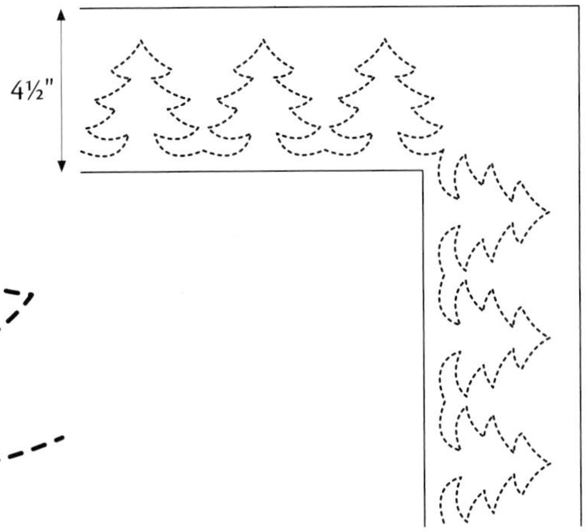

Heavenly Dove

Arrow indicates direction for continuous-line machine quilting.

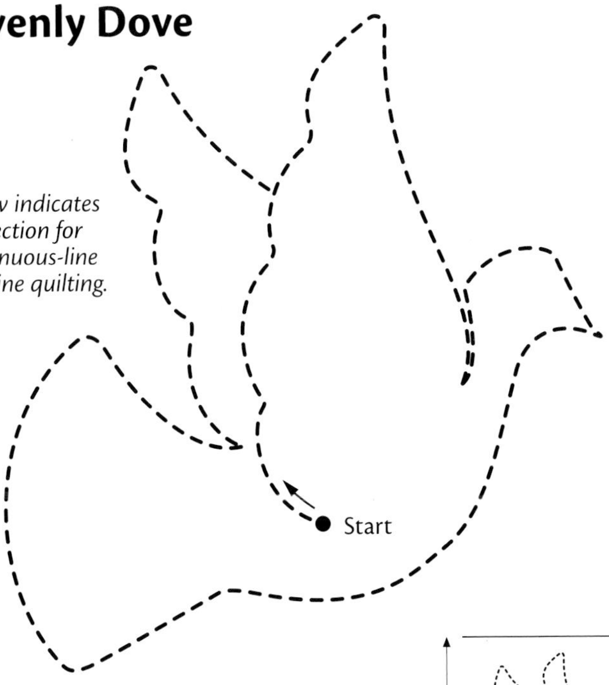

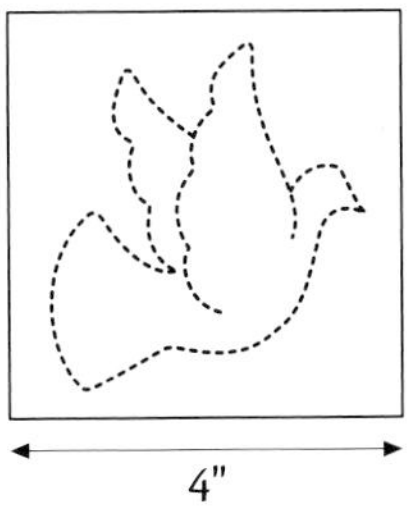

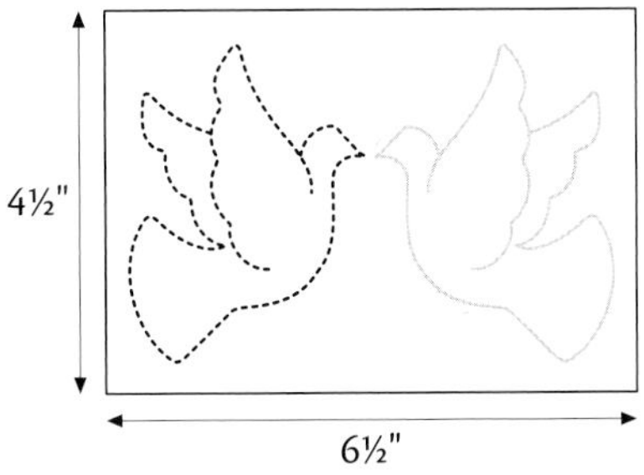

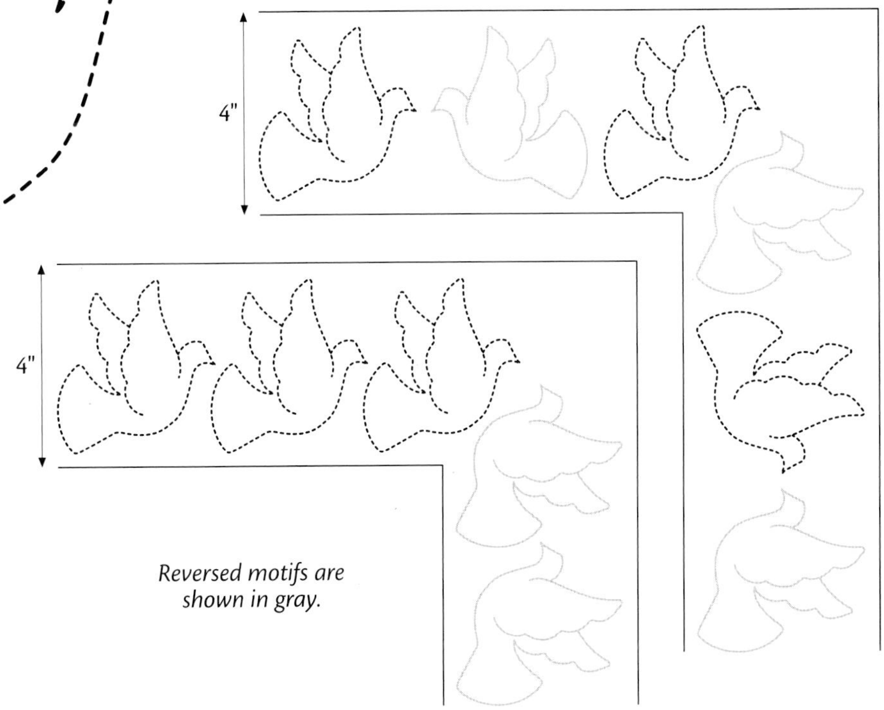

Reversed motifs are shown in gray.

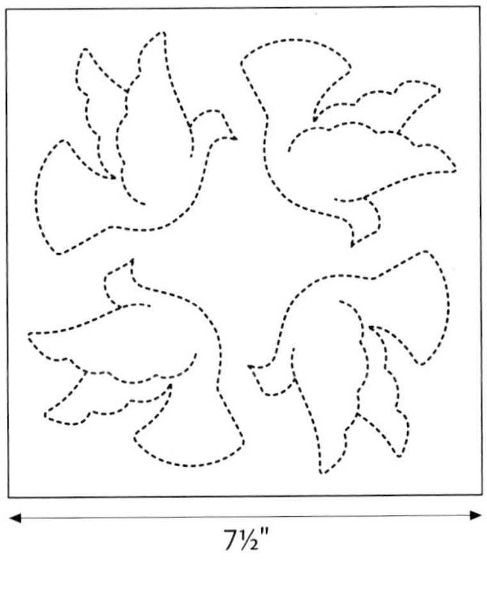

Poinsettia Garland

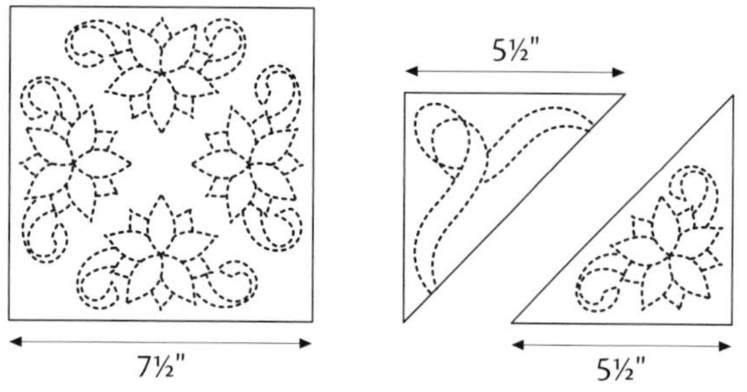

7½"
5½"
5½"

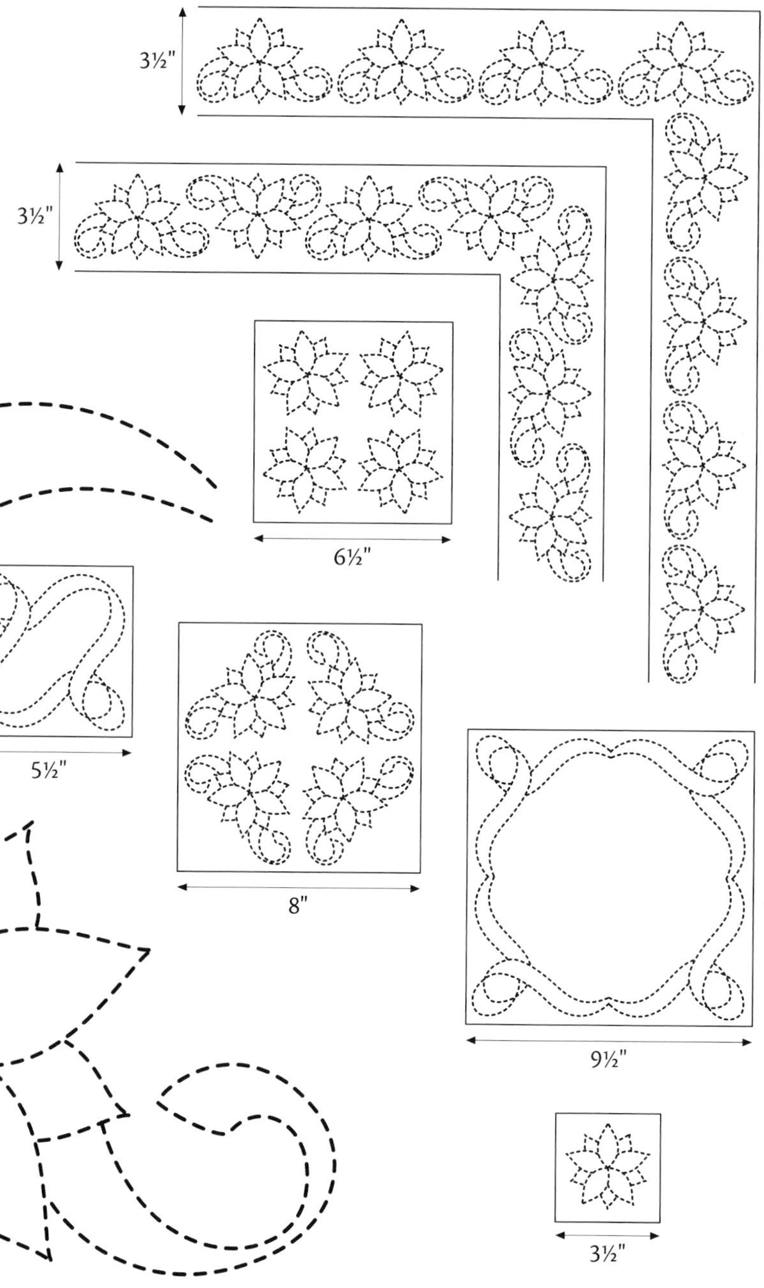

3½"
3½"
6½"
5½"
8"
9½"
3½"

Li'l Mitten

Reversed motifs are shown in gray.

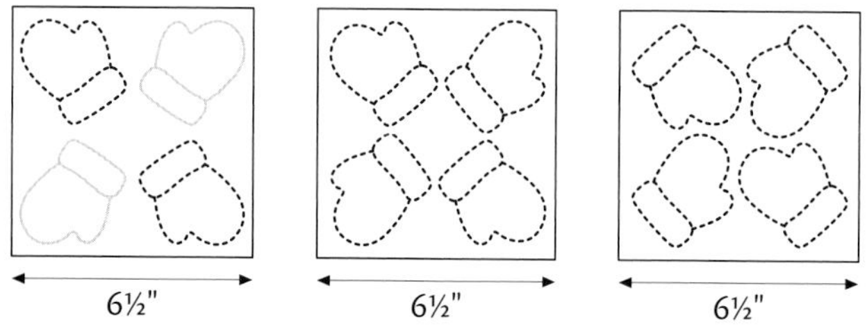

6½"
6½"
6½"

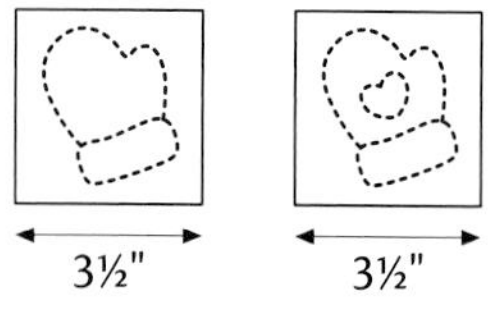

3½"
3½"

3½"

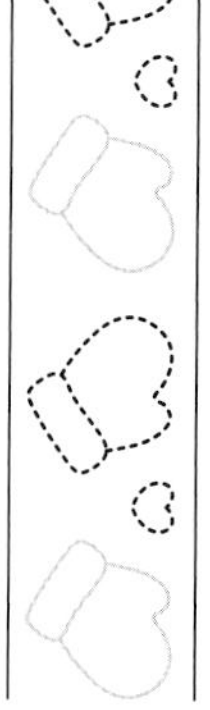

Use the heart from Hearts Abloom, page 155, to decorate the mitten or to accent the border design.

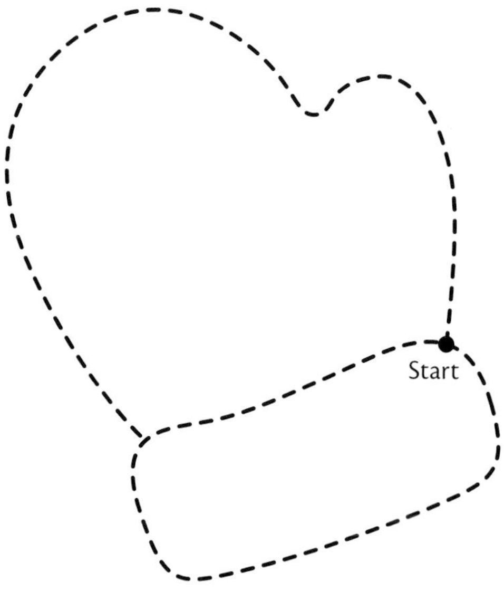

Start

Poinsettia Wreath

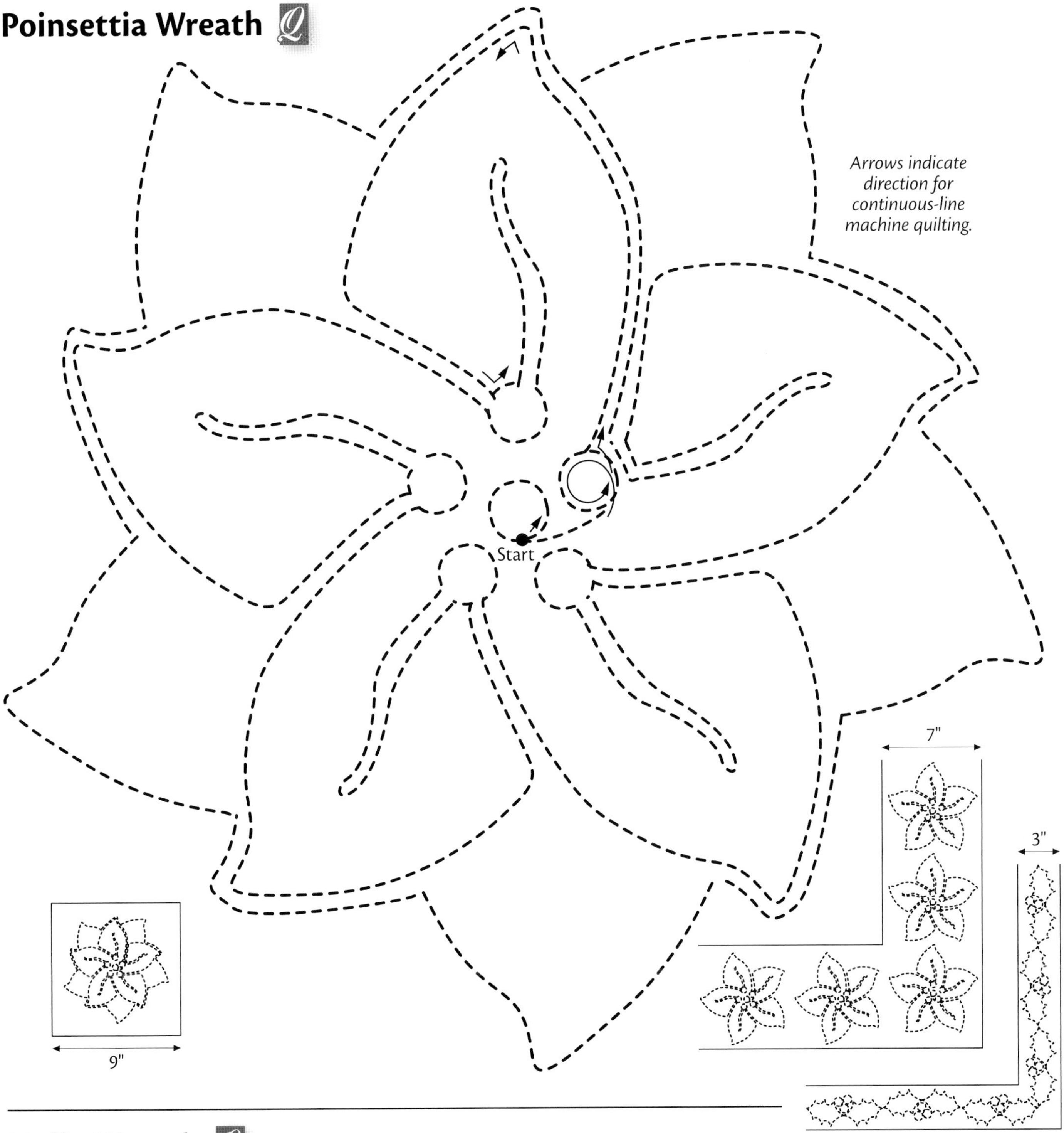

Arrows indicate direction for continuous-line machine quilting.

Holly Wreath

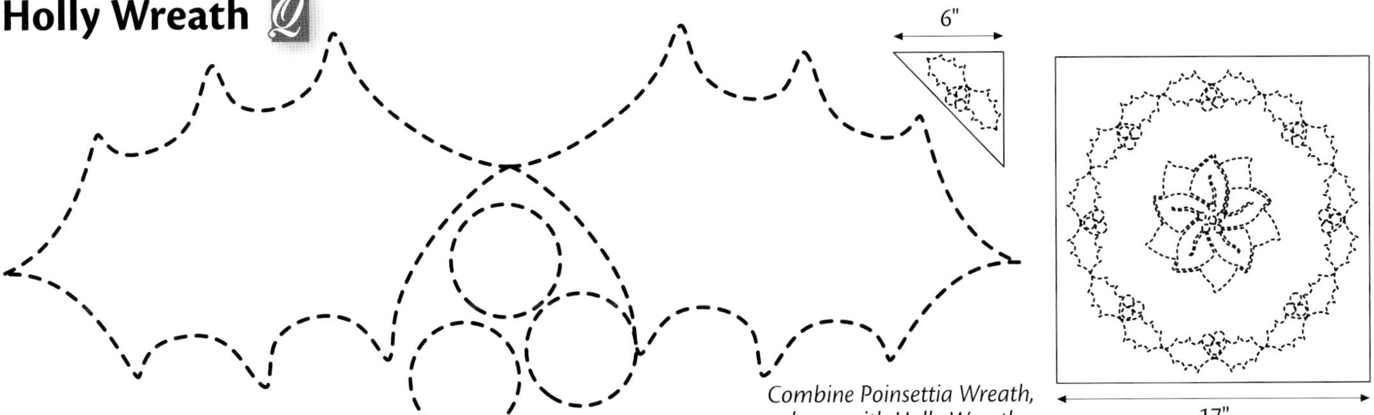

Combine Poinsettia Wreath, above, with Holly Wreath.

Holly and Ribbon

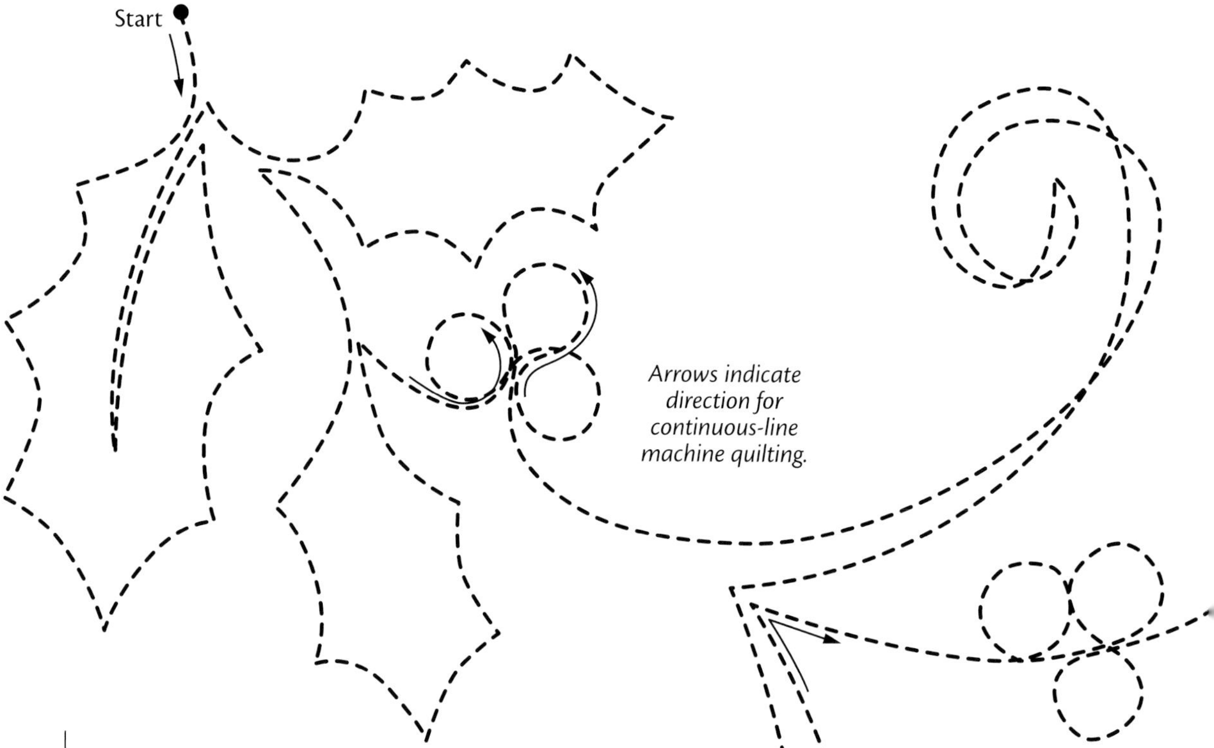

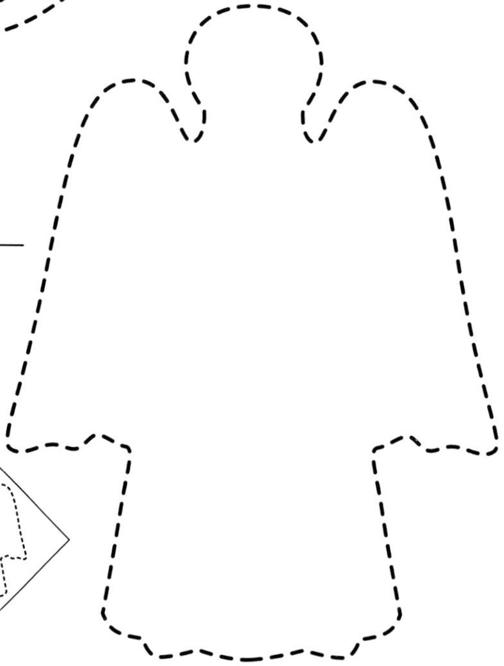

Angel

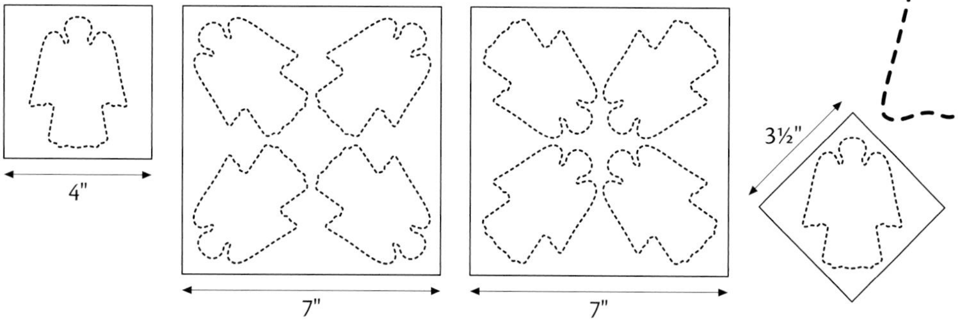

Poinsettia

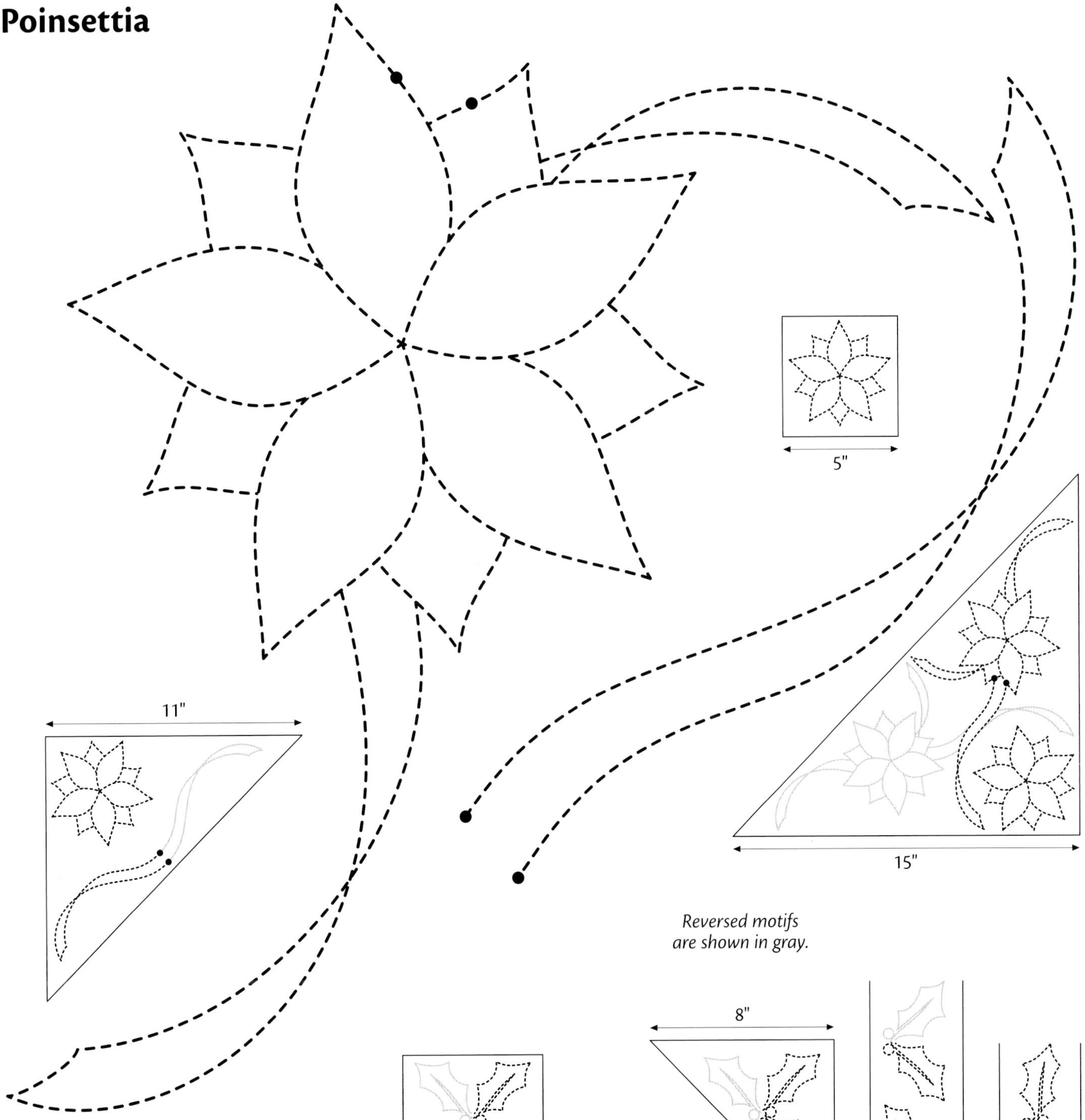

5"
11"
15"

Reversed motifs are shown in gray.

Holly

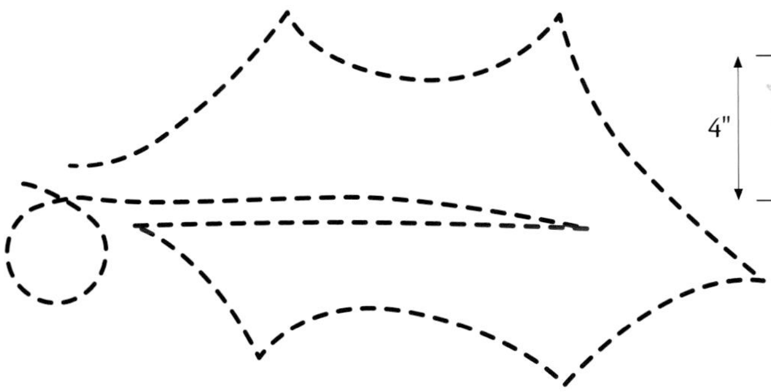

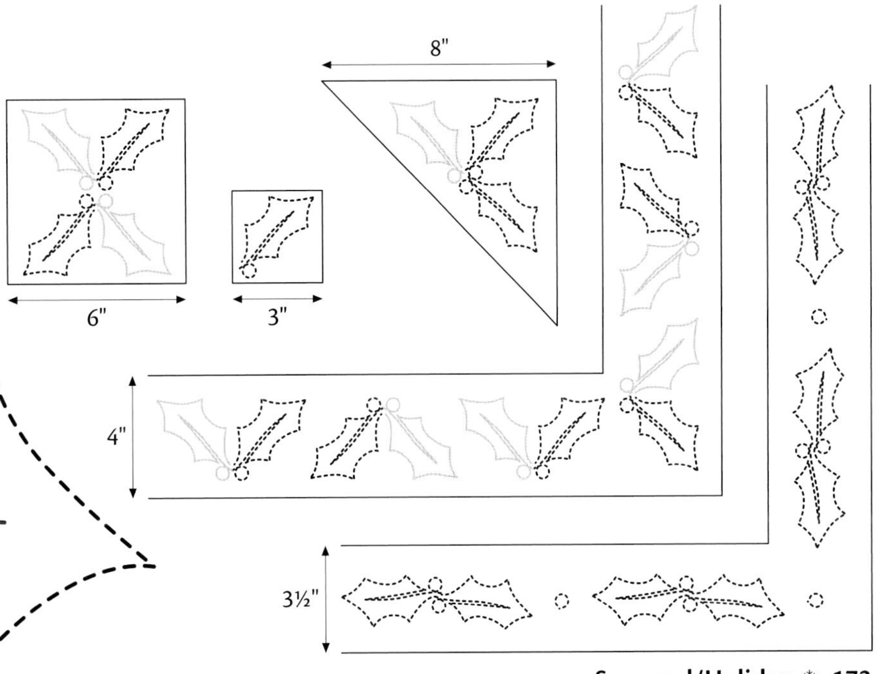

8"
6"
3"
4"
3½"

Hollyberry

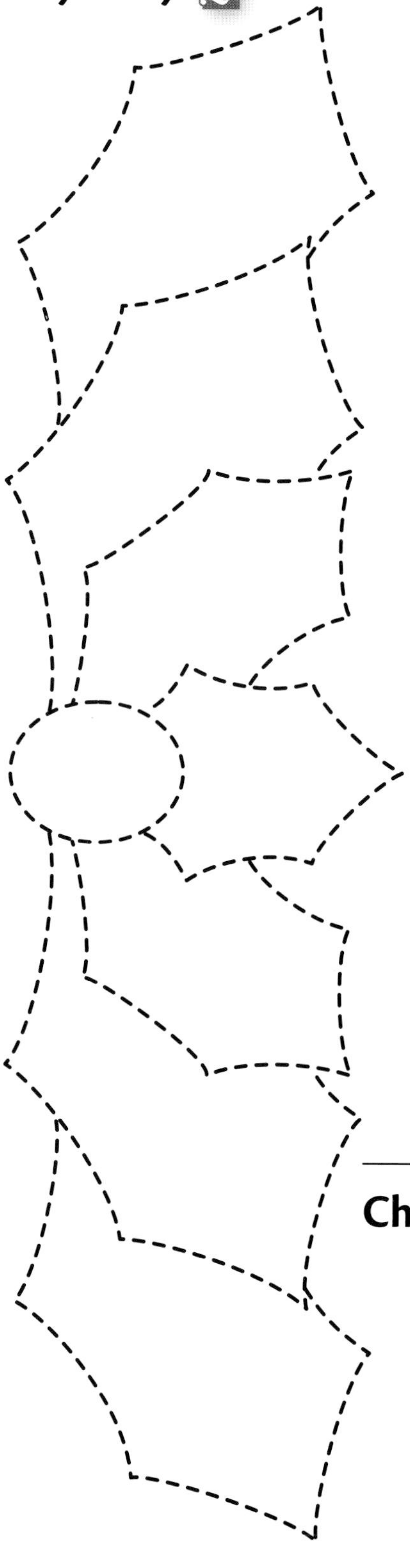

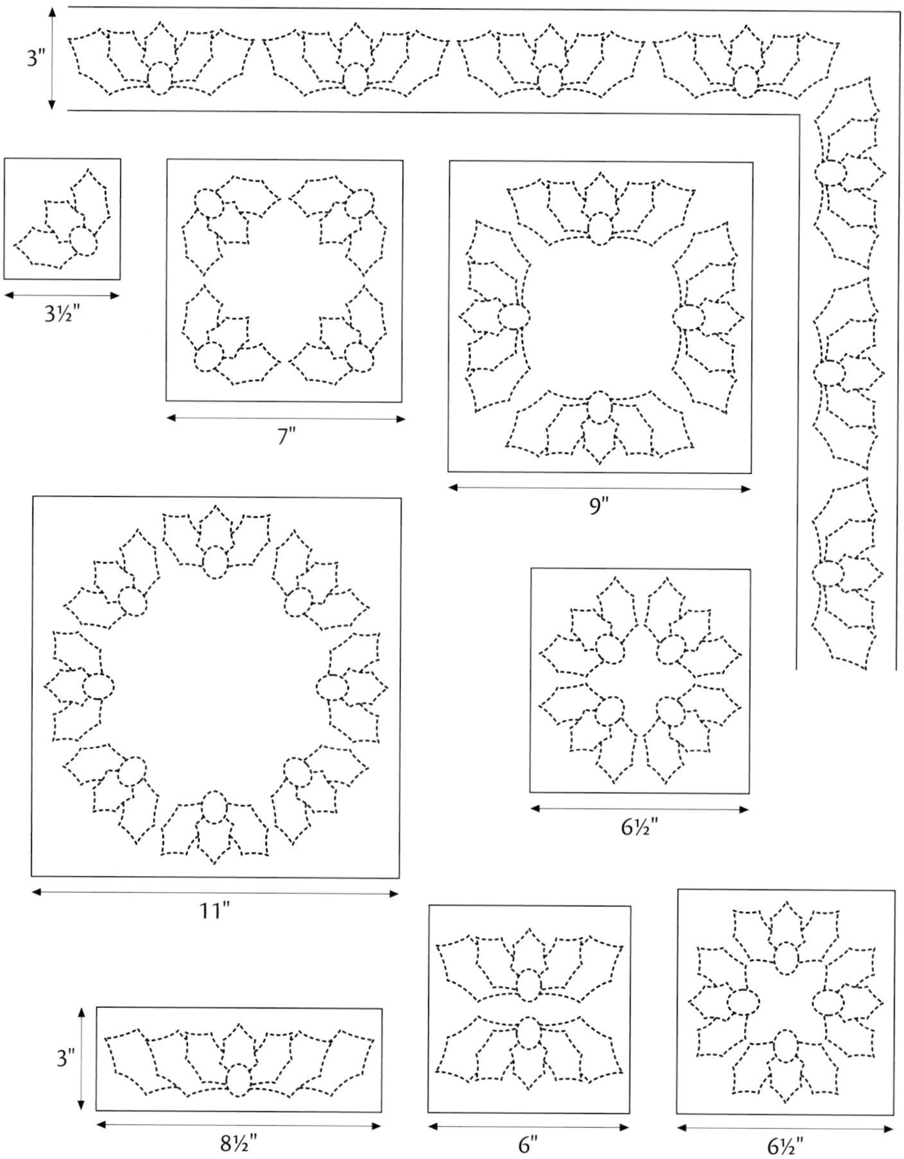
3"
3½"
7"
9"
11"
6½"
3"
8½"
6"
6½"

Christmas Lights

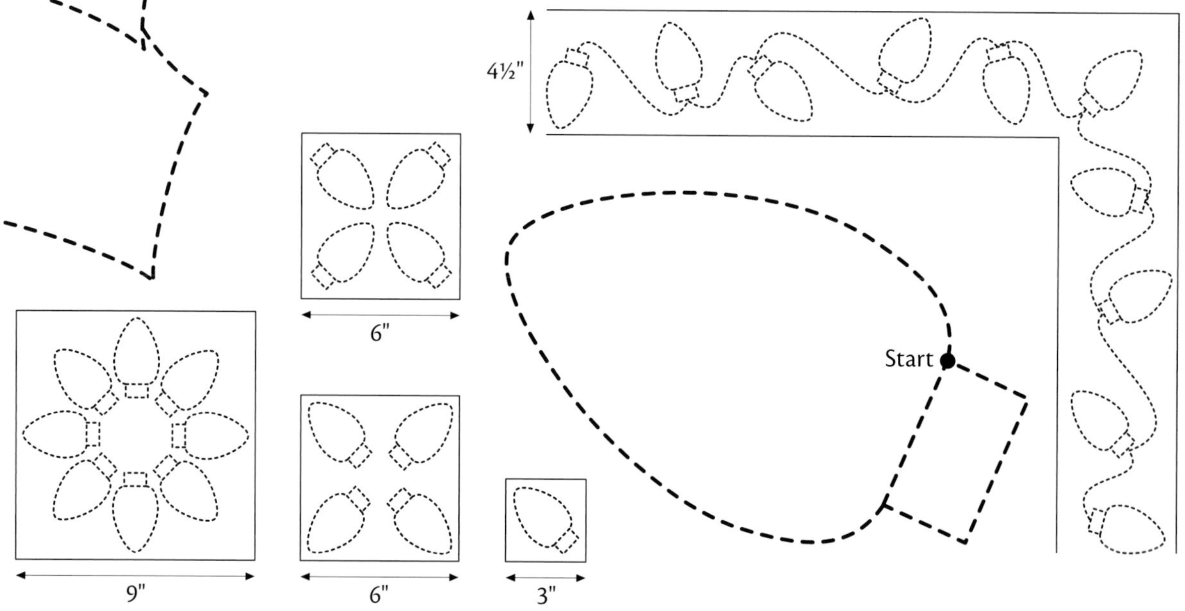
4½"
6"
Start
9"
6"
3"

Bow Tie

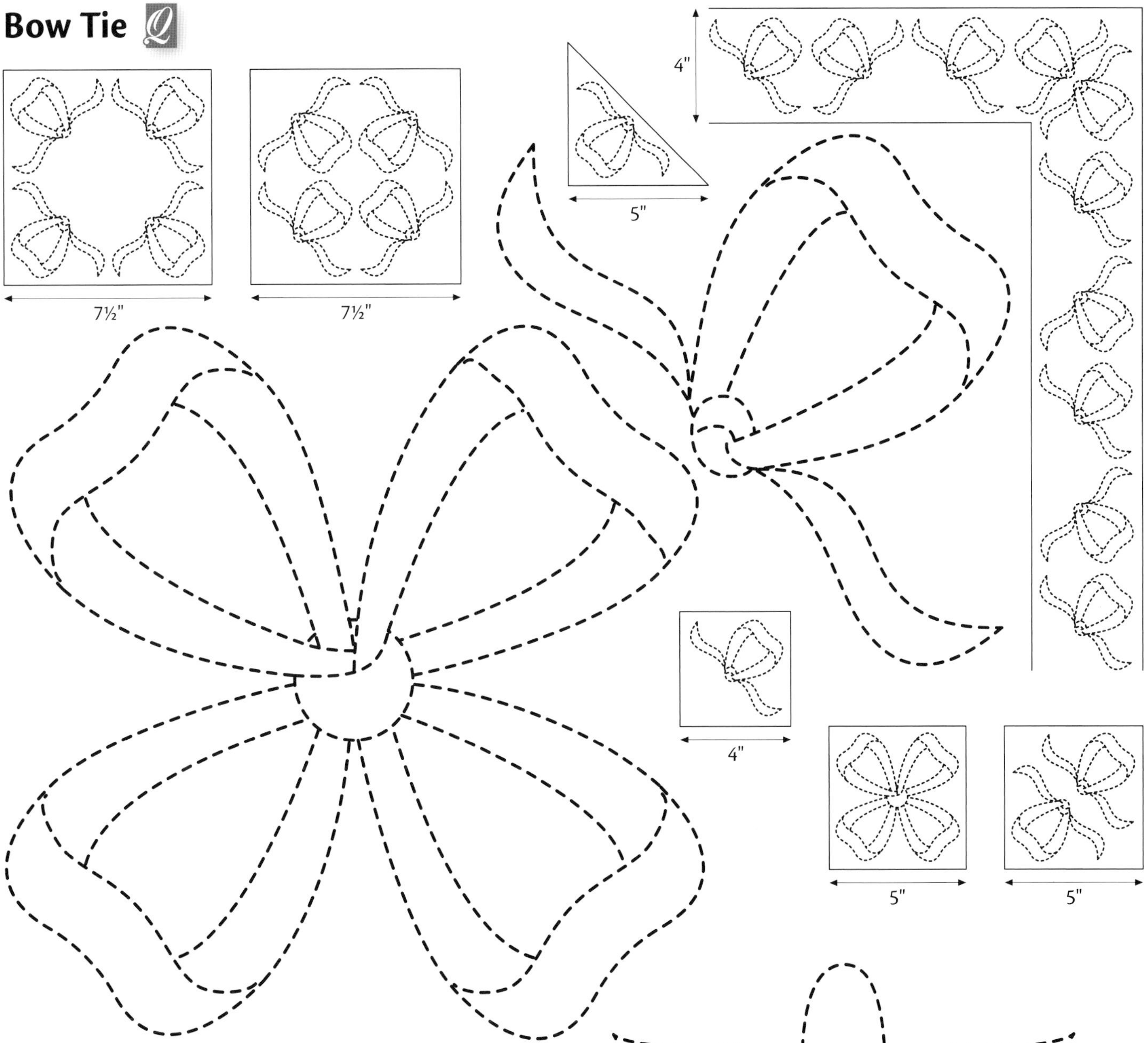
7½"
7½"
5"
4"
4"
5"
5"

Snow Crystal 1

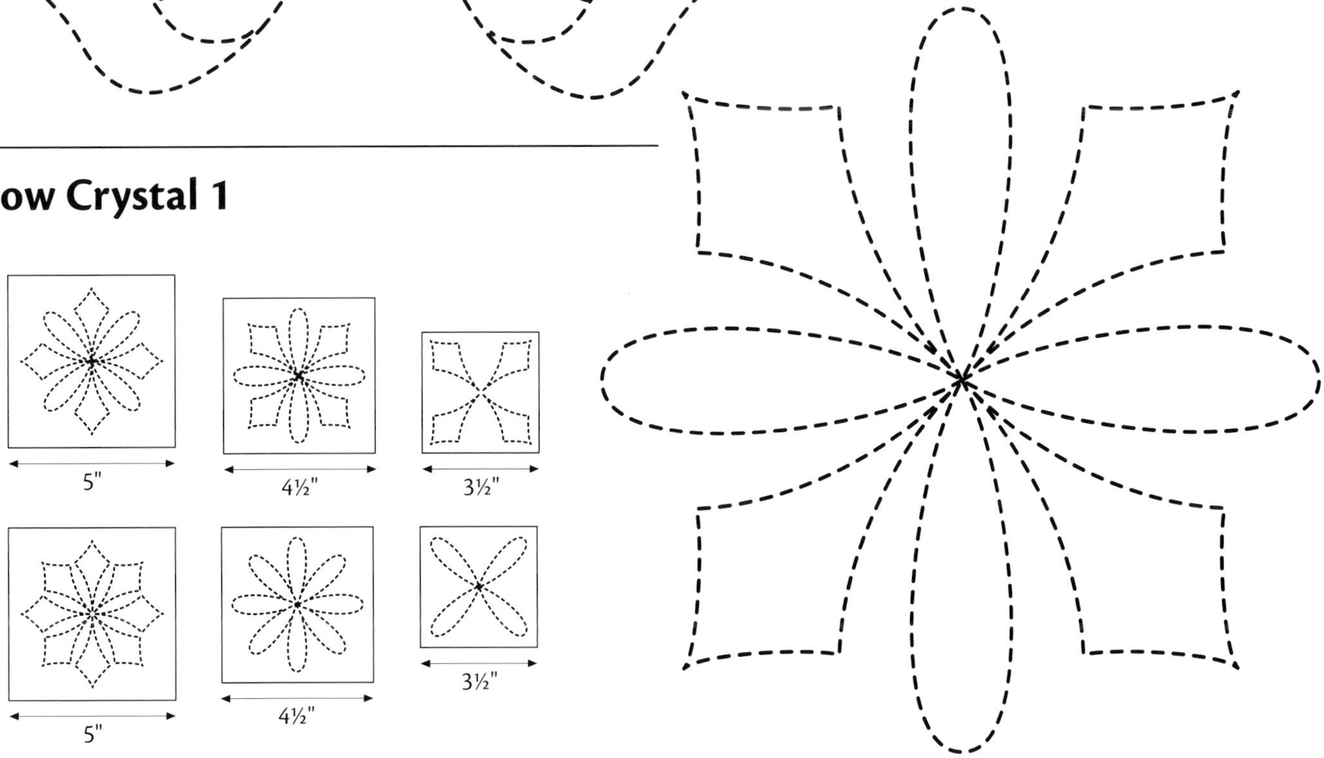
5"
4½"
3½"
5"
4½"
3½"

Snow Crystal 2

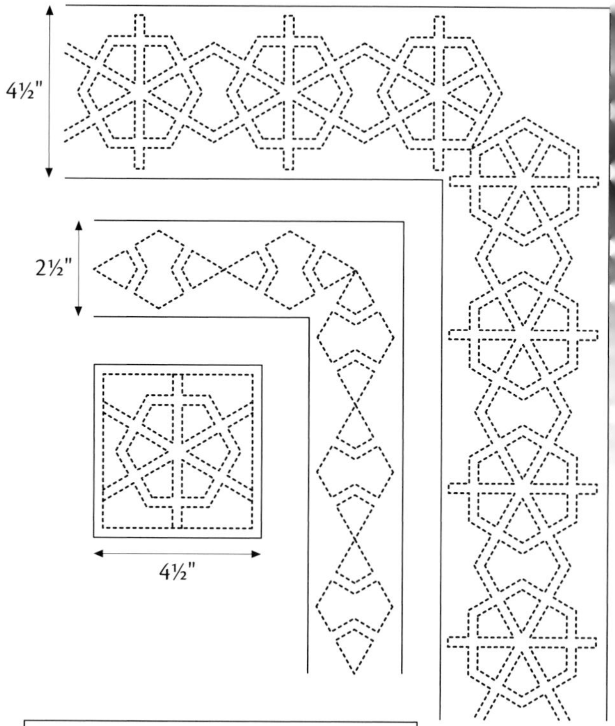

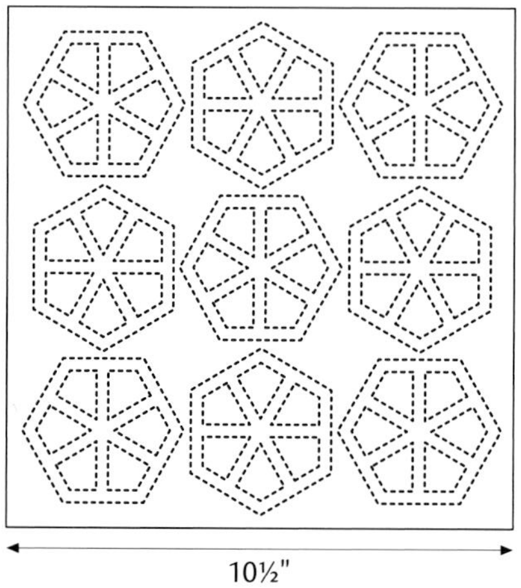

Snowflake

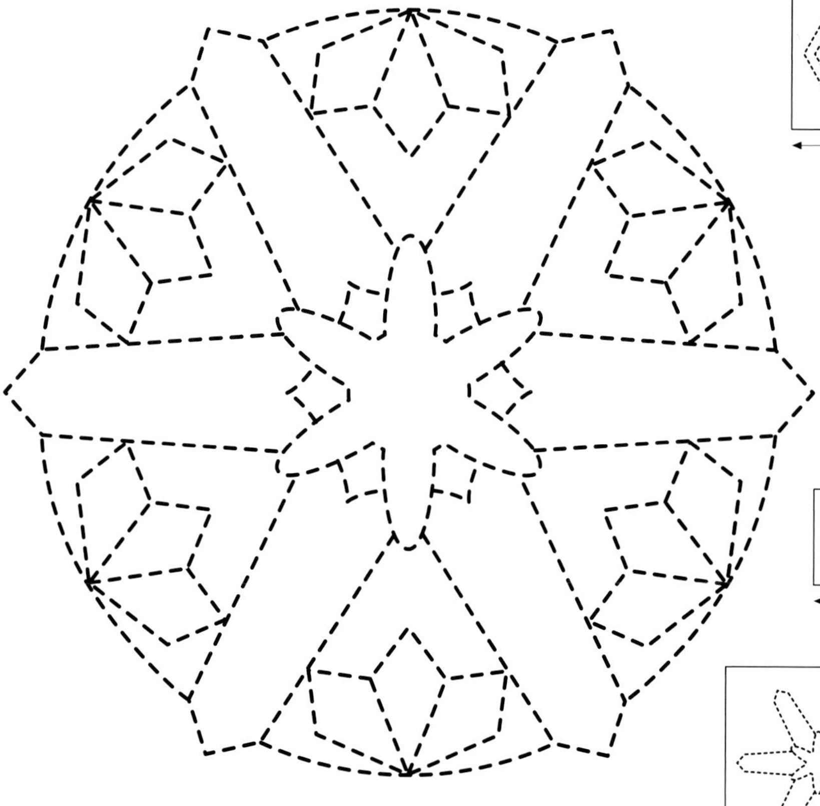

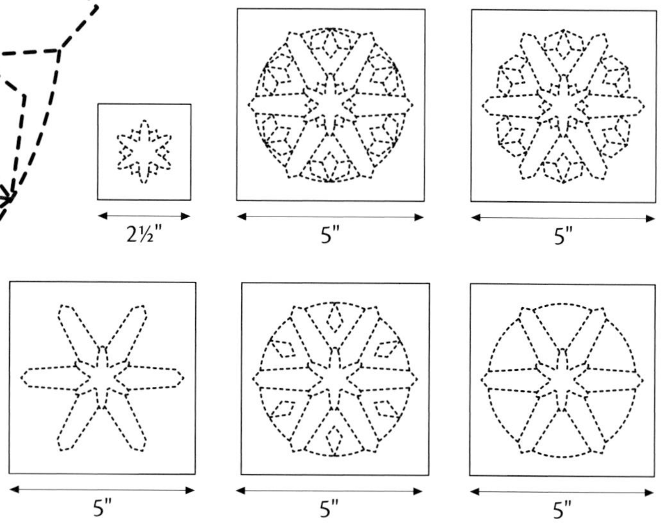

Vines and Leaves

Grapevine

Center for
3" border
3"
3"
6½"
7½"
5½"
7½"
5"
4"
3"
Arrows indicate
direction for
continuous-line
machine quilting.
Start
6"

Leafy Vine

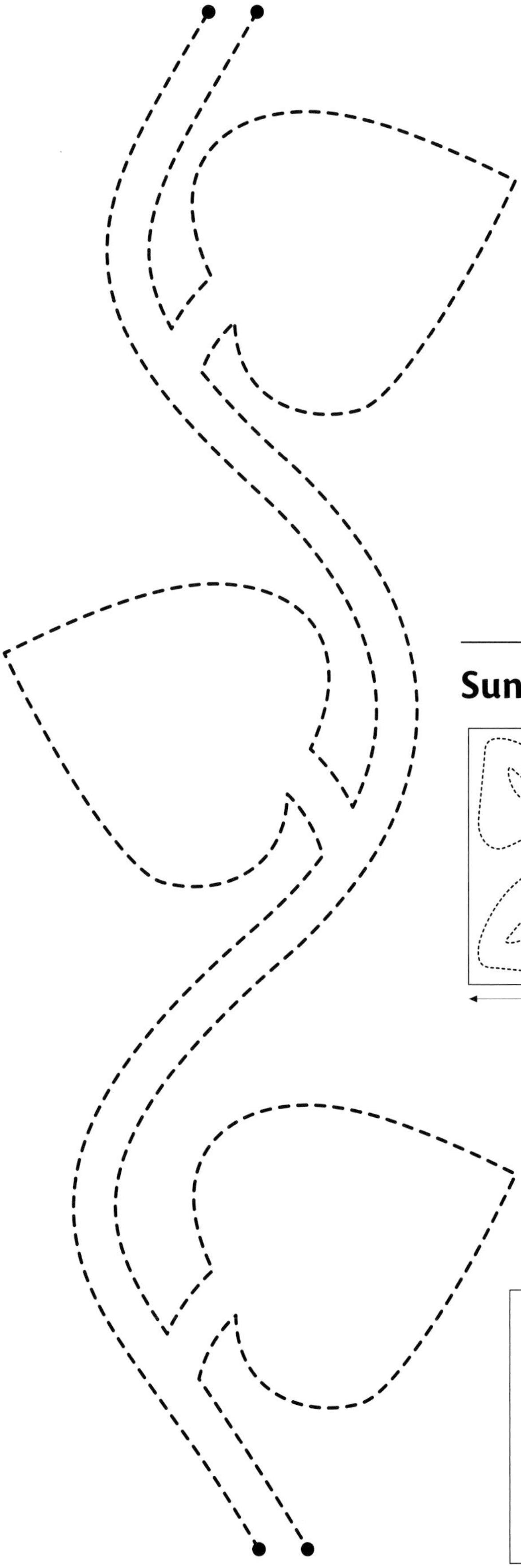

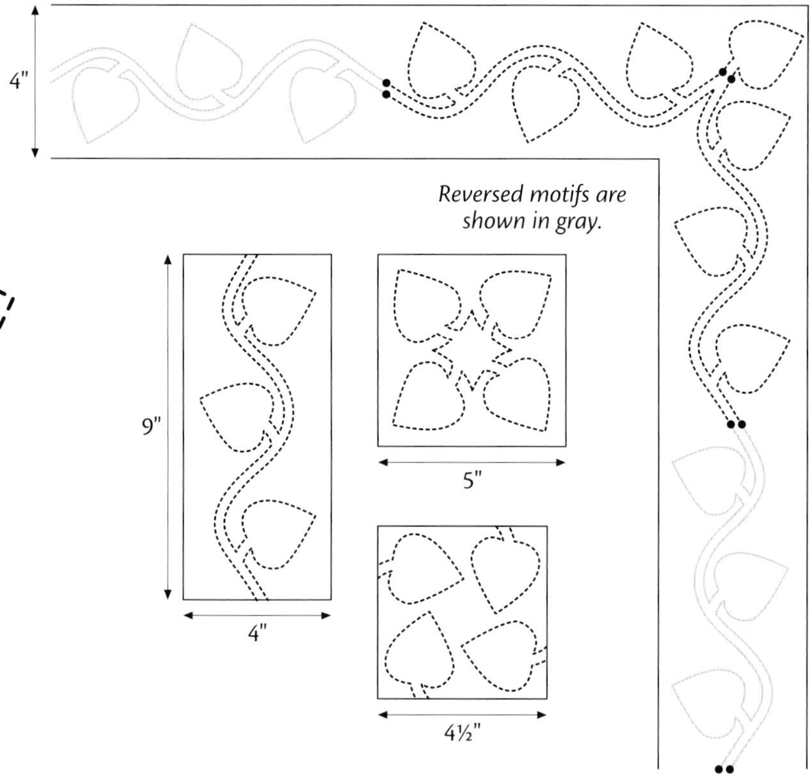

Reversed motifs are shown in gray.

Sunsprite

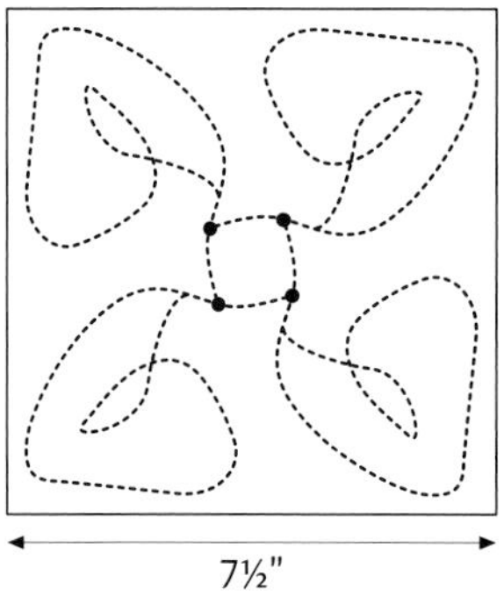

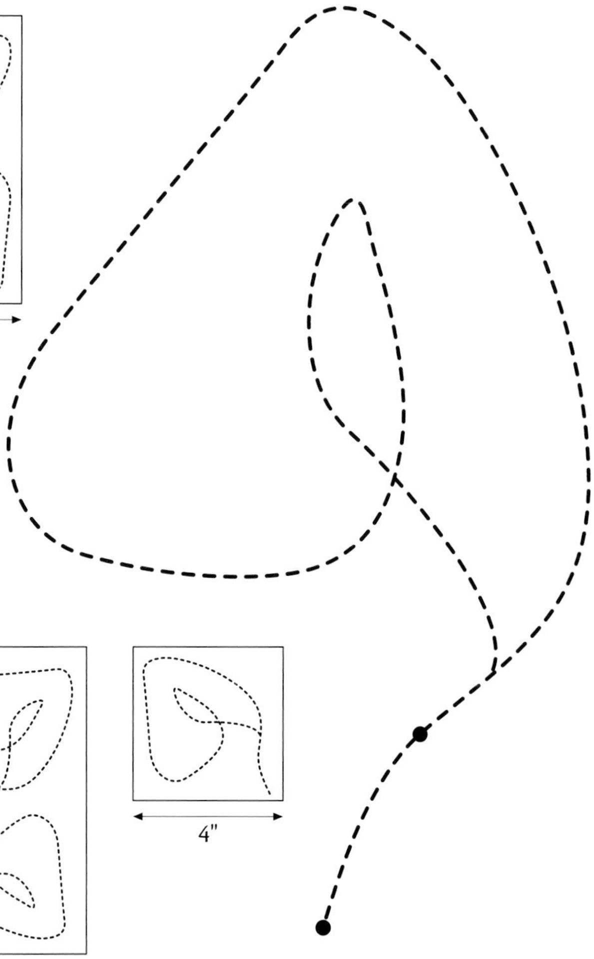

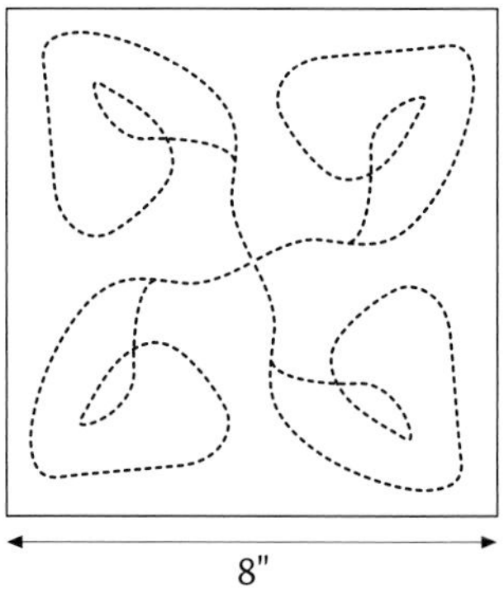

Budding Vine

3½"
12"
6"
4"
6"
5"
4"
3½"
5½"
7½"
9"
10"
7"
8" (5" circle)
10"
5"

Reversed motifs are shown in gray.

Ivy 1

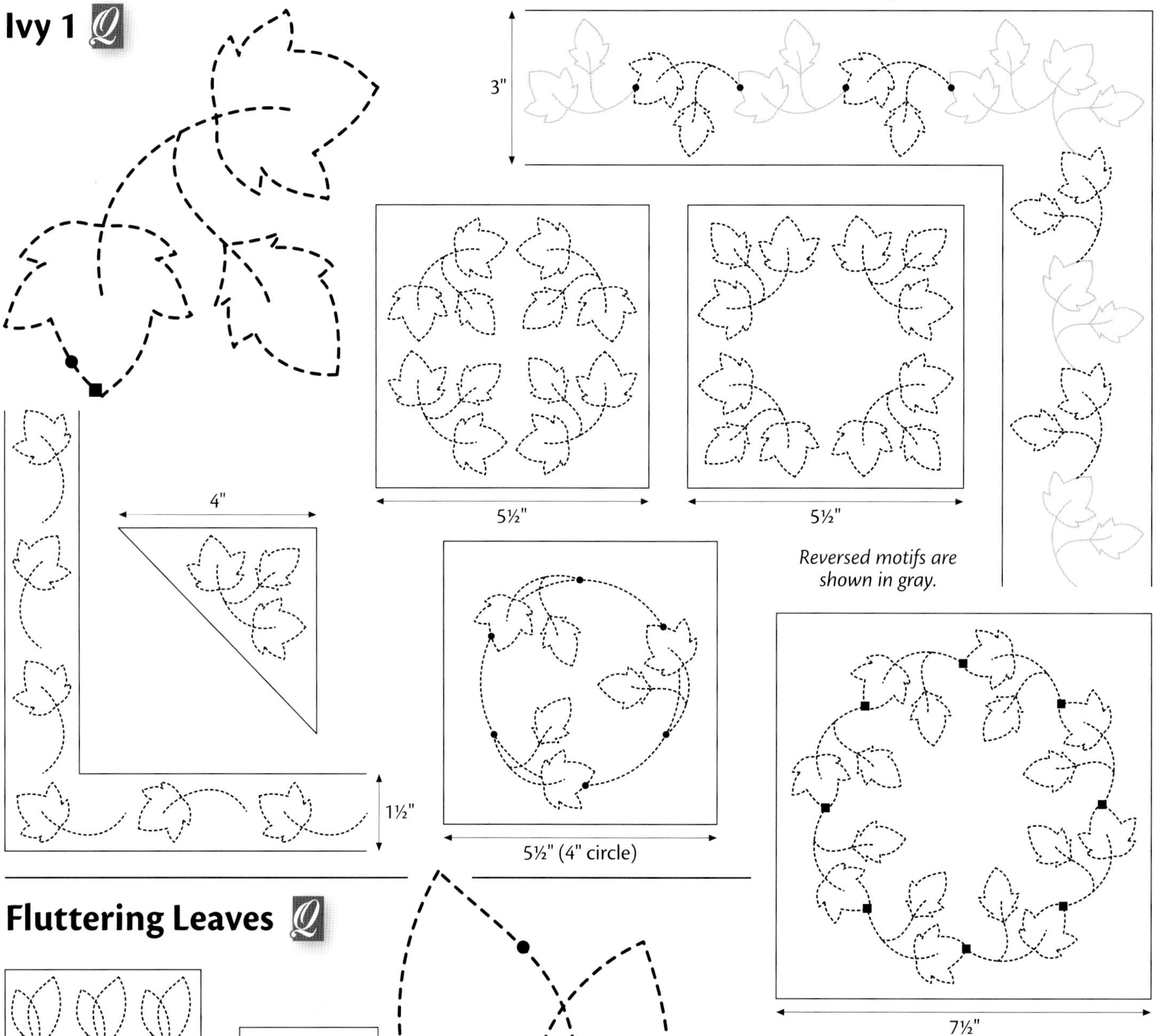

3"
5½"
5½"
4"
1½"
5½" (4" circle)
7½"

Reversed motifs are shown in gray.

Fluttering Leaves

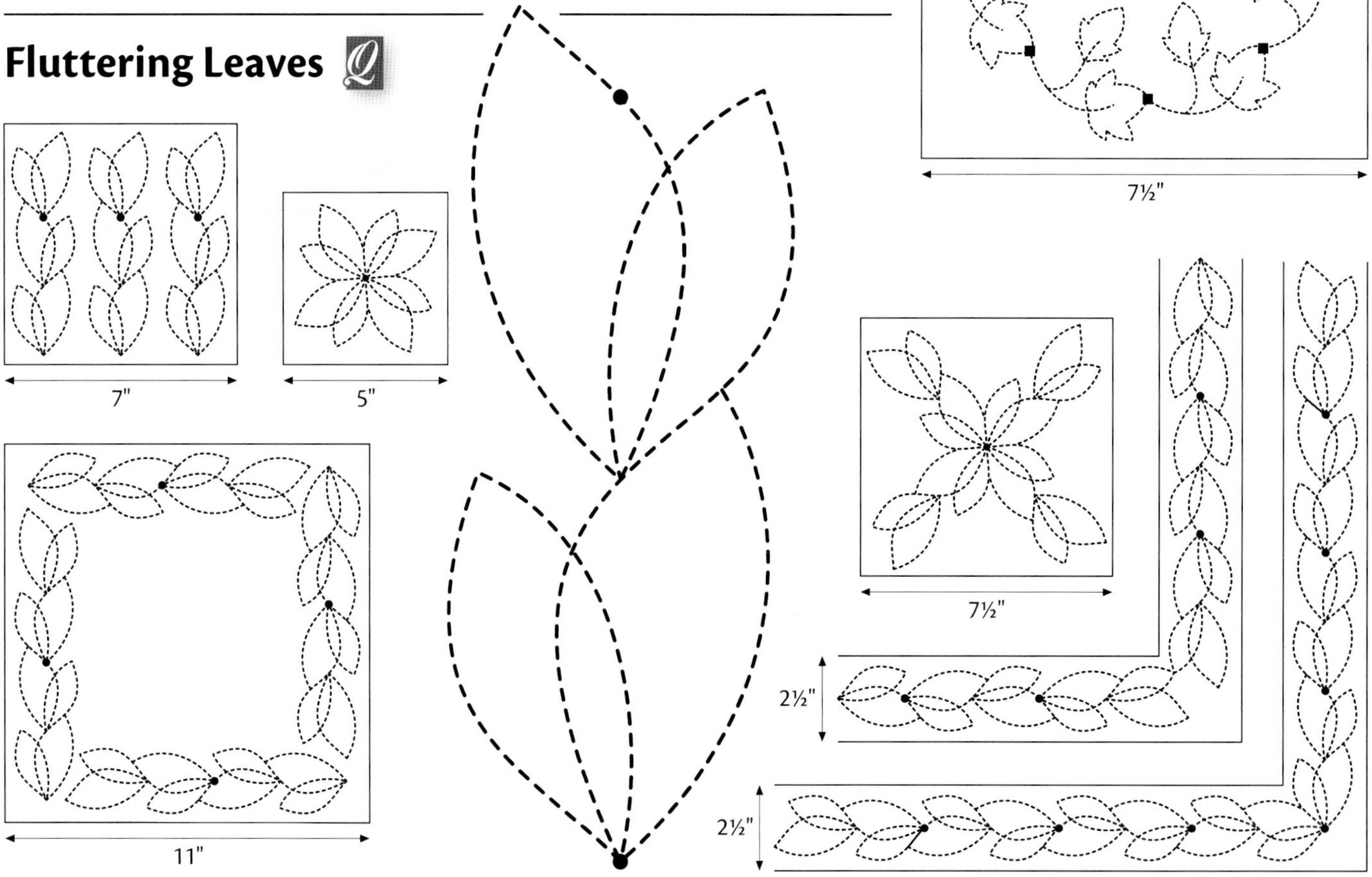

7"
5"
11"
7½"
2½"
2½"

Versatile Ivy

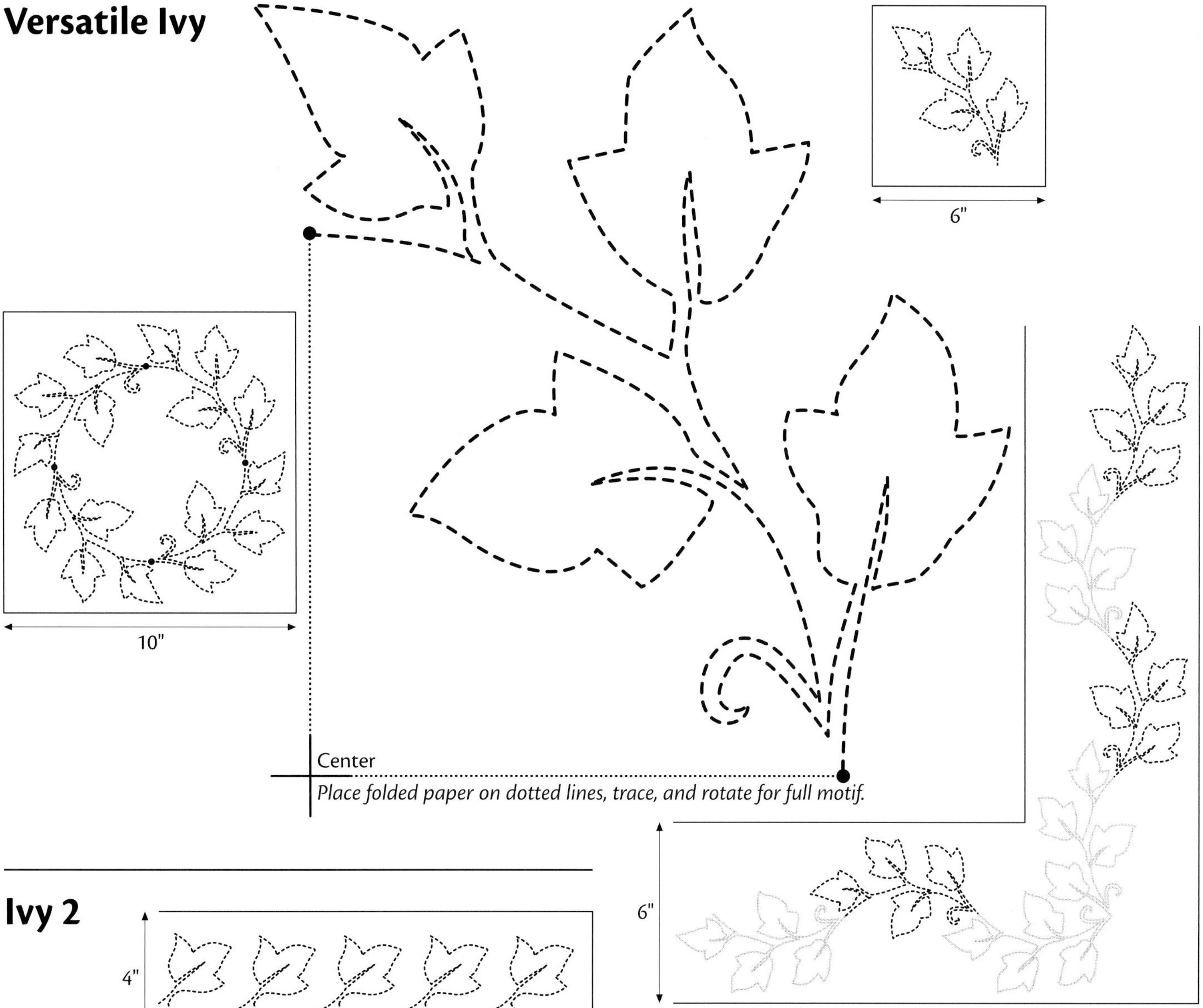
6"
10"
Center
Place folded paper on dotted lines, trace, and rotate for full motif.
6"

Reversed motifs are shown in gray.

16"

Ivy 2

4"
3"
5"
6½"

Leaf Cable

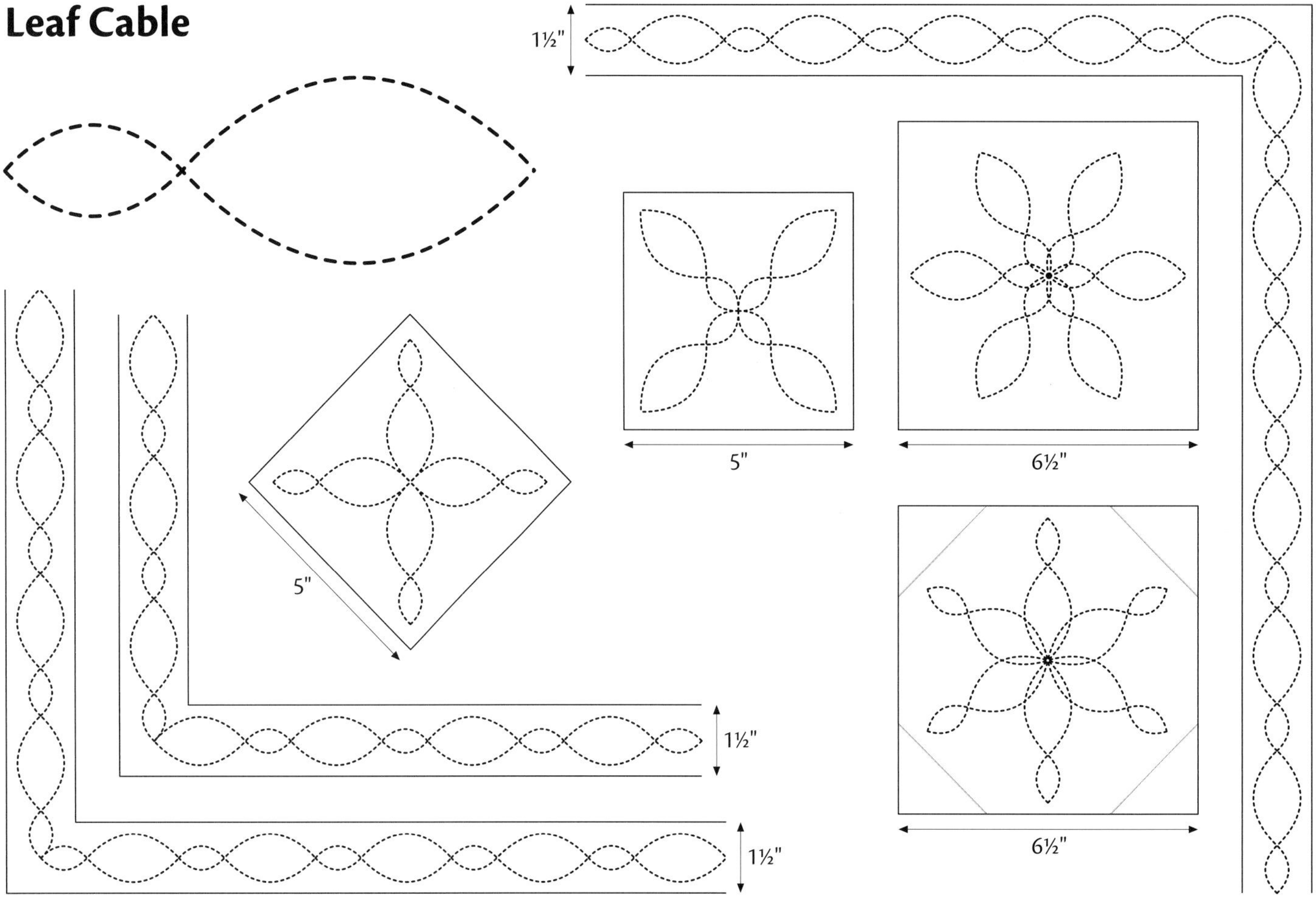
1½"
5"
6½"
5"
6½"
1½"
1½"

Mother's Garden

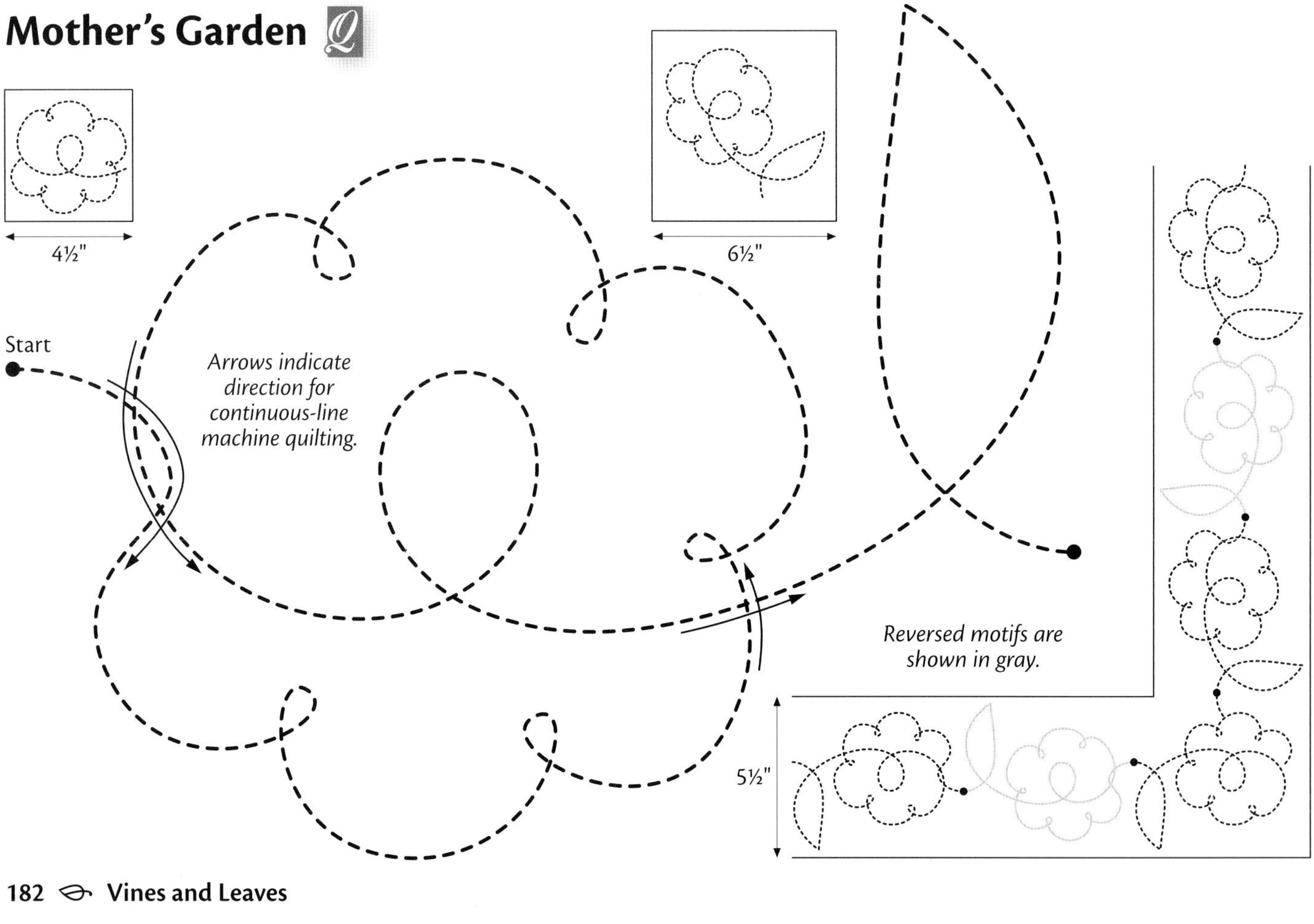
4½"
6½"
Start
Arrows indicate direction for continuous-line machine quilting.
Reversed motifs are shown in gray.
5½"

Autumn Leaves

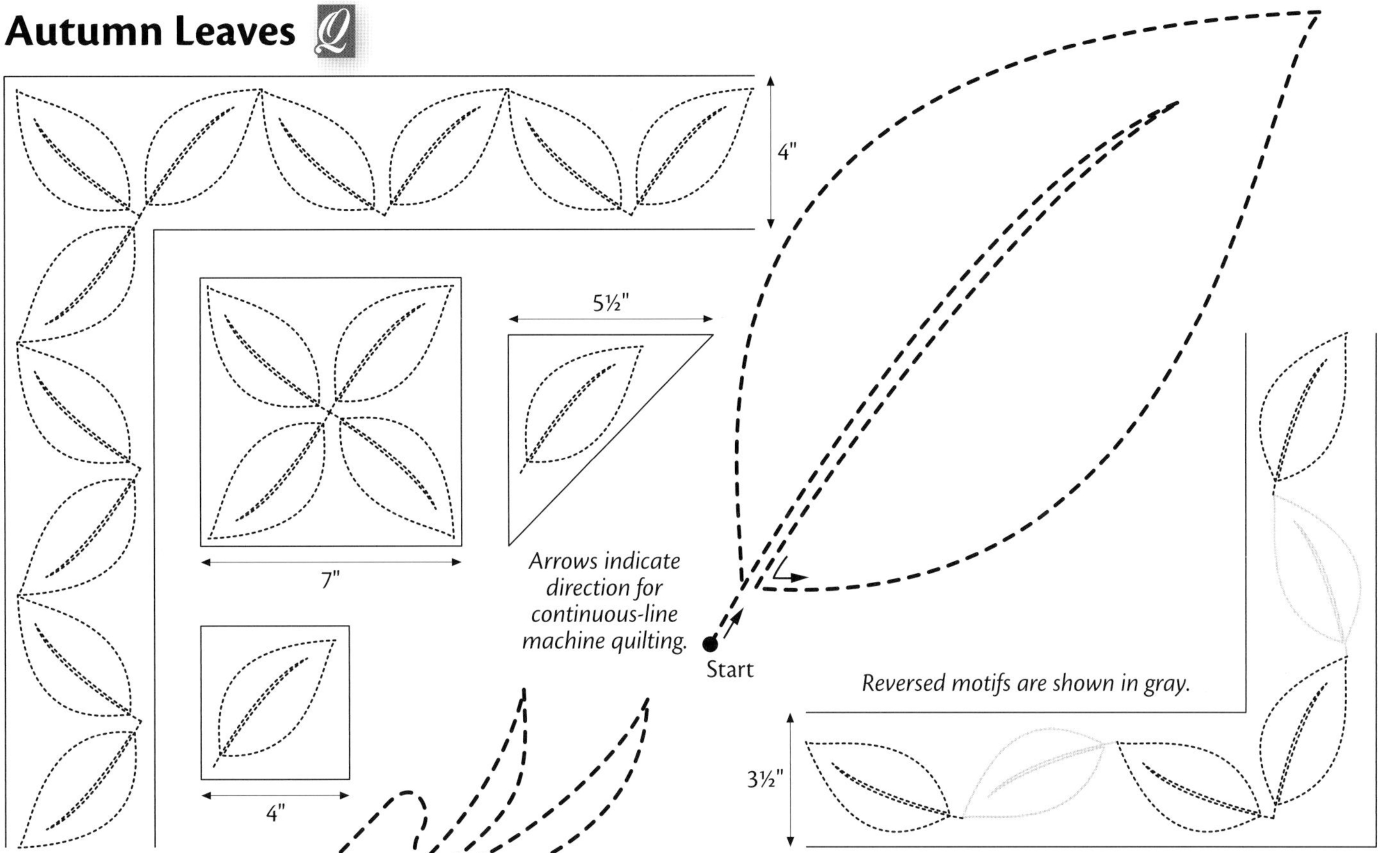
4"
7"
5½"
4"
Arrows indicate direction for continuous-line machine quilting.
Start
Reversed motifs are shown in gray.
3½"

Bamboo

4"
9"
6½"
9"

Leaf Spray

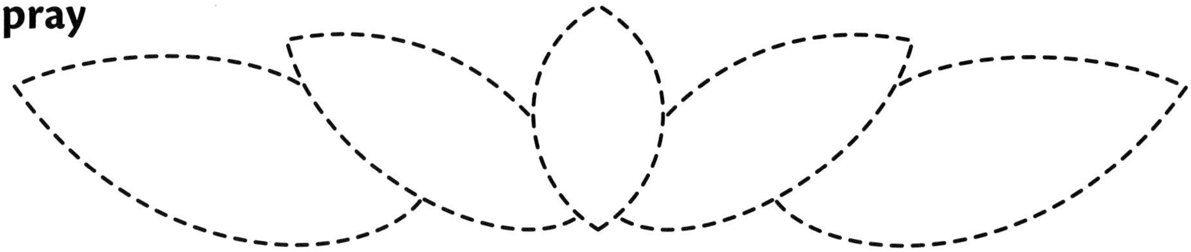

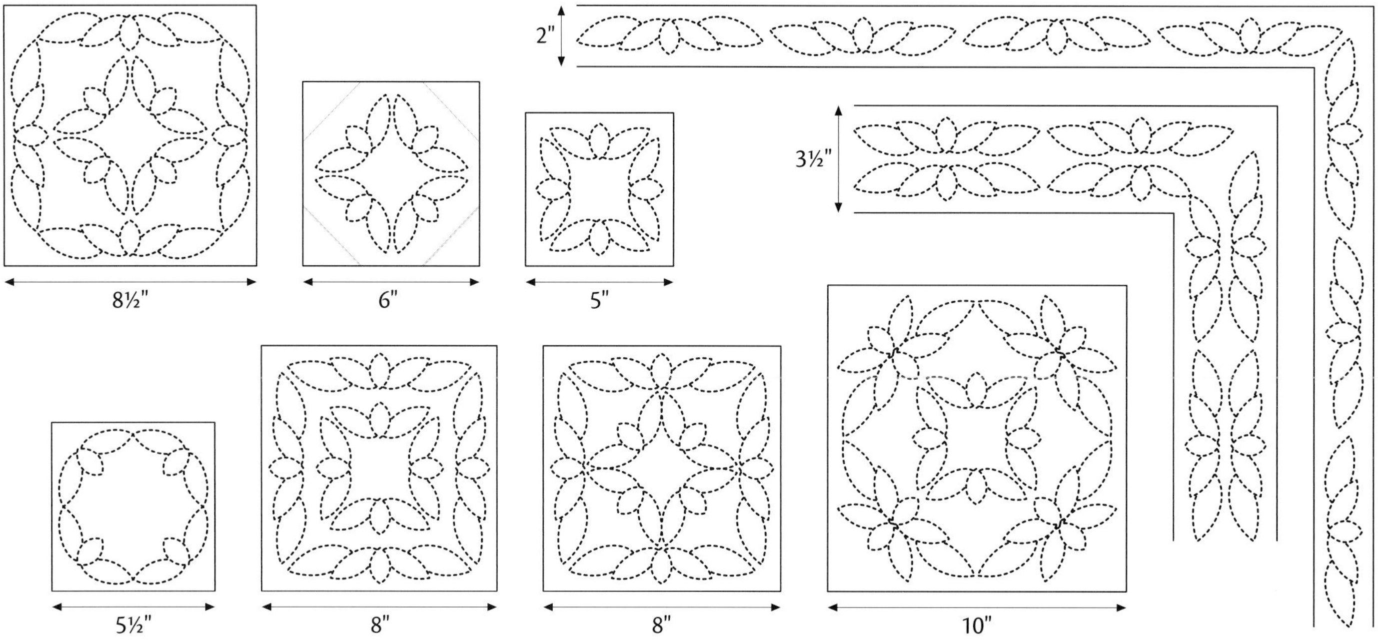

2"
3½"
8½"
6"
5"
5½"
8"
8"
10"

Tea Leaf

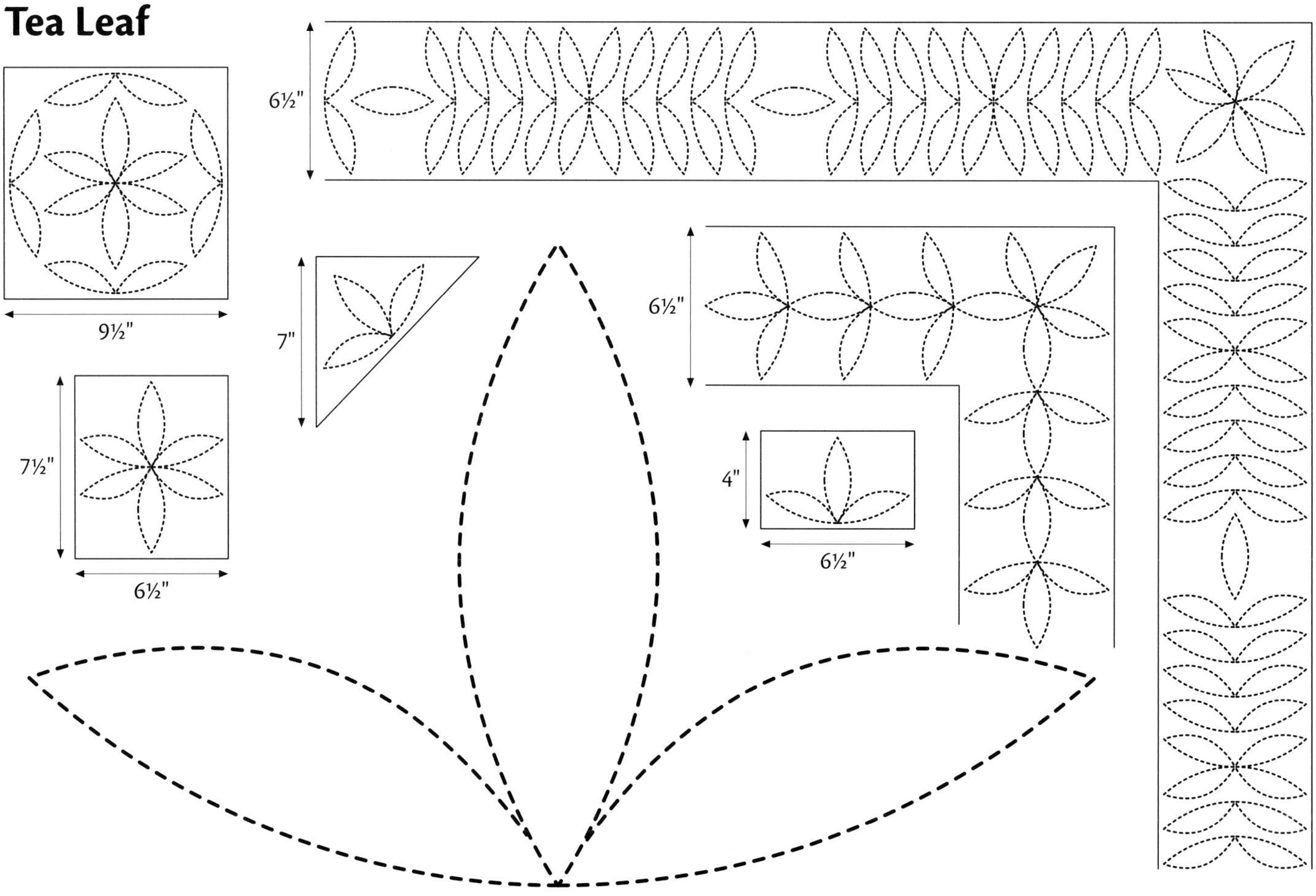

6½"
9½"
7"
6½"
7½"
6½"
4"
6½"

Woodland Sprig

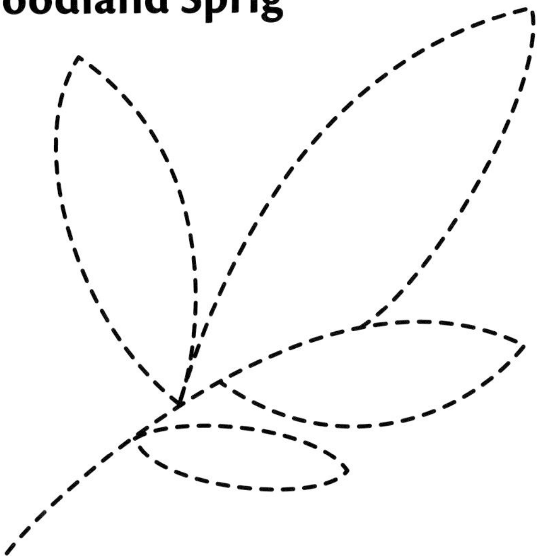

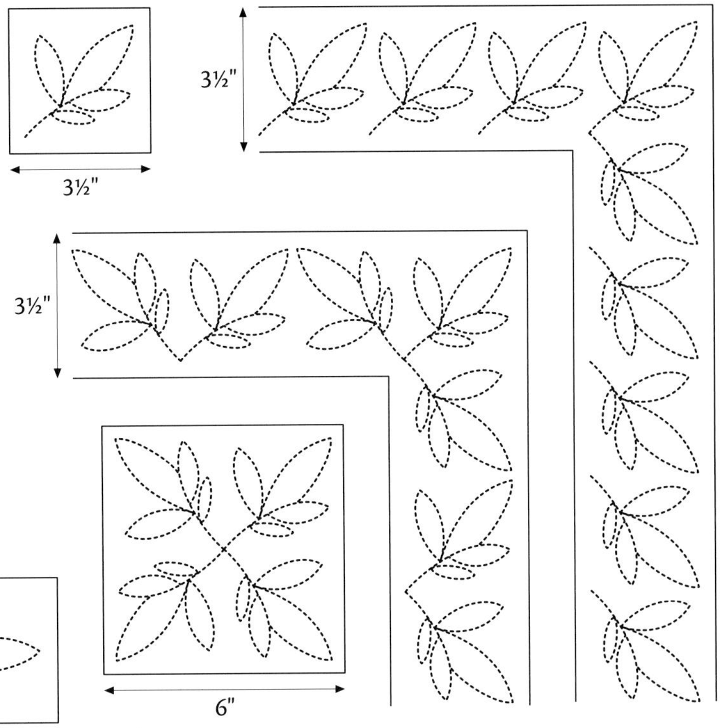
3½"
3½"
3½"
3½"
6"

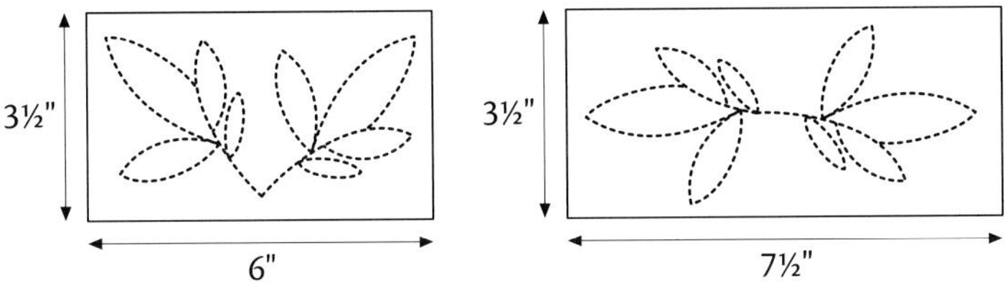
3½"
6"
3½"
7½"

Leaf Wreath

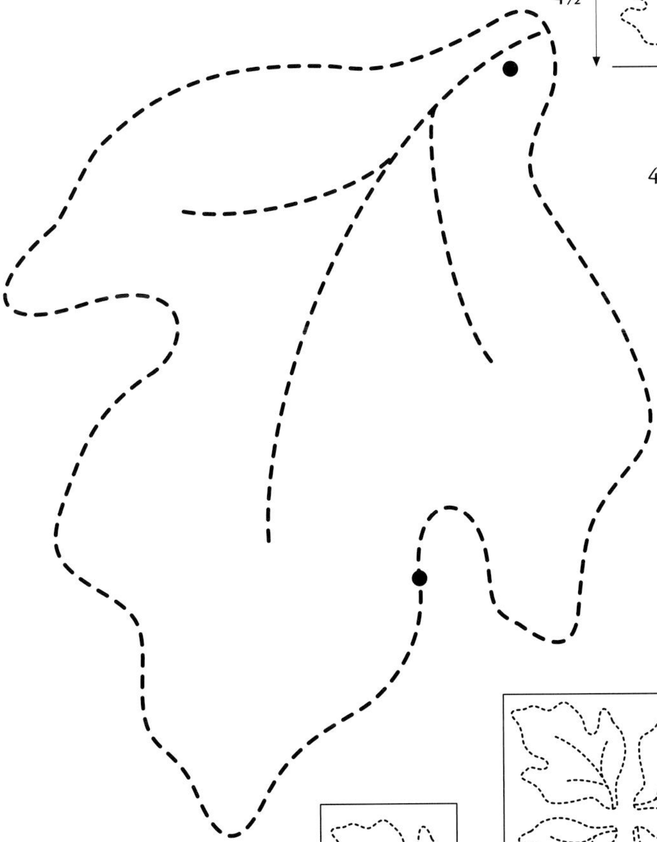

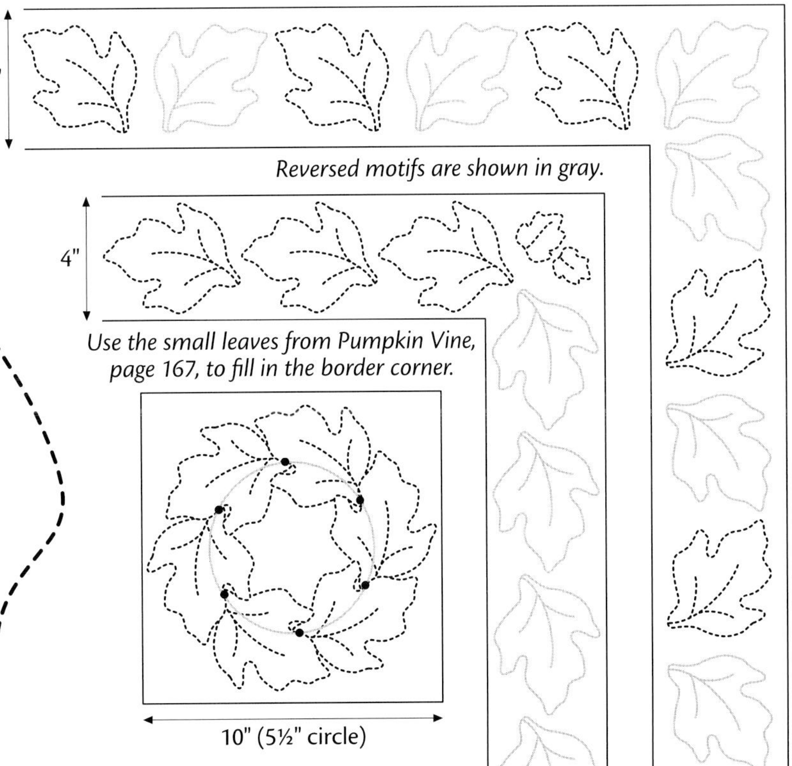
4½"
Reversed motifs are shown in gray.
4"
Use the small leaves from Pumpkin Vine, page 167, to fill in the border corner.
10" (5½" circle)

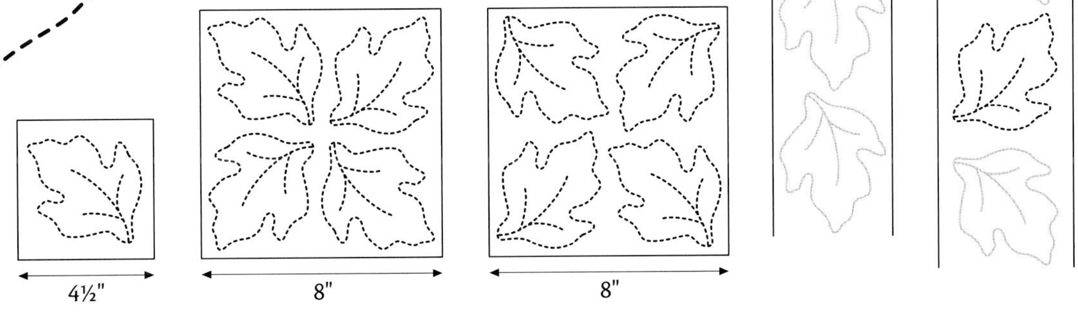
4½"
8"
8"

Lilting Leaf

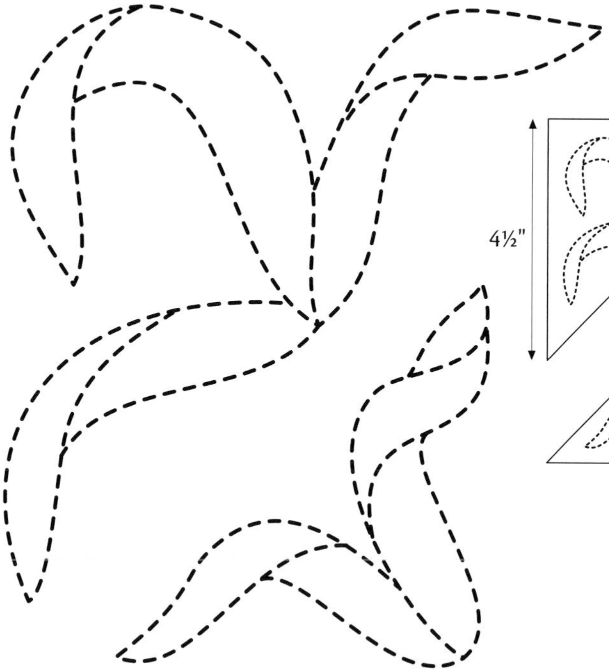

2½"
4½"
3"
7"
4"
4"

Ivy League

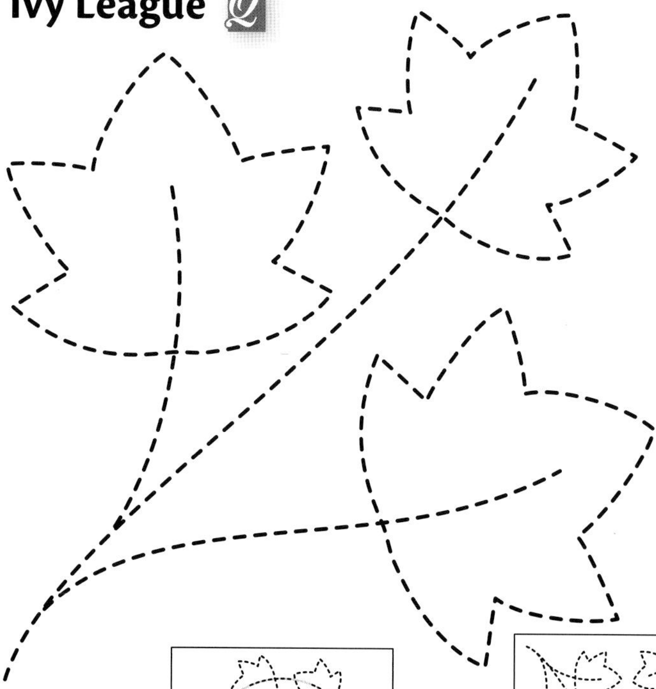

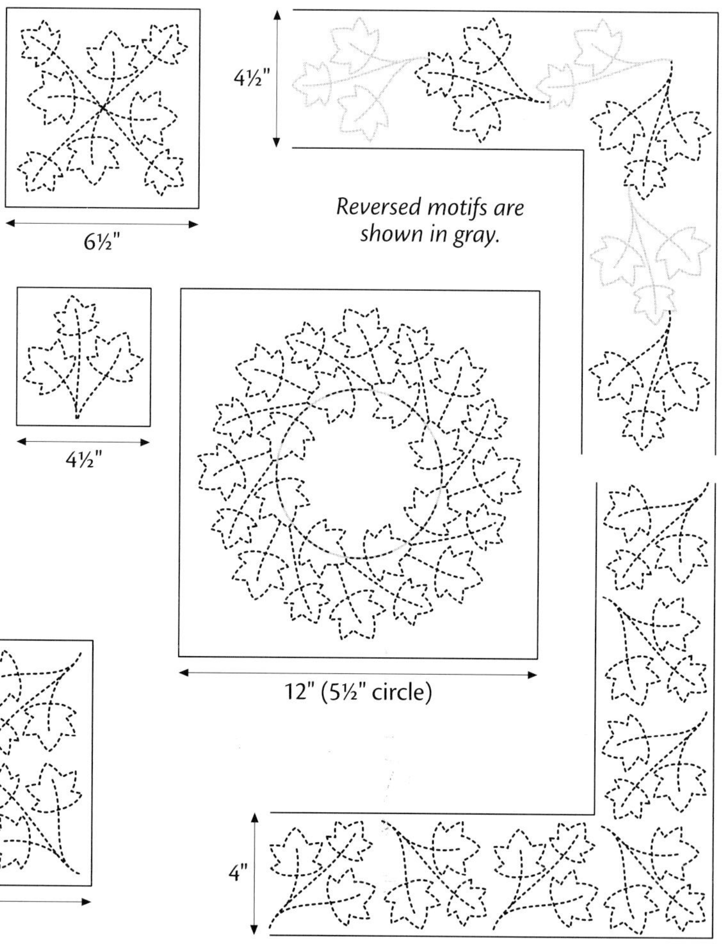
6½"
4½"
Reversed motifs are shown in gray.
4½"
12" (5½" circle)
4"

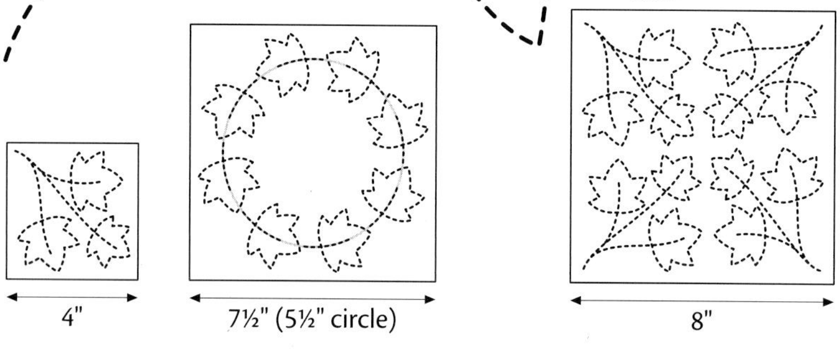
4"
7½" (5½" circle)
8"

Fall Leaf

11" (6½" circle)
4"
4"
4"
4"
4"
7½"
7½"
7"
4"
4"
4"
13"

Trailing Vine

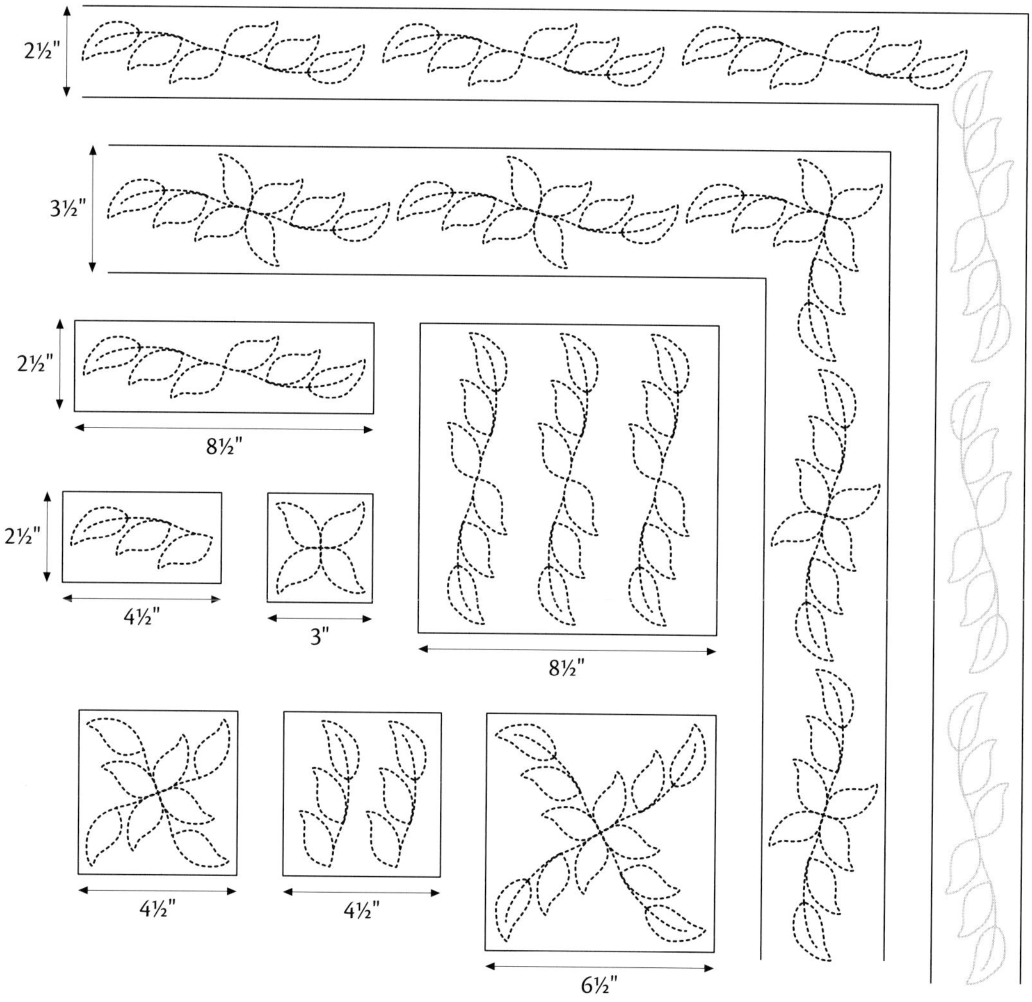

2½"
3½"
2½"
8½"
2½"
4½"
3"
8½"
4½"
4½"
6½"

Reversed motifs are shown in gray.

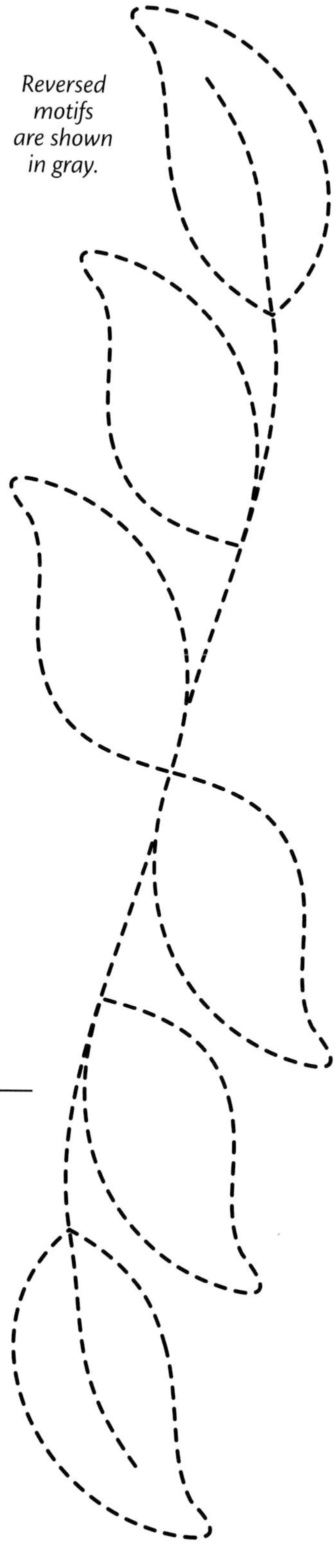

Autumn Mystery

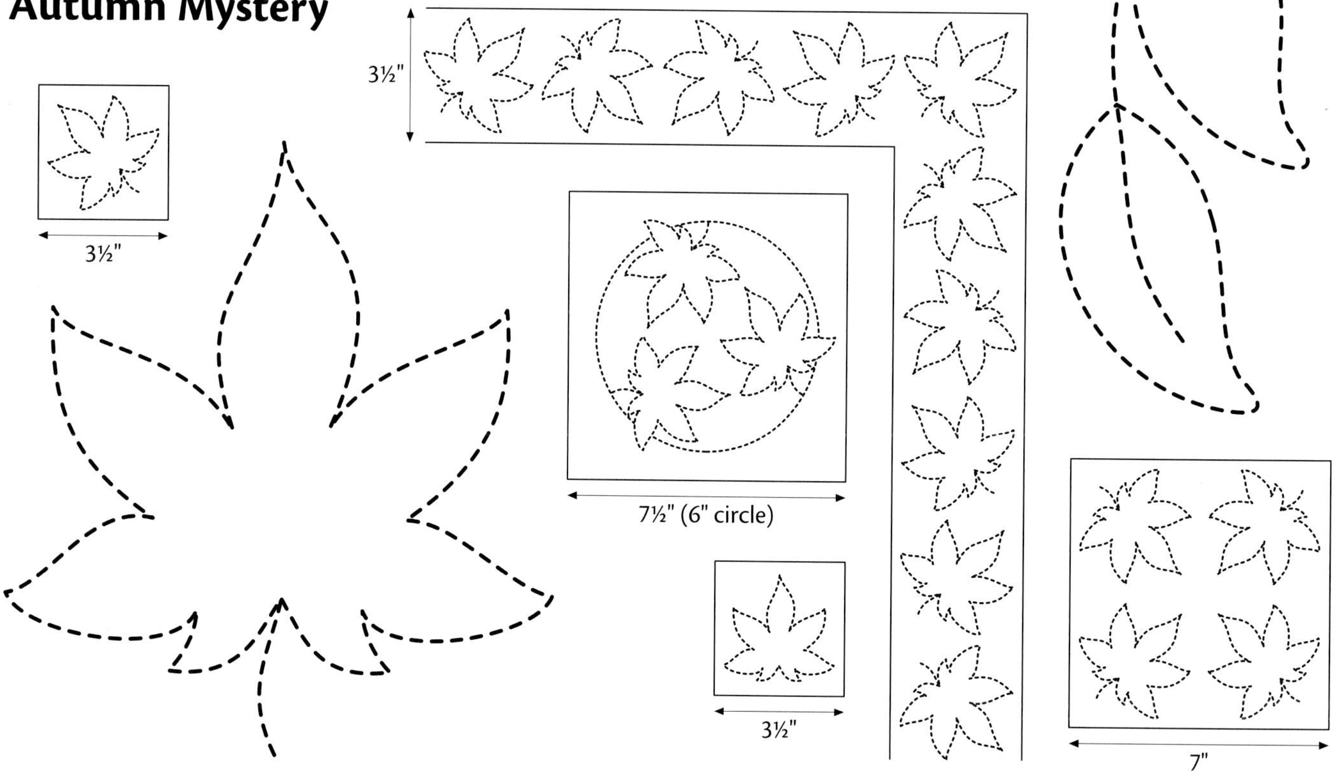

3½"
3½"
7½" (6" circle)
3½"
7"

Fizz Leaves

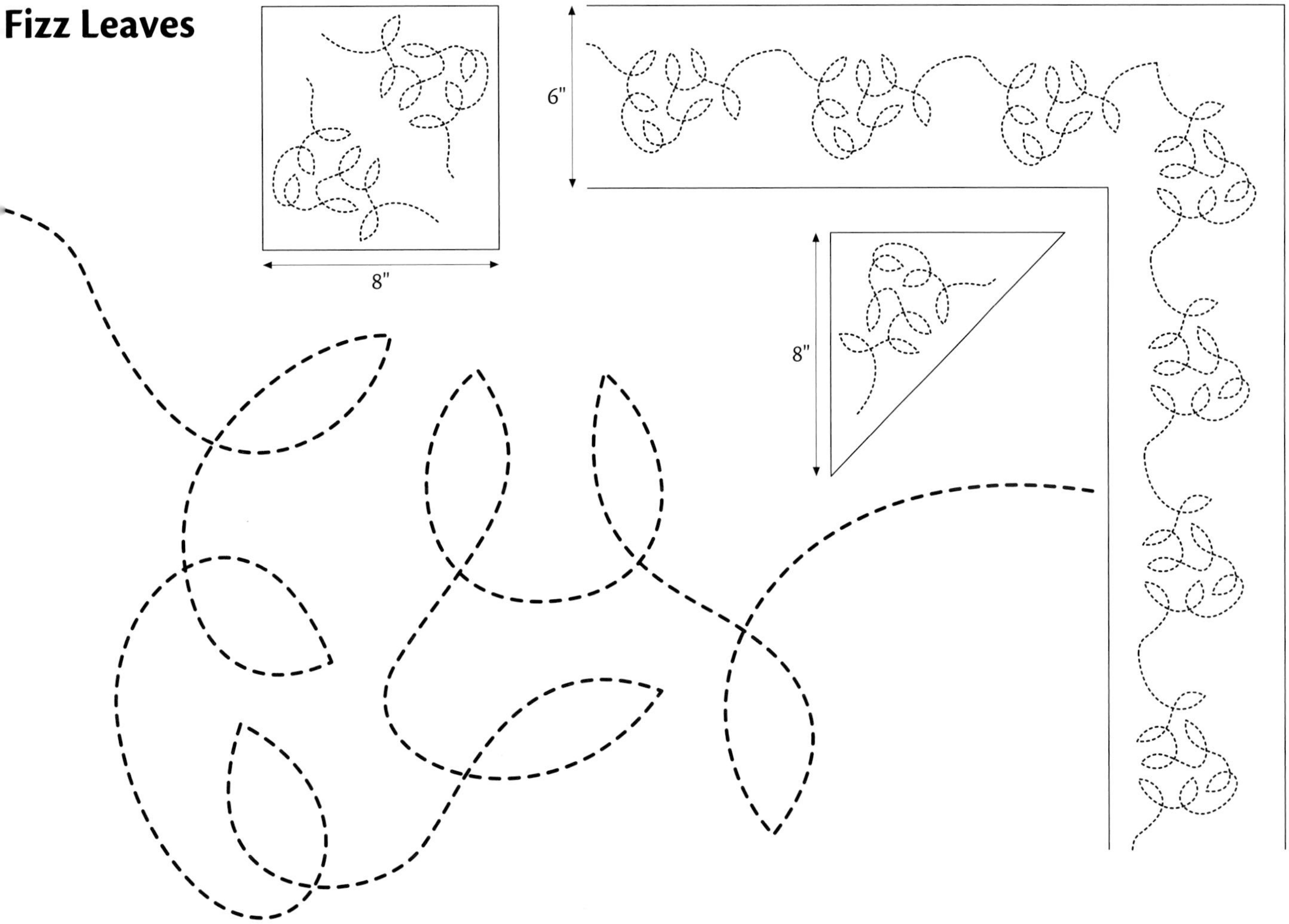

8"
6"
8"

Lucky Clover

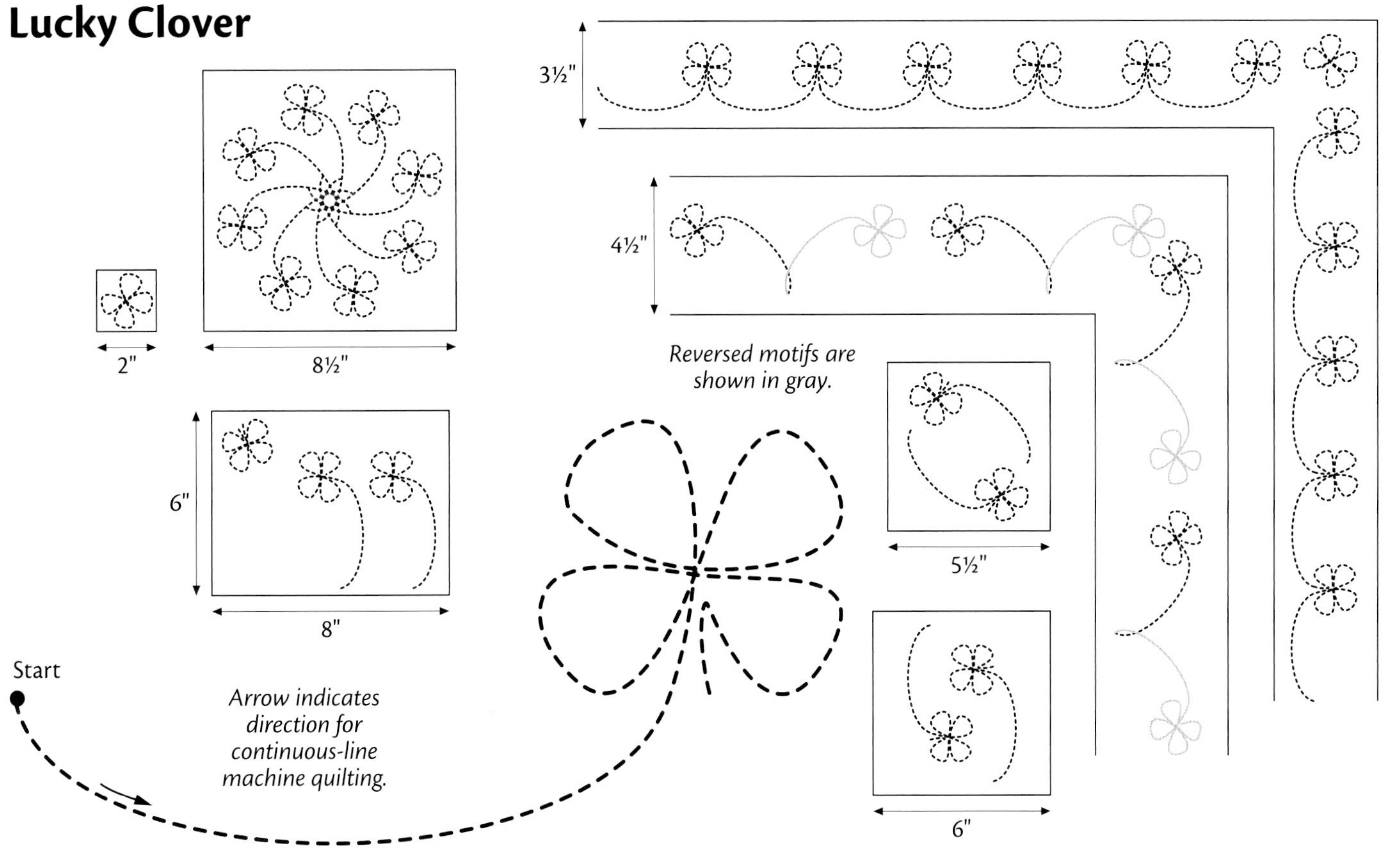

3½"
4½"
2"
8½"
6"
8"
5½"
6"
Reversed motifs are shown in gray.
Start
Arrow indicates direction for continuous-line machine quilting.

Friendship Vine 1

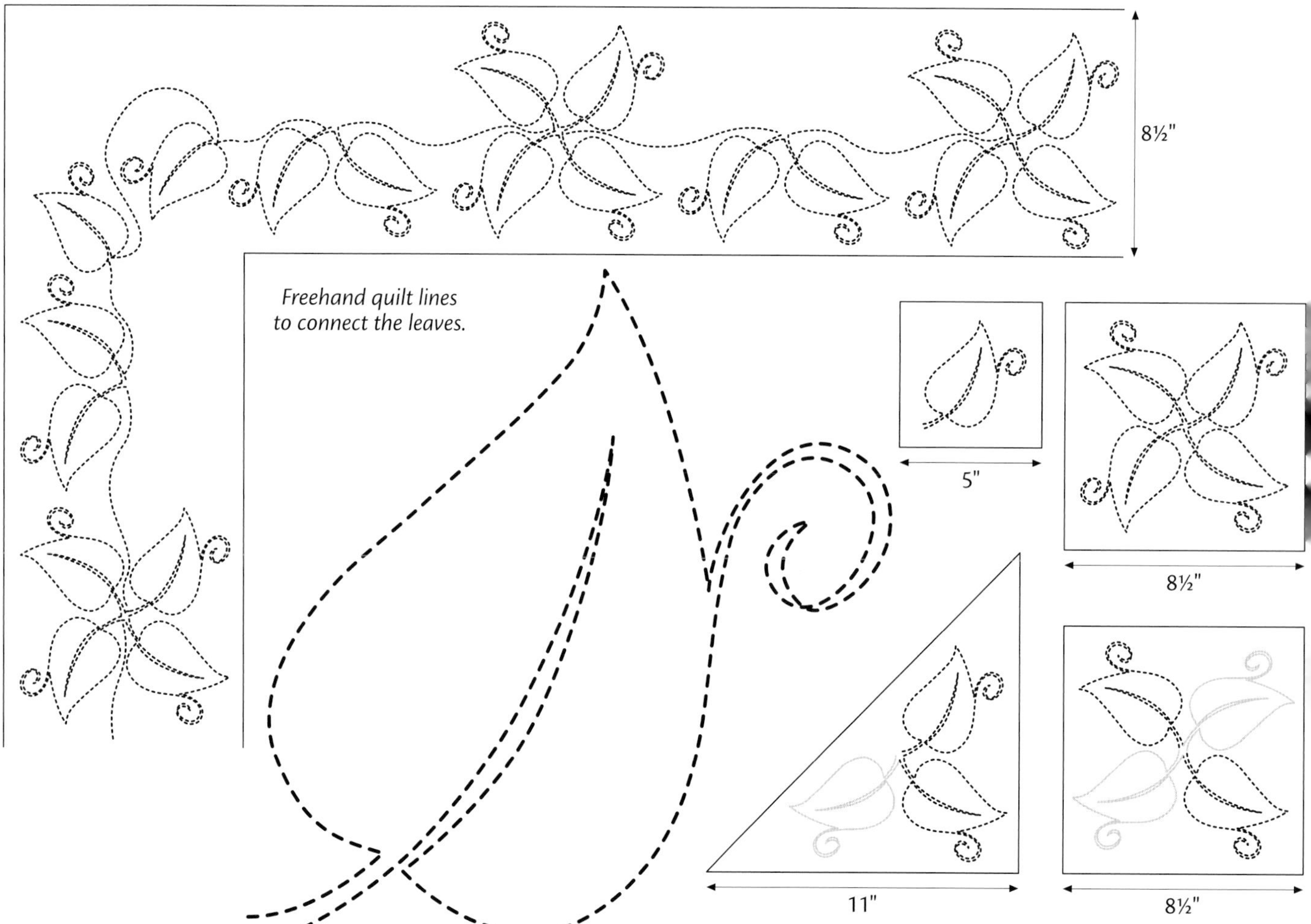
8½"
Freehand quilt lines to connect the leaves.
5"
8½"
11"
8½"

Reversed motifs are shown in gray.

Summer Leaves

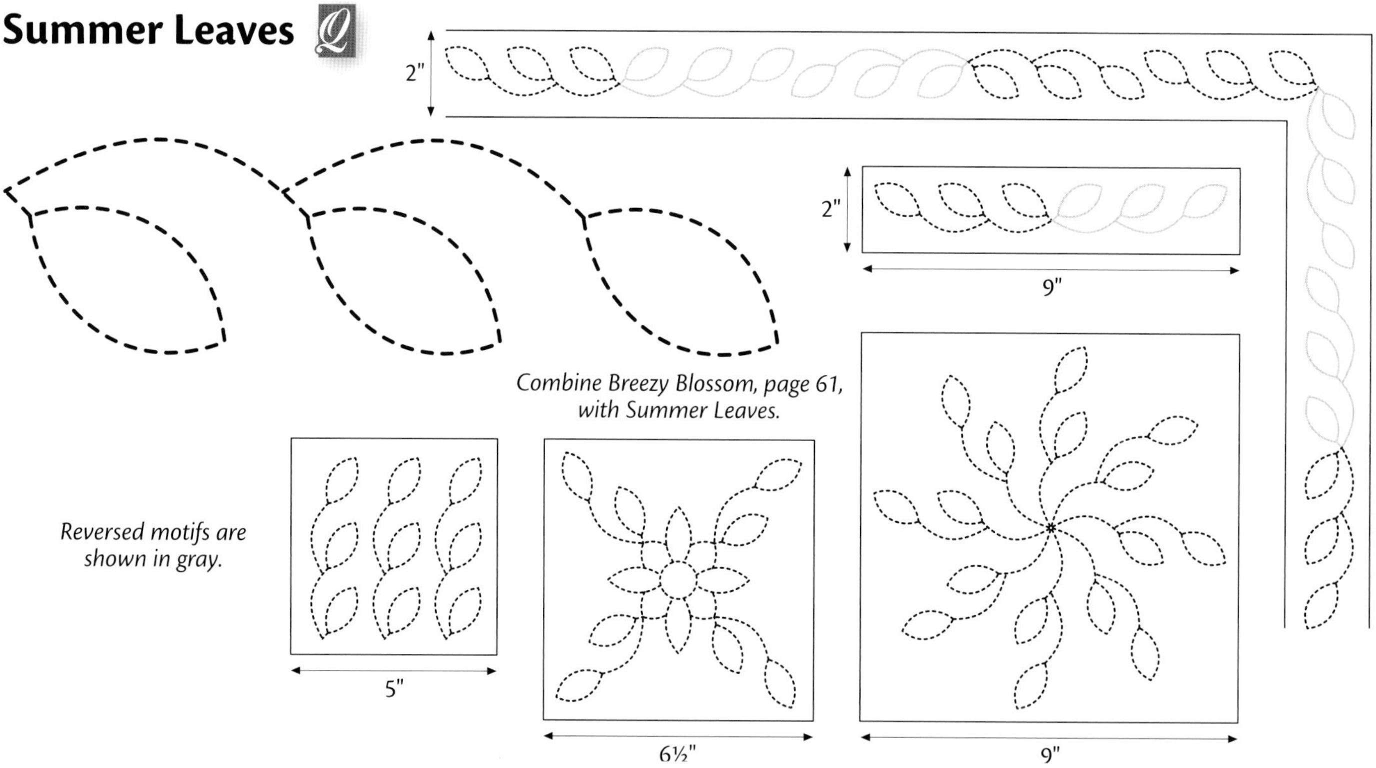
2"
2"
9"
5"
6½"
9"

Combine Breezy Blossom, page 61, with Summer Leaves.

Reversed motifs are shown in gray.

Friendship Vine 2

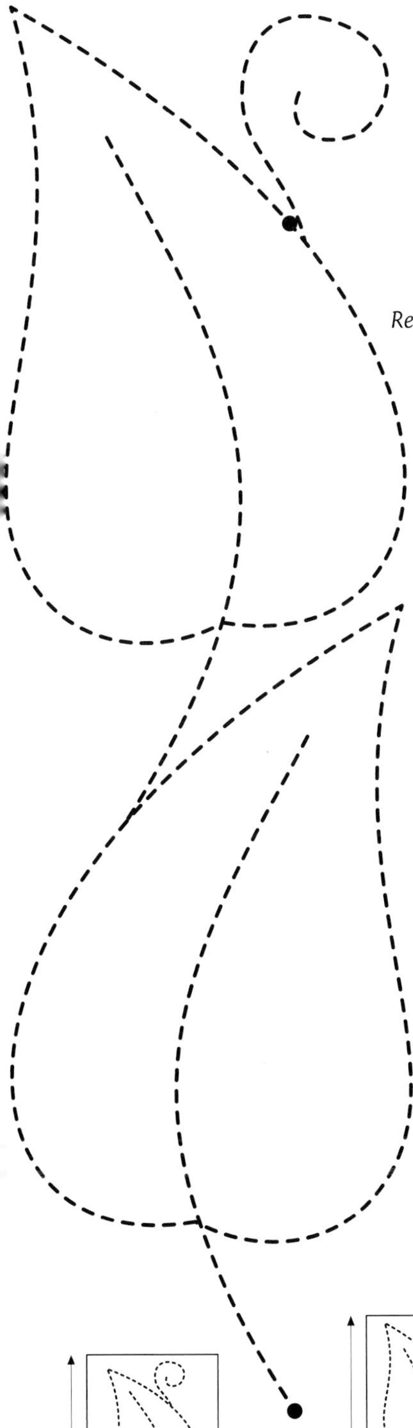

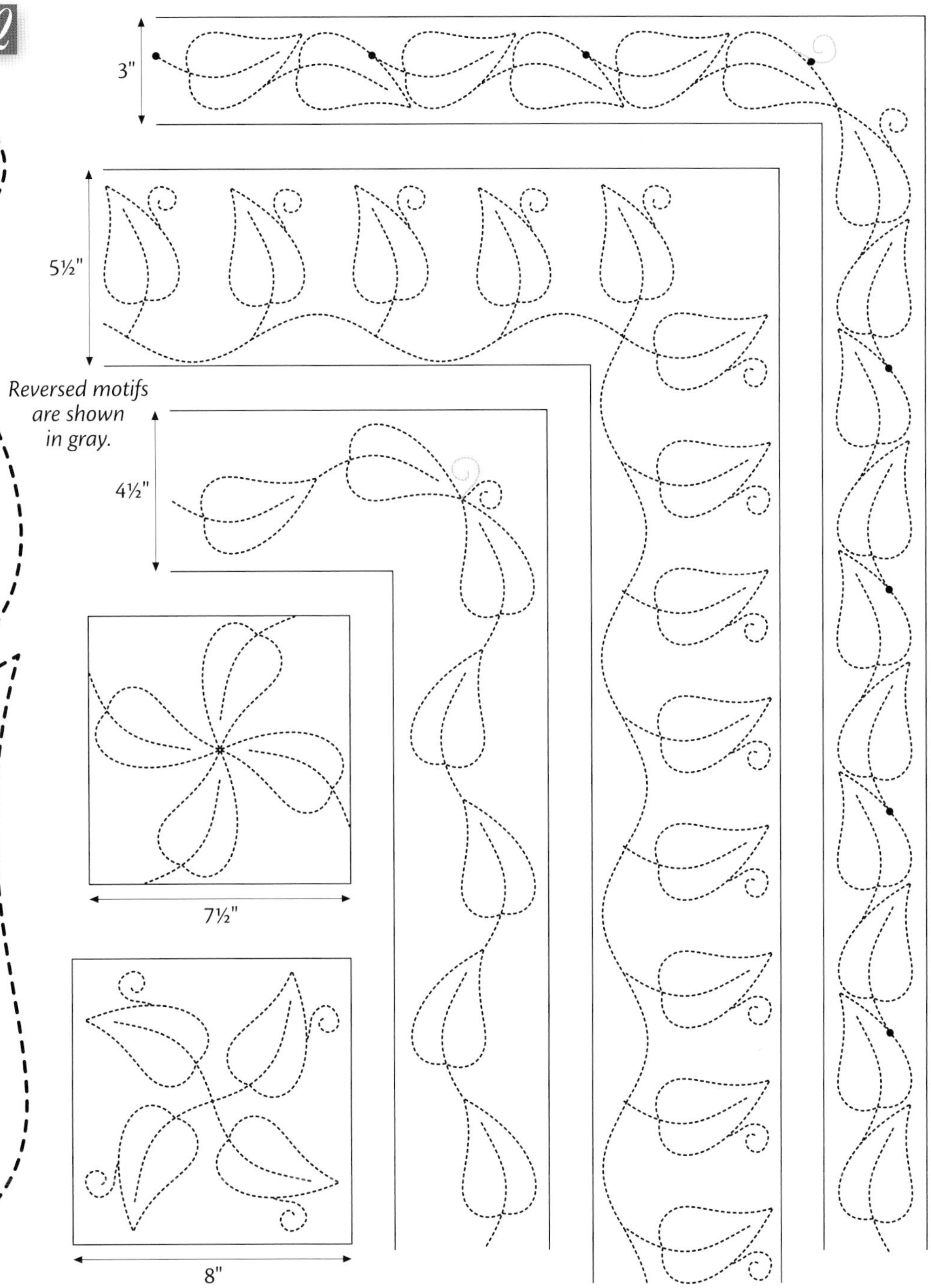

3"
5½"
Reversed motifs are shown in gray.
4½"
7½"
8"

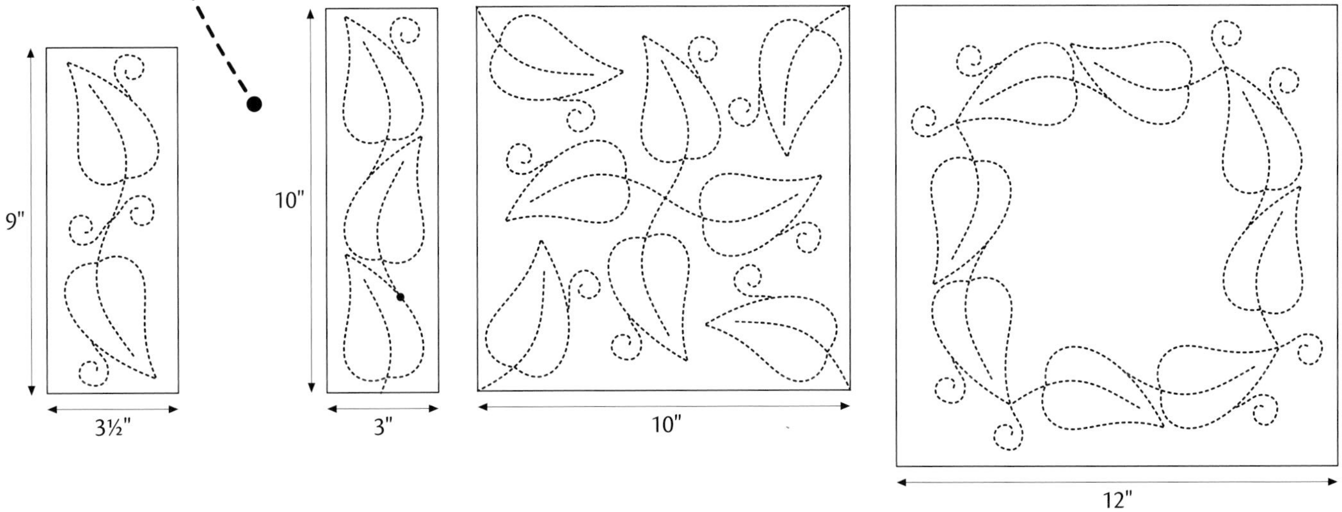

9"
3½"
10"
3"
10"
12"

Spring Leaves

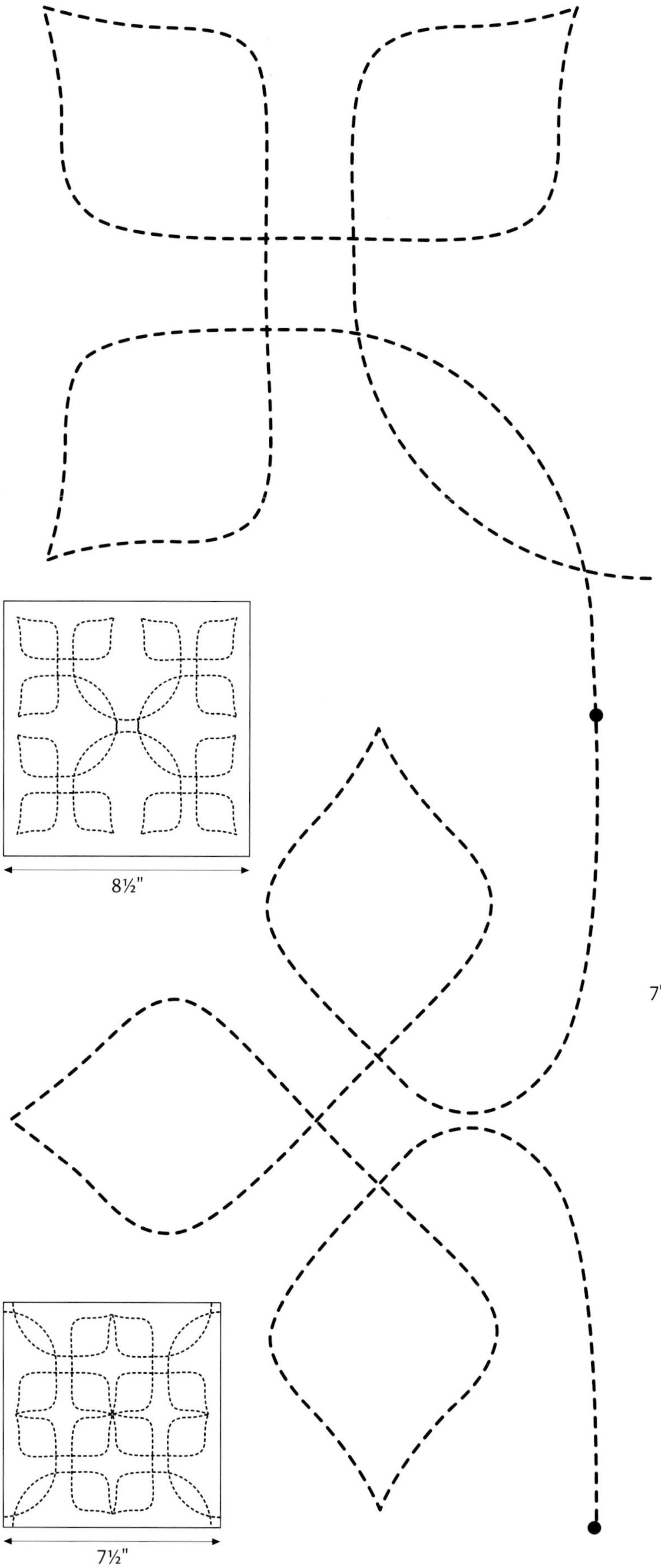

15"

Loveleaf

Ivy Leaf

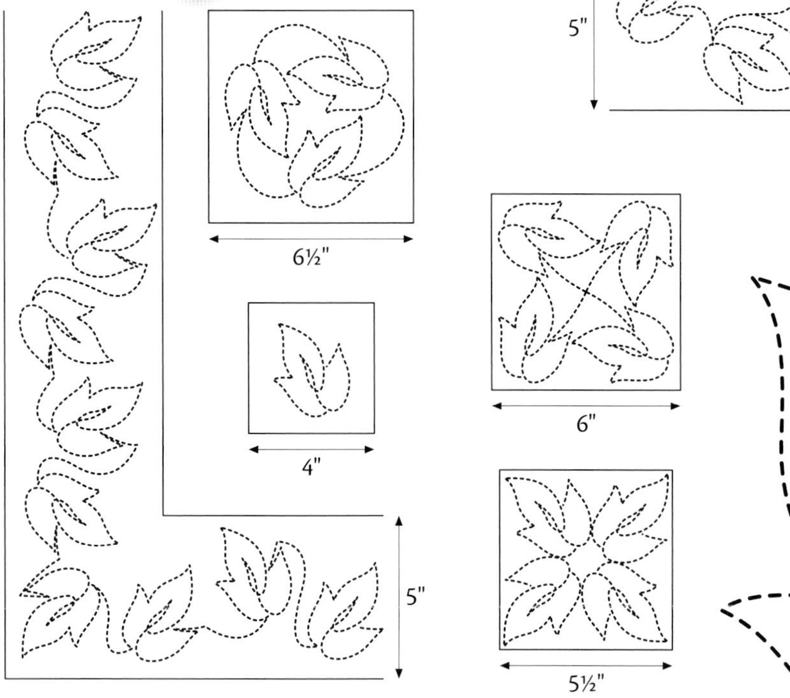
6½"
4"
6"
5"
5½"

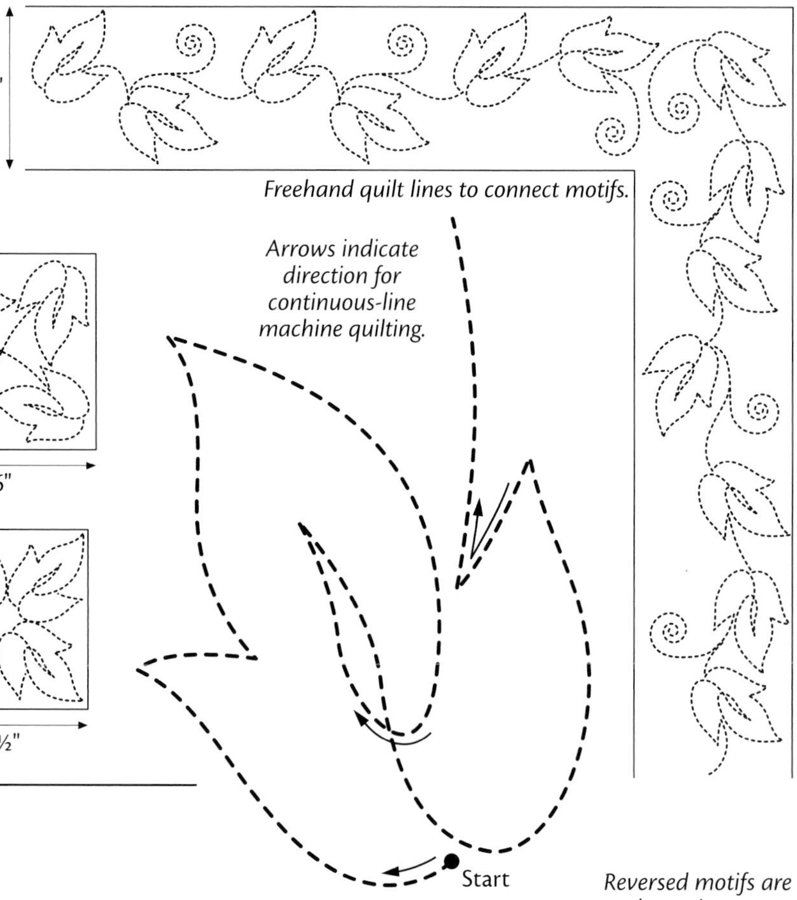
5"
Freehand quilt lines to connect motifs.
Arrows indicate direction for continuous-line machine quilting.
Start

Magic Vine

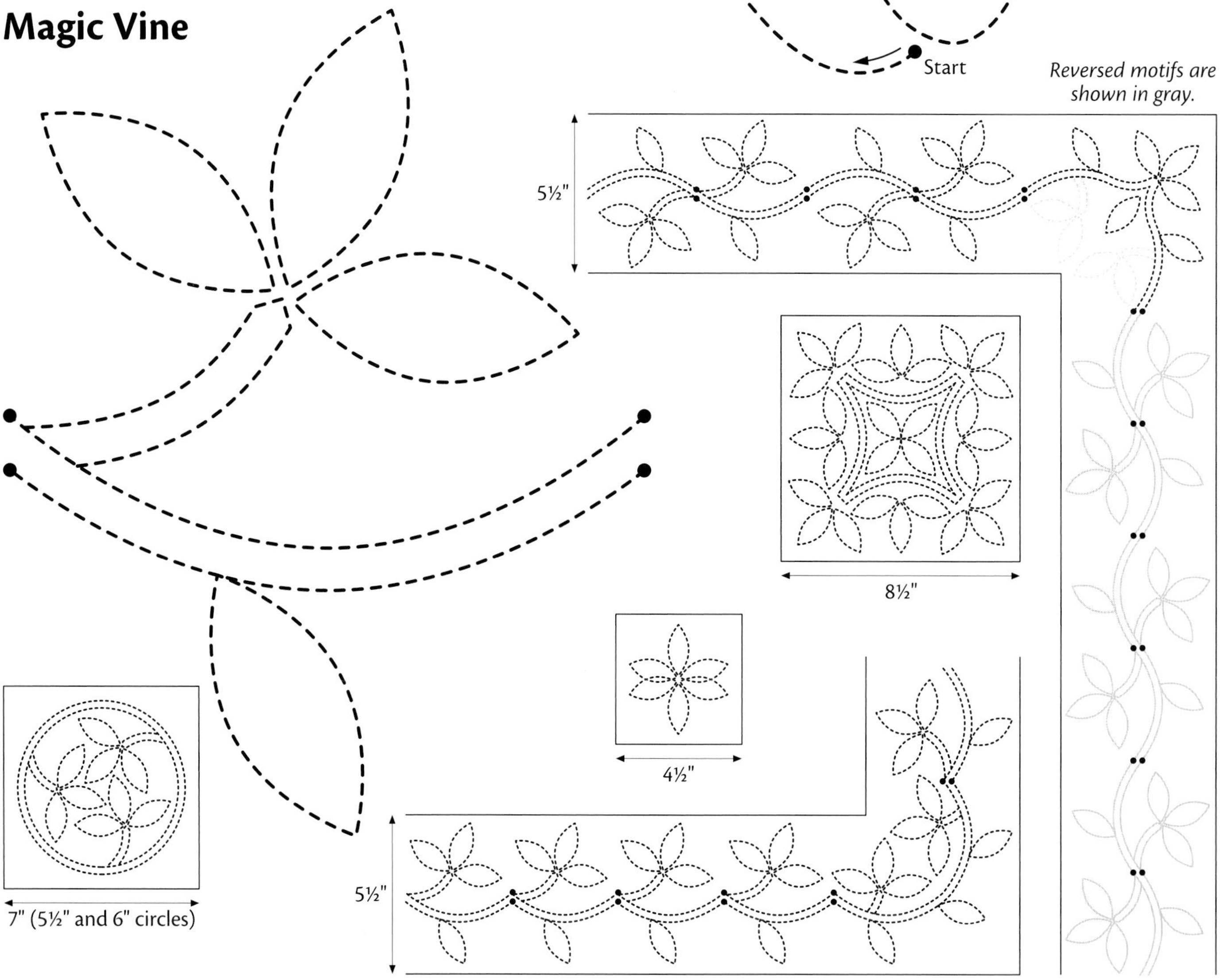
Reversed motifs are shown in gray.
5½"
8½"
4½"
7" (5½" and 6" circles)
5½"

Cloverleaf

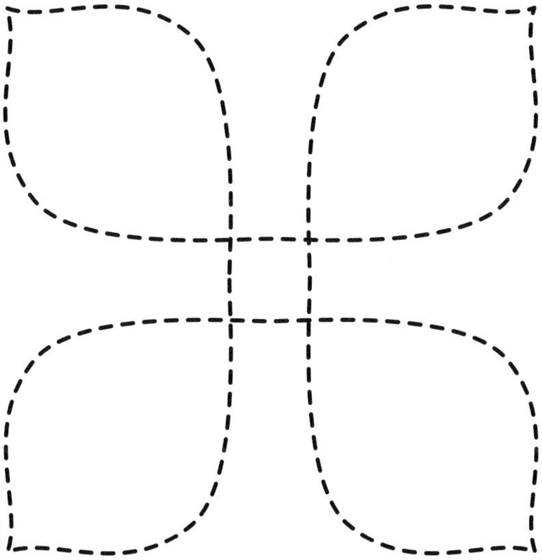

4½"

4½"

3½"

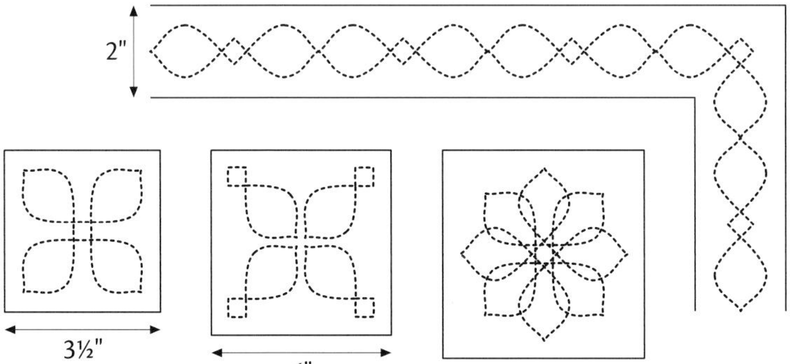

2"

3½"

4"

4½"

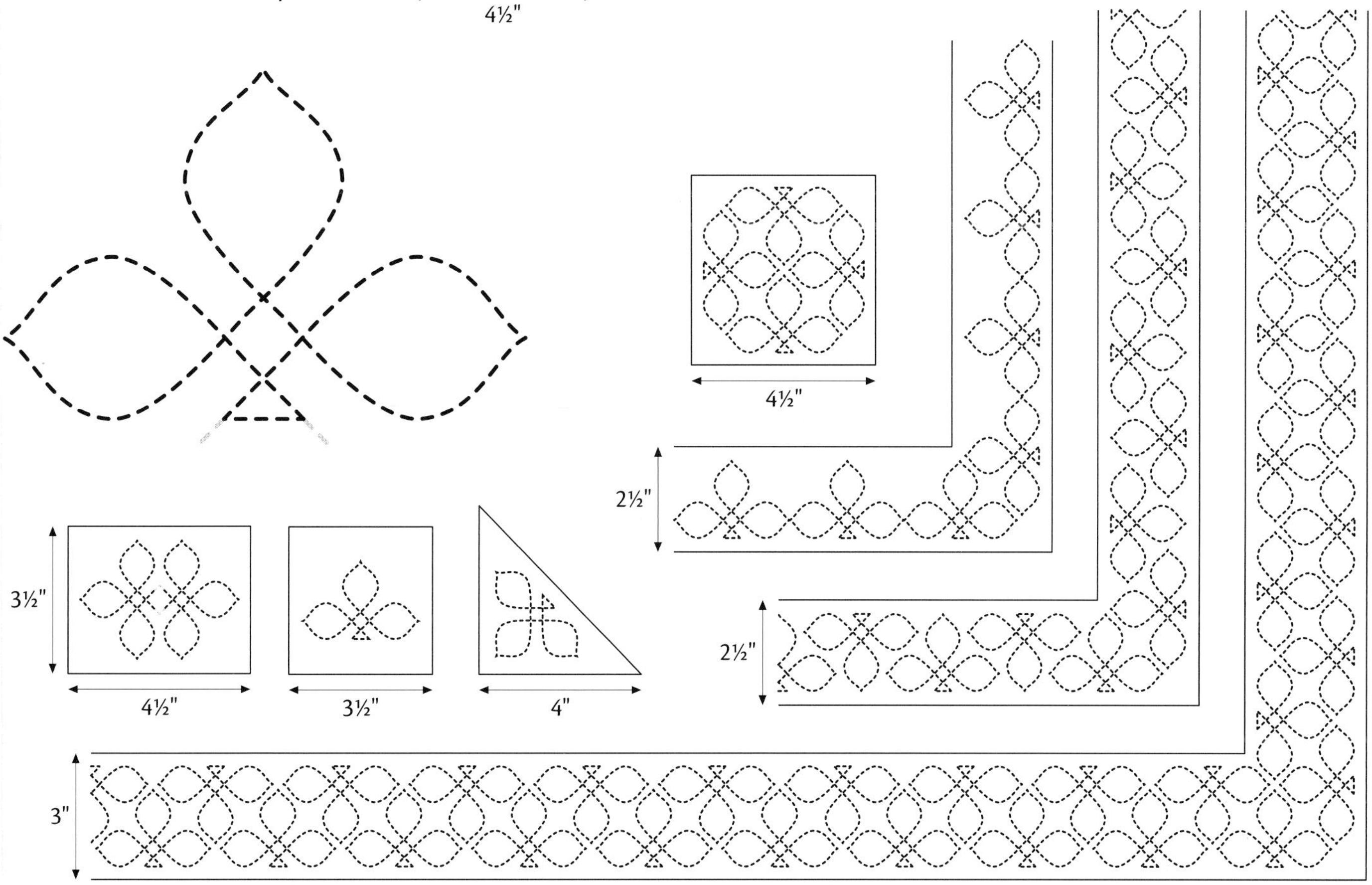

4½"

2½"

2½"

3½"

4½"

3½"

4"

3"

Trellis Vine

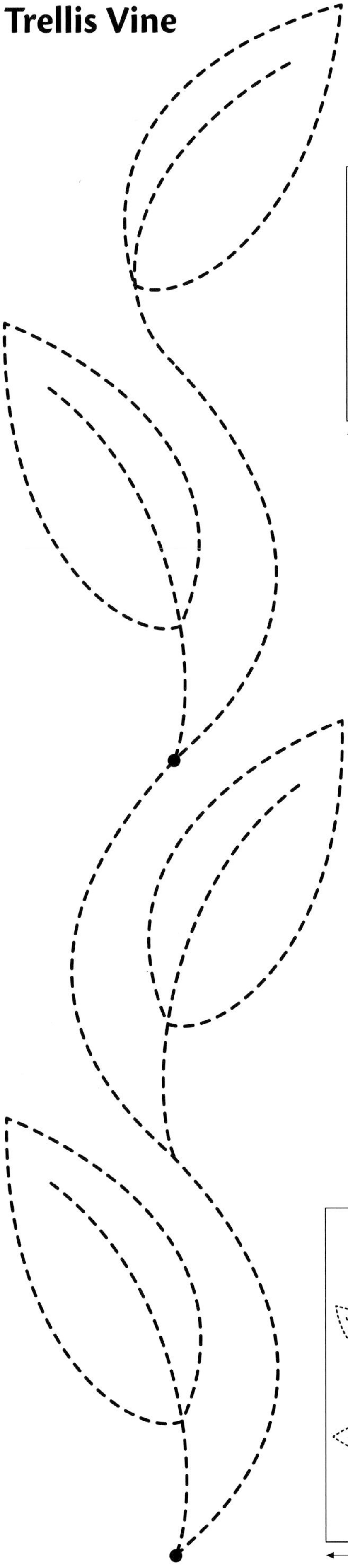

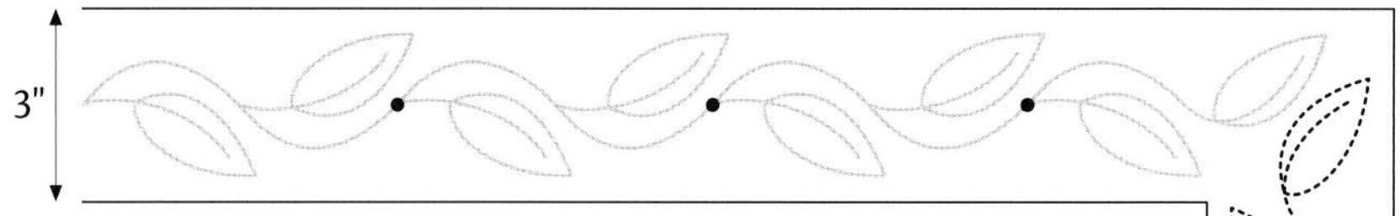
3"

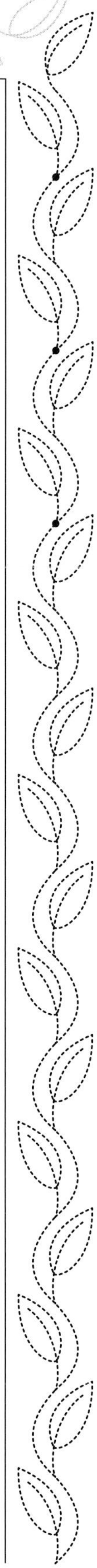

Reversed motifs are shown in gray.

8"

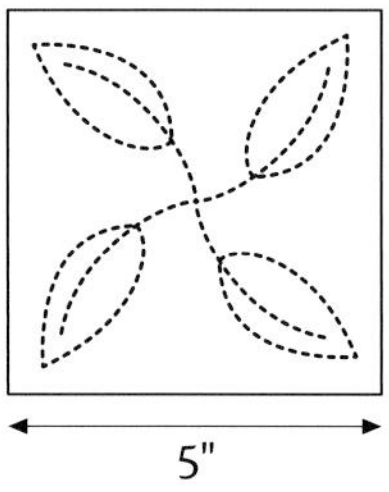
5"

6"

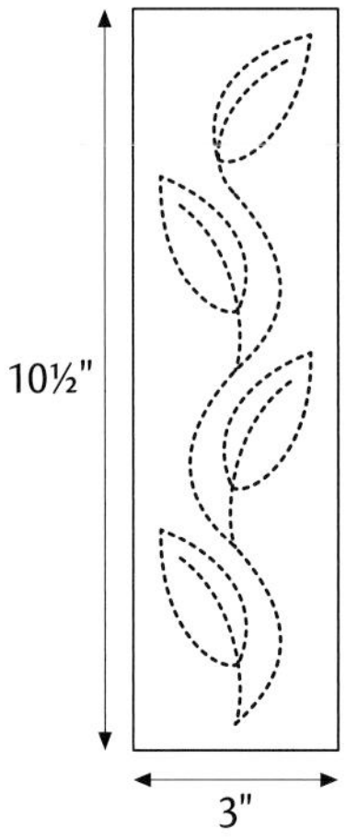
10½"
3"

12"

8"

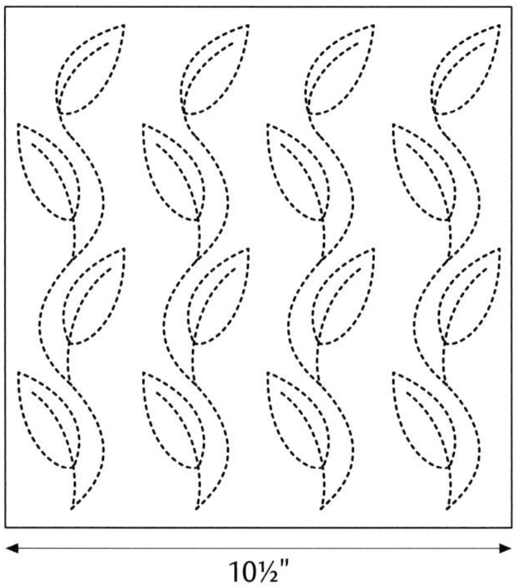
10½"

10½"

Leafy Meander 1

6"

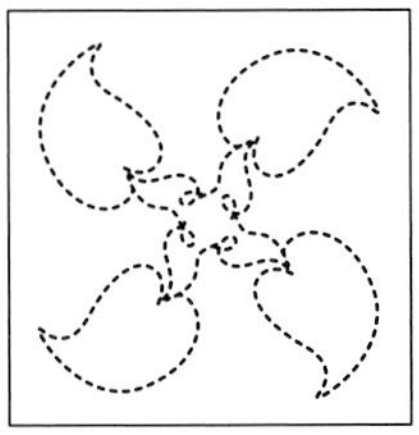

6"

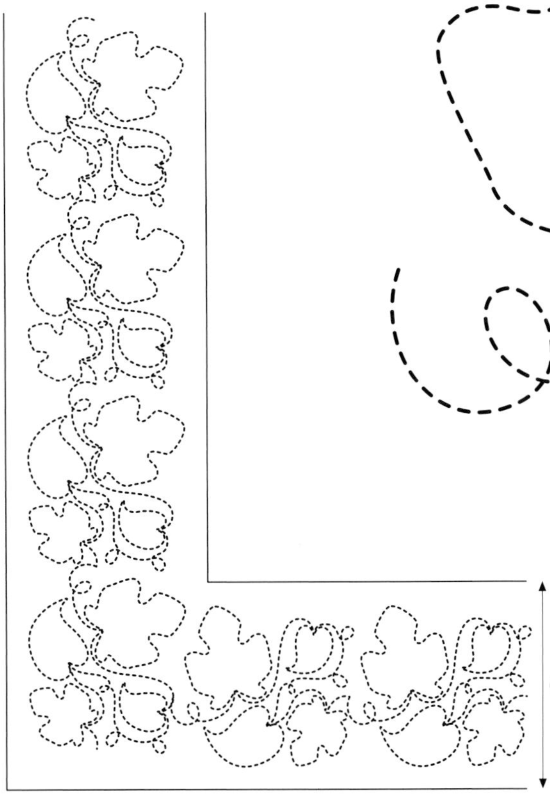

6"

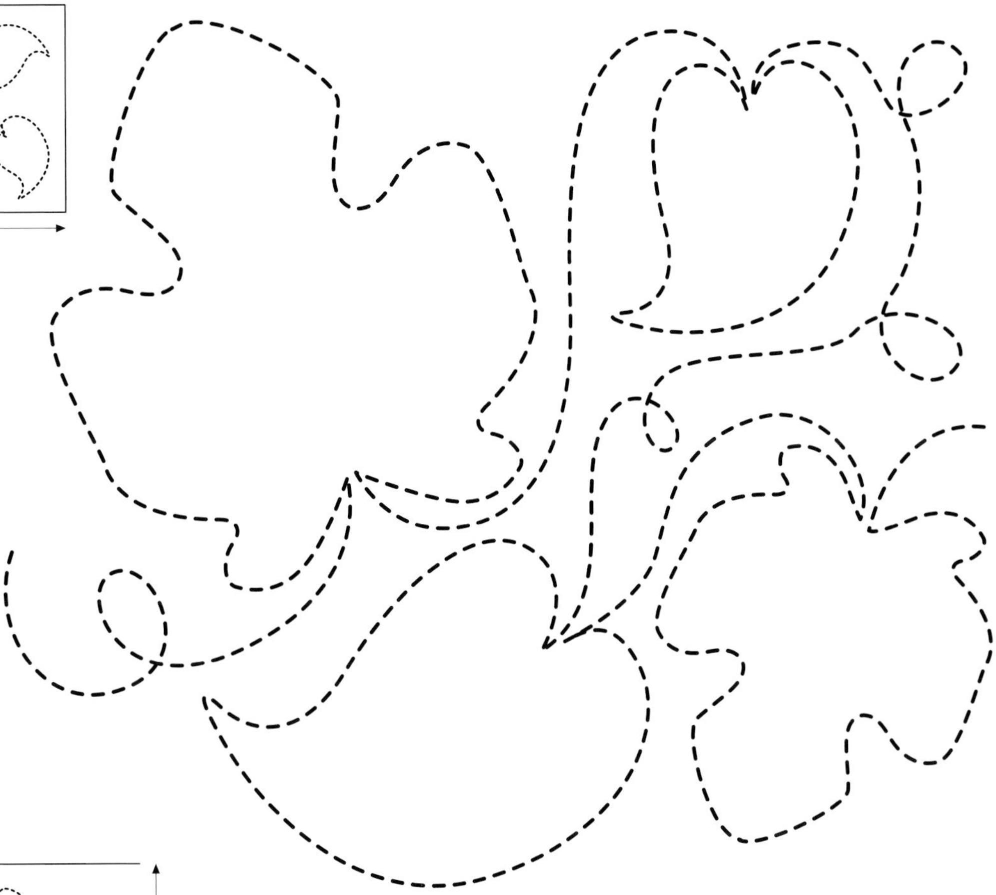

Leafy Meander 2

7"

Reversed motifs are shown in gray.

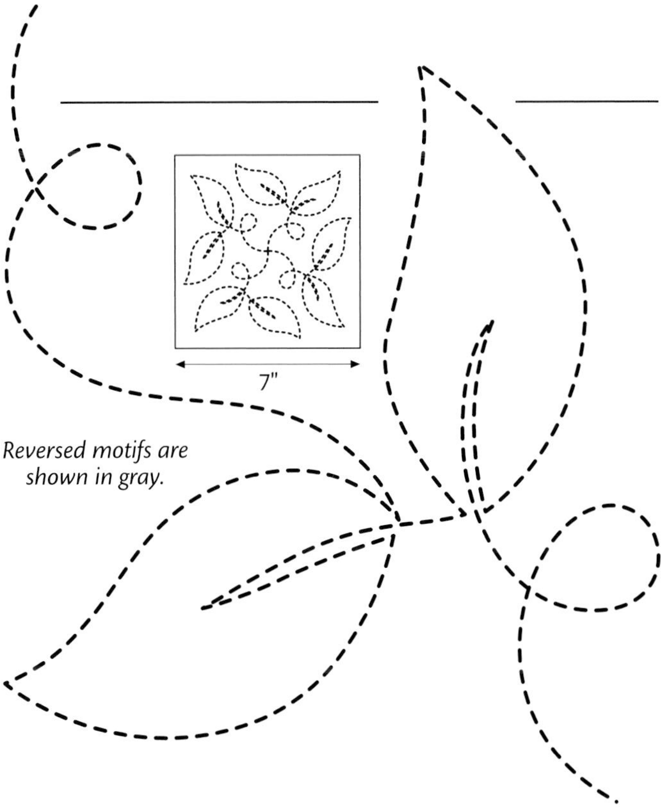

Funky Flower

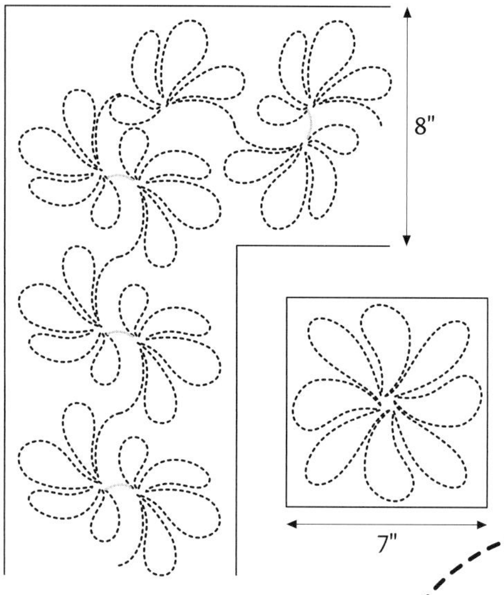

8"

7"

12"

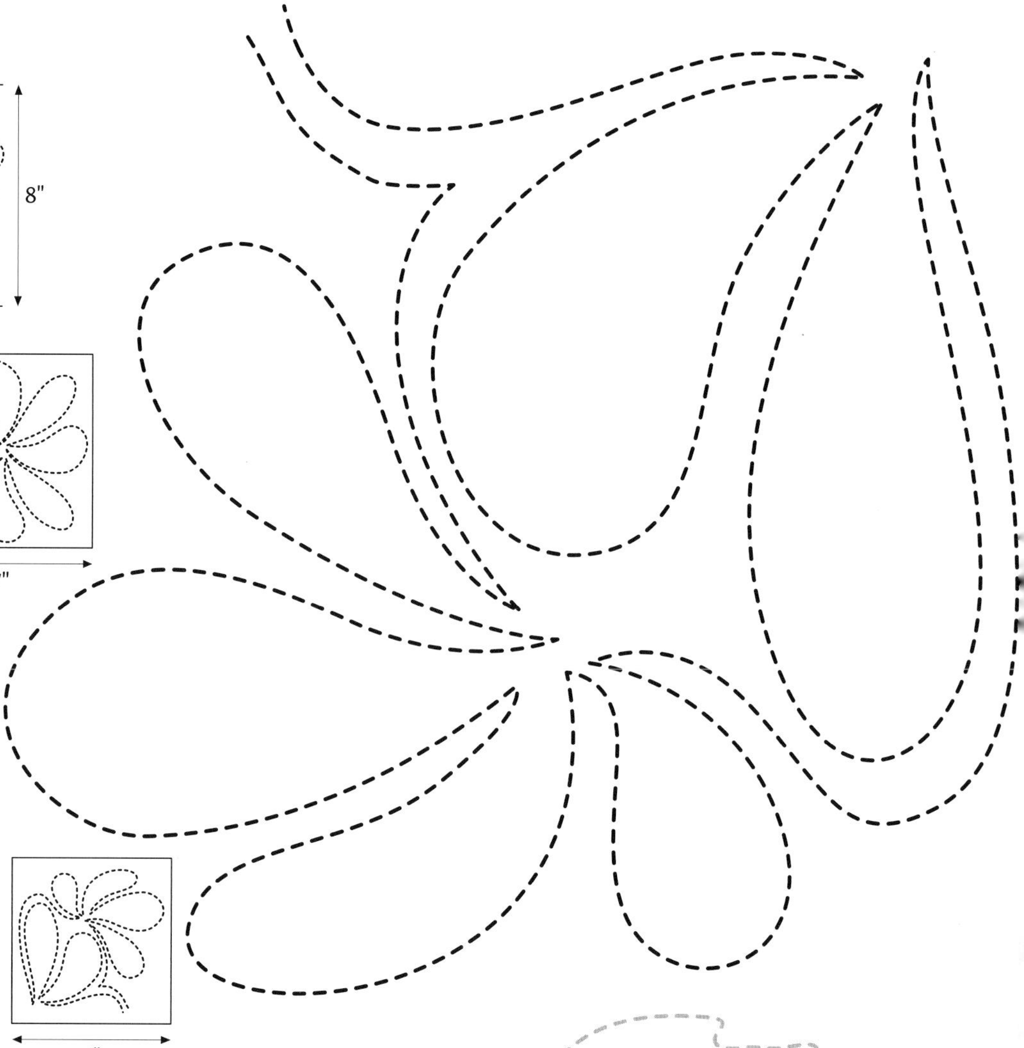

6"

Leafy Bough

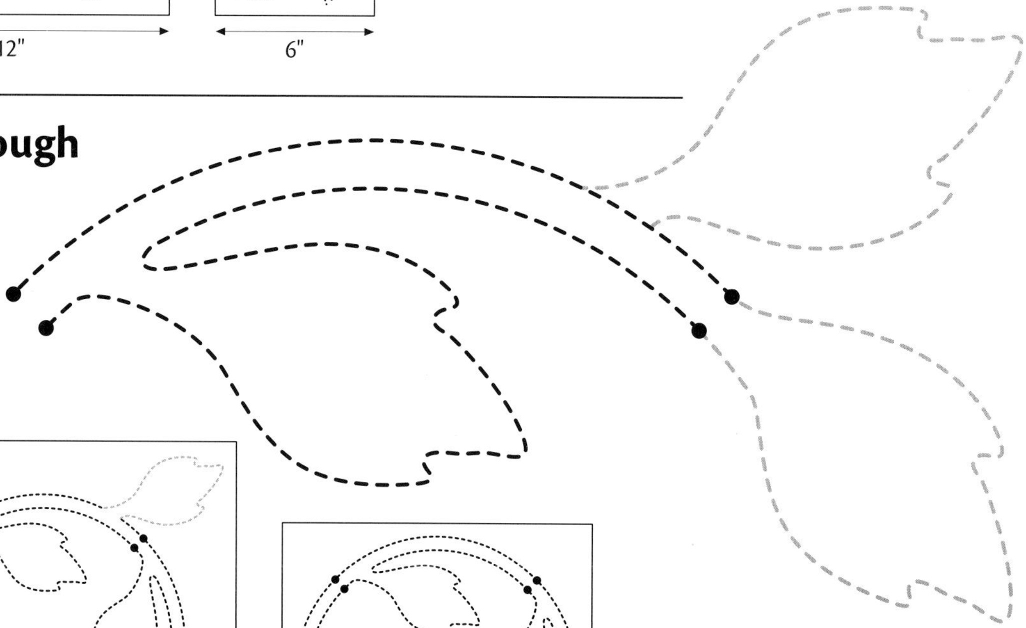

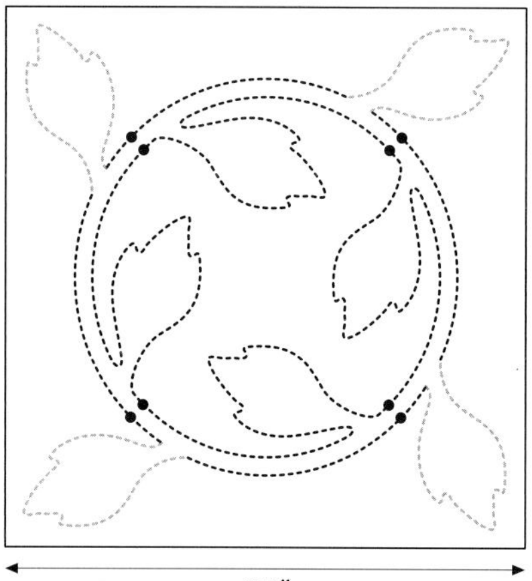

7½"

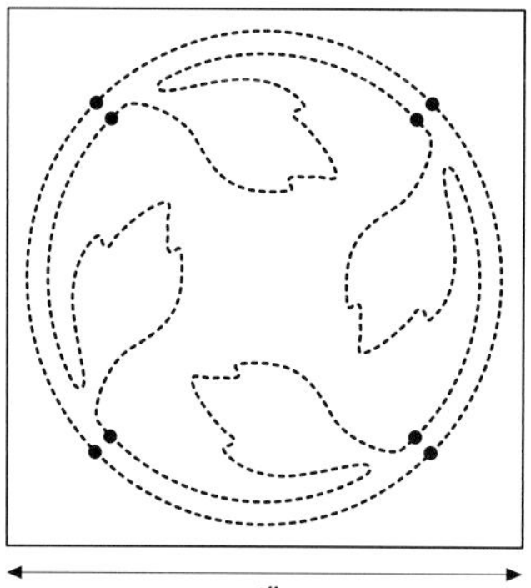

6"

Reversed motifs are shown in gray.

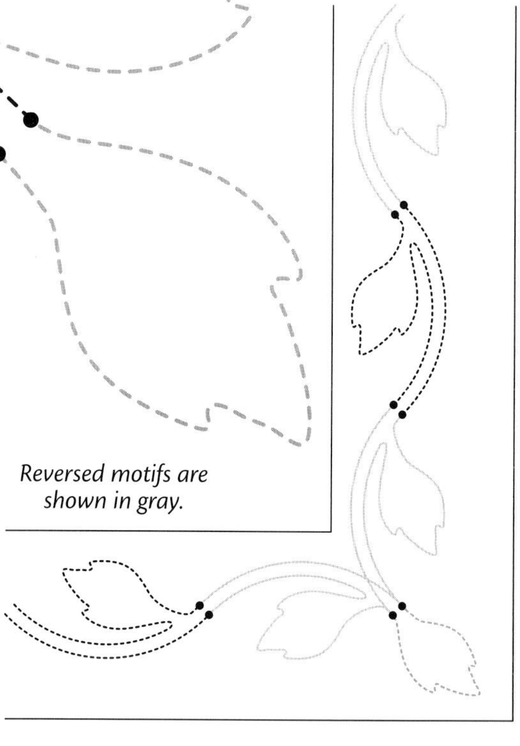

3½"

Lazy Leafy

4½"

2½"

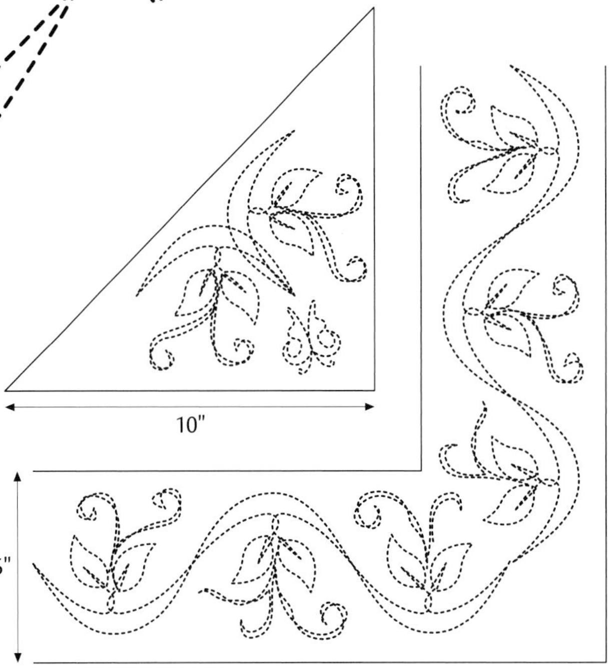

10"

5"

8"

7½"

Cotton Sprig

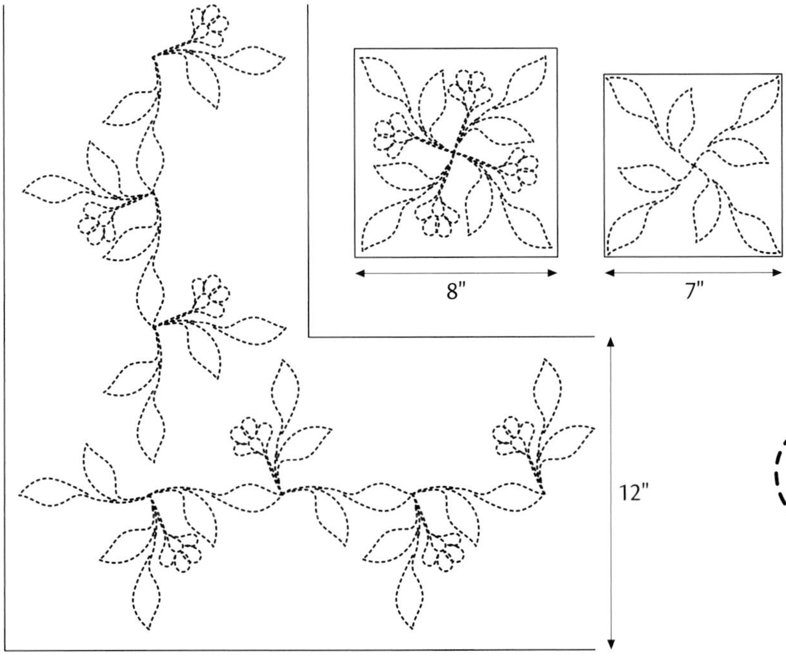

8"

7"

12"

4½"
Arrows indicate direction for continuous-line machine quilting.
Start

Lilac Leaf

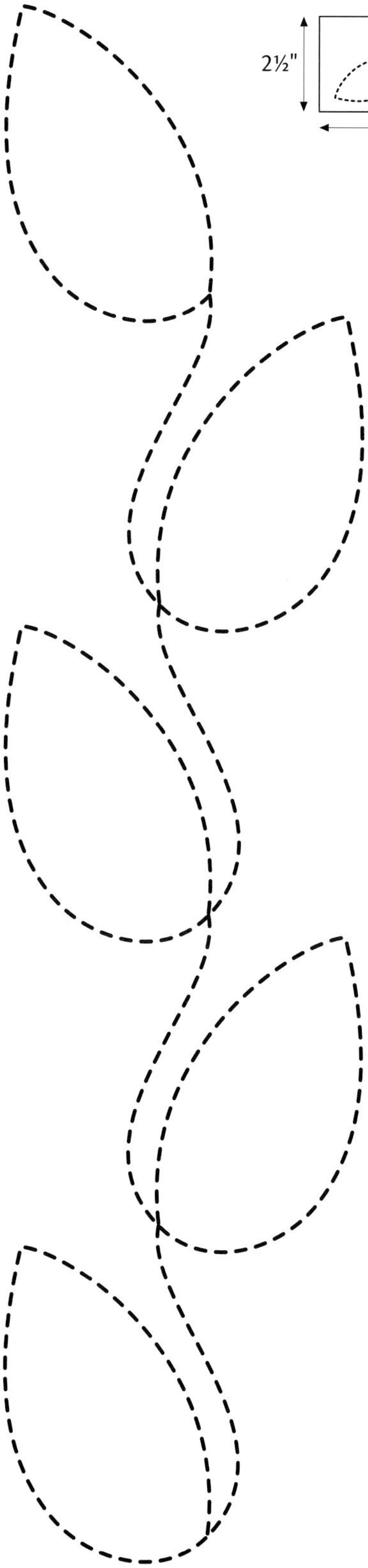

Reversed motifs are shown in gray.

Circle and Angle Patterns

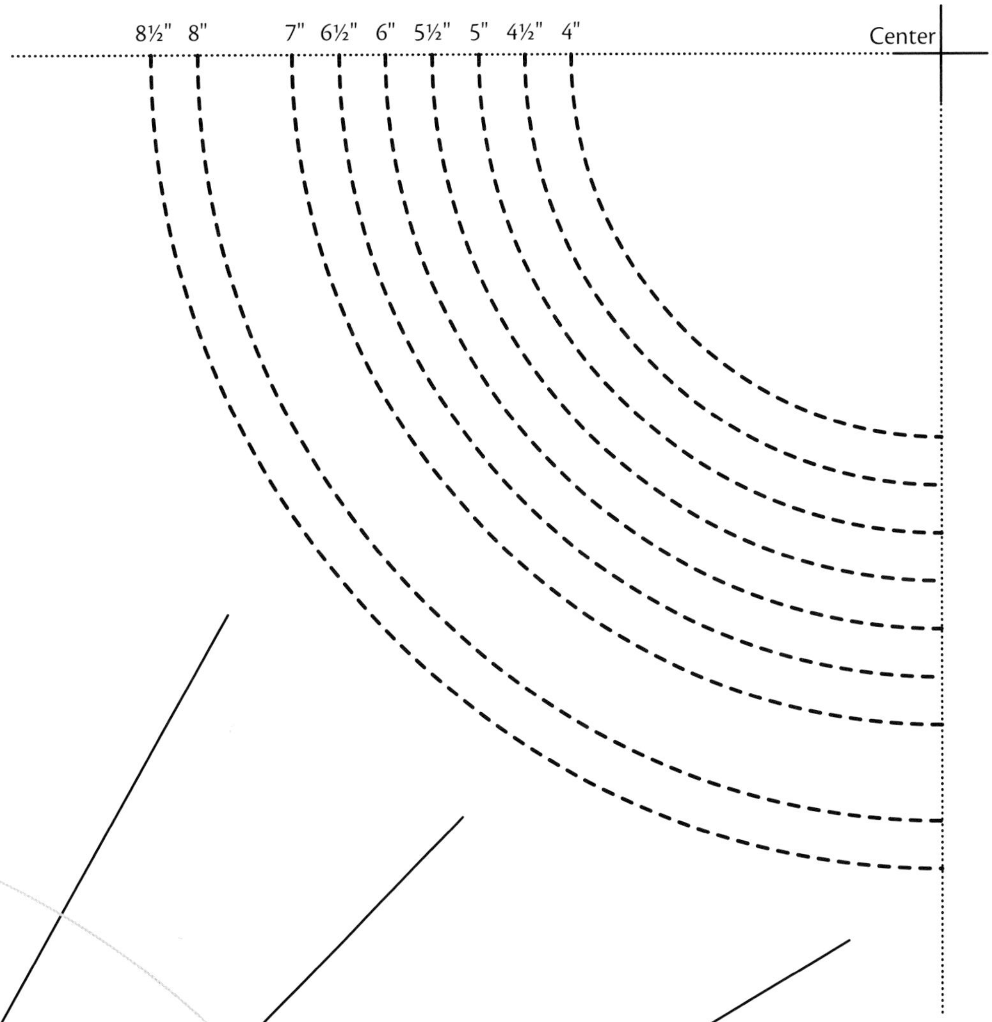
8½" 8" 7" 6½" 6" 5½" 5" 4½" 4"
Center

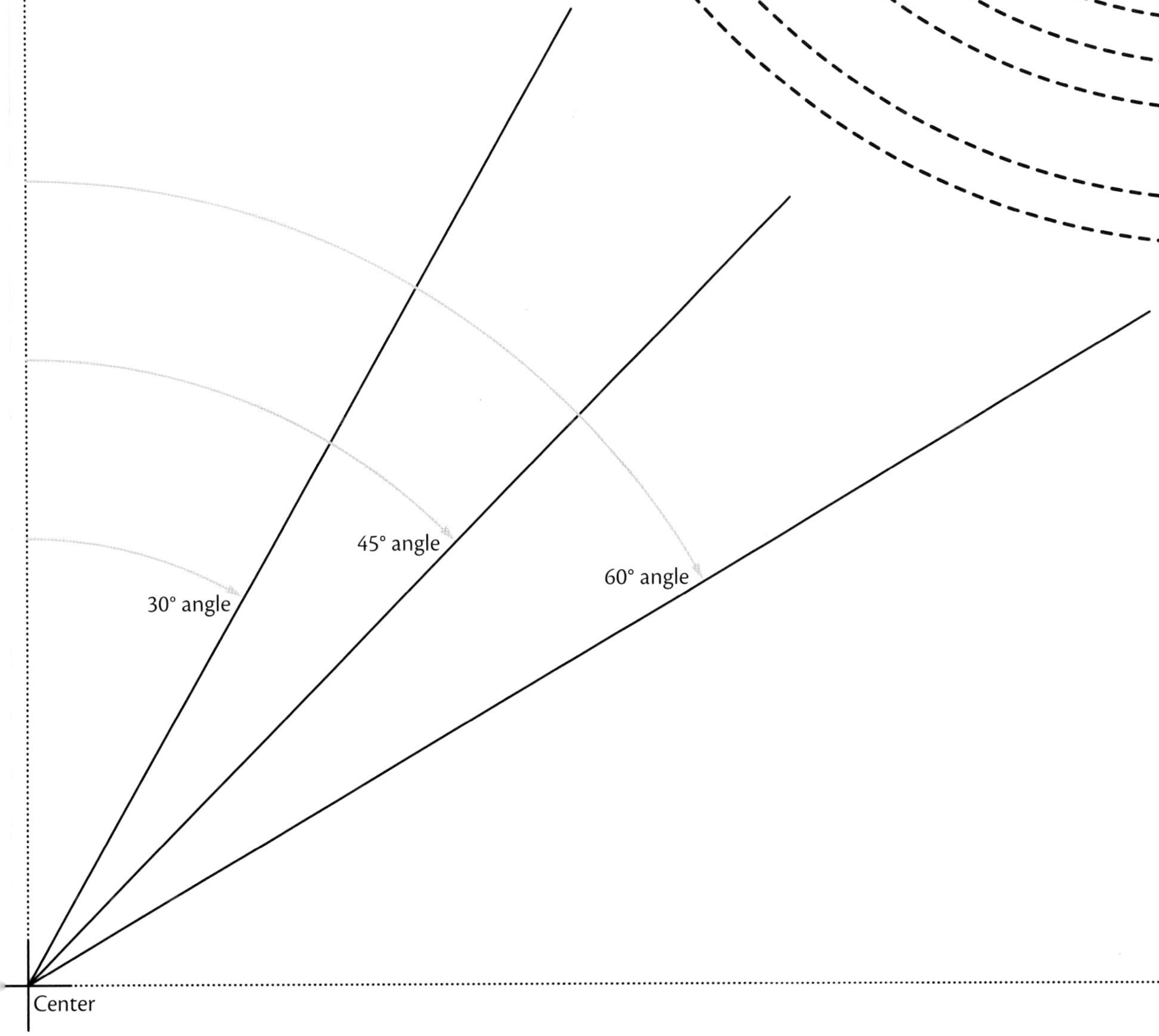
30° angle
45° angle
60° angle
Center

Size Index

Squares

Twirl Around, 132
Whirligig, 134

13"
Bows and Borders, 136
Celebration 1, 59
Celebration 2, 114
Fancy Feathers, 41
Fall Leaf, 187
Fantasia, 139
Feather Plume, 45
Floral Medley, 87
Kaleidoscope, 50
Kissing Hearts, 145
Lida Rose, 60
Lilac Leaf, 200
Rondo, 91
Sparkling Flower, 77
Sun Feathers, 51
Wandering Flower, 100

13½"
Floral Spray, 85
Limerick Waves, 55

14"
Cable Border, 128
Climbing Vine, 99
Kissing Hearts, 145
Loving Hearts, 154
Sweetheart Swag, 53

14½"
Windswept, 142

15"
Butterfly Garden, 97
Cherry, 109
Fanfare, 42
Feather Spray, 46
Garden Party, 102
Hearts and Swags, 152
Holiday Hearts, 165
Spring Leaves, 192
Washington's Wreath, 54

16"
Candle Flame, 113
Fancy Feathers, 41
Feathered Heart, 57
Ivy 2, 181
Sweetheart Swag, 53

17"
Evening Flower, 84
Feather Heart, 44
Feathered Heart, 57
Holly Wreath, 171
Sweet Talk, 58

Rectangles

If you don't find the dimensions you need, match the height of your rectangle with border motifs and see if repeats fit into your rectangle area.

2" x 3½"
Comet, 31

2" x 4"
Gibraltar, 135
Hanover, 127

2" x 4½"
Daisy Delight, 80

2" x 5½"
Gibraltar, 135
Petite Daisy, 92

2" x 6"
Shooting Stars, 30

2" x 6½"
Comet, 31
Fish Splash, 118

2" x 9"
Summer Leaves, 190

2" x 9½"
Hanover, 127

2" x 12"
Whirligig, 134

2½" x 4½"
Bows and Bells, 163
Trailing Vine, 188

2½" x 5"
Bonnie Blue Ribbon, 28
Twirl Around, 132
Wind Swirl, 116

2½" x 5½"
Lantern Lily, 60

2½" x 6½"
Bows and Bells, 163
Lemon Peel, 136

2½" x 7"
Double Feather Wreath, 40

2½" x 7½"
Wind Swirl, 116
Yukon Cable, 115

2½" x 8½"
Trailing Vine, 188

2½" x 9"
Lilac Leaf, 200

2½" x 9½"
Twirl Around, 132

2½" x 10"
Yukon Cable, 115

2½" x 10½"
Explorers, 131

2½" x 12"
Bonnie Blue Ribbon, 28

2½" x 12½"
Yukon Cable, 115

3" x 5"
Buttercup, 78
Caesar's Heart, 160
Ribbon Reel, 113

3" x 5½"
Bows and Borders, 136
Star of David, 168
Win Again, 141

3" x 6"
Double Feather Wreath, 40
Garden Party, 102
Stardust, 14

3" x 6½"
Garden Party, 102

3" x 8½"
Hollyberry, 174

3" x 9"
Sizzle, 32

3" x 10"
Friendship Vine 2, 191

3" x 10½"
Explorers, 131
Trellis Vine, 196

3" x 15"
Garden Party, 102

3½" x 4½"
Cloverleaf, 195

3½" x 5"
Spring Promise, 62

3½" x 5½"
Sweethearts, 52

3½" x 6"
Oak and Acorn, 166
Woodland Spring, 185

3½" x 6½"
Sunshine, 8

3½" x 7"
Cat Tails, 144

3½" x 7½"
Woodland Spring, 185

3½" x 9"
Friendship Vine 2, 191

3½" x 10"
Sweetheart Swag, 53

3½" x 10½"
Ritzy, 134

3½" x 11½"
Twinkling Stars, 23

3½" x 12"
Budding Vine, 179

4" x 6"
Budding Vine, 179

4" x 6½"
Tea Leaf, 184

4" x 8"
Ribbon Dance, 116

4" x 8½"
Shooting Stars, 30
Whirlabout, 112

4" x 9"
Leafy Vine, 178
Tulip, 101

4" x 9½"
Sea Serpent, 15

4" x 10"
Ribbon Dance, 116

4" x 11"
Lida Rose, 60

4" x 17½"
Tulip, 101

4½" x 6½"
Heavenly Dove, 169
Ritzy, 134

4½" x 8"
Starburst, 168

4½" x 13"
Ribbons of Love, 157

4½" x 14"
Holiday Hearts, 165

4½" x 15"
Floral Spray, 85

4½" x 16"
Ribbons of Love, 157

5" x 8"
Butterfly Garden, 97
Feathered Cable, 43

5" x 10"
Sweethearts, 52

5½" x 9"
Rhythm and Bows, 158

5½" x 9½"
Floral Heart, 153

6" x 8"
Lucky Clover, 189

6" x 10"
Best Foot Forward, 22

6½" x 7½"
Tea Leaf, 184

6½" x 10½"
Feather Plume, 45

7" x 9"
Cherry, 109

9½" x 13½"
Feather Heart, 44

Triangles
(measured on short side)

Borders

A motif that fits in a square can also be used for a border. Select one with the same measurement as the border width you wish to fill and repeat the design along the lengths.

Alphabetical Index